# THE RÁS

## A DAY BY DAY DIARY OF IRELANDS GREAT BIKE RACE

BY JIM TRAYNOR

ISBN: 978-1-905451-71-5

A CIP catalogue for this book is available from the National Library.

This book was published in cooperation with
Choice Publishing & Book Services Ltd, Drogheda, Co Louth, Ireland
Tel: 041 9841551 Email: info@choicepublishing.ie
www.choicepublishing.ie

## FOR JIM

This book tells the story of Ireland's greatest bike race which was formally named "RÁS TAILTEANN" from its beginning in 1953 but has always been informally referred to as 'The RÁS'. It is largely written by one of the sports greatest volunteers, the late Jim Traynor who died in 2003, and is now published by his wife Bridie as her tribute to Jim and their lifelong love of cycle sport.

Jim became fascinated with road racing as a teenager in Newry and joined the Newry Wheelers club. The highlight of his competitive career was his participation in RÁS TAILTEANN during the sixties and seventies. Initially his main involvement was as a competitor in road events but he then became involved in organisation and for many years was the club's main event promoter, with responsibility for the Tour of Ulster during the 1960s. He was still a member at the time of his death.

Jim began his contribution to The RÁS in the early 1970s and performed a range of useful functions until in more recent times he focussed on the position of Chief Judge, in which role his decisions were rarely questioned and hardly ever challenged. Jim's reputation on The RÁS led to him also being in demand by other event organisers all over Ireland and there was nowhere too distant for him to travel to from start to end of the year.

Like most people involved in cycling, Jim also worked for the sport in a variety of capacities. He is credited as being the man who first introduced a computer-based result system to stage racing, using a basic programme written by himself at a Tour of Ulster. He helped to set up and became a member of the Irish Cycling Tripartite Committee, the umbrella body used to first co-ordinate the three separate organisations that used to "control" cycling in Ireland, and he worked towards the eventual unity that followed in the setting up of the Federation of Irish Cyclists, now

# Acknowledgements

Bridie Traynor wishes to thank all those who helped her in bringing Jim's book to fruition. In particular she's pleased to mention the huge contribution from Dermot Dignam, Miceal Campbell and Shane Stokes.

*The Late Jim Traynor*

# Contents

Cycling Ireland. Jim won the National Cycling Association's Jim Killean Award for outstanding contribution to the sport in 1976.He was a UCI National Commissaire. He reported cycling news for several publications but principally for The Irish News, where he spent most of his working life.

His first-hand knowledge of The RÁS and the personalities involved in it, whether as organisers or competitors, make this year by year account, from the hand of a man who was there and who played an important part in the action, an invaluable document. It is Jim's own account of a race that he loved. He wrote most of it himself in the years before his sudden death. The only additions have been by some friends who have filled a few gaps in his almost-completed work, with Bridie as the driver towards publication.

For those of us privileged to know him, this book will be a treasure for us to keep.

**MBL**

# THE RÁS

## THE BEGINNING

The material in the first two chapters concerning the conception and organising of the first 8-day race in Ireland comes, largely verbatim, from the account by Kerry Sloan, one of the organisers of the first week-long RÁS TAILTEANN published in the NCA Twenty-first Birthday Book, itself edited by Sloan in 1959.
Ever since Henri Desgranges founded the fabulous Tour de France away back in the early 1900's, stage racing has caught the imagination of cyclists all over the world.
In Ireland the call came later than in most countries. Proximity to England caused the road sport to develop along Time Trial lines. However, even time-trialling was a poor relation branch of the sport for Track Racing was the big attraction.
The split in 1949 swept away all the NCA roadmen leaving the NCA predominantly a track racing association with virtually no time-triallists so what road racing there was became Massed Start.
As the NCA regained strength this branch of the sport started to thrive and a road-racing calendar became established and naturally, fed on a diet of cycling reading which highlighted the Tour de France and such legendary figures as Coppi, Kubler, etc. the roadmen started to think in terms of stage racing.
The first stage race in Ireland was held in August 1950 when the Western CC, Belfast, put on a Belfast - Dublin - Belfast Two Day for the Irish News Cup. (The Western had run a Belfast - Dublin one-day race since 1948.).
The following year, 1951, the British League of Racing Cyclists, like the NCA unrecognised by the UCI, promoted its Tour of Britain a 12-day race sponsored by the Daily Express and invited an NCA team to compete. The team was Karl McCarthy (winner of the Belfast - Dublin - Belfast), Con Carr, Eddie Hawkins, Matt Sands and Joe Lennon.
In spite of their lack of experience in long distance massed start racing and stage racing the team did very well in the event which had stages up to 150 miles. McCarthy was placed on several stages and finished ninth overall. Lennon became the hero of the race when after three crashes he finished second on the final stage in London swathed in bandages.
After this support for stage racing became greater than ever and in 1952 there were three events, a 3-day Tour of Munster, a 2-day RÁS Laighean and the Belfast - Dublin.
At this time interest in a longer Tour of Ireland type of race was at its height and two men were trying to put such a race on the road. One was Joe Christle of Dublin's Gate RC who was negotiating with the Irish Press who were interested in sponsoring such a race.
These negotiations reached an advanced stage and the 1952 Racing Calendar included a Tour of Ireland. However, just as the final contract was ready to be drawn up, a spanner was thrown into the works. The Irish Press wanted the CRE, the UCI

recognised body, to compete in the race, under terms which were completely unacceptable to the NCA, and that was that.

While Joe Christle was working in Dublin, Pat McAllister, (who organised the Belfast - Dublin - Belfast) was also working on the problem in Belfast. He had been team manager of the Irish team in the Tour of Britain and had established contacts with the Daily Express.

His aim was for a Daily Express Tour of Ireland. However, he ran into stiff opposition at home for many felt that it would be unwise for the NCA to help in promoting this newspaper in Ireland. However the Daily Express withdrew from cycle racing altogether and this probably avoided a further split in the NCA. As it was Western CC left the NCA.

# 1953

In 1953 among the increasing number of stage races being promoted was a 2-day RÁS TAILTEANN from Dublin to Enniscorthy. The inaugural RÁS was held on the weekend of September 19/20, attracting a good field of 52 riders despite being so late in the year, only a week before the end of the road-racing season.

## STAGE 1

Rain and wind were the conditions faced by the riders in the inaugural RÁS Mick Carr (Cork) probably had no idea when he won the first stage, 90 miles from Dublin to Wexford, that he was leading home the first of hundreds of RÁS stages.
It was a good decisive win, Carr coming home on his own, 34 seconds ahead. The Carrigtwohill rider broke away from the field at Enniscorthy. He was chased home by a 4-man group led in by Mick Cahill (Harps CC).
**Stage 1 Dublin - Wexford 90 Mls**. 1 M.Carr (Cork) 4.20.26 2 M.Cahill (Harps CC) at 34 secs 3 W.Scannell (National CC) s.t. 4 C.O'Reilly (Antrim) s.t. 5 C.Dunne (Harps CC) s.t.

*1953 Winner Colm Christle*

## STAGE 2

The stage back to Dublin was longer, 110 miles, and Colm Christle's stage win gave him the overall victory, and a place in the record books as the first RÁS winner.
Frank Reilly Meath) attacked shortly after the start. Five miles later he was joined by Con Carr (North Kildare) and Leo Collins (Meath) and these three had established a lead of 2 minutes at New Ross.
Colm Christle (St. James's Gate) bridged the gap to the leaders and then Kerry Sloan (North Kildare) made it across. Christle had a puncture but was able to change and get back to the leaders.

As the race entered its final stages, only Christle, Collins, Carr and Sloan remained of the original break and they had been joined by J. Moran (St. Lawrence); P. McKenna (St. James's Gate) In a close sprint Christle got the verdict from Culleton with the other Gate rider McKenna third. The top five on overall all finished in the winning break.

**Stage 2 Wexford - Dublin 110 Mls.** 1 C.Christle (St. James's Gate) 5.01.03 2 O.Cullerton (Wexford) 3 P.McKenna (St. James's Gate) 4 K.Sloan (North Kildare) 5 J.Moran (St. Lawrence) 6 P.Fitzgerald (Kerry) 7 L.Collins (Meath) 8 T.Caldwell (Belfast) 9 C.Carr (Nr Kildare) 10 C.O'Reilly (Belfast).

**General Classification:** 1 C.Christle (St. James's Gate) 9.20.39 2 P.McKenna (St. James's Gate) at 30 secs 3 K.Sloan (North Kildare) at 1.01 4 J.Moran (Wicklow) at 1.23 5 P.Fitzgerald (Kerry) at 7.40 6 L.Collins (Meath) at 11.16 7 W.Scannell (National CC) s.t. 8 C.O'Reilly (Belfast) at 11.31 9 C.Dunne (Harp CC) at 14.45 10 H.O'Toole-King (St. James's Gate) s.t.

**Team:** St.James's Gate (C.Christle, P.McKenna, H.O'Toole-King) 28.17.13.

# 1954

With sponsorship from An Tostal, Aspro and Hercules Cycles the CRE's 5-day Tostal Tour in 1953 was a big success throughout most of the country, although it had a hard time in the NCA heartlands of Kerry. The success of the event was a big blow to the NCA with 1953 the blackest year in its history.
A NCA Tour was therefore considered a must but it was widely believed that such a race without sponsors was impossible. Sloan wrote:
I was one of the few who thought that the race could be run without sponsors, although such help would be very welcome. Accordingly I called a meeting of the cyclists in Dublin and the surrounding counties in the autumn of 1953 to discuss the problem and to see what help would be forthcoming from them.
The handful who attended the meeting thought that Kerry Sloane had gone mad and their attitude showed it. The meeting decided to let me go ahead but no useful suggestions or offers of help were forthcoming.
Next morning, however, I got a phone call from Joe Christle. He had not been at the meeting but knew all about it. He had done a considerable amount of work on the subject of a stage race, during the abortive negotiations with the Irish Press, and would like to have a chat with me.
The 'chat' brought to light the fact that we both thought it worth while to chance running the race without sponsorship. We decided to go ahead and plan the race on the assumption that there would be no sponsors. At the same time every effort would be made to get a sponsor.
Only one obstacle remained to be negotiated. The NCA had to give its official blessing and the Executive Council, not very revolutionary at the best of times, was not too keen to allow a hair-brained scheme such as an unsponsored eight-day race, to go ahead.
However, thanks to President Jim Killean, who backed the scheme to the hilt, the Executive grudgingly gave its blessing on the condition that no financial burden be put on the Executive and that full details of the race would have to be put before the Council a week before the start and that if was thought that the arrangements were not satisfactory, it would call the race off.
John O'Reilly and Bernie O'Brien were added to help with the organisation and when O'Brien later withdrew due to illness in 1955 he was replaced by Frank Baird. Throughout that winter a route was selected, hotels booked subscriptions and programme advertising collected, transport borrowed, riders instruction manual compiled as the organisers, with no previous experience, discovered the enormity of the task they had embarked on.
No announcement of the proposed RÁS was made until after the CRE's 7-day Tostal Race was issued. Eighty English and 30 CRE would take part in a race of seven days

which included a rest day in the middle. The race was to be in April.
However when the RÁS was announced as a 1,000 mile 8-day in August, the CRE, fearing that their heavily sponsored showpiece would be overshadowed, significantly increased their route to seven full days with 800 miles of racing.
This was far too much for the largely inexperienced field, especially so early in the year and the field was already reduced to half when the weather broke and most of the field abandoned in a snowstorm with only a handful reaching the finish in Dublin.
Meanwhile the RÁS TAILTEANN was having its own troubles. After much hard work the necessary finance had been raised. The CRE were saying that a race without sponsors was impossible and that the organisation would collapse leaving riders stranded and that no-one in the NCA was capable of putting on such an event.
Many NCA riders also had their doubts and with three weeks to go only a dozen had entered. However after much canvassing, persuading and cajoling 39 riders were on the start line when GAA Secretary Paddy O'Keefe dropped the starting flag at the GPO in O'Connell Street, Dublin.
The Irish Independent billed the race as an 'Irish-style Tour de France', giving the preview an unprecedented amount of publicity for an NCA event. Thirty-nine riders were entered with teams from Ulster, Cork, Kildare, Louth, National CC, St. James Gate CC, Connacht, Kerry, Meath, Harp CC, Army, Tailteann, Waterford who had two riders and single entries from Tyrone, Wexford, Tipperary, Antrim and Limerick and there was also two individual entries: Paddy O'Callaghan of Kerry and Pat Murphy (Gate).
The race was to cover almost 1,000 miles and take in 23 counties. Pre-race favourites were Terry Carmody (Kerry), Con Carr (Kildare) and the Christle brothers Colm and Mick from the Gate.
The RÁS was a huge success from the start where thousands of Dubliners blocked the thoroughfares to cheer the riders and as the event wended its way round the four provinces in a triumphal procession. At one point a train actually stopped on the line as the passengers got out to watch the race go by.
It was the annual holiday fortnight and holiday-makers touring the country by car joined in with the official cavalcade, following for days. In Tralee, with the Kerry team doing so well, an estimated 20,000 lined the finishing straight for nearly a mile.

## STAGE 1

Joe O'Brien, a 19-year-old apprentice mechanic, riding for the National CC won the opening stage of the first eight-day RÁS in 1954, 103 miles from Dublin to Wexford.
Animator of the opening stage was Paddy White (Army) who had a 100-yard lead at Newland's Cross on the Naas Road. He was caught but went again with Tom Flanagan (Meath), Seamus McGreevy (Ulster), Phil Clarke (Gate) and Terry Carmody (Kerry).

After 61 miles the break was caught and it was only at Ferrycarrig Bridge, 2.5 miles from the finish when Victor Bridges (Wexford) got away. He was joined by Mick Palmer (Connacht) and O'Brien who attacked from Palmer's wheel to win by 5 seconds from a fast finishing bunch of 37 led in by Carmody just ahead of Christy Dunne (Harp CC).

Big losers on the stage were the Christle brothers, Colm, the 1953 winner who had waited for his brother Mick after a puncture.

**Stage 1 Dublin - Wexford 104 Mls.** 1 J.O'Brien (National CC) 4.37.06 2 T.Carmody (Kerry) at 5 secs 3 C.Dunne (Harp CC) 4 W.Cooper (National CC).

## STAGE 2

There were big stage bonuses in the early events the winner getting 60 seconds, second place 45 and third 30 so O'Brien started the second stage from Wexford to Cork (128 miles) with 20 seconds in hand over Carmody. Until 1960 there was also a bonus of 1 minute for retaining the yellow jersey and although this only played a role over the final few stages in 1954, it was almost certainly responsible for allowing several early RÁS winners to survive in the lead.

Mick Christle (Gate CC) was first into Cork, outsprinting Willie O'Brien (Cork) with Cecil O'Reilly (Antrim) two lengths behind in third place but the new leader by 23 seconds from P.O'Shea (Army).

The main move of the stage was started by O'Reilly and O'Brien along with P. White (Army) and Paud Fitzgerald. They were joined by Mick Christle (Gate), P.O'Shea (Army) and J.Crowe (Kildare) and by Dungarvan they held a 1 minute advantage on S. Condron (Tailteann) with the bunch at 2 minutes.

At Fermoy they were joined by three more: Steve Abbott (Harp CC), Harry O'Toole King (Gate CC) and D.Ryan (Limerick). O'Reilly took the KOM prime at Watergrass Hill. They stayed together to the finish at South Mall where Christle easily won the sprint.

**Stage 2 Wexford - Cork 128 Mls.** 1 M.Christle (Gate CC) 6.10.28 2 W.O'Brien (Cork) s.t. 3 C.O'Reilly (Antrim) s.t. 4 S.Abbott (Harp CC) s.t. 5 P.O'Shea (Army CC) s.t.

**General Classification:** 1 C.O'Reilly (Antrim) 10.47.10 2 P.O'Shea (Army) at 23 secs 3 equal P.White (Army) D.Ryan (Limerick) J.Crowe (Kildare) at 26 secs 6 J.O'Brien National) at 2.30 7 T.Carmody (Kerry) at 2.50 8 C.Dunne (Harp CC) at 3.10.

## STAGE 3

There was a huge crowd in Tralee to see Kerry rider Terry Carmody take the stage and move into the overall lead. He won the sprint from Phil Clarke (Gate CC) with another Kerry rider third, a youthful E. Mangan, better known as Gene, who was to become a RÁS legend.

The 130 miles stage was run off in torrential rain. There was an early climb at Liberty Hill taken by race leader O'Reilly from Phil Clarke and Terry Carmody. The three were caught and after 30 miles Con Carr (Kildare) made a lone break getting a 1 minute gap. He was chased and joined by Carmody and Clarke and these three had 3 minutes in hand at Bantry.
Carr was dropped on the climb after Glengariffe but the other two stayed ahead to Tralee where Carmody took the sprint with a chasing quartet led in by Mangan almost 7 minutes down and the bunch another 28 seconds back.
**Stage 3 Cork - Tralee 130 Mls.** 1 T.Carmody (Kerry) 6.1.50 2 P.Clarke (Gate CC) s.t. 3 E.Mangan (Kerry) at 6.53 4 J.O'Brien (National) s.t. 5 J.Hickey (Cork) s.t. 6 W.O'Brien (Cork) s.t. 7 F.Ward (Harp CC) at 6.59 8 P.Fitzgerald (Kerry) at 7.21.
**General Classification:** 1 T.Carmody (Kerry) 16.51.50 2 J.O'Brien (National CC) at 6.03.

## STAGE 4

Cecil Reilly was back in yellow after the fourth stage, 110 miles to Ennis. Yellow jersey Carmody fell victim to the first of what became a distinctive feature of the event down the years a RÁS special where a big break goes away to build up a huge lead, with the rest of the field losing any chance of overall honours.
Nine riders survived in the lead to the finish where Paddy White (Army CC) won a close sprint from O'Reilly but the bunch, including the yellow jersey came home over 20 minutes behind.
White and Paul Fitzgerald started the winning move right from the off and quickly raced to a six minute lead. They were chased by O'Reilly and Con Carr who dropped back leaving the Antrim rider to bridge the gap on his own over 25 miles.
Carr tried again with D. Ryan (Limerick) and seven riders eventually made it across. Also there were Steve Abbott who later had to stop with mechanical trouble, Ulster riders Pat Rogers and Seamus Devlin, C. Dunne (Harp) and Joe O'Brien (National).
The RÁS suffered its first tragedy when Andrew Christle, brother of the race director Joe and competitors Mick and Colm was killed in a motorcycle accident in Tralee. The Gate team withdrew from the race.
**Stage 4 Tralee - Ennis 110 Mls.** 1 P.White (Army CC) 4.06.04 2 C.O'Reilly (Antrim) s.t. 3 J.O'Brien (National CC) s.t. 4 P.Fitzgerald (Kerry) s.t. 5 C.Dunne (Harp CC) s.t. 6 P.Rogers (Ulster) s.t.
**General Classification:** 1 C.O'Reilly (Antrim) 21.39.55 2 P.White (Army CC) at 1.01 3 D.Ryan (Limerick) at 1.59 4 J.O'Brien (National) at 2.58 5 C.Dunne (Harp CC) at 4.42 6 P.Rogers (Ulster) at 6.38.

## STAGE 5 (a) and (b)

The RÁS had its first time-trial on the Thursday and it was to be the longest ever in the event, 40 miles from Ennis to Galway, and it undoubtedly decided the final

outcome. If that wasn't enough the riders then had an afternoon 58 miles stage to Athlone.
O'Brien won the time-trial by 56 seconds from Paddy O'Callaghan (Kerry) with Willie O'Brien (Cork) a further 13 seconds down. With O'Reilly only eighth at 3.02, O'Brien took back the jersey with O'Reilly second 2.06 in arrears.
The strain was telling on the riders, hardly any of whom had ever ridden a week-long race. Three of the Kerry team retired before the afternoon start and another rider packed during the stage.
After 30 miles Tommy Flanagan (Meath) and J. O'Meara (Waterford) went away. They were chased by Cork pair W. O'Brien and P. Hickey, Victor Bridges (Wexford) and Paud Fitzgerald (Kerry) and these four caught the leaders, the six then holding a 2 minute advantage. O'Meara and Hickey were dropped in the final miles leaving Flanagan to win the sprint from the remaining four.
**Stage 5a Ennis - Galway 40 Mls. TT:** 1 J.O'Brien (National CC) 1.38.24 2 P.O'Callaghan (Kerry) 1.39.20 3 W.O'Brien (Cork) 1.39.33 4 J.Rowe (Army) 1.40.03 5 T.Carmody (Kerry) 1.40.11 6 T.Flanagan; (Meath) 1.40.12
**Stage 5b Galway - Athlone 58 Mls.** 1 T.Flanagan (Meath) 2.10.10 2 W.O'Brien (Cork) s.t. 3 P.Fitzgerald (Kerry) s.t. 4 V.Bridges (Wexford) s.t. 5 P.Hickey (Cork) at 1.25 6 J.O'Meara (Waterford) s.t.
**General Classification:** 1 J.O'Brien (National CC) 25.33.20 2 C.O'Reilly (Antrim) at 2.06 3 P.White (Army CC) at 5.50 4 M.Palmer (Connacht) at 6.09 5 D.Ryan (Limerick) at 7.04 6 F.Ward (Harp CC) at 9.18.

## STAGE 6

The marathon event, with over 100 miles racing on every stage, except the split stage which totalled 96, continued to take its toll and two of the Army riders, White and Rowe, failed to start on the Friday. Army had been strong challengers in the team race and, barring accidents, National were now assured of victory in this category.
Willie O'Brien (Cork) won the sixth stage, 106 miles to Armagh City, in a 4-man sprint but with both Joe O'Brien and nearest challenger Cecil Reilly finishing in the main group, over 12.42 behind the stage winner, there were no changes at the top.
Willie O'Brien, Paul Fitzgerald (Kerry), with Meath pair Tommy Flanagan and Tom Gerrard started the main move of the day only four miles after the start and stayed away to the finish. On the stage into Ulster northern riders were prominent in the pursuit with Joe McIvor (Tyrone) and Seamus McGreevy (Ulster) both in groups which finished in front of the bunch.
Steve Abbott (Harp CC) and McIvor finished 5th and 6th 4.32 behind the leading four with McGreevy and Frank Ward (Harp CC) 1.02 further behind.
**Stage 6 Athlone - Armagh 106 Mls**. 1, W.O'Brien (Cork) 4.07.07 2 T.Flanagan (Meath) s.t. 3 P.Fitzgerald (Kerry) s.t. 4 T.Gerrard (Meath) s.t. 5 S.Abbott (Harp CC) at 4.32 6 J.McIvor (Tyrone) s.t.

**General Classification:** 1 J.O'Brien (National CC) 29.52.09 2 C.O'Reilly (Antrim) at 2.06 3 D.Ryan (Limerick) at 8.04 4 M.Palmer (Connacht) at 8.09 5 F.Ward (Harp CC) at 8.53 6 P.Fitzgerald (Kerry) at 10.27.

## STAGE 7

The 117 miles stage from Armagh to Newry produced the only bunch finish of the week, Willie O'Brien (Cork) taking his second stage in a row with Christy Dunne (Harp CC) and Mick Palmer (Connacht) next best of the riders who sprinted for the line on the Belfast Road. Dunne had been prominent throughout the stage launching numerous attacks but the bunch wasn't in a mood to let any serious attack develop and all were chased down.

**Stage 7 Armagh - Newry 117 Mls.** 1 W.O'Brien (Cork) 5.27.00 2 C.Dunne (Harp CC) s.t. 3 M.Palmer (Connacht) s.t. 4 C.O'Reilly (Antrim) s.t. 5 P.Hickey (Cork) s.t.

**General Classification:** 1 J.O'Brien (National CC) 35.29.09 2 C.O'Reilly (Antrim) at 2.06 3 M.Palmer (Connacht) at 7.39 4 D.Ryan (Limerick) at 8.04 5 F.Ward (Harp CC) at 8.53 6 P.Fitzgerald (Kerry) at 10.27.

## STAGE 8

The honour of winning the final stage of the first 8-day went to Dungannon's Joe McIvor, riding as the sole representative of Tyrone. Joe O'Brien finished in the bunch just 5 seconds behind maintaining his lead, and winning the first 8-day.

The 1954 RÁS has a special place in my memory as it was the first cycle race I ever saw when the race left Newry on the final Sunday. After watching the pre-race preparations at the two hotels, the Imperial and the Boulevard, opposite each other in the centre of the town, we went to the Dublin road to see the riders climb the hill.

Just in front of us a rider's frame broke and another rider gave him his bike. Now 42 years later, reading the newspaper reports, I have learned that it was Steve Abbott. That glimpse of cycle racing led to a lifetime in the sport.

After an early break they were all together at Drogheda when McIvor, Paud Fitzgerald (Kerry), and Victor Bridges (Wexford) went away. Bridges dropped back at Slane with mechanical trouble and at 50 miles the two in front were 2 minutes clear.

By Kells the gap was over 4 minutes but a spirited chase was developing behind. At Navan it was 3.5 minutes and by Clonee it was down to 1 minute. Entering the Phoenix Park McIvor attacked just before Fitzgerald was caught by the fast closing bunch. At the line McIvor had only 5 lengths in hand over Frank Ward (Harp CC) who won the sprint from Cecil O'Reilly (Antrim) and Steve Abbott (Harp CC).

The team race which had been close for the first half of the race became easier for National CC after the withdrawal of Gate and Army. With O'Brien on the National team were Paddy Edgerton and Dick Sweeney. Meath finished second over 15 minutes down.

**Stage 8 Newry - Dublin 110 Mls.** 1 J.McIvor (Tyrone) 4.44.20 2 F.Ward (Harp CC) at 2 secs 3 C.O'Reilly (Antrim) s.t. 4 S.Abbott (Harp CC) s.t. 5 P.Hickey (Cork) s.t. 6 J.O'Brien (National CC) s.t. 7 J.Whelan (Kildare) s.t. 8 C.Dunne (Harp CC) s.t.
**General Classification:** 1 J.O'Brien (National CC) 40.01.29 2 C.O'Reilly (Antrim) at 2.23 3 M.Palmer (Connacht) at 9.39 4 D.Ryan (Limerick) at 10.04 5 F.Ward (Harp CC) at 10.13 6 P.Fitzgerald (Kerry) at 12.27 7 C.Dunne (Harp CC) at 14.02 8 P.Rogers (Ulster) at 14.49 9 T.Flanagan (Meath) at 23.25 10 P.O'Callaghan (Kerry) at 24.40 11 T.Gerrard (Meath) at 26.41 12 C.Carr (Kildare) at 26.59.
**Team:** 1 National CC 121.10.52 2 Meath 121.26.07 3 Harp CC 121.27.56 4 Ulster 121.28.47 5 Kildare 121.29.27.
**King of the Mountains:** Cecil O'Reilly (Antrim).
When Kerry having won the individual and team race returned to the 'Kingdom' they were accorded a reception such as only Kerry footballers get after winning an All-Ireland. In Westport third placed Mick Palmer was met by a torchlight procession and all over the country presentations were made by towns and counties to their riders. The RÁS had taken its place among Ireland's top sporting events.

1954 Winner – Joe O'Brien

# 1955

There was a big increase in the entry for the second 8-day RÁS in 1955 with over 60 riders taking the start at the GPO in Dublin for the 107 miles stage to Newry which was won by Dennis O'Connor of Dublin, entered as an individual.
Joe Christle's publicity machine was now in full working order and the newspapers published a constant flow of team news in the weeks leading up to the race.

## STAGE 1

The opening stage was from Dublin to Newry and Brian Monaghan (Down), Christy Gurhy (Sligo), Joe Lennon (Louth), D. Collins (Meath) and Tony Halliday (Down) made the first major break of the race and at Drogheda had a lead of 1.20. They were joined by another eight riders but the group was caught after Dundalk. Three riders then went away O'Connor,
Mick Palmer (Connacht) and Malachy Denny of the Gate CC, with the county structure of the race beginning to become established, riding for the first Dublin team.
The three had 2 minutes in hand over the climb out of Newtownhamilton where Palmer attacked, opening up a gap of 30 seconds before breaking his chain and being passed by the other two. However he borrowed a bike from a spectator and managed to finish third, 25 second behind O'Connor who outsprinted his companion on the fast downhill run into the finish at Monaghan Street. Gene Mangan (Kerry) led in the bunch nearly 2 minutes down.
**Stage 1 Dublin - Newry 107 Mls.** 1 D.O'Connor (Individual) 4.17.05 2 M.Denny (Dublin) at 11 secs 3 M.Palmer (Connacht) at 26 secs 4 G.Mangan (Kerry) at 1.54 5 P.Fitzgerald (Kerry) at 1.55 6 S.Abbott (Dublin) same time.

## STAGE 2

The second stage from Newry to Sligo, won by Tommy Flanagan (Meath) at 140 miles is one of the longest ever raced in the RÁS (only exceeded by the 150 miles Clonakilty to Wexford in 1961 and equalled by the Sligo to Dublin in 1958. The 138 miles from Monaghan to Ballina in 1956 followed a 20 miles neutralisation from Armagh after the events the previous day when the race was abandoned after a riot in Cookstown, which makes it the longest distance ridden in a stage at 158 miles).
Frank Ward (indiv.), Denis O'Connor (indiv.), Sean Condron (indiv.), Denis Ryan (Limerick), Tom Flanagan (Meath), Paud Fitzgerald (Kerry) and Pat Murphy (Dublin) went away and established a lead of over 2 minutes.

Several small groups got up to the leaders and after 50 miles there were 10 in the leading group, including Brian Monaghan (Down), Joe McIvor (Tyrone), which kept increasing its lead and at Carrickmore they were 11 minutes ahead.
This had dropped to 7 minutes by Kesh but the ten stayed away to finish over 5 minutes ahead in Sligo where Flanagan took the sprint. O'Connor retained the yellow jersey with Fitzgerald next and Monaghan third. Monaghan's brother Dermot, the youngest rider in the race at 17, finished the stage with a broken collarbone but didn't start stage 3.
**Stage 2 Newry - Sligo 140 Mls.** 1 T.Flanagan (Meath) 6.41.05 2 P.Fitzgerald (Kerry) 3 D.O'Connor (Indiv.) 4 F.Ward (Indiv.) 5 D.Ryan (Limerick) 6 J.Curley (Indiv.) at 1 second.
**General Classification:** 1 D.O'Connor (Indiv.) 10.57.20 2 P.Fitzgerald (Kerry) at 2.55 3 B.Monaghan (Down) at 2.56 4 J.McIvor (Tyrone) at 4.02 5 J.Pegley (Kildare) at 7.59 6 T.Gerrard (Meath) s.t. (Times were split to 1.5 of a second but I have rounded down to the full second).

## STAGE 3

Gene Mangan (Kerry) won the first of a career total of 12 RÁS stage victories on the 75 miles stage, a sprint in those days, from Sligo to Westport. O'Connor retained the jersey, finishing in the bunch 2.01 behind the stage winner.
Mick Palmer (Connacht) a Mayo man tried hard to bring off a home win and went away on a solo effort before Castlebar which lasted for 30 miles but came to nothing when he was caught by a chasing group of eight near the finish.
Mangan and Steve Abbott (Dublin), unquestionably then the two best sprinters in the country fought out a close sprint in Westport with the Kerryman getting the victory on this occasion.
**Stage 3 Sligo - Westport 75 Mls.** 1 G.Mangan (Kerry) 2.59.09 2 S.Abbott (Dublin) 3 P.Hickey (Cork) 4 M.Palmer (Connacht) 5 R.Williams (Dublin) 6 F.Ward (Dublin) 7 L.Collins (Meath) 8 C.Clarke (Kildare) 9 T.Gerrard (Meath).
**General Classification:** 1 D.O'Connor (Indiv.) 13.57.00 2 P.Fitzgerald (Kerry) at 3.40 3 B.Monaghan (Down) at 4.26 4 J.McIvor (Tyrone) at 5.32 5 S.Abbott (Dublin) at 6.32 6 G.Mangan (Kerry) at 7.08.

## STAGE 4

Frank Ward won the 91 miles stage from Westport to Ennis ahead of Paddy O'Callaghan (Kerry); B. Reilly (Meath), and Mickey Mooney (Down). A diversion at Galway shortened the stage and the race arrived much earlier into Ennis than had been expected. O'Connor retained the yellow jersey with little change overall except for Paud Fitzgerald (Kerry) who fell and lost 4 minutes, Brian Monaghan (Down) moving up to 2nd overall.

There was an incident outside Galway when a horse reared up bringing down Ronnie Williams (Dublin) who smashed his gears but after a long chase he caught the bunch by Gort.
After 40 miles the main break of the day went away containing Gerry Keogh (Dublin), Frank Ward (indiv.), Con Carr (Kildare), Basil Reilly (Meath) Pat O'Callaghan (Kerry) and Mickey Mooney (Down). These six built up a good lead by the finish in Westport where Ward was best 2.46 ahead of the bunch led in by Gene Mangan (Kerry).
**Stage 4 Westport - Ennis 91 Mls.** 1 F.Ward (Indiv.) 3.38.30 2 P.O'Callaghan (Kerry) s.t. 3 B.Reilly (Meath) s.t. 4 M.Mooney (Down) s.t. 5 C.Carr (Kildare) s.t. 6 G.Keogh (Dublin) s.t.
**General Classification:** 1 D.O'Connor (Indiv.) 17.38.16 2 B.Monaghan (Down) at 4.26 3 P.Fitzgerald (Kerry) at 4.34 4 F.Ward (Indiv.) at 6.27 5 S.Abbott (Dublin) at 6.42 6 C. Carr (Kildare) at 6.44.

## STAGE 5

Steve Abbott (Dublin) and Gene Mangan (Kerry) resumed their sprinting duel at the finish in Tralee of the fifth stage, 89 miles from Ennis with this time the Kerryman losing out before an enormous home crowd.
Mangan looked a winner until he swerved to avoid a manhole cover some 20 yards from the line giving Abbott the opportunity to squeeze through for the narrowest of verdicts.
Seamus Healy (Tipperary), Ronnie Long (Limerick), Tom Gerrard (Meath) and Pat O'Callaghan (Kerry) went after 14 miles of racing and by Adare (33 miles) they had a lead of 1 minute. Before Newcastlewest the break was caught and passed by another quartet: Steve Abbott (Dublin), Leo Collins (Meath), Pat Rogers (Tyrone) and Pat O'Meara (Limerick) who in turn were caught by the bunch.
Although the field split into several groups on the descent of the Barna Gap, they all came together on the descent and the bunch arrived together into Tralee for a spectacular finish.
In the general classification O'Connor retained his lead from Monaghan. Mangan showed the best improvement overall moving up to 5th.
In the team race Kerry led Dublin by 3 minutes.
**Stage 5 Ennis - Tralee 89 Mls.** 1 S.Abbott (Dublin) 3.43.03 2 G.Mangan (Kerry) 3 B.O'Brien (Kildare) 4 B.Reilly (Meath) 5 P.Hickey (Cork) 6 J.O'Hare (Louth).
**General Classification:** 1 D.O'Connor (Indiv.) 21.20.19 2 B.Monaghan (Down) at 5.26 3 P.Fitzgerald (Kerry) at 5.33 4 S.Abbott (Dublin) at 6.42 5 G.Mangan (Kerry) at 7.23 6 F.Ward (Indiv.) at 7.27.

## STAGE 6

O'Connor lost his lead on the sixth stage which saw some serious climbing in Kerry

with Steve Abbott (Dublin) taking the KOM primes at Lady's View and Liberty Hill which along with a second to Gene Mangan at the Tunnel Road saw him lead the mountains classification by 8 points to 5 for Tommy Flanagan (Meath).
Over the climbs and descents an 8-man lead group formed at the front including Mangan and Abbott. At Kenmare they were chased by a seven man group 3 minutes down while the yellow jersey was 12 minutes back the road and it stayed that way to the finish with O'Connor's reign over.
Steve Abbott (Dublin) who finished fourth on the stage in the same time as the winner took over the yellow jersey by 11 seconds from Gene Mangan (Kerry). O'Connor dropped to 5th, over 4 minutes back while Brian Monaghan (Down) who had been second also missed the break slipping to 7th.
**Stage 6 Tralee - Cork 88 Mls.** 1 G.Keogh (Dublin) 5.39.05 2 G.Mangan (Kerry) at 10 secs 3 F.Ward (Indiv.) s.t. 4 S.Abbott (Dublin) s.t. 5 P.Hickey (Cork) s.t. 6 M.Palmer (Connacht) s.t.
**General Classification:** 1 S.Abbott (Dublin) 27.06.01 2 G.Mangan (Kerry) at 11 secs 3 F.Ward (Indiv) at 30 secs 4 M.Palmer (Connacht) at 1.24 5 D.O'Connor (Indiv.) at 4.48 6 C.Dunne (Indiv.) at 7.02 7 B.Monaghan (Down) at 8.24; 8, P. Fitzgerald (Kerry) at 11.22.

## STAGE 7

Gene Mangan (Kerry) had his second stage win of the week on the 129 miles stage from Cork to Wexford and took the jersey from Steve Abbott (Dublin) who finished in the bunch, well behind a big leading break.
After 28 miles there was a nine-man group with a one-minute lead. They were Mick Christle (Dublin), Mickey Mooney (Antrim), Victor Bridges (Wexford), Leo Collins (Meath), Pat O'Callaghan (Kerry), Joe Lennon (Louth), Mick Palmer (Connacht), Seamus Healy Tipperary) and Jack Crowe (Kildare).
Lennon was dropped after 60 miles and shortly afterwards they were all together. Christle went away again with Tom Ryan (Tipperary), Basil Reilly (Meath) and Mickey Mooney (Antrim) with the bunch at 1.15. Groups of riders got up to the leaders leaving a big group at the front which was over 2 minutes ahead of the bunch at Carrick-on-Suir and this group stayed away to the finish where Mangan won the sprint ahead of Mick Christle with Pat Hickey (Cork) third.
**Stage 7 Cork - Wexford 129 Mls.** 1 G.Mangan (Kerry) 5.57.50 2 M.Christle (Dublin) s.t. 3 P.Hickey (Cork) s.t. 4 A.Cassidy (Tailteann) s.t. 5 F.Ward (Indiv) s.t. 6 T.Gerrard (Meath) s.t.
**General Classification:** 1 G.Mangan (Kerry) 33.05.02 2 F.Ward (Indiv) at 1.19 3 M.Palmer (Connacht) at 2.13 4 S.Abbott (Dublin) at 6.29 5 P.Hickey (Cork) at 12.11 6 D.O'Connor (Indiv) at 13.17.

## STAGE 8

The final stage, 104 miles from Wexford to Dublin, ended in a disputed win for Sean Condon (Tailteann CC) from Seamus McGreevy (Down), the verdict first going to the Newry rider before the verdict was reversed. A photo of the finish on the esplanade at Collins Barracks published the following morning seemed to show McGreevy in front.

Shortly after the start McGreevy and Fin Healy (Cork) went away and they were joined by Jim Curley (Tailteann) and finally by Condron. Curley dropped back, the other three building up a 2.30 lead which they held for most of the way.

The yellow jersey finished in the bunch led in by Steve Abbott (Dublin) 2.07 behind the break.

**Stage 8 Wexford - Dublin 104 Mls.** 1 S.Condron (Indiv.) 4.41.10 2 S.McGreevy (Down) s.t. 3 F.Healy (Cork) s.t. 4 J.Crowe (Kildare) s.t. 5 P.Hickey (Cork) s.t. 6 S.Abbott (Dublin) at 2.07 7 G.Mangan (Kerry) s.t. 8 M.Christle (Dublin) s.t.

**Final General Classification:** 1 G.Mangan (Kerry) 37.47.19 2 F.Ward (Indiv.) at 2.19 3 M.Palmer (Connacht) at 3.12 4 S.Abbott (Dublin) at 7.29 5 P.Hickey (Cork) at 13.11 6 D.O'Connor (Indiv.) at 14.17.

**Team:** 1 Kerry (G.Mangan, P.Fitzgerald, P.O'Callaghan) 114.15.27 2 Dublin (S.Abbott, G.Keogh, M.Denny) 114.22.56 3 Cork (P.Hickey, J.Varian, F.Healy) 114.37.31.

**King of the Mountains**: S. Abbott (Dublin).

1955 Winner – Gene Mangan

# 1956

The second stage of the 1956 event had to be abandoned after a riot in Cookstown, Co. Tyrone. As a result the RÁS didn't enter Northern Ireland again until 1968. There were 58 starters.

A rule was introduced limiting the entries from any one county to a team of six. Over the next few years many riders, especially from Dublin, sought and got places on teams from counties which couldn't field their full complement. Initially there was a connection with the county, such as a grandparent, but as the years went by it became accepted practice that riders unable to get a place with their county could take up vacant places on other county teams.

## STAGE 1

The first stage in 1956 was an exact copy of the opener a year earlier from Dublin to Newry and it had a very similar result with a three-man break finishing well ahead of the field, National CC rider Cecil Donoghue, riding for Dublin outsprinting Pat O'Meara of Wicklow to take the stage.

The defending RÁS champion Gene Mangan lost almost 8 minutes due to a puncture. He had just crossed the border and the Kerry team car was held up at the customs post (at that time cars had to be stamped in and out of Northern Ireland) and Mangan had to wait nearly 5 minutes for a wheel.

Dennis O'Connor (Dublin) who won the opener a year before was in an early 6-man break which had 30 seconds at Navan where he took the first prime. They were caught after Dundalk when O'Donoghue, O'Meara and Jack Parker (Exiles) got away and while the bunch stalled they built up a big lead. Parker fell back with 10 miles to go coming home 50 seconds behind the leaders. Stephen Ryan (Limerick) led in the bunch almost 4 minutes later.

**Stage 1 Dublin - Newry 95 Mls.** 1 C.O'Donoghue (Dublin) 4.1.45 2 P.O'Meara (Wicklow) at 1 sec. 3 J.Parker (Exiles) at 50 secs 4 S.Ryan at 4.25 5 D.O'Connor (Dublin) at 4.26 6 T.Flanagan (Meath) at 4.27.

## STAGE 2

The second stage was abandoned after a riot in Cookstown. The following extract describing the events is taken from the report of Con Kenneally in the Irish Independent:

'Batons, bottles and battling bystanders came the way of the cyclists in the second stage (Newry to Armagh) of the NCA's 8-day RÁS TAILTEANN which was to have gone round Lough Neagh to Armagh yesterday. Instead of a 106 miles stage, they

raced only 24 miles to Lurgan, then 'toured' as far as Cookstown in Co. Tyrone, where the race was broken up when the cyclists were attacked by a large crowd.
'When the leading official car, driven by Mick Christle, and carrying a Tricolour, arrived a Lenaderg, near Banbridge, two constables stopped the race. Their request to have the flag taken down was refused and they did not interfere as the race continued on towards Lurgan.
'Just outside Lurgan the race was again stopped but this time the police broke the flagstaff and, in the ensuing melee, one of the occupants of the car was struck in the face with a blackthorn stick.
When the main body of cyclists and the attendant cars arrived at Lurgan the situation had every appearance of becoming serious.
Several of the cycling party had to be restrained by their companions from coming to grips with the police, and the position was not eased by the arrival of some young women who began to incite the cyclists by rendering "The Sash".
Next on the scene was a tender full of R.U.C. re-inforcements, but this time a conference between police officers and the race management was in progress a little further down the road, and the police did not leave the tender.
The authorities were adamant that the car could not continue the course carrying the flag - in fact one of the plainclothes-men present requested Bernie O'Brien of Kildare to remove a green, white and gold flash from his shoulder which, however, he refused to do.
Joe Christle, during all the excitement had the Flag and the broken staff in his hand, and when he and the N.C.A. president Jim Killeen, returned from the conference, Christle announced that the race "would not be allowed to continue."
Instead, he said, they would complete the stage as a protest run, and that it would not be included in the times for the general classification.
From Lurgan the cyclists continued right up along the Lough across through Randalstown to Magherafelt, uninterrupted. Then, when they were about four miles from Cookstown two of the cyclists tried to remove a Union Jack from a flagpole. Two policemen who were following the race foiled them, one of the cyclists being struck with a baton.
Entering Cookstown the cyclists were confronted by a line of police across the road. They were stopped and the drivers of vans which were carrying green white and gold identity discs were told to remove them.
'The cyclists were ordered to continue on while this was being done, but they had gone less than a hundred yards when a bottle was thrown into the middle of the road in front of them. The cyclists stopped to avoid the broken glass and as they did stones were thrown at them from both sides of the street. They were rushed, and a melee ensued which even the police, with drawn batons, were powerless to stop for ten minutes.
The Kerry contingent, with their green and gold colours, came in for special attention and Paddy Moriarty was the first man struck. One of their mechanics, Jimmy Leahy

was badly beaten around the face and was kicked on the ground, while Matt Fahy, of the Exiles team, was also struck.
Then the cyclists, who also collected their share of punishment from batons, remounted and got out of town. They were joined outside by their vans and as many as possible were driven the last 25 miles into Armagh, the rest following on in semi-darkness.
Today's route from Armagh to Ballina will probably be diverted through Clones, but a definite decision will not be made until this morning.'

## STAGE 3

The next morning the stage was neutralised as a protest from Armagh to Monaghan where racing proper started. Without this neutralisation this would have been the longest stage ever in the As it was near veteran at 38, Con Carr (Kildare), notable for breaking a string of long distance place-to-place records, won the 136 miles stage to Ballina and took the jersey.
There was some confusion for the first couple of hours as the route had been changes to avoid going back into the North through Enniskillen and the race went off course several times. They were back on the original route by Carrick-on-Shannon when Carr was in the leading break along with three Antrim riders Frank Thompson, Jimmy McGarry and Mickey Mooney plus John Keane (Exiles). They were joined by Brian Monaghan (Down), Denis O'Connor (Dublin) and Paud Fitzgerald (Kerry).
Others made their way up to the leaders before Carr attacked again outside Charlestown, taking with him McGarry and Fitzgerald. Over the final 20 miles the Kerryman dropped back. Carr then got rid of McGarry but his place was taken by another Antrim rider Thompson who stayed with him to the finish where the Kildare man won by 1 second.
Mickey Mooney came in 1.47 later with Malachy Denny (Dublin) with Gene Mangan leading in the next group, 2.27 behind the winner. Cecil O'Donoghue finished over 10 minutes down, his yellow jersey going to Carr who lead from Antrim pair Thompson and Mooney.
**Stage 3 Armagh (Monaghan) - Ballina 136 Mls.** 1 C.Carr (Kildare) 6.35.33 2 F.Thompson (Antrim) at 1 sec 3 M.Mooney (Antrim) at 1.47 4 M Denny (Dublin) at 1.49 5 G.Mangan (Kerry) at 2.27 6 D.O'Connor (Dublin) s.t.
**General Classification:** 1 C.Carr (Kildare) 10.42.33 2 F.Thompson (Antrim) at 16 secs 3 M.Mooney (Antrim) at 1.22 4 S.Ryan (Limerick) at 2.37 5 D.O'Connor (Dublin) at 2.38 6 T. Flanagan (Meath) at 2.39.

## STAGE 4

Gene Mangan won the fourth stage from Ballina to Nenagh but it was 20-year-old Belfast barman Mickey Mooney who took the yellow jersey, leading the 1955 winner by 1.21. A lot of interest was beginning to develop in the team race where the tactical

battle between Dublin and Kerry was influencing the race. After 4 stages, Dublin who had lost to Kerry the previous year, led by nearly 15 minutes.
Kerry had made a determined effort to wipe out their deficit but although they had the first two into Nenagh with Mangan and Paud Fitzgerald, Dublin had three well up and moved further ahead.
The deciding move of the stage came after 23 of the 132 miles when seven riders went away, Mangan, Fitzgerald, Mooney, John Keane (Exiles, Pat O'Meara (Wicklow) and Dublin pair Cecil O'Donoghue and Ronnie Williams. They were chased by Dennis O'Connor (Dublin), J. Cullen (Exiles) and Frank Thompson (Antrim) with the bunch over 2 minutes back.
At Moylough where local man Keane took the prime the bunch, steadily losing ground, was now 10 minutes down and it stayed like that to the finish. Race leader Carr tried constantly to leave the bunch to no avail and finished with the bunch 15 minutes behind Mangan. Just behind the leading six were Dennis O'Connor and Ronnie Williams (Dublin), Jack Cullen (Exiles) and Frank Thompson (Antrim) which brought Williams up to third overall.
**Stage 4 Ballina - Nenagh 132 Mls.** 1 G.Mangan (Kerry) 5.44.15 2 P.Fitzgerald (Kerry) s.t. 3 J.Keane (Exiles) s.t. 4 C.Donoghue (Dublin) s.t. 5 M.Mooney (Antrim) s.t. 6 P.O'Meara (Wicklow) s.t.
**General Classification:** 1 M.Mooney (Antrim) 16.27.54 2 G.Mangan (Kerry) at 1.21 3 R.Williams (Dublin) at 1.32 4 J.Keane (Exiles) at 1.45 5 C.Donoghue (Dublin) at 2.06 6 P.Fitzgerald (Kerry) at 3.03.

## STAGE 5

With the fifth stage finishing in Tralee, Kerry made an all-out assault and reduced their team deficit by 10 minutes. They also won the stage with Paud Fitzgerald although Dublin took over the lead, the jersey going to Ronnie William who led by 22 seconds from John Keane (Exiles). The stage winner Fitzgerald moved up to third overall.
A notable retiral was that of Natty Fahy (Exiles) who had a rib broken in Monday's melee at Cookstown. He crashed on Tuesday near Boyle and again in Ballinasloe and still managed to ride two more stages with his left arm in plaster.
The field stayed together through Limerick but after Rathluirc they started to splinter with seven minutes covering several groups. On the climb after Newcastlewest the leading break had a 5 minute lead on a chasing bunch with the next group, containing yellow jersey Mooney 10 minutes in arrears.
The big leading group lost Ryan (Tipperary), Con Carr (Kildare), Malachy Denny (Dublin) and Alec Davis (Louth) on the Barna Gap. As well as having Mangan and Fitzgerald with the leaders, Kerry had Callaghan and Moriarty with the chasers.
There was an enormous crowd at the finish in Tralee but there was almost a disaster when an oil tanker turned into the main street just before the leaders arrived. With the crowd he couldn't turn but just managed to get across the line before the cyclists.

Fitzgerald made it a great day for the home crowd winning the sprint from Colm Christle (N.S.C.) with another Kerry rider J. Switzer third.
**Stage 5 Nenagh - Tralee 106 Mls.** 1 P.Fitzgerald (Kerry) 4.21.10 2 C.Christle (N.S.C.) s.t. 3 J.Switzer (Kerry) s.t. 4 T.Flanagan (Meath) s.t. 5 J.Keane (Exiles) s.t. 6 R.Williams (Dublin) s.t.
**General Classification:** 1 R.Williams (Dublin) 21.10.30 2 J.Keane (Exiles) at 22 secs 3 P.Fitzgerald (Kerry) at 1.36 4 P.O'Meara (Wicklow) at 8.30 5 G.Mangan (Kerry) at 11.21 6 T.Flanagan (Meath) at 13.39.

## STAGE 6

The Exiles team had been reduced to a sole survivor by the end of the but that sole survivor John Keane, a 20-year-old carpenter from Moylough, Co. Galway, was the new yellow jersey leading Kerry's Paud Fitzgerald by 59 seconds.
These two fought out the sprint into Kenmare, where Fitzgerald took his second stage win in succession. All six Kerry riders were to the fore in their home territory and they took over the lead in the team race from Dublin.
The field split into three group shortly after the start and four riders: Cecil O'Donoghue (Dublin), Paud Fitzgerald (Kerry), John Keane (Exiles) and Colm Christle (N.S.C.) had a 1 minute lead at Killarney on a group of six; Brian Monaghan (Down), Alec Davis (Louth), Mick Creighton (Meath), Mick Mooney (Antrim), Tom Whelan (Tipperary) and E. Dalton (Wicklow). Then came another chasing group followed by the bunch led by leader Ronnie Williams.
After Killorglin the front two groups merged leaving 11 five minutes ahead of the bunch at Cahirciveen but Williams had left the bunch in a chasing group and had moved up considerably.
On the Coomakista Pass Fitzgerald and Keane attacked through the heavy fog and opened up a gap of 1.09 on Tom Whelan (Tipperary) by the finish in Kenmare with Mickey Mooney leading in the rest of the break over 4 minutes later.
**Stage 6 Tralee - Kenmare 112 Mls.** 1 P.Fitzgerald (Kerry) 5.18.51 2 J.Keane (Exiles) s.t. 3 T.Whelan (Tipperary) at 1.07 4 M.Mooney (Antrim) at 5.58 5 S.Ryan (Limerick) 6 B.Monaghan (Down) s.t.
**General Classification:** 1 J.Keane (Exiles) 26.28.58 2 P.Fitzgerald (Kerry) at 59 secs 3 R.Williams (Dublin) at 9.17 4 P.O'Meara (Wicklow) at 18.47 5 M.Mooney (Antrim) at 20.13 6 G.Mangan (Kerry) at 22.34.

## STAGE 7

It was another stage win for Gene Mangan on the 133 miles stage from Kenmare to Clonmel, the fourth Kerry win in a row. His Kerry teammate Paud Fitzgerald took over the yellow jersey after some very strange tactics saw him lose a lot of time on the bunch, although the race leader before the stage, John Keane (Exiles) lost even more.

Fitzgerald went off on a lone break just after the start leaving the teamless Keane to chase on his own. At one stage the gap was over 4 minutes before the bunch took up the chase and he was caught after Fermoy.
Both Fitzgerald and Keane were then dropped by the bunch but the Kerryman was the stronger and although he lost time nevertheless ended up leading the GC by over 6 minutes from Keane with Pat O'Meara of Wicklow still third, although his deficit had shrunk from over 18 to 13 minutes.
**Stage 7 Kenmare - Clonmel 133 Mls.** 1 G.Mangan (Kerry) 5.57.30 2 D.O'Connor (Dublin) s.t. 3 T.Flanagan (Meath) s.t. 4 T.Kiely (Tipperary) s.t. 5 J.McGarry (Antrim) s.t. 6 J.Gearon (Tipperary) s.t.
**General Classification:** 1 P.Fitzgerald (Kerry) 32.32.07 2 J.Keane (Exiles) at 6.03 3 P.O'Meara (Wicklow) at 13.08 4 G.Mangan (Kerry) at 15.03 5 B.Monaghan (Down) at 21.41 6 M.Denny (Dublin) at 24.29.

## STAGE 8

With Fitzgerald 6 minutes ahead of Keane leaving Clonmel and Kerry leading Dublin by 42 minutes in the team race, all the team, except Pat Moriarty, stayed together in the bunch, keeping out of trouble.
However to rub home their superiority, the one Kerryman in the break, Moriarty, took the stage winning the sprint from a five-man break ahead of Jimmy McGarry (Antrim), Cecil O'Donoghue (Dublin), J. Cullen (N.S.C.) and E. Dalton (Wicklow). Malachy Denny (Dublin) led in the chasers 3.05 behind.
A measure of Kerry's superiority was their team win by 28.24 from Dublin, even after allowing the Dubliners to claw back 14 minutes on the final stage. They won five stages, two each from Mangan and Fitzgerald as well as Moriarty's in Dublin.
John Keane's achievement of finishing second was all the more remarkable in that he had no backup, not even a team car, and that for the second half of the race he had absolutely no team support being the only member of the Exiles squad left in the race.

1956 Winner – Paudie Fitzgerald

**Stage 8 Clonmel - Dublin 112 Mls.** 1 P.Moriarty (Kerry) 4.49.05 2 J.McGarry (Antrim) s.t. 3 C.O'Donoghue (Dublin) s.t. 4 E.Dalton (Wicklow) s.t. 5 J.Cullen (N.S.C) s.t. 6 M.Denny (Dublin) at 3.05.
**General Classification:** 1 P.Fitzgerald (Kerry) 37.15.37 2 J.Keane (Exiles) at 7.33 3 P.O'Meara (Wicklow) at 14.08 4 G.Mangan (Kerry) at 15.59 5 C.O'Donoghue (Dublin) at 20.12 6 J.Gearon (Tipperary) at 23.45 7 D.O'Connor (Dublin) at 25.36 8 T.Flanagan (Meath) at 27.27 9 M.Mooney (Antrim) at 27.36 10 J.McGarry (Antrim) at 27.46.
**Team:** 1 Kerry (G.Mangan, P.Fitzgerald, P.O'Callaghan) 113.01.01 2 Dublin 113.18.19 3 Antrim 113.51.49 4 Tipperary 114.29.25.

# 1957

The 1957 RÁS was due to head north once again but the events of the previous year coupled with the outbreak of the IRA campaign in 1956 saw the race banned by the R.U.C. In the week preceding the race and a new route was hastily found for the opening stage which now became a big loop starting and finishing in Dublin.
Opening stages are generally fairly easy, but these 95 miles which included Sallygap must rank as one of the hardest opening days ever with a big climb coming in the first hour. A row over expenses saw Kerry deciding not to take part leaving the way open for Dublin who had finished behind them for the past two years.

## STAGE 1

It was Frank Ward of the Dublin team who won the opening stage and emphasing the expected Dublin supremacy he was followed home by teammate Archie Williams. Another Dublin rider Steve Abbott, the organiser of the 1957 race led in the chasers in 6th place to give Dublin first blood in the team race.
After the usual early skirmishes, the race started in earnest when they hit Sallygap after 23 miles. At this stage Archie Williams (Dublin), Billy Canning (Antrim) and John Gearon (Tipperary) had a 30 second lead on the bunch.
An early casualty was Pat O'Meara (Tipperary), third the year before who crashed at Bray and never got back into contention. It was a bad day for Tipperary as Gearon, who was in the break all day crashed with 8 miles to go. Cork were also in the wars when two of their riders Tom Scanlon and Pat Noonan crashed along with Dublin's Christy Dunne on the descent of Sallygap.
Frank Ward (Dublin), Ben McKenna (Meath) and Gerry Rea (Cork) made it up to the leaders leaving five at the front following Gearon's crash. These five finished 1.18 in front of the chasers led in by Steve Abbott (Dublin) from Frankie Thompson (Antrim).
**Stage 1 Dublin - Dublin 95 Mls.** 1 F.Ward (Dublin) 3.50.07 2 A.Williams (Dublin) s.t. 3 B.McKenna (Meath) s.t. 4 G.Rae (Cork) s.t. 5 W.Canning (Antrim) s.t. 6 S.Abbott (Dublin) at 1.18 7 F.Thompson (Antrim) s.t. 8 J.Lowth (Meath) s.t. 9 W.Heasley (Meath) s.t. 10 B.O'Brien (Kildare) s.t.

## STAGE 2

Ben McKenna, then an 18-year student riding for Meath, won his first RÁS stage on the 137 miles run from Dublin to Sligo, his first success in an astonishing RÁS career which included one outright win in 1959 and a record of consistent high finishes over the next two decades.

He won a tight sprint from Christy Dunne (Dublin), the pair finishing 1.45 ahead of a group of four led in by Gerry Keogh (Dublin). Kerry Sloan (Westmeath) was next home with the bunch led in by Steve Abbott (Dublin) a further 4 minutes back. This gave McKenna the yellow jersey by 30 seconds from Archie Williams (Dublin).
There was an early break of six riders including Jimmy McGarry (Antrim) who beat Bernie O'Brien (Kildare) for the prime at Kilcock. The leaders had 2.25 at Clonard with some riders joining the leaders and others dropping back.
On the climb of the Curlew Mountains McKenna and Dunne left the leaders. Antrim, who were mounting a strong team attack, lost McGarry with gear trouble with Seamus Doherty and Frank Thompson waiting for him. McGarrry could do nothing on the replacement machine and told the other two to chase on their own but they couldn't regain the leaders while the unfortunate McGarry finished last along with team-mate Dan McGurk.
**Stage 2 Dublin - Sligo 137 Mls.** 1 B.McKenna (Meath) 6.09.00 2 C.Dunne (Dublin) s.t. 3 G.Keogh (Dublin) at 1.45 4 B.O'Brien (Kildare) s.t. 5 G.Rea (Cork) s.t. 6 A.Williams (Dublin) s.t.
**General Classification:** 1 B.McKenna (Meath) 9.57.37 2 A.Williams (Dublin) at 30 secs 3 G.Rea (Cork) at 3.00 4 G.Keogh (Dublin) at 4.03 5 B.O'Brien (Kildare) at 4.15 6 M.Woods (Tipperary) at 4.53 7 F.Ward (Dublin) at 7.45 8 S.Abbott (Dublin) at 8.28 9 J.Lowth (Meath) at 9.18 10 W. Heasley (Meath) s.t.

## STAGE 3

Frank Ward (Dublin) who had lost the jersey the previous day, hit back on the 86 miles run from Sligo to Castlebar, winning his second stage and moving back up to 5th overall, 5.15 behind McKenna who retained the jersey, although with a much reduced margin of only 30 seconds over Dublin's Archie Williams.
The Curlew Mountains were again the catalyst being tackled in the opposite direction just after the start. A group of six went away early on including Ward and Williams along with Jimmy McGarry (Antrim), Alec Davis (Meath), Dick Barry (Cork) and E. Navagh (Meath), and these six were chased at 1 minute by Steve Abbot (Dublin), Frankie Thompson (Antrim), Bill Heasley (Meath) and Christy Dunne (Dublin).
By Castlerea the leaders had increased their lead to over 2 minutes while the chasers were back in the bunch. The break were working well and in no danger of being caught and Castlebar was reached well ahead of schedule, the 85 miles covered in just 3 and a half hours. In the sprint Ward beat McGarry with Williams just behind, the six all timed equal.
**Stage 3 Sligo - Castlebar 85 Mls.** 1 F.Ward (Dublin) 3.36.10 2 J.McGarry (Antrim) s.t. 3 A.Williams (Dublin) s.t. 4 A.Davis (Meath) s.t. 5 D.Barry (Cork) s.t. 6 E.Navagh (Meath) s.t.
**General Classification:** 1 B.McKenna (Meath) 13.37.17 2 A.Williams (Dublin) at 30 secs 3 G.Rea (Cork) at 3.45 4 G.Keogh (Dublin) at 4.03 5 F.Ward (Dublin) at

5.15 6 B.O'Brien (Kildare) at 5.18 7 W.Woods (Meath) at 5.33 8 W.Heasley (Meath) at 8.18 9 S.Abbott (Dublin) at 9.19 10 J.Lowth (Meath) s.t.

## STAGE 4

Jim Lowth, a 17-year-old apprentice fitter from Duleek won the 136 miles stage four from Castlebar to Nenagh, a ride that moved him up to sixth on GC. Ben McKenna, like so many yellow jersey holders, found himself a captive of the bunch and finished with them 11 minutes behind Lowth dropping to 8th behind the new leader Bernie O'Brien (Kildare) who had a 1.12 lead over Gerry Rea (Cork).

Second on the stage was Pat O'Meara (Tipperary) who spent a lot of effort early going off on a solo break before Tuam. He was out in front for 30 miles and when he took the prime at Moylough he was over 2 minutes in front.

A group of three went in pursuit and caught O'Meara 15 miles after Athlone. They were his Tipperary teammate Tom Whelan, Jim Lowth and Bernie O'Brien and these four had a 2.45 advantage at the finish over a group led in by Frank Ward ahead of Frankie Thompson.

**Stage 4 Castlebar - Nenagh 136 Mls.** 1 J.Lowth (Meath) 6.27.45 2 P.O'Meara (Tipperary) s.t. 3 B.O'Brien (Kildare) s.t. 4 T.Whelan (Tipperary s.t. 5 F.Ward (Dublin) at 2.15 6 F.Thompson (Antrim) s.t.

**General Classification:** 1 B.O'Brien (Kildare) 20.07.50 2 G.Rea (Cork) at 1.12 3 G.Keogh (Dublin) at 1.40 4 F.Ward (Dublin) at 2.42 5 M.Woods (Tipperary) at 3.00 6 J.Lowth (Meath) at 3.30 7 W.Hcasley (Meath) at 4.45 8 B.McKenna (Meath) at 8.10 9 T.Whelan (Tipperary) at 9.31 10 A.Williams (Dublin) at 9.47.

## STAGE 5

An incredible run of misfortune on the 112 miles stage to Tralee saw race leader Bernie O'Brien finish last while at the front Frank Ward (Dublin) won his third stage to regain the yellow jersey.

O'Brien's troubles began with a puncture. Team-mate Con Carr waited but the bunch was steaming ahead and by Rathluirc they were 11 minutes down in company of Kerry Sloan (Westmeath). Carr then punctured and O'Brien broke a gear cable his gear smashing his back wheel and Sloan towed him for 10 miles before a team car arrived.

At the front a large break of over 20 had split from the bunch and on the climb at Barna Gap six got away: Ward, Jimmy McGarry and Billy Canning (Antrim), Ben McKenna and Jim Lowth (Meath) and John Gearon (Tipperary) and these six had a 2 minute gap on the bunch at the finish.

**Stage 5 Nenagh - Tralee 113 Mls.** 1 F.Ward (Dublin) 4.43.38 2 J.McGarry (Antrim) s.t. 3 W.Canning (Antrim) s.t. 4 B.McKenna (Meath) s.t. 5 J.Lowth (Meath) s.t. 6 J.Gearon (Tipperary) s.t.

**General Classification:** 1 F.Ward (Dublin) 24.52.52 2 G.Rea (Cork) at 2.30 3 equal. J.Lowth (Meath) and G.Keogh (Dublin) at 1.48 5 M.Woods (Tipperary) at 3.18 6 W.Heasley (Meath) at 6.03 7 B.McKenna (Meath) at 6.20 8 J.Gearon (Tipperary) at 8.53 9 T.Whelan (Tipperary) at 9.49 10 A.Williams (Dublin) at 10.05.

## STAGE 6

Pat O'Meara (Tipperary) won the sixth stage to Clonakilty which saw some tough climbing. Frank Ward finished fifth, almost 6 minutes down, but retained the yellow jersey leading Gerry Rea (Cork) by 3.40, The 1 minute bonus for holding the jersey plus stage time bonuses stretching his lead.

O'Meara, Alec Davis (Meath) and Jimmy McGarry (Antrim) went away shortly after the start at Farranfore. At Killarney McGarry took the prime with the trio now 2.15 ahead. McGarry was again first at the KOM primes at Ladies View but had mechanical trouble and had to drop back.

O'Meara took the next KOM prime at The Tunnel to lead McGarry by a point in the mountains competition. The Antrim man then had a puncture and finished well down. The two leaders however stayed out in front all day and came home 2.20 ahead of a lone chasing rider Bill Heasley (Meath).

The next group, containing the yellow jersey finished 6.35 behind but although O'Meara moved up to 9th and Davis to 8th there were no changes in the top 7 on GC except that Heasley, although still in sixth place had cut his deficit on the leader by 4 minutes.

In the team race Meath had been steadily chipping away at Dublin's lead and the gap was now down to 43 seconds.

**Stage 6 Tralee - Clonakilty 109 Mls.** 1 P.O'Meara (Tipperary) 4.42.15 2 A.Davis (Meath) s.t. 3 W.Heasley (Meath) at 2.20 4 F.Thompson (Antrim) at 5.55 5 F.Ward (Dublin) s.t. 6 B.McKenna (Meath) s.t.

**General Classification:** 1 F.Ward (Dublin) 29.38.32 2 G.Rea (Cork) at 3.40 3 equal. J.Lowth (Meath) and G.Keogh (Dublin) at 3.58 5 M.Woods (Tipperary) at 4.18 6 W.Heasley (Meath) at 4.28 7 B.McKenna (Meath) at 8.20 8 A.Davis (Meath) at 8.04 9 P.O'Meara (Wicklow) at 10.43 10 J.Gearon (Tipperary) at 10.53 11 T.Whelan (Tipperary) at 11.49 12 A.Williams (Dublin) at 11.55.

## STAGE 7

Ben McKenna won the seventh stage coming home 5 seconds ahead of Gerry Keogh and the remainder of a 5-man break who along with Frank Starr (Dublin) had gone clear at Callan, 10 miles from the finish. Frank Ward who finished in the group retained the yellow jersey and led Gerry Keogh by 3.23.

The stage was run off in appalling conditions. A small group went away outside Cork: Ward, McKenna, Dan Noonan (Cork) and Frank Thompson (Antrim). Noonan

dropped back after a puncture but the other trio stayed out in front and at one stage were 6 minutes ahead.
However the bunch started chasing in earnest and the trio were caught at Callan when another break went away which again included Ward and McKenna along with Gerry Keogh, Jimmy McGarry (Antrim), and Alec Davis (Meath) and over the final 10 miles these five opened up a big gap of 3.05 on the bunch which was led in by John Gearon (Tipperary).
**Stage 7 Clonakilty - Kilkenny 108 Mls** 1 B.McKenna (Meath) 5.42.05 2 G.Keogh (Dublin) at 5 secs 3 A.Davis (Meath) s.t. 4 F.Ward (Dublin) s.t. 5 J.McGarry (Antrim) s.t. 6 J.Gearon (Tipperary) at 3.05.
**General Classification:** 1 F.Ward (Dublin) 35.19.27 2 G.Keogh (Dublin) at 3.23 3 B.McKenna (Meath) at 7.30 4 A.Davis (Meath) at 8.49 5 G.Rea (Cork) at 9.05 6 J.Lowth (Meath) at 9.23 7 M.Woods (Tipperary) at 10.53 8 W.Heasley (Meath) at 11.03 9 J.Gearon (Tipperary) at 14.13 10 P.O'Meara (Tipperary) at 14.18.

## STAGE 8

Antrim's Frank Thompson won the final stage, 100 miles from Kilkenny to Dublin but the major honours went to Dublin who took the individual with Frank Ward as well winning the team with Ward, Gerry Keogh and Archie Williams, who ended up 6 minutes ahead of the Meath trio of Ben McKenna, Alec Davis and Jim Lowth.
The animator of the final stage was Antrim's Jimmy McGarry who went off on his own. Having already tied up the King of the Mountains award he took the primes at Freshford and Monasterevan by which stage he was 1.25 in front, However his effort to win the stage came to nothing when he was captured near the finish setting the stage up for a big bunch sprint won by Thompson from Ward with Tom Whelan (Tipperary) third. Despite his solo effort McGarry had enough left to finish sixth in the sprint.
**Stage 8 Kilkenny - Dublin 100 Mls.** 1 F.Thompson (Antrim) 4.44.15 2 F.Ward (Dublin) s.t. 3 T.Whelan (Tipperary) s.t. 4 C.Dunne (Dublin) s.t. 5 R.Roe (Dublin) s.t. 6 J.McGarry (Antrim) s.t.

*Frank Ward 1957 Winner*

**General Classification:** 1 F.Ward (Dublin) 40.00.57 2 G.Keogh (Dublin) at 5.03 3 B.McKenna (Meath) at 9.15 4 A.Davis (Meath) at 10.34 5 G.Rea (Cork) at 10.34 6 J.Lowth (Meath) at 11.08 7 M.Woods (Tipperary) at 12.38 8 W.Heasley (Meath) at 12.48 9 J.Gearon (Tipperary) at 15.58 10 T.Whelan (Tipperary) at 18.39 11 A.Williams (Dublin) at 19.55 12 F.Thompson (Antrim) at 24.23.
**Team:** 1 Dublin (F.Ward, G.Keogh, A.Williams) 120.27.49 2 Meath (B.McKenna, A.Davis, J.Lowth) 120.33.48 3 Tipperary (M.Woods, J.Gearon, T.Whelan) 120.50.06; 4 Antrim (Thompson, Canning, Doherty) 121.46.02 5 Cork (Rae, Hickey, Scanlon) 122.41.27.
**King of the Mountains:** J.McGarry (Antrim).

## 1958

It was back to going round Ireland in a clockwise direction which has always been the more usual. In total there have only been eight run clockwise.
After staying out of the 1957 RÁS Kerry were back with a vengeance and led the general classification from the start. They also won six of the eight stages.
Kerry rider Gene Mangan went into the event the hottest of all favourites, having been virtually unbeatable throughout the season. As is often the way with such favourites everything didn't go to plan but he certainly left his mark on the 1958 RÁS.

### STAGE 1

It was first blood to Kerry when Dan Ahern, an 18-year-old farmer from Farranfore won the opening stage from Dublin to Wexford winning in a sprint from a 9-man group ahead of Steve Abbott (Dublin) and Eamon Ryan (Kildare).
Pre-race favourite Gene Mangan led in the chasers 30 seconds in arrears. Making his first appearance in the RÁS Results was Paddy Flanagan of Kildare, who was to write quite a few chapters in the history of the event over the next two decades.
It was a fairly uneventful stage with the field, apart from some unsuccessful breakaway attempts, staying together until Ferns when the winning 9-man move went away.
Con Kenneally noted in the Independent that the Kerry team, apart from Mangan and Pat Callaghan, were very inexperienced and not strongly fancied before the event. However with Mick Murphy finishing 8th, they now had three in the top ten and for the first time led the team race on the opening day.
**Stage 1 Dublin - Wexford 90 Mls.** 1 D.Ahern (Kerry) 4.01.00 2 S.Abbott (Dublin) 3 E.Ryan (Kildare) 4 T.Flanagan (Meath) 5 M.Denny (Dublin) 6 P.Flanagan (Kildare) 7 T.Ryan (Tipperary 8 M. Murphy (Kerry) 9 S.Walsh (Tipperary) all same time 10 G.Mangan (Kerry) at 30 secs.

### STAGE 2

Ahern had a disastrous day on the 117 miles stage to Kilkenny coming in almost 20 minutes behind with the main bunch which also included Steve Abbott. Kerry lost the team lead to Dublin but they kept the yellow jersey which moved onto the shoulders of Mick Murphy, a 25-year-old from Cahirciveen who had only taken up the sport the previous year.

Murphy came home on his own, 50 seconds ahead of Ben McKenna (Meath) after he had broken away on the bridge at Carrick-on-Suir and riding strongly all the way to the finish in Kilkenny.
Murphy was in the first break of importance which went away before New Ross along with Pat O'Meara (Tipperary) and Antrim pair Jimmy McGarry and Cormac McLynn. These four were chased and joined by Gene Mangan (Kerry), Tom Kiely, Tom Ryan and Sean Walsh (Tipperary), Ben McKenna (Meath) and Malachy Denny (Dublin).
Murphy and O'Meara broke away in Carrick but the Tipperary man soon dropped back as Murphy powered over the KOM prime at Glenbower where he was 2 minutes ahead of another Tipperary man Tom Kiely.
He too dropped back and went away to take second place with Mangan winning the sprint from the seven survivors a further 1.48 behind.
**Stage 2 Wexford - Kilkenny 117 Mls.** 1 M.Murphy (Kerry) 6.02.50 2 B.McKenna (Meath) at 50 secs 3 G.Mangan (Kerry) at 2.38 4 T.Ryan (Tipperary) 5 T.Kiely (Tipperary) 6 P.Flanagan (Kildare) all same time.
**General Classification:** 1 M.Murphy (Kerry) 10.02.50 2 B.McKenna (Meath) at 2.05 3 T.Ryan (Tipperary) at 3.23 4 equal P.Flanagan (Kildare) and G.Mangan (Kerry) at 3.58 6 T.Kiely (Tipperary) at 4.08 7 equal J.McGarry (Antrim) and R.Williams (Dublin) at 4.38 9 C.O'Reilly (Dublin) at 6.00.

## STAGE 3

The 125 miles stage from Kilkenny to Clonakilty was one of those which add to the list of RÁS legends, crammed with the sort of incidents by which races are won or lost.
The hot favourite Gene Mangan lost over 30 minutes after two punctures and a crash in Cork City where the race met the tea-time traffic resulting in chaos.
Another crash victim in Cork was the Irish senior massed-start champion Cahal O'Reilly (Dublin) riding his first RÁS. His bike was wrecked but team-mate Archie Williams gave over his machine and O'Reilly caught the leaders and went on to win the stage in a sprint from a 10-man break.
Race leader Mick Murphy was also in the wars. He was up with the leaders approaching Cork at Glanmire when he punctured with his team car up the road. He threw his bike in the ditch and grabbed an 'ancient-looking machine from a generous onlooker' and set off in pursuit although the saddle was about 6 inches too high for the diminutive Kerryman.
Outside Cork he got a more suitable machine from a team-mate and rode through a stream of stragglers to rejoin the leaders and he finished in the same time as O'Reilly to keep the jersey. Behind the 10-man break, Steve Abbott led in a chasing group 2.20 down.

**Stage 3 Kilkenny - Clonakilty 125 Mls.** 1 C.O'Reilly (Dublin) 5.32.25 2 J.McGarry (Antrim) 3 P.Flanagan (Kildare) 4 T.Ryan (Tipperary) 5 C.McLynn (Antrim) 6 S.Murphy (Dublin) all same time.
**General Classification:** 1 M.Murphy (Kerry) 15.35.15 2 J.McGarry (Antrim) at 2.53 3 P.Flanagan (Kildare) at 3.08 4 T.Ryan (Tipperary) at 3.08 5 M.Denny (Dublin) at 3.38 6 T.Kiely (Tipperary) at 4.08 7 B.McKenna (Meath) at 4.25 8 C.O'Reilly (Dublin) at 6.00 9 R.Williams (Dublin) at 6.58 10 S.Murphy (Dublin) at 8.00.

## STAGE 4

Coalisland man Seamus Devlin (Tyrone) came home on his own to win the 106 miles fourth stage to Tralee, 1.23 ahead of Jack Courtney (Meath) with Gene Mangan winning a sprint over old rival Steve Abbott (Dublin) for third, reversing the placings of their last sprint into Tralee when Abbott won the stage.
Mangan was the hero of the stage for the Kerrymen for he had given his bike to race-leader Murphy when the latter crashed coming into Glenariffe. Mangan had to wait six minutes for a spare and his recovery to finish third was remarkable. Murphy finished in the group led in by Mangan and retained his race lead.
Most of the leaders were in the Mangan/Murphy group the only real change in the top ten being Devlin's move to 10th and Jimmy McGarry dropped to 5th, Tom Ryan moving up a place to lie second, 3.08 behind Murphy. Dublin was back in the lead in the team race. They had been placed behind Tipperary the previous day but this was found to be an error.
(Note: As McGarry was credited with the same time as Ryan, one can only assume that he incurred some penalty of 2 minutes which dropped him down 2 places. Unfortunately Jimmy died of a stroke during the 1997 RÁS and I was unable to check this with him).
**Stage 4 Clonakilty - Tralee 106 Mls.** 1 S.Devlin (Tyrone) 4.51.30 2 J.Courtney (Meath) at 1.23 3 G.Mangan (Kerry) at 2.40 4 S.Abbott (Dublin) 5 T.Ryan (Tipperary) 6 J.McGarry (Antrim) all same time.
**General Classification:** 1 M.Murphy (Kerry) 20.28.25 2 T.Ryan (Tipperary) at 3.08 3 P.Flanagan (Kildare) at 4.08 4 M.Denny (Dublin) at 4.38 5 J.McGarry (Antrim) at 4.53 6 T.Kiely (Tipperary) at 5.08 7 B.McKenna (Meath) at 5.25 8 C.O'Reilly (Dublin) at 6.00 9 R.Williams (Dublin) at 7.58 10 S.Devlin (Tyrone) at 8.05.

## STAGE 5

Gene Mangan (Kerry) who had won the stage into Nenagh two years previous, and had taken the Irish senior road race title there also, completed a Tipperary treble by winning the 111 miles fifth stage from Tralee.
Having lost all hope of the overall title Mangan had now two aims. 1 To help team-mate Mick Murphy to keep the yellow jersey, and 2 to pick up as many stages as he could as a consolation prize.

There were 41 riders left in the race and they took it fairly steady for the first half of the stage. The only break of the day involved six riders: Mangan, Paddy Flanagan (Kildare) and Ben McKenna (Meath), Cahal O'Reilly and Ronnie Williams (Dublin), and Tom Kiely (Tipperary).
Mangan and McKenna attacked near Limerick and when Flanagan fought his way back, the other three dropped back to the bunch. At the finish Mangan powered away to beat the other two by 5 seconds.
Race leader Murphy rode heavily strapped after an X-ray disclosed that his accident at Glengariffe the previous day had dislocated his shoulder. He was already being dubbed the 'iron man'.
**Stage 5 Tralee - Nenagh 111 Mls.** 1 G.Mangan (Kerry) 4.39.5 2 P.Flanagan (Kildare) at 5 secs 3 B.McKenna (Meath) s.t. 4 S.Abbott (Dublin) at 1.10 5 equal T.Ryan (Tipperary) and J.McGarry (Antrim) at 1.15.
**General Classification:** 1 M.Murphy (Kerry) 25.08.05 2 P.Flanagan (Kildare) at 3.38 3 T.Ryan (Tipperary) at 4.33 4 B.McKenna (Meath) at 5.10 5 M.Denny (Dublin) at 6.03 6 J.McGarry (Antrim) at 6.18 7 T.Kiely (Tipperary) at 6.33 8 C.O'Reilly (Dublin) at 7.25 9 R.Williams (Dublin) at 9.23 10 S.Devlin (Tyrone) at 9.30.

## STAGE 6

Gene Mangan won his second stage, the very long 139 miles from Nenagh to Castlebar outsprinting a 3-man group, 1.07 ahead of the chasers. However the Kerryman was still only 17th overall, over half-an-hour behind his team mate Mick Murphy.
The original break which went away at Ballyforan, after Athlone, had five riders, Mangan, Eamon Ryan (Kildare), Cahal O'Reilly (Dublin), Ben McKenna (Meath) and the race-leader Murphy.
Coming into Tuam Ryan went off on his own and going through the town he had a 1.5 minutes lead on Mangan and O'Reilly who were in pursuit. The three eventually came together and stayed away to the finish where Mangan's great sprint gave him victory by 8 seconds over Ryan with O'Reilly a further 4 behind.
Behind them came two chasers, Jack Courtney (Meath) and yellow jersey Murphy while Steve Abbott led in the bunch a further 10 seconds in arrears. The main changes in the top ten were the retirale of Jimmy McGarry who had knee trouble and Paddy Flanagan Kildare) who finished well down and dropped from 2nd to 12th.
**Stage 6 Nenagh - Castlebar 139 Mls.** 1 G.Mangan (Kerry) 5.47.00 2 E.Ryan (Kildare) at 8 secs 3 C.O'Reilly (Dublin) at 12 secs 4 J.Courtney (Meath) at 1.07 5 M.Murphy (Kerry) at 1.08 6 S.Abbott at 1.17.
**General Classification:** 1 M.Murphy (Kerry) 30.56.25 2 T.Ryan (Tipperary) at 5.43 3 C.O'Reilly (Dublin) at 5.47 4 B.McKenna (Meath) at 6.20 5 M.Denny (Dublin) at 7.12 6 T.Kiely (Tipperary) at 7.32 7 E.Ryan (Kildare) at 10.22 8 R.Williams (Dublin) at 10.32 9 S.Devlin (Tyrone) at 10.40 10 M.Creighton (Bective) at 13.35.

## STAGE 7

Mangan continued his run of success by winning the relatively short 80 miles stage from Castlebar to Sligo. There was little change on GC with leader Murphy, still riding with heavy strapping for his dislocated shoulder, surviving another fall, this time at Castlerea but fortunately he did not further damage the shoulder.
The race leader was in an early break which came to nothing and it was on the climb of the Curlews that Mangan and Tyrone's Seamus Devlin went away, the two finishing 31 seconds in front at Sligo where Mangan won by a second from the Coalisland man who moved from 9th to 4th overall.
**Stage 7 Castlebar - Sligo 100 Mls.** 1 G.Mangan (Kerry) 3.37.10 2 S.Devlin (Tyrone) s.t. 3 S.Murphy (Dublin) at 30 secs 4 S.Abbott (Dublin) 5 T.Ryan (Tipperary) 6 B.McKenna (Meath) all same time.
**General Classification:** 1 M.Murphy (Kerry) 34.36.35 2 T.Ryan (Tipperary) at 3.37 3 B.McKenna (Meath) at 4.14 4 S.Devlin (Tyrone) at 6.56 5 C.O'Reilly (Dublin) at 7.07 6 M.Denny (Dublin) at 8.13 7 R.Williams (Dublin) at 8.27 8 T.Kiely (Tipperary) at 9.03 9 M.Creighton (Bective) at 11.29 10 D.Ryan (Kildare) at 11.43.

## STAGE 8

Gene Mangan made it 4-in-a-row on the final stage from Sligo to Dublin's Phoenix Park (133 miles) but it was his team mate Mick Murphy who took the race 4.44 ahead of Meath's Ben McKenna. Mangan's incredible run of four stages failed to get him into the top ten, he finished 12th.
Ben McKenna made his move to snatch the race from Murphy shortly after the start and by Boyle McKenna and team mate Willie Heasley were 2 minutes ahead of the bunch containing the yellow jersey.
Mangan and Murphy then went in pursuit along with Cormac McLynn (Antrim) and after a 25-mile chase the two Kerrymen caught the two Meathmen. With Mangan in superb sprinting form there wasn't much doubt as to the stage win. At the finish the quartet had 44 seconds over Dublin pair Steve Abbott and Cahal O'Reilly.
Dublin won the team race by the narrow margin of 1.07 over Tipperary with Kerry third.
**Stage 8 Sligo - Dublin 133 Mls.** 1 G.Mangan (Kerry) 6.12.15 2 B.McKenna (Meath) 3 W.Heasley (Meath) 4 M.Murphy (Kerry) all same time 5 S.Abbott (Dublin) at 44 secs 6 C.O'Reilly (Dublin) s.t.
**General Classification:** 1 M.Murphy (Kerry) 40.47.35 2 B.McKenna (Meath) at 4.44 3 C.O'Reilly (Dublin) at 9.06 4 T.Kiely (Tipperary) at 11.03 5 T.Ryan (Tipperary) at 12.17 6 E.Ryan (Kildare) at 13.43 7 M.Denny (Dublin) at 16.53 8 R.Williams (Dublin) at 19.36 9 S.Devlin (Tyrone) at 20.11 10 P.O'Meara (Tipperary) at 23.23.

**Team:** 1 Dublin (M.Denny, C.O'Reilly, R.Williams) 123.08.20 2 Tipperary (T.Kiely, T.Ryan, P.O'Meara) 123.09.27 3 Kerry (Murphy, Mangan, Lacy) 123.21.22.

*Mick Murphy – 1958 winner*

## 1959

### STAGE 1

The 1959 RÁS once more went anti-clockwise round the country with the opening stage from Dublin to Dundalk, the 104 miles taking in a route through Navan, Trim, Kells and Ardee and it was first blood to Dublin when Cecil O'Donoghue came home on his own, 45 seconds ahead of Gerry Meehan (Antrim).
Meehan led in a chasing group of five which included two more Dublin riders: Denis McGrath and Shay Murphy giving Dublin an immediate lead in the team race. Antrim's Frankie Thompson was also in this group giving the young Antrim team second place.
The previous year's winner Mick Murphy of Kerry was a big loser when his tyre blew out shortly after the start and he ended up in the ditch. He finished last on the stage almost an hour down.
O'Donoghue was in a four man break with Meehan, McGrath and Thompson which had a minute in hand at Ardee. Gerry Keogh (Meath) and Shay Murphy (Dublin) joined the leaders but with 18 miles to go O'Donoghue attacked and stayed out in front to the finish.
Among those who had bad luck on the stage was Ray Kennedy who had gear trouble in the neutralised section before the start proper at Ashtown. It was the first mention in RÁS despatches of Ray who in later years would become the race's resident announcer and the man who coined a phrase always associated with the event when he would exhort the crowd at stage finishes to applaud 'the men of the RÁS '
**Stage 1 Dublin - Dundalk 104 Mls.** 1 C.O'Donoghue (Dublin) 4.22.32 2 G.Meehan (Antrim) at 45 secs 3 G.Keogh (Meath) 4 D.McGrath (Dublin) 5 F.Thompson (Antrim) 6 S.Murphy (Dublin) all same time.

### STAGE 2

Mick Palmer (Mayo), third overall in 1954 and 1955, won the second stage, 134 miles from Dundalk to Longford and took over the yellow jersey by 25 seconds from O'Donoghue. On the opening stage Palmer had gone off course 18 miles from the finish but had recovered to come in with the main bunch.
The Mayo man had spent much of the stage in the main bunch but when it caught the break 16 miles from the finish, he broke away with another first stage casualty, Mick Murphy, and the two finished 2.15 ahead of the chasing group which contained the race leader.
O'Donoghue had tried to defend his lead by going on the attack and for 30 miles he was away with Frank Thompson, Ben McKenna (Meath), Mick O'Hare (Cork) and

Paddy Doyle (Kildare) before they were caught just as Palmer made his winning move.
**Stage 2 Dundalk - Longford 134 Mls.** 1 M.Palmer (Mayo) 5.55.40 2 M.Murphy (Kerry) s.t. 3 C.Dunne (Exiles) at 2.15 4 E.Lacy (Kerry) 5 M.O'Hare (Cork) 6 P.Flanagan (Kildare) all same time.
**General Classification:** 1 M.Palmer (Mayo) 10.19.12 2 C.O'Donoghue (Dublin) at 25 secs 3 F.Thompson (Antrim) at 50 secs 4 S.Murphy (Dublin) s.t. 5 G.Meehan (Antrim) at 1.15 6 R.Williams (Dublin) at 2.00.

## STAGE 3

Mick Murphy (Kerry) had lost any hope of a RÁS double when he lost an hour on the opening stage but he made his mark on the race as he followed up his second place on Sunday with a stage win into Westport at the end of the 120 miles stage from Longford.
The Kerryman accomplished his stage win on a bike which he had borrowed from the Antrim team as his own had become unusable following his adventures on the opening stages.
Gerry Meehan (Antrim) who finished in a group 45 seconds behind Murphy took over the lead with a slender 5 second advantage over Paddy Flanagan (Kildare).
Cecil O'Donoghue and Frank Thompson for the third day went on the offensive and at Castlebar had a minute's advantage over a group of 15 including Murphy. When they came together on a climb a few miles later Murphy made his move and opened up a 45 second gap in the final 10 miles over a group of four containing Meehan who took over the jersey.
The race was blown apart riders coming in over an hour down. Overnight race leader Mick Palmer lost 10 minutes and dropped out of contention.
**Stage 3 Longford - Westport 120 Mls.** 1 M.Murphy (Kerry) 5.50.00 2 P.Flanagan (Kildare) at 45 secs 3 B.McKenna (Meath) 4 D. Ahern (Kerry) 5 G.Meehan (Antrim) all same time 6 F.Thompson (Antrim) at 1.00.
**General Classification:** 1 G.Meehan (Antrim) 16.11.12 2 P.Flanagan (Kildare) at 5 secs 3 D.Ahern (Kerry) at 35 secs 4 F.Thompson (Antrim) at 50 secs 5 B.McKenna (Meath) at 1.30 6 C.O'Donoghue (Dublin) at 1.40 7 R.Williams (Dublin) at 2.10 8 S.Murphy (Dublin) at 3.00.

## STAGE 4

For the fourth day the lead changed, although this time it stayed with the same team, Antrim's Frankie Thompson taking the jersey from Gerry Meehan who dropped to 5th. Mick Palmer (Mayo) who had already had a stage win and a second place, took his second stage in a sprint from a 5-man group which finished 1.34 ahead at the finish in Ennis.

It was an epic break as the five: Palmer, Thompson, Shay O Hanlon (Dublin), Ben McKenna (Meath), and Shay Murphy (Dublin) had broken away shortly after the start of the 134 miles stage from Westport on the climb at Leenane. They came in ahead of a 16-man group who were two minutes down.
The stage noted the first appearance in the RÁS results of Shay O Hanlon, who would go on to win the event four times, win 24 stages, and in a remarkable run be the only rider in the three years between 1965 and 1967 to wear the leader's yellow jersey, leading all three events from start to finish.
Two riders: Dan Ahern (Kerry) and Ronnie Williams (Dublin) got away from the chasing group to take the 6th and 7th places, 1.34 behind the winning quintet after closing to within 20 seconds as one stage before dropping back.
**Stage 4 Westport - Ennis 134 Mls.** 1 M.Palmer (Mayo) 6.20.00 2 B.McKenna (Meath) 3 S.O Hanlon (Dublin) 4 F.Thompson (Antrim) 5 S.Murphy (Dublin) all same time 6 D. Ahern (Kerry) at 1.34.
**General Classification:** 1 F.Thompson (Antrim) 22.31.47 2 B.McKenna (Meath) at 10 secs 3 D.Ahern (Kerry) at 1.34 4 S.Murphy (Dublin) at 2.25 5 R.Williams (Dublin) at 3.09 6 G.Meehan (Antrim) at 4.35 7 P.Flanagan (Kildare) at 4.40 8 C.O'Donoghue (Dublin) at 6.05 9 M.Palmer (Mayo) at 7.10 10 T.Finn (Dublin) at 8.02.

## STAGE 5

Meath's Ben McKenna, who had been steadily moving up the classification, made his move on the 110 miles fifth stage from Ennis to Tralee and won the stage to take over the lead with the best margin of the week to date, 2.43 ahead of Dublin's Shay Murphy.
He won from a four-man group including Dublin pair Ronnie Williams and Shay Murphy and Tipperary's John Gearon. They were 45 seconds clear of a 10-man group led in by Cecil O'Donoghue (Dublin) from Dan Ahern (Kerry).
The leading two groups at the finish had been in the main move of the day of 14 riders which were clear of the field at Rathluirc. However it wasn't until the long drag after Newcastlewest the four broke away.
Overnight leader Frank Thompson was a prisoner of the bunch and dropped to 7th overall, just ahead of team mate Gerry Meehan. The big improvers apart from McKenna were Murphy and Williams who moved to 2nd and 4th, Ahern holding on to third.
**Stage 5 Ennis - Tralee 110 Mls** 1 B.McKenna (Meath) 4.44.35 2 J.Gearon (Tipperary) 3 S.Murphy (Dublin) 4 R.Williams (Dublin) all same time 5 C.O'Donoghue at 45 secs 6 D.Ahern (Kerry) s.t.
**General Classification:** 1 B.McKenna (Meath) 27.15.32 2 S.Murphy (Dublin)at 2.43 3 D.Ahern (Kerry) at 4.09 4 R.Williams (Dublin) at 4.44 5 P.Flanagan (Kildare) at 6.05 6 C.O'Donoghue (Dublin) at 7.40 7 F.Thompson (Antrim) at 9.00 8

G.Meehan (Antrim) at 11.05 9 M.Palmer (Mayo) at 13.50 10 T.Finn (Dublin) at 14.42.

## STAGE 6

There was little change on the 120 miles sixth stage from Tralee to Fermoy, Dermot Byrne (Wexford) slipping away from the whole field five miles from the finish to come home 20 seconds ahead of the bunch led in by Jim Ludden (Dublin).
The race leader crashed just as Byrne made his move and although he remounted he lost 1.30 over the final five miles and he was taken to hospital for abrasions. Although he kept the jersey his lead over Shay Murphy was cut to 1.35.
Another casualty was ex-race leader Frank Thompson who had been lying 7th overnight who had to retire from the race with a pulled muscle. Surprisingly for a long stage which included the climbs at Ladies View and Molls Gap early on, the field stayed together and apart from Thompson dropping out there was little change in the general classification.
**Stage 6 Tralee - Fermoy 130 Mls.** 1 D.Byrne (Wexford) 5.40.00 2 J. Ludden (Dublin) at 20 secs 3 M.O'Hare (Cork) 4 A.Cabal (Kerry) 5 G.Keogh (Dublin) all same time.
**General Classification:** 1 B.McKenna (Meath) 32.57.02 2 S.Murphy (Dublin) at 1.35 3 D.Ahern (Kerry) at 1.59 4 R.Williams (Dublin) at 2.32 5 P.Flanagan (Kildare) at 4.55 6 C.O'Donoghue (Dublin) at 6.30 7 G.Meehan (Antrim) at 9.55 8 M.Palmer (Mayo) at 12.40 9 P.O'Meara (Wicklow) at 19.50 10 T.Finn (Dublin) at 20.57.

## STAGE 7

Ronnie Williams finished 4th on the 100 miles stage from Fermoy to Waterford behind Belfastman Cormac McLynn (Antrim) and moved up to second overall, gaining 1.30 on leader McKenna and moving to within 1 second of the lead. That second was vital to McKenna as he received 1 minute bonus for retaining the jersey and went into the final stage with 1.01 in hand.
McKenna, despite nursing his injuries led the chase of the break which had been started by Mick Murphy (Kerry) and Eamon Ryan (Clare) but with other riders joining the leaders this leading group grew to 16 strong.
Williams was the only danger man with the leaders but the Meath man led the chase to limit his losses and went into the final stage in yellow. However with two Dublin riders within 3 minutes, his hold on the jersey was anything but secure.
**Stage 7 Fermoy - Waterford 100 Mls.** 1 C.McLynn (Antrim) 4.16.10 2 T.Whelan (Tipperary) 3 C.Dunne (Exiles) 4 R.Williams (Dublin) 5 P.O'Callaghan (Waterford) 5 P.Flanagan (Kildare) all same time.
**General Classification:** 1 B.McKenna (Meath) 37.16.30 2 R.Williams (Dublin) at 1 sec. 3 S.Murphy (Dublin) at 2.45 4 P.Flanagan (Kildare) at 2.37 5 D.Ahern (Kerry) at 2.59 6 C.O'Donoghue (Dublin) at 7.30 7 G.Meehan (Antrim) at 10.55 8 M.Palmer

(Mayo) at 13.40 9 P.O'Callaghan (Waterford) at 19.12 10 B.Atkinson (Cork) at 20.37.

## STAGE 8

The heavily bandaged Ben McKenna survived a tough 120 miles final stage from Waterford to Dublin which took in the climb of the Wicklow Gap to emerge victorious in Dublin with a margin of 61 seconds, by far the smallest in the history of the race to date.

Although it was close at the top with the possibility of a last stage upset, the top men of GC were closely watching each other with little change of any of them getting away. As a result when a break of seven went clear, with no danger men included, they were let go and by Gorey they had seven minutes in hand with little chance of being caught.

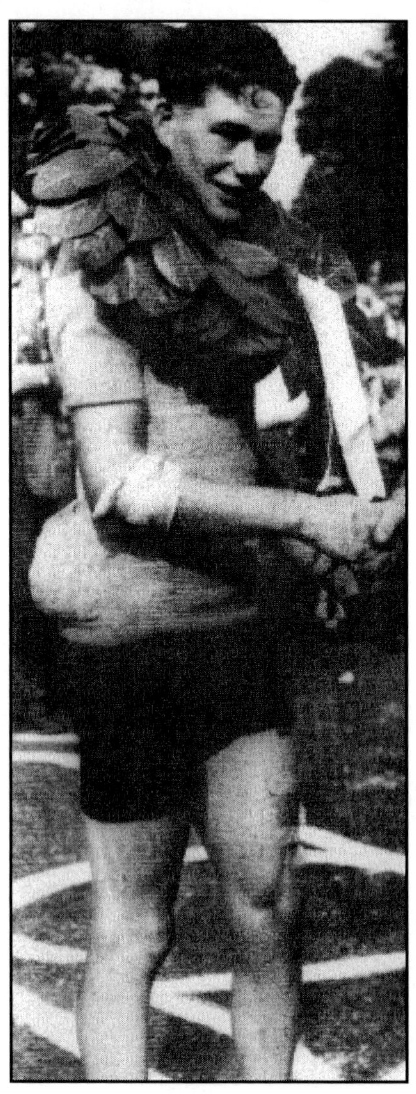

*Ben McKenna, 1959*

On the climb of the Wicklow Gap Mick Murphy, went away. He was chased by Shay O Hanlon who joined him on the descent and the two stayed away to the finish where Murphy took his second stage from the young Dubliner with Gerry Keogh next, 1.06 behind. Two stage wins were some consolation for the 1958 winner after misfortune cost him over two hours in lost time early in the week.

**Stage 8 Waterford - Dublin 120 Mls.** 1 M.Murphy (Kerry) 6.02.30 2 S.O Hanlon (Dublin) at 5 secs 3 G.Keogh (Dublin) at 1.06 4 P.McCormack (Kildare) at 50 secs 5 M.Palmer (Mayo) at 1.20 6 C.O'Donoghue (Dublin) s.t.

**General Classification:** 1 B.McKenna (Meath) 43.12.27 2 R.Williams (Dublin) at 1.01 3 S.Murphy (Dublin) at 3.35 4 P.Flanagan (Kildare) at 3.37 5 D.Ahern (Kerry) at 3.59 6 C.O'Donoghue (Dublin) at 7.40 7 G.Meehan (Antrim) at 11.55 8 M.Palmer (Mayo) at 14.40 9 P.O'Callaghan (Waterford) at 20.12 10 M.Logan (Kildare) at 24.26.

**Team:** 1 Dublin (R.Williams, S.Murphy, S.O Hanlon, C.O'Donoghue) 174.12.18 2 Kildare 175.02.09 3 Meath 175.02.09.

## 1960

### STAGE 1

Torrential rain marked the opening stage of the 1960 RÁS, 92 miles from Dublin to Cavan which was won by 19-year-old Dan Ahern (Kerry) in a sprint from an 11-man group. Shay O Hanlon (Dublin), whose performances during the season saw him start the event as many people's favourite, finished where he had in the final stage a year before, in second place.

The field of 81 stayed together early, the only action at the primes, Eddie McGrath (Antrim) winning at Navan and O Hanlon at Kells. After Kells 11 riders went away, Dublin well represented with O Hanlon, Shay Murphy and the McGrath brothers Denis and Dermot. Kerry had two: Ahern and Mick Murphy, Kildare two: Murt Logan and Eric Ryan; Meath two: Mick Collins and Machlin Gaffney and the 11 were completed by Noel Waddy (Cork).

This group got a lead of over 1 minute but the bunch weren't going to let a big gap open and at the finish the 11 were just 1.07 up on the main group.

**Stage 1 Dublin - Cavan 92 Mls.** 1 D.Ahern (Kerry) 3.22.00 2 S.O Hanlon (Dublin) 3 M.Gaffney (Meath) 4 S.Murphy (Dublin) 5 M.Collins (Meath) 6 Dermot.McGrath (Dublin) 7 Denis.McGrath (Dublin) 8 M.Murphy (Kerry) 9 M.Logan (Kildare) 10 E.Ryan (Kildare) 11 N.Waddy (Cork) all same time.

### STAGE 2

Paddy Flanagan (Kildare) won the second stage, 109 miles from Cavan to Castlebar and took over at the top of the General Classification by 14 seconds from Dundalk man Paddy Neary (Louth) who had also been second on the stage, the two finishing 1.25 ahead of the main bunch, led in by Machlin Gaffney (Meath).

Flanagan didn't make his winning move until about 25 miles from the finish when he, Neary and Patsy Wall went away. Coming through Swinford the trio were 45 seconds ahead of a small group which was in turn 1.15 ahead of the main bunch.

Wall was dropped by the other two who found the gates of a level crossing closed as they came into the finish town of Castlebar. They climbed over the gates and remounted going on to contest the sprint.

**Stage 2 Cavan - Castlebar 109 Mls.** 1 P.Flanagan (Kildare) 5.04.00 2 P.Neary (Louth) s.t. 3 M.Gaffney (Meath) at 1.25 4 M.Logan (Kildare) 5 M.Christle (Dublin) 6 W.Heasley (Meath) all same time.

**General Classification:** 1 P.Flanagan (Kildare) 8.26.07 2 P.Neary (Louth) at 14 secs 3 M.Gaffney (Meath) at 17 secs 4 S.Murphy (Dublin) at 1.03 5 M.Logan (Kildare) s.t. 6 Denis.McGrath (Dublin) at 1.18 7 M.Collins (Meath) s.t. 8 Dermot.McGrath (Dublin) s.t. 9 D Ahern (Kerry) at 2.09 10 S.O Hanlon Dublin) at 2.24.

## STAGE 3

Shay O Hanlon (Dublin) won the first of his 24 RÁS stages after the 110 miles stage from Castlebar to Tuam out sprinting Eddie Flanagan (Kildare). Forty-three seconds later race leader Paddy Flanagan came in with the remains of the break to retain his yellow jersey.

It was an epic ride for the Dubliner who, after three punctures, was over three minutes behind the leaders at one stage. Four riders: Dan Ahern, Dave Kenny (Exiles), Eamon Kelly (Dublin) and Dave O'Regan (Cork) were out in front for over 100 miles.

O Hanlon went in pursuit at Maam Cross and caught and left a chasing group of 20 including Paddy Flanagan and his brother Eddie as well as Mick Murphy. He caught the three leaders at Oughterard. The Flanagan's joined the leaders after Galway but O Hanlon attacked again taking with him Eddie Flanagan, whose earlier great riding had done much to save Paddy's yellow jersey bring him up to the leaders.

In the team race Dublin had 3 minutes in hand over Kildare with Meath almost 2 minutes further back.

**Stage 3 Castlebar - Tuam 110 Mls.** 1 S.O Hanlon (Dublin) 4.25.00 2 E.Flanagan (Kildare) s.t. 3 S.Dillon (Dublin) at 43 secs 4 P.Flanagan (Kildare) 5 D.Ahern (Kerry) all same time.

**General Classification:** 1 P.Flanagan (Kildare) 12.51.35 2 S.O Hanlon (Dublin) at 56 secs 3 S.Dillon (Dublin) at 2.10 4 P.Neary (Louth) at 2.18 5 D.Ahern (Kerry) at 2.24 6 M.Gaffney (Meath) at 2.54 7 E.Flanagan (Kildare) at 3.03 8 Denis.McGrath (Dublin) at 3.21 9 N.Waddy (Cork) at 3.24 10 S.Murphy (Dublin) at 3.40.

## STAGE 4

Dan Ahern took his second stage, 98 miles from Tuam to Thurles and moved up to second overall, although still 1.08 behind Flanagan and with the 1 minute bonus for holding the yellow jersey, the Kildare man had 2.08 in hand at the start of the fifth stage.

Dave Kenny (Exiles), who had been in a 100-mile break the previous day and Jim Lowth (Meath) went away shortly after the start and stayed out in front for over 60 miles and at Ballinasloe, after 40 miles, they were 1.25 ahead of a chasing group of 13 which was a minute clear of the main field.

However 20 miles further on at Borrisokane, the two were caught by the chasing group which included O Hanlon, Ahern and Flanagan. Ahern, Shay Murphy (Dublin), Liam Baxter (Kildare), Frank O'Rourke (Wexford) and Pat Cleary (Tipperary) broke away from the leaders who were caught by the main bunch while the five stayed away to the finish where Ahern took the sprint.

**Stage 4 Tuam - Thurles 110 Mls.** 1 D.Ahern (Kerry) 3.50.00 2 F.O'Rourke ((Wexford) 3 P.Cleary (Tipperary) 4 L.Baxter (Kildare) 5 S.Murphy (Dublin) all same time.
**General Classification:** 1 P.Flanagan (Kildare) 16.41.51 2 D.Ahern (Kerry) at 1.08 3 S.O Hanlon (Dublin) at 1.56 4 E.Flanagan (Kildare) at 2.47 5 S.Dillon (Dublin) at 2.48 6 S.Murphy (Dublin) at 2.51 7 P.Neary (Louth) at 2.57 8 M.Gaffney (Meath) at 3.54 9 M.Logan (Kildare) at 4.06 10 B.McKenna (Meath) at 4.12.

## STAGE 5

After trying long breaks for the previous two stages, Dave Kenny (Exiles) changed his tactics on the 120 miles stage from Thurles to Killorglin and was rewarded with a stage win. The Mallow-born rider who had lived most of his life in London, attacked on a hill outside Tralee with less than 20 miles to go and got away, holding on to a slender lead to the finish where he had just 10 seconds in hand.
Up until Kenny's attack it had been uneventful for 100 miles with a strong Kildare team defending Flanagan's lead by chasing down all breakaway attempts. 1959 winner Ben McKenna, who had worked his way up to 10th overall after losing time with mechanical trouble on the early stages, tried to get away with teammate Mick Collins and they had 30 seconds at Limerick only to be brought back.
At Rathkeale the field was split into three groups covered by 1 minute but by Tralee they were all together again before Kenny made his winning move. He was followed over the line by a chasing group of 10 with the bunch not far behind.
**Stage 5 Thurles - Killorglin 120 Mls.** 1 D.Kenny (Exiles) 5.05.00 2 J.Whelan (Tipperary) at 5 secs 3 L.Dunne (Meath) 4 M.Christle (Dublin) 5 V.Atkinson (Cork) 6 W.Hynes (Derry) all same time.
**General Classification:** 1 P.Flanagan (Kildare) 21.46.16 2 D.Ahern (Kerry) at 2.08 3 S.O Hanlon (Dublin) at 2.56 4 P.Neary (Louth) at 3.41 5 E.Flanagan (Kildare) at 3.47 6 S.Dillon (Dublin) at 3.48 7 S.Murphy (Dublin) at 3.50 8 Dermot.McGrath (Dublin) at 4.38 9 P.Wall (Tipperary) at 4.52 10 equal D.Kenny (Exiles) and M.Logan (Kildare) at 4.56.

## STAGE 6

Dan Ahern had his third win of the event and his most popular when he gave Kerry a home win on the 98 miles run round the Ring of Kerry to Killarney. However he remained 2.08 behind Flanagan on G.C.
It was a good day for Kerry as Mick Murphy had clinched the King of the Mountains title with second placing on both the Coomakista Pass and Moll's Gap. He beat 17-year-old Willie Hynds of Derry by 1 point.
It was a day of crashes including one by the race-leader. His brother Eddie was also in a crash, one of four riders who went off the road on the 'Round of Beef' bend on

the descent from Moll's Gap. Also in trouble was Shay O Hanlon whose pedal unscrewed 10 miles from the finish and in consequence he dropped 3 places on GC.
At the end of the stage 20 riders remained in the lead after lone breakaway Willie Heasley (Meath) punctured 1 mile from the finish allowing Ahern to win the sprint from the chasers to take the victory.
**Stage 6 Killorglin - Killarney 98 Mls.** 1 D.Ahern (Kerry) 4.10.00 2 S.Murphy (Dublin) 3 S.Dillon (Dublin) 4 C.McLynn (Antrim) 5 P.Cleary (Tipperary) 6 J.Gearon (Tipperary) all same time.
**General Classification:** 1 P.Flanagan (Kildare) 25.55.16 2 D.Ahern (Kerry) at 2.08 3 S.Murphy (Dublin) at 4.05 4 S.Dillon (Dublin) at 4.18 5 P.Neary (Louth) at 4.41 6 S.O Hanlon (Dublin) at 4.46 7 M.Murphy (Kerry) at 5.16 8 P. Wall (Tipperary) at 5.52 9 M. Collins (Meath) at 6.21 10 equal F.O'Callaghan (Waterford) and F.Ryan (Tipperary) at 6.45.

## STAGE 7

Larry Dunne (Meath) won the 131 miles seventh stage from Killarney to Kilkenny out sprinting his breakaway companion Mick Murphy (Kerry) 26 seconds ahead of the field.
Race Leader Paddy Flanagan (Kildare) came home safely in the field and went into the final stage with a lead of 3.34 over nearest rival Dan Ahern (Kerry).
Dunne and Murphy were with the leaders all day but after the race had been fragmented for nearly 40 miles, there was a general regroupment and they were all together at Callan when Dunne and Murphy went again, this time in a successful move.
**Stage 7 Killarney - Kilkenny 131 Mls.** 1 L.Dunne (Meath) 5.40.00 2 M.Murphy (Kerry) same time 3 J.Whelan (Tipperary) at 26 secs 4 M.Collins (Meath) 5 M.Christle (Dublin all same time.
**General Classification:** 1 P.Flanagan (Kildare) 31.35.16 2 D.Ahern (Kerry) at 2.34 3 M.Murphy (Kerry) at 4.32 4 S.Murphy (Dublin) at 5.15 5 S.Dillon (Dublin) at 5.18 6 S.O Hanlon (Dublin) at 5.46 7 P.Neary (Louth) at 5.51 8 P.Wall (Tipperary) 6.18 9 M. Collins (Meath) at 6.32 10 F.Ryan (Tipperary) at 7.11.

## STAGE 8

After leading from the end of Stage 2, Paddy Flanagan defended all week to win his first RÁS ahead of Kerry's Dan Ahern with a winning margin of 3.23. However the Kerryman who won three stages would have been a definite contender under modern rules when one takes into consideration the 5 minutes in daily bonuses the winner received for holding the jersey. However that was the prevailing rule and Paddy Flanagan wasn't the only RÁS winner to benefit.

The final stage went to Sean Dillon who came home with Mick Murphy and John O'Mahony (Cork) 25 seconds clear of the main field.
The race stayed intact for most of the 100 miles stage from Kilkenny to the Phoenix Park and it was only at Lucan that the three riders went away to contest the final sprint.
A last stage crash put Eddie Flanagan (Kildare) out of the race and dropped Kildare out of the team placing where they had been lying fourth. However Dublin once again took the team title ahead of Meath and Tipperary.
**Stage 8 Kilkenny - Dublin 100 Mls.** 1 S.Dillon (Dublin) 4.13.25 2 M.Murphy (Kerry) 3 J.O'Mahony (Cork) all same time 4 D.O'Regan (Cork) at 25 secs 5 M.O'Hare (Cork); 6 P.Cleary (Tipperary) all same time.
**General Classification:** 1 P.Flanagan (Kildare) 35.47.51 2 D.Ahern (Kerry) at 3.23 3 M.Murphy (Kerry) at 4.12 4 S.Dillon (Dublin) at 4.53 5 S.Murphy (Dublin) at 6.05 6 S.O Hanlon (Dublin) at 6.36 7 P.Neary (Louth) at 6.41 8 P.Wall (Tipperary) at 7.08 9 M.Collins (Meath) at 7.22 10 equal F.Ryan (Tipperary) and M.O'Callaghan (Waterford).
**Team:** 1 Dublin (S.Murphy, S.Dillon, S.O Hanlon, M.Christle) 148.17.52 2 Meath (M.Collins, B.McKenna, M.Gaffney, P.Roe) 148.33.07 3 Tipperary (P.Wall, F.Ryan, T.Kiely, J.Whelan) 144.12.34.
**King of the Mountains:** 1 M.Murphy (Kerry) 2 W.Hynds (Derry).

*Paddy Flanagan, 1960 winner*

# 1961

There were a couple of important changes for the 1961 ninth edition with the RÁS moved to the final week of June from the first week in August which had been the date of all the previous events except the 1953 2-Day in September.
With the event getting bigger (92 were entered that year) it was getting harder to find accommodation for so many people in what was the holiday fortnight for most of the Republic.
The second change was that the race leader would no longer receive a 1 minute bonus if he successfully defended the yellow jersey. The argument had been that the leader suffered the disadvantage of being the most marked man in the race and so should get some balancing advantage. However recent events had seemed to show that it was having to great an influence on the eventual race result.
However the RÁS of 1961 still had some noticeable differences from the current event. The stages started much later and generally finished around 7 p.m., the idea being to give spectators time to get their tea before going out to see the race. Years later when, due to pressure from the media for earlier results stage finishes were changed to mid afternoon, it brought about a big drop in the number of spectators at stage finishes.
One result of the late finishes was that the pressmen had to work out their own GC at the finish in order to meet deadlines. Where as now in the age of computers a short provisional GC is produced and printed on the platform within minutes of the winner crossing the line, in the early days getting out a GC with individual calculation cards meant it was often midnight before it was typed up and duplicated.
This meant that the results available in the newspapers of that time are not nearly as extensive as they are now. Judges only gave the first 6 on the stage and the GC which appeared in the next morning's papers depended on how much information was available to the journalists on the line and was certainly provisional. The only journalist from that era still on the race in the 90's, Jim McArdle of the Irish Times recalls how when they had got what information they could from the Judges, they worked out their own GC to meet deadlines.
One may notice that the stage winner's time is usually a neat minute. To aid them in their forthcoming calculations, the judges and timekeepers usually rounded up the stage winner's time to the nearest minute and timed the gaps from him to the following riders. Although nobody lost out because of this method, winning times were not of the split-second accuracy of today with electronic timing and photo-finish cameras.
Although the GC bonuses were removed, there were still big bonuses of 1 minute, 30 secs and 15 secs for stage placings. This was in line with current in the Tour de

France and it was only when Le Tour dropped or reduced its bonuses that the RÁS followed suit.

## STAGE 1

The defending Race Champion Paddy Flanagan threw down the gauntlet right away in his bid to become the first man to win the race twice. He led a group of nine into Navan after a short stage of 73 miles which didn't start until 4 P.M. because of a big Patrician Congress Mass in Croke Park.
Second in the sprint was Dermot Dignam (Dublin) ahead of pre-race favourite Shay O Hanlon. The field had stayed together for most of the way, Flanagan and O Hanlon got away together at Ardee but the bunch was not letting two such dangerous riders go and they soon reeled them in.
There was a big surprise at the finish when Belfastman Frank Mc Donald riding for Armagh, was first across the line on his own. However it transpired that he had been dropped before Ardee and had taken a wrong turning which saw him cover a shorter route than the rest of the field. He was penalised and withdrew from the race protesting his innocence.
When a break of nine eventually did get clear over the final miles, they were never allowed to build up much of a lead and the bunch were only 30 seconds down at the finish.
**Stage 1 Dublin - Navan 73 Mls.** 1 P.Flanagan (Kildare) 2 D.Dignam (Dublin) 3 S.O Hanlon (Dublin) 4 J.O'Connell (Exiles) 5 M.Logan (Kildare) 6 P.Reidy (Cork) all same time.

## STAGE 2

The 120 miles second stage from Navan to Castlebar was another of those RÁS specials which turns everything upside down. Seven riders were led into Castlebar by Mayo-born Alan Dillon, now living in Dublin but riding for his native county, His brother Sean was a member of the Dublin team

They were 8 minutes ahead of the next group but more importantly, the race favourites Flanagan and O Hanlon, prisoners of the bunch, their every move chased down, finished 18 minutes back with all hope of overall honours lost.
Shortly after the start a big group of 18 riders went away in what was to be the move of the stage and of the race. The big break would fragment over the remaining 120 miles but for anyone who did not make it into that initial 18 their race was as good as over.
At the finish seven riders remained at the front: Dillon, Ben McKenna (Meath), Tom Finn (Dublin), Mick Christle (Dublin), Tom Kiely (Tipperary) and Kildare pair Eamon Ryan and Liam Baxter.

**Stage 2 Navan - Castlebar 120 Mls.** 1 A.Dillon (Mayo) 6.03.00 2 B.McKenna (Meath) 3 T.Finn (Dublin) 4 M.Christle (Dublin) 5 T.Kiely (Tipperary) 6 E.Ryan (Kildare) all same time.
**General Classification:** 1 A.Dillon (Mayo) 9.06.35 2 B.McKenna (Meath) at 30 secs 3 T.Finn (Dublin) at 15 secs 4 equal M.Christle,(Dublin) E.Ryan,(Kildare) L.Baxter(Kildare) all same time.

## STAGE 3

Tuesday's third stage, 109 miles from Castlebar to Tuam, resulted in a second win for defending champion Paddy Flanagan and he moved up to 7th overall, but he was still a massive 15 minutes behind the new race leader Tom Finn of Dublin.
Finn finished fourth on the stage, 27 seconds behind Flanagan but it was enough for him to take the jersey from Alan Dillon who lost time and dropped from fourth, over 7 minutes behind the Dubliner. Ben McKenna remained second, 41 seconds behind with Mick Christle still third a further 30 seconds back.
A ten-man break went away shortly after the start which included O Hanlon and Sean Dillon, Shay Murphy, Tom Finn and Denis McGrath, all Dublin, the Flanagan brothers Paddy and Eddie, race leader Alan Dillon, Frank O'Rourke (Wexford) and Jim Drumm (Kerry). As they swung towards Maam Cross a strong side wind saw the leading group reduced to six with Drumm and O'Rourke, Alan Dillon, race leader and Shay Murphy all dropping back The leading group of six now led by 5 minutes.With six
miles to go Eddie Flanagan attacked but he was caught by Sean Dillon and then brother Paddy who won the 3-up sprint while Finn led home the remains of the break 27 seconds down.
**Stage 3 Castlebar - Tuam 109 Mls.** (incl. bonuses) 1 P.Flanagan (Kildare) 4.54.00 2 S.Dillon (Dublin) at 30 secs 3 E.Flanagan (Kildare) at 45 secs 4 T.Finn (Dublin) at 1.27 5 D.McGrath (Dublin) 6 S.O Hanlon (Dublin) all same time.
**General Classification:** 1 T.Finn (Dublin) 14.02.47 2 B.McKenna (Meath) at 41 secs 3 M.Christle (Dublin) at 1.11 4 A.Dillon (Mayo) at 7.20 5 E.Ryan (Kildare) at 8.20 6 D.Dignam (Dublin) at 10.01 7 P.Flanagan (Kildare) at 15.18 8 J.O'Connell (Exiles) at 15.23 9 D.McGrath (Dublin) at 16.00 10 P.Reidy (Cork) at 16.25.

## STAGE 4

Joe Lonergan (Tipperary) won the 135 miles stage from Tuam to Castleisland, 5 seconds ahead of a five-man group led by Allan Dillon (Mayo) from Shay O Hanlon (Dublin).
The first major break of the day came before Tuam when Sean Dillon (Dublin), Brother Alan riding for Mayo, Mick Hackett (Louth), Jim O'Connell (Exiles), Eamon Ryan (Kildare) and Jim Moynihan (Tipperary) got away. They stayed away

through Athenry but the Dublin team went to the front and brought them back by Craughwell.
Two miles later Jim Ludden and Alan Dillon (both Mayo), Fred Harris (Meath) and Tipperary pair J. Curry and W. Burke went clear but by Gort only Ludden Dillon and Burke were still out in front.
The Dublin team again did most of the chasing and be break was caught after Ennis. The field stayed together for most of the remainder of the stage until 8 miles from the finish when 6 went away and from these six Lonergan jumped away in the final mile.
**Stage 4 Tuam - Castleisland 135 Mls.** (incl. bonuses) 1 J.Lonergan (Tipperary) 6.34.00 2 A.Dillon (Mayo) at 35 secs 3 S.O Hanlon (Dublin) at 50 secs 4 D.Dignam (Dublin) at 1.05 5 D.McGrath (Dublin) 6 T.Ryan (Tipperary) all same time.
**General Classification:** 1 T.Finn (Dublin) 20.38.40 2 B.McKenna (Meath) at 41 secs 3 M.Christle (Dublin) at 1.11 4 A.Dillon (Mayo) at 6.02 5 E.Ryan (Kildare) at 7.20 6 D.Dignam (Dublin) at 9.13 7 D.McGrath (Dublin) at 15.12 8 P.Flanagan (Kildare) at 15.18 9 J.O'Connell (Exiles) at 15.23 10 T.Ryan (Tipperary) at 16.12.

## STAGE 5

The fifth stage also went to Tipperary, Paddy Wall who came home with Jim Whitty (Wexford) 1.25 seconds ahead of a chasing trio of Sean Dillon, Shay O Hanlon and Paddy Neary (Louth).
The stage was round the Ring of Kerry from Castleisland to Killarney and they field stayed together until after Killorglin when Sean Dillon and Dermot McGrath (both Dublin), Mick Hackett (Louth), Murt Logan (Kildare) and Pat Firman (Wexford) went away the break opening up a lead of 3 minutes by Glenbeigh.
On the descent from the Coomakista pass Shay O Hanlon and Mick Twomey (Cork) caught the leaders but the bunch, led by Finn made contact shortly after. It was then that Wall and Whitty made their move and they had a 3 minute advantage at the top of Moll's Gap but this had dropped to 1.25 seconds by the finish.
**Stage 5 Castleisland - Killarney 120 Mls.** (incl. bonuses) 1 P.Wall (Tipperary) 5.54.00 2 J.Whitty (Wexford) at 30 secs 3 S.Dillon (Dublin) at 1.55 4 S.O Hanlon (Dublin) at 1.25 5 P.Neary (Louth) s.t. 6 P. Reidy (Cork) at 3 mins.
**General Classification:** 1 T.Finn (Dublin) 26.37.05 2 B.McKenna (Meath) at 41 secs 3 M.Christle (Dublin) at 1.11 4 A.Dillon (Mayo) at 6.02 5 E.Ryan (Kildare) at 7.20 6 D.Dignam (Dublin) at 9.08 7 P.Flanagan (Kildare) at 13.53 8 P.Wall (Tipperary) at 14.16 9 S.O Hanlon (Dublin) at 14.21 10 S.Dillon (Dublin) at 14.53.

## STAGE 6 (a) and (b)

Finn retained his lead after Friday's two stages but his lead over Ben McKenna was cut to 15 seconds.

The morning's 19 miles time-trial was won by Paddy Flanagan who was 5 seconds faster than O Hanlon over the 19 miles from Killarney to Kenmare which included the climb of Moll's Gap.
O Hanlon looked on course to win the test but jammed his chain 4 miles from the finish losing an estimated 20 seconds. Third fastest was Sean Dillon who was 28 seconds behind the winner. McKenna and Finn were close together in 7th and 8th place with the Meath man having the better time by 14 seconds.
If O Hanlon missed out on victory in the TT he had the satisfaction of winning the 80 miles afternoon stage to Clonakilty and his day's efforts moved him from 9th to 4th overall. He attacked with teammate Dillon on the mountain out of Kenmare and they breasted the summit 1 minute clear of the field.
The two continued to stretch their advantage and by the finish their lead was an impressive 4.46 over the bunch.
**Stage 6(a) Killarney - Kenmare 19 Mls. TT:** 1 P.Flanagan (Kildare) 57.59 2 S.O Hanlon (Dublin) 57.34 3 S.Dillon (Dublin) 57.57 4 J.Clarke (Tipperary) 59.13 5 J.Murphy (Louth) 59.46 6 J.Whitty (Wexford) 59.50 7 B.McKenna (Meath) 59.59 8 T.Finn (Dublin) 1.00.13 9 E.Ryan (Kildare) 1.00.24 10 L.Dunne (Meath) 1.00.28.
**Stage 6(b) Kenmare - Clonakilty 80 Mls.** (incl. bonuses) 1 S.O Hanlon (Dublin) 2.59.15 2 S.Dillon (Dublin) at 34secs 3 T.Ryan (Tipperary) at 4.25 4 J.O'Connell (Exiles) at 4.40 5 J.Whitty (Wexford) 6 S.Steede (Galway) all same time.
**General Classification:** 1 T.Finn (Dublin) 30.42.19 2 B.McKenna at 15 secs 3 M.Christle (Dublin) at 4.09 4 S.O Hanlon (Dublin) at 5.56 5 S.Dillon (Dublin) at 7.25 6 P.Flanagan (Kildare) at 10.09.

## STAGE 7

O Hanlon continued his great run with another win on the long 160 miles stage from Clonakilty to Wexford but he led in a bunch containing all the favourites and there was no change at the top of the leader board with Finn taking a 27 second leads over McKenna into the final stage.
The length of the stage saw the field in no mood for any early adventures and although there were occasional breakaway attempts they all came to nothing.
As a result it was a bunch finish in Wexford where O Hanlon won by 13 seconds from Cork-born Jerome Dorgan, riding for the Exiles with local man Frank O'Rourke of Wexford third.
**Stage 7 Clonakilty - Wexford 160 Mls** (incl. bonuses) 1 S.O Hanlon (Dublin) 7.14.00 2 J.Dorgan (Exiles) at 30 secs 3 F.O'Rourke (Wexford) at 45 secs 4 M.Christle (Dublin) at 1 min. 5 H.Mulholland (Armagh) 6 D.Dignam (Dublin) all same time.
**General Classification:** 1 T.Finn (Dublin) 37.57.19 2 B.McKenna at 27 secs 3 M.Christle (Dublin) at 4.09 4 S.O Hanlon (Dublin) at 4.56 5 S.Dillon (Dublin) at 7.25 6 P.Flanagan (Kildare) at 10.09 7 D.Dignam (Dublin) at 13.29 8 D.McGrath (Dublin) at 15.35 9 P.Reidy (Cork) at 15.40 10 P.Wall (Tipperary) at 16.20.

## STAGE 8

Shay O Hanlon took this third stage in a row but Tom Finn held on to win by 27 seconds from Ben McKenna with O Hanlon finishing third at 3.56, an amazing performance when one remembered that he had lost 18 minutes on Monday.
It was a typical final stage with no break of consequence and it all ended in a spectacular mass bunch sprint which had lasted for the 500 yards of the straight in the Phoenix Park with O Hanlon winning from teammate Sean Dillon.
The stage-winner's bonus saw O Hanlon move up past his teammate Mick Christle to third overall. Dublin once more took the team race with Finn, O Hanlon, Christle and Dillon) 9 minutes ahead of Tipperary. They made it a clean sweep of the major awards as Sean Dillon won the King of the Mountains.
In seventh place came Dermot Dignam (Dublin) the highest overall placing for the man whose name would become synonymous with the RÁS as its long-time organiser.

**Stage 8 Wexford - Dublin 100 Mls.** 1 S.O Hanlon (Dublin) 5.07.00 2 S.Dillon (Dublin) 3 J.Dorgan (Exiles) 4 P.Flanagan (Kildare) 5 J.Drumm (Kerry) 6 F.O'Rourke (Wexford) all same time.

**General Classification:** 1 T.Finn (Dublin) 43.05.19 2 B.McKenna (Meath) at 27 secs 3 S.O Hanlon (Dublin) at 3.56 4 M.Christle (Dublin) at 4.09 5 S.Dillon (Dublin) at 5.55 6 P.Flanagan (Kildare) at 10.09 7 D.Dignam (Dublin) at 13.29 8 Denis.McGrath (Dublin) at 15.35 9 P.Reidy (Cork) at 15.40 10 P.Wall (Tipperary) at 16.20.

**Team:** 1 Dublin (T.Finn, S.O Hanlon, M.Christle, S.Dillon) 172.36.16 2 Tipperary (P.Wall, T.Ryan, J.Clarke, J.Moynihan) 173.45.15 3 Cork (P.Reidy, M.Twomey, N.Waddy, J.Ahern) 173.58.38.

**King of the Mountains:** S.Dillon (Dublin).

1961 winner, Tom Finn

## 1962

The RÁS moved back from June to August for the 1962 edition when 92 riders from 12 county teams plus an Exiles team were entered. When one of the pre-race favourites Paddy Flanagan and his brother Eddie failed to start it enhanced Shay O Hanlon's position as pre-race favourite for the third year.
It was the first RÁS that I went all the way with, acting as team manager for a Down team for which Newry Brothers Brian and Dermot Monaghan had come over from Leeds where they were now based. Sean O'Hare was the only home rider on the team which was augmented by two Dublin riders Dermot McGrath and Mitch McNamara and after the opening stage McGrath was race leader with Monaghan second but our glory was short-lived.

### STAGE 1

On the opening stage was 76 miles to Longford the vital move came in the first hour at Kilcock when Dermot Dignam (Dublin), Dermot Monaghan (Down), Liam Baxter (Kildare), Willie Burke and Seamus Walsh (both Tipperary) and John Goddard (Exiles) went away and by Kinnegad their lead was up to 1.30.
By Mullingar this was up to 2 minutes with Walsh having dropped back to the bunch. At Edgeworthstown a 10-man chasing group formed which included Dermot McGrath and Shay O Hanlon (Dublin) and past winner Ben McKenna (Meath).
From this group McGrath and John O'Mahony (Cork) attacked and despite a strong headwind they caught the leaders only three miles from the finish where McGrath took the sprint from team-mate Monaghan.
**Stage 1 Dublin - Longford 76 Mls.** 1 Dermot.McGrath (Down) 3.13.19 (inc. 1 min. bonus) 2 D.Monaghan (Down) at 30 secs (inc. 30s. bonus) 3 L.Baxter (Kildare) at 45 secs (inc. 15 secs bonus) 4 D.Dignam (Dublin) at 1 minute 5 J.O'Mahoney (Cork) 6 J.Goddard (Exiles) 7 F.Walsh (Tipperary) all same time 8 D.Ahern (Kerry) at 1.30 9 M.Hackett (Meath) 10 P.Fireman (Cork) 11 R.Shaw (Cork) 12 D.Sheehan (Exiles) all same time. (Bonus times deducted from the stage time on the opening stage. On subsequent stages the bonuses are given deducted from the GC times).

### STAGE 2

At the end of the second stage, 122 miles from Longford to Donegal Town, Shay O Hanlon was in a position that was to become very familiar to him over the next few years - leader of the RÁS.
O Hanlon won his fifth RÁS stage on his own, chased home at 1.10 by two past RÁS winners Tom Finn and Ben McKenna. After the stage he led the event by nearly two

minutes from McKenna and Dermot McGrath, the yellow jersey coming in with the bunch 2.35 behind O Hanlon.
McGrath had obviously decided that attack was the best means of defence and he went from the start line along 22 others. Eight miles from Roscommon this big break led by 1 minute but by the time that town was reached they had been joined by O Hanlon, Sean Mann (Antrim), Patsy Wall (Tipperary) and Eamon Ryan (Kildare) who proceeded to go right through the leaders.
The quartet was joined by several small groups and as they passed through Carrick-on-Shannon in heavy rain there were 13 in the lead. O Hanlon attacked on his own but over the next 10 miles he was joined by Tom Finn, Ben McKenna, Patsy Wall and John Goddard (Exiles) and these four had 2 minutes over the chasing group and 3 minutes over the bunch which contained the yellow jersey.
With 10 miles to go O Hanlon again went on his own and opened up a gap of over a minute by the finish.
**Stage 2 Longford - Donegal 122 Mls.** 1 S.O Hanlon (Dublin) 5.31.35 2 T.Finn (Dublin) at 1.10 3 B.McKenna (Meath) s.t. 4 S.Cullen (Dublin) at 2.07 5 A.Kiely (Tipperary) at 2.12 6 J.O'Mahoney (Cork) 7 T.Kiely (Tipperary) all same time
**General Classification:** 1 S.O Hanlon (Dublin) 8.45.34 2 equal D.McGrath (Down) and B.McKenna (Meath) at 1.55 4 D.Monaghan (Down) at 2.02 5 L.Baxter (Kildare) at 2.1 6 J.O'Mahoney (Cork) at 2.32 7 equal M.Hackett (Meath) F.O'Rourke (Wexford) and D.Ahern (Kerry) at 2.52 10 S.Cullen (Dublin) at 3.07 11 equal T.Kiely (Tipperary) E.Crosbie (Waterford) B.Monaghan (Down) and P.Wall (Tipperary) all at 3.12

## STAGE 3

Sonny Cullen (Dublin) won the 110 miles third stage to Athenry from an 8-man break but O Hanlon was right there in second place to reinforce his lead. Cullen's victory brought him up to second overall 2.37 behind his team-mate.
O Hanlon had started the action attacking from the gun and led for 20 miles chased by four riders: Dermot McGrath and Brian Monaghan (Down), Liam Baxter (Kildare) and Dave Kenny (Exiles). The four linked up with the leader but by Sligo the bunch came up and the whole field was together.
Dublin trio Cullen, Mick Christle, and Jimmy Kennedy then went away in company of John Goddard and were joined by O Hanlon, Jim Harrigan (Kildare) Bob Shaw (Cork) and Tipperary pair Patsy Wall, and Seamus Walsh. Shaw was dropped but the other eight stayed away to fight out the final sprint.
**Stage 3 Donegal - Castlebar 110 Mls.** 1 S.Cullen (Dublin) 4.44.50 2 S.O Hanlon (Dublin) 3 J.Goddard (Exiles) 4 P.Wall (Tipperary) 5 J.Kennedy (Dublin) 6 M.Christle (Dublin) 7 S.Walsh (Tipperary) 8 J.Halligan (Kildare) all same time
**General Classification:** 1 S.O Hanlon (Dublin) 13.29.54 2 S.Cullen (Dublin) at 2.37 3 P.Wall (Tipperary) at 3.42 4 B.McKenna (Meath) at 4.05 5 L.Baxter (Kildare) at 4.07 6 D.Monaghan (Down) at 4.12 7 equal F.O'Rourke (Wexford) and D.Ahern

(Kerry) at 5.02 9 R.Shaw (Cork) at 5.05 10 equal T.Kiely (Tipperary) and B.Monaghan (Down) at 5.22

## STAGE 4

Dan Ahern of Kerry won the fourth stage, 112 miles from Castlebar to Athenry with a great ride on his own for the last 14 miles. However the gaps were small at the finish and there were no big changes on GC with O Hanlon still leading Cullen by over 2 minutes.
The action started after only 4 miles when Dermot Dignam and Denis McGrath (both Dublin) and Jim Roche (Wexford) went away. They were soon joined by Tom Finn (Dublin) Bob Shaw (Cork) and Jim Halligan (Kildare) and these six soon had 1.30 of a lead on two riders: Brian Monaghan (Down) and Sonny Cullen (Dublin).
The two chasers were caught by the bunch at Letterfrack and at Clifden the six leaders were two minutes in front which was up to 2.30 at Maam Cross where Dignam and McGrath went ahead on their own. Eleven riders including the race leader went in pursuit but the field were still in close pursuit.
The remainder of the break was caught by the pursuers but the two Dublin riders stayed away through Galway before they were finally caught. With 14 miles to go first Sean Mann (Antrim) attacked and then John Goddard (Exiles). Both were brought back but when Ahern went he opened up a sizeable gap and despite a furious chase he held on all the way to the line where he still had 35 seconds in hand.
**Stage 4 Castlebar - Athenry 112 Mls.** 1 D.Ahern (Kerry) 5.02.00 2 J.Goddard (Exiles) at 35 secs 3 B.Naylor (Dublin) 4 S.O'Hare (Down) 5 J.O'Mahoney (Cork) 6 M.Hackett (Meath) 7 J.Caulfield (Louth) 8 E.Ryan (Kildare) all same time
**General Classification:** 1 S.O Hanlon (Dublin) 18.32.19 2 S.Cullen (Dublin) at 2.37 3 D.Ahern (Kerry) at 3.27 4 P.Wall (Tipperary) at 3.32 5 B.McKenna (Meath) at 3.57 6 L.Baxter (Kildare) at 3.59 7 D.Monaghan (Down) at 4.04 8 F.O'Rourke (Wexford) at 4.54 9 R.Shaw (Cork) at 5.07 10 equal P.Kelly (Tipperary) E.Crosbie (Wexford) and B.Monaghan (Down) at 5.14

## STAGE 5

Sonny Cullen (Dublin) won his second stage, the 130 miles run to Tralee and as a result moved to within 44 second of race-leader O Hanlon.
With only 11 miles to go Cullen had two minutes lead and looked like taking over the jersey. However O Hanlon managed to reduce his deficit to 53 seconds by the finish so although Cullen also got the 1 minute winner's bonus, the 1.53 still wasn't enough.
The vital move of the stage came when 20 riders including Cullen and Ben McKenna going away and by Ennis they had over 30 seconds lead. O Hanlon reacted and caught the leaders on his own. He immediately attacked taking with him Paddy Neary (Louth), and Dublin team-mates Brendan Magennis and Denis McGrath.

This break stayed out in front for 20 miles but were brought back by the 14 riders remaining of the original break after Clarecastle. On the Barna Gap Seamus Walsh (Tipperary) and Seamus McCarron (Derry) went away and they were joined by Cullen, Neary, and Denis McGrath.
Cullen and Neary then went ahead on their own and raced to a 2 minute lead before O Hanlon dug into his reserves over the final miles to remove the threat to his lead.
**Stage 5 Athenry - Tralee 130 Mls.** 1 S.Cullen (Dublin) 5.57.00 2 P.Neary (Louth) s.t. 3 J.Kennedy (Dublin) at 53 secs 4 S.O Hanlon (Dublin) 5 B.Magennis (Dublin) 6 T.Finn (Dublin) 7 B.McKenna (Meath) 8 S.McCarron (Derry) 9 L.Baxter (Kildare) all same time.
**General Classification:** 1 S.O Hanlon (Dublin) 24.30.12 2 S.Cullen (Dublin) at 44 secs 3 P.Wall (Tipperary) at 3.32 4 B.McKenna (Meath) at 4.05 5 L.Baxter (Kildare) at 4.07 6 R.Shaw (Cork) at 5.15 7 J.Kennedy (Dublin) at 5.20 8 T.Finn (Dublin) at 5.55 9 P.Neary (Louth) at 6.27 10 S.Walsh (Tipperary) at 11.56.

## STAGE 6 (a) and (b)

If O Hanlon had been made to look vulnerable on Stage 5 when he lost nearly 2 minutes, he hit back with a vengeance on Friday's double stage winning both time-trial and massed start and finishing the day over 7 minutes clear of Sonny Cullen who remained his nearest rival.
On the 20 miles morning time-trial from Tralee to Killarney O Hanlon beat team-mate Jimmy Kennedy by 1.36 with his margin over 6th placed Cullen 2.54 giving him back all he had lost to Cullen the previous day and he now led on GC by 3.50.
He might have been expected to rest on his laurels on the short 60 miles afternoon stage to Fermoy but he went from the gun with team-mate Brendan Magennis and after three miles they had 30 seconds lead.
They were joined by three Exiles riders: John Goddard, Dave Kenny and Pat Ransom, John Caulfield (Louth), Mick Twomey (Cork) and Jimmy Kennedy. Their lead at Mallow was nearly 2 minutes on a chasing bunch containing Cullen and Denis McGrath. However the leaders increased their lead all the time and they were 2.33 ahead at the finish.
**Stage 6(a) Tralee - Killarney 20 Mls. TT:** 1 S.O Hanlon (Dublin) 44.54 2 J.Kennedy (Dublin) 46.30 3 equal D.Kenny (Exiles) and S.McCarron (Derry) 46.35 5 K.O'Brien (Cork) 46.50 6 S.Cullen (Dublin) 47.00 7 P.Reidy (Cork) 47.07 8 B.Monaghan (Down) 47.20 9 B.Naylor (Dublin) 47.26 10 equal L.Baxter (Kildare) and T.Finn (Dublin) 47.30 12 P.Wall (Tipperary) 47.31.
**Stage 6(b) Killarney - Fermoy 60 Mls.** 1 S.O Hanlon (Dublin) 2.21.00 2 B.Magennis (Dublin) 3 J.Kennedy (Dublin) 4 M.Twomey (Cork) 5 J.Caulfield (Louth) 6 J.Goddard (Exiles) 7 D.Kenny (Exiles) all same time.
**General Classification:** 1 S.O Hanlon (Dublin) 27.34.36 2 S.Cullen (Dublin) at 7.23 3 J.Kennedy (Dublin) at 8.41 4 P.Wall (Tipperary) at 10.52 5 L.Baxter (Kildare) at 11.16 6 P.Neary (Louth) at 14.36 7 R.Naylor (Dublin) at 16.44 8 T.Finn (Dublin) at

18.16 9 B.McKenna (Meath) at 20.54 10 B.Magennis (Dublin) at 22.28 11 S.Walsh (Tipperary) at 22.40 12 R.Shaw (Cork) at 25.29.

## STAGE 7

**Stage 7 Fermoy - Gorey** 1 B Naylor 5.27.05
**General Classification:** 1 S O Hanlon

## STAGE 8

While there was no doubt, given the size of his lead starting the final stage, that Shay O Hanlon would win, he emphasised his dominance, unquestionably the most complete by any one rider in the history of the race, by coming home on his own on the final stage into the Phoenix Park, nearly 2 minutes clear, to win by the huge margin of 19 minutes and 4 seconds.
First to show on the final stage were Denis McGrath, Brian Monaghan, Jimmy Kennedy, Jim Goddard and Dave Kenny. When they were caught Kenny went again with Patsy Wall and gained 30 seconds before being brought back.
increasing his lead all the way. In the sprint for the minor positions Murt Logan won from Dermot Monaghan and Dermot McGrath.
**Stage 8 Gorey - Dublin 71 Mls.** 1 S.O Hanlon (Dublin) 3.5.00 2 M.Logan (Kildare) at 1.50 3 D.Monaghan (Down) 4 D.McGrath (Down) 5 D.McGrath (Dublin) 6 J.O'Mahoney (Cork) all same time.
**General Classification:** 1 S.O Hanlon (Dublin) 36.06.36 2 S.Cullen (Dublin) at 19.04 3 P.Neary (Louth) at 20.16 4 J.Kennedy (Dublin) at 20.23 5 P.Wall (Tipperary) at 22.34 6 L.Baxter (Kildare) at 22.58 7 T.Finn (Dublin) at 26.31 8 D.McGrath (Dublin) at 28.16 9 B.McKenna (Meath) at 29.11 10 S.Walsh (Tipperary) at 29.34 11 B.Magennis (Dublin) at 31.15 12 R.Shaw (Cork) at 33.11.
**Team:** 1 Dublin (O Hanlon, Cullen, Kennedy) 108.59.14 2 Tipperary (Wall, Walsh, Kiely) 110.04.27 3 Kildare (Baxter, Logan, Halligan) 110, 38.09.
**King of the Mountains:** S.O Hanlon.

*1962 winner – Sé O Hanlon, pictured with Jim Killean, President NCA and Joe Christle*

# 1963

Race director Joe Christle threw a bombshell into Irish cycling circles when, a week before the '63 RÁS he announced that a national team from Poland could be on the start line the following Sunday.
The Northern Ireland Cycling Federation immediately objected to the international body, the UCI, who, on the Thursday before the race was due to start, banned member federations from taking part in the RÁS TAILTEANN 'because it was organised by a non affiliated body'.
The media assumed that the Poles would not take part and in the Friday previews they were not mentioned, Con Kenneally in the Independent tipping Kerry's Dan Ahern, in the absence of O Hanlon, who was spending the season racing in France. After O Hanlon's dominance the previous year one can only speculate as to how he would have fared against the visitors.
However the Polish team, no doubt counting on the voting strength of the Eastern bloc at the UCI in avoiding suspension, duly lined up for the start on the opening stage from Dublin to Ballyjamesduff.

## STAGE 1

The visitors, as might have been expected of experienced internationals, were in control throughout the first stage and had two riders in the nine-man break which finished two minutes up with Jerzy Mikolajczyk winning from John Goddard (Exiles) and Dan Ahern (Kerry).
From the start the Poles marked everybody who went up the road and any break that formed had one of their team included. The first serious looking escape came after 40 miles at Dundalk when Christy Kimmage was joined by Zbgniew Glowaty and their lead grew to 30 secs. One of the Poles, Malkiewicz, punctured and had a 20 miles solo chase to get back on.
Meanwhile the two leaders were joined by a chasing group which included Ben McKenna (Meath), J. Phelan (Tipperary), Denis McGrath (Dublin), J. Brosnan (Kerry), John Goddard and Liam Baxter (Kildare) but by Shercock they were all together again. Dan Ahern then attacked and he was joined by a group of eight and it was this move which proved to be successful, the nine staying away to the finish.
**Stage 1 Dublin - Ballyjamesduff 101 Mls.** (inc. bonuses) 1 J.Mikolajczyk (Poland) 4.05.03 2 J.Goddard (Exiles) 4.5.33 3 D.Ahern (Kerry) 4.5.48 4 S.Lally (Sligo) 4.6.03 5 P.Ward (Tipperary) 6 J.Linde (Poland) 7 M.Logan (Kildare) 8 J.Kennedy (Dublin)) 9 B.Magennis (Antrim) all same time 10 C.Kimmage (Dublin) at 3.05 11 S.Cullen (Dublin) 12 M.Gaffney (Meath) same time.
**Team:** Poland 12.19.26 2 Dublin 12.22.29 3 Exiles 12.22.41.

## STAGE 2

Jerzy Linde made it two in a row for the visitors when he came home on his own, 15 seconds ahead of a four-man group led in by Mick Christle (Dublin) who had been a doubtful starter following a crash on the opening stage.

Linde, the Polish pursuit champion, who was in good form having just finished third in the Tour of Romania, made his effort over the final miles leaving the bunch on his own, catching and passing two groups who were up the road. His efforts gave him the yellow jersey by 15 seconds from his team-mate Mikolajczyk.

After the start Glowaty and Malkiewicz went away joined by Tom Finn (Dublin) and Sean Lally (Sligo) and after 15 miles at Cavan they held a 30 second lead.

At Killeshandra they were joined by Linde, Chojnacki (Poland), W. Burke (Tipperary), A. Nulty and Mick Collins (Meath) and Dan Ahern (Kerry) but by the half-way point at Mohill they were all together once again.

At Longford Ben McKenna went clear with Liam Moriarty (Kerry) and they were chased by Mick Christle and Christy Kimmage (Dublin), Johnny Lonergan (Tipperary) and the yellow jersey.

It was then that Linde left the bunch and powered to the front, coming home on his own to take the stage and the race lead.

**Stage 2 Ballyjamesduff - Mullingar 103 Mls.** 1 J.Linde (Poland) 4.05.03 2 M.Christle (Dublin) at 15 secs 3 J.Lonergan (Tipperary) 4 J.Mikolajczyk (Poland) 5 M.Chojnacki (Poland) all same time 6 G.Mangan (Kerry) at 30 secs 7 T.Reilly (Meath) 8 C.Kimmage (Dublin) all same time.

**General Classification:** 1 J.Linde (Poland) 8.10.06 2 J.Mikolajczyk (Poland) at 15 secs 3 J.Goddard (Exiles) at 1.00 4 D.Ahern (Kerry) at 1.15 5 S.Lally (Sligo) at 1.30 6 equal J.Kennedy (Dublin) B.Magennis (Antrim) J.Wall (Tipperary) M.Logan (Kildare) all at 2.27 10 J.Lonergan (Tipperary) at 3.17 11 M.Christle (Dublin) at 3.30 12 M.Chojnacki (Poland) at 3.32.

**Team:** 1 Poland 24.34.05 2 Dublin 24.39.50 3 24.40.17.

## STAGE 3

Jerzy Mikolajczyk won the third stage in a row for the Poles and took back the yellow jersey which he had worn after Sunday's stage and the Poles strengthened their grip on the race finishing 1, 2 and 4th on the stage with all their five riders now in the top ten on GC.

Mikolajczyk finished on his own covering the 105 miles from Mullingar to Tuam in 4.36.10, 17 seconds ahead of his team-mate Chojnacki. Next home, 15 seconds later were Christy Kimmage and Glowaty with the Dubliner taking the sprint?

These four had been in the vital move of the stage just after half-distance at Roscommon where the main field had split into two big groups divided by around a minute. It was then at the three Poles attacked, only Kimmage managing to stay with them.

The four built up a lead of six minutes and stayed together until the final mile when the Poles used their numerical strength to get two away to take the major placings with Kimmage only able to salvage third place.

**Stage 3 Mullingar - Tuam 105 Mls.** 1 J.Mikolajczyk (Poland) 4.36.15 2 M.Chojnacki (Poland) at 17 secs 3 C.Kimmage (Dublin) at 32 secs 4 Z.Glowaty (Poland) same time 5 B.McKenna (Meath) at 6.25 6 S.Cullen (Dublin) 7 D.Ahern (Kerry) 8 J.Linde (Poland) 9 M.Collins (Meath) all same time 10 M.Christle (Dublin) at 7.52.

**General Classification:** 1 J.Mikilajczyk (Poland) 12.45.36 2 M.Chojnacki at 4.04 3 C.Kimmage (Dublin) at 4.41 4 Z.Glowaty (Poland) at 4.56 5 J. Linde (Poland) at 5.33 6 D.Ahern (Kerry) at 8.25 7 J.Goddard (Exiles) at 10.10 8 S.Cullen (Dublin) at 10.55 9 B.McKenna (Meath) at 10.57 10 M.Malkiewicz (Poland) at 11.25 11 L.Baxter (Kildare) s.t. 12 P.Wall (Tipperary) at 11.26.

**Team:** 1 Poland 38.27.25 2 Dublin 38.44.31 3 Exiles 38.52.29.

## STAGE 4

Dubliner Sonny Cullen scored the first Irish win on a good day for the Irish with none of the Poles finishing in the first six home and on the GC John Goddard of the Exiles team was the new race leader by 31 seconds from Mikolajczyk. Cullen's efforts put him in third place on GC, at 1.45.

In an extraordinary turnaround a lot of the gains the Poles had made on the opening three stages were wiped out with their first rider home Glowaty over 5 minutes down. They still led the team with the margin over Dublin cut from 14 minutes to 3.36.

It was the bunch reaction to the Poles domination of the first three stages that saw them act as one big team against the visitors, marking every move and refusing to work in any break that included a Pole. Eventually the pressure told and they found themselves captive in the bunch while a break built up a big lead.

They may also have thought that two groups totalling 25 riders were unlikely to stay away for over 100 miles. However when the two groups eventually joined they worked fairly well and gradually built up a big lead.

Only Glowaty, who went in pursuit along with Dan Ahern, made any inroads on the lead but even so they were over 5 minutes back at the end.

**Stage 4 Tuam - Castleisland 127 Mls.** 1 S.Cullen (Dublin) 4.33.03 2 J.Kennedy (Dublin) 3 D.Kenny (Exiles) 4 J.Goddard (Exiles) 5 P.Wall (Tipperary) 6 M.Collins (Meath) all same time.

**General Classification:** 1 J.Goddard (Exiles) 18.29.49 2 J.Mikolajczyk (Poland) at 45 secs 3 S.Cullen (Dublin) at 1.14 4 L.Baxter (Kildare) at 2.13 5 P.Wall (Tipperary) at 2.16 6 Z.Glowaty (Poland) at 2.43 7 M.Collins (Meath) at 3.12 8 M.Chojnacki (Poland) at 3.37 9 D.Kenny (Exiles) at 4.11 10 J.Kennedy (Dublin) at 4.28 11 D.Ahern (Kerry) at 4.35 12 J.Linde (Poland) at 6.41.

**Team** 1 Poland 55.35.16 2 Dublin 55.38.53 3 Exiles 55.45.58.

## STAGE 5

The importance of the previous day chase by Zbigniew Glowaty and Dan Ahern became evident after Thursday's 113 miles Kerry Mountain stage from Castleisland when the two finished 1st and 2nd and took over the lead at the top of the general classification.
With these two in a three-man sprint for the line was another Pole, Jerzy Linde who finished third behind his team-mate and the Kerryman. It was almost 4 minutes before the next arrival, Archie Williams (Dublin) who beat another Pole, Marian Chojnacki to the line.
After their bad day on Wednesday the Poles seized back the initiative and went on the attack on the first climb outside Waterville. Earlier Glowaty and Chojnacki had gone away with Exiles riders L. and P.J. Doyle and Dublin's Christy Kimmage and these five were soon joined by another two Poles, Mikolajczyk, Linde, Dublin's Kennedy and Williams, Kenny (Exiles), Ahern and Dennis McGrath (Wicklow).
This was the break of the day with the bunch never looking like bringing them back and at Killorglin, where Glowaty led up the hill; they had 2 minutes lead on the bunch. After Cahirciveen the Poles made the vital attack Glowaty and Linde going clear along with Dan Ahern.
Archie Williams went in pursuit joined by another Pole, Chojnacki. Going through Kenmare the three leaders were 2 minutes ahead of the chasing pair who were chased at 10 seconds by Dennis McGrath. A minute leader came a chasing group of Jimmy Kennedy, Christy Kimmage, Sean Lally (Sligo) and Kenny and Doyle of the Exiles and Mikolajczyk (Poland) and this order was maintained over the 10 miles climb of Molls Gap and on the descent to the finish where Glowaty crashed but with his team-mate waiting was able to rejoin Ahern.
**Stage 5 Castleisland - Killarney 113 Mls.** 1 Z.Glowaty (Poland) 4.53.40 2 D.Ahern (Kerry) 3 J.Linde (Poland) all same time 4 A.Williams (Dublin) at 3.50 5 M.Chojnacki (Poland) s.t. 6 C.Kimmage (Dublin) at 5.36 7 J.Mikolajczyk (Poland) s.t.
**General Classification:** 1 Z.Glowaty (Poland) 23.25.12 2 D.Ahern (Kerry) at 2.22 3 J.Mikolajczyk (Poland) at 3.24 4 J.Linde (Poland) at 4.58 5 M.Chojnacki (Poland) at 5.42 6 P.Wall (Tipperary) at 6.09 7 D.Kenny (Exiles) at 8.04 8 C.Kimmage (Dublin) at 8.05 9 J.Kennedy (Dublin) at 8.21 10 L.Baxter (Kildare) at 9.32 11 J.Goddard (Exiles) at 9.37.

## STAGE 6

It was Ahern and Glowaty who were again involved in the sprint for the sixth stage from Killarney to Clonmel (94m.) but this time it was the Kerryman who got the verdict for the second Irish stage win of the week but the GC was unchanged except for the winner's bonus bringing Ahern to within 1.52 of the yellow jersey.

Action early on saw the field split into two groups at Rathmore, 12 miles after the start. Malkiewicz and Dave Kenny got away but even with the Pole sitting in their lead was 2 minutes over the field which had come together.
However with only one working the break was doomed and they were caught at Fermoy and at Mitchelstown Dan Ahern, Liam Baxter, Johnny Lonergan, Patsy Wall, Archie Williams, Tom Reilly (Meath) and Mick Twomey (Cork), Glowaty and Malkiewicy and another Pole Linde, who punctured and was absorbed by the chasers.
This break stayed away to the finish where they came home 1.15 ahead of the chasing group led in by Kerry's Gene Mangan with the main field at 3.40.
**Stage 6 Killarney - Clonmel 94 Mls** 1 D.Ahern (Kerry) 3.55.00 2 Z.Glowaty (Poland) 3 P.Wall (Tipperary) 4 J.Lonergan (Tipperary) 5 J.Malkiewicz (Poland) 6 L.Baxter (Kildare) all same time.
**General Classification:** 1 Z.Glowaty (Poland) 27.19.42 2 D.Ahern (Kerry) at 1.52 3 M.Chojnacki (Poland) at 6.12 4 P.Wall (Tipperary) at 6.24 5 J.Linde (Poland) at 6.43 6 J.Mikolajczyk (Poland) at 7.34 7 D.Kenny (Exiles) at 8.34 8 C.Kimmage (Dublin) at 9.50 9 L.Baxter (Kildare) at 10.02 10 J.Kennedy (Dublin) at 10.06 11 J.Goddard (Exiles) at 11.22 12 S.Cullen (Dublin) at 13.07.
**Team:** 1 Poland 82.12.01 2 Dublin 82.32.09 3 Exiles 82.51.39.

## STAGE 7

Dublin's Christy Kimmage gave the Irish their third stage win when he won the sprint into Gorey at the end of the 94 miles stage from Clonmel. There was no change overall, Glowaty holding his 52 second advantage over Ahern.
The field was content to stay together for much of the stage although there was an early break by Gene Mangan (Kerry) and when he was caught a similar effort by Cork's Pat Reidy who led through New Ross.
Frank O'Rourke led the field through his home town of Wexford, taking the prime while his team-mate Larry Doran had a similar success in Enniscorthy.
Apart from these individual efforts the field stayed intact for most of the stage, Doran's 20-mile effort ending when he was caught by Kimmage, Johnny Lonergan (Tipperary) and Marian Chojnacki (Poland).
Doran was dropped with 8 miles to go while the three leaders were joined by another Pole, Linde, these four contesting the stage sprint where Kimmage won from Linde, Lonergan and Chojnacki. The bunch were just behind Sonny Cullen (Dublin) leading them in 10 seconds later.
**Stage 7 Clonmel - Gorey 94 Mls.** 1 C.Kimmage (Dublin) 3.59.30 2 J.Linde (Poland) 3 J.Lonergan (Tipperary) 4 M.Chojnacki (Poland) all same time 5 S.Cullen (Dublin) at 10 secs. 6 J.Kennedy (Dublin 7 M.Logan (Kildare) all same time.
**General Classification:** 1 Z.Glowaty (Poland) 31.19.22 2 D.Ahern (Kerry) at 52 secs 3 M.Chojnacki (Poland) at 6.02 4 P.Wall (Tipperary) at 6.24 5 J.Linde (Poland) at 7.19 6 J.Mikolajczyk (Poland) at 7.34 7 C.Kimmage (Dublin) at 8.40 8 L.Baxter

(Kildare) at 10.02 9 J.Kennedy (Dublin) at 10.06 10 J.Goddard (Exiles) at 11.22 11 D.Kenny (Exiles) at 11.59 12 S.Cullen (Dublin) at 13.07.

## STAGE 8

It was Kimmage taking his second stage in a row on the final stage from Gorey to Dublin's Phoenix Park winning the sprint from a 4-man group which included the race leader who finished third on the stage to increase his lead on Ahern who dropped 29 seconds which included Glowaty's 15 seconds third place bonus.
Ahern had not given up his chance of the overall win without a fight and on the climb of the Wicklow Gap he attacked and went away on his own. However the yellow jersey soon went in pursuit taking with him team-mate Chojnacki, Kimmage and Kildare pair Murt Logan and Liam Baxter.
This break stayed away to the finish although Ahern, suffering from his attempts to get away, dropped back on the run-in to the finish finishing with a chasing bunch who were led in by Cork's Mick Twomey, 14 seconds behind.

*1963 winner – Poland's Glowaty, pictured in the centre*

The visitors had scored a decisive victory but the Irish, although no match for the Poles' team tactics, were by no means disgraced taking half the stages and through Ahern making the winner fight all the way for his win. The Poles finished 1st, 3rd, 4th and 10th and had a decisive win in the team classification. Their visit caused huge interest in the race and an estimated crowd of 15,000 watched the finish in the Park.

**Stage 8 Gorey - Dublin 70 Mls.** 1 C.Kimmage (Dublin) 2.50.10 2 M.Logan (Kildare) 3 Z.Glowaty (Poland) 4 N.Chojnacki 5 L.Baxter (Kildare) all same time 6 M.Twomey (Cork) at 14 secs.

**General Classification:** 1 Z.Glowaty (Poland) 34.09.17 2 D.Ahern (Kerry) at 2.17 3 M.Chojnacki (Poland) at 6.17 4 J.Linde (Poland) at 6.32 5 P.Wall (Tipperary) at 6.53 6 C.Kimmage (Dublin) at 7.55 7 L.Baxter (Kildare) at 10.17 8 J.Kennedy (Dublin) at 13.09 9 J.Goddard (Exiles) at 14.25 10 J.Mikolajczyk (Poland) at 14.30 11 D.Kenny (Exiles) at 15.01 12 S.Cullen (Dublin) at 16.10 13 M.Twomey (Cork) at 17.09 14 P.Reidy (Cork) at 17.14 15 S.Lally (Sligo) at 21.40 16 A.Williams (Dublin) at 23.04 17 R. Shaw (Cork) at 23.08.

In a footnote to the race the Polish team stayed on for a track meeting in the Eamon Ceannt Stadium, Crumlin on the following Wednesday. They easily beat an Irish quartet in a 4000 metres team pursuit after one of the Irish team, Mick Finegan punctured. Their time was 5.19.

Gene Mangan won the 1000 metres TT equalling the Irish record in 1.17, 2 seconds ahead of Jerzy Linde. Linde was also second in a 20 laps scratch behind Sonny Cullen with Finnegan third. Finegan won the 1 lap sprint.

## 1964

With the RÁS now settled into the early July date, there were no overseas team in the 1964 event and among those being mentioned as pre-race favourites were past winners O Hanlon, Mangan and McKenna.
Also strongly fancied was 19-year-old Mike O'Donoghue from Carlow who had just had a string of good results and even more prominently the other past winner in the field, Paddy Flanagan of Kildare, who had been virtually unbeatable over the previous month including the Irish 100m. MS Championship where he had dead-heated with Mick Christle the previous Sunday.
O Hanlon was back racing in Ireland and had won the only stage race of the year, the 4-day RÁS Uladh and he looked to be in top form when he rode away from the field in a 50Kms race in the Phoenix Park, a few days before the start

### STAGE 1

The four past winners in the field were all prominent on the opening stage, Flanagan and McKenna driving the main break of the day, O Hanlon prominent in the chase which brought it to an end, and Gene Mangan, after keeping quiet all day, coming through with a great sprint to take the stage in a big bunch finish.
The opening stage was a short one, only 54 miles from Dublin to Carlow and Flanagan and McKenna were immediately into action as they powered away in a break which contained Mike O'Donoghue, Pat Reidy and K. O'Brien (Cork), John Drumm and John Brosnan (Kerry) Gerry McKenna and Eddie McGrath (Antrim) and Eamon Keane (Waterford).
By the time they passed Clondalkin the break was already well established and on the Naas dual carriageway their lead was over a minute on the chasing pair of Shay O Hanlon and Meath's Mick Creighton with the bunch 30 seconds further behind.
The position was unchanged at Naas but by Kilcullen O Hanlon and Creighton were caught. The Dublin team, now with nobody away, went to the front and working well gradually reduced the lead until the break was ended eight miles from the finish, paving the way for a bunch gallop in which Mangan (riding in this RÁS for Carlow) showed all his old speed to win from three of the Dublin team: Jimmy Kennedy, Bob Naylor and Sonny Cullen.
**Stage 1 Dublin - Carlow 54 Mls.** 1 G.Mangan (Carlow) 2.02.00 2 J.Kennedy (Dublin) 3 R.Naylor (Dublin) 4 S.Cullen (Dublin) 5 J.Lonergan (Tipperary) 6 M.O'Donoghue (Carlow) all same time.

## STAGE 2

There was a surprise early on stage 2 when the race leader retired, prompting speculation that he had not the fitness for a full RÁS and never intended going all the way.
At the end of the 118 miles stage to Cork, it was Paddy Flanagan who came home on his own, 15 seconds in front of a group of nine led in by O Hanlon, which gave the Kildare man they jersey over the Dubliner with a margin of 45 seconds.
First to show were Flanagan and McKenna again along with Brendan Magennis (Antrim), Mick Creighton, Peter Sargent and Paddy Hynes (Armagh) and Bob Shaw (Derry). When they were caught it was the turn of Tom Reilly (Meath), Tommy Hughes (Armagh) and Sonny Cullen, who were chased by Ben McKenna and Jimmy Kennedy going through Kilkenny.
After another regroupment O Hanlon attacked on the hill out of Carrick-on-Suir but he too was brought back. Leaving Dungarvan O Hanlon went again taking with him Johnny Drumm (Kerry), Liam Baxter (Kildare), K. O'Brien (Cork), Mike O'Donoghue, Sonny Cullen, Paddy Flanagan and Ben McKenna and they soon were over a minute up.
This break too was caught with the field splitting up as small groups continually opened up a gap only to be brought back. Ben McKenna and Sean Lally (Dublin) led at Middleton chased by Flanagan and O Hanlon with a group of ten eventually coming together at the front from which Flanagan got away in the last half mile.
**Stage 2 Carlow - Cork 118 Mls.** 1 P.Flanagan (Kildare) 5.14.00 2 S.O Hanlon (Dublin) at 15 secs 3 M.O'Donoghue (Carlow) 4 S.Lally
(Dublin) 5 J.Drumm (Kerry) 6 G.McKenna (Antrim) all same time.
**General Classification:** 1 P.Flanagan (Kildare) 7.17.00 2 S.O Hanlon (Dublin) at 45 secs 3 M.O'Donoghue (Carlow) at 1.00 4 equal S.Lally (Dublin) G.McKenna (Antrim) B.McKenna (Meath) T.Pratt (Cork) L.Baxter (Kildare) all at 1.15.

## STAGE 3

It was Paddy Flanagan again on the 82 miles stage to Kenmare, again on his own, this time 1 minute ahead of Ben McKenna, his win increasing his lead to 2.45. McKenna was second while O Hanlon had dropped to 7th, ten minutes down.
At the start in Cork it was raining gently but as the day wore on the wind got up to near gale force, spread-eagling the field on a day so bad that there were seven retirals.
Flanagan made his opening attack on the climb out of Glengariff catching early breakaways Ben McKenna and team-mate Mick Creighton. He dropped the Meath riders on the descent of the Tunnel Road coming home a minute ahead of McKenna with Creighton a further 5 seconds back while Johnny Drumm (Kerry) led in a chasing group another 25 seconds behind.

**Stage 3 Cork - Kenmare 82 Mls.** 1 P.Flanagan (Kildare) 11.06.10 2 B.McKenna (Meath) at 1.00 3 M.Creighton (Meath) at 1.05 4 J.Drumm (Kerry) at 1.30 5 J.Lonergan (Tipperary) 6 E.Flanagan (Kildare) all same time.
**General Classification:** 1 P.Flanagan (Kildare) 11.06.10 2 B.McKenna (Meath) at 2.45 3 M.Creighton (Meath) at 7.05 4 J.Drumm (Kerry) at 7.45 5 equal J.Lonergan (Tipperary) and E. Flanagan (Kildare) at 8.20 7 S.O Hanlon (Dublin) at 10.15 8 T.Reilly (Meath) at 10.30.

## STAGE 4

Shay O Hanlon won the fourth stage, 97 miles from Kenmare to Castleisland but although he improved four places to lie third overall, he still trailed leader Flanagan by 6 minutes. The stage was something of a Dublin benefit with five riders in the first six, only Louth's Peter Sargent spoiling their clean sweep.
The opening move came from Denis McGrath (Dublin) and Gabriel Howard, a Meath man riding for Derry. (This was Gabriel's first mention in reports of the RÁS in which he would be a stage-winner and after a notable career continued his association as part of one of the permanent service crews, as did another rider who was prominent during this period, Mick Twomey.)
They were first over the Coomakista Pass, 1 minute ahead of Sonny Cullen, Kevin O'Brien (Cork), Francie Davey (Antrim) and Meath pair of Mick Creighton, Tom Reilly and Kildare's Jim Halligan. By Cahirciveen the two leaders had been caught and now at the front 30 seconds ahead of the bunch were McGrath, Cullen, Davey, Reilly, O'Brien, Howard and Halligan.
With the bunch all together again Sean Lally and Bob Naylor attacked at Killorglin and when they had a gap established Dublin team-mate O Hanlon jumped across and the three, working like clockwork, were 2 minutes ahead as they passed through Tralee.
They rode flat out on the run-in to Castleisland, Lally not able to hold the pace but hanging on to take third, just one second ahead of the fast closing bunch.
**Stage 5 Kenmare - Castleisland 97 Mls.** 1 S.O Hanlon (Dublin) 4.50.10 2 R.Naylor (Dublin) s.t. 3 S.Lally (Dublin) at 1.53 4 P.Sargent (Louth) at 1.54 5 S.Cullen (Dublin) 6 J.Kennedy (Dublin) all same time.
**General Classification:** 1 P.Flanagan (Kildare) 15.59.14 2 B.McKenna (Meath) at 2.45 3 S.O Hanlon (Dublin) at 6.21 4 M.Creighton (Meath) at 7.05 5 equal E.Flanagan (Kildare) and J.Lonergan (Tipperary) at 8.20.

## STAGE 5

Flanagan, who admitted on Wednesday to having taken too much out of himself in the rain on Stage 3, had his second bad day in a row, coming in the bunch 3.23 behind Ben McKenna, who took over the lead by 23 seconds from the Kildare rider.

The stage went to Sonny Cullen (Dublin) who won from a 4-man group on the 144 miles stage to Galway, McKenna coming in 16 seconds later.
Johnny Brosnan (Kerry) went away on his own before Ennis and going through the town he had a 1 minute lead over Sonny Cullen, Johnny Lonergan and Wexford's Larry Doran. The four came together and at one time their lead was over 2 minutes but it had been cut back to less than 20 seconds as they approached Galway city by a chasing group of 11 from which Mike O'Donoghue almost bridged the gap to the leaders with Antrim's Gerry McKenna leading in the rest of the chasers.
**Stage 5 Castleisland - Galway 114 Mls.** 1 S.Cullen (Dublin) 5 25.10 2 J.Lonergan (Tipperary) 3 J.Brosnan (Kerry) 4 L.Doran (Wexford) all same time 5 M.O'Donoghue (Carlow) at 10 secs 6 G.McKenna (Antrim) at 16 secs.
**General Classification:** 1 B.McKenna (Meath) 21.27.25 2 P.Flanagan (Kildare) at 22 secs 3 M.Creighton (Meath) at 4.20 4 J.Lonergan (Tipperary) at 4.49 5 S.O Hanlon (Dublin) at 6.41 6 M.O'Donoghue (Carlow) at 8.14 7 G.McKenna (Antrim) at 8.15 8 T.Reilly (Meath) at 9.51 9 S.Lally (Dublin) at 10.04 10 S.Cullen (Dublin) at 10.14 11 R.Naylor (Dublin) at 10.38 12 F Davey (Antrim) at 10.46.

## STAGE 6

Kildare's Liam Baxter won the sixth stage, 76 miles from Galway to Castlebar leading in a three man group from Sean Lally (Dublin) and Jim Halligan (Kildare) but the bunch, led in by Bob Naylor from Paddy Flanagan was only 52 seconds behind and there were no changes at the top. It looked that Flanagan, confident of his ability in Sunday's time-trial, was content to keep McKenna at 22 seconds.
The close marking of the Dublin and Kildare teams was causing tension in the bunch and race director Joe Christle severely cautioned the field before the start after blows had been exchanged between members of the two teams on the previous stage.
The three who were to fight out the finish, along with Kevin O'Brien (Cork) went away within 5 miles of the start in Galway and at one time their lead was over 4 minutes ahead of a chasing group containing McKenna, Flanagan, O Hanlon and Creighton.
O Hanlon gambled on a solo effort and left the chasers and got almost to within a minute of the leaders. He failed but it was a gallant effort as it took the other three 35 miles to catch him even though his lead on them never exceeded a minute.
**Stage 6 Galway - Castlebar 76 Mls.** 1 L.Baxter (Kildare) 3.14.00 2 S.Lally (Dublin) 3 J.Halligan (Kildare) all same time 4 R.Naylor (Dublin) at 52 secs 5 P.Flanagan (Kildare) at 55 secs 6 S.Cullen (Dublin) s.t.
**General Classification:** 1 B.McKenna (Meath) 24.42.20 2 P.Flanagan (Kildare) at 22 secs 3 M.Creighton (Meath) at 4.20 4 J.Lonergan (Tipperary) at 5.49 5 S.O Hanlon (Dublin) at 6.43 6 M.O'Donoghue (Carlow) at 8.14 7 S.Lally (Dublin) at 8.38 8 T.Reilly (Meath) at 9.51 9 S.Cullen (Dublin) at 10.24 10 R.Naylor (Dublin) at 10.45 11 G.McKenna (Antrim) at 12.00 12 L.Baxter (Kildare) at 14.57.

## STAGE 7

It was a home win on the Saturday stage from Castlebar to Navan (134) when local man Frank Reilly was first across the line. Fortune smiled on the Meath man as his companion in the 2-man break, Bob Naylor, an acknowledged sprinter, unshipped his chain within sight of the finish line.

The bunch containing all the top men of GC came in 1.25 behind the leaders and there was no change overall, everything coming down to the last stage time trial.

The stage had just got underway when Reilly and Naylor went away and soon had a substantial lead. At one time it was over 3 minutes but they lost 1 minute at a closed level-crossing in Castlerea. Luck was still against them when they lost 30 seconds at a wrong turning in Castlepollard but they kept going and as neither posed a big danger on GC, the bunch seemed content to let them stay out in front.

The only change in the overall position was that Naylor moved up two places to eighth. Two more riders got away from the bunch in pursuit and Jimmy Kennedy (Dublin) won the sprint for third from another Navan rider Mick Collins but Collins crashed and was unable to start the following stage.

**Stage 7 Castlebar - Navan 134 Mls.** 1 F.Reilly (Meath) 5.30.00 2 R.Naylor (Dublin) at 20 secs 3 J.Kennedy (Dublin) at 31 secs 4 M.Collins (Meath) s.t. 5 E.McGrath (Antrim) at 1.25 6 M.Logan (Kildare) s.t.

**General Classification:** 1 B.McKenna (Meath) 30.13.45 2 P.Flanagan (Kildare) at 22 secs 3 M.Creighton (Meath) at 4.20 4 J.Lonergan (Tipperary) at 5.49 5 S.O Hanlon (Dublin) at 6.43 6 M.O'Donoghue (Carlow) at 8.14 7 S.Lally (Dublin) at 8.38 8 R.Naylor (Dublin) at 8.40 9 T.Reilly (Meath) at 9.51 10 S.Cullen (Dublin) at 10.24.

## STAGE 8 (a) and (b)

Paddy Flanagan made history by becoming the first rider to win the RÁS twice. He didn't win the time-trial stage from Navan to Dublin (25 miles), that honour going to O Hanlon, but his margin over race-leader Ben McKenna was enough to turn his 22 second deficit into a victory margin of 1.29.

O Hanlon's victory on the time-trial, covering the 25 miles in 54.29, gave him the stage win by 19 seconds from Flanagan and was enough to lift him to 3rd overall.

McKenna excelled himself in the time-trial, not his favourite discipline, and actually finished 3rd on the stage, but up against two of the best riders against the watch that Ireland has ever produced, his task proved too much so it was Flanagan and not the Meath man who got the first RÁS double.

The 50 kilometre afternoon stage in the Phoenix Park was never likely to change the GC. Like the rest of the week it was a tussle between Dublin and Kildare, Jimmy Kennedy (Dublin) winning from Kildare's Murt Logan in a six-man sprint, the bunch led in by O Hanlon in 7th place.

On the third of the ten laps Logan, Larry Doran (Wexford), Tommy Hughes (Armagh) and Peter Sargent (Louth) opened up a 200 yards advantage. Next time round Hughes was gone and Johnny Drumm (Kerry) and Jim Halligan (Kildare) had joined the leaders.
Two laps later the break was still away but Drumm had dropped back and Jimmy Kennedy (Dublin) had got up, the break holding a 15 second advantage on the bunch. On lap 6 they were still away but there was a chasing group of Patsy Wall (Tipperary) and Antrim pair Francie Davey and Gerry McKenna. Johnny Drumm rejoined the leaders only to be dropped again but when the leading four had 1 minute on the bunch at the bell, it was certain they wouldn't be caught.
Kennedy won comfortable from Logan, Doran and Sargent while behind T. Pratt (Cork) and P Wall (Tipperary) got away from the bunch to take 5th and 6th.
**Stage 8a Navan - Dublin 25 Mls. TT:** 1 S.O Hanlon (Dublin) 54.29 2 P.Flanagan (Kildare) 54.48 3 B.McKenna (Meath) 56.24 4 M.O'Donoghue (Carlow) 56.35 5 S.Lally (Dublin) 56.55 6 M.Creighton (Meath) 56.58 7 R.Naylor (Dublin) 57.28 8 L.Baxter (Kildare) 57.35 9 J.Lonergan (Tipperary) 58.03 10 G.McKenna (Antrim) 58.16.
**Stage 8b Circuit Phoenix Park 30 Mls.** 1 J.Kennedy (Dublin) 1.10.16 2 M. Logan (Kildare) 3 L.Doran (Wexford) 4 P.Sargent (Louth) all same time 5 T.Pratt (Cork) at 40 secs 6 P.Wall (Tipperary) s.t.
**General Classification:** 1 P.Flanagan (Kildare) 32.19.54 2 B.McKenna (Meath) at 1.29 3 S.O Hanlon (Dublin) at 5.32 4 M.Creighton (Meath) at 6.38 5 J.Lonergan (Tipperary) at 8.12 6 M.O'Donoghue (Carlow) at 10.10 7 S.Lally (Dublin) at 10.54 8 R.Naylor (Dublin) at 11.58 9 T.Reilly (Meath) at 13.43 10 S.Cullen (Dublin) at 14.49
**Team:** 1 Meath (McKenna Creighton T Reilly) 97.21.32 2 Dublin (O Hanlon Lally Naylor) 97.28.06 3 Kildare (P.Flanagan Baxter E.Flanagan) 98.00.23.

*Paddy Flanagan, 1964 winner*

# 1965

The Rás moved to June 20th in 1965 and it was the start of the O Hanlon era. In a feat, probably unparallel in any major stage race, the Dubliner, after winning the opening stage, would be the only wearer of the leader's jersey for three years.
In keeping with his custom of following current trends in the Tour de France, race director Joe Christle decided to run a Junior RÁS (just as the Tour had its Tour de l'Avenir) in parallel with the main event. However, unlike the Tour de l'Avenir, the juniors in the RÁS rode with the seniors on all stages except the Ring of Kerry stage, when they had a rest day but they had their own general classification. The experiment was a mixed success, probably because there were not enough good standard juniors for a completely separate event, and it was not continued in later years. Some years later juniors would get their own week-long event when the Junior Tour of Ireland was created by J.J. McCormack.
After Flanagan's second win in 1964 he was again among the favourites but between him and the treble was O Hanlon who had been unbeatable during the season prior to the RÁS winning the Rás Uladh and Rás Mumhain stage races as well as the Irish 100 miles road race title which had taken place on the Sunday prior to the Rás.

## STAGE 1

O Hanlon threw down the gauntlet to all aspirants for overall honours when he won the opening stage, 84 miles from Dublin to Monaghan, 5 seconds ahead of Patsy Wall (Tipperary) with the remainder of the winning break led in by Kerry's Johnny Drumm, 4 seconds later.
O Hanlon looked in some trouble in the first hour when an 8-man break including Dublin's Jimmy Kennedy built up a 30 second lead and then were joined by a second group containing such danger men as Ben McKenna and Mick Creighton (Meath) and Tipperary's Lonergan brothers.
By Drogheda this big group at the front were still going away with their lead approaching 2 minutes. On Tullyesker hill, after Drogheda, O Hanlon went in pursuit with Drumm and Monaghan's Tony Murphy and after a hard chase they joined the leaders. With so many top men now away, those left in the bunch could say goodbye to any hope of a high placing on GC.
There were 26 entrants in the Junior RÁS and they had a tough day, the best of them coming in 3 minutes down with Tony Small (Harp) finishing best to take the lead from team-mate Paul O'Connell and Joe Lonergan (Clonmel CC).
**Stage 1 Dublin - Monaghan 84 Mls.** 1 S.O Hanlon (Dublin) 3.15.00 2 P.Wall (Tipperary) at 5 secs 3 J.Drumm (Kerry) s.t. 4 J.Kennedy (Dublin) 5 R.Shaw (Dublin) 6 A.Murphy (Monaghan) all same time.

**Junior Rás Stage 1:** 1 A.Small (Harp CC) 2 P.O'Connell (Harp CC) 3 J.Lonergan (Tipperary) 4 A.Robinson (Velo Sport) 5 B.Keane (Waterford); 6 R.McNamara (Clann Brugha).

## STAGE 2

Gabriel Howard (Meath) jumped away from the field 12 miles from the finish in Birr and held on gamely to take the stage. With no big gaps at the finish, the top six stayed unchanged.

Although the day ended with little change, the 115 miles stage had been one of constant attacks with small breaks holding on for a few miles only to be brought back by the hard chasing bunch.

After an opening attack by Dublin pair Jimmy Kennedy and Sean Lally was neutralised, this was followed by a good looking move when 17 riders built up a lead of 30 seconds only to be brought by the leader who was not prepared to let any dangerous moves develop.

Former winner Gene Mangan went away spurring the only attack of the day from leader O Hanlon who joined him and the two built up a lead of around 30 seconds but by Mullingar they were safely back in the main field.

At Kilbeggan it was the turn of Meath's Tom Reilly who stayed out in front until after Tullamore where he was joined by team-mate Mick Creighton and Tipperary's Eddie Phelan but by Kilmacormack the field was once again intact.

It was looking like a big bunch sprint when Howard slipped off with 12 miles to go and against the odds hung on to take the stage by 32 seconds while Junior RÁS rider A. Robinson led in the bunch ahead of Tommy Hughes (Louth).

**Stage 2 Monaghan - Birr 115 Mls.** 1 G.Howard (Meath) 5.35.00 2 A.Robinson (Velo Sport) at 32 secs 3 T.Hughes (Louth) at 35 secs 4 P.Connell (Harp) 5 J.Kennedy (Dublin) 6 R.Naylor (Galway) all same time.

**General Classification:** 1 S.O Hanlon (Dublin) 7.51.35 2 P.Wall (Tipperary) at 35 secs 3 J.Drumm (Kerry) at 54 secs 4 J.Kennedy (Dublin) s.t. 5 equal R.Shaw (Dublin) A.Murphy (Monaghan) M.Creighton (Meath) B.McKenna (Meath) J.Roche (Louth) T.Kiely (Tipperary) and S.Lally (Dublin) all at 1.09

## STAGE 3

O Hanlon went on the offensive on the third stage and emphasised his dominance when he came home on his own to win the stage, 39 seconds ahead of second placed Johnny Lonergan (Tipperary) opening up a big gap at the top of the class sheet of 2.35 over Patsy Wall (Tipperary).

The Dubliner was in the opening move which went from the line with 9 others including past winner Ben McKenna. Their lead went to 25 seconds but the bunch came back to them going into Roscrea.

Next on the offensive were Johnny Drumm (Kerry), Patsy Wall (Tipperary), Jimmy Kennedy (Dublin) and junior Tony Small (Harp) but they too were soon swallowed up.
Approaching Durrow O Hanlon went again in company with Tony Murphy (Monaghan), Patsy Wall and John Brosnan (Kerry) and they soon built up a 1.15 gap which had increased by 2 minutes by Urlingford.
The bunch sensed the danger and were chasing hard with Ben McKenna prominent at the front and at Borrisoleigh it looked that the break would be soon caught. However O Hanlon, realising that his companions were tiring, went off on his own just before the bunch came up.
For the final 14 miles it was a pursuit between the leader and the bunch and he held on strongly to hold his advantage to the finish where he had 39 seconds in hand over Johnny Lonergan and Denis McGrath (Dublin) who in turn had 13 seconds on Mike O'Donoghue (Carlow) while Bobby Shaw (Dublin) led in the bunch exactly a minute behind the winner.
**Stage 3 Birr - Nenagh 77 Mls** 1 S.O Hanlon (Dublin) 3.22.00 2 J.Lonergan (Tipperary) at 39 secs 3 D.McGrath (Dublin) s.t. 4 M.O'Donoghue (Carlow) at 52 secs 5 R.Shaw (Dublin) at 1.00 6 J.Kennedy (Dublin) s.t.
**General Classification:** 1 S.O Hanlon (Dublin) 11.12.35 2 P.Wall (Tipperary) at 2.35 3 equal J.Drumm (Kerry) and J.Kennedy (Dublin) at 2.54 5 equal R.Shaw (Dublin) A.Murphy (Monaghan) M.Twomey (Cork) M.Creighton (Meath) B.McKenna (Meath) T. Kiely (Tipperary) and S. Lally (Dublin) at 3.09 12 T.Hughes (Louth) at 5.15
**Junior Rás** 1 equal A.Small (Harp CC) and T.O'Connell (Harp CC) 11.18.41 3 A.Robinson (Velo Sport) at 3.36

## STAGE 4

O Hanlon had to produce something extra to retain the jersey on stage four, 94 miles from Nenagh to Killarney when he was back in the bunch at Newcastlewest, 4.30 down on a strong break. However he fought back and ended up winning the stage and with his performance surely destroying any remaining hopes his rivals may have had of overall victory.
Shortly after the start six riders went away: Sean Lally, Mick Christle and Paddy Hynes (Dublin), Joe Roche (Louth), Tony Small (Harp CC) and Johnny Drumm (Kerry). These six had a 45 second lead at Bird Hill on the main Limerick Road and shortly afterwards they were joined by the entire Meath team: Creighton, McKenna, Kennedy, Howard and Reilly as well as Phelan (Tipperary), Power (Waterford), Neary (Louth) and Sergeant (Gate RC).
It started to look ominous for the race leader when the big break was timed at 3.00 ahead with the lead steadily increasing to 4.30 at Limerick. It steadied at 4.30 until Newcastlewest when O Hanlon decided it was do or die and started to chase in company with young Monaghan rider Tony Murphy.

After a great ride they caught the leaders immediately going on the attack when only Drumm, Lally, Neary, Howard and Hynes could stay with him the sextet coming in 3.25 ahead of a chasing group of eight.

**Stage 3 Nenagh - Killarney 94 Mls.** 1 S.O Hanlon (Dublin) 5.00.00 2 J.Drumm (Kerry) 3 S.Lally (Dublin) 4 P.Neary (Louth) 5 G.Howard (Meath) 6 P.Hynes (Dublin) all same time.

**General Classification:** 1, S.O Hanlon (Dublin) 16.11.36 2 J.Drumm (Kerry) at 3.23 3 S.Lally (Dublin) at 3.53 4 equal M.Creighton (Meath) B.McKenna (Meath) and A.Murphy (Monaghan) at 7.28 7 T.Kiely (Tipperary) at 8.28 8 T.Reilly (Meath) at 10.25 9 S.Kennedy (Meath) at 10.27 10 G.Howard (Meath) at 11.14 11 equal P.Wall (Tipperary) and P.Hynes (Dublin) at 12.51

## STAGE 5

A bad day on Wednesday saw Dublin's Jimmy Kennedy drop out of contention for overall honours but he hit back next day to take the prestigious Ring of Kerry Stage with Kerry's Johnny Drumm second into Killarney for the second day in a row.

O Hanlon had some anxious moments during the stage when team-mate Sean Lally looked like he might be riding into the jersey. However the Dubliner fought back on the climbs and finished with the leaders in 4th place, the only change on overall being the improvement of Drumm, lying second overall, whose bonus moved him 30 seconds closer to the leader.

Shortly after they rolled away from Killarney Gene Mangan went on the offensive along with Dublin pair Denis McGrath and Bobby Shaw and they were joined by Lally, Tony Arthur's (Kerry) and Paddy Neary and going through Mangan's home town of Killorglin the break were over a minute up.

At Glenbeigh it was nearly 2 minutes on a chasing group of Mick Creighton (Meath), John Clark (Tipperary), Mike O'Donoghue (Carlow), and Cork pair Frank O'Sullivan and Jim Dorgan. Dorgan dropped back but the rest joined up with the leaders with Creighton and Neary going away on the Coomakista Pass.

On the climb O Hanlon left the bunch in pursuit and on the descent caught McGrath, Arthur's, O'Donoghue and the leaders Neary and Creighton, but he had to stop with a loosening headset, the signal for Lally, McGrath and Arthur's to break clear.

O Hanlon, back in the bunch waited until the next big climb where he went away with Drumm, Kennedy and Tipperary's Patsy Wall and they caught the leaders on the fast descent of Moll's Gap where Arthur's crashed.

With five miles remaining Kennedy attacked and just held on to the line ahead of the fast finishing Drumm.

**Stage 5 Killarney - Killarney 104 Mls.** 1 J.Kennedy (Dublin) 5.07.00 2 J.Drumm (Kerry) 3 P.Wall (Tipperary) 4 S.O Hanlon (Dublin) 5 P.Neary (Louth) 6 E. Phelan (Tipperary) all same time

**General Classification:** 1 S.O Hanlon (Dublin) 21.18.39 2 J.Drumm (Kerry) at 2.54 3 S.Lally (Dublin) at 7.07 4 equal B.McKenna (Meath) and M.Creighton (Meath) at

9.55 6 T.Kiely (Tipperary) at 10.27 7 P.Wall (Tipperary) at 11.53 8 G.Howard (Meath) at 12.59 9 P.Hynes (Dublin) at 15.16 10 R. Naylor (Galway) at 18.47

## STAGE 6

After their 'day off' during the ring of Kerry stage, the riders of the Junior Rás were back in the field on Friday and they must have benefited from the rest as three of them finished in the winning 5-man break, one of them, Bernard Keane (Waterford) winning the stage.

Sean Lally also finished in the break which came in 4.46 ahead of race-leader O Hanlon, Lally moving up to second overall 2.06 behind his team-mate. The other senior in the break, Jimmy Kennedy, who had dropped out of the top ten after his bad day on Wednesday, in two stages had fought back to lie 3rd overall.

It was the fresh juniors who were on the attack from the gun, Tony Small going away to be joined by fellow juniors Campbell (Velo), Sargeant (Gate), Junior Rás leader O'Connell (Harp), Keane and Power (both Waterford), Lonergan and Cummins (both Tipperary), Mills (Clan Brugha), plus seniors Lally and Kennedy and Clancy (Galway).

Perhaps it was the presence of so many juniors in the break that caught O Hanlon off-guard but when their lead stretched to over 6 minutes Lally was race-leader on the road and it was time to hit the panic button.

The big group at the front was eventually reduced to five, Kennedy, Lally, Keane, Small and O'Connell and they rode strongly with their lead continually growing. It was not until the climb of Gloccamaura that O Hanlon started to chase in earnest with a group that included Wall, Pratt, O'Sullivan, Kiely, Twomey, Naylor and McKenna and they did enough over the remaining miles to save the leader's jersey.

**Stage 6 Killarney - Clonmel 94 Mls.** 1 B.Keane (Waterford) 3.46.00 2 J.Kennedy (Dublin) 3 A.Small (Harp) 4 P.O'Connell (Harp) all same time 5 S.Lally at 15 secs 6 R.Naylor (Galway) at 4.31

**General Classification:** 1 S.O Hanlon (Dublin) 25.09.25 2 S.Lally (Dublin) at 2.06 3 J.Kennedy (Dublin) at 6.19 4 J.Drumm (Kerry) at 9.01 5 equal B.McKenna (Meath) and M.Creighton (Meath) at 9.55 7 T.Kiely (Tipperary) at 10.28 8 P.Wall (Tipperary) at 12.35 9 G.Howard (Meath) at 13.41 10 P.Hynes (Dublin) at 15.16 11 R.Naylor (Galway) at 18.31 12 P.Neary (Louth) at 22.11

## STAGE 7

Mike O'Donoghue (Carlow) won the first of his eight Rás stages on the penultimate day, the 106 miles from Clonmel to his home town but there was no change in the general classification with O Hanlon still firmly in control.

**Stage 7 Clonmel - Carlow 106 Mls** 1 M.O'Donoghue (Carlow) 4.12.00

**General Classification:** 1 S.O Hanlon (Dublin) 2 S.Lally (Dublin) at 2.06 3 J.Kennedy (Dublin) at 6.19 4 J.Drumm (Kerry) at 9.01 5 equal B.McKenna (Meath) and M.Creighton (Meath) at 9.55 7 T.Kiely (Tipperary) at 10.28 8 P.Wall (Tipperary) at 12.35 9 G.Howard (Meath) at 13.41 10 P.Hynes (Dublin) at 15.16 11 R.Naylor (Galway) at 18.31 12 P.Neary (Louth) at 22.11

## STAGE 8 (a and b)

O Hanlon duly ran out a decisive winner and like on his previous win in 1962, he emphasised his superiority by winning the final morning's time-trial while in the afternoon's circuit race in Phoenix Park he was 3rd in the same time as the winner, Bob Naylor riding for Galway.

His efforts on the day considerably stretched his lead and his margin at the end was just under 8 minutes over team-mate Sean Lally with another Dubliner, Jimmy Kennedy third to leave absolutely no doubt about the team win.

The morning TT was from Carlow to Kilcullen and there was nobody in the same league as the race leader who finished the 23 miles test in 55.41 with Meath's Mick Creighton next best with 57.09. Lally was third in 58.26 and Monaghan's Tony Murphy 4th, 58.30 while Cork riders Tom Pratt and Frank O'Sullivan completed the first six.

Tony Small (Harp CC) went into history as the winner of the one and only Junior RÁS ahead of his team-mate Paul O'Connell.

The afternoon's stage was over ten laps of the 3-mile circuit in the Park and O Hanlon made his move on the fourth lap, jumping across to an early break which included O'Callaghan (Waterford), Roche (Louth), O'Donoghue (Carlow), O'Connell (Harp), Naylor (Galway), McGrath (Dublin), Murphy (Monaghan), and Cork pair Twomey and O'Sullivan.

There was drama in the final sprint when Murphy and O'Sullivan came down 400 metres from the line, the Monaghan rider having to be taken to hospital, thus being deprived of a high overall placing following his good ride in the TT. In a blanket finish the first six all were timed at 1.08.15.

**Stage 8(a) TT Carlow - Kilcullen 23 Mls.** 1 S.O Hanlon (Dublin) 55.41 2 M.Creighton (Meath) 57.09 3 S.Lally (Dublin) 58.26 4 A.Murphy (Monaghan) 58.30 5 T.Pratt (Cork) 58.47 6 F.O'Sullivan (Cork) 58.56

**Stage 8(b) Dublin - Dublin 30 Mls.** 1 S.O Hanlon (Dublin) 1.08.15 2 M.O'Donoghue (Carlow) 3 S.O Hanlon (Dublin) 4 P.O'Connell (Harp) 5 M.O'Callaghan (Waterford) 6 M.Twomey (Cork) all same time

**General Classification:** 1 S.O Hanlon (Dublin) 31.27.20 2 S.Lally (Dublin) at 7.56 3 J.Kennedy (Dublin) at 13.22 4 M.Creighton (Meath) at 14.45 5 J.Drumm (Kerry) at 16.22 6 B. McKenna (Meath).

(A tragic footnote to the 1965 Rás was that three riders who were very prominent in that event, Bernard Keane, Waterford Johnny Drumm of Kerry and Paddy Neary of Louth, were all killed in accidents in the year before the next RÁS).

*Sé O Hanlon, Winner 1965*

## 1966

There were several major innovations in the 1966 RÁS. Most important was the increase from 8 to 10 days, the race now starting on the Friday evening. This would continue until 1974 when the Friday stage was dropped, to be used once more, in 1988 when the race began on Friday with a criterium in Dublin to mark the city's millennium celebrations.
1966 also saw the first criterium in the RÁS, a one hour event in Killarney. As a result of the success of this stage criterium were often included over the next few years before falling out of favour as this type of stage often gave a somewhat distorted result, playing an important role on GC which seemed out of proportion to the amount of racing involved compared to the rest of the week's racing.
O Hanlon, defending his title, was greatly assisted in his task by the organizers who put in a long time-trial as the opening stage from Dublin to Navan, as the Dubliner at that time was acknowledged to be almost unbeatable against the watch.
Not in his favour was the end of the big all conquering Dublin teams. To solve the problem of Dublin, which had a huge pool of riders looking for a place in the race, club teams were allowed and O Hanlon was entered for a weak-looking Clann Brugha. A strong Dublin outfit, now in opposition, was Setanta which included past winner Gene Mangan along with two other contenders for top honours Jimmy Kennedy and Sonny Cullen. Meath too were split with their previous year's star Mick Creighton on a Navan Road Club entry.
There was an international flavour again with the inclusion of a French team from the FSGT, the UCI unrecognized French association which was very strong in working class areas of France.
On a personal note it was my first RÁS as a rider and I had the distinction of finishing last on GC after a week-long battle with Gene Tetreaught, an American with the US Forces in Derry who held the lanterne rouge all week only to pack it with two days to go.
Because of the 50th anniversary of the 1916 Rising the leader's jersey was white with tricolour bands instead of the usual yellow.

### STAGE 1

As had been widely expected O Hanlon won the opening TT stage but his margin was not great, just 29 seconds over the other double winner Paddy Flanagan. O Hanlon's time for the straight out course which was just over 25 miles was 57.50.
The French team showed their quality taking the next two places and all four finished in the top ten. The other Flanagan brother, Eddie was fifth while the largely unknown Tony Arthur's of Kerry completed the top six.

After years of Dublin heading the team classification it had a different look with France leading Kildare and Setanta.

**Stage 1 Dublin - Navan 25 Mls. TT.** 1 S.O Hanlon (Clann Brugha) 57.50 2 P.Flanagan (Kildare) 58.19 3 S.Gimenos (France) 58.55 4 J.Dieuegard (France) 59.55 5 E.Flanagan (Kildare) 1.00.16 6 T.Arthur's (Kerry) 1.00.44 7 P.Robert (France) 1.00.55 8 G.Mangan (Setanta) 1.00.55 9 M.Creighton (Navan RC) 1.01.21 10 J.Bellay (France) 1.01.55

## STAGE 2

The French showed they meant business on the first road stage, a short one of 42 miles from Navan to Dundalk, when the winner was Jean Bellay with O Hanlon retaining the yellow jersey.

The stage finished in a bunch sprint where the Frenchman got the better of Bob Shaw (Clan Brugha) and Patsy Wall (Carrick-on-Suir) after the field regrouped a few miles from the finish.

There was a break shortly after the start which included Bellay and Shaw along with Tony Arthur's (Kerry), Tommy Hughes (Galway), Tony Murphy (Monaghan), Mick Kinsella (Kildare) and Pat O'Connell (Harp) and this group had a lead of over 1 minute on the bunch at Kells where they were chased by a group containing O Hanlon, Paddy Flanagan and Sonny Cullen at 30 secs.

The bunch were not letting these three go and the impetus of the chase led to the front group being mopped up as well in time for a big bunch gallop in Dundalk.

Past winner Ben McKenna had the hard luck story of the day. He had been with the break but broke a chain and eventually came in over 8 minutes down.

**Stage 2 Navan - Dundalk 42 Mls.** 1 J.Bellay (France) 1.40.00 2 R.Shaw (Clan Brugha) 3 P.Wall (Carrick-on-Suir) 4 T.Murphy (Monaghan) 5 J.Kennedy (Setanta) 6 G.Mangan (Setanta) all same time

**General Classification: 1** S.O Hanlon (Clann Brugha) 2.37.50 2 P.Flanagan (Kildare) at 29 secs 3 S.Gimenos (France) at 1.05 4 J.Dieumegard (France) at 2.05 5 E.Flanagan (Kildare) at 2.26 6 A.Arthur's (Kerry) at 2.54 7 J.Ropert (France) at 3.05 8 G.Mangan (Setanta) at 3.08 9 M.Creighton (Navan RC) at 3.31 10 M.O'Donoghue (Carlow) at 3.40

## STAGE 3

A great solo ride saw Eddie Flanagan win the third stage, 77 miles from Dundalk to Ballyjamesduff where he attacked with 12 miles of the stage remaining and held on to win by 1.36 on the bunch led in by Jean Bellay. O Hanlon retained the overall lead with the only big change on GC, the improvement of Eddie Flanagan to third.

Seven miles after the start a group of ten went away including three of French team: Bellay, Dieumegard and Gimenos, along with Eamon Breen (Kerry), Mick Creighton

(Navan RC), Jim Halligan (Kildare), Mike O'Donoghue (Carlow) and Carrick-on-Suir pair E. Phelan and J. Cummins.
They opened a gap of less than a minute but it didn't grow and O Hanlon counter-attacked in company with Monaghan's Tony Murphy, Brian Monaghan (Down) and Liam O'Connor (Limerick).
They caught the leaders but the break wouldn't work together and more and more riders joined the leaders the race eventually coming together.
There were a couple more breaks but they were both brought back and it was looking like a bunch finish when Flanagan got away with 12 miles remaining.
**Stage 3 Dundalk - Ballyjamesduff 77 Mls.** 1 E.Flanagan (Kildare) 2.59.10 2 J.Bellay (France) at 1.36 3 G.Mangan (Setanta) 4 P.Flanagan (Kildare) 5 S.Gimenos (France) 6 J.Dieumegard (France) all same time
**General Classification: 1** S.O Hanlon (Clann Brugha) 2 P.Flanagan (Kildare) at 29 secs 3 E.Flanagan (Kildare) at 50s 4 S.Gimenos (France) at 1.05 5 J.Dieumegard (France) at 2.05 6 A.Arthur's (Kerry) at 2.54 7 G.Mangan (Setanta) at 3.08 8 M.Creighton (Navan RC) at 3.35 9 M.O'Donoghue (Carlow) at 3.40 10 J.Bellay (France) s.t. 11 J.Kennedy (Setanta) at 4.13 12 T.Murphy (Monaghan) at 4.16

## STAGE 4

1955 RÁS winner Gene Mangan, riding for Setanta CC, out sprinted team-mate Jimmy Kennedy to take the fourth stage, 71 miles from Ballyjamesduff to Ballinasloe. O Hanlon, who punctured while with the leaders, had to work hard to hold on to his overall lead.
There was early drama when the bunch went off course when in pursuit of a 10-man break. The race was stopped and restarted at Finnea but the break, although set off with a time equal to their advantage when the race was stopped, had lost their rhythm and were soon caught.
Mangan went away at Mullingar but was caught and at Kilbeggan a large group got clear which included Frenchmen Bellay and Ropert, Creighton (Navan RC), Tommy Hughes (Galway), Paul Kelly (Monaghan), Brian Monaghan (Down), Tommy Pratt (Cork), Sean Walsh and Eddie Phelan (Carrick-on-Suir), Jim Halligan (Kildare), Ben McKenna (Meath) and Mike O'Donoghue (Carlow).
After O Hanlon punctured, the leaders were 30 seconds ahead of a chasing group containing Jimmy Kennedy (Setanta), Paddy Flanagan (Kildare), Tony Murphy (Monaghan), C. Kelleher (Limerick) and Gimenos of France.
At Athlone the leaders were in sight and O Hanlon, in a group which included Mangan and the two Flanagan's, set about getting across to the leaders. They succeeded and it was a 20-strong break which arrived together to contest the sprint at Ballinasloe where Mangan, who had last won a stage two years before at Carlow, showed he still had a sprint to beat the best.

**Stage 4 Ballyjamesduff - Ballinasloe 71 Mls.** 1 G.Mangan (Setanta CC) 2.50.10 2 J.Kennedy (Setanta CC) 3 J.Bellay (France) 4 E.Flanagan (Kildare) 5 T.Pratt (Cork) 6 S.Cullen (Setanta CC) all same time
**General Classification:** 1 S.O Hanlon (Clan Brugha) 8.28.46 2 P.Flanagan (Kildare) at 39 secs 3 E.Flanagan (Kildare) at 50 secs 4 S.Gimenos (France) at 1.05 5 G.Mangan (Setanta CC) at 3.08 6 M.Creighton (Navan RC) at 3.31 7 M.O'Donoghue (Carlow CC) at 3.40 8 J.Bellay (France) at 4.05 9 J.Kennedy (Setanta) at 4.13 10 T.Murphy (Monaghan) 4.16 11 B.McKenna (Meath) at 4.29 12 E.Phelan (Carrick-on-Suir) at 4.37

## STAGE 5

Jean-Claude Dieumegard gave the French their second stage win out sprinting John Dorgan (Cork) into Limerick at the end of an eventful 87 miles stage from Ballinasloe which saw big changes in the GC although the top two places remained the same.
Unluckiest man of the day was Jimmy Kennedy (Setanta) who was in a 3-man break on the outskirts of Limerick when he punctured. He led in the chasing group in third place.
Just after the start five riders went away: Kennedy and Dorgan, Tony Arthur's (Kerry), Joe Roche (Velo Sport) and Bob Shaw (Clan Brugha). Riding well together they stayed clear until Ennis they were caught by a group which included Dieumegard.
Previous day's winner Mangan chasing on his own almost made it to the leaders when his gears jammed and he saw the O Hanlon/Flanagan group ride past him and he finished with Eddie Flanagan and Santos Gimenos, 5 minutes down, the three dropping down the GC.
Behind the leaders the gaps really opened in the bunch over the windy final miles. With the Kennedy group, 33 seconds back were Mike O'Donoghue, Sonny Cullen and Brian Monaghan. Ben McKenna and Eddy Phelan came in 2.15 down and 3.30 behind the winner came O Hanlon and Paddy Flanagan. The big losers were the French with the best rider now Gimenos in 9th place.
**Stage 5 Ballinasloe - Limerick 87 Mls.** 1 J.Dieumegard (France) 3.35.10 2 J.Dorgan (Cork) at 5 secs 3 J.Kennedy (Setanta CC) at 33 secs 4 S.Cullen (Setanta CC) 5 B.Monaghan (Down) 6 M.O'Donoghue (Carlow) all same time
**General Classification:** 1 S.O Hanlon Clan Brugha) 12.07.26 2 P.Flanagan (Kildare) at 29 secs 3 M.Creighton (Navan RC) at 34 secs 4 M.O'Donoghue (Carlow) at 43 secs 5 J.Kennedy (Setanta) at 1.16 6 T.Murphy (Monaghan) at 1.19 7 B.Monaghan (Down) at 1.54 8 E.Flanagan (Kildare) at 2.25 9 S.Gimenos (France) at 2.40 10 B.McKenna (Meath) at 3.14 11 E.Phelan (Tipperary) at 3.22 12 J.Bellay (France) at 4.05

## STAGE 6

After his bad luck on Tuesday, Gene Mangan hit back by winning his second stage, the 97 miles from Limerick to Killarney, an especially sweet victory only a few miles from his home town of Killorglin.

Big loser on the day was Kildare's Paddy Flanagan who dropped from 2nd to 9th overall. He took painkillers for the pain in his leg which was injured in a crash on Saturday and they left him feeling unwell throughout the stage.

O Hanlon held on to the top position with a lead of 43 seconds over Mike O'Donoghue with Navan's Mike Creighton a further 47 back.

An early break went away started by Setanta pair Mangan and Mick Christle soon joined by their team mates Sonny Cullen and Jimmy Kennedy. Also there were Seamus Kennedy (Navan RC), Gabriel Howard (Meath), Eddie Green and Tony Arthur's (Kerry), Tommy Hughes (Galway), Tom Pratt and John Dorgan (Cork), Mike O'Donoghue (Carlow), Brian Monaghan (Down), Jean Bellay (France) and race-leader O Hanlon.

With a break this size, especially with many of them in contention, it was a question of whether they would work together and when, as on this occasion, they did, there was little chance of them being brought back. By Abbeyfeale they had over 2 minutes lead and were going away and it stayed like this to Farranfore when the vital split came in the leaders.

O Hanlon, O'Donoghue, Mangan and Bellay went away and despite all the efforts of the remainder of the break, they went nearly a minute up and stayed that way to the finish where they had 56 seconds in hand over their former companions, led in by Cullen with the main bunch at almost 5 minutes.

As well Paddy Flanagan, brother Eddie lost time when he and Ben McKenna were brought down by a runaway horse at Listowel, Flanagan dropping from 3rd to 11th and McKenna from 10th to 13th overall.

**Stage 6 Limerick - Killarney 97 Mls.** 1 G.Mangan (Setanta) 3.26.10 2 J.Bellay (France) 3 M. O'Donoghue (Carlow) 4 S.O Hanlon (Clan Brugha) all same time 5 S.Cullen (Setanta) at 56 secs 6 T.Pratt (Cork) s.t

**General Classification:** 1 S.O Hanlon (Clan Brugha) 15.33.36 2 M.O'Donoghue (Carlow) at 43 secs 3 M.Creighton (Navan RC) at 1.30 4 J.Kennedy (Setanta) at 2.15 5 B.Monaghan (Down) at 2.50 6 J.Bellay (France) at 4.05 7 G.Mangan (Setanta) at 4.43 8 J.Dorgan (Cork) at 4.50 9 P.Flanagan (Kildare) at 5.12 10 T.Murphy (Monaghan) at 6.02 11 E.Flanagan (Kildare) at 6.25 12 E.Breen (Kerry) at 7.57

## STAGE 7

An enormous crowd lined the main street in Killarney for the 1-hour criterium in which 26.5 miles were covered and it was a popular result for the Kerry crowd when Gene Mangan took his third stage in four days.

In the big bunch gallop for the line, Mangan judged his effort just right to win from Frenchman Bellay with O Hanlon third. There were no important changes in the general classification.
Man of the stage was Mick Kinsella of Kildare, riding his first RÁS, who went away on lap 15 staying out in front to take the next five lap primes only to be hauled in half way round the final circuit.
The crowd contributed generously and there were primes every lap. Paddy Flanagan, recovering from his injuries took three laps with others going to Kerrymen Mangan, Jim Brosnan and Eamon Breen, Tom Platt (Cork)(2), Tony Murphy (Monaghan), Sonny Cullen (Setanta), Bob Knowd and Tommy Hughes (Galway), Mike O'Donoghue (Carlow) and Jim Halligan (Kildare) before Kinsella took off the win the rest.
**Stage 7 Killarney - Killarney 26.5 Mls.** 1 G.Mangan (Setanta) 58.24 2 J.Bellay (France) 3 S.O Hanlon (Clan Brugha) all same time
**General Classification:** 1 S.O Hanlon (Clan Brugha) 16.32.00 2 M.O'Donoghue (Carlow) at 43 secs 3 M.Creighton (Navan RC) at 1.30 4 J.Kennedy (Setanta) at 2.15 5 B.Monaghan (Down) at 2.50 6 J.Bellay (France) at 4.05 7 G.Mangan (Setanta) at 4.43 8 J.Dorgan (Cork) at 4.50 9 P.Flanagan (Kildare) at 5.12 10 T.Murphy (Monaghan) at 6.02 11 E.Flanagan (Kildare) at 6.25 12 E.Breen (Kerry) at 7.57

## STAGE 8

O Hanlon asserted his authority on the race winning the eighth stage, in the process stretching his lead to over 4 minutes with just two days to go but he had to show all his fighting qualities when he found himself chasing alone, 1 minute behind a dangerous break containing two Frenchmen, one of whom, Jean Bellay, started the day 6th on G.C.
The race leader was in an initial break of 20 riders which went away shortly after the start of the 98 miles run from Killarney to Carrick-on-Suir. However the two Frenchmen then went away in company with John Dorgan (Cork) who lay 8th overall.
When their lead reached almost a minute, the leader decided to act and went in solo pursuit and after an 8-miles chase he caught the trio. The four stayed away for the rest of the stage enabling O Hanlon to distance himself from the four riders nearest to him at the start of the day. At the finish he was the strongest while Bellay and Dorgan had the satisfaction of moving up to 2nd and 3rd overall.
Paddy Flanagan led in a chasing group of nine riders but they were nearly 5 minutes down but the bunch with Mangan, O'Donoghue, Creighton and Kennedy were over 6 minutes back.
**Stage 8 Killarney - Carrick-on-Suir 98 Mls.** 1 S.O Hanlon (Clan Brugha) 4.00.15 2 J.Bellay (France) 3 J.Dieumegard (France) 4 J.Dorgan (Cork) all same time 5 P.Flanagan (Kildare) at 4.45 6 P.Ropert (France) s.t

**General Classification:** 1 S.O Hanlon (Clann Brugha) 20.32.15 2 J.Bellay (France) at 4.05 3 J.Dorgan (Cork) at 4.50 4 M.O'Donoghue (Carlow) at 6.41 5 M.Creighton (Navan) at 7.24 6 J.Kennedy (Setanta) at 8.22 7 B.Monaghan (Down) at 9.00 8 P.Flanagan (Kildare) at 9.57 9 T.Murphy (Monaghan) at 10.57 10 G.Mangan (Setanta) at 11.03 11 E.Flanagan (Kildare) at 12.35 12 B.McKenna (Meath) at 12.42

## STAGE 9

Bob Shaw won the penultimate stage, 72 miles from Carrick-on-Suir to Kilcullen with Clan Brugha teammate O Hanlon finishing in the main bunch 2.52 behind. As all the major contenders finished with him there were no vital changes in the general classification and the Dubliner looked all set to become the first triple winner carrying a 4.05 advantage into the final day.

Shaw won from a 9-man break which had stayed away for most of the stage while the leaders kept a close watch on each other in the bunch. All nine were timed with the winner at 3.00.15. Shaw had just missed a stage-win on the first road stage exactly a week earlier when he was pipped by Bellay but had his revenge when he beat another Frenchman, Gimenos to the line.

**Stage 9 Carrick-on-Suir - Kilcullen 72 Mls.** 1 R.Shaw (Clan Brugha) 3.00.15 2 S.Gimenos (France) 3 S.Kennedy (Navan RC) 4 T.Pratt (Cork) 5 P.Hynes (Clan Brugha) 6 P.Robert (France) all same time

**General Classification:** 1 S.O Hanlon (Clan Brugha) 22.36.58 2 J.Bellay (France) at 4.05 3 J.Dorgan (Cork) at 4.50 4 M.O'Donoghue (Carlow) at 6.53 5 M.Creighton (Navan RC) at 7.40 6 J.Kennedy (Setanta CC) at 8.20 7 B.Monaghan (Down) at 8.58 8 P.Flanagan (Kildare) at 9.57 9 J.Dieumegard (France) at 10.04 10 T.Murphy (Monaghan) at 10.47 11 G.Mangan (Setanta) at 10.53 12 S.Gimenos (France) at 11.58

## STAGE 10

Paddy Flanagan had some consolation for the illness which put him out of the race for overall honours when he won the final stage from Kilcullen which finished with five laps in the Phoenix Park. However, whereas they had been joint holders of the record for number of RÁS wins on two each, O Hanlon was now undisputed leader on three.

Mick Christle went into action from the opening mile, the long drag out of Kilcullen where he was joined by Setanta teammate Gene Mangan and Monaghan's Tony Murphy and this trio stayed out in front until the a chasing group of eight riders caught them at Rathcoole.

With a tailwind the 11-man group sped along at over 35 mph and this group were all together as they entered the Park where there were five 3-mile laps to finish the race. On the final circuit it was Christle again who made the first move. He was joined by Flanagan but they were brought back and O Hanlon had a go.

Flanagan caught him and went again and at the line he was clear by 6 seconds from the Dubliner with Kennedy winning the third place sprint from Mangan a further 4 seconds behind. The bunch, led in by John Dorgan was 1.03 behind the winner.
The French with three in the break made sure of the team prize beating Setanta who also had three in the lead group. Setanta had led most of the week until the French had two in the vital 4-man break on the Friday.
**Stage 10 Kilcullen - Dublin 42 Mls.** 1 P.Flanagan (Kildare) 1.27.10 2 S.O Hanlon (Clan Brugha) at 6 secs 3 J.Kennedy (Setanta) at 10 secs 4 G.Mangan (Setanta) 5 S.Gimenos (France) 6 T.Murphy (Monaghan) all same time
**General Classification:** 1 S.O Hanlon (Clan Brugha) 25.02.38 2 J.Bellay (France) at 4.09 3 J.Dorgan (Cork) at 5.47 4 M.O'Donoghue (Carlow) at 6.57 5 J.Kennedy (Setanta CC) at 8.36 6 M.Creighton (Navan RC) at 8.37 7 P.Flanagan (Kildare) at 9.51 8 B.Monaghan (Down) at 9.57 9 J.Dieumegard (France) at 10.07 10 T.Murphy (Monaghan) at 10.51 11 G.Mangan (Setanta) at 10.57 12 S.Gimenos (France) at 12.02 13 E.Flanagan (Kildare) at 13.32 14 B.McKenna (Meath) at 13.3915 M.Christle (Setanta) at 14.05
**Team:** 1 France (Bellay, Dieumegard, Gimenos) 75.34.13 2 Setanta CC (Kennedy, Mangan, Christle) at 6.30 3 Kildare 4 Monaghan 5 Navan RC 6 Carrick-on-Suir

*1966 winner – Sé O Hanlon, pictured with Jim Killean, President NCA and Joe Christle*

## 1967

The 1967 RÁS was very similar in format to the previous year's race. The Friday evening opening time-trial was retained and criterium in Monaghan, Carrick-on-Suir and Killarney sought to emulate the success of the criterium in the Kerry town a year earlier.
The French team from the FSGT were back again and would be regular visitors for some years to come. The race started a week earlier on June 23. Like the previous year club teams were allowed and 1996 winner O Hanlon was in a joint club entry, Clan Brugha and Velo Sport combining for the event as Clann Velo.

### STAGE 1

Seamus O Hanlon started the first stage wearing the race leader's jersey by virtue of his win the previous year and after the 25 miles time-trial in Navan on the Navan - Kells Road, he had earned the right to keep it winning by 19 seconds from Louth's Kevin Dolan with the best of the French team Felix Martin third at 41 seconds.
O Hanlon's time for the 25 broke the existing Irish 25 miles time-trial record but the course was not measured under time-trial conditions, being simply a TT stage in a multi-stage event.
The French showed that they were a strong outfit and the led the team race by 3.15 from Louth, quite a large margin after only 25 miles of racing.
**Stage 1 Navan - Navan 25 Mls. TT.** 1 S.O Hanlon (Clann Velo) 55.26 2 K.Dolan (Louth) 55.45 3 F.Martin (France) 56.07 4 A.Lombardo (France) 56.23 5 T.Arthur's (Kerry) 57.37 6 J.Roche (Clann Velo) 58.07 7 M.Creighton (Meath) 58.11

### STAGE 2(a) and (b)

O Hanlon gave his rivals no time to recover when he straight away won the first road stage, the 65 miles run from Navan to Monaghan, the first half of a split stage and when he was third in the evening's criterium there was already a real feeling that he was well on his way to three-in-a row.
All the early attacks in the morning were nullified until four riders went away at Dundalk: Ben McKenna (Meath), John Dorgan (Cork), Tommy Hughes (Louth) and Mike O'Donoghue (Carlow).
This looked like a promising break and the race leader, seeing the danger, went in pursuit with a small group which included Paddy and Eddie Flanagan (Kildare), Frenchmen Pierre Ropert and Georges Journaut, Tom Cullimore (Wexford) and Brian Connaughton (Meath A), these seven catching the leaders at Castleblayney.
Eleven riders contested the sprint and the uphill finish suited O Hanlon who won comfortably from O'Donoghue and Flanagan.

The now customary big crowd watched the evening stage on a 1-mile circuit in Monaghan. Early animator was Felix Martin (France) who took four laps primes in a row before Kildare's Mick Kinsella went off and took three. Also well up in the hunt for lap primes was Down's Brian Monaghan who also won 4 laps. Other laps went to Ropert, Lombardo, O Hanlon, and Pat McGibbon (Armagh).
With eight laps to go Eddie Flanagan (Kildare) and Benny Donnelly (Armagh) went away sharing the primes as they held on to a slender lead which was only 5 seconds at the line with the race leader leading in the bunch in third place.
**Stage 2(a) Navan - Monaghan 65 Mls.** 1 S.O Hanlon (Clann Velo) 2.27.00 2 M.O'Donoghue (Carlow) 3 P.Flanagan (Kildare) 4 G.Journaut (France) 5 P.Ropert (France) 6 E.Flanagan (Kildare) 7 J.Dorgan (Cork) 8 T.Cullimore (Wexford) 9 B.McKenna (Meath) 10 T.Hughes (Louth) 11 B.Connaughton (Meath) all same time
**Stage 2(b) Monaghan - Monaghan 27.5 Mls.** 1 E.Flanagan (Kildare) 1.01.15 2 B.Donnelly (Armagh) same time 3 S.O Hanlon (Clann Velo) at 5 secs 4 J.Bellay (France) 5 P.Ropert (France) 6 P.Flanagan (Kildare) all same time
**General Classification:** 1 S.O Hanlon (Clann Velo) 4.23.41 2 F.Martin (France) at 1.01 3 B.McKenna (Meath) at 2.59 4 P.Flanagan (Kildare) at 3.04 5 M.Creighton (Meath) at 3.06 6 J.Bellay (France) at 3.38 7 M.O'Donoghue (Carlow) at 3.47 8 J.Kennedy (Dublin) at 3.48 9 P.Ropert (France) at 3.52 10 T.Hughes (Louth) at 4.09 11 E.Flanagan (Kildare) at 4.19 12 S.Kennedy (Meath) at 4.28.

## STAGE 3

Dual RÁS winner Paddy Flanagan showed he was still a force to be reckoned with by winning the third stage, 99 miles from Monaghan to Ballinasloe, moving up to second overall. However right on his wheel was race-leader O Hanlon who completed a good day's work but seeing off some of the French threat, erstwhile 2nd overall Martin coming in over 9 minutes down.
The French tried to control the race but lost it halfway through the stage when all six of their team were in a chasing group while up the road were most of the major contenders like O Hanlon, O'Donoghue, Dorgan, and Dolan.
Paddy Flanagan had also missed the key break but in company of Frenchmen Journaut and Ropert, Benny Donnelly (Armagh) and Brian Connaughton (Meath) he started to chase strongly. The French refused to work and it was mainly due to the efforts of Flanagan and Donnelly that they finally made contact six miles after Athlone.
Meanwhile Dolan had gone off on his own and with his ability against the watch looked like he might hold out but when O Hanlon and Flanagan got together to inspire the chase they reeled him in six miles from the finish. With Frenchman Ropert sitting in on the chase this left four at the front and Flanagan took the sprint from O Hanlon with Ropert also beating the tired Dolan. The remainder of the break came in 38 seconds behind led in by O'Donoghue.

**Stage 3 Monaghan - Ballinasloe 99 Mls** 1 P.Flanagan (Kildare) 3.55.10 2 S.O Hanlon (Clann Velo) 3 P.Ropert (France) 4 K.Dolan (Louth) all same time 5 M.O'Donoghue (Carlow) at 38 secs 6 B.McKenna (Meath) 7 G.Journaut (France) 8 J.Dorgan (Cork) 9 P.Hynes (Westmeath) all same time
**General Classification:** 1 S.O Hanlon (Clann Velo) 8.18.51 2 P.Flanagan (Kildare) at 3.05 3 B.McKenna (Meath) at 3.37 4 P.Ropert (France) at 3.42 5 M.O'Donoghue (Carlow) at 4.15 6 J.Dorgan (Cork) at 5.22 7 G.Journaut (France) at 5.28 8 J.Bellay (France) at 7.04 9 J.Kennedy (Dublin) at 7.14 10 E.Flanagan (Kildare) at 7.25 11 V.Sheridan (Kildare) at 8.15 12 B.Connaughton (Meath) at 8.41

## STAGE 4

Another stage win for O Hanlon on the 114 miles run from Ballinasloe to Castleisland left him in a very strong position for another overall victory as he saw another of his main rivals, Paddy Flanagan, lose time and drop to 4th overall. Pierre Ropert of France was the new second place but his deficit on the Dubliner was 4.39.
The race leader looked to be in control throughout the stage chasing everything that went up the road. Bob Shaw went right from the start and was soon joined by O Hanlon. After them went Frenchmen Bellay and Ropert but Bellay dropped back before Portumna leaving just three at the front.
A few miles later they were joined by Martin Power (Tipperary) after a fine ride in company with Cork's John Dorgan. On the long straight roads around Nenagh the bunch could see the break but nobody seemed to want to lead the chase and their chance was gone.
By Limerick the lead was up to 3 minutes as a chasing group tried and failed to bridge the gap. On the Bearnagh Gap O Hanlon attacked and was joined by Ropert but he went again on the descent into Castleisland and this time he stayed away finishing on his own 47 seconds ahead of the rest of the break led in by Dorgan.
**Stage 4 Ballinasloe - Castleisland 114 Mls.** 1 S.O Hanlon (Clann Velo) 4.42.30 2 J.Dorgan (Cork) at 47 secs 3 P.Ropert (France) 4 M.Power (Tipperary) all same time 5 P.Flanagan (Kildare) at 3.17 6 G.Santi (France) 7 G.Journaut (France) 8 K.Dolan (Louth) 9 B.McKenna (Meath) 10 R.Shaw (Dublin) all same time
**General Classification:** 1 S.O Hanlon (Clann Velo) 13.01.21 2 P.Ropert (France) at 4.39 3 J.Dorgan (Cork) at 6.29 4 P.Flanagan (Kildare) at 6.22 5 B.McKenna (Meath) at 6.54 6 M.O'Donoghue (Carlow) at 7.44 7 G.Journaut (France) at 8.45 8 J.Bellay (France) at 11.36 9 J.Kennedy (Dublin) 11.46 10 V.Sheridan (Kildare) at 12.47 11 B.Connaughton (Meath) at 13.13 12 G.Howard (Meath) at 14.11

## STAGE 5(a) and (b)

The RÁS staged its first ever team trial on stage 5a, over 14 miles from Castleisland to Killarney. With the big variation in the quality of RÁS teams, it was wisely decided that the times would only count towards the team race.

With first three riders to count, the French used their lowest three on GC to do most of the work and when Journaut punctured, Bellay and Ropert waited for him while TT specialist Martin, Santi and Lombardo powered ahead to win the stage by 56 seconds from Meath.
The evening stage was a 'round the houses' in Killarney and like the year before it was watched by a big crowd who donated generously to lap primes. With all the top men on GC in the bunch sprint there were no changes to the overall positions.
The organiser was still experimenting with this type of stage and the distance was extended by some 20 minutes, the winner coming home in 1.20.00.
The French, on a roll after their team win in the morning, took the stage with Felix Martin who took off with 9 laps to go and with a superb solo effort put 2.20 into the field in 9 miles. He was helped by the rest of his team behind who used all their skill to stall the bunch at every opportunity. O Hanlon, was quite happy, however, as they did all the defending for him and he only had to keep an eye on second placed Ropert.
**Stage 5(a) Castleisland - Killarney 14 Mls. TTT.** 1 France 2 Meath at 56 secs
**Stage 5(b) Killarney - Killarney 33 Mls.** 1 F.Martin (France) 1.20.00 2 G.Mangan (Kerry) at 2.20 3 J.Bellay (France) 4 P.Flanagan (Kildare) 5 A.Lombardo (France) 6 S.O Hanlon (Clann Velo) all same time
**General Classification:** 1 S.O Hanlon (Clann Velo) 14.23.41 2 P.Ropert (France) at 4.41 3 J.Dorgan (Cork) at 6.11 4 P.Flanagan (Kildare) at 6.22 5 B.McKenna (Meath) at 6.56 6 M.O'Donoghue (Carlow) at 8.25 7 G.Journaut (France) at 8.45 8 J.Bellay (France) at 11.36 9 J.Kennedy (Dublin) at 11.46 10 V.Sheridan (Kildare) at 12.47

## STAGE 6

Keeping up the run of French success, Antonio Lombardo won Wednesday's sixth stage, a short run of 69 miles from Killarney to Crosshaven. He led in a 6 man break from O Hanlon but with none of his closest rivals in the break, the gap had stretched at the front where O Hanlon now led by 6.04 from Ropert who kept second place.
Although the stage was relatively short, it contained a few tough climbs and was run off in strong winds and drizzling rain. O Hanlon was in action almost from the start when seven riders went away and they would stay together for most of the stage.
With the leader and Lombardo was O'Donoghue, who was to improve his 6th place to 4th, Kevin Dolan, another French rider Gerard Santi and Westmeath pair Christy Reynolds and Colm Nulty.
Behind several chasing groups formed but lack of a serious driving force in each saw their efforts fail. Eventually most of O Hanlon's main rivals finished in a big group, 1.35 behind the stage winner.
**Stage 6 Killarney - Crosshaven 69 Mls.** 1 A.Lombardo (France) 2.38.25 2 S.O Hanlon (Clann Velo) 3 M.O'Donoghue (Carlow) 4 G.Santi (France) 5 C.Reynolds (Westmeath) 6 C.Nulty (Westmeath) 7 K.Dolan (Louth) all same time 8 T.Hughes (Louth) at 1.35 9 P.Flanagan (Kildare) 10 G.Journaut (France) all same time

**General Classification:** 1 S.O Hanlon (Clann Velo) 17.02.26 2 P.Ropert (France) at 6.04 3 J.Dorgan (Cork) at 7.44 4 M.O'Donoghue (Carlow) at 7.45 5 P.Flanagan (Kildare) at 7.57 6 B.McKenna (Meath) at 8.29 7 G.Journaut (France) at 10.20 8 J.Bellay (France) at 13.11 9 J.Kennedy (Dublin) at 13.21 10 V.Sheridan (Kildare) at 14.22 11 B.Connaughton (Meath) at 14.48 12 K.Dolan (Louth) at 15.06

## STAGE 7

Yet another of the French team won a stage when Gerard Santi, who had been in the winning break the previous day, led in a 6-strong group into Cahir at the end of a 69 miles stage from Crosshaven.
Behind Paddy Flanagan led in the bunch which contained all the contenders 1.15 down. Biggest loser on the day was Cork's Dorgan who dropped from 3rd to 6th.
The break went away around Cork city and there were 8 included. Bob McNamara (Clann Velo) fell back from the leaders when he had mechanical trouble and French rider Journaut sat up and waited for the chasers, presumably to help Ropert.
This left six at the front: Santi, Pat McGibbon and Donal Lavery (Armagh), Gabriel Howard and Mick Creighton (Meath) and Vincent Sheridan (Kildare) and while their lead fluctuated throughout the day and they were in sight of the chasers on some long straights, they held on to the end.
**Stage 7 Crosshaven - Cahir 69 Mls.** 1 G.Santi (France) 2.54.30 2 P.McGibbon (Armagh) 3 M.Creighton (Meath) 4 V.Sheridan (Kildare) 5 G.Howard (Meath) 6 D.Lavery (Armagh) all same time
**General Classification:** 1 S.O Hanlon (Clann Velo) 19.58.11 2 P.Ropert (France) at 6.04 3 M.O'Donoghue (Carlow) at 7.45 4 P.Flanagan (Kildare) at 7.57 5, B.McKenna (Meath) at 8.29 6 J.Dorgan (Cork) at 13.01 7 V.Sheridan (Kildare) at 13.07 8 F.Martin (France) at 15.31 9 G.Journaut (France) at 15.37 10 S.McGuinness (Offaly) at 15.50 11 G.Howard (Meath) at 16.11 12 B.Donnelly (Armagh) at 16.48

## STAGE 8(a) and (b)

O Hanlon suffered a rare TT defeat in the morning's 22.5 miles time-trial but the winner, Felix Martin of France who beat him by 34 seconds, was 14 minutes behind him in the overall standings and posed no threat to his overall lead.
Starting last he had caught the number two on GC Pierre Ropert, who started 2 minutes in front of him with three miles of the stage to go.
There was a big mix up in Clonmel which was chock-a-block with traffic, many riders, including the race-leader, going the wrong way up a one-was street. Some were called back by Gardai and some got through.
This lead to a spate of objections, both from riders who had been called back and those who had gone the proper route. In the end race director Christle threw out all the objections and let the finishing times stand.

Another objection was from Paddy Flanagan, third in the TT, who had moved to within 19 seconds of Ropert, whom, Kildare alleged, had taken pace from O Hanlon after he was caught. However officials said that while O Hanlon and Ropert had caught and recaught each other several times, no pace was taken.
The evening stage was a 30 lap criterium in Carrick-on-Suir on a 0.9 mile circuit where the French got their second win of the day through Antonio Lombardo who edged out breakaway companion Benny Donnelly (Armagh) in the sprint.
Although the pair finished 1.10 ahead of a chasing group there was little change to the top end of the general classification with the main contenders all in the main bunch which finished 1.25 behind Martin.
Lombardo and Donnelly were away for much of the stage and the pair won a rich haul of primes, Martin 13 and Donnelly 9. They worked well together until two laps to go when the Frenchman attacked. Although Donnelly chased and caught him by the finish, Martin stayed in front to take the stage. Pat McGibbon (Armagh) led in a chasing group to take third.
Earlier Mick Walsh (Kildare) had taken the first two laps being caught on the third where Mike O'Donoghue won the sprint. Then the French were to the fore Martin winning the 4th and Lombardo took the next three. There was now a small group away from which Donnelly won the 8th lap and team-mate McGibbon the 9th. Lombardo and Donnelly shared the next two.
McGibbon and Frank Reilly (Cavan) were with Lombardo and Donnelly at this stage with O Hanlon trying to bridge the gap on his own. However after the leading quartet split, Donnelly and Martin forged ahead stretching their lead all the way.
**Stage 8a Cahir - Carrick-on-Suir 22.5 Mls.** 1 F.Martin (France) 52.19 2 S.O Hanlon (Clan Velo) 52.54 3 P.Flanagan (Kildare) 53.21 4 T Hughes (Louth) 53.21 5 A.Lombardo (France) 53.45 6 M.Creighton (Meath) 54.01
**Stage 8b Carrick-on-Suir - Carrick-on-Suir 27 Mls.** 1 A.Lombardo (France) 1.05.30 2 B.Donnelly (Armagh) same time 3 P.McGibbon (Armagh) at 1.10 4 G.Journaut (France) 5 F.Reilly (Cavan) 6 C.Nulty (Westmeath).
**General Classification:** 1 S.O Hanlon (Clan Velo) 21.58.00 2 P.Ropert (France) at 6.03 3 P.Flanagan (Kildare) at 6.22 4 M.O'Donoghue (Carlow) at 7.49 5 B.McKenna (Meath) at 9.59 6 equal F.Martin (France) and V. Sheridan (Kildare) at 12.57 8 J.Dorgan (Cork) at 14.49 9 B.Donnelly (Armagh) at 15.38 10 S.McGuinness (Offaly) at 17.05

## STAGE 9

Mick Creighton won the 9th stage in a 3-up sprint from Tony Arthur's (Kerry) and his Meath team-mate Seamus Kennedy. They were chased home 15 seconds late by Antonio Lombardo (France) while the bunch came in together 56 seconds behind.
With the short stage and only a short circuit stage in Dublin to come, there was little chance of any worthwhile moves developing and the top men on GC all seemed

content to stay in the bunch, especially as O Hanlon, with a lead of over 8 minutes seemed to be now out of reach.

He did however have some anxious moments when he was caught up in traffic going through Kilkenny in pursuit of the break and when he narrowly missed a parked car in Leighlinbridge.

**Stage 9 Carrick-on-Suir - Carlow 67 Mls.** 1 M. Creighton (Meath) 2.35.05 2 T.Arthur's (Kerry) 3 S.Kennedy (Meath) all same time 4 A.Lombardo (France) at 15 secs 5 S.O Hanlon (Clann-Velo) at 56 secs 6 P.Flanagan (Kildare) s.t

**General Classification:** 1 S.O Hanlon (Clann-Velo) 24.34.01 2 P.Ropert (France) at 8.03 3 P.Flanagan (Kildare) at 8.42 4 M.O'Donoghue (Carlow) at 9.49 5 B.McKenna (Meath) at 11.59 6 equal V.Sheridan (Kildare) and F.Martin (France) at 14.56 8 B.Donnelly (Armagh) at 17.38 9 M.Creighton (Meath) at 18.10 10 S McGuinness (Offaly) at 19.05 11 S.Kennedy (Meath) at 19.31 12 G.Howard (Meath) 19.36

## STAGE 10

O Hanlon wore the RÁS leader's jersey for his 28th consecutive day of racing to score his third successive and fourth victory in all but he had a scare on the final day with a crash that saw him finish with a mud-splattered jersey and a gashed elbow into the Phoenix Park where Jimmy Kennedy won the final stage.

The crash happened with two laps of the Park to go when Frenchman Martin skidded on the rain-soaked surface and came down right in front of the race-leader. Both were up immediately but O Hanlon had punctured and continued on team-mate Joe Roche's machine.

Despite the strange bike he chased to such effect that he finished 6th on the stage, 21 seconds behind the winner.

The RÁS finished with a 30 miles circuit race in the Park. This developed into a tactical battle as the French tried to block the third and fourth placed riders on GC, Paddy Flanagan and Mike O'Donoghue, in defence of Ropert's second place. Their tactics just succeeded but by the narrowest of margins, Flanagan finishing just 1 second behind the Frenchman on GC.

*1967 winner Se O Hanlon*

A group of eight went away on the fifth lap: O Hanlon, Lombardo, Martin, Vincent Sheridan, Jimmy Kennedy, Joe Roche, Ben McKenna and Cyril Kevlihan. This group were 25 seconds ahead when the crash occurred.
Back in the bunch Flanagan and O'Donoghue finally shook off their French policemen and went away in the company of Louth's Kevin Dolan but they just failed to make enough time to improve their overall standing.
At the finish Kennedy and Sheridan got clear to finish 5 seconds ahead of Lombardo with Kevlihan and McKenna a further 4 and 5 seconds down with O Hanlon coming back for 6th 21 seconds behind Kennedy.
**Stage 10 Dublin - Dublin 30 Mls.** 1 J Kennedy (Dublin) 1.15.45 2 V.Sheridan (Kildare) same time 3 A.Lombardo (France) at 5 secs 4 C.Kevlihan (Louth) at 9 secs 5 B.McKenna (Meath) at 11 secs 6 S.O Hanlon (Clan Velo) at 21 secs 7 F.Martin (France) at 30 secs 8 M.O'Donoghue (Carlow) at 51 secs 9 K.Dolan (Louth) 10 P.Flanagan (Kildare) all same time
**General Classification:** 1 S.O Hanlon (Clan Velo) 25.50.07 2 P.Ropert (France) at 8.31 3 P.Flanagan (Kildare) at 8.32 4 M.O'Donoghue (Carlow) at 9.59 5 B.McKenna (Meath) at 11.49 6 V.Sheridan (Kildare) at 14.35 7 F.Martin (France) at 15.05 8 B.Donnelly (Armagh) at 18.06 9 M.Creighton (Meath) at 19.33 10 S.McGuinness (Offaly) s.t. 11 S.Kennedy (Meath) at 20.00 12 G.Howard (Meath) at 20.03 13 G.Journaut (France) at 21.10 14 E.Flanagan (Kildare) at 22.03 15 J.Dorgan (Cork) at 22.26
**Team:** 1 France 72.20.18 2 Meath 78.42.02 3 Kildare 78.44.49 4 Armagh 79.25.07 5 Westmeath 79.33.44 6 Louth 79.33.45

# 1968

The 1968 RÁS delivered a shock to Irish cyclists the likes of which they had never experienced before and demonstrated just how much the NCA was in need of real international competition.
Race director Joe Christle had an invitation to send a team accepted by the Czechoslovakian federation and it was understood that a club standard team would be sent.
However 'les evenements', the student revolution of Paris in May 1968 saw the cancellation of the amateur Tour de France: the Tour de 'Avenir
And the Czechs who had their Olympic/World Championship team in peak form after the Peace Race, with a large hole in the programme. So they sent them to Ireland.
With the French returning once more, it was decided by the NCA to select an Irish team for the first time in the RÁS giving the event three national teams. As county teams had already been organized, a compromise was reached that the six riders selected would also count for their counties in the county classification. The six were Seamus O Hanlon (Dublin), Benny Donnelly (Antrim), Kevin Dolan (Louth), Tony Ryan (Tipperary), Mike O'Donoghue (Carlow) and Seamus Kennedy (Meath).
From the opening stage the visitors showed no mercy and set out to win everything that was to be won. Unlike the Polish and later Russian teams who came to the RÁS, they remained aloof from the home riders and it wasn't long before a strong animosity developed. I remember well the early stages with the six Czechs pounding away at the front while the entire field stretched out in a long line, each rider fighting for dear life to hold the wheel in front.
After a few stages of being hammered, some late night meetings developed a strategy to deal with the Czechs and an unofficial Irish Second team was selected. With two men to mark each Czech they more or less contained them for the rest of the week, however the Irish only salvaged one stage and very little else.

## STAGE 1

Friday's Irish Press posed the question in a huge headline: Are the Czechs Invincible'. After Friday night's 65 miles stage to Newry the answer could have been given - yes! With the visitors taking the first six places, it was 3.25 before the first of the home riders arrived in Newry.
A sign of what was to come came accidentally when the flag was dropped for the ceremonial start at the GPO in O'Connell Street. The Czechs didn't realise the race was neutralized for the first six miles and took off like a rocket. The rest of the field thought they better stay with them and the race shot off up the Drumcondra Road at

full speed through the Dublin rush hour, in two single lines each side of the slow-moving traffic.
The race officials couldn't get past the traffic and it was some miles out of the city before they got to the front and stopped the race allowing everything to get together for the racing start. They might as well have let it continue for the Czechs went straight to the front riding flat out with everyone else hanging on.

Something had to give and a big split occurred at the front with the Czech team, most of the Irish team and another half-dozen riders riding away from the rest. It stayed like this until Dunleer, with 25 miles to go when Czechs Karel Vavra and Pavel Dolozel went away. The Irish tried to match them but to no avail and then it was the turn of Jiri Zelenka and Pavel Konecny to go clear, and when they had opened up a gap the other two dropped back to wait for them and then the four started working like a TTT squad.
Some miles later the other two Czechs took off and came home some 1.45 behind Zelenka who won the stage. Mike O'Donoghue was 7th at 3.25 leading in Mick Creighton (Meath), Pierre Evan (France); Seamus Kennedy (Ireland/Meath) Kevin Dolan (Ireland/Louth) and Seamus O Hanlon (Ireland/Dublin).
**Stage 1 Dublin - Newry 65 Mls.** 1 J.Zelenka 2.18.40 2 P.Konecny; 3 K.Vavra 4 P.Dolozel all same time 5 M.Hrazdira at 1.45 6 J.Havelka s.t. (all Czechoslovakia) 7 M.O'Donoghue (Ireland) at 3.25 8 P.Evan (France) 9 S.Kennedy (Ireland) 10 K.Dolan (Ireland) all same time

## STAGE 2

It was more of the same for the Irish riders on the 90 miles stage from Newry to Ballyjamesduff with the Czechs taking the first four places, all four of them ahead of the field which was led in by Mike O'Donoghue, just ahead of another Czech, Dolozel.
Stage winner was Milan Hrazdira, but the lead went to Pavel Konecny. Overnight leader Zelenka who had been followed every inch of the stage by Shay O Hanlon, finished with the bunch six minutes behind the winner and dropped to 9th overall. This man-to-man marking by the desperate Irish was a sign of things to come.
The field, with the Czechs setting the pace, stayed together on the climbs out of Newry at Newtownhamilton and Keady Mountain but the pace at the front saw the field split with 30 riders in a leading group at Cavan.
From here to the finish the Czechs used a tactic of sending riders away and by the finish four of them had gone, leaving O'Donoghue to salvage some home pride by winning the sprint for 5th.
**Stage 2 Newry - Ballyjamesduff 90 Mls.** 1 M.Hrazdira (Czechoslovakia) 3.26.30 2 J.Havelka (Czech) at 15 secs 3 K.Vavra (Czech) at 25 secs 4 P.Konecny at 30 secs 5 M.O'Donoghue (Ireland) at 1.40 6 P.Dolozel 7 S.Kennedy (Ireland) 8 B. Donnelly (Ireland) 9 T.P.Reilly (Meath) 10 C. Nulty (Meath) all same time

**General Classification:** 1 P.Konecny (Czech) 5.45.55 2 K.Vavra (Czech) at 10 secs 3 M.Hrazdira (Czech) at 30 secs 4 J.Havelka (Czech) at 1.45 5 P.Dolozel (Czech) at 1.55 6 equal M.O'Donoghue (Ireland) M.Creighton (Meath) and S.Kennedy (Ireland) at 5.50 9 J.Zelenka (Czech) at 5.55 10 S.O Hanlon (Ireland) at 9.30

## STAGE 3

Two of the Czech team: Jiri Zalenka and Milan Hrazdira jumped away from the bunch 1.5 miles after the start in Ballyjamesduff and were never seen again, Zelenka taking the stage from his team-mate in Ballinasloe, almost 6 minutes ahead. Hrazdira took over the race lead by 4 minutes from Zelenka.

The bunch, however, had obviously decided that they weren't going to let any more go and the rest of the Czechs were fiercely marked all day, every move they made chased down by up to four Irish riders. This led to frayed tempers and in one incident Havelka, closely marked by O Hanlon, dropped right back from the bunch and out the back of the cavalcade before trying, to no avail, to drop the Irish captain.

In similar fashion Mike O'Donoghue was glued to the wheel of Konecny while Jimmy and Seamus Kennedy were on Dolozel and Vavra. It was the latter two who went for home at Athlone, the two Irishmen staying with them all the way to the finish where Jimmy Kennedy was unlucky not to take third, pulling his foot out of the toe clip in the finishing straight. As it was Dolozel and Vavra finished 3rd and 4th ahead of the two Kennedy's, all in the same time.

**Stage 3 Ballyjamesduff - Ballinasloe 85 Mls.** 1 J.Zelenka (Czech) 3.06.00 2 M.Hrazdira (Czech) s.t. 3 P.Dolozel (Czech) at 5.58 4 K.Vavra (Czech) 5 J.Kennedy (Dublin B) 6 S.Kennedy (Ireland) all same time

**General Classification:** 1 M.Hrazdira (Czech) 8.53.10 2 J.Zelenka (Czech) at 4.00 3 K.Vavra (Czech) at 4.53 4 P.Dolozel (Czech) at 6.37 5 P.Konecny (Czech) at 6.57 6 J.Havelka (Czech) at 7.42 7 S.Kennedy (Ireland) at 10.08 8 M.O'Donoghue (Ireland) at 12.17 9 M.Creighton (Meath B) at 13.17 10 J.Kennedy (Dublin B) at 16.13 11 S.O Hanlon (Ireland) at 16.37 12 K.Dolan (Ireland) at 16.41

## STAGE 4

Open hostility flared up after the fourth stage form Ballinasloe to Spiddal with the Irish holding tactics resulting in three Irish riders getting into the top six. Overnight leader Hrazdira was involved in a scuffle with O Hanlon after the Irishman's tough marking saw the two of them finish over 10 minutes behind the winner Zalenka who took over the race lead.

Best of the Irish was Seamus Kennedy in 3rd place while Benny Donnelly was 5th and Mike O'Donoghue 6th and they actually managed to slightly dislodge the Czech's grip on the general classification with Seamus Kennedy taking over 5th overall.

Interviewed after the stage O Hanlon explained their tactics: "We had to do something. They were getting it far too easy. They wanted us to work with them and drop us, as they did on Friday, when it suited them. We had to work to our strength. Each man was given a Czech to mark and his job was to stay on his wheel. They did not like it and that outburst at the end showed that."
After chasing everything down all day, the Irish finally let four Czechs: Havelka, Konecny, Zelenka and Dolozel, get away at Oranmore with only O'Donoghue, Kennedy and Donnelly able to go with them.
The four visitors worked furiously and at Oughterard they had a lead of 5 minutes which was up to 7 by Costello. On the run-in to the finish the Czechs tried in turn to get away and eventually their superiority told with Zelenka, Konecny and Havelka getting away with only Kennedy sitting on. Behind them O'Donoghue contrived to get Donnelly away from Dolozel and the Antrim rider caught the leaders after a couple of miles of hard chasing.
Zelenka made use of a passing lorry to get away from the leaders and opened up a minute gap by the finish where Konecny out sprinted Kennedy after the two had gone clear. Havelka came home next having shaken off Donnelly on the run-in and 5 minutes later O'Donoghue led in Dolozel.
**Stage 4 Ballinasloe - Spiddal 94 Mls.** 1 J.Zelenka (Czech.) 3.45.10 2 P.Konecny (Czech) at 1.05 3 S.Kennedy (Ireland) s.t. 4 J.Havelka (Czech) at 1.43 5 B.Donnelly (Ireland) at 2.11 6 M.O'Donoghue (Ireland) at 4.58
**General Classification:** 1 J.Zelenka (Czech) 12.41.50 2 P.Konecny (Czech) at 4.17 3 J.Havelka (Czech) at 6.35 4 M.Hrazdira (Czech) at 6.50 5 S.Kennedy (Ireland) at 7.18 6 P.Dolozel (Czech) at 7.44 7 K.Vavra (Czech) at 12.03 8 M.O'Donoghue (Ireland) at 13.45 9 B.Donnelly (Ireland) at 16.11 10 M.Creighton (Meath B) at 24.14 11 S.O Hanlon (Ireland) at 14.44 12 K. Dolan (Ireland) at 14.48

## STAGE 5

The Irish took a stage and it was O Hanlon who won a furious 15-man downhill sprint after the 114 miles from Spiddal to Abbeyfeale. Next was Czech Vavra with the French finally also getting into the placings with Pierre Evan (France)
The Czechs, fed up with being marked by the whole bunch, must have decided to cut down the numbers early on and the whole team took off from the start, stringing out the bunch on the road into Galway. Inevitably the elastic snapped and off the front went the sextet accompanied by Dolan, O'Donoghue, Donnelly, O Hanlon and Kennedy (Ireland), Brian Monaghan (Down), Colm Nulty (Meath) and Barry Lacey (Dublin).
However behind everyone had not given up the fight. While at the front with the county team race in mind some county riders were prepared to work with the Czechs to improve their positions while the same incentive drove a chasing bunch which got up to the leaders at Newmarket-on-Fergus.

Colm Nulty (Meath) then attacked and was joined by Konecny and the two raced clear. Konecny punctured and as he waited for a wheel the break passed. Three of this team dropped back to bring him up and the Irish took the opportunity to try and distance them but after a hard chase they got back to the leaders.
Once again it was the Irish sitting on and giving the Czechs no latitude and it stayed like that to the finish where O Hanlon took a very welcome Irish victory.
**Stage 5 Spiddal - Abbeyfeale 114 Mls.** 1 S.O Hanlon (Ireland) 4.40.10 2 K.Vavra (Czech) 3 P.Evan (France) 4 P.Dolozel (Czech) 5 M.Hrazdira (Czech) 6 K.Dolan (Ireland) all same time
**General Classification:** 1 J.Zelenka (Czech) 17.25.45 2 M.Hrazdira (Czech) at 3.55 3 P.Dolozel (Czech) at 4.16 4 P.Konecny (Czech) at 4.17 5 J.Havelka (Czech) at 4.22 6 S.Kennedy (Ireland) at 7.38 7 K.Vavra (Czech) at 8.03 8 M.O'Donoghue (Ireland) at 14.00 9 J.Kennedy (Dublin B) at 15.38 10 B.Donnelly (Ireland) s.t. 11 S.O Hanlon (Ireland) at 19.32; 20 K.Dolan (Ireland) at 20.06

## STAGE 6

The hilly 76 miles stage from Abbeyfeale to Dingle saw the visitors reassert their dominance with Hrazdira coming home alone, 9 minutes before Dolozel out sprinted Jimmy Kennedy for second place.
The pattern had been as on previous days until Tralee when Hrazdira got away with his shadow O Hanlon on his wheel. They were soon joined by overnight leader Zelenka, who had slipped away from Seamus Kennedy after some confusion at the front of the bunch, and Christy Reynolds (Meath).
With Reynolds only interested in the inter-county race, he didn't help O Hanlon in marking the Czechs and with them taking it in turns to attack, eventually Hrazdira got away. This left O Hanlon now glued to Zelenka who wasn't prepared to work with the Meath rider who held out riding on his own at the front for 25 miles before they were caught.
John Mangan (Kerry) then broke away joined by Vavra and his marker Kevin Dolan as they came through Dingle for the first time with a loop of Slea Head to come. They were followed by Dolozel and Jimmy Kennedy who got up to the chasers and it stayed that way to the finish. Hrazdira's big gap saw him take over the yellow jersey.
**Stage 6 Abbeyfeale - Dingle 76 Mls.** 1 M.Hrazdira (Czech) 3.32.15 2 P.Dolozel (Czech) at 8.29 3 J.Kennedy (Dublin B) 4 K.Dolan (Ireland) 5 K.Vavra (Czech) 6 J.Mangan (Kerry) all same time
**General Classification:** 1 M.Hrazdira (Czech) 21.02.55 2 P.Dolozel (Czech) at 7.31 3 J.Zelenka (Czech) at 8.51 4 K.Vavra (Czech) at 13.30 5 P.Konecny (Czech) at 12.22 6 J.Havelka (Czech) at 16.13 7 S.Kennedy (Ireland) at 16.29 8 M.O'Donoghue (Ireland) at 18.05 9 K.Dolan (Ireland) at 23.36 10 B.Donnelly (Ireland) at 24.29 11 S.O Hanlon (Ireland) at 28.23 12 J.Kennedy (Dublin B) at 29.03

## STAGE 7

There was a change of tactics by the Irish for Stage 7, a short 51 miles run form Dingle to Killorglin. It was decided that while the close marking would continue, if they got away with a Czech, they would work with him. This greatly improved both the racing and the atmosphere in the bunch with a lifting of the siege mentality.
Winner of the stage was again a Czech, Jan Havelka who won in an uphill sprint from Benny Donnelly, described by Tom O'Shea in the Irish Press as the 8 stone 12 lbs. bundle of racing magic from Belfast.
Havelka jumped away right after the flag was dropped and was immediately joined by Donnelly. He was surprised but delighted when the Ireland rider went to the front and the two soon built up a lead.
At Farranfore Hrazdira put on the pressure and a group of six went off the front of the bunch including O Hanlon, Colm Nulty and Christy Reynolds (Meath), Barry Lacey and Jimmy Kennedy (Dublin) and Czech. Dolozel.
By Killarney this group was 30 seconds behind the two leaders but as the chasing group were joined by several other riders the impetus went out of the chase and the leaders stretched their advantage but at the Line it was only 25 seconds on Dolozel who got away near the finish.
**Stage 7 Dingle - Killorglin 51 Mls.** 1 J.Havelka (Czech) 2.15.24 2 B.Donnelly (Ireland) s.t. 3 P.Dolozel (Czech) at 22 secs 4 J.Zelenka (Czech) at 1.33 5 P.Konecny (Czech) 6 S.O Hanlon (Ireland)
**General Classification:** 1 M.Hrazdira (Czech) 23.18.04 2 P.Dolozel (Czech) at 8.08 3 J.Zelenka (Czech) at 10.51 4 K.Vavra (Czech) at 13.37 5 P.Konecny (Czech) at 16.22 6 J.Havelka (Czech) at 14.58 7 S.Kennedy (Ireland) at 18.29 8 M.O'Donoghue (Ireland) at 24.05 9 B.Donnelly (Ireland) at 24.29 10 K.Dolan (Ireland) at 25.36 11 S.O Hanlon (Ireland) at 30.23 12 J.Kennedy (Dublin B) at 31.03

## STAGE 8

The Czechs gave a superb display of climbing on Friday's 126 miles stage from Killorglin to Crosshaven finishing with three riders coming home nearly 12 minutes in front of the next group, this time Dolozel taking stage honours. Hrazdira was with the leaders and stayed in yellow.
On the first climb at Molls Gap race-leader Hrazdira went off on his own and on the descent he was joined by team mates Dolozel and Vavra and the three worked together to put the huge gap between themselves and the rest over the next 100 miles.
The next group home was led in by Mike O'Donoghue and included Czech Konecny, and three of the Meath team: Christy Reynolds, Gabriel Howard and Colm Nulty.
**Stage 8 Killorglin - Crosshaven 126 Mls.** 1 P.Dolozel (Czech) 5.37.55 2 K.Vavra (Czech) 3 M.Hrazdira (Czech) all same time 4 M.O'Donoghue (Ireland) at 11.45 5 P.Konecny (Czech) 6 C.Reynolds (Meath) 7 G.Howard (Meath) 8 C.Nulty (Meath) all same time

**General Classification:** 1 M.Hrazdira (Czech) 28.55.54 2 P.Dolozel (Czech) at 7.38 3 K.Vavra (Czech) at 13.18 4 J.Zelenka (Czech) at 24.36 5 P.Konecny (Czech) at 26.07 6 J.Havelka (Czech) at 28.23 7 S.Kennedy (Ireland) at 32.14 8 M.O'Donoghue (Ireland) at 35.50 9 B.Donnelly (Ireland) at 37.54 10 K.Dolan (Ireland) at 39.21 11 S.O Hanlon (Ireland) at 44.08 12 J.Kennedy (Dublin B) at 44.48

## STAGE 9

Dreadful weather was a major feature of the penultimate stage and the strong headwinds and torrential rain, which never eased during the 4 hours of racing, caused many retirements, some even ending up in hospital suffering from exposure.

The Czechs again took the top placings the stage going this time to Zelenka after Hrazdira had looked like the winner approaching the finish in Carrick-on-Suir only to overshoot a corner on the twisting descent leaving the way open for his compatriot.

The break of the day had gone away shortly after the start as they approached Cork City. All the Czechs were there along with most of the Ireland team as well as some county riders.

At Dungarvan an effort by Meath's T. P. Reilly was chased by Hrazdira, Zelenka and Havelka and they soon got rid of the Meath man. The trio soon built up a lead and O Hanlon set off on a lone chase. It was unsuccessful but he finished fourth after being joined by Dolozel. Just behind Mike O'Donoghue led in the remainder of the break.

**Stage 9 Crosshaven - Carrick-on-Suir 90 Mls.** 1 J.Zelenka (Czech) 4.04.55 2 J.Havelka (Czech) s.t. 3 M Hrazdira (Czech) at 25 secs 4 S.O Hanlon (Ireland) at 5.05 5 P.Dolozel (Czech) s.t. 6 M.O'Donoghue (Ireland) at 5.25

**General Classification:** 1 M.Hrazdira (Czech) 33.01.01 2 P.Dolozel (Czech) at 11.41 3 K.Vavra (Czech) at 19.11 4 J.Zelenka (Czech) at 24.04 5 J.Havelka (Czech) at 27.56 6 P.Konecny (Czech) at 31.50 7 S.Kennedy (Ireland) at 37.52 8 M.O'Donoghue (Ireland) at 41.43 9 B.Donnelly (Ireland) at 43.32 10 S.O Hanlon (Ireland) at 48.11 11 K.Dolan (Ireland) at 55.44 12 C.Reynolds (Meath) at 56.01

## STAGE 10

If the Irish harboured any hoped that the Czechs might rest on their laurels on the final stage, 100 miles from Carrick-on-Suir to Dublin they were soon dispelled and it was the story as before with two of the all-conquering visiting team coming into the Phoenix Park 4.15 ahead of the next group which was led in by another Czech.

Czechoslovakia was also the lead story on most of the front pages that Monday with the Eastern bloc countries, less Czechoslovakia, meeting in Warsaw to decide on what action they would take about the Dubcek government. This would lead to the Warsaw Pact countries invading Czechoslovakia to end the so-called 'Czech spring'.

In retrospect the situation back home was probably responsible for the aloofness of their cycling team in Ireland. Indeed Irish riders who met members of the team,

especially RÁS winner Hrazdira, during the Grand Prix l'Humanite in France the following year, found them extremely friendly.
Again it was Hrazdira who attacked soon after the start of the stage along with Ireland's Kevin Dolan. They were joined by John Mangan (Kerry), Seamus Walsh (Tipperary) and Tony Holton (Meath).
This group stayed away until after Carlow when they were caught but Hrazdira stayed out in front where he was joined by Dolozel, the two stretching their lead all the way to Dublin where the yellow jersey won the stage.
It was 4.15 later that Karel Vavra out sprinted Seamus Kennedy and another Czech Jiri Zelenka came home next 1.15 later while Ben McKenna led in an 8-man group another 30 seconds down.

**Stage 10 Carrick-on-Suir - Dublin 100 Mls.** 1 M.Hrazdira (Czech) 4.32.00 2 P.Dolozel (Czech) s.t. 3 K.Vavra (Czech) at 4.15 4 S.Kennedy (Ireland) s.t. 5 J.Zelenka (Czech) at 6.00 6 B.McKenna (Meath A) s.t.

**General Classification:**
1 M.Hrazdira (Czech) 37.33.00 2 P.Dolozel (Czech) at 1.57 3 K.Vavra (Czech) at 4.52 4 J.Zelenka (Czech) at 6.00 5 J.Havelka (Czech) at 5.27 6 P.Konecny (Czech.) at 9.21 7 S.Kennedy (Ireland) at 13.38 8 M.O'Donoghue (Ireland) at 18.54 9 B.Donnelly (Ireland) at 21.03 10 S.O Hanlon (Ireland) at 25.42

*Milan Hrazdira (Czech) 1968 Winner*

## 1969

Irish riders were no doubt happy to see no East European teams in the starting line-up of the '69 RÁS after their experience of the Czechs the previous year. The 10-day event which started on Friday, June 27, with a 52 miles stage to Dundalk, had a 5-man French team as the only visitors.
While Shay O Hanlon was still thought by most commentators to be one of the favourites, after his run of victories had only been halted by the Czechs, an Irish squad had been competing on the continent since the start of the season. The members of this squad, the brainchild of RÁS Director Joe Christle and known as the Stephens Project: Christy Reynolds and Seamus Kennedy from Meath, Andy Stynes (Dublin) and Benny Donnelly (Antrim) had returned from Belgium for the event and were highly fancied.

### STAGE 1

All except Stynes made the top ten on the opening stage. There had been much attacking riding during the first 30 miles before but it was only on the drag up Tullyesker, after Drogheda that Kennedy and Reynolds opened a sizeable gap in company with Jim McConville (Down).
When the race left the main road at Castlebellingham for a section of minor roads through Dromiskin on the run-in to the finish a couple of chasing groups got away. Kevin Dolan (Louth), Benny Donnelly, Brian Connaughton (Meath), John Mangan (Kerry) and Ben McKenna went in pursuit but were still 1.44 down at the line where Kennedy took the honours from McConville and Reynolds with local favourite Dolan leading in the chasers.
On a personal note, in my only top ten placing in a RÁS stage I was outsprinted by Frenchman Felix Martin for 9th place, 2.04 behind the winner after we got away three miles out and just managed to hold off a fast closing bunch.
**Stage 1 Dublin - Dundalk 52 Mls.** 1 S.Kennedy (Meath A) 2.00.05 (less 15 secs bonus) 2 J.McConville (Down) (s.t. less 10 secs.) 3 C.Reynolds (Meath A) (s.t. less 5 secs.) 4 K.Dolan (Louth) at 1.44 5 J.Mangan (Kerry) 6 B.Connaughton (Meath A) 7 B.Donnelly (Antrim) 8 B.McKenna (Meath B) all same time 9 F.Martin (France) at 2.04 10 J.Traynor (Down) s.t

### STAGE 2

Saturday stage was a 71 miles trip from Dundalk to Ballinamore which was won by Mike O'Donoghue (Carlow) but with him in the break was Jim McConville (Down) who took over the yellow jersey.

**Stage 2 Dundalk - Ballinamore 71 Mls.** 1 M.O'Donoghue (Carlow) 2.55.30
**General Classification:** 1 J.McConville (Down)

## STAGE 3

Johnny Lonergan (Tipperary) won the 85 miles third stage from Ballinamore to Ballina in the process taking over the race leadership.
However it was the Meath team who dominated the stage and at the finish many of the top contenders, including O Hanlon, had dropped out of contention as they came home in the main bunch, nearly 14 minutes behind the break. Of the previous top six only Benny Donnelly remained in sixth place after a complete transformation of the leader board.
While Lonergan took the stage and the lead by out sprinting a 4-man lead group which included Frenchman Jean Grini, and Meath's Larry Clark and Colm Nulty, Meath had seven riders in the first 12 home who as a result all went into the top 12 on GC and the Meath A and B teams were way ahead in the team classification.
Yet the stage had started with plenty of aggressive riding Saturday's stage winner O'Donoghue going away with Vincent Sheridan (Kildare) and Kevin Dolan (Louth). When they were caught a 14-man break went clear and stayed away over the climb of the Curlew Mountains but they were brought back by the bunch on the fast descent.
It was when they turned sharp left at Collooney with a strong breeze coming in from the sea that the race changed. Sean Walsh (Tipperary), Patsy Wall (Waterford) went away with Meath's Larry Clark and brothers Colm and John Nulty. They were joined by Gabriel Howard (Meath), Davy McLarnon (Antrim), Derek Carroll (Dublin).
As the break opened up a significant lead riders went across in ones and two including Donnelly who was the only well placed riders to escape the clutches of the Meath riders who were controlling the bunch which eventually became demoralised and toured along, dropping further and further behind.
The favourites left behind: O Hanlon, O'Donoghue and Mangan didn't combine to organise a chase playing into the hands of Meath who with two strong 6-man teams were in complete command. At the finish O Hanlon commented: 'We did this in the Dublin team in 1961, so I suppose I should be the last to complain'.
**Stage 3 Ballinamore - Ballina 85 Mls** 1 J.Lonergan (Tipperary) 3.21.32 2 J.Grini (France) 3 L.Clark (Meath A) 4 C.Nulty (Meath A) all same time 5 J.Nulty (Meath B) at 9 secs 6 D.McLarnon (Antrim) 7 B.Connaughton (Meath A) 8 T.Reilly (Meath B) 9 P.Wall (Waterford) 10 B.McKenna (Meath B) all same time
**General Classification:** 1 J.Lonergan (Tipperary) 8.21.00 2 J.Grini (France) at 5 secs 3 L.Clark (Meath A) at 10 secs 4 C.Nulty (Meath A) at 15 secs 5 J.Nulty (Meath B) at 25 secs 6 B.Donnelly (Antrim) at 34 secs 7 B.Connaughton (Meath A) at 2.14 8 B.McKenna (Meath B) at 2.19 9 equal G.Howard (Meath B) T.Reilly (Meath B) D.McLarnon (Antrim) and P.Wall (Waterford) all at 6.41
**Team:** 1 Meath A 24.59.28 2 Meath B 25.06.27 3 Antrim 25.29.40

## STAGE 4

Meath continued their domination on the 98 miles fourth stage from Ballina to Gort but the stage victory went to 18-year-old John Mangan (Kerry). Despite his age the Kerryman had been one of the pre-race favourites but, like most of the other fancied riders had lost a lot of time on the third stage.
Meath, with 12 strong riders, in two teams, went for the yellow jersey and at the end of the day Brian Connaughton of their A team was at the top of the GC with a huge advantage of 5.07 over previous leader Lonergan with France's Grini a further 5 seconds down. Mangan's great ride lifted him from 20th to 9th overall, still nearly 8 minutes in arrears.
Mangan was early on the attack along with Shay O Hanlon but were soon brought back by the Meath combination. Then Ben McKenna (Meath B) went away with Jack Lacey (Kerry), Brian Holmes (Antrim), Tom Reilly (Meath B) and Tony Holton (Louth) but after Castlebar the race came together again.
In pouring rain Mangan, Connaughton and Dublin Frankie Dames went away 10 miles after Castlebar. With Mangan doing all the driving Dames dropped back as the other two increased their lead as the Meath riders maintained their grip on the bunch behind.
After Galway Mangan attacked but was held by the Meath man. However with 5 miles remaining Mangan finally managed to open a gap and between there and the line opened up a lead of almost two minutes. It was over four minutes before the next finishers, Christy Reynolds (Meath A) and Andy Stynes (Dublin) and another 3 minutes before Jean Cabassut of France led in Brian Davey (Antrim). A minute later Frankie Dames and Tipperary's Sean Walsh came home and finally Kevin Dolan (Louth) led in a big group over 9 minutes behind Mangan. However it was 32.45 before the main peleton containing O Hanlon, Donoghue and Kennedy arrived.
**Stage 4 Ballina - Gort 98 Mls** 1 J.Mangan (Kerry) 4.3.14 2 B.Connaughton (Meath A) at 1.56 3 C.Reynolds (Meath A) at 5.58 4 A.Stynes (Dublin) s.t. 5 J.Cabassut (France) at 8.12 6 B.Davey (Antrim) s.t. 7 F.Dames (Dublin) at 8.58 8 S.Walsh (Tipperary) s.t. 9 K.Dolan (Louth) at 9.06 10 D.McLarnon (Antrim) s.t
**General Classification:** 1 B.Connaughton (Meath A) 12.28.14 2 J.Lonergan (Tipperary) at 5.07 3 J.Grini (France) at 5.12 4 L.Clarke (Meath A) at 5.17 5 B.McKenna (Meath B) at 7.16 6 equal D.McLarnon (Antrim) P.Wall (Waterford) and G.Howard (Meath B) all at 7.34 9 J.Mangan (Kerry) at 7. 37 10 T.Reilly (Meath B) at 10.12 11 S.Walsh (Tipperary) at 11.39 12 C.Reynolds (Meath A) at 12.03

## STAGE 5

For the first time since the start of the race Meath's iron grip slipped and breaks went away almost at will. Johnny Lonergan got away from the leading group 10 miles from the finish to take his second stage and he took back some time on the race leader whose margin nevertheless was a healthy 3.52 on the Tipperary man.

Seamus Kennedy (Meath A) and Mike O'Donoghue (Carlow) went away after only 2 miles and with both being well down the bunch they were let go. At Adare Michael Tinnelly (Down) and Mick Duggan (Cork) went in pursuit some 4 minutes behind the two leaders. Then it was the turn of Jim McConville (Down) and Benny Donnelly (Antrim) to leave the bunch.

As they came down off the Barna Gap Vincent Sheridan (Kildare) attacked and was quickly joined by race-leader Connaughton and John Mangan and they set off in hot pursuit of the leaders as behind them the bunch fragmented as the Meath men lost control.

By Castleisland the leading groups had merged into an 18-strong break which included all the French team. Mangan tried to get away from Connaughton but the race-leader grimly hung onto his wheel. With 10 miles left Lonergan attacked and opened up a minute's lead by the finish where O'Donoghue beat Grini to take second place.

**Stage 5 Gort - Tralee 111 Mls** 1 J.Lonergan (Tipperary) 4.55.10 2 M.O'Donoghue at 1.00 3 J.Grini (France) 4 S.Kennedy (Meath A) 5 V.Sheridan (Kildare) 6 B.Donnelly (Antrim) 7 J.McConville (Down) 8 F.Martin (France) 9 J.Mangan (Kerry) 10 B.Davey (Antrim) all same time

**General Classification:** 1 B.Connaughton (Meath A) 17.24.24 2 J.Lonergan (Tipperary) at 3.52 3 J.Grini (France) at 5.07 4 L.Clarke (Meath A) at 6.32 5 J.Mangan (Kerry) at 7.37 6 B.McKenna (Meath B) at 8.50 7 P.Wall (Waterford) at 8.59 8 T.Reilly (Meath B) at 10.12 9 D.McLarnon (Antrim) at 10.54 10 G.Howard (Meath B) at 11.19 11 S.Walsh (Tipperary) at 13.04 12 J.McConville (Down) at 15.08.

**Team:** 1 Meath A 52.15.40 2 Meath B 52.41.26 3 Tipperary 52.49.56

## STAGE 6

Shay O Hanlon won the short 42 miles stage to Cahirciveen in a sprint from Larry Clarke (Meath A) and Mike O'Donoghue (Carlow) these three finishing 10 seconds in front of the bunch so there were no changes in the overall situation.

Most of the day's drama was played out behind the bunch as first Mangan had mechanical trouble and then, with 20 miles to go Lonergan punctured and Meath tried to increase Connaughton's overall lead.

Mangan got back to the bunch after cousin Gene dropped back to help him regain the peleton. It looked serious for the Meath men as they went to the front to try and keep him from getting back. However the Tipperary man was lucky as he had not only his team mates for assistance but also Antrim's Benny Donnelly who had dropped back to help a teammate and another puncture victim George Tamortishi of France and they all combined to regain the peleton despite the furious pace being set at the front.

With the drama over it looked like a bunch sprint but O Hanlon, O'Donoghue and Clarke managed to open up a tiny gap which they held to the line where O Hanlon won his 21st RÁS stage.

**Stage 6 Tralee - Cahirciveen 42 Mls.** 1 S.O Hanlon (Dublin) 2.00.04 2 L.Clarke (Meath A) 3 M.O'Donoghue (Carlow) all same time 4 J.Cabassut (France) at 10 secs 5 S.Kennedy (Meath A) 6 G.Mangan (Kerry) 7 J.Grini (France) 8 J.Mangan (Kerry) 9 B.Connaughton (Meath A) all same time

**General Classification:** 1 B.Connaughton (Meath A) 19.05.43 2 J.Lonergan (Tipperary) at 3.52 3 J.Grini (France) at 5.07 4 L.Clarke (Meath A) at 6.32 5 J.Mangan (Kerry) at 7.37 6 B.McKenna (Meath B) at 8.50 7 P.Wall (Waterford) at 8.59 8 T.Reilly (Meath B) at 10.12 9 G.Howard (Meath B) at 11.19 10 D.McLarnon (Antrim) at 13.04 11 S.Walsh (Tipperary) at 14.14 12 C.Reynolds (Meath A) at 14.30

## STAGE 7

Mike O'Donoghue (Carlow) won his second stage of the week when he out sprinted a 14 man group to the line in Kinsale after a fast 128 miles stage from Cahirciveen.

Meath were back in control and leader Connaughton increased his lead over second placed Lonergan by nearly a minute to 4.53 and barring accidents looked odds-on to hold the jersey to Dublin.

The race started 10 minutes ahead of schedule and while most of the field were informed Shay O Hanlon and teammate Paddy Wall was still in their hotel as they saw the race leave town. Luckily for them the early pace was gentle and O Hanlon made up nearly a 4 minute deficit by the Coomikista Pass with Wall taking somewhat longer to get up.

After getting his breath back the Dubliner attacked after 60 miles on the climb of the Tunnel Road and was joined by Mike O'Donoghue. After 75 miles O'Donoghue decided O Hanlon was demanding too high a work-rate and dropped back to Colm Nulty (Meath A) and Kevin Dolan (Louth) who were chasing a minute behind later to be joined by Frenchman Cabassut and Larry Clarke (Meath A).

Cabassut made it across to O Hanlon at Drimoleague (86m.) and a couple of miles later the other four got up making six at the front. They were being chased by Jim McConville (Down), Seamus Kennedy (Meath A), Benny Donnelly (Antrim) and French riders Henri Prevost and Jean Grini and they joined the leaders at Dunmanway.

Larry Clarke, who was lying fourth, crashed into an oncoming car and his bike was wrecked but Nulty dropped back and gave him his thus saving Clarke his overall position. behind John Mangan attacked and was joined by Connaughton, Vincent Sheridan (Kildare) and T.P. Reilly (Meath A) and these four just got onto the leaders at they approached the finish where O'Donoghue took the sprint.

**Stage 7 Cahirciveen - Kinsale 128 Mls.** 1 M.O'Donoghue (Carlow) 5.32.10 2 S.Kennedy (Meath A) 3 J.Cabassut (France) 4 S.O Hanlon (Dublin) 5 K.Dolan (Louth) 6 B.Donnelly (Antrim) 7 J.McConville (Down) 8 F.Martin (France) 9 H.Prevost (France) 10 J.Grini (France) all same time

**General Classification:** 1 B.Connaughton (Meath A) 24.38.03 2 J.Lonergan (Tipperary) at 4.53 3 J.Grini (France) at 5.07 4 L.Clarke (Meath A) at 7.09 5 J.Mangan (Kerry) at 7.37 6 B.McKenna (Meath B) at 11.13 7 T.Reilly (Meath B) at 12.20 8 G.Howard (Meath B) s.t 9 P.Wall (Waterford) at 12.39 10 D.McLarnon (Antrim) at 14.05 11 J.McConville (Down) at 14.58 12 C.Reynolds (Meath A) at 15.31

## STAGE 8

The 109 miles stage from Kinsale to Waterford was notable for a race-long break by Benny Donnelly and Shay O Hanlon with the stage going to the 21-year-old Antrim rider.

The two went away just after the start and by Cork City they had a lead of 2 minutes on Tony Holton (Louth) and Peter Sargent (Cork). Their lead continued to grow and at Middleton (32m.) it was 4.30 and at Youghal (50m.) it was over 7 minutes on John O'Sullivan (Cork) who was chasing on his own.

At Dungarvan Vincent Sheridan (Kildare) and Kevin Dolan (Louth) were chasing and had brought the lead down to 5 minutes with the bunch another 2 minutes behind. It stayed that way to the finish where the diminutive Donnelly, who because of his size wasn't giving the much taller O Hanlon much shelter, was probably that much fresher and when he attacked with two miles to go he opened a small gap which he held to the line.

Back in the bunch there was drama when the race-leader punctured with only 3 miles to go. The French team, hoping to improve Grini's position went to the front and piled on the pressure but Connaughton gladly accepted teammate Colm Nulty's bike and with the Meath men all in attendance got back to the peleton before the finish. With O Hanlon and Donnelly not in overall contention there was no change overall.

**Stage 8 Kinsale - Waterford 109 Mls** 1 B.Donnelly (Antrim) 4.22.30 2 S.O Hanlon (Dublin) s.t. 3 K.Dolan (Louth) at 3.42 4 V.Sheridan (Kildare) s.t. 5 M.O'Donoghue (Carlow) at 4.45 6 J.Cabassut (France) s.t

**General Classification:** 1 B.Connaughton (Meath A) 29.03.18 2 J.Lonergan (Tipperary) at 4.53 3 J.Grini (France) at 5.07 4 L.Clarke (Meath A) at 7.09 5 J.Mangan (Kerry) at 7.37 6 B.McKenna (Meath B) at 11.13 7 T.Reilly (Meath B) at 12.20 8 G.Howard (Meath B) s.t. 9 P.Wall (Waterford) at 12.39 10 D.McLarnon (Antrim) at 14.05 11 J.McConville (Down) at 14.58 12 C.Reynolds (Meath A) at 15.31

## STAGE 9

Mike O'Donoghue won his third stage of the week, a hugely popular victory in his native Carlow. At the finish he out sprinted Jean Pierre Cabassut (France) and Jim McConville (Down) after these three had stayed away since going clear at half-distance at Wexford.

By the time they reached Bunclody the leading trio had two minutes on the peleton with only 20 miles left with strong sprinter O'Donoghue odds-on to take another stage.
By the finish their advantage had shrunk but they still had 1.05 over chasers Mick Kinsella (Carlow) and Peter Sargent (Cork) while Tony Holton (Louth B) led in the bunch 15 seconds later.
With all the main contenders safely in the bunch there was no change in the general classification and with Connaughton and Meath only having to be careful on the final stage a civic reception had already been arranged for the Square in Navan for Sunday evening to welcome the victors.
**Stage 9 Waterford - Carlow 83 Mls.** 1 M.O'Donoghue (Carlow) 3.44.00 2 J.Cabassut (France) 3 J.McConville (Down) all same time 4 M.Kinsella (Carlow) at 1.05 4 P.Sargent (Cork) s.t. 6 A.Holton (Louth) at 1.20
**General Classification:** 1 B.Connaughton (Meath A) 32.48.38 2 J.Lonergan (Tipperary) at 4.53 3 J.Grini (France) at 5.07 4 L.Clarke (Meath A) at 7.18 5 J.Mangan (Kerry) at 7.37 6 B.McKenna (Meath B) at 9.49 7 T.Reilly (Meath B) at 11.13 8 G.Howard (Meath B) at 12.20 9 P.Wall (Waterford) at 12.39 10 D.McLarnon (Antrim) at 14.05 11 J.McConville (Down) at 14.43 12 C.Reynolds (Meath A) at 15.31

## STAGE 10

Vincent Sheridan (Kildare) deprived O'Donoghue of a fourth stage win when he out sprinted the Carlow man in the Phoenix Park at the end of the 50 miles stage from Carlow after the two of them went away at Rathcoole.
At the finish they were 30 seconds in front of John Mangan who broke away in the final miles in a bid to take over 4th place from Meath's Larry Clarke. However Meath led the chase and Mangan's gain of 20 seconds was not enough for him to move up for even with the five seconds bonus he was still 4 seconds behind the Meath man.
Connaughton came home safely in the bunch to win by the 4.53 he had held since the previous Thursday but in fact, once he took the jersey on the previous Monday he looked home and dry because of the iron grip his team held on the race. Meath indeed had two strong teams who worked as one and this would give the organisers some thought of how to prevent such strong combinations dominating in future events.
Meath A won the team by nearly 30 minutes from the Meath B team with third placed France another 8 minutes behind.
**Stage 10 Carlow - Dublin 50 Mls.** 1 V.Sheridan (Kildare) 1.59.27 2 M.O'Donoghue (Carlow) s.t 3 J.Mangan (Kerry) at 30 secs 4 S.Kennedy (Meath A) at 50 secs 5 G.Mangan (Kerry) 6 K.Dolan (Louth) 7 B.Donnelly (Antrim) 8 K.Dolan (Louth) 9 S.O Hanlon (Dublin) 10 J.McConville (Down)

**General Classification:** 1 B.Connaughton (Meath A) 34.48.55 2 J.Lonergan (Tipperary) at 4.53 3 J.Grini (France) at 5.07 4 L.Clarke (Meath A) at 7.18 5 J.Mangan (Kerry) at 7.22 6 B.McKenna (Meath B) at 9.49 7 T.Reilly (Meath B) at 11.13 8 G.Howard (Meath B) at 12.20 9 P.Wall (Waterford) at 12.39 10 D.McLarnon (Antrim) at 14.05 11 J.McConville (Down) at 14.43 12 C. Reynolds (Meath A) at 15.31

*Brian Connaughton, 1969 Winner*

## 1970

After the total domination of Meath Joe Christle decided it was time for a change and it was back to the Eastern bloc with the USSR this time the guests.
After the Poles in '63 and the Czechs in '68 the Irish riders had a fair idea of what was in store, the only question being had the standard risen enough in two years for the home teams to put up more than token resistance.
There were high hopes from four Irish riders who had been racing on the continent since the start of the season: Seamus Kennedy and Christy Reynolds of Meath, Benny Donnelly of Antrim and Dublin's Andy Stynes. The four were part of the Stephens' Project, organised by Christle for the NCA aiming to give promising riders experience of racing abroad for an extensive period of time.
Also in the field was French team most of who had finished well up and in front of the Irish in the Grand Prix l'Humanite, a 3-day FSGT event contested by most of the Eastern bloc countries.

## STAGE 1

The opening stage was an evening one, 58 miles from Dublin to Oldcastle and the Russians as expected provided the winner. However it was a hard fought victory with the home riders up with the action all the way, Kennedy, Reynolds and Styles all finishing in the top six.
The Russians set a furious pace from the start and Alexander Gysiatnikov went away at Dunshaughlin but was quickly joined by Christy Reynolds. Despite the fast pace the pair stayed clear but were always in sight on the long straights and the biggest lead was 45 seconds at Kells.
As a six-man chasing group including Russians Dzharstans and Slobodenuk, Seamus Kennedy and Brian Connaughton (Meath), Andy Stynes (Dublin) and John Mangan (Kerry) closed in on the leaders at Virginia, with 10 miles to the finish, Reynolds dropped back leaving Gysiatnikov out on front on his own but he gamely held on and still had 30 seconds in hand at the finish.
His teammate, P. Dzhartans, who had been sitting in, outsprinted Seamus Kennedy for 2nd place with Russian captain Gainam Saidchushin leading in the bunch 1.35 down on the winner.
**Stage 1 Dublin - Oldcastle 58 Mls.** 1 A.Gysiatnikov (USSR) 2.02.35 2 P.Dzharstans (USSR) at 30s 3 S.Kennedy (Meath A) 4 M.Slobodenuk (USSR) 5 C.Reynolds (Meath A) 6 A.Stynes (Dublin) 7 J.Mangan (Meath) 8 B.Connaughton (Meath A) all same time 9 G.Saidchushin (USSR) at 1.35
**General classification:** As above minus bonuses of 60, 45 and 30 seconds for 1st, 2nd and 3rd.

## STAGE 2

**Stage 2 Oldcastle - Westport 110m.** 1 A.Gysiatnikov (USSR) 5.14.30
**General Classification:** 1 A Gysiatnikov (USSR)

## STAGE 3

Gysiatnikov took his third stage in a row on the 113 miles run in wind and rain from Westport to Gort and the Russians dominated the general classification holding the top four places.

After holding the visitors well for two days the top Irish riders made a bad blunder on the third day and the team from the USSR quickly took advantage and virtually tied up the race. It happened just six miles after the start on the first climb of the day. The Russians found themselves at the front and not marked and immediately attacked, all five going away.

The French team were quicker to react and got three riders into the break and that was the last time the leaders were seen all day. One of the French, Perron dropped back after 46 miles but the Russians kept up a relentless team time-trial at the front, increasing their lead despite the best efforts of the Meath team to organise a chase. By the finish the best of the home riders, Seamus Kennedy, was over 9 minutes behind the stage winner.

With Gysiatnikov already a double winner it had obviously been decided to give him the maximum bonus and he went ahead by 5 seconds to take the stage and the 1 minute extra, which he hardly needed. On GC he lead Khrapov by 4.31 and their nearest challenger was Jean Pierre Buscail of France lying 5th at 8.02.

**Stage 3 Westport - Gort 113 Mls.** 1 A.Gysiatnikov (USSR) 4.31.10 2 V.Khrapov (USSR) at 5 secs 3 P.Dzharstans (USSR) at 7 secs 4 G.Saidchushin (USSR) at 10 secs 5 Y.Lavrouchkin 6 J.P.Buscail (France) 7 J.L.Marionneau (France) all same time 8 S.Kennedy (Meath) at 9.30 9 J.Mangan (Kerry) 10 C.Nulty (Meath A) all same time

**General Classification:** 1 A.Gysiatnikov (USSR) 11.46.15 2 V.Khrapov (USSR) at 4.31 3 P.Dzharstans (USSR) at 6.47 4 Y.Lavrouchkin (USSR) at 7.13 5 J.P.Buscail (France) at 8.02 6 G.Saidchushin (USSR) at 9.03 7 J.L.Marionneau (France) at 9.05 8 C.Reynolds (Meath A) at 14.56 9 C.Nulty (Meath A) at 16.31 10 S.Kennedy (Meath A) at 16.50 11 equal J.Mangan (Kerry) and B.Connaughton (Meath A) at 17.20

## STAGE 4

The home riders improved their morale on the fourth stage, 120 miles from Gort to Thurles. Although the stage again went abroad, three of the USSR team contesting the sprint which went to Yury Lavrouchkin his only stage win of the '70 RÁS although he would return to win another four seven years later.

Seamus Kennedy, who had proved he was a match for the visitors at sprinting, was in with a chance to take the stage but crashed 300 yards from the finish. Lavrouchkin's winning margin was 7 seconds over a big break led in by Siadchushin.
Sixteen riders went away on the climb of the Corkscrew, 30 miles after the start and they stayed together all the way to the finish. The big surprise was the absence of yellow jersey Gysiatnikov who was heavily marked in the peleton. However he eventually got away with a small group at Limerick and cut his deficit on the leaders to 2.10 at the finish, more than enough to retain his jersey.
After their humiliation on Sunday the Irish launched an all-out attack, Benny Donnelly (Antrim) got away on the climb to be joined by Saidchushin and Seamus Kennedy, the Russian sitting-in.
They were caught by 13 riders including two Russians and three French along with Colm Nulty and Christy Reynolds (Meath A), Johnny Lonergan (Tipperary), Vincent Sheridan (Kildare), Michael Tinnelly (Armagh), Kevin Dolan (Louth), Noel Clarke (Meath B) and John Mangan (Kerry). Shortly afterwards Jim McConville (Armagh) joined them on his own making 17 who stayed away for the remainder of the stage.
The Russians, with the yellow jersey back in the bunch, didn't do any work but the remainder battled away trying to put some time into the jersey and were favourites to win the sprint. Seamus Kennedy moved up to challenge but was pushed into the footpath crashing heavily and losing 30 seconds. The Russians took the top three places, Yuri Lavruyshkin from Saidchuchin and Krhapov with Henri Prevost (France) just ahead of the first of the home riders Benny Donnelly.
**Stage 4 Gort - Thurles 120 Mls.** 1 Y.Lavrouchkin (USSR) 4.58.11 2 G.Saidchushin (USSR) at 7 secs 3 V.Krhapov (USSR) 4 H.Prevost (France) 5 B.Donnelly (Antrim) 6 C.Nulty (Meath A) 7 J.Lonergan (Tipperary) 8 V.Sheridan (Kildare) 9 J.L.Marionneau (France) 10 M.Tinnelly (Armagh) all same time.
**General Classification:** 1 A.Gysiatnikov (USSR) 16.46.36 2 V.Khrapov (USSR) at 2.13 3 Y.Lavrouchkin (USSR) at 4.13 4 J.P.Buscail (France) at 6.01 5 G.Saidchushin (USSR) at 6.18 6 P.Dzharstans (USSR) at 6.47 7 J.L.Marionneau (France) at 7.04 8 C.Reynolds (Meath A) at 14.53

## STAGE 5

Gainam Saidchushin the Russian team leader celebrated his 33rd birthday with a win into Killarney on the 109 miles fifth stage beating his teammate Petrov Dzharstans for the top spot at the head of a six-man break. Gysiatnikov kept the yellow jersey.
For much of the stage the Russians controlled the race keeping the bunch intact as they countered all efforts to get away. With 27 miles left John Mangan (Kerry) and Benny Donnelly (Antrim) got clear joined by the inevitable Russian, this time Lavrouchkin but the two home riders pressed on and built up a lead of two minutes with at 17 miles to go.
This brought a reaction from the USSR team with Saidchushin and Dzharstans going in pursuit accompanied by Seamus Kennedy and they caught the leaders with 7 miles

to go in time for the visitors to set up the stage as a birthday present for their leader. Despite his injuries from the preceding day's crash Kennedy came through to take 3rd place with Mangan also managing to spit the Russians in 4th.
**Stage 5 Thurles - Killarney 109 Mls.** 1 G.Saidchushin (USSR) 4.54.18 2 P.Dzharstans (USSR) 3 S.Kennedy (Meath A) 4 J.Mangan (Kerry) 5 Y.Lavrouchskin (USSR) 6 B.Donnelly (Antrim) all same time 7 J.Lonergan (Tipperary) at 1.07 8 A.Gysiatnikov (USSR) 9 V.Khrapov (USSR) 10 J.L.Marionneau (France) all same time
**General Classification:** 1 A.Gysiatnikov (USSR) 21.42.01 2 V.Khrapov (USSR) at 2.13 3 Y.Lavrouchkin (USSR) at 3.16 4 G.Saidchushin (USSR) at 4.12 5 P.Dzharstans (USSR) at 4.55 6 J.P.Buscail (France) at 6.19 7 J.L.Marionneau (France) at 7.04 8 C.Reynolds (Meath) at 13.11 9 S.Kennedy (Meath A) at 13.51 10 J.Mangan (Kerry) at 14.10 11 C.Nulty (Meath A) at 14.41 12 B.Connaughton (Meath A) at 17.31

## STAGE 6

The riders had a fairly easy day on Wednesday with only a 30-lap round-the houses race in Killarney for the sixth stage which gave Russian captain Saidchushin his second victory in a row.
He went away with Johnny Lonergan (Tipperary) with seventeen laps to go and they just held off the field to the line.
As was normal in the criterium stages which took place in Killarney several times, a huge crowd generously donated lap primes and the visitors took the lion's share. Saidchushin won nine although his breakaway companion took six.
There were no changes in the overall race except for the time bonuses of 1 minute, 45 and 30 seconds which went to the first three home.
**Stage 6 Killarney Criterium 30 Mls.** 1 G.Saidchushin 1.17.10 2 J.Lonergan (Tipperary) 3 P. Dzharstans (USSR) 4 V.Khrapov (USSR) 5 C.Reynolds (Meath A) 6 J.L.Marionneau (France) all same time
**General Classification:** 1 A.Gysiatnikov (USSR) 22.59.01 2 V.Khrapov (USSR) at 2.13 3 G.Saidchushin (USSR) at 3.12 4 Y.Lavrouchkin (USSR) at 3.16 5 P.Dzharstans (USSR) at 4.40 6 J.P.Buscail (France) at 6.19 7 J.L.Marionneau (France) at 7.04 8 C.Reynolds (Meath) at 13.11 9 S.Kennedy (Meath A) at 13.51 10 J.Mangan (Kerry) at 14.10 11 C.Nulty (Meath A) at 14.41 12 B.Connaughton (Meath A) at 17.31

## STAGE 7

If the yellow jersey had seen his lead being gradually whittled away over the previous three stages, he came back with a bang on the mountain stage from Killarney to Castletownbeare coming home with teammate Khrapov six minutes ahead of third man Christy Reynolds (Meath A).

The stage had originally been an easy 50 miles run with only one major climb but in a surprise move race director Joe Christle announced the previous day that 22 miles had been added taking in the Ring of Beara which included some very steep climbs, the worst of which saw several riders in the lead group reduced to dismounting and running up to the top.
Gysiatnikov and Khrapov went away on the descent at Lauragh after 36 miles and over the spectacular roads of Beara they opened up a huge gap over the next 36 miles. With his stage-winner's bonus Gysiatnikov is now 2.38 ahead of Khrapov and barring accidents it was between the two of the with third man Saidchushin almost 10 minutes down.
Five miles after the start the bunch began to fragment and a 20-man group formed at the front including three Russians, three French, the top Meathmen plus Lonergan, Donnelly and Jim McConville. This group was well clear when the two Russians made their move. The only consolation for the Irish was Reynolds' third place.
**Stage 7 Killarney - Castletownbeare** 1 A.Gysiatnikov (USSR) 3.3.15; 2 V.Khrapov (USSR) same time 3 C.Reynolds (Meath A) at 6.00 4 P.Dzharstans (USSR) 5 Y.Lavrouchkin (USSR) 6 J.Lonergan (Tipperary) 7 S.Kennedy (Meath A) 8 J.L.Marionneau (France) 9 J.Mangan (Kerry) 10 J. McConville (Armagh) all same time
**General Classification:** 1 A.Gysiatnikov (USSR) 26.01.50 2 V.Khrapov (USSR) at 2.38 3 G.Saidchushin (USSR) at 9.48 4 Y.Lavrouchkin (USSR) at 9.54 5 P.Dzharstans (USSR) at 10.54 6 J.P.Buscail (France) at 12.56 7 J.L.Marionneau (France) at 14.04 8 C.Reynolds (Meath A) at 19.21 9 S.Kennedy (Meath A) at 20.53 10 J.Mangan (Kerry) at 21.10 11 C.Nulty (Meath A) at 21.46 12 B.Connaughton (Meath A) 24.38

## STAGE 8

Mick Grimes, a 41-year-old steel erector from Dundalk had the greatest win of his long cycling career when he came home 37 seconds ahead of Yury Lavrouchkin to win the 132 miles eighth stage from Castletownbeare to Dungarvan.
Grimes, the oldest rider in the race had failed to get selection on the Louth team who preferred to send younger riders and got a place on the Sligo team. He also held the probably unique distinction of competing in the same RÁS as his son both in 1970 and in the previous year.
During the week the Russian team had become friendly with the Dundalk rider, somewhat bemused by his presence in the race and their masseur had been giving him the odd massage. So they probably felt there was little danger in letting him go up the road to take an early prime, after all there were still some 80 miles to go. However the Dundalk man kept on riding and at Middleton he held a lead of 4.30 over the bunch.
However after Youghal the Russians saw the gap was still over 4 minutes and sent a man off in pursuit. Up the climb and on the descent into Dungarvan Lavrouchkin

rapidly eat into Grimes lead but they had underestimated his great strength, despite his age, and he held on for a famous victory, the only one by an Irishman in the '70 event and one which saw Grimes feted like a hero on his return to Dundalk with celebrations including a parade round the town.
There was no real change overall as Christy Reynolds (Meath) led in the main bunch from Johnny Lonergan (Tipperary) and Saidchushin, 1.57 behind the stage winner.
**Stage 8 Castletownbeare - Dungarvan 132 Mls.** 1 M.Grimes (Sligo) 5.46.15 2 Y.Lavrouchkin (USSR) at 37 secs 3 C.Reynolds (Meath) at 1.57 4 J.Lonergan (Tipperary) 5 G.Saidchushin (USSR) 5 S.Kennedy (Meath A) 7 A.Gysiatnikov (USSR) 8 B.Donnelly (Antrim) 9 J.L.Marionneau (France) 10 C. Nulty (Meath A) all same time
**General Classification:** 1 A.Gysiatnikov (USSR) 31.50.37 2 V.Khrapov (USSR) at 2.38 3 Y.Lavrouchkin (USSR) at 8.04 4 G.Saidchushin (USSR) at 9.48 5 P.Dzharstans (USSR) at 10.54 6 J.L.Marionneau (France) at 14.04 8 C.Reynolds (Meath A) at 19.06 9 S.Kennedy (Meath A) at 20.53 10 J.Mangan (Kerry) at 21.10 11 C.Nulty (Meath A) at 21.46 12 B.Connaughton (Meath A) 24.38

## STAGE 9

**Stage 9 Dungarvan - Portlaoise 83 Mls.** 1 G. Saidchushin USSR) 3.23.10
**General Classification:** 1 A. Gysiatnikov (USSR)

## STAGE 10

The final stage was the fastest of the week with action right from the off on the short 52 miles run from Portlaoise to the Phoenix Park, won inevitably by the visitors, this time Dzharstans. Gysiatnikov as expected had no problems and ran out a comfortable overall winner.
Almost immediately after the start a break formed with the entire USSR team, four Meathmen and three French riders and they soon left all the rest behind.
As they approached the outskirts of Dublin Dzharstans attacked and with his four team mates doing nothing to aid the chase he raced to a 45 second lead by the finish line. The race leader was next home with Khrapov making it a 1-2-3. Frenchman Marionneau was next with Kennedy best of the Irish fifth.
The USSR easily won the team race from France with Meath third, almost an hour behind the Russians. It was a complete rout for the home riders as not only were the first five placed filled by the Russians but the next two went to France with Christy Reynolds best placed Irish rider, eighth, almost 12 minutes behind the winner.
Despite the hammering they took from the visitors, the home riders were much more competitive than they had been against the Czechs, and had learned a lot in the intervening two years.
**Stage 10 Portlaoise - Dublin 52 Mls.** 1 P.Dzharstans (USSR) 1.40.10 2 A.Gysiatnikov (USSR) at 45 secs 3 V.Khrapov (USSR) 4 J.L.Marionneau (France) 5

S.Kennedy (Meath A) 6 G.Saidchushin (USSR) 7 J.P.Buscail (France) 8 C.Nulty (Meath A) 9 Y.Lavrouchkin (USSR) 10 J.L.Perron (France) all same time

**General Classification:** 1 A.Gysiatnikov (USSR) 36.58.12 2 V.Khrapov (USSR) at 4.35 3 G.Saidchushin (USSR) at 10.33 4 Y.Lavrouchkin (USSR) at 14.03 4 5 P.Dzharstans (USSR) at 14.45 6 J.P.Buscail (France) at 15.48 7 J.L.Marionneau (France) at 16.25 8 C.Reynolds (Meath A) at 21.56 9 S.Kennedy (Meath A) at 3.23 10 C.Nulty (Meath A) at 24.02 11 J.Mangan (Kerry) at 26.13 12 B.Connaughton (Meath A) 27.08

*1970 winner – Alexander Gysiatnikov*

## 1971

After the Russian steamroller, there were no East European teams in the line up for the 1970 RÁS with the French FSGT team the only overseas representation in the 80-strong field which started on the Friday evening stage on June 25.
The race previews in the Press weren't going for any outstanding favourite but names being mentioned were past winners O Hanlon, Connaughton, in-form Mike O'ODonoghue (Carlow), Seamus Kennedy (Meath) and John Mangan (Kerry).

### STAGE 1

The opening stage was a short evening run of 40 miles from Dublin to Dunleer, Co. Louth, the distance virtually guaranteeing a very high speed and in fact the distance was covered at over 30 mph.
A stage like this looked sure to end in a big bunch sprint but three riders got away with 10 miles to go and they tenaciously held on to the narrowest of leads to the finish where they still had 14 seconds in hand over the bunch.
In the break were Ben McKenna (Meath B) T.P.Reilly (Meath A) and Batty Flynn (Kerry). McKenna, winner, in '59, hadn't won a stage since and this win gave him his fourth stage victory (two in '57 and one in '59).
Brian Monaghan (Down) led in the bunch from Robert Gauthier (France) with all the favourites finishing in the same time.
The finish was marred by a crash in the bunch during the sprint which put Sligo's Tony Mooney out of the race. Also involved were Oliver McKenna, brother of the stage winner and Daniel Lefol (France) but they were both able to finish, carrying their bikes over the line.
**Stage 1 Dublin - Dunleer 40 Mls.** 1 B.McKenna (Meath B) 1.21.10 2 B.Flynn (Kerry) 3 T.P.Reilly (Meath A) all same time 4 B.Monaghan (Down) at 14 secs 5 R.Gauthier (France) 6 G.Mangan (Kerry) 7 T.Kelly (Galway) all same time

### STAGE 2

Ben McKenna held on to his leader's jersey for less than 24 hours and it passed to Kerry's John Mangan who won the 86 miles stage from Dunleer to Clones in a three-up sprint from Colm Nulty (Meath A) and Michael Tinnelly from Rostrevor, riding for Antrim. Who finished 6 seconds adrift?
After Newry a local farmer was annoyed that the cyclists had upset his prize herd, blocked the road and some riders who had been dropped had to make a lengthy detour. There was also a problem when the RUC removed a tricolour which was on one of the accompanying cars.

McKenna looked on course to retain the jersey when he had over a minute lead along with Pat Healy (Kerry) Derek Carroll (Dublin), Nulty and Tinnelly going through Newry and they were joined after Armagh by Mangan, Gabriel Howard (Dublin) and former winner Brian Connaughton (Meath A).
At Monaghan, with only 13 miles left Mangan attacked taking with him Nulty and Tinnelly and they opened a gap of nearly two minutes by the finish.
**Stage 2 Dunleer - Clones 86 Mls.** 1 J.Mangan (Kerry) 3.40.55 2 C.Nulty (Meath A) same time 3 M.Tinnelly (Antrim) at 6 secs 4 B.Connaughton (Meath A) at 1.58 5 P.Healy (Kerry) at 2.00 6 G.Howard (Dublin) at 2.08
**General Classification:** 1 J.Mangan (Kerry) 5.00.19 2 C.Nulty (Meath A) at 15 secs 3 M.Tinnelly (Antrim) at 36 secs 4 B.McKenna (Meath A) at 1.58 5 B.Connaughton (Meath A) at 2.43 6 P.Healy (Kerry) at 2.45 7 G. Howard (Dublin) at 2.53

## STAGE 3

Meath went on the attack on the 80 miles stage from Clones to Sligo and were rewarded by taking over the lead in both the individual and team races, 22-year-old Colm Nulty, who finished second to Kerry's Batty Flynn, taking the yellow jersey by 12 seconds from the Kerryman.
John Mangan (Kerry) who started the day in yellow was involved in a crash early on. He still finished 7th on the stage but fell back to 4th overall, over 5 minutes behind the new leader. Nulty also had his problems, losing time after a puncture at half distance but he had regained the bunch before the winning move.
The Meath attack came on the Curlew mountains with 25 miles remaining when Meath's Seamus Kennedy and Nulty forged ahead taking with them Flynn who was policing the break for Mangan.
Although there was a concerted chase on the descent of the Curlews, Nulty and Kennedy set a cracking pace and by the finish they had stretched their lead to 4.52 were the victory was easy for Flynn who had not been contributing to the work.
Meath had been on the attack all day and just after the start they had McKenna, Clarke and Kennedy in a 6-man break along with Flynn, Mick Cahill (Cork) and Derek Carroll (Dublin). It was at this time that the race leader crashed but he soon was back in a chasing group with O Hanlon and Joe Roche (Dublin), John Lawlor and Peter Murphy (Carlow) and the inevitable Meath men Brian Connaughton and Nulty.
Nulty punctured but got back up and went straight through up to the leaders where Flynn dropped back to take Mangan up to the front. After this regroupment there were several breakaway attempts before the winning move on the Curlews.
**Stage 3 Clones - Sligo 80 Mls.** 1 B.Flynn (Kerry) 3.41.30 2 C.Nulty (Meath A) at 6 secs 3 S.Kennedy (Meath A) s.t. 4 B.McKenna (Meath B) at 4.52 5 J.Lawlor (Carlow) s.t. 6 M.O'Donoghue Carlow) at 5.08 7 J.Mangan (Kerry) s.t
**General Classification:** 1 C.Nulty (Meath A) 8.44.20 2 B.Flynn (Kerry) at 2.12 3 S.Kennedy (Meath A) at 2.52 4 J.Mangan (Kerry) at 5.04 5 M.Tinnelly (Antrim) at

5.35 6 B.McKenna (Meath B) at 7.14 7 B.Connaughton (Meath) at 7.37 8 G.Howard (Dublin) at 7.47 9 T.P.Reilly (Meath) at 8.02 10 equal J.McConville (Armagh) D.Carroll (Dublin) S.O Hanlon (Dublin) M.O'Donoghue (Carlow) and L.Clarke (Meath) all at 8.06

## STAGE 4

It was Meath again on stage 4, 115 miles from Sligo to Oughterard when Noel Clarke (Meath A) won, but there were no changes at the top with Colm Nulty retaining his lead.

However it could all have been very different when after 30 miles the yellow jersey was back in the bunch, over 7 minutes behind the break. This contained Mike O'Donoghue (Carlow) and Jim McConville (Armagh) who had made the first escape to be joined first by Meath's Brian Connaughton and then by a chasing group of Noel Clarke, Derek Carroll and Joe Roche (Dublin) and Peter Sargent (Cork).

When the leaders learned that their deficit was 7 minutes alarm bells rang and a chase was organised with Seamus Kennedy, O Hanlon, Mangan, Flynn and Nulty all riding hard and by half distance at Castlebar the danger was over with a group of 40 coming together at the front and it stayed this was to Connemara.

It was only on the outskirts of Oughterard that Clarke made his successful attack in company with Rene Lozingo (France) with the diminutive Meath man having the strongest sprint. Seamus Kennedy led in the bunch 35 seconds later.

**Stage 4 Sligo - Oughterard 115 Mls.** 1 N.Clarke (Meath A) 5.04.30 2 R. Lozengo (France) s.t. 3 S.Kennedy (Meath A) at 35 secs 4 S.O Hanlon (Dublin) at 40 sec 5 R.Gauthier 6 D.Lefol (France) 7 B.McKenna (Meath B) 8 B.Everitt (Meath B) 9 L.Clarke (Meath A) all same time

**General Classification:** 1 C.Nulty (Meath A) 39.49.55 2 B.Flynn (Kerry) at 2.12 3 S.Kennedy (Meath A) at 2.47 4 J.Mangan (Kerry) at 5.04 5 M.Tinnelly (Antrim) at 5.35 6 B.McKenna (Meath B) at 7.14 7 B.Connaughton (Meath) at 7.37 8 G.Howard (Dublin) at 7.47 9 T.P.Reilly (Meath) at 8.02 10 equal J.McConville (Armagh) D.Carroll (Dublin) S.O Hanlon (Dublin) M.O'Donoghue (Carlow) and L.Clarke (Meath) all at 8.06

## STAGE 5

It was a Clarke from Meath again on stage 5, 72 miles to Milltown Malbay, but this time it was Larry who took the stage. He won in a 2-up sprint from Daniel Lefol (France).

However, 1 minute later yellow jersey Colm Nulty led in the bunch which had been controlled all day by the strong Meath teams and there was no change at the top except for the stage winner who moved up to 6th from equal 10th. Because of his third place bonus Nulty increased his lead at the top by another 5 seconds.

O Hanlon tried to break the Meath grip on the race on the climb of the Corkscrew at Ballyvaughan but he soon had most of the Meath team for company and gave up the fight leaving the Meath men in control and they kept a tight rein on the race until 12 miles from the finish when they let one of their number, Clarke, escape in company of Frenchman Lefol and it was an extra bonus for them to win yet another stage.
**Stage 5 Oughterard - Milltown Malbay 72 Mls.** 1 L.Clarke (Meath A) 3.14.30 2 D.Lefol (France) s.t. 3 C.Nulty (Meath A) at 55 secs 4 G.Howard (Dublin) 5 S.Kennedy (Meath A) 6 G.Puissegur (France) 7 D.Caqueret (France) 8 R.Lozingo (France) 9 S.O Hanlon (Dublin) 10 B.Flynn (Kerry) all same time
**General Classification:** 1 C.Nulty (Meath A) 17.05.20 2 B.Flynn (Kerry) at 2.17 3 S.Kennedy (Meath A) at 2.52 4 J.Mangan (Kerry) at 5.09 5 M.Tinnelly (Antrim) at 5.40 6 L.Clarke (Meath) at 7.16 7 B.McKenna (Meath B) at 7.19 8 B.Connaughton (Meath) at 7.42 9 G.Howard (Dublin) at 7.52 10 T.P.Reilly (Meath) at 8.07 11 equal J.McConville (Armagh) D.Carroll (Dublin) S. O Hanlon (Dublin) M. O'Donoghue (Carlow) all at 8.11

## STAGE 6 (a) and (b)

Colm Nulty lost over a minute to his closest rival Batty Flynn on the Wednesday morning 17 miles time-trial from Milltown Malbay to Kilrush and then in the afternoon found himself in the bunch which was over 5 minutes down.
However the Meath man fought back and with 10 miles to go the break was caught and Nulty lived to fight another day, albeit with a reduced margin over the Kerryman.
Flynn won the morning stage by 44 seconds from '69 winner Brian Connaughton (Meath A). Nulty put up a good fight to take third, 28 seconds down while Jim McConville (Armagh) was next a further 11 seconds back, making a good start on what was to be an excellent day for the Lurgan man. Shay O Hanlon (Dublin) was fifth at 1.43 with Meath A's Larry Clarke completing the top six 1 second behind O Hanlon ad 3 ahead of team-mate Seamus Kennedy.
Clarke, Kennedy, O Hanlon, Rene Lozingo (France) and 10th placed O'Donoghue were part of a break which went away before Tralee and when their lead went to over 5 minutes, Kennedy was race leader on the road.
With Kerry not represented they led the chase behind. Cohesion went out of the break, as they were joined by a chasing group, which included Ben McKenna (Meath B) and Antrim pair Brian Davey and Michael Tinnelly, who had dropped a place to 6th overall after the TT. Their lead tumbled and with 10 miles left they were caught.
This was the signal for another attack and a big group went away from which McConville won the uphill sprint at Dunquin, the Armagh rider's efforts on the day taking him to 7th on GC.
**Stage 6a Milltown Malbay - Kilrush 17 Mls. TT.** 1 B.Flynn (Kerry) 45.46 2 B.Connaughton (Meath A) at 44 secs 3 C.Nulty at 1.12 4 J.McConville (Armagh) at

1.23 5 S.O Hanlon (Dublin) at 1.43 6 L.Clarke (Meath A) at 1.44 7 S Kennedy (Meath A) at 1.47

**Stage 6b Tarbert - Dunquin 70 Mls.** 1 J.McConville (Armagh) 3.18.15 2 G.Issegor (France) 3 G.Howard (Dublin) 4 P.Healy (Kerry) 5 B.Connaughton (Meath A) 6 J.Marionneau (France) 7 B.McKenna Meath B) all same time

**General Classification:** 1 C.Nulty (Meath A) 21.11.08 2 B.Flynn (Kerry) at 1.05 3 S.Kennedy (Meath A) at 3.27 4 B.Connaughton (Meath A) at 5.29 5 J.Mangan (Kerry) at 5.46 6 M.Tinnelly (Antrim) at 6.05 7 J.McConville (Armagh) at 6.18 8 L.Clarke (Meath A) s.t. 9 G.Howard (Dublin) at 7.20 10 S.O Hanlon (Dublin) at 7.32 11 J.Marionneau (France) at 7.52 12 B.McKenna (Meath B) at 8.13

## STAGE 7

Colm Nulty virtually wrapped up the 1971 RÁS with an epic stage win on the 116 miles mountainous stage from Dunquin to Castletownbere and at the end of the day he led the race by 6.51 over Kerry's John Mangan while Batty Flynn, who had started the day just over a minute behind dropped to eighth, 17.20 down on the Meath rider.

Nulty broke away 20 miles into the stage in company of John Mangan and Dublin duo Derek Carroll and Gabriel Howard. Mangan sat in while the other three set a fast pace and by Killarney they had seven minutes lead over the cruising bunch.

Mangan attacked several times on the climb of the Tunnel Road but each time Nulty rode back up to him. With 200 metres to go to the top Mangan went again but once more the Meath rider brought him back.

Mangan kept trying and his most promising chance came on the climb outside Glengariffe when he went clear. However he was joined by Nulty and he sat up giving Howard and Carroll the chance to rejoin the leaders.

So it stayed that way to the finish where the four leaders arrived intact with Nulty winning the sprint from Mangan, with Howard 3rd and Carroll 4th, all timed at 5.20.12. It was a long wait for the fifth man home who was Mike O'Donoghue who led in Robert Gauthier (France) and T.P. Reilly (Meath A) at 5.21. Guy Puissegur (France) was next home leading in Ben McKenna (Meath B) and Noel Clarke (Meath A) another 31 seconds down.

Two more riders, Jim McConville (Armagh) and Peter Murphy (Carlow) came in 7 minutes down and that was it until the bunch came in 16 minutes in arrears. The Meath riders in the bunch had resisted all attempts to chase and manager Louis White, who had employed similar tactics in masterminding Connaughton's win two years previously was confident saying: 'Nulty must surely win now.'

**Stage 7 Dunquin - Castletownbere 116 Mls.** 1 C.Nulty (Meath A) 5.20.12 2 J.Mangan (Kerry) 3 G.Howard (Dublin) 4 D.Carroll (Dublin) all same time 5 M.O'Donoghue (Carlow) at 5.21 6 R.Gauthier (France) 7 T.P.Reilly (Meath A) all same time 8 G.Puissegur (France) at 5.52 9 B.McKenna (Meath B) 10 N.Clarke (Meath A) all same time

**General Classification:** 1 C.Nulty (Meath A) 26.31.05 2 J.Mangan (Kerry) at 6.51 3 G.Howard (Dublin) at 8.30 4 D.Carroll (Dublin) at 8.35 5 J.McConville (Armagh) at 13.28 6 B.McKenna (Meath B) 15.33 7 T.P.Reilly (Meath A) at 15.54 8 B.Flynn (Kerry) at 17.20 9 M.Cahill (Cork) at 18.17 10 G.Puissegur (France) at 18.27 11 S.Kennedy (Meath) at 19.41 12 R. Gauthier (France) at 19.45

## STAGE 8 (a) and (b)

Batty Flynn, whose challenge for the RÁS was wiped out in the Meath blitzkrieg on Thursday, had some consolation with a home stage win into Killarney on the first of two stages on the Friday, the evening criterium going to Frenchman Robert Gauthier. However the yellow jersey was active on both stages and made Flynn fight all the way to get his stage win finishing the closest of seconds while he was 7th in the big bunch sprint in the evening in the same time as the winner.

Indeed it was Nulty who was first on the attack in the morning going away shortly after the start in Castletownbere quickly joined by Flynn and another Meath A rider Brian Connaughton.

The three stayed away finishing 1.26 ahead of a chasing group of seven which included John Mangan so Nulty increased his lead to 8.26. With Mangan was team-mate Pat Healy, Meath's Seamus Kennedy, Jim McConville (Armagh), Mick Kinsella (Carlow) and Daniel Caqueret (France).

Also there was Dublin's Derek Carroll but he crashed. Shay O Hanlon was in the process of getting across to the break when he came upon the crashed Carroll and gave his better placed team-mate his bike and as a result he lost over 12 minutes.

The usual immense crowd turned out to watch the 25 Mls criterium in Killarney which although it provided some fast and furious racing with prime sprints every lap, nevertheless produced no changes in the overall, Robert Gauthier winning the big gallop from team-mate Rene lozingo with Seamus Kennedy third.

**Stage 8a Castletownbere - Killarney 54 Mls.** 1 B.Flynn (Kerry) 2.21.16 2 C.Nulty (Meath A) 3 B.Connaughton (Meath A) all same time 4 S.Kennedy (Meath) at 1.21 5 J.Mangan (Kerry) 6 P.Healy (Kerry) 7 T.P.Reilly (Meath A) 8 D.Caqueret (France) 9 J.McConville (Armagh) 10 M.Kinsella (Carlow) all same time

**Stage 8b Killarney Criterium 25 Mls** 1 R.Gauthier (France) 1.14.25 2 L.Lozingo (France) 3 S.Kennedy (Meath A) 4 B.Flynn (Kerry) 5 J.Mangan (Kerry) 6 B.Connaughton (Meath A) 7 C.Nulty (Meath A) 8 G.Puissegur (France) 9 P.Sargent (Cork) all same time

**General Classification:** 1 C.Nulty (Meath A) 28.52.07 2 J.Mangan (Kerry) at 8.26 3 G.Howard (Dublin) at 13.25 4 J.McConville (Armagh) at 15.18 5 B.Flynn (Kerry) at 16.05 6 T.P.Reilly (Meath A) at 17.29 7 B.McKenna (Meath B) at 20.28 8 S.Kennedy (Meath A) at 21.17 9 B.Connaughton (Meath A) at 22.52 10 P.Hyland (Mayo) at 25.31 11 J.Murphy (Louth) at 26.03 12 M.O'Donoghue (Carlow) 26.08

**Team:** 1 Meath A 84.30.52 2 Kerry 84.57.42 3 France 85.20.39

## STAGE 9

Mike O'Donoghue (Carlow), one of the pre-race favourites, whose chance of overall honours was now gone, had the consolation of a stage win when he out sprinted Shay O Hanlon (Dublin) and Noel Clarke (Meath A)in a group of ten which came home 2.02 in front of the main group.

This contained yellow jersey Colm Nulty who now looked, barring accidents, that he was assured of victory with only the final stage to come.

O'Donoghue was an early attacker and he was joined by O Hanlon. These two stayed out in front for some miles before they were joined by Clarke, Jim McConville (Armagh), Pat Healy (Kerry), D. Caqueter (France), Brian Davey (Antrim), Mick Kinsella (Carlow), Gabriel Howard (Dublin) and Tony Gavin (Galway).

This was the move of the day and they stayed out in front for the remainder of the stage although their lead never posed any major threat to those behind.

**Stage 9 Killarney - Roscrea 109 Mls.** 1 M.O'Donoghue (Carlow) 4.38.00 2 S.O Hanlon (Dublin) 3 N.Clarke (Meath A) 4 J.McConville (Armagh) 5 P.Healy (Kerry) 6 D.Caqueret (France) all same time

**General Classification:** 1 C.Nulty (Meath A) 34.47.49 2 J.Mangan (Kerry) at 8.26 3 G.Howard (Dublin) at 12.23 4 J.McConville (Armagh) at 13.51 5 B.Flynn (Kerry) at 15.54 6 T.P.Reilly (Meath A) at 18.18 7 S.Kennedy (Meath A) at 21.01 8 B.McKenna (Meath B) at 21.17 9 B.Connaughton (Meath A) at 22.52 10 M.O'Donoghue (Carlow) at 24.50 11 P.Hyland (Mayo) at 26.31 12 D.Caqueret (France) at 26.35

## STAGE 10

The final stage was won by Batty Flynn just ahead of Kerry team-mate John Mangan with Robert Gauthier (France) third.

Little could happen on this final stage to upset the overall positions. They were racing on wide, flat and fast roads where the strong Meath combinations could wipe out any dangerous move.

Early on Flynn, Seamus Kennedy, Daniel Caqueret and Noel Clarke went away but their bid was ended by Shay O Hanlon and Jean Paul Marionneau who brought the bunch up coming into Naas.

Finally around Kill on the Naas dual carriageway the vital move came when eight riders went away and they built up a 1.15 lead by the finish.

**Stage 10 Roscrea - Dublin 76 Mls.** 1 B.Flynn (Kerry) 2.50.15 2 J.Mangan (Kerry) at 2 secs 3 R.Gauthier (France) 4 C.Nulty (Meath A) 5 N.Clarke (Meath A) 6 D.Caqueret (France) 7 J.Murphy (Louth) 8 B.Connaughton (Meath) all same time

**General Classification:** 1 C.Nulty (Meath A) 37.38.06 2 J.Mangan (Kerry) at 8.16 3 G.Howard (Dublin) at 13.48 4 J.McConville (Armagh) at 15.50 5 B.Flynn (Kerry) s.t. 6 T.P.Reilly (Meath A) at 19.33 7 S.Kennedy (Meath A) at 22.16 8 B.McKenna (Meath B) at 19.49 9 B.Connaughton (Meath A) at 22.52 10 M.O'Donoghue

(Carlow) at 24.50 11 D.Caqueret (France) at 26.35 12 N.Clarke (Meath A) at 26.59 13 J.Murphy (Louth) at 27.06 14 P.Hyland (Mayo) at 27.47 15 R.Gauthier (France) at 27.59

**Team:** 1 Meath A 110.46.37 2 Kerry 111.15.27 3 France 111.42.04 4 Meath B 111.47.21 5 Carlow 112.00.49 6 Antrim 112.18.07

*1971 Winner – Colm Nulty*

## 1972

There were 74 entries for the 1972 RÁS with the French FSGT team the only visiting selection. There were some innovations with two double stages, on the opening Saturday and on the Tuesday, while on Wednesday there were also two stages, one of them a 25 miles time-trial.

This was balanced out to some extent when on the Thursday, for the first and only time in the RÁS, there was a rest day. The top three from the previous year were there, however defending champion Colm Nulty only squeezed on to the Meath 'B' team as a late selection (he had not been expected to return from France where he had been racing) and Kerry's John Mangan was not on the county team but on a team entered by Dublin club Setanta. As well as this the 1971 third placed rider Gabriel Howard, from Meath, was once more riding on the Dublin team!

### STAGE 1

It was first blood to Meath A when Seamus Kennedy won a ten-man sprint into Dundalk, his second RÁS stage; coincidentally his previous win had also been into Dundalk three years previously.

The 50 miles stage on the main road from Dublin was always going to be fast and likely to discourage any serious breaks until ten riders got away after about half-an-hour of racing and they stayed in front to the finish.

The bunch chased all the way the pace causing the bunch to split and while a chasing group of about 20 came in only 50 seconds down, the remainder of the bunch lost a huge 3.28 in the final 30 miles.

In the sprint Kennedy edged out Pat Healy (Kerry) with John Mangan (Setanta) third. French riders Daniel Lefol and Pierre Merklen took the next two places to give France a 35 second lead over Meath A in the team classification. Defending champion Colm Nulty came home in sixth place.

**Stage 1 Dublin - Dundalk 50 Mls** 1 S.Kennedy (Meath A) 1.52.00 2 P.Healy (Kerry) 3 J.Mangan (Setanta) 4 D.Lefol (France) 5 P.Merklen (France) 6 C.Nulty (Meath B) 7 D.Mangan (Kerry) 8 G.Howard (Dublin) 9 B.McKenna (Meath B) 10 D.Caqueret (France) all same time

**Team:** 1 France 5.36.00 2 Meath A at 35 secs 3 Dublin at 1.40

### STAGE 2 (a) and (b)

Meath A had their second win in a row when Noel Clarke won the sprint from a group of 18 into Belturbet at the end of the morning's 50 miles stage from Dundalk. It was a dramatic finish with Clarke colliding with Carlow's Mike O'Donoghue in the sprint and falling heavily. However he was able to start on the afternoon stage.

Seamus O Hanlon (Dublin) was third in the same time and Seamus Kennedy finished just behind in fourth place to retain the yellow jersey.

**Stage 2a Dundalk - Belturbet 50 Mls.** 1 N.Clarke (Meath A) 2.13.10 2 M.O'Donoghue (Carlow) 3 S.O Hanlon (Dublin) 4 S.Kennedy (Meath A) 5 J.Mangan (Setanta) 6 P.Healy (Kerry) 7 C.Nulty (Meath B) 8 D.Lefol (France) 9 B.McKenna (Meath B) 10 B.Dupin (France) all same time

Mike O'Donoghue, who thought he had won the morning stage and had appealed, losing the verdict to Noel Clarke, made amends on the afternoon 79 miles stage to Donegal town winning from a five man group.

He won the sprint from Brian Connaughton (Meath A), John Mangan (Setanta), Noel Clarke and Eddie Flanagan (Kildare). Shay O Hanlon who had been with the group punctured near the finish and lost 57 seconds. However it was over six minutes until the next group arrived led in by Ben McKenna (Meath B). Mangan who had finished in the same time as the winner on all three stages took over the yellow jersey.

**Stage 2b Belturbet - Donegal Town 78 Mls.** 1 M.O'Donoghue (Carlow) 3.35.45 2 B.Connaughton (Meath A) 3 J.Mangan (Setanta) 4 N.Clarke (Meath A) 5 E.Flanagan (Kildare) all same time 6 S.O Hanlon (Dublin) at 57 secs 7 B.McKenna (Meath B) at 6.30

**General Classification:** 1 J.Mangan (Setanta) 7.40.55 2 M.O'Donoghue (Carlow) at 35 secs 3 N.Clarke (Meath A) at 45 secs 4 B.Connaughton (Meath A) at 50 secs 5 E.Flanagan (Kildare) s.t. 6 S.O Hanlon (Dublin) at 1.52 7 B.McKenna (Meath B) at 6.50

## STAGE 3

Tragedy struck on Sunday morning when young Dunleer rider Noel McGuill who had been riding with the Louth team, died in Ballyshannon hospital from head injuries received on Saturday when he crashed at Ballintra, just a few miles from the finish in Donegal. The 25-year-old rider was the reigning Irish cyclo-cross champion. The Louth team withdrew from the race and as a mark of respect the leader's jersey was not presented before the third stage and a minute's silence was observed.

In the following years, until road works removed the stretch of road and the stone bridge where the crash had occurred, RÁS officials laid a floral tribute at the spot whenever the race passed that way.

Meath continued to dominate on the 80 miles stage to Dungloe with Kennedy taking another stage. However Mangan still led O'Donoghue at the top of the GC with the best Meath man Noel Clarke third at 45 secs.

The decisive break came shortly after the start when Larry Clarke (Meath A) and John McNally (Meath B) went away on the Barnesmore Gap. They were chased by Gabriel Howard (Dublin), and Gene Mangan (Setanta) but these were caught by the bunch.

Then Colm Nulty and Seamus Kennedy got away and at Letterkenny they were 35 seconds behind the leaders with the bunch at 55 seconds. A few miles further on the

four Meath riders got together and worked well to the finish where they had an advantage of 41 seconds on a group of 11 containing all the top six on GC except Eddie Flanagan who dropped one place to sixth, behind O Hanlon.
**Stage 3 Donegal - Dungloe 80 Mls** 1 S.Kennedy (Meath A) 3.43.30 2 C.Nulty (Meath B) 3 L.Clarke (Meath A) 4 J.McNally (Meath B) all same time 5 N.Clarke (Meath A) at 41 secs 6 B.Dupin (France) 7 P.Healy (Kerry) 8 B.Connaughton (Meath A) 9 P.Merklen (France) 10 D.Caqueret (France)
**General Classification:** 1 J.Mangan (Setanta) 11.24.56 2 M.O'Donoghue (Carlow) at 35 secs 3 N.Clarke (Meath A) at 45 secs 4 B.Connaughton (Meath A) at 50 secs 5 S.O Hanlon (Dublin) at 1.52 6 E.Flanagan (Kildare) at 4.37 7 C.Nulty (Meath B) at 6.01 8 D.Caqueret (France) at 7.57 9 B.McKenna (Meath B) at 9.12 10 S.Kennedy (Meath A) at 10.56
**Team:** 1 Meath A 34.21.08 2 Meath B 34.32.12 3 France 34.35.40

## STAGE 4

Yet another stage went to Meath when Noel Clarke out sprinted a 17-strong group at the end of the 88 miles stage from Dungloe to Sligo. John Mangan finished with the leaders and retained the yellow jersey.
Ten miles out it looked odds on for a French 1/2 when Bernard Dupin and Daniel Cliqueret held a 1 minute lead but the work of the Meath riders and Dublin's Shay O Hanlon in the 15-man chase group saw the French pair recaptured before the finish.
The vital move of the day came after only 16 miles at Glenties when 12 riders went clear including the race leader, Clarke, the two Frenchman, O Hanlon and Gabriel Howard (Dublin) as well as Meath riders Brian Connaughton, Seamus Kennedy and the Nulty brothers Colm and Mick.
Their lead went to 1.30 by Donegal Town when they were caught by a chasing group which included Daniel Lefol and Pierre Merklen (France).
Connaughton went away on his own but by Ballyshannon they were all together again. Then O Hanlon, Dupin and Nulty had a go but they too were brought back before the two French riders attacked and looked to be on course to stay away only for the hard work behind.
**Stage 4 Dungloe - Sligo 88 Mls.** 1 N.Clarke (Meath A) 3.52.10 2 G.Howard Dublin A) 3 D.Mangan (Kerry) 4 S.O Hanlon (Dublin A) 5 G.Mangan (Setanta) 6 B.Dupin (France) 7 C.Nulty (Meath B) 8 M.Nulty (Meath A) 9 B.Connaughton (Meath A) 10 D. Cliqueret (France) all same time
**General Classification:** 1 J.Mangan (Setanta) 15.17.21 2 N.Clarke (Meath A) at 30 secs 3 M.O'Donoghue (Carlow) at 35 secs 4 B.Connaughton (Meath A) at 50 secs 5 S.O Hanlon (Dublin A) at 1.08 6 C.Nulty (Meath A) at 5.51

## STAGE 5 (a) and (b)

Another double stage saw the riders cover a total of 134 miles with a morning run of

65 miles to Tuam won by Bernard Dupin of France while Colm Nulty had a superb solo win by over 2 minutes on the 69 miles leg to Ennistymon.
The morning stage was fairly uneventful except for an 11-man group which went away at Tubercurry, 17 miles from the start. This group built a substantial lead by the finish where Dupin won the sprint from John McNally (Meath B) and Seamus Kennedy (Meath A).
Derek Carroll (Dublin A) led in the bunch 4.05 later but despite the gap there were no big changes at the top of the GC with most of the main contenders finishing in the bunch.
**Stage 5a Sligo - Tuam 64 Mls.** 1 B.Dupin (France) 2.43.20 2 J.McNally (Meath B) 3 S.Kennedy (Meath A) 4 M.McKenna (Meath A) 5 G.Howard (Dublin A) 6 L.Clarke (Meath A) 7 P.Healy (Kerry) 8 M.Moore (Armagh) 9 D. Caqueret (France) 10 H.Prevost (France) all same time
In the afternoon there was a 25-man break after 25 miles but it was brought back by the bunch. The main action came in the final hour of the stage on the climb of the Corkscrew after Ballyvaughan where Nulty went away on his own.
Over the top he had a lead of 2 minutes on a six-man group including O Hanlon, Mangan, Meathmen Brian Connaughton and Noel Clarke, Mike O'Donoghue (Carlow) and Bernard Caqueret (France).
These six were caught but Mangan went away again accompanied by Connaughton and Dermot Dignam (Dublin) but when Mangan led the trio across the line there were 2.24 behind the stage winner who moved up to 5th overall. However apart from Connaughton, Mangan had strengthened his position in relation to his rivals.
**Stage 5b Tuam - Ennistymon 68 Mls.** 1 C.Nulty (Meath B) 3.7.30 2 J.Mangan (Setanta) at 2.24 3 B.Connaughton (Meath A) 4 D.Dignam (Dublin A) all same time 5 M.Lacey (Kerry) at 4.13 6 C.Reynolds (Meath B) 7 J.Lena (France) 8 S.O Hanlon (Dublin A) 9 P.Merklen (France) all same time
**General Classification:** 1 J.Mangan (Setanta) 21.14.13 2 B.Connaughton (Meath A) at 50 secs 3 N.Clarke (Meath A) at 1.12 4 M.O'Donoghue (Carlow) at 2.53 5 C.Nulty (Meath B) at 3.26 6 S.O Hanlon (Dublin A) at 3.51

## STAGE 6 (a) and (b)

Mike O'Donoghue (Carlow) won the morning's 26 miles time-trial from Ennistymon to Tarbert by 23 seconds from Shay O Hanlon (Dublin A) but the race-leader was in touch finishing third a further seven seconds back to strengthen his hold on the race.
O'Donoghue's time brought him up to second overall 2.04 behind Mangan but without a strong team he was not the same threat to the Killorglin rider as the Meath challengers especially as the county had two strong teams.
O Hanlon was the only other rider to improve his position finishing the day fourth overall, 3.44 in arrears. Connaughton slipped a place to third but instead of being 50 seconds behind he was now 2.15.

**Stage 6a Ennistymon - Tarbert 26 Mls. TT:** 1 M.O'Donoghue (Carlow) 1.11.31 2 S.O Hanlon (Dublin A) 1.11.54 3 J.Mangan (Setanta) 1.21.1 4 B.Connaughton (Meath A) 1.13.31 5 D.Caqueret (France) 1.13.54 6 E.Flanagan (Kildare) 1.14.11
The afternoon stage was only 44 miles from Tarbert to Kilorglin and there was action from the start and after 4 miles Shay O Hanlon and T.P. Reilly (Meath B) quickly opened a useful gap which was 1 minute at Castlemaine.
However despite their all out efforts they were caught and passed by a 10 man group to finish with the race leader in the bunch, 59 seconds behind the winner.
In a thrilling sprint for the stage Seamus Kennedy won by a wheel from Christy Reynolds (Meath B) to take his third stage of the week. He was steadily climbing up the GC sheet and would eventually finish 9th, 9 minutes down, emphasising just how costly to him had been Saturday's stage to Donegal when he lost over 11 minutes.
**Stage 6b Tarbert - Killorglin 44 Mls.** 1 S.Kennedy (Meath A) 1.54.35 2 C.Reynolds (Meath B) 3 C.Nulty (Meath B) 4 P.Healy (Kerry) 5 D.Caqueret (France) 6 B.Dupin (France) 7 D.Mangan (Kerry) 8 P.Hyland (Galway) 9 G.Howard (Dublin A) 10 M.McKenna (Meath A) all same time
**General Classification:** 1 J.Mangan (Setanta) 24.33.05 2 M.O'Donoghue (Carlow) at 2.04 3 B.Connaughton (Meath A) at 2.15 4 S.O Hanlon (Dublin A) at 3.44 5 C.Nulty (Meath B) at 4.05 6 D.Caqueret (France) at 4.27 7 N. Clarke (Meath A) at 7.40

## STAGE 7

After Thursday's rest day the two Meath teams made an all out effort to overhaul leader John Mangan on the tenth stage, 111 hilly miles from Killorglin to Kinsale which included the climbs at Moll's Gap and Tunnel Road, but the yellow jersey, although finishing 4.41 behind the stage winner Bernard Dupin of France, kept in touch with his closest challengers and looked to be strong enough to keep his lead to Dublin.
Dupin took his second stage of the week out sprinting breakaway companions Martin McKenna (Meath A) and Brian Davey (Antrim) with Padraic Hyland (Mayo) just tailed off six seconds further back. These were followed 4.10 later by a small group led in by Mick Nulty (Meath B) with the bunch containing all the main contenders finishing just 27 seconds later.
Early on there was a break by Dupin, and Meath riders Noel Clarke, Seamus Kennedy and Gabriel Howard who was riding for Dublin A, and although they had opened a good gap at Killarney they were caught just after Glengariff. Dupin however was soon back in the action going away with McKenna and Davey to take his second stage.
**Stage 7 Killorglin - Kinsale 111 Mls** 1 B.Dupin (France) 4.48.20 2 M.McKenna (Meath A) 3 B.Davey (Antrim) all same time 4 P.Hyland (Mayo) at 6 secs 5 M.Nulty (Meath B) at 4.16 6 J.Lena (France) s.t.

**General Classification:** 1 J.Mangan (Setanta) 29.16.06 2 M.O'Donoghue (Carlow) at 2.04 3 B.Connaughton (Meath A) at 2.15 4 S.O Hanlon (Dublin A) at 3.44 5 C.Nulty (Meath B) at 4.07 6 D.Caqueret (France) at 5.55

## STAGE 8

Jean Lena of France won the penultimate stage of the 1972 RÁS out sprinting Seamus Kennedy to deprive the Meath man of his fourth stage of the week, the 91 miles run from Kinsale to Carlow.

The yellow jersey came home safely in the main group with his main challengers, 1.34 behind the 3-man break which also contained double stage winner Bernard Dupin (France).

These three had gone away at Fermoy, with 60 miles to go but as none of the three were a serious threat overall they were 'permitted' to stay away as long as the gap did not become too great.

**Stage 8 Kinsale - Carrick on Suir 91 Mls.** 1 J.Lena (France) 3.44.05 2 S.Kennedy (Meath A) 3 B.Dupin (France) all same time 4 C.Reynolds (Meath B) at 1.34 5 S.O Hanlon (Dublin A) 6 J.Mangan (Setanta) 7 D.Lefol (France) 8 D. Carroll (Dublin A) 9 J.Lacey (Kerry) all same time

**General Classification:** 1 J.Mangan (Setanta) 35.01.45 2 M.O'Donoghue (Carlow) at 2.04 3 B.Connaughton (Meath A) at 2.15 4 S.O Hanlon (Dublin A) at 3.44 5 C.Nulty (Meath B) at 4.07 6 D.Caqueret (France) at 5.55

## STAGE 9

After a week in the yellow jersey 20-year-old Killorglin rider John Mangan came home in triumph, finishing 7th on the final stage, 1.22 behind winner Bernard Dupin (France,) to take overall victory by 2.04 from Carlow's Mike O'Donoghue with past winner Brian Connaughton (Meath) third only 11 seconds further back.

The final stage, 99 miles from Carrick-on-Suir to Dublin was something of a formality for the race leader who stayed in the bunch keeping an eye on his main rivals.

Shortly after the start Dupin T.P. Reilly (Meath), Brian Davey (Antrim) and john Lawlor (Carlow) opened up a lead which was half-a-minute at Kilkenny. Then the gap started to grow and by Leighlinbridge it was 2.15 before the bunch started to chase and the lead was slowly reduced.

At Kilcullen it was still 2 minutes when Reilly broke a chain and dropped back to the bunch while the leaders were joined by Vincent Sheridan (Kildare) and Derek Carroll (Dublin) and these five stayed at the front to the Park where Dublin beat Sheridan by half-a wheel to take his third stage of the week.

As a result of his win 'Jacko' was invited to spend some months racing in France where he was eventually to spend many years becoming something of a legend in Brittany and Northern France and although he never turned professional he had an extremely successful career there. Many years later when the Tour de France came to Ireland, the famous 'speaker' of the Tour, Daniel Mangeas, several times referred to him during his commentary on the Irish Tour stages.

**Stage 9 Carrick-on-Suir - Dublin 99 Mls.** 1 B.Dupin (France) 3.55.20 2 V.Sheridan (Kildare) 3 B.Davey (Antrim) 4 J.Lawlor (Carlow) 5 D.Carroll (Dublin A) all same time 6 H.Prevost (France) at 1.22 7 J.Mangan (Setanta) 8 S.O Hanlon (Dublin A) 9 C.Reynolds (Meath B) 10 J.Lena (France) all same time

**General Classification:** 1 J.Mangan (Setanta) 36.58.33 2 M.O'Donoghue (Carlow) at 2.04 3 B.Connaughton (Meath A) at 2.15 4 S.O Hanlon (Dublin A) at 3.44 5 C.Nulty (Meath B) at 4.07 6 D.Caqueret (France) at 5.55 7 B.Dupin (France) at 7.02 8 N.Clarke (Meath A) at 7.17 9 S.Kennedy (Meath) at 9.21 10 E.Flanagan (Kildare) at 14.11 11 M.Nulty (Meath A) at 17.37 12 G.Howard (Dublin A) at 24.35 13 B.Davey (Antrim) at 26.03 14 C.Reynolds (Meath B) at 27.36 15 J.Lena (France) at 37.25

**Team:** 1 Meath A 110.54.31 2 France 111.21.24 3 Meath B 111.38.59

*John Mangan, winner 1972*

## 1973

The '73 RÁS which started on June 29 was back to a more traditional format with no rest days or split stages. However there were some very long stages with the Wednesday and Thursday runs almost 200 kilometres each.
Sixty-eight riders entered and as in the previous year France was the only visiting team and it looked that Meath with three teams would again be very strong. However '72 winner Mangan had returned from France and started as favourite, although he was on a weak Kerry team with only his brother Denis Mangan and Denis Clifford for support.
Others being tipped by the papers were Seamus Kennedy, Brian Connaughton, Larry and Noel Clarke and the Nulty brothers, all from Meath, and '64 winner Paddy Flanagan who had been having a great season. Also fancied was '72 runner-up Mike O'Donoghue of Carlow and the ever-present Shay O Hanlon (Dublin).

### STAGE 1

The opening stage was the second shortest of the week at 48 miles, the shortest being the final run from Navan to Dublin, and as usual on short stages the pace was high for most of the way.
Just after Naas Paddy Flanagan (Kildare) and Maurice Bann Lavery (Armagh) got away and they were soon joined by Shay O Hanlon, Giles Sabourin (France), Brian Davey (Antrim), Mick Nulty and Mick Kennedy (Meath Flora), Noel Clarke (Meath Discover Ireland) and the two Mangan's, John and Denis.
The group worked well together and soon had a minute's lead. Subourin and Kennedy dropped back as the bunch closed to within 15 seconds at Moone. However the lead started to grow again and when the eight fought out a thrilling sprint in Carlow where Denis Mangan won by half a wheel from O Hanlon with Clarke third, the gap over the bunch was 1.10.
**Stage 1 Dublin - Carlow 48 Mls.** 1 D.Mangan (Kerry) 2.05.10 2 S.O Hanlon (Dublin) 3 N.Clarke (Meath Disc Ireland) 4 P.Flanagan (Kildare) 5 J.Mangan (Kerry) 6 B.Davey (Antrim) 7 M.Nulty (Meath Flora) 8 M.Bann Lavery (Armagh-Louth-Down) all same time 9 M.Cahill (Cork) at 1.10 10 J.McNally (Dublin) s.t.

### STAGE 2

Mike O'Donoghue (Carlow) won the second stage, 87 miles from Carlow to Waterford but as he hadn't been in the break on Friday evening the yellow jersey passed to Shay O Hanlon (Dublin), equal on time with Paddy Flanagan (Kildare) and Brian Davey (Antrim) but leader because of better stage placings.

For 28-year-old O'Donoghue it was his eighth RÁS stage. He joined the leaders only 20 miles from the finish and was best in the 10-man sprint.
There were early attacks by first ten riders and then six but before Kilkenny Tom Lane (Cork) went away on his own chased by T.P.Reilly (Meath Red Island). Lane stayed clear through the climb at Ninemilehouse but the headwind took its toll and he was joined by Brian Connaughton (Meath Discover Ireland) who took the prime at Carrick-on-Suir.
Next to get across to the leaders was Jack Murphy of the Louth, Armagh, Down combination team and other came across as the wind swung behind them on the final run in to the finish.
**Stage 2 Carlow - Waterford 87 Mls.** 1 M.O'Donoghue (Carlow) 4.10.00 2 P.Flanagan (Kildare) 3 S.O Hanlon (Dublin) 4 M.Cahill (Cork) 5 T.P.Reilly (Meath Red Island) 6 S.Castagnet (France) 7 C.Lafforgue (France) 8 G.Sabourdin (France) 9 B.Davey (Antrim) 10 S.Kennedy (Meath Disc Ireland) all same time
**General Classification:** 1 S.O Hanlon (Dublin) 6.16.20 2 P.Flanagan (Kildare) 3 B.Davey (Antrim) all same time 4 M.O'Donoghue (Carlow) at 1.10 5 M.Cahill (Cork) 6 S.Castagnet (France) 7 S.Kennedy (Meath Disc Ireland) all same time

## STAGE 3

The 107 miles stage to Macroom, run off in atrocious conditions, was won by Mick Nulty (Meath Flora) after him and Kildare's Paddy Flanagan went away with 12 miles to the finish to open a lead of 1.22 which gave Flanagan the yellow jersey by 1.22 from his long-time rival O Hanlon.
Flanagan knew he could take the jersey and promised Nulty the stage if the Meath man worked with him and true to his word he made no effort in the final sprint.
In the atrocious conditions of wind, rain, fog and even floods, where at times visibility was down to a few years, there wasn't much action early on as the race round wound the coastal road to Dungarvan although there was a short-lived six-man break.
After Dungarvan Flanagan and Nulty went away and had a lead of 30 seconds at Youghal when they were joined by Noel Clarke with some 10 riders spread out between the break and the bunch.
As they entered Cork Seamus Kennedy (Meath Disc Ireland), Larry Clarke (Meath Disc Ireland) and French pair Lafforgue and Leroy joined up with the leading trio. As more riders made it across to the leaders the main bunch was losing time and was over four minutes behind the leaders.
**Stage 3 Waterford - Macroom 107 Mls.** 1 M.Nulty (Meath Flora) 4.59.45 2 P.Flanagan (Kildare) same time 3 M.O'Donoghue (Carlow) at 1.22 4 D.Mangan (Kerry) 5 C.Reynolds (Meath Red Island) 6 B.Dupin (France) 7 G.Sabourin (France) 8 S.Castagnet (France) 9 N.Clarke (Meath Disc Ireland) 10 G.Howard (Dublin) all same time

**General Classification:** 1 P.Flanagan (Kildare) 11.14.55 2 S.O Hanlon (Dublin) at 1.22 3 M.O'Donoghue (Carlow) at 2.32 4 S.Castagnet France) 5 S.Kennedy (Meath Disc Ireland) all same time 6 B.Davey (Antrim) at 2.38 7 D.Mangan (Kerry) at 2.56 8 N.Clarke Meath Disc Ireland) s.t. 10 M.Cahill (Cork) at 3.48

## STAGE 4

Mike O'Donoghue won the 106 miles stage from Macroom to Tralee in a sprint from a 5-man group which finished 42 seconds ahead of the main bunch which contained Paddy Flanagan (Kildare) who retained his overall lead. O'Donoghue's win moved him up to third overall at 1.50.

Although the weather had improved considerable from Sunday, this was a hard stage with plenty of climbing and there were groups finishing up to 20 minutes after the winner.

It was all out attacking from the drop of the flag and almost immediately a seven-man group got clear including O'Donoghue, John Mangan (Kerry), Dupin and Castignet (France), and from Meath Mick Creighton, Seamus Kennedy and Christy Reynolds.

Working extremely well they quickly built up a big lead and by Ballylickey, 30 miles into the stage, their lead was 4 minutes. Over the climb and down into Glengariff saw this grow to 6 minutes and a further minute was added on the climb of the Tunnel Road.

This was the maximum lead as the bunch started to pull them back from Kenmare. Outside Killarney on the Killorglin Road it was down to 2 minutes but they held out to the finish where their margin was only 42 seconds as Denis Mangan (Kerry) led in the chasers.

**Stage 4 Macroom - Tralee 106 Mls.** 1 M.O'Donoghue (Carlow) 4.42.30 2 C.Reynolds (Meath Red Island) 3 B.Dupin (France) 4 J.Mangan (Kerry) 5 S.Kennedy (Meath Disc Ireland) 6 S.Castagnet (France) 7 M.Creighton (Meath Disc Ireland) all same time 8 D.Mangan (Kerry) at 42 secs 9 J.Murphy (Armagh/Down/Louth) 10 S.O Hanlon (Dublin) all same time

**General Classification:** 1 P.Flanagan (Kildare) 15.58.07 2 S.O Hanlon (Dublin) at 1.22 3 M.O'Donoghue (Carlow) at 1.50 4 S.Castignet (France) s.t. 5 S.Kennedy (Meath Disc Ireland) s.t. 6 B.Davey (Antrim) at 2.38 7 D.Mangan (Kerry) at 2.56 8 N.Clarke (Meath Disc Ireland) s.t.

## STAGE 5

There was virtually no change at the top of the GC after the 105 miles stage from Tralee to Gort, won by Noel Clarke (Meath Discover Ireland) as all the top placed riders, except Serge Castagnet (France) were in an 18-man group which finished nearly 11 minutes ahead of the next bunch on the road.

Castagnet had the misfortune to puncture twice and lost al hope of catching the leading group as their lead continued to grow. The split had occurred after only two miles of the stage and with so many top men included most of them prepared to work; they simply left the rest of the race behind.
Three miles from the finish Clarke attacked chased by O Hanlon and Flanagan but the Meath man held on to take the stage. Despite the gap which some estimated as around 60 yards, all the 18 riders were given the same time for the stage?
Apart from Castagnet the only other rider to disappear from the top ten was Mick Creighton (Meath Discover Ireland) who had been disqualified for allegedly taking a tow on the previous stage, a decision strenuously denied by his team who refused to take up position behind team leaders France in the pre-race parade. Team captain Brian Connaughton said it was the only way they would express their disagreement with the decision to disqualify their rider.
**Stage 5 Tralee - Gort 105 Mls.** 1 N.Clarke (Meath Disc Ireland) 4.18.10 2 S.O Hanlon (Dublin) 3 P.Flanagan (Kildare) 4 J.Mangan (Kerry) 5 S.Kennedy (Meath Disc Ireland) 6 J.Murphy (Armagh/Down/Louth) 7 B.Dupin (France) 8 D.Mangan (Kerry) 9 M.Leroy (France) 10 B.Connaughton (Meath Disc. Ireland)
**General Classification:** 1 P.Flanagan 20.16.17 2 S.O Hanlon (Dublin) at 1.22 3 M.O'Donoghue (Carlow) at 1.50 4 S.Kennedy (Meath Disc Ireland) s.t. 5 B.Davey (Antrim) at 2.38 6 D.Mangan (Kerry) at 2.56 7 N.Clarke (Meath Disc Ireland) s.t. 8 B.Dupin (France) at 3.18 9 M.Cahill (Cork) at 3.48 10 T.P.Reilly (Meath Red Island) at 4.07 11 B.Connaughton (Meath Disc Ireland) s.t. 12 M.McKenna (Meath Red Island) s.t.

## STAGE 6

There was a complete reshuffle at the top of the classification after Wednesday's long sixth stage, 120 miles from Gort to Belmullet which was won by Larry Clarke (Meath Discover Ireland).
With race leader Flanagan finishing over 10 minutes behind and second placed O Hanlon and most of the other main favourites over 8 minutes back, Mike O'Donoghue (Carlow) took over the yellow jersey with a margin of 1.28 from Bernard Dupin (France) with Cork's Mick Cahill a further 30 seconds behind.
Immediately after the start O'Donoghue, Dupin and Tim Lane (Cork) went away and they were joined by John McNally (Dublin), Christy Reynolds (Meath Red Island) and Martin Lydon (Galway/Sligo).
At Galway they were joined by another seven: Jack Murphy (Louth/Armagh/Down), Larry Clarke (Meath Disc Ireland), Joe McAloon (Antrim), Mick Cahill (Cork), Denis Clifford (Kerry), and Dublin pair Gabriel Howard and Terry Campbell.
These thirteen worked well together and by Castlebar, where Reynolds took the prime, they had an advantage of over six minutes. As the gap grew to 11 minutes Campbell and McNally dropped back followed later by McAloon and Lydon but the remaining nine stayed together and at the finish, where Clarke took his first stage

since 1971, they still had a huge lead of 10.47. Flanagan, who tried his heart out with little help dropped to 7th, over 8 minutes down.

**Stage 6 Gort - Belmullet 120 Mls.** 1 L.Clarke (Meath Disc Ireland) 5.00.41 2 C.Reynolds (Meath Red Island) 3 B.Dupin (France) 4 J.Murphy (Louth) 5 M.O'Donoghue (Carlow) 6 M.Cahill (Cork) 7 T.Lane (Cork) 8 D.Clifford (Kerry) 9 G.Howard (Dublin) all same time 10 J.McAloon (Antrim) at 2.45

**General Classification:** 1 M.O'Donoghue (Carlow) 25.18.48 2 B.Dupin (France) at 1.28 3 M.Cahill (Cork) at 1.58 4 J.Murphy (Armagh/Louth/Down) at 3.16 5 S.O Hanlon (Dublin) at 6.59 6 S.Kennedy (Meath Disc Ireland) at 7.27 7 P.Flanagan (Kildare) at 8.22 8 D.Mangan (Kerry) at 8.33 9 N.Clarke (Meath Disc Ireland) s.t. 10 B.Davey (Antrim) at 11.00

## STAGE 7

After losing the lead on Wednesday, Paddy Flanagan had some consolation on the following stage into Donegal Town which he won coming home on his own, 17 seconds ahead of Charles Lafforgue (France).

However O'Donoghue came in with a 12-strong group 21 seconds behind the winner to maintain his lead over Bernard Dupin who was also in the group. Flanagan made a slight improvement on GC moving up a place to sixth at 8.01.

The first 14 home had gone away at Ballisoadare, with 43 miles to go. Seamus Kennedy, lying sixth overall fell but despite the best efforts of his Meath Discover Ireland team they could not get up to the leaders whose lead at Sligo was seven minutes. As well as Kennedy, Brian Davey (Antrim) didn't make the break and dropped out of the top ten.

**Stage 7 Belmullet - Donegal 122 Mls.** 1 P.Flanagan (Kildare) 5.16.37 2 C.Lafforgue (France) at 17 secs 3 J.Murphy (Armagh/Down/Louth) at 21 secs 4 D.Mangan (Kerry) 5 S.O Hanlon (Dublin) 6 J.Mangan (Kerry) 7 D.Clifford (Kerry) 8 B.Connaughton (Meath Disc Ireland) 9 M.O'Donoghue (Carlow) 10 N.Clarke (Meath Disc Ireland) all same time

**General Classification:** 1 M.O'Donoghue (Carlow) 30.35.46 2 B.Dupin (France) at 1.28 3 M.Cahill (Cork) at 1.58 4 J.Murphy (Armagh/Louth/Down) at 3.16 5 S.O Hanlon (Dublin) at 6.59 6 P.Flanagan (Kildare) at 8.01 7 D.Mangan (Kerry) at 8.33 8 N.Clarke (Meath Disc Ireland) s.t. 9 B.Connaughton (Meath Disc Ireland) at 9.43 10 M.McKenna (Meath Red Island) at 9.44 11 M.Nulty (Meath Flora) at 11.10 12 J.Mangan (Kerry) at 12.42

## STAGE 8

Mick Nulty (Meath Flora) won the 90 miles stage from Donegal to Clones, coming home on his own 2.02 ahead but on overall it only moved him up from 11th to 7th.

Martin McKenna (Meath Red Island) and Frenchman Charles Lafforgue were next home with John McNally (Dublin) 4 seconds later. John Mangan led in the bunch

containing all the top places riders 52 seconds later with O'Donoghue looking more and more like a RÁS winner.
Story of the day was that of Antrim rider Joe McAloon who crashed and was taken to hospital in Manorhamilton. So determined was he to finish that when he was discharged he returned to the spot where he had crashed and rode the remainder of the stage, coming home 3 hours behind the winner. In the days before time percentage cut-offs, he was able to start the next day and despite being in quite a lot of pain he finished the race on Sunday.
There was controversy over an alliance that Donoghue, who had little team support of his own, had forged with Flanagan and the Kildare team who agreed to work for him for the remainder of the race. When he punctured with 35 miles to go he was helped back to the bunch by Flanagan and Christy Reynolds of the Meath team.
The race stayed together for much of the way and Nulty's successful attack on the mountain at Glangevlin was the only break of note.
**Stage 8 Donegal - Clones 90 Mls.** 1 M.Nulty (Meath Flora) 3.56.08 2 M.McKenna (Meath Red Island) at 2.02 3 C.Lafforgue France) s.t. 4 J.McNally (Dublin) at 2.06 5 J.Mangan (Kerry) at 2.58 6 D.Devin (Meath Flora) 7 S.O Hanlon (Dublin) 8 S.Kennedy (Meath Disc Ireland) 9 J.Murphy (Louth) 10 M.Leroy (France) all same time
**General Classification:** 1 M.O'Donoghue (Carlow) 34.34.56 2 B.Dupin (France) at 1.28 3 M.Cahill (Cork) at 1.58 4 J.Murphy (Armagh/Louth/Down) at 3.16 5 S.O Hanlon (Dublin) at 6.59 6 P.Flanagan (Kildare) at 8.01 7 M.Nulty (Meath Flora) at 7.56 8 D.Mangan (Kerry) at 8.33 9 N.Clarke (Meath Disc Ireland) s.t. 10 M.McKenna (Meath Red Island) at 9.44 11 B.Connaughton (Meath Disc Ireland) at 10.44 12 J.Mangan (Kerry) at 12.42

## STAGE 9

John Mangan (Kerry), who lost the chance to retain his RÁS title when he dropped back on stage suffering from a chest complaint, had been gradually climbing up the GC starting the stage in 12th position. He set the seal on his recovery with a fine stage win into Navan.
He got the verdict over local rider Noel Clarke in a 2-up sprint after the two had been away for the last 35 miles. However a group of 20, with all the top men present, came home 42 seconds later and the Kerryman had to be content with his stage win for he stayed 12th overall.
After six miles of the stage Joe Roche (Dublin) and Gerard Sabourin (France) got away and built up a lead of 1 minute by Cavan. However by Virginia they had been caught by the main bunch that stayed together until Mangan and Clarke went clear at Kingscourt.
**Stage 9 Clones - Navan, 84 Mls.** 1 J.Mangan (Kerry) 3.31.45 2 N.Clarke (Meath Disc Ireland) s.t. 3 D.Mangan (Kerry) at 42 secs 4 C.Reynolds (Meath Red Island) 5 M Leroy (France) 6 P.Flanagan (Kildare) 7 S.Kennedy (Meath Disc Ireland) 8 S.O

Hanlon (Dublin) 9 J.Murphy (Armagh/Louth/Down) 10 C.Lafforgue (France) all same time

**General Classification:** 1 M.O'Donoghue (Carlow) 38.07.33 2 B.Dupin (France) at 1.28 3 M.Cahill (Cork) at 1.58 4 J.Murphy (Armagh/Louth/Down) at 3.16 5 S.O Hanlon (Dublin) at 6.59 6 N.Clarke (Meath Disc Ireland) at 7.41 7 P.Flanagan (Kildare) at 8.01 8 M.Nulty (Meath Flora) at 7.56 9 D.Mangan (Kerry) at 8.33 10 M.McKenna (Meath Red Island) at 9.44 11 B.Connaughton (Meath Disc Ireland) at 10.44 12 J.Mangan (Kerry) at 11.59

## STAGE 10

John Mangan (Kerry) won his second successive stage, the short 47 miles run from Navan to the Phoenix Park but it was Mike O'Donoghue who followed the Kerryman, to whom he had been runner up a year earlier, into the RÁS history books as he maintained the 1.28 margin over Bernard Dupin of France which he had held since he took the yellow jersey on the long stage to Belmullet on Wednesday, without doubt the vital break of the week.

The bunch stayed together on the run in from Navan and it was only at the entrance to Phoenix Park that Seamus Kennedy and Charles Lafforgue went away and led first time over the finish line by 50 seconds.

Mangan went in pursuit catching the leading two and then jumping away to win by 20 seconds from the Frenchman who beat Kennedy in the sprint. 22 seconds later Shay O Hanlon led in the chasers.

*1973 winner, Mike O'Donoghue*

**Stage 10 Navan - Dublin 47 Mls.** 1 J.Mangan (Kerry) 2.54.45 2 C.Lafforgue (France) at 20 secs 3 S.Kennedy (Meath Disc Ireland) s.t. 4 S.O Hanlon (Dublin) at 42 secs 5 C.Reynolds (Meath Red Island) 6 N.Clarke (Meath Disc Ireland) 7 G.Sabourdin (France) 8 P.Flanagan (Kildare) 9 M.Leroy (France) 10 B.Dupin (France) all same time

**General Classification:** 1 M.O'Donoghue (Carlow) 41.04.16 2 B.Dupin (France) at 1.28 3 M.Cahill (Cork) at 1.58 4 J.Murphy (Armagh/Louth/Down) at 3.16 5 S.O Hanlon (Dublin) at 6.59 6 N.Clarke (Meath Disc Ireland) at 7.41 7 P.Flanagan (Kildare) at 8.01 8 M.Nulty (Meath Flora) at 8.04 9 D.Mangan (Kerry) at 8.33 10 M.McKenna (Meath Red Island) at 8.43 11 J.Mangan (Kerry) at 8.50 12 B.Connaughton (Meath Disc Ireland) at 9.51 13 S.Kennedy (Meath Disc Ireland) at 19.49 14 B.Davey (Antrim) at 24.38 15 T.P.Reilly (Meath Red Island) at 26.04

**Team:** 1 Meath Discover Ireland 123.24.34 2 Kerry 124.00.39 3 France 124.03.58

## 1974

The 1974 RÁS was a historic one with an Irish Cycling Federation team taking part for the first time. The ICF has been invited before but had declined. However on this occasion they asked for, and received, permission from the international ruling body, the Union Cycliste International to take part.
There is no doubt that this first taste of intercompetition in no small way led to the Irish Tripartite Agreement between the NCA, ICF and NICF five years later which provided for full intercompetition.
Their team included Tour of Ireland winner Peter Doyle along with McQuaid brothers Pat and Kieron, Sean Lally, Brendan Madden and Mick Toolan. The build-up to the race in the Press concentrated on the clash between NCA star and four-time winner O Hanlon and Doyle.
There was also a sign of things to come with a big financial contribution from An Bord Failte. In a few years this would lead to the first full sponsorship of the RÁS by the tourist authority in the Discover Ireland RÁS TAILTEANN.
Also in the event were regular visitors France and teams from Algeria and Germany, the largest international participation to date.

### STAGE 1

First blood went to the ICF when Peter Doyle pulled on the first yellow jersey after winning the sprint into Carrick-on-Shannon after a very fast stage from Dublin, with the 90 miles covered in 10 minutes over 3 hours.
Doyle won from an eight-man break which finished 5 minutes ahead of the bunch, putting many big names with a lot to do to get in with any chance of overall honours. Past winners Shay O Hanlon and Mike O'Donoghue were not there and neither were any riders from the French, German or Algerian teams.
**Stage 1 Dublin - Carrick-on-Shannon 90 Mls.** 1 P.Doyle (Irish Cycling Federation) 3.10.35 2 C.Nulty (Meath C) 3 S.Lally (ICF) 4 B.Connaughton (Meath Destination Donegal) 5 P.Flanagan (Kildare) 6 J.McNally (Dublin) 7 M.McKenna (Meath A) 8 M.Nulty (Meath C) all same time

### STAGE 2

Sunday's second stage, 83 miles from Carrick-on-Shannon to Westport went to Seamus Kennedy (Meath Dest Donegal) who out sprinted a four-man break which finished 20 seconds ahead of the bunch, led in by Pat McQuaid (ICF), which included Peter Doyle who retained the race lead. He remained tied on time with the seven other riders who had finished in the break on Saturday.

The ICF spent all day chasing down breaks in defence of the yellow jersey. There were plenty of attacks. At Frenchpark Mickey Kennedy (Meath C) was away but along for the ride was Mick Toolan and Pat McQuaid (IFC).
At Ballaghadereen it was the turn of Gabriel Howard (Dublin) and Sean O'Hare (Down) but they too were brought back only for Brian Connaughton (Meath Dest Donegal) and Mick Cahill (Cork) to try their luck with the inevitable ICF 'passenger" Mick Toolan.
At Swinford Toolan again went along, this time with Mickey Kennedy again but once more they were not allowed to build up a workable gap.
So it continued until 10 miles from the finish at Newport where Seamus Kennedy attacked taking with him Pat McGarrigle (Antrim) and French paid Jean Marionneau and Marc Pauwells and these four managed to hold off the chasers to the finish where Kennedy won his fifth RÁS stage half-a-wheel ahead of Pauwells.
**Stage 2 Carrick-on-Shannon - Westport 83 Mls.** 1 S.Kennedy (Meath Destination Donegal) 3.13.20 2 M.Pauwells (France) 3 J.Marionneau (France) 4 P.McGarrigle (Antrim) all same time 5 P.McQuaid (ICF) at 20 secs 6 J.David (France) 7 S.O Hanlon (Dublin) 8 M.Toolan (ICF) 9 M.O'Donoghue (Carlow) 10 S. Lally (ICF)
**General Classification:** 1 P.Doyle (ICF) 6.25.35 2 C.Nulty (Meath C) 3 S.Lally (ICF) 4 B.Connaughton (Meath Dest Donegal) 5 P.Flanagan (Kildare) 6 J.McNally (Dublin) 7 M.McKenna (Meath A) 8 M.Nulty (Meath C) all same time 9 S.Kennedy (Meath Dest Donegal) at 4.40 10 J.Marionneau (France) 11 J.Pauwells (France) 12 P.McGarrigle (Antrim) all same time

## STAGE 3

Pat McQuaid of the ICF team won Monday's 95 miles stage from Westport to Galway in a big bunch sprint with fifth riders getting the same time. There was no change overall Doyle retaining the jersey with seven riders still on the same time at the top of the GC.
At the start Doyle and the ICF team had made a supreme effort to split up the race and the went from the off up the hill in Westport and for the first 10 miles the field were stretched out in a long line with quite a few gaps as riders fought to hold the wheel in front. However when it became obvious that the bunch was not going to let anyone go the pace went off and there was a general regroupment.
For most of the rest of the stage the ICF team played a defensive role chasing down a succession of breakaway attempts. The most likely break came between Letterfrack and Clifden when Gabriel Howard (Meath A), Seamus Kennedy (Meath Dest Donegal) and Mick Nulty (Meath C) went away with the inevitable ICF man in attendance, this time Sean Lally.
When their lead got to a minute Nulty looked like a threat to the leader and the ICF launched an all-out chase which saw the break brought back to the bunch which stayed together to the finish where McQuaid won a thrilling sprint from Horst Schultz (Germany) and Noel Clarke (Meath Dest Donegal). Despite two punctured

Doyle still finished eighth. When the break was caught, Nulty, who had been working flat out in the hoping of taking over the lead, dropped back and lost two minutes although he stayed in 8th place overall

**Stage 3 Westport - Galway 95 Mls.** 1 P.McQuaid (ICF) 4.02.30 2 H.Schultz (Germany) 3 N.Clarke (Meath Dest Donegal) 4 S.Lally (ICF) 5 D.Floegel (Germany) 6 S.O Hanlon (Dublin) 7 K.McQuaid (ICF) 8 P.Doyle (ICF) 9 J.Murphy (Louth) 10 A.Chibane (Algeria) all same time

**General Classification:** 1 P.Doyle (ICF) 10.28.05 2 C.Nulty (Meath C) 3 S.Lally (ICF) 4 P.Flanagan (Kildare) 5 B.Connaughton (Meath Dest Donegal) 6 J.McNally (Dublin) 7 M.McKenna (Meath A) 8 M.Nulty (Meath C) at 2.00 9 S.Kennedy (Meath Dest Donegal) at 4.40 10 J.Marionneau (France) 11 J.Pauwells (France) 12 P.McGarrigle (Antrim) all same time

## STAGE 4

The fourth stage, 84 miles from Galway to Kilkee, was a good one for the ICF who took the first two places with Mick Toolan and Brendan Madden with their lead in the team race now over ten minutes.

They also kept the yellow jersey, Sean Lally taking over from teammate Doyle by virtue of stage placings but the top six on general were still all tied on time. John McNally (Dublin) who had also been lying equal on time had a series of punctures and finished down the field, dropping out of contention for the overall honours.

Immediately after the start Mick Cahill (Cork) jumped away and he was joined by Christy Reynolds (Meath A) and Mick Toolan (ICF) along as policeman for Doyle. Their lead was 1.30 at Kilcolgan and as they came into Ballyvaughan they were joined by Gabriel Howard (Meath A), Jim Keogh (Cork), Henry Prevost (France) and Brendan Madden (ICF).

As they reached Lahinch the lead was up to 5.30 but the bunch was starting to chase and at Milltown Malbay with 20 miles to go the gap was down to 4 minutes.

The break split on the run-in and the two ICF riders, freshest from sitting in all day, jumped clear to take the major placings. Prevost was third at 5 seconds, 2 seconds ahead of Howard and the remainder of the break.

Chibane of Algeria finished 5 seconds ahead of the bunch containing all the leaders except McNally which was timed at 3.10 down on Toolan who moved up to 8th overall at 3.30 with Howard the other main improver of the day moving to 9th at 3.54.

**Stage 4 Galway - Kilkee 87 Mls** 1 M.Toolan (ICF) 3.27.45 2 B.Madden (ICF) s.t. 3 H.Prevost (France) at 5 secs 4 G.Howard (Meath A) at 7 secs 5 M.Cahill (Cork) 6 J.Keogh (Cork) all same time 7 A.Chibane (Algeria) at 3.05 8 D.Devin (Meath C) at 3.10 9 M.Pauwells (France) 10, D.Floegel (Germany) all same time

**General Classification:** 1 S.Lally (ICF) 13.59.07 2 P.Doyle (ICF) 3 C.Nulty (Meath C) 4 P.Flanagan (Kildare) 5 B.Connaughton (Meath Dest Donegal) 6 M.McKenna (Meath A) all same time 7 M.Nulty (Meath C) at 2.14 8 M.Toolan (ICF) at 3.30 9

G.Howard (Meath A) at 3.54 10 M.Pauwells (France) at 4.40 11 S.Kennedy (Meath Dest Donegal) 12 J.Marionneau (France) 13 P.McGarrigle (Antrim) all same time

## STAGE 5 (a) and (b)

After Wednesday's two stages Peter Doyle was back in the lead but this time he was out on his own with a 20 second advantage over teammate Lally.
The morning stage, 47 miles from Tarbert to Killarney, won by Kieron McQuaid (ICF) had produced no big changes on the overall although Colm Nulty (Meath C) and Martin McKenna (Meath A) failed to make the 10-man break and dropped out of the top six.
The action started at Listowel when ICF pair Brendan Madden and Sean Lally went away. They were joined by Noel Clarke (Meath Dest Donegal), Paddy Flanagan (Kildare), Brian Connaughton (Meath Dest Donegal), John McNally (Meath C), Dieter Floegel (Germany), M. Pauwells (France) as well as Kieron McQuaid and Doyle.
By Tralee these ten had a lead of over 5 minutes and the race for the rest was effectively over. On GC Lally still led from McQuaid with Flanagan and Connaughton still equal on time.
**Stage 5a Tarbert - Killarney 47 Mls.** 1 K.McQuaid (ICF) 1.45.45 2 P.Doyle (ICF)) 3 D.Floegel (Germany) 4 S.Lally (ICF) 5 M.Pauwells (France) 6 N.Clarke (Meath Dest Donegal) 7 P.Flanagan (Kildare) 8 J.McNally (Meath C) 9 B.Madden (ICF) 10 B.Connaughton (Meath Dest Donegal) all same time
Thousands lined the 1-mile circuit in Killarney for the 20 lap criterium which saw Colm Nulty (Meath C) lead for several early laps before he was replaced at the front by Doyle, making a determined bid to gain some time.
However he was caught on the 14th lap but was still in front as a group of eight went away. At the line Dieter Floegal won the sprint from teammate Horst Schultz, Pauwells of France and O Hanlon (Dublin). However Doyle finished in the same time and gained 20 seconds over the three who had been equal with him on time since the end of the opening stage in Carrick-on-Shannon.
**Stage 5b Killarney Criterium 20 Mls.** 1 D.Floegel (Germany) 55.42 2 H.Schultz (Germany) 3 M.Pauwells (France) 4 S.O Hanlon (Dublin) 5 K.McQuaid (ICF) 6 C.Nulty (Meath C) 7 P.Doyle (ICF) 8 M.O'Donoghue (Carlow) all same time 9 P.McQuaid (ICF) at 20 secs
**General Classification:** 1 P.Doyle (ICF) 16.40.34 2 S.Lally (ICF) at 20 secs 3 P.Flanagan (Kildare) 4 B.Connaughton (Meath Dest Donegal) all same time 5 M.Pauwells (France) at 4.40 6 C.Nulty (Meath C) at 4.46 7 M.McKenna (Meath A) at 5.06 8 N.Clarke (Meath Dest Donegal) at 6.50 9 J.McNally (Meath C) s.t. 10 M.Nulty (Meath C) at 7.20 11 M.Toolan (ICF) at 8.09 12 G.Howard (Meath A) at 8.33

## STAGE 6

Martin McKenna (Meath A), who had dropped back on overall on Wednesday morning's stage, came back to win the 78 miles seventh stage from Killarney to Cobh. There was no change at the top of the GC.
The ICF team were determined to defend Doyle's lead and when things looked dangerous they rode flat out at the front for an 8-mile stretch during which they cut the advantage of the leading group by over a minute.
From the start there were continuous attempts to break away and eventually eight riders: john Sullivan (Cork), Meath Destination Donegal trio Noel Clarke, Seamus Kennedy and Emmanuel Thackaberry, Henry Prevost (France), Pat McGarrigle (Antrim) and from the ICF Brendan Madden and Pat McQuaid.
Despite the ICF men sitting in the lead grew with only the remaining ICF team members prepared to contribute to the chase. The lead reached a maximum of 1.30 at Coachford but then started to come down and they were eventually caught going into Blarney.
Four riders then went away. McGarrigle was there again along with Marionneau (France), Martin McKenna and Madden again along as policeman for the yellow jersey. They rode hard to stay clear and at the finish, where McKenna won a thrilling sprint, they had 17 seconds in hand over Jack Murphy (Louth) while Doyle headed the bunch three seconds later.
**Stage 6 Killarney - Cobh 78 Mls.** 1 M.McKenna (Meath A) 3.2.20 2 J.Marionneau (France) 3 B.Madden (ICF) 4 P.McGarrigle (Antrim) all same time 5 J.Murphy (Louth) at 17 secs 6 P.Doyle (ICF) at 20 secs 7 P.Sabourin (France) 8 M.Pauwells (France) 9 P.McQuaid (ICF) 10 D.Floegel (Germany) all same time
**General Classification:** 1 P.Doyle (ICF) 19.43.14 2 S.Lally (ICF) at 20 secs 3 P.Flanagan (Kildare) 4 B.Connaughton (Meath Dest Donegal) all same time 5 M.Pauwells (France) at 4.40 6 C.Nulty (Meath C) at 4.46 7 M.McKenna (Meath A) at 4.46 8 N.Clarke (Meath Dest Donegal) at 6.50 9 J.McNally (Meath C) s.t. 10 M.Nulty (Meath C) at 7.20 11 M.Toolan (ICF) at 8.09 12 G.Howard (Meath A) at 8.33

## STAGE 7

Pat McQuaid (ICF) took his second victory of the week, the 73 miles stage from Cobh to Tramore and a 5-up sprint, just pipping Shay O Hanlon (Dublin), John Keogh (Cork) and Noel Clarke (Meath Dest Donegal).
O Hanlon and Clarke had been the main movers in a move to break the ICF stranglehold on the race and for a long time during the stage it looked like they might succeed. They went away just after the start along with Gabriel Howard (Meath A), John Keogh (Cork) and the inevitable ICF man keeping a watching brief for the leader, this time Pat McQuaid.

The four working riders working like demons opened up an incredible gap of almost six minutes bring Clarke very close to taking the lead on the road. They held on to much of their big lead at Dungarvan with only around 20 miles to go.
Behind the ICF were working flat out at the front but they were getting no help from the rest of the bunch. Nevertheless their efforts told as the break tired on the tough coastal road and at Bunmahon, with 10 miles left the gap was down to just over 2 minutes and the danger was over for Doyle.
McQuaid, with an armchair ride all day was the freshest of the five and as expected took the sprint. The overall was unchanged with Doyle still leading teammate Lally by those 20 seconds gained in the Killarney criterium.
**Stage 7 Cobh - Tramore 73 Mls.** 1 P.McQuaid (ICF) 3.17.55 2 S.O Hanlon (Dublin) 3 J.Keogh (Cork) 4 N.Clarke (Meath Dest Donegal) 5 G.Howard (Meath A) all same time 6 S.Kennedy (Meath Dest Donegal) at 5 secs 7 J.Marionneau (France) 8 M.Nulty (Meath C) all same time 9 P.Floegel (Germany) at 17 secs 10 J.Murphy (Louth) all same time
**General Classification:** 1 P.Doyle (ICF) 21.1.27 2 S.Lally (ICF) at 20 secs 3 P.Flanagan (Kildare) 4 B.Connaughton (Meath Dest Donegal) all same time 5 M.Pauwells (France) at 4.40 6 M.McKenna (Meath A) at 4.46 7 C.Nulty (Meath C) at 4.46 s.t. 8, N. Clarke (Meath Dest Donegal) at 6.22 9 J.McNally (Meath C) s.t. 10 M.Nulty (Meath C) at 7.20 11 M.Toolan (ICF) at 8.09 12 G.Howard (Meath A) at 8.15

## STAGE 8

Kieron McQuaid emulated Brother Pat in winning two stages when he was first into Carlow after the 94 miles run from Tramore. There were no changes overall.
**Stage 8 Tramore - Carlow 94 Mls.** 1 K. McQuaid (ICF) 3.40.15
**General Classification:** 1 P.Doyle (ICF) 2 S.Lally (ICF) at 20 secs 3 P.Flanagan (Kildare) 4 B.Connaughton (Meath Dest Donegal) all same time 5 M.Pauwells (France) at 4.40 6 M.McKenna (Meath A) at 4.46 7 C.Nulty (Meath C) at 4.46 s.t. 8, N. Clarke (Meath Dest Donegal) at 6.22 9 J.McNally (Meath C) s.t. 10 M.Nulty (Meath C) at 7.20 11 M.Toolan (ICF) at 8.09 12 G.Howard (Meath A) at 8.15

## STAGE 9

The final stage, a fairly easy run of 70 miles from Carlow to the Phoenix Park was won by Shay O Hanlon, his 22nd RÁS stage when he came home at the head of a 10-man group, none of whom were a danger to yellow jersey Doyle who came home safely in the bunch 20 seconds later.
Doyle had led for most of the week although his teammate Sean Lally, then equal on time, took the jersey for a couple of days by virtue of a better point's total. Doyle had been equal with seven other riders on time after the opening stage and one by one these fell away until he moved out on his own by 20 seconds on the shortest stage of

the week, the round-the-houses in Killarney and the strong ICF team defended that 20 seconds to the finish.
It was inevitable that this first competitive encounter between the two controlling bodies would develop into a NCA versus ICF encounter and it resulted in a fairly dull race based largely on defence. It was one of the closest finishes in the history of the event with three riders 20 seconds behind the winner
The final stage saw no successful breaks on the 50 miles up from Carlow to Dublin where there were 10 laps of the 2 mile circuit in the Park where a huge crowd was waiting. With teammate Lally in second place, the only riders who could threaten the leader were Kildare's Paddy Flanagan and Meath's Brian Connaughton, both like Lally only 20 seconds in arrears, but it was never likely they would escape from the ICF's grasp.
Connaughton tried on the fourth lap but immediately found Doyle on his wheel where he stayed to the finish. With five laps to go ten riders opened a gap which, although it was never allowed to grow to more than half-a-minute, the ten still had 20 seconds at the line where O Hanlon out sprinted Meath's Seamus Kennedy and Christian Dorrie of France adding to his long list of RÁS stage victories. The ICF won the team classification by a big margin.
**Stage 9 Carlow - Dublin 70 Mls.** 1 S.O Hanlon (Dublin) 2.38.10 2 S.Kennedy (Meath Dest Donegal) 3 C.Dorrie (France) 4 P.McGarrigle (Antrim) 5 B.Madden (ICF) 6 M.Nulty (Meath C) 7 W.Thomann (Germany) 8 A.Madji (Algeria) 9 J.Murphy (Louth) 10 A.Chibane (Algeria) all same time
**General Classification:** 1 P.Doyle (ICF) 29.21.32 2 S.Lally (ICF) at 20 secs 3 P.Flanagan (Kildare) s.t. 4 B.Connaughton (Meath Dest Donegal) s.t. 5 C.Nulty (Meath) at 4.26 6 M.Pauwells (France) at 4.40 7 M.McKenna (Meath A) at 4.46 8 N.Clarke (Meath Dest Donegal) at 6.04 9 J.McNally (Meath C) at 6.31 10 M.Nulty (Meath C) at 6.50 11 M.Toolan (ICF) at 8.09 12 G.Howard (Meath A) at 8.15 13 J.P.Marionneau (France) at 8.27 14 P.McGarrigle (Antrim) at 8.40 15 S.Kennedy (Meath Dest Donegal) at 8.57 16 S.O Hanlon (Dublin) at 9.06
In a postscript efforts towards reconciliation between the cycling bodies continued when in August an NCA team for the first time took part in the ICF's 8-day Tour of Ireland. Shay O Hanlon, Seamus Kennedy, Mick Nulty and Mick Cahill with Kennedy and Nulty finishing a creditable joint 12th in an international field. The race was won by Tony Lally riding for the Irish Olympic Squad which included a youthful Sean Kelly, soon to be a professional and unfortunately, unlike Stephen Roche, Martin Earley and Paul Kimmage, never to ride the RÁS.

*1974 Winner, Ireland's Peter Doyle*

## 1975

It was confidently expected that the ICF would again take part in the 1975 RÁS but in a surprising about-face, the world controlling body, which had given permission a year previously, told the ICF that it would be against the rules to compete.
An appeal by the ICF was turned down. The UCI's response to the appeal was: 'In answer to your cable of May 15 it is not possible for us to permit any participation for non affiliated cyclists (NCA) with affiliated cyclists in the same race.
'It is not our intention to put in front of you any difficulties but I have to say no when the rules say no'.
There was then an even more surprising turn of events when the NICF announced that they would take part in the RÁS subject to a number of conditions. These were that the event could be confined to riders from the NCA, ICF or NICF, or riders who are domiciled in Ireland.
This put the race director Dermot Dignam in a quandary as invitations had already been accepted by France, Algeria and Germany.
The RÁS Committee met and came up with a proposal to run the RÁS as two simultaneous events, one for international riders and one domestic, which would mean that the invited foreign teams would not be competing in the same event as the ICF and NICF. However this compromise was turned down by the Northern body who, like the ICF, decided not to risk UCI sanctions by taking part.
So the race got underway, on Saturday, June 9, with teams from France, Germany, Algeria, Ireland (NCA), and ten county teams making up the 76-strong field. A 5-man team from Bavaria failed to start although they were reported to have arrived in Dublin before the race.

### STAGE 1

The opening 76 miles stage to Monaghan was won by Seamus Kennedy (Ireland) from a group of eight which got away 10 miles after the start and built up a huge lead of 6.48 by the finish.
He won in an uphill sprint from D. Zekri (Algeria), J. Zebisch (Germany) with Paddy Flanagan (Kildare) fourth and Mick Cahill (Cork) fifth. Two more of the original break came home 2.05 later: John Lawlor (Carlow) and John McNally (Dublin) with Mick Nulty (Ireland) 10 seconds further back.
With such a big gap opened up on the opening stage, it was looking like many of the favourites were already out of contention but even bigger time deficits had been made up before.
**Stage 1 Dublin - Monaghan 76 Mls.** 1 S.Kennedy (Ireland) 2.55.30 2 D.Zekri (Algeria) 3 J.Zebisch (Germany) 4 P.Flanagan (Kildare) 5 M.Cahill (Cork) all same

time 6 J.Lawlor (Carlow) at 2.05 7 J.McNally (Dublin) s.t. 8 M.Nulty (Ireland) at 2.15 9 T.Murphy (Monaghan) 4.45 10 W.Thomann (Germany) s.t.

## STAGE 2

Wolfgang Thomann (Germany), who had been 10th on the opening stage, won the 81 miles stage to Letterkenny in an uphill sprint which saw him open a 2 second gap on Gabriel Howard (Meath A) and Noel Clarke (Ireland).
It was hard and fast racing all the way with continual breaks going away and holding slender leads for some miles before being brought back and with only 26 miles remaining less than a minute covered the field from front to back.
The most promising move of the day saw 15 riders with a 30 second lead at Omagh. However they were caught before the border crossing at Strabane when Zebisch and Bobby Power (Ireland) had a lead of just 15 seconds on a 4-man group with another six riders between them and the bunch.
However on the run-in they all came together for a big bunch sprint with the German jumping out of the pack up the final hill to the line. There was little change on the overall classification except for Thomann who moved up from 10th to 9th. The leading riders had to be split on points leaving Kennedy in the jersey on equal time with Flanagan (2nd) and Zebisch (3rd). Zekri and Cahill both lost time and the Cork man was now 4th at 1.43 with the Algerian 5th at 1.47.
**Stage 2 Monaghan - Letterkenny 81 Mls.** 1 W.Thomann (Germany) 3.11.30 2 G.Howard (Meath A) at 2 secs 3 N.Clarke (Ireland) 4 S.Kennedy (Ireland) 5 P.Flanagan (Kildare) 6 J.Zebisch (Germany) 7 M.Hamza (Algeria) 8 J.Stitner (Germany) 9 T.Murphy (Monaghan) 10 J.McNally (Dublin)
**General Classification:** 1 S.Kennedy (Ireland) 6.07.05 2 P.Flanagan (Kildare) 3 J.Zebisch (Germany) all same time 5 M.Cahill (Cork) at 1.43 5 D.Zekri (Algeria) at 1.47 6 J.McNally (Dublin) at 2.05 7 M.Nulty (Ireland) at 2.15 8 J.Lawlor (Carlow) at 3.20 9 W.Thomann (Germany) at 5.13 10 T.Murphy (Monaghan) at 5.45

## STAGE 3

It was a good day for the Ireland team on the hilly 85 miles run through the Donegal hills to Donegal Town as the took first and second on the stage with Noel Clarke and Shay O Hanlon while their man in yellow, Seamus Kennedy kept the jersey.
On an extremely warm day which saw tourists throw buckets of water over the perspiring riders, several well placed riders fell out of contention. Mick Nulty (Ireland) who had been 6th overall retired from the race sick with 15 miles to go. Another retiral was John Lawlor (Carlow) who had been eighth. He had to receive medial treatment for exhaustion. Mick Cahill (Cork) who was 5th suffered a series of punctures and lost over 6 minutes.

Immediately after the start Colm Nulty (Meath A) and teammate Denis Devin got away and opened up a lead of 1 minute on a chasing group of 20 at Fintown, after 19 miles of racing.
At Ardragh Nulty led from Devin and Bobby Power (Ireland) 40 seconds ahead of Christian Dory (France) with the main bunch at 1.40. Power dropped back on the fierce climb of Glengesh but the other two stayed out in front until Glencolmcille, with 32 miles left, when they were joined by Kennedy, Flanagan, Zebisch and Zekri.
With 15 miles to go the leaders were joined by Noel Clarke, and Meath A pair Martin McKenna and Eamon Connolly. Connolly and Devin punctured and in a great ride Gabriel Howard (Meath A) closed a 2 minute gap to the leaders on his own.
Clarke then attacked and was joined by O Hanlon, Zebisch, Kennedy, Zekri and Flanagan and they finished in that order, all timed at 4.30. Martin McKenna was 5 seconds down with the Howard and Devin coming home 30 seconds later.
**Stage 3 Letterkenny - Donegal Town 85 Mls.** 1 N.Clarke (Ireland) 4.30.00 2 S.O Hanlon (Ireland) 3 J.Zebisch (Germany) 4 D.Zekri (Algeria) 5 S.Kennedy (Ireland) 6 P.Flanagan (Kildare) all same time 7 M.McKenna (Meath A) at 5 secs 8 G.Howard (Meath A) at 35 secs 9 D.Devin (Meath A) s.t. 10 W.Thomann (Germany) at 2.45
**General Classification:** 1 S.Kennedy (Ireland) 10.10.35 2 J.Zebisch (Germany) 3 P.Flanagan (Kildare) all same time 4 D.Zekri (Algeria) at 1.47 5 J.McNally (Dublin) at 6.23 6 N.Clarke (Ireland) at 6.45 7 S.O Hanlon (Ireland) at 6.48 8 G.Howard (Meath A) at 8.20 9 W.Thomann (Germany) at 9.08 10 M.McKenna (Meath A) at 9.38 11 E.Thackaberry (Kildare) at 9.48 12 B.Power (Ireland) at 9.50

## STAGE 4

Colm Nulty (Meath A) was leading the sprint into Castlebar when he crossed a white line 30 yards from the finish and sat up thinking he had won. However the line was a street marking and both Shay O Hanlon (Ireland) and Tony Murphy (Monaghan) passed him before the actual finish line.
Paddy Flanagan was another who saw a mistake cost him dearly. He punctured and took a wheel from another team car and was fined a minute. he stayed in third place overall but was now that minute behind race leader Kennedy who finished the stage in the bunch, 3.15 down on the 9-man break but none of whom were a danger to his overall lead. Biggest improvement on the day went to stage-winner O Hanlon who moved up just one place on GC but who was now only 3.23 behind.
First serious break of the day went at Ballyshannon, after 14 miles, when Colm Nulty, Tony Murphy and Tony McGovern (Sligo) went clear to be joined by Eamon Connolly (Meath A) and Mickey Kennedy (Meath B). At Bundoran the five held a 30 second lead on Tony Mooney (Sligo) who was caught by the bunch a few miles later.
Before Sligo the leaders were joined by O Hanlon, Mick Cahill (Cork), John McNally (Dublin) T.P.Reilly (Meath B) and Zebisch but the German punctured and

dropped back to the bunch which was 2.30 behind at Charlestown and this gap grew by a further minute over the final 20 miles.

**Stage 4 Donegal - Castlebar 95 Mls.** 1 S.O Hanlon (Ireland) 3.59.30 2 T. Murphy (Monaghan) 3 C.Nulty (Meath A) 4 M.Cahill (Cork) 5 J.McNally (Dublin) 6 M.Kennedy (Meath B) 7 E.Connolly (Meath A) 8 T.P.Reilly (Meath B) 9 M.McKenna (Meath A) all same time 10 C.Dory (France) at 3.15

**General Classification:** 1 S. Kennedy (Ireland) 14.13.20 2 J.Zebisch (Germany) s.t. 3 P.Flanagan (Kildare) at 1.00 4 D.Zekri (Algeria) at 1.57 5 J.McNally (Dublin) at 3.08 6 S.O Hanlon (Ireland) at 3.23 7 M.McKenna (Meath A) at 6.23 8 N.Clarke (Ireland) at 6.45 9 E.Connolly (Meath A) at 7.28 10 G.Howard (Meath A) at 8.00 11 W.Thomann (Germany) at 9.08 12 equal E.Thackaberry (Kildare) and B.Power (Ireland) at 10.18

## STAGES 5 (a) and (b)

A 50 miles morning stage to Galway was followed by a 20 miles criterium that evening. Noel Clarke (Ireland) won the road stage in a sprint from a seven man group and almost pulled off a double in the criterium where he lost the out to Mick Nulty but the day's racing produced no change at the top of the GC.

The day started with an appeal by Paddy Flanagan which succeeded in getting his 1 minute penalty from stage 5 removed putting him back on equal time with Kennedy and Zebisch.

In the morning's stage Noel Clarke took the prime at Ballinrobe after 18 miles and went ahead being joined by Martin McKenna (Meath A), Alain Gentilhomme (France) and Aziz Merzoug (Algeria). After a chase they were caught by Algerian pair Malek Hamza and Ahmed Haouas and Bobby Power (Ireland).

The seven worked well together and at Headford, with 10 miles to go they held a lead of 1.10 and they kept their lead to the finish where Clarke won in a hectic sprint from the Algerian rider Hamza and Bobby Power.

**Stage 5a Castlebar - Galway 50 Mls.** 1 N.Clarke (Ireland) 2.00.10 2 M.Hamza (Algeria) 3 B.Power (Ireland) 4 A.Haous (Algeria) 5 A.Gentilhomme (France) 6 M.McKenna (Meath A) 7 A.Merzoug (Algeria) all same time 8 D.Devin (Meath A) at 2.15 9 S.Kennedy (Ireland) 10 P.Flanagan (Kildare) all same time

The second stage on Wednesday was an evening criterium watched by a big crowd in Galway city centre. Noel Clarke just failed to bring off the double when he finished second to Mick Nulty.

It was a good stage for the Ireland team as they also took third and fourth places with Seamus Kennedy and Shay O Hanlon. There were no changes on overall.

Haous of Algeria was the animator of the first half of the race taking the opening four laps and then, after Noel Clarke took the next two Haous came back to win the next three.

On the 11th circuit Nulty attacked and opened a small gap which he held to the finish winning 10 primes in all and he still managed to hold off the fast finishing bunch to win the stage with the entire bunch credited with the same time as the winner.
**Stage 5b Galway Criterium 20 Mls.** 1 M.Nulty (Ireland) 45.00 2 N.Clarke (Ireland) 3 S.Kennedy (Ireland) 4 S.O Hanlon (Ireland) 5 W.Thomann (Germany) 6 F.Krun (Germany) 7 C.Dory (France) 8 J.Zebisch (Germany) 9 A.Haous (Algeria) all same time
**General Classification:** 1 S.Kennedy (Ireland 17.00.45 2 J.Zebisch; 3 P.Flanagan, all same time 4 D.Zekri (Algeria) at 1.57 5 J.McNally (Dublin) at 3.08 6 S.O Hanlon (Ireland) at 3.23 7 M.McKenna (Meath A) at 6.23 8 N.Clarke (Ireland) at 6.45 9 E.Connolly (Meath A) at 7.28 10 G.Howard (Meath A) at 8.00 11 W.Thomann (Germany) at 9.08 12 equal E.Thackaberry (Kildare) and B.Power (Ireland) at 10.18

## STAGE 6

There was a surprise winner of Thursday's 81 miles sixth stage from Galway to Limerick when Tipperary's Joe Cashin went away with 27 miles of the stage remaining and at the finish he had 1.24 in hand over the chasers.
The first break of the day was a solo effort by another Tipperary rider, Billy Kennedy, who was holding a 45 second lead when the race was stopped by a closed level-crossing at Craughwell after 16 miles.
They were re-started with Kennedy given his 45 seconds but by Woodford, 30 miles, they were again all together.
Then Mick Nulty (Ireland) and Driss Zekri (Algeria) went away and built up a 1 minute lead before being brought back before Scariff where Cashin made his successful bid for victory.
Another hero of the day was Meath's Gabriel Howard who after a series of mishaps the previous day was continuing in the race with a broken Arm. Before the crash which resulted in this injury he had sustained another injury. In the very hot weather spectators had been throwing buckets of water over the riders. Unfortunately one let go of the bucket which hit Gabriel on the nose.
Despite his injuries he only lost 1.45 on the sixth stage, slipping from 9th to 12th.
**Stage 6 Galway - Limerick 81 Mls.** 1 J.Cashin (Tipperary) 3.14.55 2 P.Flanagan (Kildare) at 1.24 3 C.Dory (France) 4 S.Kennedy (Ireland) 5 P.Sabourin (France) 6 A.Haous (Algeria) 7 W.Thomann (Germany) 8 M.Hamza (Algeria) 9 J.Zebisch (Germany) 10 T. Mannion (Galway)
**General Classification:** 1 S.Kennedy (Ireland) 20.16.04 2 J.Zebisch; 3 P.Flanagan, all same time 4 D.Zekri (Algeria) at 1.57 5 J.McNally (Dublin) at 3.08 6 S.O Hanlon (Ireland) at 3.23 7 M.McKenna (Meath A) at 6.23 8 N.Clarke (Ireland) at 6.45 9 E.Connolly (Meath A) at 7.28 10 A.Gentilhomme (France) at 8.51 11 W.Thomann (Germany) at 9.08 12 G. Howard (Meath A) at 9.45

## STAGE 7

It was almost another surprise win after a long, lone break on the stage to Kilkenny but Meath A rider Eamon Connolly was caught and passed with just 800 metres to go by Malek Hamza (Algeria).

86 miles earlier at the start in Limerick another Algerian Haous broke his chain and gears just as the flag was dropped but after a chase he managed to get back to the bunch.

Various early attempts came to nothing until Connolly raced away with 45 miles still to go. With only six miles to go and the main bunch still intact it looked like the Meath man was home and dry until Hamza and Martin O'Hara (Sligo) went in pursuit.

They were joined by Salvador Campomones (France) but O'Hara couldn't match the fierce pace they were setting and dropped back to the bunch. At the 1 kilometre to go sign they had Connolly in sight and the Algerian made a huge final effort and caught him just before the home straight and went right past and Connolly was fortunate to be able to hang on his wheel to take second with the Frenchman just 5 seconds back in third place.

The bunch had also been closing in and Paddy Flanagan led them in only 15 seconds down on the stage winner.

**Stage 7 Limerick - Kilkenny 86 Mls** 1 M.Hamza (Algeria) 3.40.15 2 E.Connolly (Meath A) s.t. 3 S.Campomones (France) at 5 secs 4 P.Flanagan (Kildare) at 15 secs 5 S.O Hanlon (Ireland) 6 C.Dory (France) 7 B.Power (Ireland) 8 S.Kennedy (Ireland) 9 D.Devin (Meath A) 10 W.Kennedy (Tipperary) all same time

**General Classification:** 1 S.Kennedy (Ireland) 23.56.34 2 P.Flanagan (Kildare) 3 J.Zebisch (Germany) all same time 4 D.Zekri (Algeria) at 1.57 5 J.McNally (Dublin) at 3.08 6 S.O Hanlon (Ireland) at 3.23 7 M.McKenna (Meath A) at 6.23 8 N.Clarke (Ireland) at 6.45 9 E.Connolly (Meath A) at 7.28 10 A.Gentilhomme (France) at 8.51 11 W.Thomann (Germany) at 9.08 12 G.Howard (Meath A) at 9.45

## STAGE 8

After a week with three riders tied together on time at the top of the general classification the connection was finally broken on the 86 miles stage through the Wicklow Mountains to Naas with Paddy Flanagan ending the day on his own in the lead.

Flanagan, a two-times RÁS winner and four-times winner O Hanlon, two of the older men in the race, were in the break of the day along with Cork's Mick Cahill and they came home 1.10 ahead of a chasing group of three, led in by Haous (Algeria), which contained Zebisch who went to second overall, 1.10 behind Flanagan.

Seamus Kennedy, who had been in yellow all week, came home 11th in a group of five, over a minute further back, to drop to third.

The mountains started around half-distance and on the steep climb at Aughavannagh Flanagan went away on his own. After a chase he was joined by O Hanlon and Cahill and these three stayed out in front to the finish where O Hanlon won the sprint.
**Stage 8 Kilkenny - Naas 86 Mls.** 1 S.O Hanlon (Ireland) 4.11.15 2 M.Cahill (Cork A) 3 P.Flanagan (Kildare) all same time 4 A.Haous (Algeria) at 1.10 5 J.Zebisch (Germany) s.t. 6 D.Zekri (Algeria) at 1.12 7 N.Clarke (Ireland) at 2.13 8 M.Hamza (Algeria) 9 A.Mahdi (Algeria) 10 A.Gentilhomme (France) 11 S.Kennedy (Ireland) all same time
**General Classification:** 1 P.Flanagan (Kildare) 28.07.49 2 J.Zebisch (Germany) at 1.10 3 S.Kennedy (Ireland) at 2.13 4 D.Zekri (Algeria) at 3.10 5 S.O Hanlon (Ireland) at 3.35 6 N.Clarke (Ireland) at 6.43 7 A.Gentilhomme (France) at 11.03 8 J.McNally (Dublin) at 11.06 9 M.Cahill (Cork A) at 14.40 10 A.Mahdi (Algeria) at 16.03

## STAGE 9 (a) and (b)

Paddy Flanagan showed that even had it gone down to the final day he would still have won his third RÁS when he won the Sunday morning time-trial with 9 seconds advantage over second placed Zebisch who had been equal with him on time all week.
Bobby Power (Ireland) was third another 13 seconds down, 12 seconds ahead of teammate Michael Nulty. The Ireland team emphasised their grip on the team race by finishing all five riders in the top eight places.
Seamus Kennedy, who had been in yellow for most of the week finished 7th, but his 63 deficit on Flanagan would have dropped him out of contention even if he had been able to hold the Kildare man over the climbs the previous day.
The afternoon stage was a short one over ten laps of the 2-mile circuit in Phoenix Park and unlikely to cause any upsets.
A small group managed to get a few seconds off the front over the final miles and Noel Clarke out sprinted Frenchman Christian Dory to take his third stage of the week.
Flanagan came home safely leading in the bunch in 9th place, 14 seconds behind Clarke and there were no changes on General Classification.
Ireland comfortably beat Algeria in the team race and Meath A had 15 minutes in hand over Kildare in the inter-county team competition.
Gabriel Howard, who incredibly had ridden the last six days with a broken arm, had his courage rewarded by the organisers who gave him a week's holiday for two anywhere in Ireland.
**Stage 9a Naas 7 Mls. TT:** 1 P.Flanagan (Kildare) 14.30 2 J.Zebisch (Germany) 14.39 3 B.Power (Ireland) 14.51 4 M.Nulty (Ireland) 15.01 5 S.O Hanlon (Ireland) 15.24 6 M.Hamza (Algeria) 15.28 7 S.Kennedy (Ireland) 15.33 8 equal A.Gentilhomme (France) and N.Clarke (Ireland) 15.39 10 A.Haous (Algeria) 15.41

**Stage 9b Phoenix Park Dublin 30Mls.** 1 N.Clarke (Ireland) 46.26 2 C.Dory (France) 3 A.Haous (Algeria) 4 C.Nulty (Meath A) 5 M.Cahill (Cork A) all same time 6 E.Thackaberry (Kildare) at 3 secs 7 S.Camponmones (France) at 5 secs 8 S.O Hanlon (Ireland) at 9 secs 9 P.Flanagan (Ireland) at 14 secs 10 W.Thomann (Germany) s.t.
**General Classification:** 1 P.Flanagan (Kildare) 29.08.59 2 J.Zebisch (Germany) at 1.19 3 S.Kennedy (Ireland) at 3.16 4 D.Zekri (Algeria) at 4.02 5 S.O Hanlon (Ireland) at 4.22 6 N.Clarke (Ireland) at 7.38 7 A.Gentilhomme (France) at 12.11 8 M.Cahill (Cork A) at 15.48 9 J.McNally (Dublin) at 16.13 10 A.Mahdi (Algeria) at 17.49 11 B.Power (Ireland) at 17.51 12 W.Thomann (Germany) at 18.17
**International Team:** 1 Ireland 87.33.07 2 Algeria 87.51.02 3 Germany 88.05.46
**County Team:** 1 Meath A 88.16.41 2 Kildare 89.31.49 3 Cork A. 89.35.18

Paddy Flanagan, Winner 1975

## 1976

History was made in the 1976 RÁS with the first ever start outside the greater Dublin area when Sligo was chosen to host the opening stage. French, German, Dutch, Algerian and Belgian teams appeared on the start list and although the Belgian squad pulled out at the last minute the race had its most international field to date with an Irish team selected to face the foreign challenge.

### STAGE 1 (a) and (b)

The opening day was a tough one with two stages, a 2 miles prologue TT in the morning and 105 miles run down the west coast to Clifden in the afternoon. Although both stages went to Irish riders, the TT to Denis Devin and the road race to Seamus Kennedy, it was Dutchman Fons Steuten who led the general classification at the end of the opening day.

Steuten had been fifth, 3 seconds behind Devin in the time trial which the Meath rider won by 1 second from another Dutch rider Jan Beurskens with Ireland's Bobby Power and H.Krins (Holland) joint third another second behind. Completing a cosmopolitan opening stage W.Liebe (Germany) was sixth at 5 seconds.

In the afternoon Bobby Power (Ireland) made the first real break at Charlestown, 30 miles after the start. He stayed out in front on his own and at Swinford he led by 1.30. At the half-way mark Power was joined by Steuten, Ben McKenna (Meath), Tony Murphy (Antrim) and some distance later Kennedy by at Westport, 63 miles their lead was down to 40 seconds.

With the bunch closing Kennedy tried a solo effort but he was brought back. Then Devin made an effort but the yellow jersey was too closely marked. With 15 miles to go Steuten, Kennedy, Brian Connaughton (Meath Collins) and Heinz Briemrieder (Germany) opened a gap and they held it to the finish where they had 43 seconds in hand over a chasing trio led in by Shay O Hanlon (Dublin) while J.J.Cornet (France) led in the bunch 21 seconds later.

**Stage 1a Sligo 2 Mls. TT:** 1 D.Devin ((Ireland) 4.17 2 J.Beurskens (Holland) 4.18 3 equal B.Power (Ireland) and H.Krins (Holland) 4.19 5 F.Steuten (Holland) 4.20 6 W.Leibe (Germany) 4.22

**Stage 1b Sligo - Clifden 105 Mls.** 1 S.Kennedy (Meath Collins) 5.00.16 2 H.H.Briemrieder (Germany) 3 B.Connaughton (Meath Collins) 4 F.Steuten (Holland) all same time 5 S.O Hanlon (Dublin) at 43 secs 6 F.Perez (France) 7 L.Clarke (Meath Collins) all same time 8 J.J.Cornet (France) at 1.04 9 J.Beurskend (Holland) 10 P.Hoffert (France) all same time

**General Classification:** 1 F.Steuten (Holland) 5.4.26 2 S.Kennedy (Meath Collins) at 4 secs 3 H.H.Briemrieder (Germany) at 7 secs 4 B.Connaughton (Meath Collins) at 17 secs

## STAGE 2

38-year-old Paddy Flanagan, winner the previous year, won the 90 miles stage from Clifden to Lisdoonvarna and took over the lead by 46 seconds from Seamus Kennedy (Meath Tayto).

Flanagan won on his own after a great ride over the last 10 miles from Ballyvaughan. He dropped Eamon Connolly (Meath Tayto) and Dinny O'Connell (Cork) who finished in that order behind him.

There was a strong cross-wind over the first 50 miles which thwarted the many breakaway attempts. After Galway the wind changed and so did the tempo of the race. A 3-man break which went away at Galway was caught and at the 71 mile mark Eamon Connolly attacked. He opened a 1-minute gap but a few miles later he was joined by Flanagan and O'Connell.

Coming up the Corkscrew Flanagan pulled away from the other two and between there and the finish, 6 miles later, he opened up a lead of 1.26 on his breakaway companions who stayed clear of the bunch led in by J.J. Cornet (France), 39 seconds behind them.

**Stage 2 Clifden - Lisdoonvarna 90 Mls.** 1 P.Flanagan (Kildare) 4.01.20 2 E.Connolly (Meath Tayto) at 1.26 3 D.O'Connell (Cork) s.t. 4 J.J.Cornet (France) at 2.05 5 F.Perez (France) 6 S.Kennedy (Meath Tayto) 7 J.C.Breure (France) 8 B.Power (Ireland) 9 S.O Hanlon (Dublin) 10 C.Rolland (France) all same time

**General Classification:** 1 P.Flanagan (Kildare) 9.07.17 2 S.Kennedy (Meath Collins) at 46 secs 3 H.H. Briemrieder (Germany) at 49 secs 4 equal D.O'Connell (Cork) and F.Perez (France) both at 1.29 6 S.O Hanlon (Dublin) at 1.36 7 E.Connolly (Meath) at 1.41 8 D.Devin (Ireland) at 1.45 9 B.Power (Ireland) at 1.47 10 J.C.Breure (France) at 1.53 11 C.Rolland (France) at 1.54 12 J.J.Cornet (France) at 1.57

**Mountains:** 1 P.Flanagan 2 E.Connolly 3 D.O'Connell

**Team:** 1 France 27.27.03 2 Ireland 27.27.28 3 Germany 27.28.20

**County Team:** 1 Meath Collins 27.26.26 2 Meath Nulty 27.29.29 3 Meath Tayto 27.31.51

## STAGE 3

Paddy Flanagan's hopes of equalling Shay O Hanlon's four victories were ended in a huge pile-up five miles after the start of the third stage which saw the Kildare man break his arm.

25 riders came down including the race leader who remounted and incredibly completed the stage ignoring the pleas of his team to retire. Also out of the race with arm injuries went Heinz Briemrieder (Germany) who had been lying third overall.

Seamus Kennedy (Meath Collins) finished sixth on the stage behind Bobby Power (Ireland) but took over the jersey with a 56 second advantage over Denis Devin (Ireland).

After the crash it took some time for the field to sort itself out but there were no early breaks of any consequence on the flat roads.
At 46 miles 14 riders went away and although they made little headway at first they persisted and gradually their lead grew and in the latter stages the bunch seemed to lost interest and came home over 7 minutes down.
In the sprint Power got the verdict from Herman Krins (Holland) with Denis Devin taking third.
**Stage 3 Lisdoonvarna - Listowel 90 Mls.** 1 B.Power (Ireland) 3.40.00 2 H.Krins (Holland) 3 D.Devin (Ireland) 4 J.C.Breure (France) 5 F.Steuten (Holland) 6 S.Kennedy (Meath Collins) 7 J.J.Cornet (France) 8 C.Nulty (Meath Nulty) 9 W.Zebisch (Germany) 10 B.McKenna (Meath Tayto) all same time
**General Classification:** 1 S.Kennedy (Meath Collins) 12.48.06 2 D.Devin (Ireland) at 54 secs 3 B.Power (Ireland) at 56 secs 4 J.C.Breure (France) at 1.02 5 J.J.Cornet (France) at 1.06 6 C.Nulty (Meath Nulty) at 1.24 7 H.Krins (Holland) at 1.56 8 W.Leivel (Germany) at 1.59 9 W.Zebisch (Germany) at 2.06 10 M.Nulty (Meath Nulty) at 2.24
**Mountains:** 1 M.Nulty 2 S.Kennedy 3 B.Power
**International Team:** 1 Holland 38.29.03 2 France 38.34.14 3 Ireland 38.34.39
**County Team:** 1 Meath Collins 38.33.46 2 Meath Tayto 38.49.19 3 Cork 38.56.13

## STAGE 4

Jean Claude Breure (France) won the 80 miles stage from Listowel to Valencia and took over the overall lead while his teammate Jean Jacques Cornet moved into second, 4 seconds behind. Colm Nulty (Meath Nulty) who finished 7th on the stage, in the same time as the winner now lay 3rd at 21 seconds.
Yellow jersey Seamus Kennedy (Meath Collins) finished 12th on the stage but was 2.19 behind the winner and he dropped to 5th overall.
Mick Nulty was active early on, first on his own and then with brother Colm and Eamon Connolly (Meath Tayto) but they were brought back.
Just before Tralee Colm Nulty went again with Martin McKenna (Meath Tayto), Brian Connaughton (Meath Collins) going with them to look after the leader's interests.
They had a minute's lead going through Tralee. Connaughton was sitting in but nevertheless their lead had grown to 2.50 at Glenbeigh.
The bunch started chasing and at Cahirciveen, with 18 miles left, Ahmed Chabane (Algeria) and J.J.Cornet went in pursuit. They were joined by Abdel Boudoukane (Algeria), Ben McKenna (Meath Tayto), Van der Hayden (Holland) and Breure.
The leaders were still nearly 3 minutes in front but the chasing group worked well together and the gap was down to 40 seconds as they crossed the bridge to Valencia Island and they caught the leaders with only 2 miles to the finish.
**Stage 4 Listowel - Valentia 82 Mls.** 1 J.C.Breure (France) 3.20.00 2 B.Connaughton (Meath Collins) 3 B.McKenna (Meath Tayto) 4 F.Steuten (Holland) 5 M.van der

Hayden (Holland) 6 A.Chabane (Algeria) 7 C.Nulty (Meath Nulty) 8 J.J.Cornet (France) 9 M.McKenna (Meath Tayto) all same time 10 A.Boudoukane (Algeria) at 1.07

**General Classification:** 1 J.C.Breure (France) 16.09.08 2 J.J.Cornet (France) at 4 secs 3 C.Nulty (Meath Nulty) at 21 secs 4 F.Steuten (Holland) at 1.34 5 S.Kennedy (Meath Collins) at 1.37 6 D.Devin (Ireland) at 1.35 7 B.Power (Ireland) at 1.37 8 M.van der Hayden (Holland) at 2.52 9 N.Clarke (Meath Collins) at 3.01 10 B.McKenna (Meath Tayto) at 3.17 11 H.Krins (Holland) at 3.33 12 W.Leibel (Germany) at 3.37

**Mountains:** 1 C. Nulty; 2 F. Steuten; 3 B. Connaughton.

**International Team:** 1 Holland 48.31.42 2 France 48.36.53 3 Ireland 48.32.36

**County Team:** 1 Meath Collins 48.38.58 2 Meath Nulty 48.41.58 3 Meath Tayto 48.48.58

## STAGE 5

A foggy morning saw the race leave Valencia Island and tackle the steep climb of Coomanaspig and on the treacherous descent Brian Connaughton crashed and had to be taken to hospital. Another Meath rider Tony Booth was also detained in hospital overnight after a crash.

The stage was won by Bobby Power (Ireland) who took over the yellow jersey from Breure, another crash victim on the treacherous descent which included five sharp hairpins, made even more dangerous by the heavy mist and rain. Despite the damage caused by the stage the position at the top of the GC had closed up considerably with 45 seconds covering the top four.

Power and Mick Nulty (Meath Nulty) went away on the first climb, before they left the island, and Nulty was first over the top as he was to be over all the climbs of the day, taking a commanding lead in the mountains classification.

Nulty had 30 seconds in hand as they crossed the bridge to the mainland over Power who in turn was chased by Colm Nulty and Seamus Kennedy at the head of the bunch.

Power got up to Nulty after Coomanaspig and at 28 miles they had a lead of nearly three minutes on a chasing group of 14 while behind the bunch were strung out all over the place.

With 16 miles to go Seamus Kennedy, Fons Steuten and F. Perez (France) left the chasers and this trio came home 1.12 behind Power who was 2 seconds in front of Nulty at the line.

**Stage 5 Valentia - Kenmare 67 Mls.** 1 B.Power (Ireland) 3.00.00 2 M.Nulty (Meath Nulty) at 2 secs 3 F.Perez (France) at 1.12 4 S.Kennedy (Meath Collins) 5 F.Steuten (Holland) 6 J.Murphy (Louth) at 2.59 7 H.de Hay (Holland) 8 D.Devin (Ireland) 9 C.Rolland (France) 10 N.Clarke (Meath Collins) all same time

**General Classification:** 1 B.Power (Ireland) 19.11.43 2 F.Steuten (Holland) at 11 secs 3 S.Kennedy (Ireland) at 14 secs 4 C.Nulty (Meath Nulty) at 45 secs 5 M.Nulty

(Meath Nulty) at 1.22 6 D.Devin (Ireland) at 2.57 7 N.Clarke (Meath Collins) at 3.25 8 J.J.Cornet (France) at 3.49 9 F.Perez (France) at 8.05 10 E.Connolly (Meath Tayto) at 10.04 11 H.de Hay (Holland) at 11.18 12 B.McKenna (Meath Tayto) at 13.50
**Mountains:** 1 M.Nulty 2 B.Power 3 C.Nulty.
**Points:** 1 S.Kennedy 36 2 F.Steuten 34 3 B.Power 29
**International Team:** 1 Holland 57.49.47 2 France 57.52.45 3 Ireland 57.59.29
**County Team:** 1 Meath Nulty 57.57.57 2 Meath Tayto 58.17.53 3 Cork 58.31.08

## STAGE 6

For the first time since the start a race leader managed to hang on to the yellow jersey as Power finished in the main bunch along with all his main rivals.
The stage was won by Josef Zebisch (Germany) after he rode the final 25 miles on his own to come home 13 seconds ahead of a six-man chasing group led in by Jean Claude Breure (France) just ahead of John McNally (Antrim).
The first important move of the day came after 32 miles at Macroom when John McNally, Mick Cahill (Cork) and Larry Clarke (Meath Collins) went away.
Back with the main bunch Mick Nulty (Meath Nulty) was making valiant efforts to drag them up to the leaders but he got little help and all his work was in vain.
After ten miles in front the break's lead was 50 seconds which soon grew to 1.10. Then Zebisch made his move from the chasers quickly catching the three leaders. He stayed with them for a few miles before making his winning move with 25 miles still remaining.
Behind more riders joined the chasing group from which Breure and McNally got away before the finish.
**Stage 6 Kenmare - Mitchelstown 91 Mls.** 1 J.Zebisch (Germany) 3.20.00 2 J.C.Breure (France) at 13 secs 3 J.McNally (Antrim) s.t. 4 F.Perez (France) at 1.33 5 L.Clarke (Meath Collins) 6 A.Chabane (Algeria) 7 M.Nulty (Meath Nulty) 8 E Deady (Cork) all same time 9 J.J.Cornet (France) at 1.34 10 J.Beurskens (Holland s.t.
**General Classification:** 1 B.Power (Ireland) 22.33.20 2 F.Steuten (Holland) at 11 secs 3 S.Kennedy (Ireland) at 14 secs 4 C.Nulty (Meath Nulty) at 45 secs 5 M.Nulty (Meath Nulty) at 1.18 6 D.Devin (Ireland) at 2.57 7 N.Clarke (Meath Collins) at 3.25 8 J.J.Cornet (France) at 3.49 9 F.Perez (France) at 8.05 10 E.Connolly (Meath Tayto) at 10.04 11 H.de Hey (Holland) at 11.18 12 M.van der Hayden (Holland) at 13.15

## STAGE 7

Noel Clarke (Meath Collins) out sprinted Henk de Hey (Holland) by half-a-wheel to take the 90 miles seventh stage from Mitchelstown to Carlow.
They were in a group of five, all timed at 3.30.00 which finished 51 seconds ahead of the main bunch containing yellow jersey Power who kept his lead of 11 seconds over Fons Steuten (Holland) going into the crucial mountain stage.

Clarke, who scored his eighth stage win, did most of the work at the front. Shortly after Cahir he broke away and rode for a time on his own before being caught by four chasers: De Hey, Billy Kennedy (Tipperary), Christian Roland (France) and Abdel Lagab (Algeria).
With 45 miles to go their lead was 1.30 as the Irish team rode at the front of the bunch keeping the gap from becoming dangerous to the leader.
The lead reached a maximum of 1.55 at Carrick-on-Suir where Colm Nulty was chasing on his own but was soon back in the bunch. The lead started coming down and with 10 miles to go it was down to 1 minute but the leaders managed to hang on to most of this over the final miles.
**Stage 7 Mitchelstown - Carlow 91 Mls.** 1 N.Clarke (Meath Collins) 3.30.00 2 H.de Hey (Holland) 3 C.Rolland (France) 4 W.Kennedy (Tipperary) 5 A.Lagab (Algeria) all same time 6 J.J.Cornet (France) at 51 secs 7 S.Kennedy (Meath Collins) 8 F.Steuten (Holland) 9 F.Perez (France) 10 J.Beurskens (Holland) all same time
**General Classification:** 1 B.Power (Ireland) 26.04.11 2 F.Steuten (Holland) at 11 secs 3 S.Kennedy (Meath Collins) at 12 secs 4 C.Nulty (Meath Nulty) at 45 secs 5 M.Nulty (Meath Nulty) at 1.18 6 N.Clarke (Meath Collins) at 2.34 7 D.Devin (Ireland) at 2.57 8 J.J.Cornet (France) at 3.49 9 F.Perez (France) at 8.01 10 H.de Hey (Holland) at 10.27 11 E.Connolly (Meath Tayto) at 11.11 12 M.van der Hayden (Holland) at 13.15
**Points:** 1 S.Kennedy 44 2 F.Steuten (Holland) 39 3 F.Perez (France) 34
**International Team:** 1 Holland 78.26.20 2 France 78.28.50 3 Ireland 78.36.53
**County Team:** 1 Meath Nulty 78.35.17 2 Meath Tayto 78.55.17 3 Meath Collins 79.32.43

## STAGE 8

Fons Steuten (Holland) who wore the yellow jersey on the stage from Clifden to Lisdoonvarna finished second on the 77 miles penultimate stage into Bray behind German Josef Zebisch to go back into the lead by 33 seconds from Colm Nulty (Meath Nulty) but with a climb of the Sally Gap on the final stage the race still looked open.
Yellow jersey Power lost any chance of defending his lead when he punctured just before the first climb and he dropped to 5th overall.
A large group went away at Laragh and this break dominated the stage. Included were Steuten, Zebisch and the two Nultys along with Denis Devin (Ireland), Christian Rolland (France) and this sextet forged ahead over the climbs eventually coming home almost 4 minutes clear.
Seamus Kennedy (Meath Collins) lying in third place before the stage was in this chasing group and dropped to sixth and his teammate Noel Clarke also dropped three places to seventh.
**Stage 8 Carlow - Bray 78 Mls.** 1 J.Zebisch (Germany) 3.20.00 2 F.Steuten (Holland) 3 D.Devin (Ireland) 4 C.Nulty (Meath Nulty) 5 C.Rolland (France) 6

M.Nulty (Meath Nulty) all same time 7 J.Hoffert (France) at 3.58 8 J.Chabane (Algeria) 9 S.Kennedy (Meath Collins) 10 F.Perez (France) all same time

**General Classification:** 1 F.Steuten (Holland) 29.24.22 2 C.Nulty (Meath Nulty) at 34 secs 3 M.Nulty (Meath Nulty) at 1.10 4 D.Devin (Ireland) at 1.19 5 B.Power (Ireland) at 4.10 6 S.Kennedy (Meath Collins) at 4.18 7 N.Clarke (Meath Collins) at 6.38 8 F.Perez (France) at 11.31 9 C.Rolland (France) at 13.34 10 E.Connolly (Meath Tayto) at 18.30 11 H.de Hey (Holland) at 18.48 12 A.Chabane (Algeria) at 18.58

## STAGE 9

Fons Steuten came home in 11th place, 1.09 behind Franz Perez (France) on the 67 miles final stage from Bray to Dublin to successfully defend the jersey and add Holland to the nations on the RÁS roll of honour.

The 38-year-old builder from Eindhoven had been in contention all week and was lying just 11 seconds behind Bobby Power going into Saturday's mountain stage which always looked like being the one which would decide the winner.

He finished second on that stage to move into the lead by 34 seconds from Colm Nulty (Meath Nulty) and he made sure the Meath man never became a danger to him on the final stage.

Although there was a climb of the Sally Gap shortly after the start in Bray all the damage was done to the weaker riders who went out the back but no serious threats came at the head of the field.

French riders Perez and J.P.Hoffert got away and finished 44 seconds ahead of a chasing group of four led in by. Cornet to give France the top three on the stage. These four were 25 seconds ahead of the main bunch where Steuten and the Dutch team were keeping a close watch on the Nulty brothers lying second and third and Denis Devin (Ireland), 4th at 1.19, the only riders within striking distance.

By winning the stage Perez won the overall points classification by just 1 point from Steuten. Mick Nulty won the mountains classification. France won the team race from Holland, Ireland and Germany while Meath teams took the top three places in the County team classification.

**Stage 9 Bray - Dublin 67 Mls.** 1 F.Perez (France) 2.40.00 2 J.P.Hoffert (France) s.t. 3 J.J.Cornet (France) at 44 secs 4 E.Deady (Cork) 5 W.Zebisch (Germany) 6 B.Power (Tipperary) all same time 7 N.Clarke (Meath Collins) at 1.09 8 T.Murphy (Antrim) 9 C.Rolland (France) 10 A.Lagab (Algeria) all same time

**General Classification:** 1 F.Steuten (Holland) 32.05.31 2 C.Nulty (Meath Nulty) at 34 secs 3 M.Nulty (Meath Nulty) at 1.10 4 D.Devin (Ireland) at 1.19 5 B.Power (Ireland) at 3.39 6 S.Kennedy (Meath Collins) at 4.18 7 N.Clarke (Meath Collins) at 6.38 8 F.Perez (France) at 10.56 9 C.Rolland (France) at 13.34 10 E.Connolly (Meath Tayto) at 18.30 11 H.de Hey (Holland) at 18.48 12 A.Chabane (Algeria) at 18.58 13 P.Hoffert (France) at 19.01 14 J.Zebisch (Germany) at 19.43 15 J.Spitzner (Germany) at 19.49

**Mountains:** 1 M.Nulty 37 2 E.Connolly and B.Power 19
**Points:** 1 F.Perez 53 2 F.Steuten 52 3 S.Kennedy 48
**International Team:** 1 France 98.38.15 2 Holland 98.57.35 3 Ireland 100.04.54
**County Team:** 1 Meath Nulty Providers) 99.59.03 2 Meath Tayto 100.45.53 3 Meath Collins Joinery 101.03.47

*Fons Steuten, Netherlands, 1976 Winner*

# 1977

The 1977 RÁS was sponsored by Bord Failte's 'Home Holidays' Campaign and the Irish Health Education Authority's 'Be Active Be Alive' drive.
The line up included the USSR, last in Ireland seven year's previously when they won 9 of the 10 stages. One of that team Yury Lavrouchkin was back again.
Also included were Holland with defending champion Fons Steuten, France, who included the Grand Prix l'Humanite winner Jean Claude Breure, Belgium, Ireland, a French regional and 10 county teams.

## STAGES 1(a) and (b)

On the opening Saturday there was a split stage with a 2 miles prologue TT in Phoenix Park which was won by Helmut WIller (Germany), a late substitution who was on his sixth visit to the race.
Two seconds behind was Sergei Chelpakov of the USSR with Denis Devin (Ireland), winner of the prologue the previous year in third place.
The afternoon stage was to Carrickmacross and past winner Brian Connaughton (Meath White's Construction) was early on the attack leading through his home village of Clonee. When he was caught another Navan rider Noel Clarke went away but he was soon back in the bunch. Through Navan it was Connaughton again with Russian Chelpakov and Herman Krins (Holland).
Connaughton took the prime and on the other side of the town they were joined by another USSR rider Ildar Gubaidulin, Breure (France) and Devin (Ireland). At the Oldcastle KOH prime the Dutchman was dropped and the remaining five kept increasing their lead. At Kingscourt with 10 miles to go Connaughton punctured as Chelpakov took the prime.
At the finish it was Chelpakov again from his teammate with Breure 3rd and Devin 4th. Yellow jersey Willer came in 4 minutes down just ahead of the bunch. The extreme cold and rain saw 12 retirals, unprecedented for a first stage in the RÁS.
**Stage 1a Dublin Phoenix Park 2 Mls. TT:** 1 H.Willer (Germany) 3.49 2 S.Chelpakov (USSR) 3.51 3 D.Devin (Ireland) 3.55 4 S.Kennedy (Ireland) 3.56 5 A.Kesters (Belgium) 3.58 6 G. Costello (Cork) 4.00.
**Stage 1b Dublin - Carrickmacross 89 Mls.** 1 S.Chelpakov (USSR) 3.31.00 2 I.Gubaidulin (USSR) 3 J.C.Breure (France) 4 D.Devin (Ireland) all same time 5 B.Connaughton (Meath) at 3.24 6 Y.Lavrouchkin (USSR) at 9.11 7 H.Willer (Germany) s.t. 8 B.Power (Ireland) at 9.35 9 P.Flanagan (Ireland) 10 P.McHugh (Antrim) all same time

## STAGE 2

The rain and cold had departed when the 90 miles second stage set off for Boyle on Sunday. There was a surprise at the start when Chelpakov and Gubaidulin turned up without their yellow and pink (KOH) jerseys. They were penalised 20 seconds costing Chelpakhov the lead.
At the first prime in Cavan a group of 15 went away, Seamus Kennedy (Ireland) taking the sprint. However the break kept splitting and they were soon all back in the bunch.
The next serious break was by Lavouchkin who went off on his own and soon had over a minute on a chasing trio: Kennedy, Willer and Paddy Flanagan (Ireland).
The three joined the Russian after the prime at Drumshambo and he proceeded to sit on the back of the group for the next 20 miles waiting for the final sprint where he had a couple of lengths in hand over Willer and Flanagan with Kennedy, who hit the hill at the finish in too high a gear losing 5 seconds.
The bunch was led in by the Belgian Albert Kesters 3.31 later. Because of Chelpakov's penalty, Denis Devin was the new race leader.
**Stage 2 Carrickmacross - Boyle 92 Mls.** 1 Y.Lavrouchkin (USSR) 3.51.00 2 H.Willer (Germany) 3 P.Flanagan (Ireland) 4 S.Kennedy (Ireland) at 5 secs 5 A.Kesters (Belgium) at 3.31 6 J.C.Breure (France) 7 B.Reval (France) 8 D.Devin (Ireland) 9 N.Struver (Germany) 10 P.Noel (France), all same time
**General Classification:** 1 D.Devin (Ireland) 7.29.28 2 S.Chelpakov (USSR) at 14 secs 3 J.C.Breure (France) at 16 secs 4 I.Gubaidulin (USSR) at 55 secs 5 B.Connaughton (Meath White's Construction) at 4.01 6 H.Willer (Germany) at 5.32 7 Y.Lavrouchkin (USSR) at 5.46 8 P.Flanagan (Ireland) at 6.36 9 S.Kennedy (Ireland) at 6.37 10 G.Costelloe (Cork) at 9.40
**Points:** 1 Y.Lavrouchkin 19 2 H.Willer 17 3 J.C.Breure 17

## STAGE 3

Stage 3 was the longest of the event, over 102 miles of mostly flat roads to Nenagh.
The stage started out like the previous day with a big group going away in a promising move only to be caught because they were not working together. There were four each from the Dutch and USSR teams but while the Dutch were prepared to work the Russians unaccountably just sat in and the break was doomed.
After Revola (France) took the prime at Roscommon (27 miles) the bunch came up fast and they were all together. Juraslev (USSR) attacked taking with him Krins (Holland) and Brian Connaughton.
At first the Russian worked hard, the team obviously not realising that the Navan rider was a real threat on GC. It was not until after the feed at Ballinasloe that the Russian manager realised the danger and order his rider to stop working, but by now they had 4 minutes lead over a chasing group and 8 on the bunch.

Connaughton and Krins kept working strongly and they held on to most of their lead over the final 20 miles. After sitting in for 20 miles Juralev was expected to win the sprint but he pulled his foot out and the stage went to Krins. Connaughton, happy to take the yellow jersey sat up and came in at 8 seconds.
The day's drama was not over for four teams including Russia, Meath and France were penalised 2 minutes per rider for unauthorised feeding from cars. However this was lifted on appeal and replaced with a severe warning.
In an interesting footnote Brian Monaghan of Newry, riding on the AIF Veterans team which included past winners Gene Mangan and Ben McKenna, made it into the top 12 on GC, 23 years after he competed in the first RÁS in 1954.
**Stage 3 Boyle - Nenagh 102 Mls.** 1 H.Krins 3.58.00 2 S.Juralev USSR) s.t. 3 B.Connaughton (Meath) at 8 secs 4 H.Willer (Germany) at 3.20 5 Y.Lavrouchkin (USSR) 6 S.Kennedy (Ireland) 7 A.Kesters (Belgium) 8 P.Noel (France) 9 C.Salentijn (Holland) 10 P.Flanagan (Ireland) all same time
**General Classification:** 1 B.Connaughton (Meath/White's Construction) 11.32.09 2 H.Willer (Germany) at 4.11 3 Y.Lavrouchkin (USSR) at 4.25
4 D.Devin (Ireland) at 4.50 5 S.Chelpakov (USSR) at 5.03 6 J.C.Breure (France) at 5.05 7 P.Flanagan (Ireland) at 5.15 8 S.Kennedy (Ireland)
at 5.16 9 I.Gubaidulin (USSR) at 5.44 10 H.Krins (Holland) at 5.49 11 A.Kesters (Belgium) at 8.44 12 B.Monaghan (AIF Veterans) at 9.55

## STAGE 4

The Soviets hit back on the 81 miles fourth stage to Castleisland placing three riders in the first six, Chelpakov climbing back to second overall only 1.41 down on Connaughton after dropping four minutes on the previous day.
Three riders went away early on: Lavrouchkin (USSR), Krins (Holland), Revoal (France) and Jack Murphy (AIF Veterans). Krins took two primes in Limerick city while Lavrouchkin took two hot spot but they were caught before the prime at Newcastle-West.
Another four then went away: Chelpakhov, Seamus Kennedy) Ireland, Franz Kroon (Belgium) and Eamon Connolly (Meath/Tayto) who took the prime.
On the climb at Barnagh Gap Kennedy was first over from Chelpakov and over the next climb at Knockakip it was Chelpakov from Kennedy. Kroons was dropped but rejoined on the descent.
At the finish in Castleisland it was Kennedy by half a wheel from the Russian with Connolly third and Kroons 4th. Gubaidulin came home on his own 1.16 later, 25 seconds ahead of 11 riders led in by Lavrouchkin. Bruere, Willer, Krins and Flanagan were all in this group and made up time on race-leader Connaughton and 5 minutes now covered the top 10 on GC.
**Stage 4 Nenagh - Castleisland 81 Mls.** 1 S.Kennedy (Ireland) 3.18.00 2 S.Chelpakov (USSR) 3 E.Connolly (Meath Tayto) 4 F.Kroons (Belgium) all same time 5 I.Gubaidulin (USSR) at 1.16 6 Y.Lavrouchkin (USSR) at 1.41 7 J.C.Breure

(France) 8 H.Krins (Holland) 9 H.WIller (Germany) 10 B.Revoal (France) all same time

**General Classification:** 1 B.Connaughton (Meath White's Construction) 14.53.28 2 S.Chelpakov (USSR) at 1.56 3 S.Kennedy (Ireland) at 2.09 4 H.Willer (Germany) at 2.35 5 Y.Lavrouchkin (USSR) at 2.49 6 J.C.Breure (France) at 3.29 7 P.Flanagan (Ireland) at 3.37 8 I.Gubaidulin (USSR) at 3.41 9 H.Krins (Holland) at 4.11 10 D.Devin (Ireland) at 4.45

**Points:** 1 Y. Lavrouchkin 24 2 H.Willer 30 3 S.Kennedy 28

**International Team:** 1 USSR 44.38.57 2 Ireland 44.49.48 3 Holland 45.04.35

**County Team:** 1 Meath Whites 45.10.19 2 Meath Tayto 45.15.25 3 AIF Veterans 45.17.31

## STAGE 5

Although the gap between standards in Ireland and the east European teams like the USSR had obviously narrowed since 1970, any illusions about the Russians vulnerability were removed after the 95 miles stage to Macroom when the Russians took the stage and the top two places on GC as well as the lead in the points, mountains and Hot Spots classifications.

The first prime in Killarney was taken by Bobby Power (Ireland) who had gone away with Juralev and Martin McKenna (Meath Tayto). They in turn were caught by five: Durelle (French Regional), Revoal (France), Chelpakov, Gubaidulin (USSR) and Henk de Hey (Holland),

On the first climb De Hey and Gubaidulin went ahead and on the next climb at the Tunnel Road the Dutchman was also dropped. However over the top Gubaidulin waited for him.

The two worked well together and at Ballylickey, where De Hey took the prime, they were 5 minutes ahead of Power, Chelpakov and Juralev with a big group a further 5 minutes back.

Gubaidulin took the final climb at Keimaneigh Pass making it maximum KOM points for the day. De Hey took the final prime at Inchigeela where their lead was fast coming down on a flying bunch, spurred on the Ireland team who had been badly caught out.

At the finish, where the Russian took the stage they had 2.43 in hand over the chasing trio who had just held off the bunch which had taken back 5 minutes of their deficit in the final 30 miles.

**Stage 5 Castleisland - Macroom, 95 Mls.** 1 I.Gubaidulin (USSR) 3.48.00 2 H.de Hey (Holland) s.t. 3 S.Chelpakov (USSR) at 2.43 4 S.Juralev (USSR) at 2.56 5 B.Power (Ireland) 6 P.Noel (France) 7 J.Madden (Galway) 8 Y.Lavrouchkin (USSR) 9 A.Kesters (Belgium) 10 J.C.Breure (France) all same time

**General Classification:** 1 I.Gubaidulin (USSR) 18.45.09 2 S.Chelpakov (USSR) at 46 secs 3 S.Kennedy (Ireland) at 3.45 4 H.Willer (Germany) at 4.21 5 Y.Lavrouchkin (USSR) at 4.35 6 J.C.Breure (France) at 5.15 7 P.Flanagan (Ireland)

at 5.25 8 H.de Hey (Holland) at 5.31 9 H.Krins (Holland) at 5.59 10 D.Devin (Ireland) at 6.33 11 S.Juralev (USSR) at 9.23 12 A.Kesters (Belgium) at 10.27
**Points:** 1 Y.Lavrouchkin 39 2 S.Chelpakov 33 3 H. Willer 30
**Mountains:** 1 I.Gubaidulin 15 2 H.de Hey 11 3 S.Chelpakov 10
**International Team:** 1 USSR 56.08.36 2 Ireland 56.27.41 3 Holland 56.39.35
**County Team:** 1, Meath Tayto 56.55.52; 2, AIF Veterans 57.14.09; 3, French Reg. 57.16.29.

## STAGE 6

The 97 mile stage to Clonmel saw an attempt by three times winner Paddy Flanagan to take the jersey but although he pulled back 5.05 on Gubaidulin, he failed to take 2nd place by just 20 seconds. However at one stage when they were over 7 minutes ahead the Kildare man was leader on the road.
That his efforts were in vain was mainly due to the Irish county riders in the break not working and Flanagan, who had done more than his share, had no answer when Lavourchkin, fresh from sitting on, jumped away with 15 miles to go.
The action as usual started early and at the first prime in Cork city (27m.) Lavourchkin beat Flanagan and Martin McKenna, 1.30 ahead of four chasers: Larry Clarke (Meath Whites), Tommy Mannion (Galway), Franx Kroons (Belgium) and Gerard Costelloe (Cork). The bunch was at 3 minutes.
At Carrigtowhill (34m.) the Russian was instructed to stop working as the race leader was now over 4 minutes back. The chasers then caught the leaders. The gap continued to increase with Flanagan, helped by McKenna, doing all the work and at Clashmore, where Lavourchkin took the prime, their lead was 6.30.
Lavourchkin went away with 15 miles to go and none could go with him. By the time the tired Flanagan had summoned up his remaining reserves and went in pursuit, the Russian was over a minute clear.
Only Kroon and Costello could stay with Flanagan. They closed the gap to 45 seconds by the finish but it was enough for Lavourchkin to take over the jersey.
Kroons beat Flanagan for second with Costelloe fourth, Clarke leading in McKenna and Mannion 21 seconds later.
**Stage 6 Macroom - Clonmel 97 Mls.** 1 Y.Lavrouchkin (USSR) 3.59.00; 2 F.Kroon (Belgium) at 45 secs 3 P.Flanagan (Ireland) 4 G.Costelloe (Cork) all same time 5 L.Clarke (Meath Whites) at 3.06 6 M.McKenna (Meath Tayto) 7 T.Mannion (Galway) all same time 8 J.C.Breure (France) at 5.40 9 P.Noel (France) 10 A.Kesters (Belgium) all same time
**General Classification:** 1 Y. Lavrouchkin (USSR) 22.48.44 2 I.Gubaidulin (USSR) at 1.15 3 P.Flanagan at 1.35 4 S.Chelpakov (USSR) at 2.01 5 S.Kennedy (Ireland) at 5.00 6 H.Willer (Germany) at 5.36 7 J.C.Breure (France) at 6.30 8 H.de Hey (Holland) at 6.46 9 H.Krins (Holland) at 7.14 10 D.Devin (Ireland) at 7.48 11 S.Juralev (USSR) at 10.38 12 A.Kesters (Belgium) at 11.42
**Points:** 1 Y. Lavrouchkin 51 2 S.Chelpakov 33 3 I.Gubaidulin 32

**Mountains:** 1 I.Gubaidulin 15 2 H.de Hey 11 3 S.Chelpakov 10
**Hot Spots:** 1 S. Juralev 11 2 Y.Lavrouchkin
**International Team:** 1 USSR 68.17.16 2 Ireland 68.37.06 3 Holland 68.54.05
**County Team:** 1 Meath Tayto 69.07.41 2 AIF Veterans 69.28.39 3 French Regional 69.35.09

## STAGE 7

Lavrouchkin notched up his third win on the 88-miles stage to Courtown. With 14 others he had come up to two riders: Chelpakov and G. Sannen (Belgium) who had been away for 72 miles.
The pair had a lead of 2.40 at one time but the chasing group cut into their lead as they battled against a stiff headwind.
With Lavourchkin in the group of 15 were three from Holland, two French, and another Belgian. The rest were Irish county riders except Paddy Flanagan (Ireland) who had a good day, moving to second ahead of Gubaidulin who finished in the main group nearly 6 minutes behind.
In the final sprint Lavourchkin edged out the Belgian Kesters and Cork's Gerard Costello.
**Stage 7 Clonmel - Courtown 88 Mls.** 1 Y.Lavrouchkin (USSR) 3.52.00 2 A.Kesters (Belgium) 3 G.Costello (Cork) 4 J.C.Breure (France) 5 P.Flanagan (Ireland) 6 P.Noel (France) 7 S.Chelpakov (USSR) 8 C.Salentijn (Holland) 9 E.Connolly (Meath Tayto) 10 L.Clarke (Meath Whites) all same time
**General Classification:** 1 Y.Lavrouchkin (USSR) 26.40.44 2 P.Flanagan (Ireland) at 1.35 3 S.Chelpakov (USSR) at 2.01 4 J.C.Breure (France) at 6.20 5 I.Gubaidulin (USSR) at 7.50 6 A.Kesters (Belgium) at 11.42 7 S.Kennedy (Ireland) at 11.44 8 E.Connolly (Meath Tayto) at 11.54 9 H.Willer (Germany) at 12.20 10 P.Noel (France) at 13.24 11 H.de Hey (Holland) at 15.30 12 H.Krins (Holland) at 15.58
**Points:** 1 Y.Lavrouchkin 63 2 J.C.Breure (France) 40 3 S.Chelpakov (URRS) 39
**Mountains:** 1 I.Gubaidulin 15 2 H.de Hey 11 3 S.Chelpakov 10
**International Team:** 1 USSR 80.00.00 2 Ireland 80.26.34 3 Holland 80.36.49
**County Team:** 1 Meath Tayto 80.57.09 2 AIF Veterans 81.18.05 3 French Regional 81.27.06

## STAGE 8

Saturday's penultimate stage may have been only 82 miles but it included four 1st and one 2nd category climb in the final 50 miles so it was always going to be the final decider.
The first 25 flat miles were very lively as riders tried to get some time in hand before the mountains but too many had the same idea and at Woodenbridge, just before the first climb the last of these breakaway attempts was brought back and they hit the first climb at Aughavanna with the bunch intact.

It didn't stay that way for long as Gubaidulin went on the attack on the 1 in 12 gradient and he went over the top on his own, chased by a 12-man group which included Flanagan and most of the top men on GC with the exception of German Willer who was suffering with stomach trouble and who abandoned the race on the climb.
Gubaidulin stayed away on the fast descent and over the 1,240 ft Drumgoff the positions stayed the same but at the top he was 2 minutes ahead.
After another fast descent there was 8 miles of flat before the 1 in 9 Luggala leading to the 2nd cat Sally Gap (1,640 ft.). Here Chelpakov got away from the chasers with Meath's Eamon Connolly. At the top of the Gap they had cut their deficit to 1.30 on Gubaidulin.
Although the two chasers were closing on the leader, he led over the final climb at Ballysmutton, taking maximum King of the Mountains points as he had on the mountain stage in Kerry.
On the run-in to the finish the leading three came together and with the two Russians working they took Chelpakov over Flanagan on GC. In fact another 7 seconds would have given him the yellow jersey. Connolly was unlucky not to win the stage, just pipped by Gubaidulin after he hit a pothole, losing all momentum as he started to sprint. The yellow jersey led in the chasers from Flanagan who got a tremendous welcome in his home town.
**Stage 8 Courtown - Newbridge 82 Mls.** 1 I.Gubaidulin (USSR) 3.37.00 2 E.Connolly (Meath Tayto) 3 S.Chelpakov (USSR) all same time 4 Y.Lavrouchkin (USSR) at 1.54 5 P.Flanagan (Ireland) 6 F.Steuten (Holland) 7 N.Struver (Germany) 8 H.de Hey (Holland) all same time 9 D.Devin (Ireland) at 2.00 10 A.Kesters (Belgium) at 6.03.
**General Classification:** 1 Y. Lavrouchkin (USSR) 30.19.40 2 S.Chelpakov at 6 secs 3 P.Flanagan (Ireland) at 1.35 4 I.Gubaidulin (USSR) at 6.02 5 E.Connolly (Meath Tayto) at 9.57 6 H.de Hey (Holland) at 13.38 7 D.Devin (Ireland) at 14.35 8 A.Kesters (Belgium) at 15.21 9 S.Kennedy (Ireland) at 17.44 10 J.C.Breure (France) at 19.35 11 H.Krins (Holland) at 19.58 12 H.Neuberger (Germany) at 21.44

## STAGE 9

The final stage comprised of a 44 miles run in from Newbridge to Dublin onto a 2 mile circuit in the Phoenix Park which was covered ten times.
The run-in was something of a parade but when they hit the circuit racing began in earnest, spurred on by Hot Spot primes every lap and it was Juralev, who was defending the Hot Spots jersey who took the first two sprints.
Although he scored no more this was enough to give him an outright win in this category with 19 points to Lavrouchkin's 12 with Frenchman Revoal scoring 11.
A big break got away and it included Chelpakov and when the lead went to over 10 seconds he was leader on the road. However the yellow jersey went in pursuit and

bridged the gap to the break and just to emphasise his right to the jersey he won the final sprint, taking his tally of stages to four (he had also won a stage in 1970).
It was a good week for the Moscow physical instructor with the overall win, 4 stages, point's winner and second in the hot spots. In the post-race interview he said he thought the standard of racing in the RÁS had improved a lot since his visit seven years before.

**Stage 9 Newbridge - Dublin 64 Mls.**
1 Y.Lavrouchkin (USSR) 2.26.49 2 H.Krins (Holland) 3 S.Kennedy (Ireland) 4 S.Chelpakov (USSR) 5 J.Cornet (France) 6 E.Connolly (Meath Tayto) 7 D.Deruelle (French Reg.) 8 E.Magennis (Antrim) 9 G.Soimmon (Belgium) 10 A.O'Halloran (Kerry) all same time

**General Classification:** 1 Y.Lavrouchkin (USSR) 32.46.30 2 S.Chelpakov (USSR) at 7 secs 3 P.Flanagan (Ireland) at 1.46 4 I.Gubaidulin (USSR) at 6.13 5 E.Connolly (Meath Tayto) at 9.50 6 H.de Hey (Holland) at 13.41 7 D.Devin (Ireland) at 14.35 8 A.Kesters (Belgium) at 15.32 9 S.Kennedy (Ireland) at 17.44 10 J.C.Breure (France) at 19.35 11 H.Krins (Holland) at 19.58 12 H.Neuberger (Germany) at 21.55 13 P.Noel (France) at 22.21 14 N.Struver (Germany) at 23.16 15 S.Juralev (USSR) at 23.33

**Points:** 1 Y.Lavrouchkin 72 2 S.Chelpakov (USSR) 58 3 P.Flanagan and I.Gubaidulin 43

**Mountains:** I.Gubaidulin

**International Team:** 1 USSR 19.13.38 2 Ireland 98.50.39 3 Holland 99.00.59 4 Belgium 99.20.06 5 Germany 99.28.39 6 France 99.29.12

**County Team:** 1 Meath Tayto 99.40.02 2 AIF Veterans 100.31.34 3 Meath White's Construction 100.34.23 4 Kildare 103.43.08

*Yuri Lavrouchkin USSR, 1977 winner*

## 1978

The Health Education Board came in as full sponsors for the 1978 event which was called the Health Race RÁS TAILTEANN.
There were 105 entries with teams from Belgium, Holland, France, Germany, Ireland, a regional German team from Bavaria and 15 county teams. There were five previous winners in the line-up: defending champion Fons Steuten, Paddy Flanagan, Shay O Hanlon, Mike O'Donoghue and Ben McKenna whose win had been 19 years beforehand in 1959.
There was another out-of-Dublin start, this time in Shannon town where there would be a prologue time-trial and a 65 miles afternoon road stage to Listowel

### STAGE 1 (a) and (b)

Wolfgang Von Hacht (Bavaria) won the 2 miles prologue in Shannon but it was Helmut Willer (Germany) winner of the afternoon stage to Listowel who would be in yellow at the end of the first day.
Von Hacht won by 3 seconds from Axel Hilgert (Germany) with the next two riders H. De Hey (Holland) and L. Swerts (Belgium) on the same time but separated by hundredths.
With a distance of only 2 miles there were no substantial gaps with the afternoon's 65 miles run always likely to really affect the classification.
There was a stiff headwind when they left Shannon and this served to discourage attacks and those who did were soon back in the bunch
After Adare, Willer and Galway's Tommy Mannion got away and managed to build up a lead of 2 minutes. The bunch then started to chase in earnest and it looked like the two breakaways might be caught but they still had 23 seconds in hand at the finish where Willer took the sprint.
Albert Kesters (Belgium) eighth overall in '77, led in the bunch just ahead of Seamus Kennedy, the Meath man riding for Kerry, and Stephen Crotty, a Monaghan rider riding for Antrim.
Willer had 2 seconds in hand over Mannion at the line but the Galway rider had been one second faster in the prologue so Willer too the jersey by a 1 second margin.
**Stage 1a Shannon 2 Mls. TT:** 1 W.von Hacht (Bavaria) 2.38 2 A.Hilgert (Germany) 2.41 3 H.de Hey (Holland) 2.41 4 L.Swerts (Belgium) 2.41 5 J.Walter (Germany) 2.43 6 L.Clarke (Meath White) 2.44 7 D.Devin (Meath Sheerin) 2.44 8 H.Krins (Holland) 2.45 9 A.O'Halloran (Kerry AIF) 2.45 10 R.Decoup (France) 2.46
**Stage 1b Shannon - Listowel 65 Mls.** 1 H.Willer (Germany) 2.20.35 2 T.Mannion (Galway North) at 2 secs 3 A.Kesters (Belgium) at 23 secs 4 S.Kennedy (Kerry AIF) 5 S.Crotty (Antrim) 6 P.Power (Tipperary) 8 H.Krins (Holland) all same time

**General Classification:** 1 H.Willer (Germany) 2.23.21 2 T.Mannion (Galway) at 1 sec 3 W.von Hacht (Bavaria) at 15 secs 4 equal A.Hilgert (Germany) H.de Hey (Holland) L.Swerts (Belgium) all at 18 secs 7 A.Kesters (Belgium) at 19 secs 8 J.Walter (Germany) at 20 secs 9 L.Clarke (Meath White) at 21 secs 10 D.Devin (Meath Sheerin) at 22 secs
**Mountains:** 1 H. Willer 2 T. Mannion 3 A.O'Halloran

## STAGE 2 (a) and (b)

Albert Kesters (Belgium) won the 74 miles stage from Listowel to Galway and then took fifth place in the evening criterium to take over the overall lead with a margin of six seconds over Noel Clarke (Ireland) and Seamus Kennedy (Kerry AIF), Clarke getting the better placing on points count back.
The morning stage was neutralised to Tarbert where the race took the Shannon ferry. When racing started there were continual attacks but none were successful until Anthony O'Halloran (Kerry AIF) went away with 17 miles to go. He was joined by John O'Sullivan (Ireland) and then by Kesters, Kennedy, Clarke, Bobby Power (Tipperary Cidona), Fons Steuten (Holland) and Larry Clarke (Meath Whites). These eight worked hard and with 12 miles to go their lead was 1.10.
Wolfgang von Hacht came up to the leaders as Steuten and O'Sullivan dropped back leaving seven still at the front. In the final miles Von Hacht and O'Halloran dropped back leaving five to contest the final sprint. Helmut Willer (Germany) led in the bunch 2.27 down.
Kennedy was a faller in the evening race round Galway city centre but was able to rejoin to finish in the bunch.
A 4-man group got away and Cork rider Pat Crowley won 11 of the 20 laps but was pipped in the final sprint by Axel Hilgert (Germany). Willer was third and Herman Krins (Holland) fourth and these four were timed 9 seconds in front of the bunch led in by Kesters.
**Stage 2a Listowel - Galway 74 Mls.** 1 A.Kesters (Belgium) 3.01.05 2 S.Kennedy (Kerry AIF) 3 B.Power (Tipperary Cidona) 4 N.Clarke (Ireland) all same time 5 L.Clarke (Meath Whites) at 4 secs 6 A.O'Halloran (Kerry AIF) at 1.37 7 W.von Hacht (Bavaria) at 1.57 8 H.Willer (Germany) at 2.27 9 G.Costello (Limerick Kentucky) 10 H.Krins (Holland) all same time
**Stage 2b Galway Criterium 20 laps.** 1 A.Hilgert (Germany) 30.05 2 P.Crowley (Cork) 3 H.Willer (Germany) 4 H.Krins (Holland) all same time 5 A.Kesters (Belgium) at 9 secs 6 H.de Hey (Holland) 7 N.Clarke (Ireland) 8 G.Costello (Limerick Kentucky) 9 J.C.Lavignac (France) 10 J.Walsh (Carlow) all same time
**General Classification:** 1 A.Kesters (Belgium) 5.54.59 2 N.Clarke (Ireland) at 6 secs 3 S.Kennedy (Kerry AIF) s.t. 4 B.Power (Tipperary Cidona) at 25 secs 5 W.von Hacht (Bavaria) at 1.53 6 H.Willer (Germany) at 2.19 7 A.O'Halloran (Kerry AIF) at 2.30 8 A.Hilgert (Germany) at 2.37 9 T.Mannion (Galway North) at 2.39 10

L.Swerts (Belgium) at 2.46 11 H.de Hey (Holland) s.t. 12 D.Devin (Meath Sheerin) at 2.49

## STAGE 3

The lead changed again after the 87 miles stage from Galway to Clifden which was won by 22-year old Drogheda rider Denis Devin (Meath Sheerin) but it was Helmut Willer of Germany who took over at the top of the G.C.

The two were in a six-man group which finished 4.19 ahead of a chasing group of eleven on a day which saw the field cut to shreds. With Devin and Willer in the break were Seamus O Hanlon (Dublin), Herman Krins (Holland), Paddy Flanagan (Ireland) and H. Bernreider (Bavaria).

This sextet were in the first break of the day which was started by Pat Crowley (Cork) C. Reynolds (Meath PT White) after 20 miles and they were joined by Devin, O Hanlon, Krins, Willer and Bernreider while they in turn were chased by a 12-man group including the race leader.

Behind them a strong crosswind was blowing the field to shreds and over half-an-hour covered them at the finish.

**Stage 3 Galway - Clifden 87 Mls.** 1 D.Devin (Meath Sheerin) 3.52.00 2 H.Willer (Germany) 3 equal P.Flanagan (Ireland) and H. Bernreider (Bavaria) 5 H.Krins (Holland) 6 S.O Hanlon (Dublin) all same time 7 A.Hilgert (Germany) at 4.19 8 A.Kesters (Belgium) 9 W.von Hacht (Bavaria) 10 S.Kennedy (Kerry AIF) all same time

**General Classification:** 1 H.Willer (Germany) 9.49.18 2 H.Krins (Holland) at 22 secs 3 D.Devin (Meath Sheerin) at 30 secs 4 P.Flanagan (Ireland) at 41 secs 5 H.Bernreider (Bavaria) at 43 secs 6 S.O Hanlon (Dublin) at 46 secs 7 A.Kesters (Belgium) at 2.00 8 S.Kennedy (Kerry AIF) at 2.06 9 N.Clarke (Ireland) s.t. 10 B.Power (Tipperary) at 2.24 11 W. Von Hacht (Germany) at 3.53 12 A.Hilgert (Germany) at 4.37

**International team:** 1 Germany 29.37.20 2 equal Ireland and Holland 29.37.54

**County Team:** 1 Meath Sheerin 29.52.03 2 Meath Tayto 29.58.09 3 Dublin 30.00.56

## STAGE 4

20-year-old soldier Jochem Wochter (Germany) won the 74-mile fourth stage from Clifden to Castlebar coming home on his own 38 seconds ahead of his three erstwhile breakaway companions led in by his teammate Axel Hilgert.

These three in turn were 20 seconds in front of the bunch led in by Kesters which contained all the top men on GC so Willer maintained his 22 second lead over Krins while the top ten remained unchanged.

Over the first ten miles there were a series of splits in the bunch which looked that it would disintegrate like on the previous day but there was a general regroupment and at Leenane the bunch was mainly intact not far behind a 5-man break.

At Westport there was a six man break not far ahead of the bunch with Eamon Connolly (Meath Tayto) the only Irish rider along with five continentals. Connolly attacked first and when he was brought back Wochter had a go and opened a half-minute lead which he held to the finish.

**Stage 4 Clifden - Castlebar 74 Mls.** 1 J.Wochter (Germany) 3.14.21 2 A.Hilgert (Germany) at 38 secs 3 W.von Hacht (Bavaria) 4 E.Connolly (Meath Tayto) all same time 5 A.Kesters (Belgium) at 58 secs 6 J.Privain (France) 7 D.Devin (Meath Sheerin) 8 S.Kennedy (Kerry AIF) 9 H.Krins (Holland) 10 H.Bernreider (Bavaria) all same time

**General Classification:** 1 H. Willer (Germany) 13.04.38 2 H.Krins (Holland) at 22 secs 3 D.Devin (Meath Sheerin) at 30 secs 4 P.Flanagan (Ireland) at 41 secs 5 H.Bernreider (Bavaria) at 43 secs 6 S.O Hanlon (Dublin) at 46 secs 7 A.Kesters (Belgium) at 2.00 8 S.Kennedy (Kerry AIF) at 2.06 9 N.Clarke (Ireland) at 2.22 10 B.Power (Tipperary) at 2.24 11 W.von Hacht (Bavaria) at 3.53 12 A.Hilgert (Germany) at 4.37

**Points:** 1 A.Kesters 42 2 H.Willer 38 3 S.Kennedy 36

**Mountains:** 1 A.Hilgert 2 H.Willer 3 H.Krins

**International Team:** 1 Germany 39.22.00 2 Ireland 39.24.10 3 Holland 39.24.40

**County Team:** 1 Meath Tayto 39.45.40 2 Kerry AIF 39.59.58 3 Meath Sheerin 40.00.44

## STAGE 5

Bobby Power (Tipperary) won his sixth RÁS stage, the 87 miles from Castlebar to Bundoran and came within 21 seconds of taking the jersey. He moved up from 10th overnight to 2nd overall.

He won the sprint from a 7-man group which came in nearly a minute ahead. Several more riders came in before the bunch which arrived 3 minutes after the stage winner.

The move of the day came at Ballina, 22 miles after the start and included Power, Leo Swerts (Belgium), Christy Reynolds (Meath PJ White), Sean O'Hare (Dublin), John O'Sullivan (Ireland), T.P. Reilly (Meath Tayto) and Ben McKenna (Meath Sheerin).

When their lead went over 3.20 Power was leader on the road but this sparked off efforts by the German riders behind to cut back their deficit which they just managed to do.

John O'Sullivan's ride in the break improved Ireland's position enough for them to take over the lead in the team classification.

**Stage 6 Castlebar - Bundoran 87 Mls** 1 B.Power (Tipperary Cidona) 3.25.25 2 C.Reynolds (Meath PJ White) 3 L.Swerts (Belgium) 4 J.O'Sullivan (Ireland) 5 S.O'Hare (Dublin) all same time 6 T.P.Reilly (Meath Tayto) at 3 secs 7 B.McKenna (Meath Sheerin) at 8 secs 8 G.Costello (Limerick Kentucky) at 49 secs 9 P.Crowley (Cork) 10 R.Decaup (France) all same time

**General Classification:** 1 H.Willer (Germany) 16.33.03 2 B.Power (Tipperary Cidona) at 20 secs 3 H.Krins (Holland) at 22 secs 4 D.Devin (Meath Sheerin) at 30 secs 5 P.Flanagan (Ireland) at 41 secs 6 H.Bernreider (Bavaria) at 45 secs 7 S.O Hanlon (Dublin) at 46 secs 8 A.Kesters (Belgium) at 2.00 9 S.Kennedy (AIF) at 2.06 10 N.Clarke (Ireland) at 2.22 11 W.von Hacht (Bavaria) at 3.32 12 A.Hilgert (Germany) at 4.16
**Points:** 1 A.Kesters 42 2 H.Willer 38 3 S.Kennedy 36
**International Team:** 1 Ireland 49.46.34 2 Germany 49.47.15 3 Bavaria 50.00.52
**County Team:** 1 Meath Tayto 50.07.50 2 Meath Sheerin 50.19.59 3 Dublin 50.24.05

## STAGE 6

Albert Kesters (Belgium) won his second stage when he escaped with 10 miles to go and finished 16 seconds ahead of a 10-man chasing group into Letterkenny at the end of a tough 96 miles stage which saw some riders finish almost an hour down.
Race leader Helmut Willer was in the break behind Kesters and reinforced his position as several of his main rivals lost time including second placed Bobby Power who came in 3.08 down dropping to 9th overall. The remains of the main bunch came home 1.28 behind Kesters.
Despite narrow, twisty roads, ideal for breaks to go out of sight, the field stayed together until Killybegs, 37 miles after the start.
Then Pat Crowley (Cork), Gearoid Costello (Limerick) and Peer Jansens (Holland) opened a gap but Jansens punctured. Three more riders: Kesters, Fons Steuten and Seamus Kennedy then got up to the leaders.
Steuten punctured and when Costello and Crowley dropped back there were only two at the front with a lead of some 2 minutes.
With 10 miles to go Kesters attacked and Kennedy was caught by a 7-man chasing group and the Belgian held his slender lead to the finish.
**Stage 6 Bundoran - Letterkenny 96 Mls.** 1 A.Kesters (Belgium) 4.10.05 2 W.von Hacht (Bavaria) at 16 secs 3 D.Devin (Meath Sheerin) 4 W.Schwingel (Germany) 5 H.Willer (Germany) 6 H.Krins (Holland) 7 S.O Hanlon (Dublin) 8 H.Bernreider (Bavaria) 9 P.Carey (Cork) all same time 10 S.Kennedy (Kerry AIF)) at 20 secs
**General Classification:** 1 H.Willer (Germany) 20.43.24 2 H.Krins (Holland) at 22 secs 3 D.Devin (Meath Sheerin) at 30 secs 4 H.Bernreider (Bavaria) at 43 secs 5 S.O Hanlon (Dublin) at 46 secs 6 A.Kesters (Belgium) at 1.44 7 P.Flanagan (Kildare) at 1.53 8 S.Kennedy (Kerry AIF) at 2.10 9 B.Power (Tipperary Cidona) at 3.12 10 W.von Hacht (Bavaria) at 3.32 11 N.Clarke (Ireland) at 4.58 12 W.Schwingel (Germany) at 5.49
**Mountains:** 1 P.Crowley 8 2 equal P.Jansens A.Hilgert and H.Willer 6
**Points:** 1 A.Kesters 54 2 H.Willer 46 3 S.Kennedy 39
**International Team:** 1 Germany 62.21.10 2 Holland 62.28.18 3 Ireland 62.22.53
**County Team:** 1 Meath Tayto 62.52.28 2 Kerry 63.01.26 3 Tipperary Cidona 63.15.42

## STAGE 7

Seamus Kennedy, from Trim in County Meath but riding for the Kerry AIF team, won the 101 miles stage from Letterkenny to Warrenpoint and in a complete rearrangement of the general classification jumped from 8th at 2.10 into the lead with a 1.02 margin over Tipperary's Bobby Power. Helmut Willer, who overnight had looked secure in yellow, came in with the main bunch over 7 minutes in arrears and dropped back to third overall, 5.44 behind Kennedy.

Early in the stage it looked like four times winner Shay O Hanlon might cause an upset as he went clear with four other riders to take the lead on the road. However the reaction from behind saw them caught before Omagh and the field stayed together for the next 15 miles.

It was Monaghan's Stephen Crotty, riding on the Antrim team, who started what was to be the move of the day and perhaps of the race. He went away on his own at the 42-mile mark and after a time he was joined by Bobby Power and teammate Paddy Power and Louth's Jack Murphy.

A few miles later a group including Kennedy went in pursuit and they caught the leaders at Armagh with 30 miles to go.

There were now 14 at the front and they rode strongly, especially Kennedy and the four Tipperary riders, Bobby Sheehan and the three Powers: Bobby, Paddy and Larry, and their lead kept growing. The Germans claimed they didn't receive adequate time checks and the gap was too big by they time they became aware of the danger. However had they been defending properly such a large and dangerous break should never have been allowed to get established.

There were some riders who dropped off the back of the break in the final miles leaving 11 timed equal with Kennedy who won the thirteenth RÁS stage of his career.

The Irish team were well represented in the break and took over at the top of the international team classification. Despite the presence of nearly all the Tipperary team, Meath Tayto was there as well and maintained their lead in the county team table.

**Stage 7 Letterkenny - Warrenpoint 101 Mls.** 1 S.Kennedy (Kerry AIF) 3.39.24 2 C.Reynolds (Meath White) 3 J.O'Sullivan (Ireland) 4 B.Power (Tipperary Cidona) 5 J.Murphy (Louth) 6 T.Mannion (Galway) 7 K.Reilly (Meath Tayto) 8 P.Power (Tipperary Cidona) 9 S.Crotty (Antrim) 10 L.Power (Tipperary Cidona) all same time

**General Classification:** 1 S.Kennedy (Kerry AIF) 24.24.58 2 B.Power (Tipperary Cidona) at 1.02 3 H.Willer (Germany) at 5.44 4 H.Krins (Holland) at 6.06 5 D.Devin (Meath Sheerin) at 6.14 6 H.Bernreider (Bavaria) at 6.27 7 S.O Hanlon (Dublin) at 6.30 8 J.O'Sullivan (Ireland) at 7.14 9 A.Kesters (Belgium) at 7.28 10 P.Flanagan (Ireland) at 7.33 11 W.von Hacht (Bavaria) at 9.16 12 N.Clarke (Ireland) at 10.42

**Points:** 1 A.Kesters 54 2 S.Kennedy 51 3 H.Willer 46

**Mountains:** 1 P.Crowley 8 2 equal P.Jansens, A.Hilgert and H.Willer, 6.

**International Team:** 1 Ireland 73.36.53 2 Germany 73.42.42 3 Holland 73.44.12

## STAGE 8

Albert Kesters (Belgium) won his third stage of the week, 88 miles from Warrenpoint to Balbriggan but Seamus Kennedy maintained his position in yellow and with over a minute in hand over Bobby Power looked fairly comfortable with only the final stage to go to win the RÁS.

The leader kept a close watch at the front and was up with the leaders all the way. He was just behind Willer who led over the first climb of the day at Windy Gap. It stayed that way all the way through Ardee, Collon and Navan, Duleek and over the final climb of the race at Bellewstown.

The winding roads over the final 20 miles were made for breakaways but Kennedy was letting nothing go and they all came together in the finish at Balbriggan where Kesters took the sprint from Von Hacht and Willer with Kennedy right up there in fourth place.

**Stage 8 Warrenpoint - Balbriggan 88 Mls.** 1 A.Kesters (Belgium) 3.27.36 2 W.von Hacht (Bavaria) 3 H.Willer (Bavaria) 4 S.Kennedy (Kerry AIF) 5 H.de Hey (Holland) 6 S.O Hanlon (Dublin) 7 G.Costello (Limerick Kentucky) 8 E.Connolly (Meath Tayto) 9 W.Laechel (Bavaria) 10 R.Decaup (France) all same time

**General Classification:** 1 S.Kennedy (Kerry AIF) 27.52.34 2 B.Power (Tipperary Cidona) at 1.02 3 H.Willer (Bavaria) at 5.44 4 H.Krins (Holland) at 6.06 5 D.Devin (Meath Sheerin) at 6.14 6 H.Bernreider (Bavaria) at 6.27 7 S.O Hanlon (Dublin) at 6.30 8 J.O'Sullivan (Ireland) at 7.14 9 A.Kesters (Belgium) at 7.28 10 P.Flanagan (Ireland) at 7.33 11 W.von Hacht (Bavaria) at 9.16 12 N.Clarke (Ireland) at 10.42

**Points:** 1 A.Kesters 66 2 S.Kennedy 60 3 H.Willer 56

**International Team:** 1 Ireland 83.59.41 2 Germany 84.05.30 3 Holland 84.07.00

**County Team:** 1 Meath Tayto 84.21.38 2 Tipperary Cidona 84.36.42 3 Kerry AIF 84.41.198

## STAGE 9

The final stage saw little action and the 77 riders left in the race came into Phoenix Park together. The only break of consequence was by Dutchman Henk de Hey who opened up a lead of 1 minute at Dunshaughlin but he was soon back in the bunch.

There were 15 laps of the 2 mile circuit scheduled but as roadworks had necessitated an extra nine miles on the run-in the organisers decided to cut the circuits to ten because of the wet and greasy condition of the circuit.

In the end it came down to a bunch sprint which went to Wolfgang von Hacht (Bavaria) from Henk de Hey (Holland) and point's leader Albert Kesters (Belgium).

Seamus Kennedy was safely in the bunch with no real threat to his yellow jersey during the stage. The 32-year-old's RÁS victory had come at his thirteenth attempt, 13 proving a lucky number for the Trim man as he also chalked up his 13th stage win during the week. He said at the finish that he had now won everything that he could and that he would retire at the end of the season.

After taking the lead in the team competition on Saturday, Ireland defended it over the last two stages and the efforts of Paddy Flanagan and Noel Clarke in that respect were of no small assistance to Kennedy in keeping the field together. Meath Tayto easily kept the county team title with a 15 minute lead over Tipperary Cidona.

Helmut Willer had some consolation for the loss of the yellow jersey running out an easy winner in the King of the Mountains while triple stage winner Albert Kesters had a decisive win the points.

**Stage 9 Balbriggan - Dublin 66 Mls.** 1 W.von Hacht (Bavaria) 2.30.00 2 H.de Hey (Holland) 3 A.Kesters (Belgium) 4 J.Wolter (Germany) 5 J.C.Lavignac (France) 6 R.Decaup (France) 7 J.Piavin (France) 8 E.Larrissey (Louth) 9 G.Costelloe (Limerick) 10 W.Lachel (Bavaria).

**General Classification:** 1 S.Kennedy (Kerry AIF) 30.22.34 2 B.Power (Tipperary Cidona) at 1.02 3 H. Willer (Bavaria) at 5.44 4 H.Krins (Holland) at 6.06 5 D.Devin (Meath Sheerin) at 6.14 6 H.Bernreider (Bavaria) at 6.27 7 S.O Hanlon (Dublin) at 6.30 8 J.O'Sullivan (Ireland) at 7.14 9 A.Kesters (Belgium) at 7.28 10 P.Flanagan (Ireland) at 7.33 11 W.von Hacht (Bavaria) at 9.16 12 N.Clarke (Ireland) at 10.42 13 F.Steuten (Holland) at 12.40 14 J.Wolter (Germany) at 12.55 15 H.Schwinger (Germany) at 12.09

**Points:** 1 A.Kesters 76 2 S.Kennedy 60 3 H.Willer 56

**Mountains:** 1 equal H.Willer 2 A.Kesters, Willer wins with better GC placing 3 equal D.Devin and S.Kennedy

**International Team:** 1 Ireland 91.29.41 2 Germany 91.35.30 3 Holland 91.37.00

**County Team:** 1 Meath Tayto 91.51.28 2 Tipperary Cidona 92.06.42 3 Kerry AIF 92.11.19

*Seamus Kennedy, 1978 Winner*

## 1979

There was a change of name in 1979 when the RÁS obtained overall sponsorship from the Health Education Bureau and the event was renamed the Health Race. However to most people, especially those involved it was still the RÁS.
It was a momentous year in the history of the event because of the agreement on intercompetition earlier in the year between the NCA, ICF and NICF and all three cycling associations had entered representative teams.
Rising star Stephen Roche on the ICF team was one of the pre-race favourites with some commentators going for Ballymena's Billy Kerr, riding for the NICF who had been second for the previous two years in the Tour of Ireland.
Also being mentioned as potential winners were defending champion Seamus Kennedy who was on the Ireland (NCA) team along with another past winner Paddy Flanagan.
The other visiting teams in the field were France, Belgium, Holland with past winner Fons Steuten and Germany who included Helmut Willer, the unlucky loser to Kennedy a year earlier.

### STAGE 1

Albert Penant, a 27-year-old builder from Charleroi won the opening stage comfortably beating Tony Lally (ICF) in a sprint from a group of eleven which went away after 30 miles of the 73 miles stage from Dublin to Longford.
From the racing start at Lucan the 114 starters had to contend with a strong headwind all the way as well as occasional heavy showers.
The race passed through the finish in Longford and then went on a 10 mile loop back to the town and it was only then that a chase was organised from the bunch and a group including Stephen Roche (ICF) and Shay O Hanlon (Dublin Erickson) and Dutchman T.V. Boxtel who just got to within a few second of the leaders at the finish with Boxtel taking eleventh place on the stage in the same time as the original break.
The bunch, including race favourite Billy Kerr (NICF) came home 1.36 behind stage winner Penant.
**Stage 1 Dublin - Longford 73 Mls.** 1 A.Penant (Belgium) 2.54.06 2 T.Lally (ICF) 3 C.Nulty (Wicklow) 4 D.Devin (NCA Ireland) 5 J.Shortt (ICF) 6 equal S.Lally (Meath/Navan) P.Crowley (Cork) S.Kennedy (NCA Ireland) J.P.van Spauwen (Holland) J.Hegarty (Galway) T.V.Boxtel (Holland) all same time

## STAGE 2

Drogheda's Colm Nulty, riding for Wicklow, took over the lead after the 92 miles stage from Longford to Westport won by 19-year-old Stephen Roche (ICF) who won from a 5-man break which finished 24 seconds ahead of a 5-man chasing group.

The field fragmented over the final 12 miles and yellow jersey Albert Penant (Belgium) came in with a group 1.15 behind Roche dropping to eighth overall.

Nulty was equal on time overall with John Shortt (ICF) but took the jersey on stage placings. After his win Roche moved up to 3rd overall at 22 seconds.

Six riders went away just after the start including Alan McCormack (ICF), Ritchie McCormack (Dublin Erickson), and Cork riders Pat and Donal Crowley.

Pat Crowley punctured and dropped back and at Strokestown the leaders had 45 seconds on a chasing group with Roche, Mick Nulty (Wicklow) and Tony Lally (ICF).

The two groups merged and an 8-man group was 2.30 at Frenchpark but a few miles later this was down to 1.30 with Denis Devin, Paddy Flanagan and Billy Kerr doing much of the work in the bunch and a few miles further on they were all back in the bunch.

Aidan McKeown (NICF) attacked and went over a minute clear but he was caught at Ballinvary. Ten riders then went away and had a minute's lead at Castlebar. With 14 miles remaining Bernie McCormack (Wicklow) attacked and he was joined six miles later by Denis Brennan (Wicklow) and Pat Healy (Kerry) with the field closing fast.

With only three miles left five riders managed to break clear and they opened up a half-minute gap by the finish where Roche won the uphill sprint.

**Stage 2 Longford - Westport 92 Mls.** 1 S.Roche (ICF) 3.56.14 2 D.Brennan (Wicklow) 3 B.Kerr (NICF) 4 P.Healy (Kerry) all same time 5 A.McKeown (NICF) at 2 secs 6 C.Nulty (Wicklow) at 24 secs 7 J.Moloney (Meath) 8 J.Shortt (ICF) 9 S.O Hanlon (Dublin Erickson) 10 R.McCormack (Dublin Erickson) all same time

**General Classification:** 1 C.Nulty (Wicklow) 6.50.42 2 J.Shortt (ICF) s.t. 3 S.Roche (ICF) at 22 secs 4 A.McKeown (NICF) at 24 secs 5 T.Lally (ICF) at 38 secs 6 S.Lally (Meath Navan) s.t. 7 S.O Hanlon (Dublin Erickson) at 46 secs 8 A.Pennant (Belgium) at 48 secs 9 J.P.van Spauwen (Belgium) at 1.01 secs 10 B.Kerr (NICF) at 1.12 11 D.Devin (Ireland) at 1.16 12 S.Kennedy (Ireland) s.t.

## STAGE 3

John Shortt, the '78 Tour of Ireland winner, took over the yellow jersey after finishing 9th into Ennis, with the same time as stage winner Bernie McCormack (Wicklow), and led the race by 12 seconds from ICF team-mate Stephen Roche.

The pair was part of an 8-man break which was away for the final 54 miles of the 94 miles stage from Westport. This leading eight were joined by a chasing group of seven, including the stage winner, at Gort, with 20 miles to go.

The stage was over mainly flat roads and the field had the wind on their backs all the way. Five riders: Anthony O'Halloran and Michael Breen (Kerry B), Peter Morton (Wicklow), Billy Kennedy (Tipperary) and John McCormack (Dublin Kellys) went away early on and they had a 40 second lead over three chasers: John Shortt, Michael Nulty (Wicklow) and Brian Stevenson (NICF) at the Partry prime, taken by Peter Morton (ICF). A few miles further on the two groups merged
After 30 miles their lead was 2 minutes and going through Galway at half distance is was up to 2.45 with Short race-leader on the road as his team mates Tony Lally and Alan McCormack controlled any attacks out of the bunch.
However after 65 miles a group of seven did get away including Roche and Bernie McCormack and they got up to the leaders with 20 miles to go. At Crusheen, with 12 miles left the big leading group's lead was 2.20 and they were working well.
Over the final miles the pace told on some of the leading group and gaps opened with only the first five finishing in the same time as the winner although 10 seconds covered the first ten.
In a very fast sprint McCormack got the verdict from Peter Morton with Brian Stevenson third.
**Stage 3 Westport - Ennis 94 Mls.** 1 B.McCormack (Wicklow) 3.25.38 2 P.Morton (Wicklow) 3 B.Stevenson (NICF) 4 S.Roche (ICF) 5 P.Flanagan (Ireland) all same time 6 A.Kesters (Belgium) at 3 secs 7 M.Nulty (Wicklow) 8 E.Connolly (Meath Tayto) 9 J.Shortt (ICF) 10 K.Reilly (Meath Tayto) all same time
**General Classification:** 1 J.Shortt (ICF) 10.16.30 2 S.Roche (ICF) at 12 secs 3 P.Morton (Wicklow) at 1.37 4 P.Flanagan (Ireland) at 2.04 5 B.Stevenson (NICF) at 2.42 6 E.Connolly (Meath Tayto) at 2.52 7 M.Nulty (Wicklow) s.t. 8 A.Kesters (Belgium) at 3.05 9 M.Breen (Kerry) at 3.09 10 T.Lally (ICF) at 4.15 11 S.Lally (Meath Navan) s.t. 12 J.Maloney (Meath Navan) at 4.23
**Points:** 1 S.Roche 27 2 J.Shortt 26 3 C.Nulty 23
**National Teams:** 1 Ireland 31.01.20 2 Belgium 31.03.00 3 Holland 31.08.21
**Regional Teams:** 1 ICF 30.00.52 2 NICF A 30.03.00 3 NICF B 31.35.48
**County Teams:** 1 Wicklow 30.52.09 2 Meath Sherlock 31.00.37 3 Kerry B 31.01.36

## STAGE 4

Former professional Alan McCormack (ICF) was first home on the 95 miles fourth stage from Ennis to Cahirciveen winning in a three-man sprint to the line from Billy Kerr (NICF). McCormack's teammate Stephen Roche was third but took over the race lead.
The three came home 3.24 over three chasers, Robbie Phillips (Galway), Helmut Willer (Germany) and Mick Nulty (Wicklow). The yellow jersey, John Shortt (ICF), came in next in a seven man group, led in by Paddy Flanagan (Ireland) a further 1.14 behind.
With a very strong headwind and two big climbs at Knockawaddera and Coomanaspig, the field was completely broken up.

Roche got away on the Knockawadders climb, after Tralee and was joined by Kerr and McCormack.Willer, Phillips and Nulty went in pursuit but were never able to get up to the strong leading trio who increased their advantage all the way to the finish.
**Stage 4 Ennis - Cahirciveen (neutralised to Tarbert) 95 Mls.** 1 A.McCormack (ICF) 3.55.44 2 B.Kerr 9NICF) 3 S.Roche (ICF) all same time 4 R.Phillips (Galway) at 3.24 5 H.Willer (Germany) 6 M.Nulty (Wicklow) all same time 7 P.Flanagan at 4.38 8 J.C.Breure (France) 9 C.Nulty (Wicklow) 10 B.McCormack (Wicklow) all same time
**General Classification:** 1 S.Roche (ICF) 14.12.26 2 J.Shortt (ICF) at 4.26 3 A.McCormack (ICF) at 4.58 4 B.Kerr (NICF) at 5.36 5 M.Nulty (Wicklow) at 6.04 6 P.Flanagan (Ireland) at 6.30 7 E.Connolly (Meath Tayto) at 7.56 8 A.Kesters (Belgium) at 7.58 9 B.McCormack (Wicklow) at 8.55 10 B.Stevenson (NICF) at 9.48

## STAGE 5

Peter Morton (Wicklow) led in an 11-man group at the end of the 90 miles stage from Cahirciveen to Mallow but with race leader Roche finishing in third place in the same time there was no change in the overall classification. Hands off the bars as he crossed the line, an offence at that time in the NCA. There was a warning from race director Dignam that the next time it happened the offending rider would be placed last on GC.
The group finished 2.41 ahead of a chasing group of three with the bunch at 5.05, Roche increasing his advantage over most of the field with 7th overall Paddy Flanagan now over 9 minutes back.
He defended well going with every break and was looking very much like a winner even with four stages still remaining. One of his main rivals and pre-race favourite, Billy Kerr (NICF) punctured with 14 miles to go and broke his glasses when hit with a stone thrown up from the road but he quickly rejoined the break finishing 8th. JC Breure (France) also punctured and rejoined the break.
A casualty was Paudi O'Shea (Kerry) who crashed on the dangerous descent from Ballaghasheen and had to be taken to hospital. One of the Dutch riders came down in the same crash and retired from the race.
On the descent the field was fragmented but there was a general regroupment as the roads levelled out. At Killarney there were 21 riders 1.45 ahead of the bunch. Alan McCormack and Colm Nulty went away but were soon joined by Roche and Kerr with several other groups coming up to what became the break of the day.
**Stage 5 Caherciveen - Mallow 90 Mls.** 1 P.Morton (Wicklow) 3.32.37 2 T.Lally (ICF) 3 S.Roche (ICF) 4 J.Shortt (ICF) 5 J.C.Breure (France) 6 C.Nulty (Wicklow) 7 A.McCormack (ICF) 8 B.Kerr (NICF) 9 A.McKeown (NICF) 10 M.Nulty (Wicklow) all same time
**General Classification:** 1 S.Roche (ICF) 17.45.03 2 J.Shortt (ICF) at 4.26; 3 A.McCormack (ICF) at 4.58 4 B.Kerr (NICF) at 5.36 5 M.Nulty (Wicklow) at 6.04 6

E.Connolly (Meath Tayto) at 7.56 7 P.Flanagan (Ireland) at 9.35 8 J.C.Breure (France) at 10.05 9 A.McKeown (NICF) at 10.25 10 T.Lally (ICF) at 10.41
**Points:** 1 S.Roche 53 2 J.Shortt 41 3 C.Nulty 40
**Mountains:** 1 A.McCormack 7 2 C.Nulty 5 3 B.Kerr and O.McQuaid 4

## STAGE 6

Frenchman Jean Claude Breure won the sixth stage from Mallow to Carrick on Suir after Oliver McQuaid (ICF) gave him a perfect lead-out from the 1 km. mark. Breure was with two ICF riders, McQuaid and Alan McCormack who should have had the stage sewn up but McQuaid thought the finish was closer and went too early gifting the stage to the Frenchman.
McCormack, who finished second, moved up on GC taking over second place from teammate Shortt. Roche still led but his margin over the second placed rider dropped from 4.26 to 3.13 but with the ICF holding the top three places overall he still looked comfortable.
With a tailwind the riders had a comparatively easy day. Just after the start Bernie McCormack (Wicklow) and Denis McCarthy went and after 30 miles they led the bunch by 2.20. McCormack led over the Vee and continued on his own 2.15 ahead of the bunch but by Cahir he was joined by Eugene Smith (Wexford).
With Roche and the ICF team chasing the lead came down and at Clonmel the leading two were just in front and on the climb outside the town they were caught and dropped as Oliver McQuaid went away to be joined by McCormack and Breure, the three going clear and by the bottom of the descent they had 1.20 in hand which they held to the finish.
**Stage 6 Mallow - Carrick-on-Suir 90 Mls.** 1 J.C.Breure (France) 3.28.00 2 A.McCormack (ICF) 3 O.McQuaid (ICF) all same time 4 T.Lally (ICF) at 1.45 5 D.Devin (Ireland) 6 F.Riordan (Dublin Kellys) 7 A.Hilgert (Germany) 8 J.Shortt (ICF) 9 S.Kennedy (Ireland) 10 S.Roche (ICF) all same time
**General Classification:** 1 S.Roche (ICF) 21.14.18 2 A.McCormack (ICF) at 3.13 3 J.Shortt (ICF) at 4.26 4 B.Kerr (NICF) at 5.36 5 M.Nulty (Wicklow) at 6.04 6 E.Connolly (Meath Tayto) at 7.56 7 J.C.Breure (France) at 8.50 8 C.Nulty (Wicklow) at 9.32 9 P.Flanagan (Ireland) at 9.35 10 A.McKeown (NICF) at 10.55
**Points:** 1 S.Roche 58 2 J.Shortt 48 3 T.Lally 44
**Mountains:** 1 O.McQuaid 11 2 A.McCormack 10 3 C.Nulty and B.McCormack 5

## STAGE 7

Bernard McCormack (Wicklow) had his second stage win into Tullamore after a 93 miles stage from Carrick-on-Suir coming home on his own 2.42 ahead of German Axel Hilgert with a bunch of 33 led in by Tony Lally (ICF) another 2 minutes behind.

With Roche and most of his rivals in this group there was no change overall as McCormack was well back in 54th place overall. The bunch sprint was so close that in those pre photo-finish days only 5 were placed.
The bunch was still all together until the climb at The Butts where Billy Kerr (NICF) was first over from Alan McCormack (NICF) and Mick Nulty (Wicklow).
These three were joined by a group of 18 just before the 40 mile mark and with all the top men there it looked like they would stay away. But by Abbeyleix the field had regrouped.
Brendan Madden (Galway) went away and was joined by Bernie McCormack and they were being chased by Hilgert on his own.
On the climb over the Cones, Madden dropped back leaving McCormack to continue on his own to take the stage with the German also doing a solo ride to take second.
**Stage 7 Carrick-on-Suir - Tullamore 93 Mls.** 1 B.McCormack (Wicklow) 4.14.10 2 A.Hilgert (Germany) at 2.42 3 T.Lally (ICF) at 4.27 4 O.McQuaid (ICF) 5 J.Shortt (ICF) 6 D.Devin (Ireland) 7 A.Kesters (Belgium) all same time (Only 7 placed)
**General Classification:** 1 S.Roche (ICF) 25.33.15 2 A.McCormack (ICF) at 3.13 3 J.Shortt (ICF) at 4.26 4 B.Kerr (NICF) at 5.36 5 M.Nulty (Wicklow) at 6.04 6 E.Connolly (Meath Tayto) at 7.56 7 J.C.Breure (France) at 8.50 8 C.Nulty (Wicklow) at 9.32 9 P.Flanagan (Ireland) at 9.35 10 A.McKeown (NICF) at 10.55
**Points:** 1 S.Roche 59 2 J.Shortt 59 3 T. Lally 57
**Mountains:** 1 A.McCormack 16 2 O.McQuaid 11 3 B.McCormack 10

## STAGE 8

Jean Claude Breure (France) won Saturday's 93 miles stage from Tullamore to Navan but yellow jersey Stephen Roche finished fourth to increase his overall lead going into the final day to 4.10 over teammate Alan McCormack.
McCormack went away on his own after 17 miles and going through Mullingar after 25 miles he had a lead of 40 seconds on the bunch but they were all back together at the start of the only climb of the day after Oldcastle.
Breure took off on the climb and was joined by Pat Healy (Kerry) and Roget Kesters (Belgium) closely followed by Tommy Mannion (Galway) and Paddy Flanagan (NCA Ireland).
Healy punctured and dropped back to a chasing group which included Roche and did well to finish 5th, just behind the Dubliner. However the two leaders stayed out in front eventually coming home 2.36 ahead of the chasers led in by Bernie McCormack (Wicklow) from Roche and Healy and these three in turn were 57 second ahead of a big chasing group of around 30 riders.
**Stage 8 Tullamore - Navan 93 Mls.** 1 J.C.Breure (France) 3.19.11 2 R.Kesters (Belgium) s.t. 3 B.McCormack (Wicklow) at 2.36 4 S.Roche (ICF) 5 P.Healy (Kerry) all same time 6 T.Lally (ICF) at 3.33 7 N.Clarke (Meath/Navan) 8 O.McQuaid (ICF) 9 J.Shortt (ICF) 10 D.Devin (NCA Ireland) all same time

**General Classification:** 1 S.Roche (ICF) 28.55.32 2 A.McCormack (ICF) at 4.10 3 equal J.Shortt (ICF) and J.C.Breure (France) at 5.11 5 B.Kerr (NICF A) at 6.24 6 M.Nulty (Wicklow) at 6.52 7 E.Connolly (Meath Tayto) at 8 C.Nulty (Wicklow) at 10.00 9 R.Kesters (Belgium) at 11.09 10 A.McKeown (NICF) A at 11.13 11 T.Lally (ICF) at 11.29 12 P.Flanagan (Ireland) at 12.17
**Points:** 1 S.Roche 72 2 T.Lally 67 3 J.Shortt and J.C.Breure 51
**Mountains:** 1 A.McCormack 16 2 O.McQuaid 11 3 B.McCormack 10

## STAGE 9 (a) and (b)

Billy Kerr at the time time-trial king was expected to take the Sunday morning 24 kms TT but Roche, showing the ability against the watch that would within a few years take him to victories in the Tour of France and Giro beat the Ballymena rider by 11 seconds with another multi time-trial championship winner Aidan McKeown (NICF) third 26 seconds behind the Dubliner.
Roche finished the trial with a broken spoke and buckled wheel. Peader O'Brien wrote in the Irish Press: 'It showed the determination of this young rider from whom much more will be heard!'
The afternoon stage was only 50 miles, starting in Navan and finishing with twelve laps of the 2-mile circuit in Phoenix Park and, barring accidents, was a formality for Roche who had increased his lead overall from 4.10 to 6.38 on Frenchman J.C. Breure who had finished fourth in the TT and moved up to second ahead of Alan McCormack.
The final stage went to Axel Hilgert (Germany) from Bernie McCormack (Wicklow) while Roche was third, the three finishing 40 seconds ahead. The main interest during the stage was the lap primes with two each going to Bernie McCormack and Roche. McCormack was first into the Park followed by Roche and Hilgert and the three worked to open a gap of nearly 1 minute on the bunch, easily off slightly on the final lap.
The ICF with 1st, 3rd and 5th easily took the Regional team award, 48 minutes better than France who won the International team while Wicklow were best county team.
Roche also won the point's classification and Alan McCormack the mountains.
**Stage 9a Navan 16 Mls. TT:** 1 S.Roche (ICF) 36.47 2 B.Kerr (NICF) 36.58 3 A.McKeown (NICF) 37.13 4 J.C.Breure (France) 37.31 5 M.Nulty (Wicklow) 38.02 6 J.Shortt (ICF) 38.09 7 H.WIller (Germany) 39.00 8 A.McCormack (ICF) and E.Connolly (Meath Tayto) and S.O Hanlon (Dublin Ericsson) all 39.15
**Stage 9b Navan - Dublin 50 Mls.** 1 A.Hilgert (Germany) 1.54.13 2 B.McCormack (Wicklow) 3 S.Roche (ICF) all same time 4 K.McInerney (Wexford) at 40 secs 5 H.de Hey (Holland) 6 F.Steuten (Holland) s.t. 7 W.Werner (Germany) at 43 secs 8 J.Shortt (ICF) 9 O.McQuaid (ICF) 10 B.Kerr (NICF) all same time
**General Classification:** 1 S.Roche (ICF) 31.26.23 2 J.C.Breure (France) at 6.54 3 A.McCormack (ICF) at 7.25 4 B.Kerr (NICF) at 7.31 5 J.Shortt (ICF) at 7.32 6 M.Nulty (Wicklow) at 9.13 7 E.Connolly (Meath Tayto) at 12.14 8 A.McKeown

(NICF) at 12.15 9 C.Nulty (Wicklow) at 13.48 10 R.Kesters (Belgium) at14.49 11 P.Flanagan (Ireland) at 16.15 12 T.Lally (ICF) at 17.12
**Points:** 1 S.Roche 85 2 J.Shortt 82 3 T.Lally 70
**Mountains:** 1 A.McCormack 16 2 O.McQuaid 11 3 B.McCormack 10
**International Teams:** 1 France 95.19.48 2 Ireland 95.20.24 3 Germany 95.45.00
**Regional:** 1 ICF 94.31.32 2 NICF A 94.47.59 3 NICF B 100.03.33
**County:** 1 Wicklow 94.42.21 2 Meath Sherlock 95.42.58

*Ireland's Stephen Roche, winner 1979*

## 1980

The Health Education Bureau sponsorship continued in 1980 with the RÁS again to be known as 'The Health Race'.
Over 100 riders were entered with five national teams. The fruits of the Tripartite Agreement were obvious in the first Ireland team in the race comprised of a joint selection from the three ruling bodies.
'99 winner Roche was refused permission to take part by his French club for whom he recorded a third win in five races that week. The Irish team was Billy Kerr, third the previous year, past winner Paddy Flanagan, Pat Healy of Killorglin and John Walsh of Carlow.
The international challenge was made up of Denmark Aer Lingus, Germany BMW, Scotland and Wales. The Kerry team included past winner John Mangan who had been racing in France for some years and a strong Dublin Kelly Carpets team included past winner Shay O Hanlon, and ICF internationals Alan McCormack and Pat McQuaid.
With the intercompetition well established, a large percentage of the entrants came from the greater Dublin area and there were entries from no less than eight Dublin teams while Meath, so long the dominant force, had three.

### STAGE 1

Alan McCormack (Dublin Kelly's Carpets) won the opening stage to Monaghan, seven seconds clear of Sean Lally (Dublin Kalkhoff) after he slipped away from the leading group in the final miles.
There was a crash with an oncoming car shortly after the start with about 20 riders coming down. The strong headwinds and frequent showers kept the field together despite continual breakaway attempts. There was a split in the field at Dundalk with a large front group forming which included about 45 riders and it was from this group that a break went away in the final 10 miles.
Ruairi O'Coilean (Meath Tirolia) a son of former RÁS rider Leo was on his own going through Castleblaney with 15 miles to go. He was chased by Sean Lally and Pat Healy (Ireland) just off the front of a group of 37.
With 10 miles to go McCormack. Lally, Healy and John Mangan (Kerry) got up to O Coilean. Healy dropped back to a chasing group of six while ex-pro. McCormack jumped away from the other three opening up a 7 second gap on Lally who led in the other three.
The chasers came in 38 seconds but the bunch, led in by Germany's Willer were 2.30 behind.
**Stage 1 Dublin - Monaghan 83 Mls.** 1 A.McCormack (Dublin Kellys Carpets) 3.13.00 2 S.Lally (Dublin Kalkhoff) at 7 secs 3 J.Mangan (Kerry) s.t. 4 R.O'Coilean

(Meath Tirolia) at 9 secs 5 A.Cunningham (Antrim) at 38 secs 6 W.Gibb (Scotland) 7 T.Lally (Dublin Kalkhoff) 8 B.Power (Tipperary) 9 P.Flanagan (Ireland) 10 P.Healy (Ireland) 11 J.Peterson (Germany BMW) all same time 12 H.Willer (Germany BMW) at 2.30
**Mountains:** 1 W. Gibb (Scotland) 2 J.Kynd (Denmark Aer Lingus)
**International Team:** 1 Ireland 9.42.19 2 Germany BMW 9.43.44 2 Denmark Aer Lingus 9.45.09
**County Team:** 1 Dublin Kellys Carpets 9.43.06 2 Meath Tirolia 9.43.15 3 Tipperary 9.46.31

## STAGE 2

Birmingham rider Neil Martin, riding for the Dublin South team, won the 98 miles stage to Strabane. He led in a group of three from Pat McQuaid (Dublin Kellys Carpets) and Billy Kerr (Ireland).
Sixteen seconds later Willy Gibb (Scotland) out sprinted his teammate Alistair Adams for fourth place while yellow jersey McCormack came home in sixth place, 42 seconds behind, to retain the lead.
It was a hard day with wind and rain and a fair amount of climbing along the Glenelly valley in the Sperrins with most of the real racing taking place over the final 30 miles.
Martin was in an early break of five riders which were away for 30 miles before being caught.
As the riders began the climb at Leaghsbridge, the good climbers were to the fore: Billy Kerr, Helmut Willer (Germany), John Mangan (Kerry), McCormack, McQuaid and Tony Lally who was unfortunate to puncture and drop back.
Willer took the KOH prime and on Koram Mountain, a few miles further on, Martin was first over from McQuaid and Kerr and these three forged ahead with the field well strung out behind them on the descent.
The trio stayed away to the finish with several small groups in pursuit and at the finish the other two had no answer to Martin's sprint.
**Stage 2 Monaghan - Strabane 98 Mls.** 1 N.Martin (Dublin South) 3.49.00 2 P.McQuaid (Dublin Kellys Carpets) 3 B.Kerr (Ireland) all same time 4 W.Gibb (Scotland) at 16 secs 5 A.Adams (Scotland) s.t. 6 A.McCormack (Dublin Kellys Carpets) at 42 secs 7 H.Willer (Germany BMW) at 43 secs 8 J Peterson (Germany BMW) s.t. 9 T.Lally (Dublin Kalkhoff) at 45 secs 10 J.Mangan (Kerry) s.t.
**General Classification:** 1 A.McCormack (Dublin Kellys Carpets) 7.02.42 2 W.Gibb (Scotland) at 12 secs 3 J.Mangan (Kerry) at 20 secs 4 J.Peterson (Germany BMW) at 49 secs 5 T.Lally (Dublin Kalkhoff) at 50 secs 6 equal B.Kerr (Ireland) and P.McQuaid (Dublin Kellys Carpets) at 1.21 8 H.Willer (Germany BMW) at 2.14 9 J.Walsh (Ireland) 2.33 10 T.Mannion (Galway) at 2.35
**Points:** 1 A.McCormack 26 2 W.Gibb 21 3 J.Mangan 18
**Mountains:** 1 N. Martin 4 2 equal H.Willer and P.McQuaid 3.

**International Team:** 1 Ireland 21.15.35 2 Germany 21.16.51 3 Scotland 21.20.56
**County Team:** 1 Dublin Kelly Carpets 21.14.50 2 Galway 21.20.21 3 Meath Tirolia 21.22.21

## STAGE 3

The first good weather of the week saw the riders racing through Donegal on an 86 miles stage to Dungloe which was won by Bobby Power (Tipperary) but with race leader McCormack 8th, only 8 seconds down, he retained the yellow jersey.
One of the pre-race favourites John Mangan of Kerry, who started the day in third place, had a series of misfortunes which saw him change bikes three times and he ended up losing over 5 minutes.
Shortly after the start a break of 13 went away and at Letterkenny, after 17 miles, the previous day's stage winner Neil Martin (Dublin South) left the leaders and went ahead on his own and opened up a gap of over 3 minutes.
It was a brave effort but there was too much power behind and by half distance at Dunfanaghy he was caught by the chasing group which contained McCormack, Kerr and McQuaid.
At Gweedore, with 26 miles to go, eight riders went away including Tony and Sean Lally (Dublin Kalkhoff), Jorg Peterson (Germany BMW), Dave Folland (Wales), John McQuaid (Dublin Falcon), Archie Cunningham (Antrim), Bernie McCormack (Dublin Kellys Carpets) and Power.
McCormack and Peterson punctured leaving six at the front and they were chased by a group which included Alan McCormack, Kerr and McQuaid who were at 1 minute with 8 miles to go but they had cut back the gap to a few seconds at the line where Power won the sprint up the long hill which is Dungloe's main street.
**Stage 3 Strabane - Dungloe 86 Mls.** 1 B.Power (Tipperary) 3.28.00 2 S.Lally (Dublin Kalkhoff) 3 J.McQuaid (Dublin Falcon) 4 T.Lally (Dublin Kalkhoff) all same time 5 A.Cunningham (Antrim) at 3 secs 6 D.Folland (Wales) at 4 secs 7 H.Willer (Germany) at 8 secs 8 A.McCormack (Dublin Kellys Carpets) 9 P.McQuaid (Dublin Kellys Carpets) 10 J.McManus (Scotland) all same time
**General Classification:** 1 A.McCormack (Dublin Kellys Carpets) 10.30.50 2 T.Lally (Dublin Kalkhoff) at 43 secs 3 equal B.Kerr (Ireland) and P.McQuaid (Dublin Kellys Carpets) at 1.21 5 equal H.Willer (Germany BMW) and J.Peterson (Germany BMW) at 2.14 7 B.Power (Tipperary) at 2.51 8 A.Cunningham (Antrim) at 2.54 9 S.Lally (Dublin Kalkhoff) at 3.19 10 T.Mannion (Galway) at 3.43
**Points:** 1 A.McCormack 34 2 equal T.Lally and S.Lally 28
**Mountains:** 1 N.Martin 4 2 equal H.Willer W. Gibb, P.McQuaid 3.
**International Team:** 1 Ireland 31.41.49 2 Scotland 31.50.14 3 Germany 31.56.42
**County Team:** 1 Dublin Kellys Carpets 31.40.39 2 Dublin Falcon 31.53.10 3 Dublin Kalkhoff 31.55.55

## STAGE 4

It seems ridiculous looking back after some 20 years but the issue of riders taking their hands off the bars in a victory salute, in contravention of the NCA's rule at the time, was a hot potato and generated many a controversy.
It came to prominence again on the fourth RÁS stage from Dungloe to Donegal Town when race leader and stage winner Alan McCormack comfortably won a 3-man sprint and when he crossed the line took both arms off and was promptly disqualified.
An appeal was lodged as riders were talking of possible protests and to everyone's relief the appeal was upheld.
The 74-mile stage had taken the riders over some very hilly country. An early break of 20 riders formed and they stayed out in front until the serious climbing started with the notorious Glengesh Pass.
Neil Martin (Dublin South) led over the top and on the descent was joined by McCormack, Billy Kerr (Ireland) and Jorg Peterson (Germany BMW).
These four were together at Glencolmcille, the half-way point of the stage but his early efforts took their toll on Martin and he dropped back.
The three stretched out their lead with the only real chase coming from Alistair Adams (Scotland) who was nearly four minutes behind the trio at the finish while John Mangan led in a 6-man group 4.13 behind the stage winner.
**Stage 4 Dungloe - Donegal 74 Mls.** 1 A.McCormack (Dublin Kellys Carpets) 3.02.00 2 J.Peterson (Germany BMW) 3 B.Kerr (Ireland) all same time 4 A.Adams (Scotland) at 3.39 5 J.Mangan (Kerry) at 4.13 6 D.Folland (Wales) 7 B.McCormack (Dublin Kellys Carpets) 8 J.Hansen (Denmark) 9 N.Martin (Dublin South) 10 M.Nulty (Meath Kellys) all same time
**General Classification:** 1 A.McCormack (Dublin Kelly Carpets) 13.32.50 2 B.Kerr (Ireland) at 1.21 3 J.Peterson (Germany BMW) at 2.14 4 T.Lally (Dublin Kalkhoff) at 6.33 5 P.McQuaid (Dublin Kelly Carpets) at 7.11 6 H.Willer (Germany BMW) at 8.04 7 A.Cunningham (Antrim) at 7.44 8 M.Nulty (Meath Kellys) at 8.03 9 J.Mangan (Kerry) at 8.35 10 J.Walsh (Ireland) at 9.48 11 J.Hansen (Denmark) at 10.02 12 J.McManus (Scotland) at 10.14
**Points:** 1 A.McCormack 49 2 T.Lally 33 3 B. Kerr 32
**Mountains:** 1 N.Martin 13 2 A.McCormack 8 3 B.Kerr 6
**International Team:** 1 Ireland 41.00.29 2 Scotland 41.13.23 3 Germany BMW 41.14.12
**County Team:** 1 Dublin Kellys Carpets 40.56.42 2 Dublin Kalkhoff 41.20.31 3 Meath Kellys 41.20.57

## STAGE 5

There was a major upset on the 94 miles run to Roscommon as race leader Alan McCormack dropped off the back at Sligo, half-way through the stage and obviously

in great distress toiled on to finish 40 minutes down. Second-placed Billy Kerr took over the yellow jersey.
Earlier a similar fate seemed to be happening to another favourite, John Mangan but he managed to recover and fight his way back to the bunch.
At Ballyshannon, about 12 miles after the start, 15 riders went away with Pat McQuaid (Dublin Kellys Carpets) the only highly placed rider there. Going through Sligo their lead was 1.30 on the chasing group where Kerr and a now recovered Mangan were doing most of the work.
Shortly afterwards McCormack dropped back to his team car for a hot drink and it looked as though he was going to abandon but he decided to carry on.
Up front the leaders still had 1.30 in hand but when McQuaid was informed of McCormack's illness he started to work and the break looked destined to succeed. Ruairi O'Coilean (Meath Tirolia) and Werner Forster (Germany BMW) dropped back leaving 13 at the front.
So it stayed to the finish where McQuaid won the sprint as the 13 finished 1.30 ahead of the chasers led in by Jan Hansen (Denmark Aer Lingus) from John Mangan.
**Stage 5 Donegal - Roscommon 94 Mls.** 1 P.McQuaid (Dublin Kellys Carpets) 3.28.00 2 K.Fisch (Denmark Aer Lingus) 3 J.Walsh (Ireland) 4 B.Madden (Galway) 5 T.Mannion (Galway) 6 P.Tansey (Dublin B.L.) 7 equal W.Gibb (Scotland) D.Folland (Wales) S.Lally (Dublin Kalkhoff) T.Murphy (Dublin Kalkhoff) M.Kelly (Dublin Falcon) M.Nulty (Meath Kellys) and B.Power (Tipperary) all same time
**General Classification:** 1 B.Kerr (Ireland) 17.03.41 2 J.Peterson (Germany BMW) at 53 secs 3 P.McQuaid (Dublin Kellys Carpets) at 4.20 4 M.Nulty (Meath Kellys) at 6.12 5 J.Walsh (Ireland) at 6.57 6 A.Cunningham (Antrim) at 7.23 7 S.Lally (Dublin Kalkhoff) at 7.31 8 B.Power (Tipperary) at 11.33 9 J.Mangan (Kerry) at 8.13 10 J.Hansen (Denmark Aer Lingus) at 8.41 11 J.McManus (Scotland) at 8.53 12 W.Gibb (Scotland) at 10.03
**Points:** 1 A.McCormack 49 2 P. McQuaid 37 3 S.Lally 34
**Mountains:** 1 N.Martin 13 2 A.McCormack 8 3 B.Kerr 7
**International Team:** 1 Ireland 51.27.29 2 Scotland 51.40.23 3 equal Germany and Wales 51.49.59
**County Team:** 1 Dublin Kalkhoff 51.53.08 2 Galway 51.54.13 3 Meath Kellys 51.55.14

## STAGE 6

The hand-off controversy would not go away and this time it was Pat McQuaid who was penalised after winning the 105 miles stage to Thurles.
He was initially disqualified but this was reduced to a 3 minute penalty and loss of the stage win which went to second placed John Mangan (Kerry). Billy Kerr retained the yellow jersey.
McQuaid was part of a 17 man group which went away at the half-way point. Also there were highly placed John Mangan (Kerry), Mick Nulty (Meath Kellys) and John

Walsh (Ireland) and as well as Mangan, three other past RÁS winners: Shay O Hanlon (Dublin Kelly Carpets); Colm Nulty (Meath Kellys) and Brian Connaughton (Meath Tirolia).
Earlier Mangan, Nulty and Walsh were away with Alan McCormack who seemed to have recovered from the sickness which lost him the jersey the previous day but it soon became apparent that he was still weak and he retired from the race.
Around Birr (55 miles) the leaders were joined by a 15-man chasing group who in turn were 1.30 ahead of a second chasing group of eight.
Ruairi O'Coilean, who had been plagued with punctures during the week suffered another deflation and lost his place with the leaders. Nulty also punctured but got a bike from teammate Phil Cassidy who did well to get back up to the leaders at Thurles, with 30 miles to go.
The bunch containing Kerr and Peterson finally woke up to the danger when the break went to five minutes and a chase began in earnest which cut the lead to three minutes at the finish.
McQuaid looked out of it when he punctured with 10 miles to go but he got back to the break with just a mile to the finish in time to launch a winning sprint although he was somewhat lucky as Mangan pulled his foot out of the pedal 50 metres from the line.
His effort was in vain. He would have known, after the warnings from the race officials following McCormack's hand-off earlier in the week, that he risked disqualification but the adrenalin charge following his successful chase and sprint win, must have caused him to throw caution to the winds. As a result of the penalty he dropped from 3rd to 5th place on the general classification with the same time gap as he had starting the day instead of becoming a real threat to the jersey. He also lost out on taking the lead in the point's classification.
**Stage 6 Roscommon - Thurles 105 Mls.** 1 J.Mangan (Kerry) 3.40.00 2 M.Kelly (Dublin Falcon) 3 D.Folland (Wales) 4 A.Adams (Scotland) 5 J.Walsh (Ireland) 6 B.Connaughton (Meath Tirolia) 7 M.Nulty (Meath Kellys) 8 equal K.Jones (Wales) J.O'Sullivan (Cork) P.Mahon (Dublin South) S.O Hanlon (Dublin Kellys Carpets) B.Madden (Galway) K.Dowd (Kerry) E.Connolly (Meath Tayto) C.Nulty (Meath Kellys) P.Cassidy (Meath Kellys)
**General Classification:** 1 B.Kerr (Ireland) 20.46.39 2 J.Peterson (Germany BMW) at 53 secs 3 M.Nulty (Meath Kellys) at 3.14 4 J.Walsh (Ireland) at 3.59 5 P.McQuaid (Dublin Kellys Carpets) at 4.20 6 J.Mangan (Kerry) at 5.16 7 A.Cunningham (Antrim) at 7.23 8 A.Adams (Scotland) at 7.25 9 S.Lally (Dublin Kalkhoff) at 7.31 10 B.Power (Tipperary) at 7.33 11 J.Hansen (Denmark Aer Lingus) at 8.41 12 J.McManus (Scotland) at 8.53
**Points:** 1 J. Mangan 46 2 A.Adams 39 3 P.McQuaid 37
**Mountains:** 1 N.Martin 13 2 B.Kerr 7 3 M.Nulty 4
**International Team:** 1 Ireland 62.33.25 2 Scotland 62.46.19 3 Wales 62.52.57
**County Team:** 1 Meath Kellys 62.55.14 2 Galway 63.00.09 3 Dublin Kalkhoff 63.02.02

## STAGE 7

Birmingham rider Neil Martin, riding for the Dublin South team, winner of stage 2, who had continued in the race against doctor's advice after dislocating his shoulder on Wednesday's stage, had his reward when he came home on his own to win the seventh stage, from Thurles to Gorey.

He finished 15 seconds ahead of a 3-man group led in by Bernie McCormack (Dublin Kellys Carpets) but race-leader Kerr came home with the main bunch that sprinted for 7th place, 30 seconds behind the stage winner so there were no big changes on overall.

Kerr was happy to sit near the front all day, countering breakaway attempts and ensuring that those who did manage to get clear never got too far away and neither Peterson nor Nulty, his closest challengers, were ever out of his sight.

The high speed of the stage also helped to keep the field together and the 92 miles were covered in 3.18. Donal Crowley (Cork) bravely went off on his own early on and although his effort was doomed he stayed away long enough to take the prime at Kilkenny.

Galway pair Brendan Madden and Tommy Mannion went away with Sean Lally (Dublin Kalkhoff) and Paul Tansey (Dublin BL Cars) then had a go but their gap hovered around the 30 second mark for a long time before they too were brought back and the field was all together with 10 miles to go.

Bernie McCormack then went and was chased by John Mangan and Phil Cassidy in turn pursued by Neil Martin and Eamon Connolly. As they came together with 4 miles to go Martin went for home and opened a 15 second gap by the finish.

**Stage 7 Thurles - Gorey 92 Mls.** 1 N.Martin (Dublin South) 3.18.00 2 B.McCormack (Dublin Kellys carpets) at 15 secs 3 J.Mangan (Kerry) at 16 secs 4 E.Connolly (Meath Tayto) s.t. 5 P.Cassidy (Meath Kellys) at 23 secs 6 P.Tansey (Dublin BL Cars) s.t. 7 M.Kelly (Dublin Falcon) at 30 secs 8 W.Gibb (Scotland) 9 T.Lally (Dublin Kalkhoff) s.t.

**General Classification:** 1 B.Kerr (Ireland) 24.05.09 2 J.Peterson (Germany BMW) at 53 secs 3 M.Nulty (Meath Kellys) at 3.14 4 J.Walsh (Ireland) at 3.59 5 P.McQuaid (Dublin Kellys Carpets) at 4.20 6 J.Mangan (Kerry) at 5.03 7 A.Cunningham (Antrim) at 7.23 8 A.Adams (Scotland) at 7.25 9 S.Lally (Dublin Kalkhoff) at 7.31 10 B.Power (Tipperary) at 7.33 11 J.Hansen (Denmark Aer Lingus) at 8.41 12 E Connolly (Meath Tayto) at 8.51

**Points:** 1 J.Mangan 59 2 T.Lally 40 3 equal A.Adams and D.Folland 39

**Mountains:** 1 N.Martin 13 2 B.Kerr 7 3 M.Nulty 4

**International Team:** 1 Ireland 72.33.30 2 Scotland 72.41.49 3 Wales 72.48.27

**County Team:** 1 Meath Kellys 72.50.30 2 Galway 72.55.39 3 Dublin Kalkhoff 72.57.32

## STAGE 8

Billy Kerr not only held on to his yellow jersey, with just one day to go, but he did it in the best possible way, winning the stage from his closest rival Jorg Peterson (Germany BMW) and he maintained his lead over the German by 53 seconds. With a fairly straightforward final stage from Carlow to Phoenix Park on the Sunday, it looked all over, barring accidents.
Despite three tough climbs in the Wicklow Mountains nearly all the top riders on GC finished with the leaders with the exception of John Walsh (Ireland) who dropped back to 8th overall.
John Mangan looked on his way to a stage win when he was out on his own with just 10 miles to go but he crashed on a corner and was caught by the field.
Kerr then went away with Peterson and Mick Nulty (Meath Kellys) and they opened up a gap of 43 seconds by the finish where the chasers were led in a blood stained John Mangan.
Earlier Kerr brushed aside any pretenders to his crown when he and Peterson got up to a leading quartet including Scottish pair Alistair Adams and Jim McManus along with Brendan Madden (Galway) and Colm Nulty (Meath Kellys) on the climb at Drumgoff.
Kerr went straight past with the German struggling to hold him and he was first over the top. He and Peterson stayed out in front and hit the foot of the Wicklow Gap together. Kerr was again first to the top, clinching the mountains classification but then, with all the major difficulties over, he relaxed and the leading pair was joined by a chasing group of 11 with 25 miles to go.
Scotland was rewarded for their aggression by taking over the lead from Ireland in the team race. Double stage winner Neil Martin finally succumbed to his injuries and pulled out of the race.
**Stage 8 Gorey - Carlow 86 Mls.** 1 B.Kerr (Ireland) 3.48.00 2 J.Peterson (Germany BMW) s.t. 3 M.Nulty (Meath Kellys) at 2 secs 4 J.Mangan (Kerry) at 43 secs 5 H.Willer (Germany BMW) 6 P.McQuaid (Dublin Kelly Carpets) 7 D.Folland (Wales) 8 E.Connolly (Meath Tayto) 9 A.Adams (Scotland) 10 J.McManus (Scotland) all same time
**General Classification:** 1 B.Kerr (Ireland) 27.53.09 2 J.Peterson (Germany BMW) at 53 secs 3 M.Nulty (Meath Kellys) at 3.16 4 P.McQuaid (Dublin Kelly Carpets) at 5.03 5 J.Mangan (Kerry) at 5.45 6 A.Cunningham (Antrim) at 8.06 7 A.Adams (Scotland) at 8.09 8 J.Walsh (Ireland) at 9.15 9 E.Connolly (Meath Tayto) s.t. 10 J.McManus (Scotland) at 9.56 11 D.Folland (Wales) at 10.09 12 C.Nulty (Meath Kellys) at 11.01
**Points:** 1 J.Mangan 71 2 D.Folland 48 3 equal B.Kerr and P.McQuaid 47
**Mountains:** 1 B.Kerr 17 2 J.Peterson 11 3 A.Adams 8
**International Team:** 1 Scotland 84.10.34 2 Ireland 84.13.37 3 Wales 84.21.55
**County Team:** 1 Meath Kellys 84.18.34 2 Galway 84.31.43 3 Dublin Kellys Carpets 84.36.16

## STAGE 9

It was a victory procession for Kerr on the 50 miles run in from Carlow to the Phoenix Park with Peterson never getting as much as a few yards ahead of the Ballymena man.

As they entered the Park with twelve 2-mile laps to complete the 1980 RÁS a group of six went away: Noel Clarke (Meath Tirolia), Archie Cunningham (Antrim), Anthony O'Halloran (Kerry); Brendan Madden (Galway); Jim McManus (Scotland) and Neil Hodge (Wales).

The lead stayed at around 40 seconds as some riders joined the leaders and others dropped back to the bunch but entering the final lap Paul Tansey (Dublin BL Cars), Madden, Kevin McInerney (Dublin South), Phillip Evans (Wales) and Martin Kelly (Dublin Falcon) were in the lead and stayed out in front to contest the sprint where Kelly took the sprint.

Sean Lally led in the bunch containing all the contenders just 10 seconds later with Kerr adding the RÁS to his impressive list of victories which included the Sealink International the previous year.

John Mangan won the points classification from Pat McQuaid, Kerr won the mountains, and Scotland maintained their lead over Ireland in the International Team while Meath Kellys beat Galway in the County Team classification.

**Stage 9 Dublin - Carlow 74 Mls.** 1 M.Kelly (Dublin Falcon) 3.09.12 2 K.McInerney (Dublin South) 3 P.Tansey (Dublin BL Cars) 4 P.Evans (Wales) 5 B.Madden (Galway) all same time 6 S.Lally (Dublin Kalkhoff) at 10 secs 7 K.Frisch (Germany BMW) 8 C.Moylan (Cork) 9 H.Willer (Germany BMW) 10 P.McQuaid (Dublin Kellys Carpets)

**General Classification:** 1 B.Kerr (Ireland) 31.02.31 2 J.Peterson (Germany BMW) at 53 secs 3 M.Nulty (Meath Kellys) at 3.16 4 P.McQuaid (Dublin Kelly Carpets) at 5.03 5 J.Mangan (Kerry) at 5.45 6 A.Cunningham (Antrim) at 8.06 7 A.Adams (Scotland) at 8.09 8 J.Walsh (Ireland) at 9.15 9 E.Connolly (Meath Tayto) s.t. 10 J.McManus (Scotland) at 9.56 11 D.Folland (Wales) at 10.09 12 C.Nulty (Meath Kellys) at 11.01

*Billy Kerr, winner '80*

**Points:** 1 J.Mangan 71 2 D.Folland 48 3 equal B.Kerr and P.McQuaid 47

**Mountains:** 1 B.Kerr 17 2 J.Peterson 11 3 A.Adams 8

**International Team:** 1 Scotland 93.38.40 2 Ireland 93.41.43 3 Wales 93.49.51

**County Team:** 1 Meath Kellys 93.46.40 2 Galway 93.59.39 3 Dublin Kellys Carpets 93.04.22

**Phoenix Park Primes:** P. Tansey (2); N. Clarke, A. O'Halloran, B. Madden, P. Evans

## 1981

There were 91 riders entered for the '81 RÁS which had a new sponsor and was known as the Tirolia RÁS. The previous year's winner Billy Kerr was not entered and two of the riders who had been prominent that year were being made pre-race favourites by the Press: Kerry's John Mangan and Belfast's Archie Cunningham, 5th and 6th respectively in 1980.

Mangan, a past winner who had raced successfully in France for a decade had rode the race for the first time in years the year before and in an all-out effort for victory was bringing his French club over to support him

Cunningham had also been something of a comeback rider but went on to win the '80 Tour of Ireland and the race was expected to be a duel between the two.

Mangan's team, riding as France, and Scotland, led by Jamie McGahan were the only visiting teams. Cunningham was leading an Ireland team which included another Tour of Ireland winner John Shortt and two other Ulster riders Aidan McKeown and Brendan Graham.

### STAGE 1

Norman Lindsay of Scotland won the opening stage, 80 miles from Dublin to Birr out sprinting Paddy Flanagan, riding for Meath Fiat, the 43-year-old past double winner showing he still was a force to be reckoned with.

The pair finished 35 seconds ahead of a group of seven led in by John Mangan from Archie Cunningham, justifying their mantle of pre-race favourites.

As usual on an opening stage it was all out action but nothing had been decided when Flanagan broke away with 35 miles to go. After a few miles he was joined by Martin Kelly (Dublin Falcon) and Adrian Byrne (Garda Beaver Bosch).

The three stayed out in front with their lead rising to a maximum 1.30. Then on the climb of Slieve Bloom the leaders were joined by Lindsay and John Shortt (Ireland) but Flanagan decided it was time to go again and he went away along with Lindsay and they opened a gap of 1 minute by the top of the climb which they held until near the finish when it was cut back by the seven chasers.

Behind the pursuing group the bunch was led in by Tony Lally (Dublin Kalkhoff) 1.51 behind the winner.

**Stage 1 Dublin - Birr 80 Mls.** 1 N.Lindsay (Scotland) 3.01.01 2 P.Flanagan (Meath Fiat) s.t. 3 J.Mangan (France) at 35 secs 4 A.Cunningham (Ireland) 5 G.Costelloe (Dublin Kalkhoff) 6 D.Gilleran (Dublin Falcon) 7 J.McGahan (Scotland) 8 A.Byrne (Beaver Bosch) 9 A.McKeown (Ireland) all same time 10 T.Lally (Dublin Kalkhoff) at 1.51

**International team:** 1 Scotland 9.5.26 2 Ireland 9.6.00 3 France 9.8.36.

**County team:** 1 Dublin Kalkhoff 9.7.50 2 Meath Tirolia 9.8.36 3 Galway 9.9.08

## STAGE 2

If few had thought of Norman Lindsay as a favourite before the race he was certainly much talked about after the 95 miles second stage to Listowel when he made it two in a row. However despite two stage wins he was still equal on time with Paddy Flanagan, the two of them 34 seconds ahead of eight riders all on equal time which included John Mangan and Archie Cunningham.

After his win on Saturday on a stage which included a stiff climb, Lindsay said he was surprised to be in the lead as he was mainly a sprinter and it was his sprinting which brought him his second success when he won a bunch sprint into a packed Listowel.

Kieran McQuaid (Dublin Falcon) was third ahead of Cousin John McQuaid (Cork Clonakilty) with Meath Tirolia pair Paul Tansey and Seamus Kennedy 4th and 5th and in the hectic bunch sprint in the days before photo-finish the judges could only place the first five with everyone else placed equal 6th.

Nine riders went away early on and stayed out in front for 65 miles. Present were Seamus Kennedy Bobby Power (Tipperary), Mick Nulty (Meath Fiat), Dermot Gilleran (Dublin Falcon); Ritchie McCormack (Meath Tayto), Fran Riordan (Dublin Dishgleam), John O'Sullivan (Cork Clonakilty), Michael McKenna (Dublin Kalkhoff) and Brendan Madden (Galway).

At the 35 miles mark they were over 5 minutes up and were working well. Going through Limerick, the half-way point their rhythm had gone and the lead started dropping and they were finally caught with 30 miles to go at Foynes.

John McQuaid went off on his own with 20 miles remaining and at Tarbert he was joined by five more including Pat McQuaid (Dublin Falcon), Tommy Mannion (Galway) and Tony Lally (Dublin Kalkhoff). With just six miles to go they had 40 seconds but they started to mess about with the inevitable result that they bunch closed and caught them with just one mile to go setting up a cavalry charge into the town where Lindsay proved that indeed he was a sprinter.

**Stage 2 Birr - Listowel 95 Mls.** 1 N.Lindsay (Scotland) 3.52.00 2 K.McQuaid (Dublin Falcon) 3 J.McQuaid (Cork Clonakilty) 4 P.Tansey (Meath Tirolia) 5 S.Kennedy (Meath Tirolia) all same time

**General Classification:** 1 N.Lindsay (Scotland) 6.53.00 2 P.Flanagan (Meath Fiat) s.t. 3 equal A.Cunningham (Ireland) A.McKeown (Ireland) J.Mangan (France) J.McGahan (Scotland) D.Gilleran (Dublin Falcon) G.Costello (Dublin Kalkhoff) A.Byrne (Garda Beaver Bosch) all at 34 secs 10 equal J.Shortt (Ireland) B.Graham (Ireland) O.Lafond (France) all at 52 secs

**International team:** 1 Scotland 20.41.26 2 Ireland 20.42.00 3 France 20.44.36

**County team:** 1 Dublin Kalkhoff 20.43.50 2 Meath Tirolia 20.44.36 3 Galway 20.45.08

## STAGE 3

It was Dublin Kalkhoff's day on stage 3 to Killorglin which was won by their rider Tony Lally while another of their riders, Gearoid Costelloe took over the yellow jersey.

Lally won a 10-up sprint from Paul Mahon (Dublin Dishgleam) and Seamus Kennedy (Meath Tirolia). Costelloe and Aidan McKeown (Ireland) were both in the break and they are equal on time at the top of the GC, 51 second ahead of ex-leader Norman Lindsay.

There was action from the start with two breaks brought back before Tralee but they were all together again after 20 miles at Tralee when 15 went away before the climb of the Conor Pass. On the climb the group split with Kevin McInerney (Dublin South), Paul Tansey and Seamus Kennedy (Meath Tirolia) and Tony Lally (Dublin Kalkhoff) moving ahead.

Gabriel Howard (Meath Tayto) and Philip Cassidy (Meath Fiat) left the bunch and got up to Lally and Kennedy while McInerney and Tansey went ahead over the top of the climb, McInerney taking the prime. Larry Power (Tipperary) also climbed well to get up to the leaders and on the descent they regrouped with seven at the front.

The bunch behind had also split on the climb and regrouped on the descent and from it Costelloe and Mahon went in pursuit of the leaders while behind them Aidan McKeown was chasing on his own. All three got across and the ten worked well together to build up a lead of 1.25 by the finish where Mahon led out the sprint only to be attacked on either side by Lally and Kennedy and while he held off Kennedy he just failed to beat Lally for the stage.

**Stage 3 Listowel - Killorglin 82 Mls.** 1 T.Lally (Dublin Kalkhoff) 3.15.00 2 P.Mahon (Dublin Dishgleam) 3 S.Kennedy (Meath Tirolia) 4 P.Tansey (Meath Tirolia) 5 K.McInerney (Dublin South) 6 L.Power (Tipperary) 7 G.Costelloe (Dublin Kalkhoff) 8 G.Howard (Meath Tayto) 9 A.McKeown (Ireland) 10 P.Cassidy (Meath Fiat) all same time

**General Classification:** 1 G.Costelloe (Dublin Kalkhoff) 10.08.34 2 A.McKeown (Ireland) s.t. 3 N.Lindsay (Scotland) at 51 secs 4 P.Flanagan (Meath Fiat) s.t. 5 S.Kennedy (Meath Tirolia) at 1.18 6 P.Tansey (Meath Tirolia) 7 T.Lally (Dublin Kalkhoff) all same time 8 J.Mangan (France) at 1.25 9 A.Cunningham (Ireland) 10 D.Gilleran (Dublin Falcon) 11 J.McGahan (Scotland) 12 A.Byrne (Garda) all same time

**Points:** 1 N.Lindsay 34 2 S.Kennedy 29 3 P.Tansey 24

**Mountains:** 1 equal N.Lindsay and K.McInerney 5 3 equal P.Flanagan and P.Tansey 3

**International team:** 1 Ireland 30.29.50 2 Scotland 30.30.41 3 France 30.43.51

**County team:** 1 Meath Tirolia 30.31.01 2 Cork 30.35.27 3 Dublin Falcon 30.46.45

## STAGE 4

John McQuaid (Cork Clonakilty) won the 104 miles stage to Clonakilty in a sprint finish from a 4-man group which included Ireland Aidan McKeown in fourth place and the Belfast man took over the lead with an advantage of 52 seconds over Gearoid Costelloe who lost the yellow jersey. After four stages around 2 minutes covered a top 10 which included most of the favourites.

The 104 miles stage to Bantry started with the Ring of Kerry and after a succession of unsuccessful early breaks it was not until the second major climb of the day at the Tunnel Road, just 20 miles from the finish, that the important action took place.

At that point Martin Kelly (Dublin Falcon), Mick Nulty (Meath Fiat) and Brendan Madden (Galway) were holding a 1 minute lead on the bunch. McKeown went to the front and started driving hard and by the top of the climb only Archie Cunningham, John Mangan and Jamie McGahan were still with him.

This quartet caught the three leaders on the descent, Nulty and Kelly unable to stay with them while John McQuaid with a courageous descent managed to bridge across to the front.

Mangan and Madden both punctured on the descent and were picked up by the chasing group. This left four at the front from which McQuaid won the sprint for the stage. The Dubliner had not been thought to have good enough pre-race form for his own Dublin Falcon team and had accepted the offer of a place on the Cork team.

**Stage 4 Killorglin - Bantry 104 Mls.** 1 J.McQuaid (Cork Clonakilty) 4.12.00 2 A.Cunningham (Ireland) s.t. 3 J.McGahan (Scotland) at 1 sec 4 A.McKeown (Ireland) at 5 secs 5 T.Mannion (Galway) at 54 secs 6 N.Lindsay (Scotland) at 57 secs 7 W.Gibb (Scotland) 8 S.Kennedy (Meath Tirolia) 9 P.McQuaid (Dublin Falcon) 10 R.McFarlane (Tipperary) all same time

**General Classification:** 1 A.McKeown (Ireland) 14.20.39 2 G.Costelloe (Dublin Kalkhoff) at 52 secs 3 A.Cunningham (Ireland) at 1.12 4 J.McGahan (Scotland) at 1.21 5 N.Lindsay (Scotland) at 1.43 6 P.Flanagan (Meath Fiat) s.t. 7 S.Kennedy (Meath Tirolia) at 2.10 8 P.Tansey (Meath Tirolia) s.t. 9 J.Mangan (France) at 2.17 10 D.Gilleran (Meath Falcon) s.t. 11 K.McInerney (Dublin South) at 2.42 12 T.Mannion (Galway) at 3.32

**Points:** 1 N.Lindsay 42 2 S.Kennedy 35 3 P.Tansey 24

**Mountains:** 1 P.Flanagan 8 2 equal N.Lindsay, M.Kelly and K.McInerney 5

**International Team:** 1 Ireland 43.07.52 2 Scotland 43.08.36 3 France 44.01.16

**County Team:** 1 Meath Tirolia 43.12.29 2 Dublin Falcon 43.15.36 3 Meath Fiat 43.23.31

## STAGE 5(a) and (b)

Aidan McKeown lost the lead to Paddy Flanagan on Wednesday morning's 65 miles stage to Clonakilty but Flanagan's hold on the yellow jersey was short as he in turn

lost it to Gearoid Costelloe after the evening criterium in the town, Costelloe regaining the jersey he had worn the previous day.
The morning's stage was won by Sean Lally (Dublin Kalkhoff) and Brother Tony, the stage winner on Monday, made it a family double when he won the evening stage.
It was veterans to the fore in the morning, 40-year-old Lally the stage winner and 43-year-old Flanagan taking the jersey. Six riders went away early but they never looked like staying away and they appeared to accept they were about to be caught at Skibbereen, the half-way point.
It was then they were joined by Flanagan and John O'Sullivan (Cork Clonakilty) and they put new life into the break which started to draw away.
With nine miles to go Mick Nulty and Paul Mahon dropped back from the leaders leaving six at the front. Brendan Madden (Galway) and John O'Sullivan also were dropped from the break but came home in front of the bunch. From the four survivors Lally out sprinted Seamus Reynolds (Meath Tirolia) for the stage win. Race leader McKeown dropped back to third.
**Stage 5a Bantry - Clonakilty 65 Mls.** 1 S.Lally (Dublin Kalkhoff) 2.42.00 2 S.Reynolds (Meath Tirolia) 3 P.Flanagan (Meath Fiat) 4 R.McCormack (Meath Tayto) all same time 5 B.Madden (Galway) at 1.02 6 J.O'Sullivan (Cork Clonakilty) at 1.04 7 J.McQuaid (Cork Clonakilty) at 1.57 8 J.Mangan (France) 9 P.Mahon (Dublin Dishgleam) 10 S.O Hanlon (Meath Tirolia)
Unlike most stage race criterium which end in bunch finishes with no big changes, on this occasion a big break which contained major contenders Archie Cunningham, Gearoid Costelloe Tony Lally and John Mangan caught lone breakaway Martin Kelly and they put enough time into the bunch for Costelloe to take back the jersey.
The others in the break all improved their positions and McKeown, who had started the day in yellow, dropped back to 7th.
In the sprint Tony Lally edged out Mangan Kennedy and Kelly to take his second stage victory.
**Stage 5b Clonakilty Criterium 25 Mls.** 1 T.Lally (Dublin Kalkhoff) 52.55 2 J.Mangan (France) 3 S.Kennedy (Meath Tirolia) 4 M.Kelly (Dublin Falcon) 5 P.Crowley (Cork Clonakilty) 6 P.McQuaid (Dublin Falcon) 7 A.Cunningham (Ireland) 8 J.McKenna (Louth/Meath) 9 T.Mannion (Galway) all same time
**General Classification:** 1 G.Costelloe (Dublin Kalkhoff) 17.57.58 2 P.Flanagan (Meath Fiat) at 28 secs 3 A.Cunningham (Ireland) s.t. 4 J.McGahan (Scotland) at 1.08 5 J.Mangan (France) at 1.25 6 S.Kennedy (Meath Tirolia) at 2.20 7 A.McKeown (Ireland) at 2.22 8 N.Lindsay (Scotland) at 2.32 9 P.Tansey (Meath Tirolia) at 3.11 10 P.McQuaid (Dublin Falcon) at 2.34
**Points:** 1 N.Lindsay 44 2 S.Kennedy 37 3 equal A.Cunningham and P.Flanagan 31.
**Mountains:** 1 P.Flanagan 9 2 equal N.Lindsay, K.McInerney, M.Kelly 5
**International Team:** 1 Ireland 51.21.19 2 Scotland 51.22.29 3 France 51.15.43
**County Team:** 1 Meath Tirolia 51.24.35 2 Dublin Falcon 51.30.03 3 Meath Fiat 51.35.41

## STAGE 6

Yet another yellow jersey change and again it went to a previous wearer when Ireland's Aidan McKeown retook the lead after losing it the previous day.
McKeown finished 10th on the stage in a 9-man group which finished 17 seconds behind stage winner Brendan Madden (Galway) who came in with Phil Cassidy (Meath Fiat). These pair, like McKeown, was part of a group of 12 which went away after only 2 miles of the stage and were never caught.
McKeown rode aggressively throughout the day and it was he who went up the road just 1 mile after the start. He was joined by 11 others and working well opened a 3 minute gap in only 20 miles.
McKeown Norman Lindsay and Pat McQuaid, having the most to gain were contributing most to the break but also present were three riders from the Tipperary team who were hoping to improve the team's standing in the County team classification. By Cork the lead was up to over 4 minutes despite the best efforts behind of Mangan and Cunningham and yellow jersey Costelloe.
At Dungarvan Cassidy attacked from the break and looked on course for the stage win but he overshot a hairpin bend on the descent which allowed Madden to join him and the Galway man had the edge in the sprint.
It was 3.30 before the bunch came home and Costelloe dropped to 5th overall, 1.11 behind the new leader.
**Stage 6 Clonakilty - Dungarvan 90 Mls.** 1 B.Madden (Galway) 3.23.00 2 P.Cassidy (Meath Fiat) s.t. 3 N.Lindsay (Scotland) at 17 secs 4 T.Lally (Dublin Kalkhoff) 5 P.Tansey (Meath Tirolia) 6 P.Mahon (Dublin Dishgleam) 7 J.Wall (Tipperary) 8 P.McQuaid (Dublin Falcon) 9 R.McFarlane (Tipperary) 10 A.McKeown (Ireland) 11 J.Bidwell (Louth) all same time 12 B.Power (Tipperary) at 25 secs
**General Classification:** 1 A.McKeown (Ireland) 21.23.37 2 N.Lindsay (Scotland) at 10 secs 3 P.Tansey (Meath Tirolia) at 34 secs 4 P.McQuaid (Dublin Falcon) at 53 secs 5 G.Costelloe (Dublin Kalkhoff) at 1.11 6 A.Cunningham (Ireland) at 1.39 7 P.Flanagan (Meath Fiat) s.t. 8 J.McGahan (Scotland) at 2.19 9 T.Lally (Dublin Kalkhoff) at 2.39 10 J.Mangan (France) at 2.40 11 R.McCormack (Meath Tayto) at 4.03 12 S.Kennedy (Meath Tirolia) at 4.10
**Points:** 1 N.Lindsay 2 T.Lally 3 P.Tansey.
**Mountains:** 1 P.Flanagan 9 2 equal K.McInerney N.Lindsay M.Kelly 5
**International Team:** 1 Ireland 64.18.05 2 Scotland 64.18.38
**County Team:** 1 Meath Tirolia 64.20.41 2 Dublin Falcon 64.24.52 3 Dublin Kalkhoff 64.31.18

## STAGE 7

There was no change overall after the 87 miles stage from Dungarvan to Courtown which was won by Bernie McCormack who got away from the leaders with 7 miles

to go and held on to win the stage.
With the mountain stage looming next day the main players were content to stay out of the action and a 4-man break which contained no threats to the overall was permitted to go away
It was McCormack who started the move after 12 miles and he was joined by Gabriel Howard (Meath Tayto), Joe Wall (Tipperary) and Brian Connaughton (Garda Beaver Bosch) before the race passed through Waterford. By Slieverue their advantage was 1 minute, at New Ross it was 2 and by Enniscorthy, with 20 miles remaining, it had grown to 4 minutes.
However they began to tire and with the bunch now chasing hard the lead started to come down. With 7 miles to go McCormack decided to go it alone and he opened a small gap of around 10 seconds at Gorey and riding strongly he increased this to 51 seconds by the finish.
Wall won the second place sprint from the remains of the break that still had over a minute in hand on the chasers. The main bunch came in 2.45 down just behind third placed Paul Tansey who had managed to slip away and steal 4 seconds.
**Stage 7 Dungarvan - Courtown 87 Mls.** 1 B.McCormack (Meath Fiat) 3.47.00 2 J.Wall (Tipperary) at 51 secs 3 B.Connaughton (Garda Beaver Bosch) 4 G.Howard (Meath Tayto) all same time 5 B.Power (Tipperary) at 2.19 6 B.Madden (Galway) 7 M.Nulty (Meath Fiat) all same time 8 P.Tansey (Meath Tirolia) at 2.41 9 M.Kelly (Dublin Falcon) at 2.45 10 G.Costelloe (Dublin Kalkhoff) all same time
**General Classification:** 1 A.McKeown (Ireland) 25.13.22 2 N.Lindsay (Scotland) at 10 secs 3 P.Tansey (Meath Tirolia) at 30 secs 4 P.McQuaid (Dublin Falcon) at 53 secs 5 G.Costelloe (Dublin Kalkhoff) at 1.11 6 A.Cunningham (Ireland) at 1.39 7 P.Flanagan (Meath Fiat) s.t. 8 J.McGahan (Scotland) at 2.19 9 T.Lally (Dublin Kalkhoff) at 2.39 10 J.Mangan (France) at 2.40 11 R.McCormack (Meath Tayto) at 4.03 12 S.Kennedy (Meath Tirolia) at 4.10
**Points:** 1 N.Lindsay 61 2 T.Lally 54 3 P.Tansey 53
**Mountains:** 1 P.Flanagan 9 2 equal K.McInerney, N.Lindsay, M.Kelly 5
**International Team:** 1 Ireland 75.47.20 2 Scotland 75.47.53
**County Team:** 1 Meath Tirolia 79.49.52 2 Dublin Falcon 75.54.07 3 Meath Fiat 75.58.00

## STAGE 8

Jamie McGahan (Scotland) who had started the day in 8th position was the surprise new leader after the eighth stage from Courtown to Trim through the Wicklow mountains.
McGahan won the stage in a 2-up sprint from Paul Mahon (Dublin Dishgleam), the two coming home 2.54 in front of a group led in by past yellow jersey and teammate of McGahan, Norman Lindsay. McGahan's lead was 36 seconds over Aidan McKeown (Ireland) and the question was would it be enough to hold off noted time-triallists McKeown on Sunday morning's 5 miles time-trial.

Notable casualty of the day was Archie Cunningham who broke his crank on the climb of the Sally Gap, fell heavily and had to be taken to hospital.
The expected attack came from John Mangan and although he jumped from 10th to 5th it was not enough to put him in a challenging position for top honours at this late stage of the race.
Just after the start there was a series of attacks as riders sought to gain some time before the first of the four climbs.
A group of seven including Seamus Kennedy managed to build up a lead of 4 minutes with the Meath Tirolia rider on the verge of becoming race leader on the road. When they hit the Devil's Glen, Fran Riordan went away from the other six and the Dublin Dishgleam rider stayed out in front over all the climbs, stitching up the King of the Mountains classification en route. Just after the second climb at Luggala Riordan was joined by McGahan and Mahon and the three started working together.
Over the Sally Gap they had a minute's advantage over a 10-man chasing group which included Paddy Flanagan (Meath Fiat), Pat McQuaid (Dublin Fosters), John Mangan (France) and Aidan McKeown, just having lost Cunningham after his crash. His loss was a bad blow to McKeown's chances for with Cunningham working, even if the break hadn't been caught, the gap would certainly have been smaller at the finish. The other rider who could have saved the day for the Irish was John Mangan, but having been marked out of the race all week by the Irish riders he declined their request to help bring McGahan back.
Having climbed superbly Riordan had given his all and he was dropped by the other two at Blessington, at which point the two leaders were 1.30 ahead and they increased this all the way to the finish.
**Stage 8 Courtown - Trim 98 Mls.** 1 J.McGahan (Scotland) 4.00.01 2 P.Mahon (Dublin Dishgleam) s.t. 3 N.Lindsay (Scotland) at 2.54 4 R.McFarlane (Tipperary) 5 J.Mangan (France) 6 P.Flanagan (Meath Tirolia) 7 C.Fraser (Scotland) 8 J.Foley (Dublin East) all same time 9 M.Walsh (Wicklow) at 2.55 10 A.McKeown (Ireland) s.t.
**General Classification:** 1 J.McGahan (Scotland) 29.16.41 2 A.McKeown at 36 secs 3 N.Lindsay (Scotland) at 45 secs 4 P.Flanagan (Meath Tirolia) at 2.14 5 J.Mangan (France) at 3.11 6 P.Tansey (Meath Tirolia) at 4.05 7 P.McQuaid (Dublin Falcon) s.t. 8 G.Costelloe (Dublin Kalkhoff) at 4.23 9 P.Mahon (Dublin Dishgleam) at 4.34 10 R.McFarlane (Tipperary) at 6.00
**Points:** 1 N.Lindsay 74 2 P.Tansey 56 3 T.Lally 54
**Mountains:** 1 F.Riordan 18 2 equal J.McGahan and P.Mahon 11
**International team:** 1 Scotland 87.56.41 2 Ireland 88.25.16
**County team:** 1 Meath Tirolia 88.09.25 2 Tipperary 88.21.32 3 Meath Fiat 88.29.40

## STAGE 9 (a) and (b)

Aidan McKeown won the morning's time-trial in Trim but at 5 miles, the shortest ever TT in the RÁS apart from prologue stages, it wasn't enough and he stayed in second place, 12 seconds behind McGahan. Having caught 25 seconds in 5 miles another 3 miles would probably have been enough for the Belfast rider to have taken back the jersey.

Pat McQuaid was second in the TT, just 2 seconds slower than McKeown and Paul Tansey was third at 4 seconds. McGahan finished 9th but had done enough in those 5 miles to ensure his overall victory.

**Stage 9a Trim 5 Mls. TT:** 1 A.McKeown (Ireland) 11.05 2 P.McQuaid (Dublin Falcon) 11.07 3 P.Tansey (Meath Tirolia) 11.09 4 P.Cassidy (Meath Fiat) 11.13 5 D.Crowley (Cork Clonakilty) 11.17 6 P.Mahon (Dublin Dishgleam) 11.20 7 B.Madden (Galway) 11.25 8 A.Byrne (Garda Beaver Bosch) 11.26 9 J.McGahan (Scotland) 11.29 10 B.Power (Tipperary) 11.31

The afternoon stage was a triumph for '69 RÁS winner Brian Connaughton riding the last stage of his last RÁS and he went out in the grand manner winning the stage before a big crowd in the Phoenix Park.

Bobby Power (Tipperary) and Bernie McCormack (Meath Fiat) got away on the run in from Trim but on entering the Park they were joined by six riders. After three laps of the Park circuit Connaughton, Paul Mahon (Dublin Dishgleam) and Oliver McQuaid (Dublin Falcon) had fought their way across to the leaders.

Into the long finishing straight for the final time Michael McKenna (Dublin Kalkhoff) attacked. Connaughton was the only one to respond and he came past to take the victory.

**Stage 9b Trim - Dublin 50 Mls.** 1 B.Connaughton (Garda Beaver Bosch) 1.45.00 2 M.McKenna (Dublin Kalkhoff) at 2 secs 3 B.McCormack (Meath Fiat) at 8 secs 4 F.Riordan (Dublin Dishgleam) 5 T.Mannion (Galway) 6 O.McQuaid (Dublin Falcon) 7 B.Power (Tipperary) 8 P.Mahon (Dublin Dishgleam) 9 B.McMahon (Wicklow) 10 R.McFarlane (Tipperary) all same time

**General Classification:** 1 J.McGahan (Scotland) 31.14.01 2 A.McKeown (Ireland) at 12 secs 3 N.Lindsay (Scotland) at 1.00 4 P.Flanagan (Meath Fiat) at 2.19 5 J.Mangan (Kerry) at 3.19 6 P.Tansey (Meath Tirolia) at 3.21 7 P.Mahon (Dublin Dishgleam) at 3.41 8 P.McQuaid (Dublin Falcon) at 3.43 9 G.Costelloe (Dublin Kalkhoff) at 4.32 10 R.McFarlane (Tipperary) at 5.26 11 R.McCormack (Meath Tayto) at 7.30 12 S.Kennedy (Meath Tirolia) at 7.58

**Points:** 1 N.Lindsay 74 2 P.Mahon 57 3 P.Tansey 56

**Mountains:** 1 F.Riordan 18 2 equal J.McGahan and P.Mahon

**International Team:** 1 Scotland 93.49.33 2 Ireland 94.18.46

**County Team:** 1 Meath Tirolia 94.07.52 2 Tipperary 94.12.50 3 Meath Fiat 93.30.50

*1981 winner, Jamie McGahan (Scotland)*

## 1982

Tirolia were again the sponsors of the 1982 RÁS and while Stephen Roche (1979) had gone on to greater things, three of the previous four winners were on the 92-strong entry list: Seamus Kennedy ('78), Billy Kerr ('80) and defending champion Jamie McGahan who once more led the Scotland team.
Kerr was on the Ireland team along with Paul Tansey, Dermot Gilleran and another rider soon to make a name for himself in the pro ranks Martin Earley.
There was a new race director, Billy Archibold of Carlow who had stepped into the breech when Dermot Dignam decided he needed a break. With finances the tightest for many years the only visiting teams were Scotland and West of England.

## STAGE 1

Billy Kerr, who had missed the '81 RÁS, started off where he had left off the year before by winning the 75 miles opening stage from Dublin to Abbeyleix.
While Stephen Roche was not in the field he was there to flag the riders off at the racing start in Tallagh. Defending champion McGahan was soon in action and he initiated a break after 24 miles of racing and he was joined by six others. In the break were Kerr, Mark Graham (Antrim), Philip Cassidy (Meath Tirolia), Paul Tansey (Raleigh Ireland and Dublin Kalkhoff pair Paddy Flanagan and Michael McKenna...
The seven were 1.30 ahead at 50 miles and just afterwards Tansey got cramp and dropped back. however after treatment he managed to get back and eventually finished in the second group.
After Castlecomer (60 miles), there was a long drag and Kerr put on the pressure which saw Cassidy and Graham lose contact. Once back on flat roads the four worked well together for the final 20 miles to Abbeyleix where Kerr got the better of McGahan in the sprint after McKenna led out followed by the Scot but the Ballymena man judged his effort to perfection edging past in the final yards.
**Stage 1 Dublin - Abbeyleix 75 Mls.** 1 B.Kerr (Ireland) 2.59.52 2 J.McGahan (Scotland) 3 M.McKenna (Dublin Kalkhoff) 4 P.Flanagan (Dublin Kalkhoff) all same time 5 E.Madden (Dublin South) at 1.45 6 D.Crowley (Cork) at 1.50 7 O.McQuaid (West of England) 8 M.Earley (Raleigh Ireland) 9 A.O'Gorman (Tipperary Cidona) 10 D.Flynn (Dublin North) 11 L.Power (Tipperary Cidona) 12 E.Keehan (Limerick Kalkhoff) all same time
**Mountains:** 1 R.McSherry (Dublin South West) 2 O.McQuaid (West of England) 3 M.Earley (Raleigh Ireland)
**Team:** 1 Dublin Kalkhoff 9.01.26 2 equal Raleigh Ireland and Scotland 9.03.16

## STAGE 2

It was a home town win into Clonmel for 27-year-old Bobby Power (Tipperary Cidona) and to make the home fans even happier he took over the yellow jersey.
There were 13 riders in the break and nine of them took over the top nine places on G.C., all of them on equal time. Yellow jersey Kerr, who finished 2.01 behind dropped to 10th but because none of the nine were with him on the opening stage he was only 11 seconds behind the new leader on equal time with his stage one breakaway companions with the exception of Tony Lally who lost 8 minutes on the stage winner.
Limerick Kalkhoff riders Gearoid Costelloe and Eddie Keehan along with Christian Blandin (Waterford) went away early on and stayed out in front for 15 miles but the Ireland team's Earley and Gilleran sat on the back doing no work and the break was caught.
Kerr and the Ireland team were marking any perceived threats but an innocuous break of 13 went away at the 25 miles mark and 25 miles later at Johnstown they had a lead of 5 minutes.
Kerr reacted with an attack and went away with McGahan and Paddy Flanagan (Dublin Kalkhoff) and they were joined by a succession of small groups until there was a chasing bunch of 15 which quickly eat into the advantage of the leaders.
Despite the chase the break never looked like being caught. Fagan tried several times in the closing miles to get away on his own but was always brought back setting up a sprint finish where Power just got the closest of verdicts from the Englishman.
**Stage 2 Abbeyleix - Clonmel 87 Mls.** 1 B.Power (Tipperary Cidona) 3.26.25 2 I.Fagan (West of England) 3 P.Colleran (Clare) 4 D.Gilleran (Raleigh Ireland) 5 R.Melrose (Scotland) 6 S.Dunphy (West of England) 7 N.Madden (Dublin South West) 8 C.Blandin (Waterford Yoplait) all same time
**General Classification:** 1 B.Power (Tipperary Cidona) 6.27.57 2 I.Fagan (West of England) 3 equal D.Gilleran (Raleigh Ireland) and D.Flynn (Dublin North) 5 R.Melrose (Scotland) 6 N.Madden (Dublin South West) 7 C.Blandin (Waterford Yoplait) 8 S.O Hanlon (Meath Tayto) 9 J.O'Sullivan (Cork) all same time 10 B.Kerr (Raleigh Ireland) at 11 secs 11 J.McGahan (Scotland) 12 M.McKenna (Dublin Kalkhoff) 13 P.Flanagan (Dublin Kalkhoff) all same time
**Mountains:** 1 D.Flynn; 2 R.McSherry (Dublin South West) 3 O.McQuaid (West of England)
**Teams:** 1 Raleigh Ireland 19.26.03 2 Dublin Kalkhoff 19.26.14 3 equal Dublin South West, Tipperary Cidona and Meath Tayto 19.27.53

## STAGE 3

The Ireland team showed their strength dominating the third stage, 91 miles to Middleton with Dermot Gilleran winning the stage and also taking over the lead.

Their dominance was emphasised by the stage result with three of the team taking the top three places while Kerr moved up to second overall behind his team-mate, but defending champion McGahan was still there in third place equal on time with the Ballymena man.
It was a day for climbers and Ireland had three on the team who were part of a six-man break which stayed away for the last 50 miles. Also there were McGahan, Gearoid Costelloe (Limerick Kalkhoff) and Philip Cassidy (Meath Tirolia).
After only 3 miles Cassidy and Brendan Madden (Dublin South West) went away and opened a useful gap of 2 minutes by Carrick-on-Suir after 20 miles.
On the long climb to Powers O'The Pot Madden dropped back and Cassidy was joined by Gilleran, Kerr, Martin Earley and Gearoid Costelloe and they Cassidy led them across the KOH prime at the top 1 minute ahead of a chasing group of around 20 with McGahan in no man's land in between and after a valiant chase he made contact with the five leaders at the 40-mile mark.
Despite the best efforts of the pursuers, notably a four-man group led by Paddy Flanagan who had a long but fruitless chase, the six had two much power to be caught. Early took the prime at The Vee and Kerr the climb at Tallow.
Early had a back wheel puncture with only 16 miles to go but team mates Gilleran and Kerr made sure he got back on. However Costelloe was not so lucky puncturing 10 miles from the finish and losing almost 3 minutes.
Kerr attacked with two miles to go causing McGahan to expend valuable energy to bring him back and playing into the Irish team's hands setting them up to take the first three placings.
**Stage 3 Clonmel - Middleton 91 Mls.** 1 D.Gilleran (Raleigh Ireland) 3.50.59 2 M.Earley (Raleigh Ireland) 3 B.Kerr (Raleigh Ireland) 4 J.McGahan (Scotland) 5 P.Cassidy (Meath Tirolia) all same time 6 G.Costelloe (Limerick Kalkhoff) at 2.58 7 D.Crowley (Cork) at 3.10 8 P.Flanagan (Dublin Kalkhoff) 9 V.Kelly (Tipperary Cidona) 10 M.Killeen (Clare) all same time
**General Classification:** 1 D.Gilleran (Raleigh Ireland) 10.18.56 2 B.Kerr (Raleigh Ireland) at 13 secs 3 J.McGahan (Scotland) s.t. 4 M.Earley (Raleigh Ireland) at 2.01 5 P.Cassidy (Meath Tirolia) s.t. 6 P.Flanagan (Dublin Kalkhoff) at 3.21 7 I.Fagan (West of England) at 3.23 8 J.O'Sullivan (Cork) at 3.47 9 G.Costelloe (Limerick Kalkhoff) at 4.59 10 B.Madden (Dublin South West) at 5.11 11 B.O'Callaghan (Wicklow) at 5.13 12 P.Tansey (Raleigh Ireland) at 5.26
**Teams:** 1 Raleigh Ireland 30.59.00 2 Scotland 31.06.05 3 Tipperary Cidona 31.13.48

## STAGE 4

Martin Earley, who would go on to win stages in the Tour de France and the Giro d'Italia, won his only RÁS stage coming into Tralee on his own, 41 seconds ahead of a chasing group of five, led in by his teammate Paul Tansey.
Although he remained 4th overall, he had cut his deficit to 48 seconds on the yellow jersey which moved from the shoulders of one teammate, Dermot Gilleran, to those

of another with Billy Kerr regaining the lead. Gilleran dropped to third behind Jamie McGahan and with the gaps so tight at the top it was still anybody's race.
An early crash involving eight riders saw Padraig O'Grady (Galway) and Liam McLoughlin (Dublin North) taken to hospital, O'Grady suffering a broken collar-bone.
Meanwhile at the front a break went away after only six miles including race-leader Gilleran and going through Cork their lead had grown to 1.30, mainly due to the driving of Cassidy.
At 45 miles they were being chased by Brendan Madden (Dublin South West) and Paddy Flanagan (Dublin Kalkhoff) with another chasing group of 12 just behind. Five miles further on Madden and Flanagan joined the leaders just before they had to paddle their way through a flooded road.
Cassidy attacked again going away with Flanagan and the two opened a 30 second gap as the remainder of the original break were caught by the 12 chasers. After they came together Earley attacked and along with Tommy Mannion (Meath Tayto) set off in pursuit of the two leaders.
After Killarney the four came together but Earley only rode with them for three miles before attacking again with 20 miles of the stage still to go but riding strong he maintained his lead all the way to the finish.
**Stage 4 Middleton - Tralee 107 Mls.** 1 M.Earley (Raleigh Ireland) 4.29.40 2 P.Tansey (Raleigh Ireland) at 41 secs 3 S.Lally (Dublin Kalkhoff) 4 E.Madden (Dublin South) 5 B.Madden (Dublin South West) all same time 6 T.Lally (Dublin Kalkhoff) at 53 secs 7 B.Power (Tipperary Cidona) 8 T.Mannion (Meath Tayto) all same time 9 W.Gibb (Scotland) at 1.00 10 C.Blandin (Waterford Yoplait) s.t.
**General Classification:** 1 B.Kerr (Raleigh Ireland) 14.49.51 2 J.McGahan (Scotland) s.t. 3 D.Gilleran (Raleigh Ireland) at 39 secs 4 M.Earley (Raleigh Ireland) at 46 secs 5 P.Cassidy (Meath Tirolia) at 1.50 6 P.Flanagan (Dublin Kalkhoff) at 3.10 7 J.O'Sullivan (Cork) at 3.26 8 I.Fagan (West of England) at 4.02 9 B.Madden (Dublin South West) at 4.37 10 P.Tansey (Raleigh Ireland) at 4.52 11 S.Lally (Dublin Kalkhoff) at 4.55 12 A.O'Gorman (Tipperary Cidona) at 5.27
**Mountains:** 1 P. Cassidy 11 2 D. Gilleran 10
**Team:** 1 Raleigh Ireland 44.29.45 2 Scotland 44.38.17 3 Dublin Kalkhoff 44.44.07

## STAGE 5 (a) and (b)

There was a split stage on the Wednesday with almost a sprint in the morning, 41 miles to Ballybunion, won by Raleigh Ireland's Paul Tansey and after crossing the Shannon by ferry in the afternoon there was 67 miles from Kilrush to Kilkee which went to Scotland's Willie Gibb.
However the day belonged to Phil Cassidy (Meath Tirolia) who broke the Raleigh Ireland stranglehold to take the yellow jersey.

Although Billy Kerr had started the day in yellow he lost the lead on the morning's stage and there was criticism of his riding on the afternoon stage from team manager Pat McQuaid when he worked with Cassidy putting the Meath man into yellow.
Kerr's argument would be that he could take back the 15 second deficit on the time-trial to come but McQuaid, used to being in control, did not appreciate the strengthening of the position of dangerous rivals Cassidy and Jamie McGahan, and the discussions that followed had a significant effect on the eventual outcome of the race.
It was on the morning stage that Raleigh Ireland slipped up letting Cassidy away in an early break that didn't contain any other danger men. The 10-man break got a minute's advantage which stayed at that for most of the short stage but when the bunch relaxed in the final miles the lead went out to 2.05 putting the Meath Tirolia rider into yellow. There was some consolation for the Raleigh squad when Paul Tansey won the sprint to take the stage.
**Stage 5a Tralee - Ballybunion 41 Mls.** 1 P.Tansey (Raleigh Ireland) 1.42.50 2 J.McKenna (Antrim) 3 O.McQuaid (West of England) 4 W.Gibb (Scotland) 5 M.McKenna (Dublin Kalkhoff) 6 P.Cassidy (Meath Tirolia) 7 G. Howard (Meath Tayto) 8 M.Drain (Antrim) 9 E.Keehan (Limerick Kalkhoff) 10 J.Bidwell (Louth) all same time
Attack was the best method of defence for Cassidy in the afternoon and he went with an early 12-man break which included Kerr.
The pace of the race saw the 12 reduced to 6 by the finish where Scotland's Willie Gibb, who had also been in the morning break, won the sprint to take the stage ahead of Earley, Kerr and McGahan with Cassidy 5th in the same time. The 6th survivor of the original break Tommy Mannion (Meath Tayto) came in 25 seconds behind.
**Stage 5b Kilrush - Kilkee 67 Mls.** 1 W.Gibb (Scotland) 2.41.22 2 M.Earley (Raleigh Ireland) 3 B.Kerr (Raleigh Ireland) 4 J.McGahan (Scotland) 5 P.Cassidy (Meath Tirolia) all same time 6 T.Mannion (Meath Tayto) at 25 secs 7 D.Gibson (Scotland) at 35 secs 8 D.Gilleran (Raleigh Ireland) s.t. 9 S.Lally (Dublin Kalkhoff) at 48 secs 10 P.Flanagan (Dublin Kalkhoff) s.t.
**General Classification:** 1 P.Cassidy (Meath Tirolia) 19.16.02 2 B.Kerr (Raleigh Ireland) at 15 secs 3 J.McGahan (Scotland) s.t. 4 D.Gilleran (Raleigh Ireland) at 55 secs 5 M.Earley (Raleigh Ireland) at 1.01 6 P.Flanagan (Dublin Kalkhoff) at 4.41 7 J.O'Sullivan (Cork) at 4.43 8 I.Fagan (West of England) at 5.02 9 P.Tansey (Raleigh Ireland) at 5.16 10 S.Lally (Dublin Kalkhoff) at 5.48 11 M.McKenna (Dublin Kalkhoff) at 6.18 12 B.O'Callaghan (Wicklow) at 6.46
**Team:** 1 Raleigh Ireland 57.46.50 2 Scotland 57.56.01 3 Dublin Kalkhoff 57.57.00

## STAGE 6

The result of the Raleigh Ireland team talk after Wednesday's stage saw Kerr sacrificing himself to mark Cassidy out of the race while teammate Gilleran took the imitative and ended the day back in yellow with a 1.15 advantage over Jamie

McGahan with Cassidy dropping out of contention and Kerr falling back to 9th overall.
It was not without drama however for Gilleran as he crashed and finished the stage bloody but unbowed, having to receive hospital treatment after the stage for his numerous cuts.
The team tactics saw Kerr marking Cassidy and Early marking McGahan and the plan worked well. After 10 miles a break went away which included McGahan and his three Scottish team-mates. Of the Raleigh Ireland riders Gilleran was the only one in the break but with the Scots doing all the work he was given an armchair ride.
At the Cross of Spancilhill, 33 miles, the lead was 3.30 and McGahan was a clear leader on the road and the Ireland plan was looking decidedly shaky. Cassidy was towing the bunch along but with little help the gap was growing and the race leader was a spent force.
With Raleigh seeing that McGahan was now the greater threat they entered into the chase and the break was caught by a chasing group at around the 70n miles mark.
McGahan and the Scots, tired after their efforts now had to watch both Earley and Gilleran and when the latter got away in a 15-strong group, McGahan, with his attentions on Earley, never saw him go. Having had an easy day so far Gilleran gave it everything and the break raced to a 1.30 lead by the finish where the Scots had the consolation of another stage win by Gibb.
The day was nearly ruined for the Raleigh team when Gilleran and Brendan Madden touched wheels and came down at Kilcormac, just 8 miles from the finish. Gilleran immediately got back on the bike and although he didn't make it back up to the front where the break was fragmenting, he finished with enough time advantage to take back the jersey.
**Stage 6 Kilrush - Tullamore 112m Mls.** 1 W.Gibb (Scotland) 4.49.17 2 S.Lally (Dublin Kalkhoff) at 1 sec 3 J.McKenna (Antrim) at 2 secs 4 T.Lally (Dublin Kalkhoff) at 5 secs 5 T.Mannion (Meath Tayto) 6 E.Keehan (Limerick Kalkhoff) 7 E.Madden (Dublin South) all same time 8 M.Drain (Antrim) at 9 secs 9 S.Dunphy (West of England) 10 J.O'Sullivan (Cork) all same time
**General Classification:** 1 D.Gilleran (Raleigh Ireland) 24.06.28 2 J.McGahan (Scotland) at 1.17 3 M.Earley (Raleigh Ireland) at 2.03 4 J.O'Sullivan (Cork) at 3.38 5 P Flanagan (Dublin Kalkhoff) at 3.41 6 S.Lally (Dublin Kalkhoff) at 4.50 7 W.Gibb (Scotland) at 6.08 8 B.Madden (Dublin South West) at 6.59 9 B.Kerr (Raleigh Ireland) at 7.14 10 P.Cassidy (Meath Tirolia) at 6.59 11 S.O Hanlon (Meath Tayto) at 7.27 12 M.McKenna (Dublin Kalkhoff) at 7.30
**Team:** 1 Raleigh Ireland 72.25.14 2 Scotland 72.28.14 3 Dublin Kalkhoff 72.29.55

## STAGE 7

Cork rider Donal Crowley won into Drogheda 10 seconds clear from a break of twelve which finished 2 minutes ahead of the bunch. There were no major changes to the overall as Gilleran and his main rivals finished in the bunch.

Raleigh Ireland had Billy Kerr and Paul Tansey in the winning break but the race leader with the help of Martin Earley was able to contain the best efforts of McGahan to get away.
The opening 50 miles were quiet but then there were some anxious moments as a horse, frightened by the noise and colour of the peleton, got out of a field and galloped along at the front of the riders causing some consternation to lone breakaway Martin Kelly (Limerick Kalkhoff) who was closest to the animal who galloped along for five miles, knocking over a parked Garda motorcycle along the way.
Unfortunately as the horse was being herded off the course, Kelly was sent the wrong direction, losing some 30 seconds which allowed Jimmy Phelan (Waterford Yoplait) to join him.
Coming into Navan the two leaders were joined by ten more and this turned out to be the winning break. On the KOM prime at the Hill of Slane Willie Gibb (Scotland) went away with Kerr and Tansey but they were brought back by the others after two miles.
Over the final five miles Kerr made several unsuccessful attempts to get away but it was an attack by Crowley which succeeded and Noel Clarke (Meath Tirolia) also opened up a small gap before the line. Another 2 seconds back came Kerr with the remainder of the twelve led in by Paul Tansey a further 30 seconds behind.
**Stage 7 Tullamore - Drogheda 85 Mls.** 1 D.Crowley (Cork) 3.26.44 2 N. Clarke (Meath Tirolia) at 10 secs 3 B.Kerr (Raleigh Ireland) at 12 secs 4 P.Tansey (Raleigh Ireland) at 42 secs 5 W.Gibb (Scotland) 6 R.Melrose (Scotland) 7 M.Kelly (Limerick Kalkhoff) 8 B.Madden (Dublin South West) 9 T.G.Carey (Tipperary Cidona) 10 M.McKenna (Dublin Kalkhoff) 11 J.Phelan (Waterford Yoplait) 12 G.Howard (Meath Tayto) all same time
**General Classification:** 1 D.Gilleran (Raleigh Ireland) 27.35.06 2 J.McGahan (Scotland) at 1.17 3 M.Earley (Raleigh Ireland) at 2.03 4 J.O'Sullivan (Cork) at 3.38 5 P.Flanagan (Dublin Kalkhoff) at 3.41 6 S.Lally (Dublin Kalkhoff) at 4.50 7 W.Gibb (Scotland) at 4.56 8 B.Kerr (Raleigh Ireland) at 5.32 9 B.Madden (Dublin South West) at 5.44 10 M.McKenna (Dublin Kalkhoff) at 6.18 11 P.Cassidy (Meath Tirolia) at 6.59 12 S.O Hanlon (Meath Tayto) at 7.27
**Mountains:** 1 M.Earley 2 B.Kerr 3 P.Cassidy
**Team:** 1 Raleigh Ireland 82.48.14 2 Scotland 82.51.44 2 Dublin Kalkhoff 82.54.36

## STAGE 8 (a) and (b)

Billy Kerr won Saturday morning's 8 miles time-trial from Dunleer to Drogheda by 20 seconds from Jamie McGahan. Gilleran was fifth, 50 seconds behind McGahan which meant that he only had a lead of 27 seconds going into the afternoon stage which was over five laps of a 12-mile circuit with the climb of Tullyesker each time.
**Stage 8a Dunleer - Drogheda 8 Mls. TT:** 1 B.Kerr (Raleigh Ireland) 17.16 2 J.McGahan (Scotland) 17.36 3 B.Madden (Dublin South West) 18.09 4 I.Fagan

(West of England) 18.25 5 D.Gilleran (Raleigh Ireland) 18.26 6 D.Crowley (Cork) 18.29 7 P.Cassidy (Meath Tirolia) 18.32 8 M.Earley (Raleigh Ireland) 18.33 9 A.O'Gorman (Tipperary Cidona) 18.35 10 W.Gibb (Scotland) 18.36

McGahan, with such a small deficit between him and a second successive RÁS, attacked just after the start on the first climb up the long drag at Tullyesker. However Gilleran and the rest of the Raleigh Ireland team where straight onto his wheel and he was obviously going nowhere.

The pattern was maintained over the successive laps until the penultimate lap when McGahan's driving drew away an 8-man break which included Gilleran and Kerr. As they pulled away from the bunch Gilleran hit a stone with his back wheel and crashed heavily. However he was quickly back on his feet and with Kerr waiting for him he set off in pursuit on the Ballymena man's much too big bike.

Up front McGahan had only to keep the break away for a lap and the jersey was his. However he informed the other riders that he wasn't going to take advantage of Gilleran's misfortune. With the others still working McGahan was still leader on the road but then Gilleran had a stroke of luck when McGahan punctured and although he got a wheel from teammate David Gibson, the break was gone.

Gilleran joined the bunch and changed bikes with his more equally sized teammate Paul Tansey. McGahan also got back to the bunch as did Kerr after a bike-change and a chase.

With all the drama over a break of four quietly slipped away from which Anthony O'Gorman (Tipperary Cidona) won the sprint for the stage from Eddie Keehan (Limerick Kalkhoff).

**Stage 8b Drogheda - Drogheda 60 Mls.** 1 A.O'Gorman (Tipperary Cidona) 2.21.31 2 E.Keehan (Limerick Kalkhoff) 3 M.Killeen (Clare) 4 P.Curtis (Dublin Kalkhoff) all same time 5 I.Fagan (West of England) at 27 secs 6 G.Costelloe (Limerick Kalkhoff 7 C.Drovet (Waterford Yoplait) 8 O.McQuaid (West of England) 9 D.Crowley (Cork) 10 B.O'Callaghan (Wicklow) all same time

**General Classification;** 1 D.Gilleran (Raleigh Ireland) 30.06.30 2 J.McGahan (Scotland) at 27 secs 3 M.Earley (Raleigh Ireland) at 2.10 4 B.Kerr (Raleigh Ireland) at 4.22 5 J.O'Sullivan (Cork) at 4.36 6 W.Gibb (Scotland) at 4.46 7 S.Lally (Dublin Kalkhoff) at 5.24 8 P.Flanagan (Dublin Kalkhoff) at 5.26 9 B.Madden (Dublin South West) at 5.27 10 M.McKenna (Dublin Kalkhoff) at 5.34 11 P.Cassidy (Meath Tirolia) at 5.45 12 S.O Hanlon (Meath Tayto) at 5.52

**Mountains:** 1 M.Earley 18 2 B.Kerr 12 3 P.Cassidy 10

**Team:** 1 Raleigh Ireland 90.21.23 2 Scotland 90.26.02 3 Dublin Kalkhoff 90.29.52

## STAGE 9

Donal Crowley (Cork) won his second stage beating Gearoid Costelloe (Limerick Kalkhoff) in a sprint from a group of five who came home 1.39 ahead at the end of the 88 miles stage into Dublin.

There was a go-slow by the field for the first 15 miles in protest against the rejection of an appeal against the decision to cut the prize money for Stage 8 by 50 per cent. because the riders refused to take part in the pre-race parade during a downpour.
During this go-slow period Gabriel Howard (Meath Tayto) and Pat Whitney (Garda Beaver Bosch) were allowed to go up the road and contest the prime after 5 miles in Howard's home village of Stamullen which Howard won in front of a huge crowd.
The two stayed out in front by 1 minute as the bunch ambled along until after 15 miles they decided they had made their protest and at Navan the race was on.
A group of 17 then went clear and quickly established a 2 minute lead which had dropped to 1.30 by Maynooth. Martin Drain (Antrim) crashed out of the break while at the front Crowley, Costelloe and Joe Wall (Waterford Yoplait) broke from the leading group.
Phillip Cassidy (Meath Tirolia) and Tommy Mannion (Meath Tayto) went in pursuit and joined the leaders after a 3-mile chase. The five stayed away to the finish opening up a useful gap. In the sprint Crowley was clearly the strongest winning in style. Cassidy was the big beneficiary jumping from 11th to 4th overall.
In the bunch Gilleran only had to keep an eye on McGahan but the Scot realised his task was hopeless and the two crossed the line together in the bunch, McGahan being the first to congratulate the winner.
**Stage 9 Drogheda - Dublin 88 Mls.** 1 D.Crowley (Cork) 3.35.49 2 G.Costelloe (Limerick Kalkhoff) 3 J.Wall (Waterford Yoplait) 4 T.Mannion (Meath Tayto) 5 P.Cassidy (Meath Tirolia) all same time 6 P.Tansey (Raleigh Ireland) at 1.39 7 S.O Hanlon (Meath Tayto) 8 J.McKenna (Antrim) 9 O.McQuaid (West of England) 10 J.Carey (Tipperary Cidona) all same time
**General Classification:** 1 D.Gilleran (Raleigh Ireland) 33.46.22 2 J. McGahan (Scotland) at 27 secs 3 M.Earley (Raleigh Ireland) at 2.10 4 P.Cassidy (Meath Tirolia) at 3.02 5 B.Kerr (Raleigh Ireland) at 4.22 6 J.O'Sullivan (Cork) at 4.36 7 G.Costelloe (Limerick Kalkhoff) at 4.55 8 W.Gibb (Scotland) at 4.46 9 S.Lally (Dublin Kalkhoff) at 5.24 10 P.Flanagan (Dublin Kalkhoff) at 5.26 11 B.Madden (Dublin South West) at 5.27 12 M.McKenna (Dublin Kalkhoff) at 5.34 13 S.O Hanlon (Meath Tayto) at 5.52 14 R.Melrose (Scotland) at 6.02 15 J.McKenna (Antrim) at 6.37
**Mountains:** 1 M.Earley 18 2 B.Kerr 12 3 P.Cassidy 10
**Team:** 1 Raleigh Ireland 101.17.22 2 Scotland 101.23.14 3 Dublin Kalkhoff 101.28.20

*Dermot Gilleran, 1982 winner*

*Fons Steuten, Netherlands*
*Winner 1976*

*Eamon Byrne, 1993*

*Philip Cassidy, 1983 &1999*

*Tommy Evans, 1996*

*Andrew Roche, 1997*

*Ciaran Power, 1998 & 2002*

*Julian Winn (Wales ) 2000*

*Chris Newton, 2003 & 2005*

*Kristian House, 2006*

*David McCann, 2004*

*Tony Martin (Germany) 2007*

*Declan Lonergan 1994*

*Stephen Gallagher, 2008 winner*

## 1983

There was a new sponsor for the 1983 RÁS, the National Dairy Council had come in with substantial support and they were to be associated with the RÁS either as sole or co-sponsor for a very long time, as would race director Dermot Dignam who was back in charge.
The 1983 race was to be known as the Dairy RÁS TAILTEANN and the race would be the biggest to date in terms of riders with 145 entered. Visiting teams were entered from France, Scotland, Belgium and England West and as well as the Ireland team, again sponsored by Irish Raleigh, there were 20 county teams and a Garda selection.
A month earlier Dublin rider Paul Kimmage had led the 2-week long British Milk Race for a week and looked set for overall victory when a crash on the penultimate stage put him out of the running. As a result he went into the Milk RÁS as a strong favourite. Others tipped by the Press were his Raleigh Ireland teammate Philip Cassidy and past winner Jamie McGahan of Scotland and his teammate David Whitehall along with defending champion Dermot Gilleran, with Kimmage, Cassidy and Garry Thompson on the Raleigh Ireland team.

## STAGE 1

Tony Murphy (Dublin B) won the opening stage of the Dairy RÁS TAILTEANN an 88 miles run from Dublin to Killeshandra... He went clear of a group of 11 riders in the final mile. It was his 11th win of the season.
Most of the favourites, with the notable exception of Paul Kimmage, got into the break that mattered, a huge group of 46 which went away after 65 miles. Kimmage however managed to limit his losses to 2.20 when he went in pursuit over the closing miles.
The big leading group was always liable to fragment and it split with 8 miles to go eight riders going clear and quickly opening a gap of over half-a-minute. These eight were joined by Murphy in company with two Scottish riders: Jamie McGahan and David Whitehall. McGahan attacked with 1 mile to go. he was caught and Murphy made his effort holding on to win by 3 seconds from Paul Tansey (Dublin A) with Raphael Kimmage (Dublin C) a further 6 seconds back.
**Stage 1 Dublin - Killeshandra 88 Mls.** 1 T.Murphy (Dublin B) 3.27.55 2 P.Tansey (Dublin A) at 3 secs 3 R.Kimmage (Dublin C) at 9 secs 4 F.Relf (Waterford) at 10 secs 5 J.McGahan (Scotland) 6 G.Thompson (Raleigh Ireland) 7 D.Whitehall (Scotland) 8 J.McQuaid (Dublin B) 9 S.Kennedy (Meath West) 10 B.Madden (Galway) 11 A.Byrne (Garda) all same time 12 D.Flynn (Waterford) at 25 secs
**Mountains:** T.Murphy
**Team:** 1 Dublin B 10.24.20 2 Dublin A 10.24.28; 3 Dublin C 10.24.44

## STAGE 2

Philip Cassidy (Raleigh Ireland) won Sunday's 96 miles race from Killeshandra to Tuam by the substantial margin of 2.40 over second placed Jamie McGahan (Scotland) and took over the yellow jersey with a lead of 2.24 over the Scot.
It was a magnificent performance by the 21-year-old Meath rider. He went away at Ballyfarnon, after 35 miles, with two Antrim riders, Martin Drain and Pat McHugh and over the Curlew Mountains the trio had a lead of just over 1 minute.
Behind race leader Tony Murphy, who had defended well in the early stages started to let the breaks go and he eventually trailed in over 5 minutes down to drop out of the top ten.
With 23 miles to go at Ballymoe Cassidy decided to go it alone and increased the speed, dropping his companions who fell back to be caught by the chasers.
Cassidy never faltered and whereas a rider on his own, who had been away for much of the day, might have been expected to weaken, it was the reverse in this case and riding strongly he increased his lead all the way to the finish.
In the 20 strong group which was chasing behind McGahan, aware of the danger was doing most of the driving, but it was to no avail as Cassidy maintained his advantage.
The Raleigh Ireland team had Paul Kimmage and Gary Thompson in the chasing group and they were giving no assistance in the chase.
McGahan eventually got away from the chasers and opened a gap of 23 seconds on the group who were led in by Raphael Kimmage (Dublin C).
**Stage 2 Killeshandra - Tuam 96 Mls.** 1 P.Cassidy (Raleigh Ireland) 3.50.00 2 J.McGahan (Scotland) at 2.40 3 R.Kimmage (Dublin C) at 3.03 4 G.Sonnen (Belgium) 5 G.Thompson (Raleigh Ireland) 6 J.McCormack (Dublin C) 7 J.McQuaid (Dublin B) 8 S.Lally (Dublin A) 9 P.Tansey (Dublin B) 10 T.Lally (Dublin A) all same time
**General Classification:** 1 P.Cassidy (Raleigh Ireland) 7.18.15 2 J.McGahan (Scotland) at 2.24 3 P.Tansey (Dublin B) at 2.46 4 R.Kimmage (Dublin C) at 2.50 5 equal G.Thompson (Raleigh Ireland) D.Whitehall (Scotland) J.McQuaid (Dublin B) F.Relf (Waterford) all at 2.52 9 equal G.Sonnen (Belgium) M.Drain (Antrim) S.Lally (Dublin A) A.Harrison (Dublin A) T.Lally (Dublin A) B.McCormack (Dublin B) J.McCormack (Dublin C) P.Mahon (Dublin C) all at 3.07
**Points:** 1 R.Kimmage 26 2 J.McGahan 35 3 G.Thompson and P.Tansey 21
**Mountains:** 1 equal T. Murphy and P. Cassidy
**Team:** 1 Raleigh Ireland 22.00.46 2 Dublin A 22.03.47 3 Dublin C 22.03.52

## STAGE 3

Tony Murphy won his second stage of the week in a sprint from seven riders, the remains of a break of 12 which went away after 16 miles and stayed out in front to the finish.

Race leader Cassidy, his teammate Gary Thompson and second placed Jamie McGahan all finished with the winner so there was no change overall but all three, who had done the bulk of the work in the 78-mile break were critical of the sit-in tactics of stage-winner Murphy who hadn't worked all day, which no doubt contributed to his easy victory.
Murphy, however, was unrepentant saying that it wasn't up to him to work in a break which contained the yellow jersey.
The other controversy un a relatively uneventful stage was when Paul Kimmage, riding with the Raleigh Ireland team, dropped back to help brother Raphael who had a series of problems. With Raphael on a different team this was a break of the rules and it resulted in an official caution from the commissaires.
The break which went away in the first hour of racing never opened up a huge lead but stayed over a minute clear all day eventually finishing 2 minutes ahead. They lost five riders along the way including Aidan Harrison (Dublin A), who didn't get back after a puncture and Eddie Connolly (Meath East) who was brought down by the RTE camera car. Fortunately he didn't sustain any serious injuries.
**Stage 3 Tuam - Nenagh 94 Mls.** 1 T.Murphy (Dublin B) 3.27.55 2 R.Melrose (Scotland) at 3 sec 3 G.Thompson (Raleigh Ireland) at 5 secs 4 J.McGahan (Scotland) at 6 secs 5 L.Blagojevic (France) 6 M.Westwood (England West) 7 P.Cassidy (Raleigh Ireland) all same time 8 T.McManus (Dublin C) at 1.26 9 R.Kimmage (Dublin C) at 2.15 10 B.McCormack (Dublin B) s.t.
**General Classification:** 1 P.Cassidy (Raleigh Ireland) 10.46.16 2 J.McGahan (Scotland) at 2.27 3 G.Thompson (Raleigh Ireland) at 2.52 4 R.Kimmage (Dublin C) at 5.00 5 R.Melrose (Scotland) at 5.05 6 equal A.Harrison (Dublin A) B.McCormack (Dublin B) J.McCormack (Dublin C) all at 5.17 9 T.Murphy (Dublin B) at 5.29 10 P.Tansey (Dublin B) at 5.52 11 equal J.McQuaid (Dublin B) F.Relf (Waterford) at 5.59
**Points:** 1 J.McGahan 37 2 G.Thompson 34 3 R.Kimmage 33.
**Mountains:** 1 G.Thompson 5 2 P.Cassidy 4 3 J.McGahan 3
**Team:** 1 Raleigh Ireland 32.26.57 2 Dublin C 32.33.33 3 Dublin B 32.34.27

## STAGE 4

The Raleigh Ireland team appeared in control throughout the 112 miles fourth stage from Nenagh to Tralee and although a break of five, which went away after 55 miles, was allowed to increase its lead to over 2 minutes, it contained no real danger man and over the final miles its lead was cut back to less than half a minute.
Winner of the stage was 38-year-old Gaston Sonnen (Belgium) who despite his years was the fastest of the leading dozen. Highest placed riders in the break were Aidan Harrison (Dublin A) and Robert Melrose (Scotland) who improved their position on GC by a place moving to 4th and 5th respectively but they were both almost five minutes down on race-leader Cassidy.

From the start it was obvious that the Ireland team were not going to let any riders away who were a threat to the jersey. Paul Kimmage, who had been warned the previous day for helping a rider from another team (his brother), was a tower of strength to the team, driving at the front for much of the day.
Most of the interest in the stage came in the final 12 miles. Stephen Delaney (Tipperary) and John McCormack (Dublin C) dropped back and Sean Lally (Dublin A) punctured. Then a group of ten got away from the bunch and got up to the two leaders leaving ten to sprint for the stage.
**Stage 4 Nenagh - Tralee 112 Mls.** 1 G.Sonnen (Belgium) 4.47.00 2 L.Power (Tipperary) 3 O.McQuaid (Dublin B) 4 M.Westwood (England West) 5 P.Mahon (Dublin C) 6 R.Melrose (Scotland) 7 A.Byrne (Garda) 8 A.Harrison (Dublin A) 9 B.O'Callaghan (Wicklow) 10 Jim.McQuaid (Garda) 11 F.Relf (Waterford) all same time
**General Classification:** 1 P.Cassidy (Raleigh Ireland) 15.33.39 2 J.McGahan (Scotland) at 2.40 3 G.Thompson (Raleigh Ireland) at 2.52 4 R.Melrose (Scotland) at 4.42 5 A.Harrison (Dublin A) at 4.54 6 R.Kimmage (Dublin C) at 5.00 7 B.McCormack (Dublin B) at 5.17 8 J.McCormack (Dublin C) s.t. 9 T.Murphy (Dublin B) at 5.30 10 F.Relf (Waterford) at 5.46 11 P.Mahon (Dublin C) at 5.51 12 John.McQuaid (Dublin B) at 5.59
**Points:** 1 J.McGahan 37 2 G Thompson 36 3 R.Kimmage 33
**Mountains:** 1 G.Thompson 5 2 P.Cassidy 4 3 M.Westwood 4
**Team:** 1 Raleigh Ireland 46.49.06 2 Dublin C 46.55.19 3 Dublin B 46.56.13

## STAGE 5

John McQuaid (Dublin B) won the 95 miles stage from Tralee to Blarney coming home on his own, 1.;26 ahead of M. Westwood (England West) and Dave Whitehall (Scotland)
Phil Cassidy retained his race lead but there was trouble in the Raleigh Ireland camp after it looked that teammate Gary Thompson had tried to take the jersey.
Both Cassidy and Thompson were in a 20-strong break which went away around 45 miles into the stage. Also there was Jamie McGahan who had three team-mates.
Thompson attacked on the climb at Inchee and was joined by two Scots riders, Dave Whitehall and Robert Melrose, lying 4th on general.
This was according to Ireland team manager Pat McQuaid's orders, hoping to leapfrog Thompson up the classification. However when it appeared that Thompson was riding into the race lead, Cassidy started to chase and with several allies in the group, especially Raphael Kimmage and John McQuaid they succeeded in bring back the Thompson group with 14 miles to go.
McQuaid then attacked with 10 miles to go and riding strongly he opened up a good gap by the finish as several small groups went in pursuit.
Pat McQuaid defended his tactics saying that had Thompson's attack succeeded Raleigh Ireland would have tied up the race for his team and that Cassidy was wrong

to chase. Asked if it was safe to leave the race leader isolated with four Scots riders in the break he said it was worth the risk.
In the team race it was a bad day for the Raleigh Ireland team as with only two riders up the road they lost the lead dropping to 4th behind Dublin B.
**Stage 5 Tralee - Blarney 95 Mls.** 1 J.McQuaid (Dublin B) 3.37.00 2 M.Westwood (England West) at 1.26 3 D.Whitehall (Scotland) s.t. 4 G.Sonnen (Belgium) at 1.38 5 T.Murphy (Dublin B) 6 L.Blagojevic (France) 7 R.Kimmage (Dublin C) 8 B.McCormick (Dublin B) 9 R.Melrose (Scotland) 10 V.Kelly (Tipperary) all same time
**General Classification:** 1 P.Cassidy (Raleigh Ireland) 19.12.04 2 J.McGahan (Scotland) at 3.07 3 G.Thompson (Raleigh Ireland) at 3.32 4 J.McQuaid (Dublin B) at 4.34 5 R.Melrose (Scotland) at 5.13 6 R.Kimmage (Dublin C) s.t. 7 T.Murphy (Dublin B) at 5.42 8 B.McCormick (Dublin B) at 5.48 9 A.Harrison (Dublin A) at 5.56 10 J.McCormack (Dublin C) at 5.57 11 D.Whitehall (Scotland) at 7.19 12 G.Sonnen (Belgium) at 7.23
**Points:** 1 R.Kimmage and G.Sonnen both 42 3 T.Murphy, J.McGahan, and G.Thompson all 41
**Mountains:** 1 G.Thompson 13 2 O.McQuaid 7 3 D.Whitehall 5
Team: 1 Dublin B 57.50.47 2 Scotland 57.52.51 3 Dublin C 57.55.22

## STAGE 6

Raphael Kimmage (Dublin C) was first into Carrick-on-Suir denying local rider Vinnie Kelly (brother of Sean) a home town win.
The pair was part of a 9-man break which went away at the top of the Gurteen Wood climb, 11 miles from the finish. Included in the break was second placed Jamie McGahan and as race leader Cassidy missed the break, claiming a slipped gear change as it went away, he lost 42 seconds on the Scot, his lead reduced to 1.45 with McGahan confident he could take the jersey from the Raleigh Ireland rider. However stage-winner Kimmage, who improved to 4th overall, asked who he thought would win said he thought he could take them both on Saturday's mountain stage.
Earlier Claude Costelloe (Limerick) and Tony Murphy (Dublin B) were away for 27 miles with their lead at one time over 2 minutes with Murphy looking a danger to the yellow jersey. However the Raleigh Ireland team went to the front and caught the pair at the top of the Gurteen climb. With the Ireland team at their most vulnerable after their chase McGahan chose this moment to launch an attack along with team-mates Melrose and Whitehall and they were joined by six more, the Scots riding flat out to hold off the chase to the finish where Kimmage went before the final corner opening a good gap which he maintained to the line.
**Stage 6 Blarney - Carrick-on-Suir 92 Mls.** 1 R.Kimmage (Dublin C) 3.48.00 2 V.Kelly (Tipperary) 3 L.Blagojevic (France) 4 R.Melrose (Scotland) 5 A.Harrison (Dublin A) 6 N.Troy (Offaly) 7 S.Cole (England West) 8 J.McGahan (Scotland) 9 D.Whitehall (Scotland) all same time 10 G.Sonnen (Belgium) at 42 secs

**General Classification:** 1 P.Cassidy (Raleigh Ireland) 23.01.26 1 J.McGahan (Scotland) at 1.45 3 G.Thompson (Raleigh Ireland) at 2.52 4 equal R.Kimmage (Dublin C) and R.Melrose (Scotland) both at 3.51 6 J.McQuaid (Dublin B) 7 A.Harrison (Dublin A) at 4.34 8 T.Murphy (Dublin B) at 5.02 9 B.McCormick (Dublin B) at 5.08 10 J.McCormack (Dublin C) at 5.17 11 D.Whitehall (Scotland) at 6.57 12 G.Sonnen (Belgium) at 7.43
**Points:** 1 R.Kimmage 57 2 J.McGahan 49 3 G.Sonnen 48
**Mountains:** 1 G.Thompson 13 2 O.McQuaid 7 3 equal D.Whitehall and T.Murphy 5
**Team:** 1 Scotland 69.16.51 2 Dublin B 69.16.53 3 Dublin C 69.20.46

## STAGE 7

Despite riding with his right arm in plaster (the result of breaking a bone in his hand in a pre- RÁS crash), Bernie McCormick, lying 9th overall before the stage, won the 70 miles stage from Carrick-on-Suir to Wexford, jumping to 3rd overall in the process, just 2.44 behind Phil Cassidy who maintained his position at the top of the classification.
McCormick was the only top-ten rider in the 8-man break which finished 2.24 in front of the bunch. With the next day's big mountain stage very much in mind the top men had taken it easy giving the lower-placed riders a chance to grab some of the glory.
Early on a patch of road works caused so many punctures that Commissaire President Ben McKenna decided to neutralise the race and restart it when the race regained normal roads. Shortly after this Brendan Madden (Galway) attacked and was joined by seven more to make the break of the day.
Also there were McCormick, Stephen Delaney (Tipperary), Terry McManus (Dublin City); Brendan Murray (Westmeath); Barry Fullerton and Antrim pair Brendan Graham and John McKenna.
The eight worked well together and at one time their advantage was over 3 minutes but when McCormick began to look like a threat on overall the Raleigh Ireland team took up the chase and reduced their lead over the final miles.
As the approached Wexford there was a succession of attempts to get away, the last coming from Madden who was caught and passed by McCormick just before the line.
**Stage 7 Carrick-on-Suir - Wexford 70 Mls.** 1 B.McCormick (Dublin B) 2.37.00 2 B.Madden (Galway) 3 J.McKenna (Antrim) 4 B.Fullerton (Armagh) 5 S.Delaney (Tipperary) 6 T.McManus (Dublin City) 7 B.Graham (Antrim) 8 B.Murray (Westmeath) all same time 9 G.Sonnen (Belgium) at 2.42 10 R. Kimmage (Dublin C) s.t.
**General Classification:** 1 P.Cassidy (Raleigh Ireland) 25, 40.50 2 J.McGahan (Scotland) at 1.45 3 B.McCormick (Dublin B) at 2.44 4 G.Thompson (Raleigh Ireland) at 2.52 5 equal R.Kimmage (Dublin C) and R.Melrose (Scotland) both at 3.51 7 J.McQuaid (Dublin B) 8 A.Harrison (Dublin A) at 4.34 9 T.Murphy (Dublin

B) at 5.02 10 J.McCormack (Dublin C) at 5.17 11 D.Whitehall (Scotland) at 6.57 12 G.Sonnen (Belgium) at 7.43
**Points:** 1 R.Kimmage 63 2 G.Sonnen 55 3 T.Murphy 49
**Mountains:** 1 G.Thompson 13 2 O.McQuaid 7 3 equal D.Whitehall and T.Murphy 5
**Team:** 1 Dublin B 77.12.41 2 Scotland 77.15.03 3 Dublin C 77.16.34

## STAGE 8

David Whitehall (Scotland) won the all-important mountain stage from Waterford which finished at the top of the Wicklow Gap.
However race-leader Phil Cassidy was 6th on the stage, 1.54 behind the winner but having survived the mountains with a lead of 2.44 over Raleigh Ireland teammate Gary Thompson it looked all over bar accidents with only a short stage into Dublin on Sunday.
It had been forecast that McGahan would out climb Cassidy in the mountains and take the lead but the Meath man was always equal to the task.
For the first 50 miles of the stage, over flat roads, riders tried to gain some time before the climbing started and of the 12-man break that became established, only one, John McQuaid, posed any threat to the yellow jersey and this became a distinct possibility when their lead reached 3.30.
However their lead soon started to shrink and before the first climb at Aughavannagh the stragglers from the break were being caught.
McGahan was sitting at the front looking comfortable but when Gary Thompson attacked, taking with him Cassidy, Raphael Kimmage (Dublin C) and Aidan Harrison (Dublin A) McGahan was not able to stay with them and the RÁS was virtually over.
The four rode through the remnants of the break over that climb and the next at Drumgoff when of the original break only Whitehall was still in front.
The Scot was riding strongly and indeed increased his lead between there and the finish but the Raleigh Ireland team were not worried about him and although he improved his position overall at the end of the day he was in 7th place, nearly 5 minutes behind Cassidy.
A massive crowd was on the top of the Gap for the first mountain-top finish to a RÁS stage and saw Whitehall come home 1.46 ahead of Thompson who led in Blagojevic (France) who had managed to stay with them, Harrison and Kimmage, all on the same time with Cassidy, having done all he needed, taking the last few metres easy to finish 8 seconds further back.
**Stage 8 Wexford - Wicklow Gap 76 Mls.** 1 D.Whitehall (Scotland) 3.19.00 2 G.Thompson (Raleigh Ireland) at 1.46 3 L.Blagojevic (France) 4 A.Harrison (Dublin C) 5 R.Kimmage (Dublin C) all same time 6 P.Cassidy (Raleigh Ireland) at 1.54 7 Jim.McQuaid (Garda) at 3.12 8 9 10 J. McCormack (Dublin C)
**General Classification:** 1 P.Cassidy (Raleigh Ireland) 29.01.44 2 G.Thompson (Raleigh Ireland) at 2.44 3 J.McGahan (Scotland) at 3.03 4 R.Kimmage (Dublin C) at

3.43 5 J.McQuaid (Dublin B) at 3.54 6 A.Harrison (Dublin A) at 4.26 7 D.Whitehall (Scotland) at 5.03 8 R.Melrose (Scotland) at 5.09 9 B.McCormick (Dublin B) at 5.25 10 T.Murphy (Dublin B) at 6.20 11 J.McCormack (Dublin C) at 7.35 12 L. Blagojevic (France) at 8.05
**Points:** 1 R.Kimmage 74 2 G.Thompson 60 3 T.Murphy 54
**Mountains:** 1 D.Whitehall 23 2 G.Thompson 21 3 L.Blagojevic 13
**Team:** 1 Scotland 83.19.07 2 Dublin B 83.20.30 3 Dublin C 83.24.19

## STAGE 9

The final stage looked like being something of a formality for Cassidy with a straightforward run into Dublin from Blessington finishing with 15 laps in the Phoenix Park.
However Cassidy took the initiative and on the approach to the Park at Tinkers Hill he broke away to join lone leader Oliver McQuaid (Dublin B) and the pair stayed out in front, McQuaid taking the stage from Cassidy who increased his overall lead by 34 seconds.
Behind, five riders broke away from the bunch in pursuit of the leaders getting to within 21 seconds. Tony Murphy (Dublin B) beat Fran Riordan (Dublin C) for third place ahead of Norman Campbell (Down); Gearoid Costello (Limerick) and M. O'Grady (Galway) with Robert Melrose (Scotland) leading home the bunch 14 seconds later.
Scotland just kept their lead in the team classification ahead of Dublin B, who gained 49 seconds on the stage, with Dublin C third and Raleigh Ireland fourth.
Raphael Kimmage had a nine point advantage in the Points Classification while his superb display of climbing on Saturday gave Scot Dave Whitehall the mountains jersey by 2 points from Gary Thompson.
**Stage 9 Blessington - Dublin 64 Mls.** 1 O.McQuaid (Dublin B) 2.30.00 2 P.Cassidy (Raleigh Ireland) at 1 sec 3 T.Murphy (Dublin B) at 21 secs 4 F.Riordan (Dublin C) 5 N.Campbell (Down) 6 C.Costelloe (Limerick) 7 M.O'Grady (Galway) all same time 8 R.Melrose (Scotland) at 35 secs 9 G.Sonnen (Belgium) 10 G.Thompson (Raleigh Ireland)
**General Classification:** 1 P.Cassidy (Raleigh Ireland) 31.31.45 2 G.Thompson (Raleigh Ireland) at 3.18 3 J.McGahan (Scotland) at 3.37 4 R.Kimmage (Dublin C) at 4.17 5 John.McQuaid (Dublin B) at 4.44 6 A.Harrison (Dublin A) at 5.00 7 D.Whitehall (Scotland) at 5.37 8 R.Melrose (Scotland) at 5.43 9 B.McCormick (Dublin B) at 5.59 10 T.Murphy (Dublin B) at 6.40 11 J.McCormack (Dublin C) at 7.09 12 L.Blagojevic (France) at 9.39 13 B.Graham (Antrim) at 10.34 14 Jim.McQuaid (Garda) at 10.55 15 S.Cole (England West) at 13.49
**Points:** 1 R.Kimmage 74 2 G.Thompson 65 3 T.Murphy 64
**Mountains:** 1 D.Whitehall 23 2 G.Thompson 21 3 L.Blagojevic 13
**Team:** 1 Scotland 94.50.12 2 Dublin B 94.50.34 3 Dublin C 94.54.38

*Philip Cassidy, Winner 1983*

## 1984

The 1984 RÁS was the first with the title FBD Milk RÁS, a name it would retain for at least the next 18 years (at time of writing). The FBD Insurance Company, which specialises in Agricultural insurance, came in as a partner with the Dairy Council, a partnership which would provide one of the longest sponsorships of a major Irish sporting event.

The '84 event came a fortnight after the two week long British Milk Race which had been absolutely dominated by a team from the USSR. Raleigh Ireland's Gary Thompson was one of the few riders to get on equal terms with the Soviets taking a stage and a second place. The Irish National Team Director Pat McQuaid said he hoped his team would dominate the RÁS in a way comparable with the Russian team in the British event. Unfortunately Thompson had to withdraw two days before the event with dental problems. His place was taken by Raphael Kimmage and the team was completed by Dermot Gilleran, Seamus Downey and David Gardiner, the latter being installed by the Press as pre-race favourite.

There were a couple of novel innovations for the opening stage. It was run off as a kilometre TT prologue on the Eamonn Ceannt track in Dublin and top Irish professional Sean Kelly, who pundits were making a favourite for the coming Tour of France, would ride the prologue as a guest. There was an echo of the bad old days of Irish cycling politics when a letter from Karl McCarthy, secretary of the ICF, was published in the Press. It sought to have Kelly reconsider his participation on the opening stage. Race director Dermot Dignam expressed disbelief that such a prominent official "should attempt to prevent Irish people from a rare opportunity to see the number one cyclist in the world in action here.''

The ''84 race also heralded a new era in the race results procedure in that a computer was used for the first time to produce the general classification. Earlier in the year the Ulster Council had obtained the services of Dr. Mike Pringle at Queens University to write a programme, running on an Apple II, for their Tour of Ulster and I was asked to operate it on the RÁS. Despite a few teething problems it worked quite well and speeded up things considerably.

The following year I recommended that Seamus Shortall, who had written his own programme, should take over doing the results for the RÁS and he has been with it ever since, constantly improving and adding to his programme which has since been used on major races all over the world.

### STAGE 1 (a) and (b)

Kelly didn't disappoint his fans and indeed recorded the fastest time of 1.15.47 for the two and a half laps of the track, despite it being a wet and windy morning.

1.16 seconds slower than Kelly, 1982 winner Dermot Gilleran (Raleigh Ireland) was fastest of the official entries taking the first yellow jersey by 0.18 of a second from Stephen Porter (Isle of Man) with Wicklow's John Brady third in 1.17.08. However with so short a test the event was only a showpiece serving only to provide an early leader with no real gaps being opened.

**Stage 1a Dublin 1km TT:** 1 D.Gilleran (Raleigh Ireland) 1.16.63 2 S.Porter (Isle of Man) 1.16.81 3 J.Brady (Wicklow) 1.17.07 4 M.Kelly (Dublin Skil) 1.17.27 5 J.McQuaid (Dublin Skil) 1.17.87 6 S.Mangan (Kerry) 1.18.00

Gilleran was into action right from the start of the 80 miles afternoon stage to Monaghan. Stephen Delaney (Dublin Leyland) and Paddy Power (Waterford Foundry) went from the gun and stayed out in front to Ashbourne where Delaney took the first prime of the race.

There were joined by five others and it this seven stayed away all the way to the finish where they had a lead of 40 seconds over a chasing group of 22. Indeed at one time, around Carrickmacross, their lead was up to 3 minutes but when the 22 went in pursuit this quickly came down and was only 1.30 at Castleblayney and in the end they were somewhat lucky to survive but they did and Gilleran did the double out sprinting Armagh pair Gerald Irvine and Joe Barr for the stage.

**Stage 1b Dublin - Monaghan 80 Mls.** 1 D.Gilleran (Raleigh Ireland) 2.58.45 2 G.Irvine (Armagh) 3 J.Barr (Armagh) 4 P.Tansey (Dublin Skil) 5 B.Power (Tipperary) 6 P.Power (Waterford Foundry) 7 S.Delaney (Dublin Leyland) all same time 8 J.McQuillan (Armagh) at 39 secs 9 S.Finnegan (Scotland) 10 S.Downey (Raleigh Ireland) all same time

**General Classification:** 1 D.Gilleran (Raleigh Ireland) 3.00.02 2 P.Tansey (Dublin Skil) at 2 secs 3 B.Power (Tipperary) at 3 secs 4 equal J.Barr (Armagh) and S.Delaney (Dublin Leyland) s.t. 6 equal G.Irvine (Armagh) and P.Power (Waterford Foundry) at 6 secs 8 S.Porter (Isle of Man) at 43 secs 9 equal R.Kimmage (Raleigh Ireland) B.Madden (Galway Rosengrens)) and J.McQuillan (Armagh) at 45 secs

## STAGE 2

Pre-race favourite Davy Gardiner crashed out of the race (and Olympic participation) when he came down heavily after 78 miles. He had a previous skull fracture and as a result the crash ended Gardiner's career at the top level although he returned to the sport years later as a veteran.

His fall came as he went to the head of a chasing group outside Roscommon when his gears slipped throwing the Lurgan rider on to the road at speed. He was taken to hospital.

The Raleigh Ireland team had some consolation when Seamus Downey won the stage and took over the yellow jersey. Downey would also benefit from Gardiner's misfortune as first reserve on the Olympic team he was to make it to the Los Angeles games.

After an initial break of five riders was overhauled 17 miles after the start, a big break of 21 riders went clear. Despite a stiff headwind Andy Hurford (Nottingham) and Brendan O'Callaghan (Galway) went off on their own before Roscommon and stayed out in front until they were caught by ten chasers at Athleague.
Downey was in this chasing group and with five miles to go he jumped away opening up a gap of 49 seconds by the finish with Jimmy McQuillan (Armagh) winning the sprint from the chasers to take over the points jersey.
**Stage 2 Monaghan - Ballinasloe 114 Mls.** 1 S.Downey (Raleigh Ireland) 4.21.30 2 J.McQuillan (Armagh) at 49 secs 3 J.McQuaid (Dublin Skil) 4 B.O'Callaghan (Galway Rosengrens) 5 T.Mannion (Galway Rosengrens) 6 A.Hurford (Nottingham) 7 J.McSharry (Galway Rosengrens) 8 B.Power (Tipperary Super Stanley) 9 P.Tansey (Dublin Skil) all same time 10 J.Ford (Wales at 2.30
**General Classification:** 1 S.Downey (Raleigh Ireland) 7.22.18 2 P.Tansey (Dublin Skil) at 5 secs 3 B.Power (Tipperary Super Stanley) at 6 secs 4 J.McQuillan (Armagh) at 28 secs 5 A.Hurford (Nottingham) at 30 secs 6 B.O'Callaghan (Galway Rosengrens) at 32 secs 7 T.Mannion (Galway Rosengrens) at 34 secs 8 D.Gilleran (Raleigh Ireland) at 38 secs 9 equal J.Barr (Armagh) and S.Delaney (Dublin Leyland) at 43 secs 11 J.Ford (Wales) at 2.411 12 J.McQuaid (Dublin Skil) at 2.422
**Points:** 1 J.McQuillan 22 2 S.Downey 21 3 P.Tansey and B.Power 19
**Team:** 1 Galway Rosengrens 22.09.24 2 Armagh 22.11.47 3 Dublin Skil 22.14.12

## STAGE 3

'78 Tour of Ireland winner John Shortt (Galway Rosengrens) won the third stage into Nenagh from breakaway companion Stephen Delaney (Dublin Leyland) but race leader Seamus Downey improved his position, finishing 9th and increasing his margin over second placed Bobby Power to 35 seconds.
However the loss of Davy Gardiner was showing on the Raleigh Ireland team and they had a hard day chasing down breaks with only three riders.
The break of the day came after 50 miles of racing on the approach to the climb at Tuamgraney where Shortt, Delaney and Limerick's Claude Costelloe went away from a leading group of 24 riders which went clear after an early break of 12 had been brought back.
The three stayed together until the hills approaching Portroe when Costelloe dropped back to be picked up by Jamie McGahan (Dublin Skil) who had just dropped Downey but the Scot was unable to maintain his momentum.
Delaney, aware of Shortt's superior finishing sprint tried repeatedly to get away on the run-in but to no avail and in the finishing sprint he sat up knowing he couldn't win.
Peter Stewart (Dublin Skil) led in a chasing group of nine riders 59 seconds later. This group included a somewhat shattered looking Downey.
**Stage 3 Ballinasloe - Nenagh 98 Mls.** 1 J.Shortt (Galway Rosengrens) 3.49.30 2 S.Delaney (Dublin Leyland) s.t. 3 P.Stewart (Dublin Skil) at 59 secs 4 J.Ford

(Wales) 5 J.McGahan (Dublin Skil) 6 A.Harrison (Dublin Leyland) 7 C.Costelloe (Limerick) 8 D.Gilleran (Raleigh Ireland) 9 S.Downey (Raleigh Ireland) 10 G.Irvine (Armagh) all same time

**General Classification:** 1 S.Downey (Raleigh Ireland) 11.12.47 2 B.Power (Tipperary Super Stanley) at 35 seconds 3 S.Delaney (Dublin Leyland) at 1.04 4 J.Shortt (Galway Rosengrens) at 1.51 5 P.Tansey (Dublin Skil) at 1.57 6 D.Gilleran (Raleigh Ireland) at 1.58 7 J.Ford (Wales) at 2.41 8 A.Hurford (Nottingham) at 2.42 9 B.O'Callaghan (Galway Rosengrens) at 2.44 10 T.Mannion (Galway Rosengrens) at 2.46 11 J.McGahan (Dublin Skil) at 2.56 12 J.McQuillan (Armagh) at 3.32

**Points:** 1 S.Downey 28 2 S.Delaney and D.Gilleran 23

**Team:** 1 Galway Rosengrens 33.43.16 2 Raleigh Ireland 33.44.44 3 Armagh 33.47.07

## STAGE 4 (a) and (b)

Gearoid Costelloe (Limerick) and Stephen Finnegan (Scotland) won Tuesday's two stages but Seamus Downey held onto his yellow jersey but his lead was down to a mere 8 seconds over a rampant Stephen Delaney (Dublin Leyland).

Delaney made his bid for yellow on the afternoon's 61 miles stage to Limerick while Downey and the Raleigh Ireland team could do no more than limit their losses with the result that Delaney just missed out but moved 56 seconds closer to the top of the GC.

Tony Murphy (Dublin West) made the initial move breaking away at Newcastlewest after 25 miles. He was joined by six riders including Delaney and Costelloe and although their lead never exceeded 1 minute they stayed away to the finish where Costelloe edged out Murphy and Tommy Mannion in the sprint.

Downey tried to get away in the closing miles but was hampered by a rubbing wheel. Peter Stewart (Dublin Skil) did manage to get away from the bunch to take 8th place with his teammate John McQuaid leading in the bunch for 9th place.

**Stage 4a Limerick - Tralee 61 Mls.** 1 G.Costelloe (Limerick) 2.28.30 2 T.Murphy (Dublin West) 3 T.Mannion (Dublin Rosengrens) 4 R.Sherry (Galway Rosengrens) 5 A.Harrison (Dublin Leyland) 6 E.Madden (Dublin West) 7 S.Delaney (Dublin Leyland) all same time 8 P.Stewart (Dublin Skil) at 46 secs 9 J.McQuaid (Dublin Skil) at 56 secs 10 B.O'Callaghan (Galway Rosengrens) s.t.

The evening criterium in Killarney was dominated by the visiting riders, Scotland's Finnegan followed home by Stephen Porter (Isle of Man) and Kenny Grey (Nottingham) with virtually the whole field close behind.

The 25 miles race was over 23 laps of the town-centre circuit and John McQuaid and Jamie McGahan both made unsuccessful attempts to get away but in the end it came down to a huge bunch gallop with Bernard Cunningham (Louth) best of the Irish riders in 4th place.

**Stage 4b Killarney Criterium 25 Mls.** 1 S.Finnegan (Scotland) 1.03.00 2 S.Porter (Isle of Man) 3 K.Grey (Nottingham) 4 B.Cunningham (Louth) 5 J.McQuillan (Armagh) 6 D.Gilleran (Raleigh Ireland) all same time
**General Classification:** 1 S.Downey (Raleigh Ireland) 14.45.13 2 S.Delaney (Dublin Leyland) at 8 secs 3 B.Power (Tipperary) at 35 secs 4 T.Mannion (Galway Rosengrens) at 1.46 5 J.Shortt (Galway Rosengrens) s.t. 6 P.Tansey (Dublin Skil) at 1.47 7 D.Gilleran (Raleigh Ireland) at 2.13 8 B.O'Callaghan (Galway Rosengrens) at 2.34 9 J.Ford (Wales) at 2.37 10 J.McGahan (Dublin Skil) at 2.46
**Points:** 1 S.Delaney, J.McQuillan and D.Gilleran 33 points each

## STAGE 5 (a) and (b)

Stephen Finnegan (Scotland) took his second stage in a row on the 52 miles morning stage from Killarney to Castletownbere and Stephen Delaney (Dublin Leyland) kept up his challenge by taking the afternoon 6 miles mountain time-trial up the Healy Pass.
However it was Tipperary's Bobby Power who took over the lead after the leading break on the morning stage, which included third, placed Power, finishing over 3 minutes ahead of Downey.
Power, weighing 12 stone, was not expected to be a serious challenger in the mountain stages but he got across to the break after the descent into Kenmare. There had been eight in the break at Moll's Gap but on the descent Power was among several riders who bridged the gap to leave 13 at the front.
It was during this period of hectic activity that Stephen Finnegan (Scotland) went away and stayed out in front to finish on his own 1.21 ahead. In fact not all those in the leading group realised that he was out in front and when Aidan Harrison (Dublin Leyland) came home he raised his hand in triumph thinking he had won the stage.
**Stage 5a Killarney - Castletownbere 52 Mls.** 1 S.Finnegan (Scotland 1.59.00 2 A.Harrison (Dublin Leyland) at 1.21 3 D.Gilleran (Raleigh Ireland) s.t. 4 P.Hodge (Wales) at 1.37 5 P.Stewart (Dublin Skil) 6 M.Coll (Scotland) 7 B.O'Callaghan (Galway Rosengrens) 8 J.McQuaid (Dublin Skil) 9 J.McQuillan (Armagh) 10 G.Irvine (Armagh) all same time
The afternoon's 3.75 miles time trial was up the Healy Pass with the famous hairpins not such a problem to individual riders climbing as to a bunch descending but giving spectators at the top a great view of the event all the way up.
Delaney had an emphatic win confirming the good form he had been showing all week and his winning margin over Jason Ford (Wales) was 22 seconds. Seamus Downey was third but his big time loss on the short morning stage saw him drop to sixth overall. His teammate Dermot Gilleran now lay second, 1.04 down on Power.
**Stage 5b Healy Pass 3.75 Mls. TT:** 1 S.Delaney (Dublin Leyland) 14.45 2 J.Ford (Wales) 15.07 3 S.Downey (Raleigh Ireland) 15.26 4 D.Gibson (Scotland) 15.28 5 J.McGahan (Dublin Skil) 15.34 6 M.Kelly (Isle of Man) 15.37 7 equal D.Gilleran

(Raleigh Ireland) and R.Kimmage (Raleigh Ireland) 15.51 9 S.Porter (Isle of Man) 15.53 10 P.Stewart (Dublin Skil) 15.54

**General Classification:** 1 B.Power (Tipperary Super Stanley) 17.02.34 2 D.Gilleran (Raleigh Ireland) at 1.04 3 J.McGahan (Dublin Skil) at 1.36 4 S.Delaney (Dublin Leyland) at 1.45 5 B.O'Callaghan (Galway Rosengrens) at 2.12 6 S.Downey (Raleigh Ireland) at 2.18 7 T.Mannion (Galway Rosengrens) at 3.51 8 P.Stewart (Dublin Skil) at 4.07 9 R.McSherry (Galway Rosengrens) at 4.22 10 J.Ford (Wales) at 4.36 11 J.Shortt (Galway Rosengrens) at 4.50 12 R.Kimmage (Raleigh Ireland) at 4.51

**Points:** 1 D.Gilleran 46 2 J.McQuillan 40 3 S.Finnegan 37

**Mountains:** 1 equal S.Finnegan and S.Delaney 6 3 J.Ford 5

**International Team:** 1 Raleigh Ireland 15.14.36 2 Wales 51.30.16 3 Isle of Man 51.32.11

**County Team:** 1 Galway Rosengrens 15.12. 28

## STAGE 6

Armagh's Jimmy McQuillan won the stage into Mallow in a sprint from a 12-man group which included Stephen Delaney (Dublin Leyland) who took over the yellow jersey from Bobby Power (Tipperary Super Stanley) who finished in the main bunch as did several other top contenders including Seamus Downey, Dermot Gilleran and Jamie McGahan.

Delaney ended the day with a useful margin of over 3 minutes from John Shortt (Galway Rosengrens) with the best Raleigh Ireland rider now Raphael Kimmage in third place a further 7 seconds back.

A ten strong break went away after only 5 miles. Delaney went in pursuit but when he joined them the break seemed doomed as they only held a lead of about 30 metres on the field.

Delaney went to the front and the break was rejuvenated and started to draw clear. Three more riders got across from the bunch and with Delaney and John Shortt doing most of the work the 14-strong group had 1.15 in hand at Glengariff.

At Ballingeary this was up to 3 minutes when another group left the bunch in pursuit. remarkably Power and the other favourites were not involved in this either and they eventually came home in the bunch 9 minutes behind the Delaney group. Downey did make several attempts to g away but he was hampered by a painful boil which made it difficult to sit on the saddle.

McQuillan's stage win put him into the point's jersey with 55 points to the 46 of Gilleran and his efforts brought Armagh to the top of the team GC.

**Stage 6 Castletownbere - Mallow 88 Mls.** 1 J.McQuillan (Armagh) 3.34.00 2 R.Kimmage (Raleigh Ireland) 3 P.Tansey (Dublin Skil) 4 J.Shortt (Galway Rosengrens) 5 K.Walsh (Meath) 6 Jim.McQuaid (Garda Bosch) 7 J.Barr (Armagh) 8 D.McCarthy (Tipperary Super Stanley) 9 M.Lawson (Scotland) 10 B.Hodges (Wicklow) 11 S.Delaney (Dublin Leyland) all same time

**General Classification:** 1 S.Delaney (Dublin Leyland) 20.38.19 2 J.Shortt (Galway Rosengrens) at 3.05 3 R.Kimmage (Raleigh Ireland) at 3.12 4 P.Tansey (Dublin Skil) at 3.23 5 J.McQuillan (Armagh) at 3.25 6 J.Barr (Armagh) 6.26 7 B.Power (Tipperary Super Stanley) at 7.13 8 B.Hodges (Wicklow) at 7.37 9 B.O'Callaghan (Galway Rosengrens) at 8.10 10 D.Gilleran (Raleigh Ireland) at 8.17 11 N.Madden (Garda Bosch) s.t. 12 J.Ford (Wales) at 8.21
**Points:** 1 J.McQuillan 55 2 D.Gilleran 46 3 S.Delaney 38
**International Team:** 1 Raleigh Ireland 62.14.30 2 Scotland 3 Wales
**County Team:** 1 Armagh 62.02.05 2 Galway Rosengrens 62.09.54 3 Dublin Skil 62.12.58

## STAGE 7

John McQuaid (Dublin Skil) won stage seven, 109 miles from Mallow to Enniscorthy when he out sprinted Armagh's Gerald Irvine after the two of them had gone away just 10 kms from the finish.
Delaney kept his place at the top of the G.C. and with a margin of 2.59 over John Shortt he looked more and more like a RÁS winner With sixth placed Joe Barr over 6 minutes down it meant the 21-year-old Dubliner essentially only had to keep an eye on four riders who might pose a threat to his jersey.
Seamus Downey who had led for several days was forced to retire because of the saddle boil that had been troubling him for several days. However he had the consolation of getting selection for the Olympics after Davy Gardiner's skull fracture ruled him out.
Ten riders went away after going through Ballyporeen and they stayed out in front until the stiff climb approaching Carrick-on-Suir when the field, led by Delaney, closed up on the leaders and the break started to disintegrate.
As they were caught McQuaid, Irvine and Brendan O'Callaghan (Galway Rosengrens) went again and they were joined by Gearoid Costelloe (Limerick) and Michael Kinsella but again they were brought back.
With 7 miles remaining Irvine went and was joined by McQuaid and the two held a slender lead of around 15 seconds to the finish where McQuaid easily won the sprint.
**Stage 7 Mallow - Enniscorthy 109 Mls.** 1 J.McQuaid (Dublin Skil) 4.15.00 2 G.Irvine (Armagh) at 1 second 3 G.Costelloe (Limerick) at 18 secs 4 J.Ford (Wales) 5 B.O'Callaghan (Galway Rosengrens) 6 M.O'Grady (Meath) 7 M.Kinsella (Longford) all same time 8 J.Shortt (Galway Rosengrens) at 26 secs 9 A.Hurford (Nottingham) 10 B.Madden (Galway Rosengrens) all same time
**General Classification:** 1 S.Delaney (Dublin Leyland) 2.54.11 2 J.Shortt (Galway Rosengrens) at 2.59 3 R.Kimmage (Raleigh Ireland) at 2.12 4 P.Tansey (Dublin Skil) at 3.23 5 J.McQuillan (Armagh) at 3.25 6 J.Barr (Armagh) at 6.26 7 B.Power (Tipperary Super Stanley) at 7.13 8 B.O'Callaghan (Galway Rosengrens) at 7.39 9 B.Hodges (Wicklow) at 7.40 10 J.Ford (Wales) at 7.50 11 N.Madden (Garda Bosch) at 8.17 12 J.McGahan (Dublin Skil) at 8.49

**Points:** 1 J.McQuillan 60 2 J.McQuaid 44 3 G.Irvine 42
**International Team:** 1 Scotland 75.14.26 2 Wales 75.20.32
**County Team:** 1 Armagh 74.47.50 2 Galway Rosengrens 75.56.44 3 Dublin Skil 74.59.42

## STAGE 8 (a) and (b)

A team time-trial was an unusual event for the RÁS with its big variation in abilities and it was probably a mistake to have it so late in the race when many teams had lost riders. However its impact on the GC was minimal as times only counted toward bonuses; a formula which was also tried, and later abandoned by the Tour de France.
Dublin Skil won the TTT by 39 seconds from Scotland and Armagh who were on equal time. This gave Paul Tansey a bonus of 15 seconds which brought him past Raphael Kimmage into third place.
**Stage 8a Enniscorthy - Gorey 18 Mls. TTT:** 1 Dublin Skil 40.54 2 Scotland 41.33 3 Armagh 41.37 4 Dublin Leyland 42.44 5 Limerick 43.15 6 Galway Rosengrens 43.35
’81 winner Jamie McGahan won the penultimate stage, a tough 84 miles from Gorey to Carlow which saw the hardest climbs of the week. Race leader Delaney finished eighth, last of the winning break and maintained his hold on the jersey.
Second-placed Short tried all day to drop the race leader but found him impossible to shake off and he remained 2.59 down with only one stage left.
Tony Murphy broke away just after the start and typically Delaney took up the chase along with four others including Shortt. Other rider came across and by Aughrim the lead group had grown to 15 with another group chasing, led by McGahan.
As they hit the first climb at Aughavannagh Delaney piled on the pressure and many of the leaders dropped back. After 40 miles, on the ascent of the Wicklow Gap, McGahan had joined the leaders who now numbered seven who were soon joined by another Dublin Skil rider Peter Stewart.
Delaney had an anxious moment when his chain started to click but he couldn’t stop to change bikes as Shortt and McGahan were on the attack. The eight stayed ahead of a chasing group led by Raphael Kimmage who had missed the break, losing all hope of a challenge for the jersey.
The eight stayed out in front coming into Carlow with 2.30 on the Kimmage group, McGahan winning the sprint to take his total tally of RÁS stage wins to three.
**Stage 8b Gorey - Carlow 84 Mls.** 1 J.McGahan (Dublin Skil) 3.24.00 2 A.Hurford (Nottingham) 3 J.Shortt (Galway Rosengrens) 4 G.Evans (Wales) 5 M.Coll (Scotland) 6 C.Costelloe (Limerick) 7 P.Stewart (Dublin Skil) 8 S.Delaney (Dublin Leyland) all same time 9 G.Costelloe (Limerick) at 2.35 10 S. Reynolds (Meath) s.t.
**General Classification:** 1 S.Delaney (Dublin Leyland) 28.18.11 2 J.Shortt (Galway Rosengrens) at 2.59 3 R.Kimmage (Raleigh Ireland) at 5.47 4 J.McQuillan (Armagh) at 5.55 5 J.McGahan (Dublin Skil) at 8.34 6 B.Power (Tipperary Super Stanley) at 9.48 7 M.Coll (Scotland) at 10.07 8 B.O’Callaghan (Galway Rosengrens) at 10.11 9

B.Hodges (Wicklow) at 10.12 10 J.Ford (Wales) at 10.32 11 A.Hurford (Nottingham) at 10.43 12 N.Madden (Garda Bosch) at 11.02
**Points:** 1 J.McQuillan 64 2 J.Shortt 50 3 equal S.Delaney and B.O'Callaghan 46
**Mountains:** 1 M.Coll (Scotland) 19 2 S.Delaney 18 3 equal C.Costelloe and J.Shortt 10.
**County Team:** 1 Armagh 2 Galway Rosengrens 3 Dublin Skil

## STAGE 9

John McQuaid took his second stage win of the week making it four stages in a row for the Dublin Skil team. However there was no challenge to the leader and 21-year-old Dubliner Stephen Delaney ran out a comfortable overall winner. His immediate comments were that it was 'the reject's revenge', referring to his being dropped from the Olympic squad.
Six miles after the start 10 riders went away and they were soon pursued by another 14 who caught them at the 20 mile mark of the 87 miles stage into the Phoenix Park. When Seamus Reynolds had a puncture it left 23 in front and by Newbridge their lead had grown to 3 minutes. Delaney was happy to let them stay out there as long as their lead didn't reach 4 minutes and his judgement was proved sound when the large break started to disintegrate and they were all back in the bunch by Clane.
Four riders then went clear: McQuaid, John Brady, Andy Hurford and Noel Madden but the last two punctured leaving McQuaid and Brady on their own as they entered the Park with a 50 second lead, hardly enough to hold off the bunch with 12 2-mile laps still to go. They managed to stay out in front for the next 10 laps before being reeled in but McQuaid had another go before the finish taking with him Armagh's Gerald Irvine and Longford's John McCormack and they finished in that order, McQuaid comfortably winning the sprint from Irvine with McCormack at 4 seconds, Andy Nicholson (Isle of Man) leading in the next group 19 seconds down.
Four times winner Shay O Hanlon marked the end of a glittering career coming home at the head of the bunch, just in front of the yellow jersey which he had worn more than any other RÁS rider.
**Stage 9 Carlow - Dublin 87 Mls.** 1 J.McQuaid (Dublin Skil) 3.14.33 2 G.Irvine (Armagh) s.t. 3 J.McCormack (Longford) at 4 secs 4 A.Nicholson (Isle of Man) at 19 secs 5 P.Tansey (Dublin Skil) 6 J.McGahan (Dublin Skil) 7 T.Mannion (Galway Rosengrens) 8 J.Barr (Armagh) 9 J.Brady (Wicklow) 10 A.Hurford (Nottingham) all same time
**General Classification:** 1 S.Delaney (Dublin Leyland) 31.34.00 2 J.Shortt (Galway Rosengrens) at 2.59 3 R.Kimmage (Raleigh Ireland) at 5.47 4 J.McQuillan (Armagh) at 5.55 5 J.McGahan (Dublin Skil) at 8.34 6 B.Power (Tipperary Super Stanley) at 9.48 7 M.Coll (Scotland) at 10.07 8 B.O'Callaghan Galway Rosengrens) at 10.11 9 B.Hodges (Wicklow) at 10.12 10 J.Ford (Wales) at 10.32 11 A.Hurford (Nottingham) at 10.43 12 N.Madden (Garda Bosch) at 11.02
**Points:** 1 J.McQuillan 64 2 J.McQuaid 59 3 G.Irvine 56

**Mountains:** 1 M.Coll (Scotland) 19 2 S.Delaney 18 3 equal C.Costelloe and J.Shortt 10
**International Team:** 1 Scotland 95.59.37 2 Wales 96.09.00 3 Isle of Man 96.16.19
**County Team:** 1 Armagh 95.40.34 2 Galway Rosengrens 95.43.59 3 Dublin Skil 95.45.40

*1984 winner, Stephen Delany*

## 1985

The 1985 RÁS once more had Irish professionals taking part in the opening prologue which was a 2 kilometre climb up the Hill of Howth, Kelly this time was joined by past RÁS winner Stephen Roche.
The USSR were back for the first time since 1977 and the question on everyone's minds was would they be able to dominate to event to the same extent in a field which had several riders with considerable international experience.
Scotland and the Isle of Man were back and Great Britain also had a team which included Chris Lillywhite on his first international outing, never having ridden a race longer than 3 days previously. The Putney rider would go on to an illustrious career in the professional ranks with a Tour of Britain win and King of the Mountains in the Nissan Classic among his palmares.

### STAGE 1 (a) and (b)

Stephen Roche was fastest up the Hill of Howth in 3.33 beating his professional rival Sean Kelly by 16 seconds.
Of the official starters, however, Irish Triathlon Champion Mick Walsh was fastest in 3.42, 3 seconds faster than Viktor Zveriuk and the strength of the Soviets was obvious from the start with three riders in the top five. Also prominent was defending champion Stephen Delaney (Dublin Leyland) who was in fourth place just five seconds behind Walsh and his teammate Mick Kinsella also made the top six with a time of 3.52.
**Stage 1a Howth Prologue 2kms. TT:** 1 M.Walsh (Galway Rosengrens) 3.42 V.Zveriuk (USSR) 3.45 3 V.Chubiakov (USSR) 3.46 4 S.Delaney (Dublin Leyland) 3.47 5 N.Kosiakov (USSR) 3.48 6 M.Kinsella (Dublin Leyland) 3.52
19-year old Chris Lillywhite won the afternoon's 67 miles stage from Dublin to Navan out sprinting John McQuaid (Raleigh Ireland) and two USSR riders in atrocious weather conditions.
The Soviets took over the race lead with Nicolai Kosiakov fourth on the stage which, with his fifth place in the prologue, saw him take the jersey with a margin of 3 seconds over Lillywhite.
An eight-man group went away after only five miles of the stage and included with three USSR riders: Antonovich, Zveriuk and Chubiakov while team-mate Kosiakov did his best to block the pursuit at the head of the 118 strong bunch riding in a deluge. Dubliner John Brady took the prime in Balbriggan before the break was reeled in at Julianstown.
On the drag up Tullyesker, after Drogheda, it was Kosiakov on the attack and he was joined by several small groups until by Dunleer there were nine in front including

Antonovich and Zveriuk with a five-man group led by Lillywhite and Stephen Spratt (Raleigh Ireland) in pursuit.
The pursuers got up to the break after Slane and a few miles later Lillywhite attacked again taking with him Kosiakov and they were joined by McQuaid and Antonovich where surprisingly the two USSR riders were left with the minor placings.
In the post stage interviews it transpired that new leader Kosiakov had ridden against Sean Kelly with a USSR team in that year's Vuelta and this gave the home riders some idea of just what quality of riders they were up against in the week to come.
**Stage 1b Dublin - Navan 67 Mls.** 1 C.Lillywhite (Great Britain) 2.10.22 2 J.McQuaid (Raleigh Ireland) 3 E.Antonovich (USSR) 4 N.Kosiakov (USSR) all same time 5 S.Cope (Great Britain) at 5 secs 6 M.O'Grady (Dublin Leyland) at 24 secs 7 D.Findlayson (Scotland) 8 J.Barr (Armagh) 9 T.McManus (Dublin Leyland) 10 V.Chubiakov (USSR) all same time
**General Classification:** 1 N.Kosiakov (USSR) 2.14.10 2 C.Lillywhite (G.B.) at 3 secs 3 E.Antonovich (USSR) at 4 secs 4 J.McQuaid (Raleigh Ireland) at 9 secs 5 S.Cope (G.B.) s.t. 6 V.Zveriuk (USSR) at 20 secs 7 V.Chubiakov (USSR) at 22 secs 8 T.McManus (Dublin Leyland) at 28 secs 9 P.Coll (Meath Navan) at 40 secs 10 M.O'Grady (Dublin Leyland) at 45 secs 11 J.Barr (Armagh) at 46 secs 12 D.Findlayson (Scotland) at 47 secs

## STAGE 2

The Soviet team dominated the 86 miles second stage from Navan to Warrenpoint placing their four riders in the top five places, only Michael Kinsella (Dublin Leyland) in fourth place preventing a clean sweep. However the team now held the top four places on GC with ex-yellow jersey Chris Lillywhite dropping to 5th; already 2 minutes behind Kosiakov who retained the lead he had taken on the first road stage.
The 26-year-old from Moscow attacked in the final mile of the stage and came home 6 seconds clear of his three team-mates and Kinsella.
There was a lot of climbing in the final 30 miles of the stage starting on the Windy Gap in the Cooley Mountains where a 12 man break, which included only one of the Soviets: Chubikov had just over a minute at the start of the climb. Also in the group were three former RÁS winners, Stephen Delaney (Dublin Leyland), Dermot Gilleran (Raleigh Ireland) and Philip Cassidy (Meath Speedwell).
In a chasing group Antonovich punctured but such was the class of the Russian that within 15 miles he had caught and dropped most of the break.
Chubikov led over the top of the Windy Gap from Bernie McCormick who had come up in the group with Stephen Spratt, Gerald Irvine and the rest of the Soviets and on the descent and the flat run through Newry the lead group grew to 23 riders.
Cassidy, Irvine and Spratt went away but almost immediately were caught by Antonovich who not long after went clear on his own. behind the rest of the Soviets attacked and only Kinsella could stay with them. On the climb from Hilltown they

caught and soon dropped Spratt, Cassidy and Irvine and they came up to their teammate on the descent into Rostrevor and with just a short flat run-in to the finish there was nothing the large group of chasers could do to bring them back.

**Stage 2 Navan - Warrenpoint 86 Mls.** 1 N.Kosiakov (USSR) 3.19.20 2 V.Chubiakov (USSR) at 6 secs 3 V.Zveriuk (USSR) 4 M.Kinsella (Dublin Leyland) 5 E.Antonovich (USSR) all same time 6 C.McCann (Armagh) at 1.51 7 C.Lillywhite (G.B.) 8 N.Barnes (G.B.) 9 S.Cope (G.B.) 10 J.McQuaid (Raleigh Ireland), all same time

**General Classification:** 1 N.Kosiakov (USSR) 5.33.30 2 E.Antonovich (USSR) at 13 secs 3 V.Zveriuk (USSR) at 27 secs 4 V.Chubiakov (USSR) at 28 secs 5 C.Lillywhite (G.B.) at 2.00 6 J.McQuaid (Raleigh Ireland) at 2.06 7 S.Cope (G.B.) s.t. 8 M.Kinsella (Dublin Leyland) at 2.10 9 T.McManus (Dublin Leyland) at 2.25 10 S.Spratt (Raleigh Ireland) at 2.36 11 M.O'Grady (Dublin Leyland) at 2.42 12 M.Coll (Antrim) at 2.53

**Points:** N.Kosiakov.

**Mountains:** 1 equal N.Kosiakov; 2 V.Chubiakov 20 pts

**International Team:** 1 USSR 16.41.01 2 Great Britain 16.48.59 3 Raleigh Ireland 16.49.09

**County Team:** 1 Dublin Leyland 16.47.24 2 Armagh 16.51.42 3 Tipperary 16.54.06

## STAGE 3

After Sunday's stage memories of previous total domination by teams from Eastern Europe were very prominent but four Irish riders made all the running on the third stage, 102 miles from Warrenpoint to Enniskillen and Irish pride was salvaged, at least for the time being.

At the end of the day the USSR still held the top two places overall with Antonovich the new yellow jersey. However Terry McManus (Dublin Leyland), who had been 4th on the stage, moved up six places on GC to 3rd overall while overnight leader Kosiakov dropped to seventh.

It was a terrible day for the Raleigh Ireland team with Dermot Gilleran and John McQuaid both sick coming home 19 minutes down with the best Ireland rider Stephen Spratt now 20th, nearly 7 minutes down.

A ten-man break formed early on and at the prime of Keady Mountain Chubiakov led Antonovich and Martin Coll (Antrim).

Behind them Joe Barr (Armagh) was chasing along with Bernie McCormick (Dublin Leyland), Phil Cassidy (Meath Speedwell) and Denis McCarthy and after a long pursuit they got up to the break at Dungannon.

With 30 miles to go McManus, McCormick, Barr and Ian Chivers (Armagh) left the leaders and stayed out in front to the finish. However on the final climb of the day, Five-mile Mountain before Fintona, Antonovich set off in pursuit and managed to get up to the leaders with just three miles to go but his efforts left him unable to contest the sprint for the stage which went to McCormick from Barr and Chivers, all five getting the same time. Chubiakov led in the remainder of the original break 1.45 down.

**Stage 2 Warrenpoint - Enniskillen 102 Mls.** 1 B.McCormick (Dublin Leyland) 4.13.11 2 J.Barr (Armagh) 3 I.Chivers (Armagh) 4 T.McManus (Dublin Leyland) 5 E.Antonovich (USSR) all same time 6 V.Chubiakov (USSR) at 1.45 7 M.Kelly (Isle of Man) 8 D.Whitehall (Scotland) 9 M.Coll (Antrim) all same time 10 R.McSherry (Galway Rosengrens) at 2.04

**General Classification:** 1 E.Antonovich (USSR) 9.46.56 2 V.Chubiakov (USSR) at 1.58 3 T.McManus (Dublin Leyland) at 2.12 4 V.Zveriuk (USSR) at 2.32 5 J.Barr (Armagh) at 3.53 6 B.McCormick (Dublin Leyland) at 3.53 7 N.Kosiakov (USSR) at 4.05 8 I.Chivers (Armagh) at 4.09 9 M.Coll (Antrim) at 4.42 10 S.Delaney (Dublin Leyland) at 5.50 11 D.Whitehall (Scotland) at 5.56 12 E.Madden (Dublin Westinghouse) at 6.02

**Mountains:** 1 V.Chubiakov 35 2 B.McCormick 30 3 E.Antonovich 20

**Points:** 1 E.Antonovich 35 2 V.Chubiakov 30 3 N.Kosiakov 27

**International Team:** 1 USSR 29.24.21 2 Great Britain at 14.55 3 Isle of Man at 18.51

**County Team:** 1 Dublin Leyland 29.29.08 2 Armagh at 6.27 3 Tipperary Super Stanley at 11.31

## STAGE 4

Vladimir Zveriuk won the 90 miles fourth stage from Enniskillen to Athlone winning the sprint from a seven-man group ahead of Nick Barnes (G.B.) and Cormac McCann (Armagh). Eugene Antonovich kept the yellow jersey 2.13 ahead of Terry McManus (Dublin Leyland) but the Soviet team looked unstoppable,

The leader and his teammate and previous yellow jersey Nicolai Kosiakov also finished in the break as did McManus who moved up a place as the other Russian; Vladimir Chubiakov had mechanical trouble and lost his second place, eventually coming home 27 minutes down. However with a big lead in the KOM competition he looked likely to give this competition his main attention for the rest of the race.

It was on the category one climb at Glengevlin that the Russian took control, putting on the pressure and splitting up the bunch with Chubiakov leading across the prime line at the top. Behind him was Barnes and Stephen Spratt (Raleigh Ireland). Also there was Spratt's teammate Dermot Gilleran who along with John McQuaid and Anthony O'Gorman was suffering from food poisoning. A weakened Gilleran dropped back from the break while O'Gorman finished 28 minutes down.

The race winning move developed from the leading group on the climb although it lost several riders like Gilleran and Chubiakov. The seven man break came home 1.14 ahead of a 4-man chasing group led in by Chris Lillywhite (G.B.) 1.14 later.

**Stage 4 Enniskillen - Athlone 90 Mls.** 1 V.Zveriuk (USSR) 3.49.23 2 N. Barnes (G.B.) 3 C.McCann (Armagh) 4 N.Kosiakov (USSR) 5 E.Antonovich (USSR) 6

T.McManus (Dublin Leyland) 7 P.Healy (Kerry) all same time 8 C.Lillywhite (G.B.) at 1.14 9 J.McQuaid (Raleigh Ireland) 10 I.Chivers (Armagh)

**General Classification:** 1 E.Antonovich (USSR) 13.36.19 2 T.McManus (Dublin Leyland) at 2.12 3 V.Zveriuk (USSR) at 2.32 4 N.Kosiakov (USSR) at 4.05 5 B.McCormick (Dublin Leyland) at 5.07 6 I.Chivers (Armagh) at 5.23 7 J.Barr (Armagh) at 5.40 8 M.Coll (Antrim) at 6.18 9 N.Barnes (G.B.) at 6.33 10 C.Lillywhite (G.B.) at 7.19 11 D.Whitehall (Scotland) at 7.32 12 M.Kelly (Isle of Man) at 7.39

**Mountains:** 1 V.Chubiakov 65 2 B.McCormick, N.Kosiakov and E.Antonovich all 30 points

**Points:** 1 E.Antonovich 46 2 N.Kosiakov 39 3 C.Lillywhite 32

**International Team:** 1 USSR 40.52.50 2 Great Britain at 18.0 3 Isle of Man at 28.18.

**County Team:** 1 Dublin Leyland 41.00.26 2 Armagh at 6.27 3 Tipperary Super Stanley at 14.07

## STAGE 5

Wednesday's 110 miles stage from Athlone to Kilkee was the longest of the '85 RÁS and although the Soviets continued to dominate the stage honours evaded them going instead to Londoner Simon Cope (G.B.), a contender for the British World Championship track team.

Big loser on the stage was second placed Dubliner Terry McManus who finished six minutes down and dropped to 6th overall. With his Dublin Leyland team stricken with a stomach bug (Stephen Delaney finishing an hour behind) McManus fought bravely but failed to make it into the vital break.

In a tough headwind the Russians made light of the conditions which were causing havoc behind and the four of them rode along at over 27 mph with the result that the 9-man winning break came home 4.30 ahead of 10th placed Chris Lillywhite (G.B.).

When Gerald Irvine (Armagh) attacked just after Ballinasloe he was quickly joined by Chubiakov, then Kosiakov and before long there were 14 in the leading group. Chubiakov strengthened his KOM lead when he was second over the Corkscrew behind Phil Cassidy who had gone off on his own before the climb.

When Chubiakov and Kosiakov crossed the summit they sat up and waited for yellow jersey Antonovich who had been 3.30 behind at the foot of the climb.

When the four Russians got together at Ennistymon they quickly swept up all in front of them dropping Cassidy, Claud Costelloe and Nick Barnes leaving nine riders in the leading group which stormed away as the field was blown to smithereens behind.

**Stage 5 Athlone - Kilkee 110 Mls.** 1 S.Cope (G.B.) 5.6.20 2 N.Kosiakov (USSR) 3 V.Zveriuk (USSR) 4 S.Spratt (Raleigh Ireland) 5 E.Antonovich (USSR) 6 M.Coll (Antrim) 7 V.Chubiakov (USSR) 8 D.Gilleran (Raleigh Ireland) 9 I.Chivers (Armagh) all same time 10 C.Lillywhite (G.B.) at 4.30

**General Classification:** 1 E.Antonovich (USSR) 18.42.39 2 V.Zveriuk (USSR) at 2.32 3 N.Kosiakov (USSR) at 4.05 4 I.Chivers (Armagh) at 5.23 5 M.Coll (Antrim) at 6.18 6 T.McManus (Dublin Leyland) at 8.12 7 S.Cope (G.B.) at 10.42 8 S.Spratt (Raleigh Ireland) at 11.12 9 J.Barr (Armagh) at 11.17 10 C.Lillywhite (G.B.) at 11.49 11 N.Barnes (G.B.) at 11.51 12 M. Kelly (IOM) at 12.09
**Mountains:** 1 V.Chubiakov 80 2 N.Kosiakov 40 3 E.Antonovich 30
**Points:** 1 E.Antonovich 57 2 N.Kosiakov 53 3 V.Zveriuk 44
**International Team:** 1 USSR 56.11.50 2 Great Britain at 27.48 3 Isle of Man at 43.47
**County Team:** 1 Armagh at 56.37.07 2 Dublin Leyland at 2.22 3 Galway Rosengrens at 18.46

## STAGE 6

Thursday's 73 miles stage to Caherciveen saw a repeat of the first two the previous day as Simon Cope out sprinted Nicolai Kosiakov at the head of an 11-man break. Cope used his trackman's speed to win from the Russian and one of the fast sprinters of the home riders John McQuaid (Raleigh Ireland) who was placed third.
After his win at Kilkee he was seen as the danger man of the break and the Soviets worked him over on the way in with successive attacks which he had to counter. Cope, like teammate Lillywhite, had never ridden a race longer than four days before and the two were coping admirably.
Most of the contenders were in the 11-strong break and there were no big changes on overall. although Kosiakov and Zveriuk moved closer to the yellow jersey.
There were two main attacks on the stage, one coming before the climb of Slieve Mish which overlooks Tralee. Gerald Irvine (Armagh) again was the early attacker and when he was caught on the descent he went again and was joined by John McQuaid. After the prime at Killorglin, taken by McQuaid, the two leaders were joined by Cope, Andrew Nicholson (Isle of Man) and Pat Healy (Kerry), Joe Barr (Armagh) and Kosiakov..
Dermot Gilleran (Raleigh Ireland), Joe McSherry and Tommy Mannion (Galway Rosengrens), Zveriuk and David Cassidy joined the break which lost Mannion with a puncture leaving 11 to sprint for the stage.
**Stage 6 Kilkee (Tarbert) - Caherciveen 73 Mls** 1 S.Cope (G.B.) 2.54.13 2 N.Kosiakov (USSR) 3 J.McQuaid (Raleigh Ireland) 4 P.Healy (Kerry) 5 V.Zveriuk (USSR) 6 A.Nicholson (Isle of Man) 7 D.Gilleran (Raleigh Ireland) 8 D.Cassidy 9 J.Barr (Armagh) 10 G. Irvine (Armagh) all same time
**General Classification:** 1 E.Antonovich (USSR) 22.39.27 2 V.Zveriuk (USSR) at 1.57 3 N.Kosiakov (USSR) at 3.30 4 I.Chivers (Armagh) at 5.23 5 M.Coll (Antrim) at 6.18 6 T.McManus (Dublin Leyland) at 8.12 7 S.Cope (G.B.) at 10.07 8 J.Barr (Armagh) at 10.32 9 S.Spratt (Raleigh Ireland) at 11.12 10 C.Lillywhite (G.B.) at 11.49 11 N.Barnes (G.B.) at 11.51 12 M.Kelly (IOM) at 12.09
**Mountains:** 1 V.Chubiakov 80 2 N.Kosiakov 67 3 E.Antonovich 30

**Points:** 1 E.Antonovich 57 2 N.Kosiakov 53 3 V.Zveriuk 44
**International Team:** 1 USSR 65.01.04 2 Great Britain at 27.48 3 Isle of Man at 44.22
**County Team:** 1 Armagh at 65.26.21 2 Dublin Leyland at 3.32 3 Galway Rosengrens at 20.07

## STAGE 7

**Stage 7 Caherciveen-Bantry 86 Mls.** 1 N.Kosiakov 3:43:04
**General Classification:** 1 E.Antonovic

## STAGE 8 (a) and (b)

John McQuaid (Raleigh Ireland) won the stage from Bantry to Blarney in a sprint from a six-man break. Antonovich stayed in yellow but only after teammate Kosiakov, the form rider of the race, for the second day in a row, spurned the chance to take the lead.
Kosiakov had gone as policeman with an attack by Stephen Delaney who went away after the climb at Duke's Wood, leaving a 17-man group.
He refused to work with the Dubliner even when their lead had grown to over 4 minutes and he was race leader on the road. He told Delaney: 'Sorry, Eugene is in very good form and I do not want to lead'.
He told Delaney that he wouldn't sprint for the stage but it was to no avail as the pair was caught by John McQuaid, Richie McSherry, Michael Kinsella and Zveriuk inside the last 5 kilometres with McQuaid winning the sprint.
Back in the bunch Antonovich cut 47 seconds off the deficit on his teammate and thereby held onto the jersey by 13 seconds from Kosiakov.
**Stage 8a Bantry - Blarney 68 Mls.** 1 J.McQuaid (Raleigh Ireland) 2.36.08 2 V.Zveriuk (USSR) 3 N.Kosiakov (USSR) 4 R.McSherry (Galway Rosengrens) 5 M.Kinsella (Dublin Leyland) all same time 6 S.Delaney (Dublin Leyland) at 16 secs
The evening criterium in the centre of Cork City was run off in a downpour which made the streets treacherous and the distance was cut by the commissaires to 40 minutes plus 5 laps.
With ten minutes of racing plus five laps to go four riders went away including double stage-winner Simon Cope (G.B.), Mike Kelly (IOM), Chubikov and Anthony O'Gorman but Kelly punctured.
Cope won the sprint from Chubiakov and O'Gorman but the commissaires reported that when O'Gorman had punctures and took a lap out he had rejoined the break and not the bunch and he was relegated. Chris Lillywhite led in the bunch 13 seconds behind the break and there were no significant changes in the classification.
**Stage 8b Cork Criterium 40 minutes plus 5 laps:** 1 S.Cope (G.B.) 1.09.05 2 V.Chubiakov s.t. 3 C.Lillywhite (G.B.) at 13 secs 4 N.Kosiakov (USSR) 5 N.Barnes (G.B.) 6 A.Nicholson (Isle of Man) 7 J.Barr (Armagh) 8 V.Zveriuk (USSR)

**General Classification:** 1 E.Antonovich (USSR)29.11.14 2 N.Kosiakov (USSR) at 13 secs 3 V.Zveriuk (USSR) at 1.58 4 I.Chivers (Armagh) at 8.37 5 S Spratt (Raleigh Ireland at 11.12 6 S.Cope (G.B.) at 14.07

**STAGE 9 (a) and (b)**

**9a Monasterevan - Dublin 54 Mls.** 1 N Kosiakov 1:48:49
**GC** 1 N Kosiakov
**9b Dublin Criterium 20 Mls.** 1 S Spratt 0:46:06
**General Classification:** 1 N.Kosiakov (USSR) 31.47.25 2 E.Antonovich (USSR) at 2.23 3 V.Zveriuk (USSR) at 4.13 4 I.Chivers (Armagh) at 9.28 5 S.Spratt (Raleigh Ireland) at 10.49 6 S.Cope (G.B.) at 10.30 7 M.Kelly (IOM) at 17.25 8 C.Lillywhite (G.B.) at 18.10 9 M.Coll (Scotland) at 18.46 10 M.Kinsella (Dublin Leyland) at 19.19 11 D.Windsor (Dublin Leech) at 21.54 12 T.McManus (Dublin Leyland) at 23.02 13 J.Barr (Armagh) at 25.25 14 R.McSherry (Galway Rosengrens) at 26.36 15 R.Fletcher (IOM) at 28.19
**International Team**: 1 USSR 95.22.44 2 Great Britain at 50.51 3 Raleigh Ireland at 1.20.02

*1985 winner, Nicolai Kosiakov (USSR)*

# 1986

A good line-up of 150 riders was due to take part in the 1986 edition of the RÁS, including strong foreign teams from Germany, Canada, the Netherlands, the Isle of Man and Britain. The Ireland Snowcream line-up of Cormac McCann, Anthony O'Gorman, Aidan Harrison and Mick Kinsella would lead the home charge, with Laurence Roche, Brian Osbourne, Julian Dalby and Philip Stewart also posing a threat in the colours of the Young Ireland selection.
However, as things turned out, one of those county teams would play the most significant role in the battle for the yellow jersey

## Prologue

Dublin Carlsberg team rider Dermot Gilleran was quickest of all the starters in the 1.2 mile Howth time trial, covering the distance in 3 minutes and 45 seconds. He was three seconds quicker than team-mate Gary Thompson and Anthony O'Gorman (Tipperary-Yoplait). The effort earned comparisons with his prologue win in the Eamonn Ceannt stadium two years earlier, plus his overall RÁS success in 1982, and suggested he would be one of the challengers for the 1986 edition.
Stephen Delaney was best of the Ireland Snowcream riders in fourth, while Peter Moeck (Germany Hamburg) was the first of the mainland European riders, placing seventh.
It had been hoped that Sean Kelly would ride the time trial, repeating what he and Stephen Roche had done one year earlier and gaining great publicity for the race. However the world number one unfortunately crashed on the final stage of the Tour of Switzerland and was forced to cancel those plans.
**Stage 1a Howth TT:** 1 D.Gilleran (Dublin Carlsberg) 1.2 miles in 3 mins 45 secs 2 G.Thompson (Dublin Carlsberg) at 3 secs 3 A.O'Gorman (Tipperary-Yoplait) same time 4 S.Delaney (Ireland Snowcream) at 4 secs 5 J.Healy (Dublin Carlsberg) at 5 secs 6 E.Madden (Dublin Westinghouse) at 6 secs 7 P.Moeck (Germany Hamburg) at 8 secs 8 Cormac.McCann (Ireland Snowcream) 9 I.Chivers (N.I.C.F. Antrim) 10 B.Osborne (Cork D.Dennehy Hino) all same time
**General Classification:** 1 D Gilleran (Dublin Carlsberg) 3.45 2 G.Thomson (Dublin Carlsberg) 3.48 3 A.O'Gorman (Ireland Snowcream) 3.48 4 S.Delaney (Tipperary Yoplait) 3.49 5 J.Healy (Dublin Carlsberg) 3.50 6 E.Madden (Dublin Westinghouse) 3.51 7 P.Moeck (Germany Hamburg) 3.53 8 C.McCann (Ireland Snowcream) 3.53 9 I.Chivers (N.I.C.F. Antrim) 3.53 10 B.Osborne (Cork D.Dennehy Hino) 3.53

## Stage 1

Guesting with the Tipperary-Yoplait team, Englishman Andy Hitchens outsprinted his compatriot Dave Spencer (East Midlands) at the end of stage 1b of the FBD Milk RÁS The duo hit the line 1 minute and 14 seconds clear of another Englishman, Dave Ferguson (Bowland-Lancashire), who led home a chase group of eight riders. Ciarán McKenna (Dublin Carlsberg), Cormac McCann (Ireland Snowcream) and Dave McCall (N.I.C.F. Antrim) rounded out the top six.

Fourteen riders were clear before Slane and on the first of two ascents of Tullyesker, McKenna led over the top. Twelve were left in contention at that point, but Hitchens and Spencer attacked soon afterwards and left the others behind. Ireland Snowcream's Aidan Harrison was dropped from this chase group.

The finale of the stage saw the riders complete five one-mile laps in Drogheda. Lapped groups came together due to the shortness of the circuit, causing confusion for the judges, but there was no doubting the result of the top riders. The main bunch finished over four minutes back.

Hitchens got the gallop and the lead in the mountains and points classifications, but Spencer ended the day in the yellow jersey of race leader. He had been two seconds faster than the Tipperary-Yoplait rider in the Howth time trial, and this performance earned him a place at the very top of the leader board.

**Stage 1 Dublin - Drogheda** 1 Andy Hitchens (Tipperary-Yoplait) 69 miles in 2.11.33 2 D.Spencer (East Midlands) same time 3 D.Ferguson (Bowland Lancashire) at 1.14 4 C.McKenna (Dublin Carlsberg) 5 C.McCann (Ireland Snowcream) 6 D.McCall (N.I.C.F. Antrim) 7 R.Fletcher (Isle of Man) 8 M.Quinn (N.I.C.F. Antrim) 9 A.Cranshaw (Bowland-Lancashire) 10 F.Wasmutr (Germany Hamburg) all same time

**General Classification:** 1 Dave Spencer (East Midlands) 2.15.30 2 A. Hitchens (Tipperary-Yoplait) at 2 secs 3 Cormac McCann (Ireland Snowcream) at 1.10 4 D.Ferguson (Bowland-Lancashire) at 1.12 5 F.Wasmutr (Germany Hamburg) at 1.13 6 D.McCall (N.I.C.F. Antrim) at 1.19 7 M.Quinn (N.I.C.F. Antrim) at 1.28 8 A.Cranshaw (Bowland-Lancashire) at 1.31 9 C.McKenna (Dublin Carlsberg) at 1.38 10 T.McManus (Kerry) at 2.08

**Points:** 1 A.Hitchens 2 D.Spencer 3 D.Ferguson

**Mountains:** 1 A.Hitchens 2 C.McKenna 3 D.Spencer

**International Team:** 1 Bowland-Lancashire 6.52.49 2 East Midlands at 44 secs 3 Ireland Snowcream at 2.58

**County Team:** 1 Tipperary-Yoplait 6.50.39 2 N.I.C.F. Antrim at 2.10 3 Dublin Carlsberg at 6.11

## Stage 2

Having suffered a puncture on the first day of racing, Eddie Madden (Dublin Westinghouse) bounced back to take stage two of the FBD Milk RÁS. He came in towards the finish in Galway with twelve other riders and then jumped away inside the final kilometre, beating Gary Thompson (Dublin Carlsberg) and Jamie McGahan (Cork D.Dennehy Hino) to the line.

Dave Ferguson (Bowland-Lancashire) and Sean Kelly's brother Vincent (Tipperary-Yoplait) were fourth and fifth, with the former taking over at the head of the general classification. Previous race leader Dave Spencer (East Midlands) lost out, ending the day nine seconds back overall.

Ferguson and Mike Kelly (Isle of Man) were on the attack for much of the stage and had a decent lead over those behind. They were finally caught by eleven chasers just six miles from the end of the stage, this merging enabling Madden to take the win.

Frank Wasmutr (Germany Hamburg) finished the day one second behind Ferguson in the general classification. Dave McCall (N.I.C.F. Antrim) was seven seconds back with the overnight leader Spencer in fourth, a further two seconds in arrears.

**Stage 2 Mullingar - Galway** 1 Eddie Madden (Dublin Westinghouse) 85.2 miles in 2.58.15 2 G.Thompson (Dublin Carlsberg) at 2 secs 3 J.McGahan (Cork D.Dennehy Hino) 4 D.Ferguson (Bowland-Lancashire) 5 V.Kelly (Tipperary-Yoplait) 6 D.McColl (N.I.C.F. Antrim) 7 M.Kelly (Isle of Man) 8 S.Triebsees (Germany Hamburg) 9 M.Young (Cork D.Dennehy Hino) 10 M.Kinsella (Ireland Snowcream) all same time

**General Classification:** 1 Dave Ferguson (Bowland-Lancashire) 5.14.59 2 F.Wasmutr (Germany Hamburg) at 1 sec 3 D.McCall (N.I.C.F. Antrim) at 7 secs 4 D.Spencer (East Midlands) at 9 secs 5 A.Hitchens (Tipperary-Yoplait) at 11 secs 6 A.Cranshaw (Bowland-Lancashire) at 35 secs 7 C.McKenna (Dublin Carlsberg) at 42 secs 8 M.Kelly (Isle of Man) at 58 secs 9 L.Power (Tipperary-Yoplait) at 1.09 10 S.Spratt (Tipperary-Yoplait) at 1.12; 11 C.McCann (Ireland Snowcream) at 1.19; 12 M.Quinn (N.I.C.F. Antrim) at 1.37

**Points:** 1 Dave Ferguson 25 2 D.McCall 20 3 A.Hitchens and E.Madden 15

**Mountains:** 1 Andy Hitchens 3 2 C.McKenna 2 3 D Spencer 1

**International team:** 1 Britain – Bowland 15.48.12 2 Ireland at 2.41 3 British East Midlands at 4.15

**County team:** 1 Tipperary 15.45.48 2 N.I.C.F. Antrim at 11 secs 3 Dublin-Carlsberg at 7.30

## Stage 3

Stage 1b winner Andy Hitchens (Tipperary-Yoplait) landed another victory when he beat five others into Kanturk at the end of the third stage of the race. The Englishman outsprinted Stephen Spratt (Tipperary-Yoplait), Mike Kelly (Isle of Man), Cormac McCann (Ireland Snowcream), Philip Cassidy (Meath) and Dave Spencer (British

East Midlands) to the line, with the next finisher Mick Kinsella (Ireland Snowcream) a further four seconds back.
Overnight race leader Dave Ferguson (Bowland-Lancashire) defended his lead for most of the 134 mile stage, the longest in the race, but cracked in the final hour of racing and finished over seven minutes back. He dropped to 29th overall, 6'57 down. The yellow jersey reverted to Spencer, who had held the lead after stage 1b.
Given the length of the day's race, it was of little surprise that the pace was relatively steady early on. A group of 16 got clear 25 miles into the stage, however, and by the 50 mile mark they were two and a half minutes ahead. Spencer, Spratt and Laurence Roche (Young Ireland) were there, as were three members of the Ireland-Snowcream team - Kinsella, Anthony O'Gorman and Aidan Harrison – plus other strong riders. However, with the danger of the break apparent, Ferguson and the main bunch got back on terms shortly after the 75 mile mark.
Spencer was on a good day and attacked once again, being caught by 20 others 96 miles into the stage. McCann, Cassidy and Roche then surged clear four miles later and opened up a good lead over the rest, with McCann riding into virtual yellow due to an exhausted Ferguson's slump.
With two laps remaining of the near-four mile finishing circuit (to be covered six times in all), the three leaders were joined by Spencer, Spratt, Hitchens and Kelly. Roche slipped back on the last lap and was overtaken by chasers Kinsella and Madden. They got close to the first group but were unable to close the last few seconds in order to fight it out with Hitchens for the stage win. Spencer finished at the back of the lead group but took over once again at the top.
**Stage 3 Galway - Kanturk** 1 Andy Hitchens (Tipperary-Yoplait) 133 miles in 5.04.19 2 S.Spratt (Tipperary-Yoplait) 3 M.Kelly (Isle of Man) 4 C.McCann (Ireland Snowcream) 5 P.Cassidy (Meath) 6 D.Spencer (British East Midlands) all same time 7 M.Kinsella (Ireland Snowcream) at 4 secs 8 P.Madden (Dublin-Westinghouse) at 9 secs 9 L.Roche (Young Ireland) at 31 secs 10 G.Irvine (N.I.C.F. Antrim) at 1.47
**General Classification:** 1 Dave Spencer (British East Midlands) 10.09.27 2 A.Hitchens (Tipperary-Yoplait) at 2 secs 3 M.Kelly (Isle of Man) at 49 secs 4 S.Spratt (Tipperary-Yoplait) at 1.03 5 C.McCann (Ireland Snowcream) at 1.10 6 L.Roche (Young Ireland) at 2.30 7 C.McKenna (Dublin-Carlsberg) 8 L.Power (Tipperary-Yoplait) at 3.19 9 P.Cassidy (Meath) at 3.34 10 M.Kinsella at 3.35 11 A.Harrison (Ireland-Snowcream) at 3.55 12 A.Johnston (East Midlands) at 4.09
**Points:** 1 D.Hitchens 30 2 D.Ferguson (Bowland-Lancashire) at 2 secs 3 D.Spencer (East Midlands) 24
**Mountains:** 1 D.Hitchens 3 2 C.McKenna 2 3 D.Spencer (East Midlands) 1

## Stage 4

Stage four of the race may have brought the third successive victory for British riders, Andy Johnston (British East Midlands) taking the honours, but Irish

supporters had good reason to cheer at the finish. After 123 hard kilometres from Kanturk to Dingle, Stephen Spratt took over at the top of the general classification, ending the day 28 seconds ahead of his Tipperary Yoplait team-mate Andy Hitchens. Mike Kelly (Isle of Man) was third, 56 second down, while the previous yellow jersey Dave Spencer (British East Midlands) lost almost eight minutes and dropped to 23rd overall. Things were even more bleak for the rider he succeeded as race leader, with Dave Ferguson pulling out due to tendonitis.
Ian Chivers (N.I.C.F. Antrim) sparked off the crucial break after just six miles of racing. He was joined by Spratt, Dermot Gilleran (Dublin-Carlsberg), John Shortt (Louth), Johnston, Phil Leigh (Bowland Lancashire), Norman Campbell (Dublin Rentokill) and Stephen Delaney (Ireland Snowcream). The latter duo lost contact early on, Delaney going south 37 miles after the start and Campbell succumbing to the pace and the gradient on the first category Connor Pass.
Johnston was sitting on the break due to the fact that his team-mate had the race lead, but raced for the prime at the top of the mountain. He beat Gilleran and Chivers for the points, taking over at the top of the KOM classification, and this trio stayed clear to fight it out for the finish. Leigh, Shortt, Spratt and Kinsela were next over the top of the climb, the latter bridging across from break to bunch before the summit, and went on to sprint it out for places four through seven. Ger Madden (Cork D.Dennehy Hino) was one of several riders who also got clear of the peleton on the Connor Pass and he went on to take eighth, 53 seconds off the winning time.
**Stage 4 Kanturk - Dingle** 1 Andy Johnston (British East Midlands) 84 miles in 3.20.29 2 D.Gilleran (Dublin-Carlsberg) at 2 secs 3 I.Chivers (N.I.C.F. Antrim) at 4 secs 4 J.Shortt (Louth) at 13 secs 5 M.Kinsella (Ireland Snowcream) 6 P.Leigh (Bowland Lancashire) 7 S.Spratt (Tipperary-Yoplait) all same time 8 G.Madden (Cork D.Dennehy Hino) at 53 secs 9 B.Osbourne (Cork D.Dennehy Hino) at 1.16 10 M.Kelly (Isle of Man) at 1.23
**General Classification:** 1 Stephen Spratt (Tipperary-Yoplait) 13.41.12 2 A.Hitchens (Tipperary-Yoplait) at 28 secs 3 M.Kelly (Isle of Man) at 56 secs 4 C.McCann (Ireland Snowcream) at 1.26 5 M.Kinsella (Ireland Snowcream) at 2.32 6 A.Johnston (British East Midlands) at 2.53 7 I.Chivers at 3.34 8 P.Leigh at 3.48 9 A.Harrison (Ireland Snowcream) at 4.21 10 G.Madden (Cork D.Dennehy Hino) at 4.44 11 Osborne (Cork D.Dennehy Hino) at 4.48 12 P.Madden (Dublin – Westinghouse) at 5.02
**Points:** 1 A.Hitchens 30 2 M.Kelly 29 3 C.McCann 28
**Mountains:** 1 A.Johnson 6 2 D.Gilleran 5 3 I.Chivers 4
**International team:** 1 Ireland 41.10.59 2 British East Midlands at 9.40 3 Bowland Lancashire at 12.26
**County team:** 1 Tipperary 44.06.05 2 Antrim at 8.35 3 Cork at 13.12

## Stage 5

Andy Hitchens (Tipperary-Yoplait) added the yellow jersey to his two previous stage wins when he rode strongly on stage 5a of the race. Finishing second, 5 seconds adrift of the victor Cormac McCann (Ireland Snowcream), the British rider ended the stage 28 seconds ahead of Mike Kelly (Isle of Man).

Overnight leader Stephen Spratt (Tipperary-Yoplait) kept tabs on his rivals for much of the stage but lost out inside the final 30 miles, finishing over five minutes back.

The 71.3 mile stage took the riders from Dingle to Killorglin, once again crossing the Connor Pass along the way. Towards the end of the Slea Head loop, Aidan Harrison (Ireland Snowcream) and Dermot Gilleran (Dublin Carlsberg) broke clear, with the latter going on to take top points at the summit of the big climb.

Hitchens, Kelly, Dave Spencer (British East Midlands) and Anthony O'Gorman (Ireland Snowcream) caught and passed Harrison before the top, crossing the prime line in that order. However there was a regrouping of sorts about 30 miles from the finish, with 40 riders joining up at the front.

Fifteen riders pressed on after this merging, with four then surging ahead on the hill after Tralee. These were McCann, Hitchens, Kelly and Spencer, and Roche then got across by himself. McCann was clearly best at the end, crossing the line well clear of the new yellow jersey Hitchens.

Spratt was disappointed to lose the race lead, ending the day 4 minutes 45 seconds back in the general classification and dropping to fifth. Mick Kinsella (Ireland Snowcream) also conceded time, going from fifth to 13th overall.

**Stage 5 Dingle - Killorglin** 1 Cormac McCann (Ireland Snowcream) 71.3 miles in 2.56.58 2 A. Hitchens (Tipperary-Yoplait) at 5 secs 3 L.Roche (Young Ireland) 4 D.Spencer (British East Midlands) 5 M.Kelly (Isle of Man) all same time 6 B.Osbourne (Cork D.Dennehy Hino) at 1.27 7 A.O'Gorman (Ireland Snowcream) 8 G.Madden (Cork D.Dennehy Hino) J.Healy (Dublin-Carlsberg) 10 P. Leigh (Bowland Lancashire) all same time

**General Classification** 1 Andy Hitchens (Tipperary-Yoplait) 16.38.40 2 M.Kelly (Isle of Man) at 28 secs 3 C.McCann (Ireland-Snowcream) at 56 secs 4 L.Roche (Young Ireland) at 4.43 5 S.Spratt (Tipperary-Yoplait) at 4.45 6 P.Leigh (Bowland Lancashire) same time 7 A.Harrison (Ireland-Snowcream) at 5.18 8 G.Madden (Cork D.Dennehy Hino) at 5.41 9 B.Osbourne (Cork D.Dennehy Hino) at 5.43 10 P.Madden (Dublin Westinghouse) at 5.59 11 D.Spencer (British East Midlands) at 6.08 12 E.Madden (Dublin Westinghouse) at 6.19

**Points:** 1 A.Hitchens 47 2 C.McCann 43 3 M.Kelly 40

**Mountains:** 1 D. Gilleran (Dublin Carlsberg) 2 A.Hitchens 8 3 A.Johnston (British East Midlands) 6

**International Team:** 1 Ireland Snowcream 50.04.47 2 East Midlands at 16.04 3 Bowland Lancashire at 21.29

**County Team:** 1 Tipperary Yoplait 50.07.32 2 Cork D.Dennehy Hino at 10.49 3 N.I.C.F. Antrim at 12.35

## Stage 6

Steve Porter (Isle of Man) beat 1983 FBD Milk RÁS winner Philip Cassidy (Meath) to win the stage 5b criterium in Tralee. The duo broke away after the halfway point of the 28 mile circuit race, then sprinted it out for the honours.
John Shand (VC d'Or London) was third, finishing 14 seconds down. Race leader Andy Hitchens (Tipperary-Yoplait) came in alongside his main rivals and retained his race lead. Mike Kelly (Isle of Man) and Cormac McCann (Ireland-Snowcream) remained his closest rivals in the general classification, 28 and 56 seconds back respectively.
**Stage 6 Tralee Criterium** 1 Steve Porter (Isle of Man) 28 miles in 58 mins 55 secs P.Cassidy (Meath) same time 3 J.Shand (VC D'Or London) at 14 secs 4 F. Wasmuth (West Germany) at 16 secs 5 P.Stewart (Young Ireland) 6 G.Irvine (N.I.C.F. Antrim) both same time 7 D.Spencer (British East Midlands) at 42 secs 8 C.McCann (Ireland-Snowcream) at 48 secs 9 P.Mosck (West Germany) 10 E. Rooney (VC D'Or London) both same time
**General Classification** 1 Andy Hitchens (Tipperary-Yoplait) 17.38.23 2 M.Kelly (Isle of Man) at 28 secs 3 C.McCann (Ireland-Snowcream) at 56 secs 4 L.Roche (Young Ireland) at 4.43 5 S.Spratt (Tipperary-Yoplait) at 4.45 6 P.Leigh (Bowland Lancashire) at 4.56 7 A.Harrison (Ireland-Snowcream) at 5.18 8 B.Osborne (Cork D.Dennehy Hino) at 5.43 9 G.Madden (Cork D.Dennehy Hino) at 5.52 10 P.Madden (Dublin Westinghouse) at 6 mins 11 D.Spencer (British East Midlands) at 6.08 12 E.Madden (Dublin Westinghouse) at 6.19
**Points:** 1 A.Hitchens 52 2 Cormac.McCann 51 3 D.Spencer 45
**Mountains:** 1 D.Gilleran 11 2 A.Hitchens 8 3 A.Johnston 6
**International Team:** 1 Ireland Snowcream 53.03.56 2 East Midlands at 17.06 3 Bowland Lancashire at 21.29
**County Team:** 1 Tipperary Yoplait 53.06.52 2 Cork D.Dennehy Hino at 10.38 3 N.I.C.F. Antrim at 11.52

## Stage 7

Laurence Roche (Young Ireland) followed in the wheel tracks of his elder brother Stephen seven years earlier when he seized the yellow jersey of the FBD Insurance Rás. The 18 year old jumped from fourth to first overall on a decisive day's racing from Killorglin to Blarney, while Stephen Spratt (Tipperary-Yoplait) showed his own FBD Milk RÁS challenge was still alive when he won a big group sprint, landing stage 6a.

Spratt outsprinted Ciarán McKenna (Dublin Carlsberg), Ger Madden (Cork D.Dennehy Hino), Mick Kinsella (Ireland Snowcream) plus many others at the end of the 64 mile leg.

An eight-man group had gone clear after Killarney and these were later joined by nine other riders, including Roche and Spratt. Those present finished three minutes 32 seconds ahead of a chase group of 15, with the main bunch trailing in six minutes 16 seconds down. This latter group contained the now-dethroned yellow jersey Andy Hitchens (Tipperary-Yoplait), Mike Kelly (Isle of Man) and Cormac McCann (Ireland Snowcream), causing a big shake-up in the general classification.

**Stage 7 Killorglin - Blarney** 1 Stephen Spratt (Tipperary-Yoplait) 64 miles in 2.40.54 2 C.McKenna (Dublin Carlsberg) 3 G.Madden (Cork D.Dennehy Hino) 4 M.Kinsella (Ireland Snowcream) 5 A.Irvine (Louth) 6 P.Cassidy (Meath) 7 N.Campbell (Dublin Rentokill) 8 D.Spencer (British East Midlands) 9 A.Dineen (Cork D.Dennehy Hino) 10 P.Leigh (Bowland Lancashire)

**General classification** 1 Laurence Roche (Young Ireland) 20.24.00 2 S.Spratt (Tipperary-Yoplait) at 2 secs 3 P.Leigh (Bowland Lancashire) same time 4 G.Madden (Cork D.Dennehy Hino) at 58 secs 5 D.Spencer (British East Midlands) at 1.19 6 A.Hitchens (Tipperary-Yoplait) at 1.33 7 M.Kelly (Isle of Man) at 2.01 8 C.McCann (Ireland Snowcream) at 2.29 9 M.Kinsella (Ireland Snowcream) at 2.34 10 I.Chivers (N.I.C.F. Antrim) at 3.35 11 A.Harrison (Ireland Snowcream) at 4.07 12 B.Osbourne (Cork D.Dennehy Hino) at 4.42

## Stage 8

Ireland Snowcream rider Aidan Harrison drew on his climbing ability to win the 6b stage of the race, a short 20 mile evening leg from Blarney to Cobh. He, Stephen Delaney (Tipperary-Yoplait), Paul Madden (Dublin Westinghouse), Gerald Irvine (Antrim) and Norman Campbell (Dublin Rentokill) got clear before the first ascent of the Westview climb in Cobh, with Gary Thompson (Dublin Carlsberg) and John Shand (VC D'Or London) in pursuit.

Harrison, Madden, Irvine, Campbell, Thompson and Shand then pressed on, with Harrison flying up the final ascent of the hill to hit the line seven seconds clear of Madden. Irvine was a further 16 seconds back.

Race leader Laurence Roche finished 14th on the stage, crossing the line in the same time as his main rivals Stephen Spratt (Tipperary-Yoplait) and Phil Leigh (Bowland Lancashire) and thus maintaining his two second advantage over both.

**Stage 8 Blarney - Cobh** 1 Aidan Harrison (Ireland Snowcream) 20 miles in 38 mins 48 secs 2 P.Madden (Dublin Westinghouse) at 7 secs 3 G.Irvine (N.I.C.F. Antrim) at 30 secs 4 G.Thompson (Dublin Carlsberg) at 46 secs 5 J.Shand (VC D'Or London) at 50 secs 6 N.Campbell (Dublin Rentokill) at 59 secs 7 P.Moeck (W. Germany) at 1 min 1 sec 8 S.Delaney (Tipperary-Yoplait) at 1 min 5 secs 9 F.Fahy (Wicklow) at 1 min 20 secs 10 A.Hitchens (Tipperary-Yoplait) same time

**General Classification:** 1 Laurence Roche (Young Ireland) 21.04.12 2 S.Spratt (Tipperary-Yoplait) at 2 secs 3 P.Leigh (Bowland Lancashire) same time 4 G.Madden (Cork D.Dennehy Hino) at 58 secs 5 D.Spencer (British East Midlands) at 1.24 6 A.Hitchens (Tipperary-Yoplait) at 1.27 7 M.Kelly (Isle of Man) at 1.59 8 C.McCann (Ireland Snowcream) at 2.23 9 M.Kinsella (Ireland Snowcream) at 2.34 10 A.Harrison (Ireland Snowcream) at 2.41 11 P.Madden (Dublin Westinghouse) at 3.29 12 I.Chivers (N.I.C.F. Antrim) at 3.36
**Points:** 1 Andy Hitchens 58 2 C.McCann 58 3 D.Spencer 53
**Mountains:** 1 D.Gilleran (Dublin Carlsberg) 11 2 A.Hitchens 8 3 D.Spencer and A.Johnston (East Midlands) 6
**International Team:** 1 Ireland Snowcream 63.15.30 2 East Midlands at 20.14 3 Bowland Lancashire at 22.33
**County Team:** 1 Tipperary Yoplait 63.19.18 2 N.I.C.F. Antrim at 1.48 3 Cork D.Dennehy Hino at 5.02

## Stage 9

Reclaiming the yellow jersey he lost on stage 5a, Stephen Spratt (Tipperary-Yoplait) showed that he meant business as the FBD Milk RÁS neared its conclusion. Scottish rider Jamie McGahan (Cork D.Dennehy Hino) won the seventh stage, a 100 mile slog from Cobh to Kilkenny, but Spratt took twelve seconds out of Roche to move ten ahead in the general classification. Equally importantly for his chances, he took the same amount of time out of the rider he had started the day level with, Phil Leigh (Bowland Lancashire). Roche and Leigh dropped to third and fourth overall, with former race leader Andy Hitchens (Tipperary-Yoplait) moving up to second.
A group of ten was clear early on during the stage and then O'Gorman, Bobby Power and Eddie Madden led through Clonmel. With 20 miles remaining 17 riders pushed ahead and had built a 90 second lead by the time they started the three laps of the finishing circuit in Kilkenny.
McGahan then attacked the break and built a strong lead over the others. Behind, Spratt had a gap over Roche and Leigh starting the finishing circuit and, in line with the rules for the stage, the time differences at this point were used to determine the general classification status. The Tipperary-Yoplait rider consequently moved back into the race lead. Roche vowed to fight on and do what he could to get back on terms.
One prominent rider was missing from the general classification that evening. Dermot Gilleran (Dublin Carlsberg) had ended the previous stage as leader in the King of the Mountains classification but was forced to retire. His team-mates Gary Thompson and Peter Stewart also pulled out. Points leader Hitchens consequently took over at the top of the KOM competition, as well as moving from sixth to second overall.

**Stage 9 Cobh - Kilkenny** 1 Jamie McGahan (Cork D.Dennehy Hino) 100 miles in 3.49.05 2 A.Johnston (British East Midlands) at 6 secs 3 A.Harrison (Ireland Snowcream) 4 S.Porter (Isle of Man) 5 T.Schools (Bowland Lancashire) 6 A.Irvine (N.I.C.F. Antrim) 7 N.Campbell (Dublin Rentokill) 8 A.O'Gorman (Ireland Snowcream) 9 A.Hitchens (Tipperary-Yoplait) 10 V.Kelly (Tipperary-Yoplait) all same time

**General Classification:** 1 Stephen Spratt (Tipperary-Yoplait) 24.54.47 2 A.Hitchens (Tipperary-Yoplait) at 3 secs 3 L.Roche (Young Ireland) at 10 secs 4 P.Leigh (Bowland Lancashire) at 12 secs 5 G.Madden (Cork D.Dennehy Hino) at 1 min 8 secs 6 A.Harrison (Ireland Snowcream) at 1 min 17 secs 7 D.Spencer (British East Midlands) at 1.34 8 M.Kelly (Isle of Man) at 2.09 9 I.Chivers (N.I.C.F. Antrim) at 2.12 10 M. Kinsella (Ireland – Snowcream) at 2.32 11 C. McCann (Ireland Snowcream) at 2.33 12 B.Osbourne (Cork D.Dennehy Hino) at 3.06

**Points:** 1 Andy Hitchens 65 2 C.McCann 58 3 D.Spencer 53

**Mountains:** 1 A.Hitchens 8 2 D.Spencer and A.Johnston (East Midlands) 6 4 M.Kinsella 5

**International Team:** 1 Ireland Snowcream 74.44.25 2 East Midlands at 21.48 3 Bowland Lancashire at 25.54

**County Team:** 1 Tipperary Yoplait 74.48.13 2 N.I.C.F. Antrim at 3.22 3 Cork D.Dennehy Hino at 5.08

## Stage 10

Taking FBD Milk RÁS stage success four years after his last such triumph, Anthony O'Gorman (Tipperary-Yoplait) beat Mick Kinsella (Ireland Snowcream) at the end of the 77 mile mountain leg from Tullow to Naas.

Kinsella jumped seven places to third overall but he fell 18 seconds short of taking the yellow jersey.

Race leader Stephen Spratt's place at the top of the leader board came under fierce attack by Kinsella, who surged ahead on the first of five climbs in Wicklow and split the main bunch into several pieces. He went over the top of Aughavannagh and Drumgoff just behind Mike Kelly (Isle of Man). A regrouping took place after the descent into Laragh, with Spratt making it into the 17-man group despite a puncture.

O'Gorman then attacked and was clear over the top of Luggala. He was joined by Kinsella and the two of them worked together to extend their lead, finishing a considerable 2.14 clear of Andy Hitchens (Tipperary Yoplait) plus most of the other big names.

Spratt was helped by team-mate Hitchens in the chase and managed to limit his losses to that margin, despite the blocking attempts by Kinsella's Ireland Snowcream team-mates Cormac McCann and Aidan Harrison. Hitchens led home the chase bunch of 12 riders, with Spratt finishing last in the group but holding on to the yellow jersey with just two stages to go.

**Stage 10 Tullow – Naas:** 1 Anthony O'Gorman (Tipperary-Yoplait) 77 miles in 3.16.47 2 M.Kinsella (Ireland Snowcream) same time 3 A.Hitchens (Tipperary-Yoplait) at 2.14 4 M.Kelly (Isle of Man) 5 P.Rogers 6 K.Davies 7 A.Harrison (Ireland Snowcream) 8 B.Osborne (Cork D.Dennehy Hino) 9 D.Spencer (British East Midlands) 10 P.Madden (Dublin Westinghouse) all same time

**General classification:** 1 Stephen Spratt (Tipperary-Yoplait) 28 hours 13 mins 48 secs 2 A.Hitchens (Tipperary-Yoplait) at 3 secs 3 M.Kinsella (Ireland Snowcream) at 18 secs 4 A.Harrison (Ireland Snowcream) at 1.17 5 D.Spencer (British East Midlands) at 1.34 6 M.Kelly (Isle of Man) at 2.09 7 C.McCann (Ireland Snowcream) at 2.33 8 B.Osborne (Cork D.Dennehy Hino) at 3.08 9 P.Madden (Dublin Westinghouse) at 3.27 10 A.O'Gorman (Tipperary-Yoplait) at 6.02

**Points:** 1 A.Hitchens 78 2 C.McCann 61 3 D.Spencer 60

**Mountains:** 1 M.Kinsella 28 2 M.Kelly 22 3 A.O'Gorman 18

**International Team:** 1 Ireland Snowcream 84.37.00 2 East Midlands at 33.11 3 Bowland Lancashire at 51.07

**County Team:** 1 Tipperary Yoplait 84.49.22 2 Cork D.Dennehy Hino at 14.52 3 N.I.C.F. Antrim at 17.45

## Stage 11

Coping best with the wet conditions, Terry McManus (Kerry) took the penultimate stage, a tough race from Naas to Enniskerry. The 46 mile leg was run off in dire weather and heavy rain fell for most of the day. Laurence Roche (Young Ireland) was one of the most active, leading over the top of the Wicklow Gap, and while he was caught on the descent he then forged ahead again with McManus and Frank Wasmuth (Germany). The three fought it out for the stage win, with McManus beating the 18 year old Irishman in the sprint. Paul Fahy (Wicklow) was next over the line, finishing 24 seconds down in fourth place and nine ahead of a chase group led in by Cormack McCann (Ireland Snowcream)

Behind, 16 riders crashed on the descent of the Long Hill. Race leader Stephen Spratt stayed out of trouble, however, and would start the final stage that afternoon with a three second gap over his Tipperary Yoplait team-mate Andy Hitchens. Given that the two would work together, Mick Kinsella (Ireland Snowcream) was his closest threat. However the 18 second advantage Spratt had took the pressure off somewhat.

**Stage 11 Naas – Enniskerry:** 1 Terry McManus (Kerry) 46 miles in 1.50.33 2 L.Roche (Young Ireland) same time 3 F.Wasmuth (Germany) same time 4 P.Fahy (Wicklow) at 24 secs 5 C.McCann (Ireland Snowcream) at 33 secs 6 A.Johnston (British East Midlands) 7 A.Hitchens (Tipperary-Yoplait) 8 S.Porter (Isle of Man) 9 P.Rogers (VC D'Or London) 10 D.Tiernan (Louth Drogheda Dundalk Dairies) all same time

**General classification:** 1 Stephen Spratt (Tipperary Yoplait) 30.04.54 2 A.Hitchens (Tipperary Yoplait) at 3 secs 3 M.Kinsella (Ireland Snowcream) at 18 secs 4

A.Harrison (Ireland Snowcream) at 1.17 5 D.Spencer (East Midlands) at 1.34 6 M.Kelly (Isle of Man) at 2.09 7 Cormac.McCann (Ireland Snowcream) at 2.33 8 B.Osborne (Cork D.Dennehy Hino) at 3.08 9 P.Madden (Dublin Westinghouse) at 3.27 10 A.O'Gorman (Ireland Snowcream) at 6.02
**Points:** 1 A.Hitchens 87 2 Cormac.McCann 72 3 M.Kelly 62
**Mountains:** 1 M.Kinsella 29 2 M.Kelly 23 3 A.O'Gorman 23

## Stage 12

Stephen Spratt faced down attacks from closest rival Mick Kinsella (Ireland Snowcream) on the final stage, holding on to win his first FBD Milk RÁS. The riders covered 29.2 miles in the Dun Laoghaire criterium and, as expected, there were many attacks from the off.
Eventual stage winner John Shand (VC D'Or London) sparked off the crucial break and was joined in the move by Laurence Roche (Young Ireland), Andy Cranshaw (Bowland Lancashire) and the third-placed rider overall, Mick Kinsella (Ireland Snowcream). The latter's presence in the move spelt danger for Spratt but he also made it into the break and marked his rival for the rest of the stage.
Shand attacked inside the final five laps and hit the line 25 seconds ahead of solo chaser Roche. Cranshaw was five seconds further back in third. Spratt's Tipperary-Yoplait team-mate Andy Hitchens had started the day second overall but finished a further 30 seconds behind in the main bunch, with Kinsella moving past him and taking second overall.
Hitchens had the consolation of taking the points jersey, though, finishing the day six points clear despite McCann's seventh place on the final stage. Kinsella took the mountains jersey and his Ireland Snowcream squad was best international team. Spratt's Tipperary Yoplait line-up came out tops in the county team prize.
**Stage 12 Dun Laoghaire Criterium:** 1 John Shand (VC D'Or London) 29.2 miles in 1.12.03 2 L.Roche (Young Ireland) at 19 secs 3 A.Cranshaw (Bowland Lancashire) at 24 secs 4 M. Kinsella (Ireland Snowcream) at 26 secs 5 Stephen Spratt (Tipperary-Yoplait) at 27 secs 6 P.Moeck (Germany) at 56 secs 7 C.McCann (Ireland Snowcream) 8 C.Bracken (Sligo) 9 F.Wesmuth (Germany) 10 J.Nolan (Meath John McCann TV) all same time **General classification:** 1 Stephen Spratt (Tipperary-Yoplait) 31.17.24 2 M.Kinsella (Ireland Snowcream) at 17 secs 3 A.Hitchens (Tipperary-Yoplait) at 32 secs 4 A.Harrison (Ireland Snowcream) at 1.46 5 D.Spencer (British East Midlands) at 2.03 6 M.Kelly (Isle of Man) at 2.38 7 C.McCann (Ireland Snowcream) at 3.02 8 B.Osborne (Cork D.Dennehy Hino) at 3.37 9 P.Madden (Dublin Westinghouse) at 3.56 10 L.Roche (Young Ireland) at 6.24 11 A.O'Gorman (Ireland Snowcream) at 6.31 12 P.Leigh (Bowland Lancashire) at 7.35
**Points:** 1 A.Hitchens 87 2 Cormac.McCann 81 3 M.Kelly 66
**Mountains:** 1 M.Kinsella 29 2 M.Kelly 23 3 A.O'Gorman 23

**International Team**: 1 Ireland Snowcream 93.48.45 2 East Midlands at 33.41 3 C.C. Bowland at 51.05
**County Team:** 1 Tipperary Yoplait 94.01.08 2 Cork D.Dennehy Hino at 15.21 3 N.I.C.F. Antrim at 40.15

*1986 winner, Stephen Spratt*

## 1987

1987 was the year of Stephen Roche's magnificent triple of Giro d'Italia, Tour de France and world championships, and several of the articles detailing his career that season pinpointed his 1979 RÁS win as the first big indicator of his ability.
In fact, the race was known for many years as an important way of determining up-and-coming talent. The length of the event, the well-balanced collection of international and county teams and the physiological demand of the race all highlighted those with the ability to go on to big things. This was the case in 1987, but the RÁS title ultimately went to a slightly older competitor who came from one of Ireland's famous cycling families, and who combined brain and brawn to overcome those riding with stronger teams.

### STAGE 1

Back in the limelight: twelve months previously the Tipperary-Yoplait team had won the FBD Milk RÁS with Stephen Spratt, and the county team took up where it left off when guest rider Greg Oravetz soloed to a clear victory on the opening stage of the 1987 RÁS, seizing the first yellow jersey.
The US rider attacked three miles from the finish of the 98 mile stage from Dublin to Killeshandra, hitting the line 19 seconds ahead of a nine man chasing group. Niall McWilliams (Young Ireland) was second, with Laurence Roche (Young Ireland) third.
The crucial break was established approximately fifteen miles into the stage and while Oravetz and Roche missed the initial selection, they joined forces to get across. The American then showed his strength when he beat all bar Gerald Irvine (Ireland-Snowcream) to the top of the day's sole categorised climb, Slieve na Caillaigh.
Their 25-man break co-operated to hold its advantage over the other main contenders, then towards the end Frank Relf (Dublin South) brought that truce amongst rivals to an end when he fired off an attack. Oravetz and his Tipperary-Yoplait team-mate Bobby Power got up to him but then Relf crashed on a bend, also causing Power to fall.
Oravetz put his head down and motored to a solo victory, while Relf finished with a nine-man chasing group. Power trailed in a further 13 seconds back, having been picked up by the remnants of that 25-man break. A number of big names were in this chasing bunch, including former race winner Philip Cassidy (Meath-Viking).
**Stage 1 Dublin - Killeshandra 98 Mls.** 1 G.Oravets (Tipperary Yoplait) 3.37.05 2 N.McWilliams (Young Ireland) at 19 secs 3 L.Roche (Young Ireland) s.t. 4 R.Harrington (Plancoet Lec France) s.t. 5 K.Kimmage (Ireland Snowcream) s.t. 6

G.Irvine (Ireland Snowcream) s.t. 7 S.Delaney (Tipperary Yoplait) s.t. 8 P.Leigh (CC Bowland) s.t. 9 P.Cassidy (Meath Viking Cycles) s.t. 10 F.Relf (Dublin South) s.t.
**General Classification:** 1 G.Oravets (Tipperary Yoplait) 2 N.McWilliams (Young Ireland) at 19 secs 3 L.Roche (Young Ireland) s.t. 4 R.Harrington (Plancoet Lec) s.t. 5 K.Kimmage (Ireland) s.t. 6 G.Irvine (Ireland) s.t. 7 S.Delaney (Tipperary Yoplait) s.t. 8 P.Leigh (CC Bowland) s.t. 9 P.Cassidy (Meath Viking Cycles) s.t. 10 F.Relf (Dublin South) s.t.
**Points:** 1 G.Oravets 15 2 N.McWilliams 14 3 L.Roche 13
**Mountains:** 1 G.Irvine 3 2 G.Oravets 2 3 S.Delaney 1
**International Team:** 1 Ireland Snowcream 10.52.25 2 Young Ireland at 3.29 3 Plancoet Lec at 3.42
**County Team:** 1 Tipperary Yoplait 10.52.06 2 Down at 45 secs 3 Dublin Panasonic at 4.14

## STAGE 2

Philip Cassidy (Meath Viking) took both the stage win and the overall lead when he triumphed at the end of the 91 mile second stage from Killeshandra to Derry. The 1983 FBD Milk RÁS winner rode aggressively throughout the stage and made his winning move with about a mile to go. Heavy rain was falling and while his rear wheel skidded while crossing the bridge close to the line, he stayed upright and gave it everything on the rise up to the finish at The Diamond.
Cassidy's effort saw him cross the line a full nine seconds clear of Ray Keane (Young Ireland), Gerald Irvine (Tipperary-Yoplait) and the rest of the chase group. Crucially, overnight leader Greg Oravetz (Tipperary-Yoplait) missed the move and finished in the main bunch, over four minutes back.
As a result Cassidy took over at the top, ending the day nine seconds clear of Irvine and 22 ahead of both Andy Cranshaw (Bowland Lancashire) and Mick Walsh (Dublin Panasonic). Fifth-placed rider Niall McWilliams (Young Ireland) was 1 minute 26 seconds in arrears.
Earlier in the stage, Oravetz's Tipperary-Yoplait team had tried to defend the lead and brought back an early break. However Irvine got clear shortly after the race crossed the border into the North and was joined by seven others, Cassidy, Walsh and Keane included. Oravetz's team-mate Stephen Spratt was there but was under no obligation to work as the team were trying to protect the yellow jersey. However he did dig in on the Seraghy Mountain climb, beating Irvine to the top.
A few extra riders joined up, including Cranshaw and his team-mate Tim Schools, and the group drove onwards through Strabane. Plancoet Lec France rider Philip Hodge then had some bad luck, puncturing out of the move and eventually finishing 1 minute 30 seconds behind the stage winner, but the others raced on towards the finish.
There Cassidy made his move on the run-in to the line, prospering in dire weather to take both the stage victory and the yellow jersey. Keane, Irvine, Schools, Cranshaw,

Martin Quinn (Down), Bill Reid (Kerry Lee Strand), Spratt, Walsh and Gary Thomson (Longford) finished nine seconds back.

**Stage 2 Killeshandra – Derry 91 Mls** 1 P.Cassidy (Meath Viking Cycles) 3.26.35 2 R.Keane (Young Ireland) at 9 secs 3 G.Irvine (Ireland Snowcream) 4 T.Schools (C.C. Bowland) 5 A.Cranshaw (C.C. Bowland) 6 M.Quinn (Down) 7 B.Reidy (Kerry Lee Strand) 8 S.Spratt (Tipperary Yoplait) 9 M.Walsh (Dublin Panasonic) 10 G.Thompson (Longford) all same time

**General Classification:** 1 P.Cassidy (Meath Viking Cycles) 7.03.59 2 G.Irvine (Ireland Snowcream) at 9 secs 3 A.Cranshaw (C.C. Bowland) at 22 secs 4 M.Walsh (Dublin Panasonic) s.t. 5 N.McWilliams (Young Ireland) at 1.26 6 Cormac.McCann (Ireland Snowcream) at 1.39 7 R.Rutgers (Holland) s.t. 8 John.McQuaid (Dublin Carlsberg) at 1.43 9 F.Relf (Dublin South) at 1.47 10 P.Leigh (C.C. Bowland) at 1.57

**Points:** 1 G.Irvine 23 2 P.Cassidy 22 3 N.McWilliams 18

**Mountains:** 1 G.Irvine 5 2 S.Spratt 3 G.Oravets 2

**International Team:** 1 Ireland Snowcream 21.15.32 2 C.C. Bowland at 2.59 3 Young Ireland 4.16

**County Team:** 1 Tipperary Yoplait 21.16.10 2 Down at 31 secs 3 Dublin Panasonic at 3.39

## STAGE 3

After losing the race lead on day two of the race, Greg Oravetz bounced back when he won the third stage of the FBD Milk RÁS into Buncrana. The 82 mile leg crossed the gruelling Gap of Mamore and, as expected, the mountain stage led to a reshuffling of the general classification. Oravetz made his move on that final climb, overhauling breakaway riders Anthony O'Gorman (Limerick Burgerland) plus Paul McCormack (Longford) and then cresting the top first. He, McCormack and Mick Kinsella (Dublin-Panasonic) joined up on the descent and blasted in to the finish, where they finished in that order.

Irvine and Philip Cassidy (Meath Viking) were next in, conceding 40 seconds. However the latter had enough time in hand to retain his yellow jersey, ending the day 9 seconds ahead of Irvine and 1 minute 30 seconds up on McCormack. The Longford rider had started the day outside the top ten overall but was very much in the running for the yellow after the mountainous stage. Others went the opposite direction; Andy Crawshaw (Bowland Lancashire) dropped from third to 24th, Niall McWilliams (Young Ireland) from fifth to 18th and Cormac McCann (Ireland-Snowcream) from sixth to twelfth. The previous year's winner Stephen Spratt cracked and went to over seven minutes down in the general classification.

The 82 mile race began in Derry and looped around Malin Head. Five riders went clear before the climb there, namely McCormack, O'Gorman, Dave Ferguson, Olivier Heuze and Russell Harrington (both Plancoet Lec France). Ferguson was first to the top of the Malin climb, beating McCormack across the prime line, and the quintet had 50 seconds lead after 50 miles of racing.

The group stuck together but once those chasing behind started to close, McCormack and O'Gorman decided it was all or nothing and pushed ahead. The latter was then dropped on the Mamore climb, then McCormack was himself caught and passed by Oravetz and then Kinsella. However the three joined up on the descent and stayed together to the finish, where they fought it out for the stage victory.
Irvine tried to shake off Cassidy on several occasions but was marked by the race leader, the two finishing fourth and fifth. Mick Walsh (Dublin Panasonic) had been running sixth but unfortunately punctured and came home in a group 2 minute and 17 seconds back. This caused him to drop one place to fifth in the general classification, as well as concede some time to his GC rivals.
**Stage 3 Derry – Buncrana 77 Mls.** 1 G.Oravets (Tipperary Yoplait) 3.06.41 2 P.McCormack (Longford) s.t. 3 M.Kinsella (Dublin Panasonic) s.t. 4 G.Irvine (Ireland Snowcream) at 40 secs 5 P.Cassidy (Meath Viking Cycles) s.t. 6 P.Goodwin (Manchester) at 1.13 7 F.Relf (Dublin South) at 1.20 8 G.Thompson (Longford) s.t. 9 P.Keogh (Kerry Lee Strand) s.t. 10 J.Barr (Down) s.t.
**General Classification:** 1 P.Cassidy (Meath Viking Cycles) 2 G.Irvine (Ireland Snowcream) at 9 secs 3 P.McCormack (Longford) at 1.30 4 M.Kinsella (Dublin Panasonic) at 1.42 5 M.Walsh (Dublin Panasonic) at 1.59 6 R.Rutgers (Holland) at 2.19 7 F.Relf (Dublin South) at 2.27 8 G.Madden (Cork) at 2.40 9 S.Downey (Down) s.t. 10 G.Oravets (Tipperary Yoplait) at 2.58
**Points:** 1 G.Irvine 35 2 P.Cassidy 33 3 G.Oravets 30
**Mountains:** 1 G.Oravets 13 2 G.Irvine 10 3 P.McCormack 10
**International Team:** 1 Ireland Snowcream 30.40.41 2 C.C. Bowland at 7.30 3 Plancoet Lec France at 9.18
**County Team:** 1 Down 30.43.06 2 Dublin Panasonic at 1.20 3 Tipperary Yoplait at 4.03

## STAGE 4

Laurence Roche bounced back from two disappointing stages when he won the fourth leg of the race, a 92 mile stage from Buncrana to Sligo. The Young Ireland rider had begun well on day one when he was third into Killeshandra but things went somewhat astray after that, with the Dubliner lying 59th, 14 minutes and 36 seconds back after the Buncrana stage. Taking the victory in Sligo was therefore a considerable boost to morale.
Roche used his bike handling skill to good effect on the damp and slippery finishing circuit, taking more risks than his three breakaway companions and sprinting in ahead of Thierry Delorme (Plancoet Lec France), Claude Costello (Limerick Burgerland) and Stephen Delaney (Tipperary Yoplait). Rik Rutgers (Holland), Tim Schools (Bowland Lancashire), Paul McCormack (Longford) and Ger Minihan (Cork) were next across the line, losing 13 seconds, while race leader Philip Cassidy was a further 11 seconds back. He retained the yellow jersey by nine seconds from

closest rival Gerald Irvine (Ireland Snowcream) but third-placed McCormack reduced his deficit slightly to 1 minute 19 seconds.
The stage was marked by an early attack which included big guns such as Andy Crawshaw (Bowland Lancashire), Mick Walsh (Dublin Panasonic), Gary Thomson (Longford) and Paul Madden (Dublin Westinghouse). Crawshaw took the prime at Ballybofey but by the time the riders hit Bundoran the peleton had essentially regrouped. Bernie McCormack (Garda Lada) took the prime there.
Delaney sparked off the stage-winning break when he kicked clear with ten miles remaining. Six miles later Delorme, Costello and Roche got across, the latter then going on to win the sprint. Most of the other big name riders finished relatively close on time, although Cormac McCann came in five minutes back and dropped to 21st overall. The Ireland Snowcream rider had started the day 12th but was losing all chance of winning the race.
**Stage 4 Buncrana – Sligo 92 Mls.** 1 L.Roche (Young Ireland) 3.55.25 2 T.Delorme (Plancoet Lec France) s.t. 3 C.Costello (Limerick Burgerland) s.t. 4 S.Delaney (Tipperary Yoplait) s.t. 5 R.Rutgers (Holland) at 13 secs 6 T.Schools (C.C. Bowland) s.t. 7 P.McCormack (Longford) s.t. 8 G.Minihan (Cork) s.t. 9 D.McCaul (Down) at 24 secs 10 S.Spratt (Tipperary Yoplait) S.t.
**General Classification:** 1 P.Cassidy (Meath Viking Cycles) 14.07.09 2 G.Irvine (Ireland Snowcream) at 9 secs 3 P.McCormack (Longford) at 1.19 4 M.Kinsella (Dublin Panasonic) at 1.42 5 M.Walsh (Dublin Panasonic) at 1.59 6 R.Rutgers (Holland) at 2.08 7 F.Relf (Dublin South) at 2.27 8 S.Downey (Down) at 2.52 9 J.Barr (Down) at 3.02 10 P.Leigh (C.C. Bowland) at 3.34
**Points:** 1 G.Irvine 37 2 P.Cassidy 33 3 G.Oravets 30
**Mountains:** 1 G.Oravets 13 2 G.Irvine 10 3 P.McCormack 10
**International Team:** 1 Ireland Snowcream 42.32.43 2 C.C. Bowland at 2.44 3 Plancoet Lec France at 8.54
**County Team:** 1 Down 42.30.33 2 Tipperary Yoplait at 3.39 3 Dublin Panasonic at 4.26

## STAGE 5

The fifth day of the 1987 FBD Milk RÁS was one of drama, with race leader Philip Cassidy (Meath Viking) and his closest rival Gerald Irvine (Ireland-Snowcream) being far behind for most of the stage, then riding back into contention close to the finish in Tipperary. They consequently held on to their first two places overall.
Niall McWilliams emulated the previous day's victory by Young Ireland team-mate Laurence Roche, out-sprinting Bernie McCormack (Garda Lada), Thierry Delorme (Plancoet Lec France) and Greg Oravetz (Tipperary-Yoplait) to the line. Paul Madden (Dublin Westinghouse) was a further five seconds back.
The 104 mile stage started in Roscommon and, six miles later, fifteen riders clipped away. They had a minute and a half after nine miles working together and this was

almost enough for the best-placed rider there, Mick Kinsella (Dublin Panasonic), to become the race leader on the road.
Fifteen others bridged after 30 miles of racing, amongst them Paul McCormack (Longford), Mick Walsh (Dublin Panasonic) and Frank Relf (Dublin South). McCormack had started the day 1 minute and 19 seconds down in third place, and with the peleton containing Cassidy and Irvine over five minutes back after 80 miles, McCormack was surely thinking that the yellow jersey would be his that evening.
Andy Crawshaw and Tim Schools (both Bowland Lancashire) attacked before Nenagh and led up the Bollingbrook climb. However Kevin Kimmage (Ireland-Snowcream) was on a good day, having earlier taken the prime in Ballinasloe, and he went clear of the others and got across to the two team-mates.
Cassidy and Irvine were finally chasing behind, joining with others such as Cormac McCann (Ireland Snowcream) and Laurence Roche (Young Ireland) in a successful bid to reduce the gap to the other general classification riders.
The three leaders were mopped up by the large front group and, approximately seven kilometres from the end of the stage, McWilliams, Bernie McCormack, Delorme, Oravetz and Madden slipped away to fight it out for the stage win.
Kimmage led in ten riders some 24 seconds later, taking sixth. Joe Barr (Down) and Relf were in this group, and with Cassidy and Irvine finishing a further 1 minute 29 seconds in arrears, the two narrowed the gap to 58 seconds and 1 minute 33 seconds respectively. They also moved to third and fifth overall.
**Stage 5 Roscommon - Tipperary 97 Mls.** 1 N.McWilliams (Young Ireland) 3.59.36 2 B.McCormick (Garda Lada) s.t. 3 T.Delorme (Plancoet Lec France) s.t. 4 G.Oravets (Tipperary Yoplait) s.t. 5 P.Madden (Dublin Westinghouse) at 5 secs 6 K.Kimmage (Ireland Snowcream) at 24 secs 7 C.Maye (Offaly Scully Kitchens) s.t. 8 R.Keane (Young Ireland) s.t. 9 J.Barr (Down) s.t. 10 A.Cranshaw (C.C. Bowland) s.t.
**General Classification:** 1 P.Cassidy (Meath Viking Cycles) 18.08.38 2 G.Irvine (Ireland Snowcream) at 9 secs 3 F.Relf (Dublin South) at 58 secs 4 P.McCormack (Longford) at 1.29 5 J.Barr (Down) at 1.33 6 M.Kinsella (Dublin Panasonic) at 1.52 7 R.Rutgers (Holland) at 2.08 8 M.Walsh (Dublin Panasonic) at 2.09 9 S.Downey (Down) at 3.02 10 G.Oravets (Tipperary Yoplait) at 3.16
**Points:** 1 G.Oravets 42 2 G.Irvine 37 3 P.Cassidy 33
**Mountains:** 1 G.Oravets 13 2 G.Irvine 10 3 P.McCormack 10
**International Team:** 1 Ireland Snowcream 54.35.41 2 C.C. Bowland at 1.25 3 Plancoet Lec France at 8.50
**County Team:** 1 Down 54.33.41 2 Tipperary Yoplait at 3.05 3 Dublin Panasonic at 6.15

## STAGE 6

Defending champion Stephen Spratt may have had a less than perfect start to his campaign for a second FBD Milk RÁS success, but the Tipperary-Yoplait rider

bounced back when he won the sixth stage of the race.
At the end of a 97 mile leg from Tipperary to Mallow, he soloed in 1 minute and 3 seconds ahead of team-mate Greg Oravetz, Gary Thomson and Paul McCormack (both Longford), taking a dominant victory. Laurence Roche (Young Ireland) and Ger Madden (Cork) led home a chasing break, some eight seconds later.
McCormack was as satisfied as Spratt with the day's result, given that he moved to the head of the general classification. Overnight leader Philip Cassidy (Meath-Viking) and second-placed rider Gerald Irvine (Ireland Snowcream) finished a massive 19 minutes and 58 seconds in arrears, the duo having pressed the self-destruct button to their RÁS campaigns when they got caught up in an argument about who should and should not work. Many laid the blame at the door of the Ireland team, with criticism flying that some bad decisions were made during the stage. Both Shane Clarke and Cormac McCann went on the attack during the stage, meaning that Irvine had only Kevin Kimmage for support.
Whoever was most at fault, the fact remained that both Cassidy and Irvine were well out of the running by the end of the stage. The same applied to Frank Relf (Dublin South), third at the start of the day, plus the riders who had been lying sixth, seventh and eighth overall. This trio - Mick Kinsella (Dublin Panasonic), Rik Rutgers (Holland) and Kinsella's team-mate Mick Walsh - were also stranded behind and lost out.
Four miles after the stage start, Spratt had showed his good sensations when he took the first King of the Mountains prime at Slieve na Muc. Philip Hodge (Plancoet Lec France) was second ahead of Oravetz and Cassidy, but the latter was then missing from a 22 man group which went away twelve miles later. Several other GC contenders were also left behind and their chances went up in smoke when the bunch stopped racing.
The gap was over sixteen minutes 50 miles into the stage and while several groups had succeeded in getting across before it opened up too wide, there was clearly no question of a recovery by the others. Spratt was flying and took the primes on each of the day's four climbs. The last of these, Mushera Mountain, copper fastened his hold on the KOM jersey and was also the springboard for his stage-winning attack.
He hit the line well clear of Oravetz and the other two, ending the day 10$^{th}$ overall. McCormack was delighted to take the yellow jersey, even if the advantage of nine seconds over Joe Barr (Down) was a slim one. Seamus Downey, Oravetz and Madden were all within two minutes one second, keeping things tight at the top.
**Stage 6 Tipperary – Mallow 97 Mls.** 1 S.Spratt (Tipperary Yoplait) 4.03.11 2 G.Oravets (Tipperary Yoplait) at 1.03 3 G.Thompson (Longford) s.t. 4 P.McCormack (Longford) s.t. 5 L.Roche (Young Ireland) at 1.11 6 G.Madden (Cork) s.t. 7 S.Clarke (Ireland Snowcream) s.t. 8 A.O'Gorman (Limerick Burgerland) s.t. 9 S.Delaney (Tipperary Yoplait) s.t. 10 T.Delorme (Plancoet Lec France) s.t.
**General Classification:** 1 P.McCormack (Longford) 22.14.21 2 J.Barr (Down) at 12 secs 3 S.Downey (Down) at 1.41 4 G.Oravets (Tipperary Yoplait) at 1.47 5 G.Madden (Cork) at 2.01 6 P.Leigh (C.C. Bowland) at 2.23 7 N.McWilliams (Young

Ireland) at 2.35 8 O.Heuze (Plancoet Lec France) at 2.48 9 G.Thompson (Longford) at 4.14 10 S.Spratt (Tipperary Yoplait) at 4.45
**Points:** 1 G.Oravets 56 2 L.Roche 39 3 G.Irvine 37
**Mountains:** 1 S.Spratt 31 2 G.Oravets 28 3 P.Hodge 19
**International Team:** 1 Plancoet Lec France 66.57.37 2 C.C. Bowland at 32 secs 3 Young Ireland at 9.44
**County Team:** 1 Tipperary Yoplait 66.48.33 2 Down at 6.11 3 Longford at 24.48

## STAGE 7

One day after he lost the chance to win the FBD Milk RÁS, Gerald Irvine showed a strong fighting spirit in winning the 91 mile seventh stage from Mallow to Tramore. The Ireland Snowcream rider attacked just before the start of the two-mile finishing circuit and soloed in sixteen seconds clear of Rik Rutgers (Holland) and Anthony O'Gorman (Limerick-Burgerland). Gary Thomson (Longford) and Brendan Graham (Garda-Lada) were a further three seconds back.

The general classification only saw small changes, with Paul McCormack (Longford) riding strongly to defend his yellow jersey. Joe Barr (Down) remained second overall but conceded a further three seconds. His team-mate Seamus Downey stayed one minute 41 seconds back in third, while Greg Oravetz (Tipperary-Yoplait) remained fourth in the overall standings. Thomson's ranking was the day's biggest change, moving from ninth to fifth.

Irvine was on the go throughout the stage. He was one of ten riders who was clear going through Kildorrery then, after their recapture, clipped away with another eight after twenty miles of racing. A regrouping saw 27 riders lead as the race passed through Ballyporeen and continued on to the climb of The Vee, where Spratt beat Oravetz to bolster his King of the Mountains lead.

The crucial break went after the descent into Lismore. Here, 47 miles into the stage, Irvine pushed ahead with John McQuaid (Dublin Carlsberg), Stephen Delaney (Tipperary Yoplait) and Claude Costello (Limerick Burgerland). These were joined a couple of miles later by the Australian Mark Cooper (Dublin Panasonic), and knuckled down to open up a lead of over one minute.

Several chasers combined and were able to bridge the gap, including former race leader Phil Cassidy (Meath Viking), O'Gorman and Graham. Thomson and Rutgers then made the junction 70 miles after the start, and the enlarged group had over two minutes lead heading along the coast road to Tramore.

Delaney sparked off the final break when he surged towards the end of the stage. O'Gorman and Irvine got across and the latter then countered, starting the finishing circuit 21 seconds clear and holding on to take the win.

**Stage 7 Mallow – Tramore 92 Mls.** 1 G.Irvine (Ireland Snowcream) 3.39.54 2 R.Rutgers (Holland) at 16 secs 3 A.O'Gorman (Limerick Burgerland) s.t. 4 G.Thompson (Longford) at 19 secs 5 B.Graham (Garda Lada) s.t. 6 P.Goodwin (Manchester) at 21 secs 7 S.Delaney (Tipperary Yoplait) s.t. 8 John.McQuaid

(Dublin Carlsberg) at 28 secs 9 J.McGahan (Garda Lada) s.t. 10 R.Keane (Young Ireland) s.t.
**General Classification:** 1 P.McCormack (Longford) 25.56.51 2 J.Barr (Down) at 12 secs 3 S.Downey (Down) at 1.41 4 G.Oravets (Tipperary Yoplait) at 1.45 5 G.Thompson (Longford) at 1.57 6 G.Madden (Cork) at 2.01 7 P.Leigh (C.C. Bowland) at 2.23 8 O.Heuze (Plancoet Lec France) at 2.32 9 N.McWilliams (Young Ireland) at 2.35 10 S.Spratt (Tipperary Yoplait) at 4.45
**Points:** 1 G.Oravets 56 2 G.Irvine 52 3 L.Roche 39
**Mountains:** 1 S.Spratt 36 2 G.Oravets 32 3 P.Hodge 19
**International Team:** 1 Plancoet Lec France 78.04.51 2 C.C. Bowland at 48 secs 3 Young Ireland at 7.52
**County Team:** 1 Tipperary Yoplait 77.53.46 2 Down at 8.28 3 Longford at 24.48

## STAGE 8

Mick Walsh (Dublin-Panasonic) and Paul McCormack (Longford) were both celebrating at the end of the penultimate day of racing, a tough stage in the heart of the Wicklow Mountains. Walsh landed the honours as the stage victor, while McCormack took time out of his closest rivals and ensured he had a comfortable buffer of two and a half minutes after the 107.5 miles from Tramore to Wicklow Town.
Walsh was regarded as one of the best climbers heading into the race and while his overall challenge came apart on stage six to Mallow, he highlighted his ability with a fine ride in the big mountains. He got clear with three others and then forged ahead of these inside the final mile. Anthony O'Gorman (Limerick-Burgerland) finished six seconds back, while McCormack and Olivier Heuze (Plancoet Lec France) came in a further three seconds later.
There was then a big gap back to the next group, with Rik Rutgers (Holland), Laurence Roche (Young Ireland), Thierry Delorme (Plancoet Lec France), Joe Barr (Down) and Gary Thomson (Longford) all two minutes and six seconds in arrears.
Barr had started the day second overall but was unable to match McCormack on the slopes, cracking early on. Whilst he finished the day still in second, he was a full two minutes and 32 seconds behind the yellow jersey in the general classification, and was by then level on time and placing with Heuze.
The mountains weren't the only things wreaking havoc. Tipperary Yoplait riders Greg Oravetz, Stephen Spratt and Stephen Delaney had started the stage in fourth, tenth and twelfth places overall and were expected to pose a threat to McCormack's lead. They were also clear leaders in the county team classification. However things went badly wrong for them due to a bad case of food poisoning; Oravetz and Spratt were well below power during the stage and dropped out of the top ten, while Delaney was forced to retire from the FBD Milk RÁS.
For those in better health, McCormack, Barr and many of the other contenders were part of a 32 man lead group which was clear ten miles into the stage. Walsh attacked

on the Aughavannagh climb and split the front bunch into several sections, the Dublin Panasonic rider taking the prime. Ten seconds later McCormack led an eight man chase group over the summit, with Barr already suffering and losing time.
There was a regrouping of sorts on the descent but Barr headed south once more on the climb of Drumgoff. Walsh, McCormack, O'Gorman and Heuze pushed ahead and raced on towards the finish, with the first of these attacking close to the line and finishing six seconds ahead of O'Gorman. McCormack and Heuze were nine seconds back, the former copper fastening his hold on the yellow jersey and the latter moving level with Barr into second place.
**Stage 8 Tramore – Wicklow 108 Mls.** 1 Mick Walsh (Dublin-Panasonic) 107.5 miles in 3 hours 59 mins 40 secs 2 A.O'Gorman (Limerick-Burgerland) at 6 secs 3 P.McCormack (Longford) at 9 secs 4 O.Heuze (Plancoet Lec France) same time 5 R.Rutgers (Holland) at 2 mins 6 L.Roche (Young Ireland) 7 T.Delorme (Plancoet Lec France) 8 J.Barr (Down) 9 G.Thomson (Longford) all same time 10 G.Irvine (Ireland Snowcream) at 3 mins 30 secs
**General Classification:** 1 P.McCormack (Longford) ) 29.56.40 2 Joe Barr (Down) at 2.32 3 O.Heuze (Plancoet Lec France) same time 4 G.Thomson (Longford) at 4.17 5 N.McWilliams (Young Ireland) at 5.56 6 T.Delorme (Plancoet Lec France) at 7.35 7 P.Leigh (Bowman Lancashire) at 8.30 8 A.O'Gorman (Limerick-Burgerland) at 8.44 9 B.Power (Tipperary Yoplait) at 10.58 10 S.Clark (Ireland-Snowcream) at 11.05
**Points:** : 1 G.Irvine 58 2 G.Oravetz 56 3 Roche 49
**Mountains:** 1 S.Spratt 36 2 G.Oravetz and A.McCormack 32
**International Team:**
**County Team:**

## STAGE 9

Showing a remarkable turnaround from their illness, Stephen Spratt and Tipperary-Yoplait team-mate Greg Oravetz dominated the 2.5 mile Devil's Glen time trial on the final morning of the race. The hill climb test was one of two split stages and saw the duo finish just two seconds apart, Spratt being the quicker of the two. Anthony O'Gorman (Limerick Burgerland) was 19 seconds behind in third while Mick Walsh (Dublin Panasonic) was a further six seconds down in fourth.
Race leader Paul McCormack defended well on the steep slopes, placing fifth and beating Olivier Heuze (Plancoet Lec France) by twelve seconds. This stretched his advantage over him to 2 minutes 44. Joe Barr (Down) was a further seven seconds back and dropped to third as a result.
As for the next rider in the general classification, Gary Thomson, the Longford rider was level on time with his team-mate McCormack, retaining both his fourth place overall and his 4 minute 17 second deficit. With just one stage left in the 1987 FBD Milk RÁS  McCormack was looking more and more certain to hang on, although he'd have to safely get through the afternoon criterium to make sure of that.

**Stage 9 Ashford TT 2.5 Mls.** 1 S.Spratt (Tipperary Yoplait) 9.33 2 G.Oravets (Tipperary Yoplait) 9.35 3 A.O'Gorman (Limerick Burgerland) 9.52 4 M.Walsh (Dublin Panasonic) 9.58 5 P.McCormack (Longford) 10.00 6 G.Thompson (Longford) 10.00 7 T.Delorme (Plancoet Lec France) 10.12 8 O.Heuze (Plancoet Lec France) 10.12 9 G.Irvine (Ireland Snowcream) 10.14 10 N.McWilliams (Young Ireland) 10.15
**General Classification** 1 P.McCormack (Longford) 30.06.40 2 O.Heuze (Plancoet Lec France) at 2.44 3 J.Barr (Down) at 2.51 4 G.Thompson (Longford) at 4.17 5 N.McWilliams (Young Ireland) at 6.11 6 T.Delorme (Plancoet Lec France) at 7.47 7 A.O'Gorman (Limerick Burgerland) at 8.36 8 P.Leigh (C.C. Bowland) at 9.15 9 S.Clarke (Ireland Snowcream) at 11.23 10 B.Power (Tipperary Yoplait) at 11.35
**Points:** 1 G.Oravetz 67 2 G.Irvine (Ireland Snowcream) 65 3 G.Thomson 55
**Mountains:** 1 S.Spratt 44 2 G.Oravets 39 3 P.McCormack 36
**International Team:** 1 Plancoet Lec France 93 hours 21 mins 13 secs 2 Ireland Snowcream at 23.27 3 Young Ireland at 27.14
**County Team:** 1 Down 93.38.45 2 Longford at 33.21 3 Tipperary at 35.50

## STAGE 10

Paul McCormack survived a crash in the closing minutes of the Dun Laoghaire criterium to race to FBD Milk RÁS success, finishing the nine-day event a comfortable 2 minutes 44 seconds ahead of Olivier Heuze (Plancoet Lec France) and 2 minutes 51 ahead of Joe Barr (Down).
The final stage was less than an hour in length, was run off at high speeds and was won by Frank Relf (Dublin South). He attacked with two of the 25 miles remaining and finished 14 seconds ahead of the next three riders, namely last year's FBD Milk RÁS champion Stephen Spratt (Tipperary-Yoplait), Cormac McCann (Ireland Snowcream) and Paul Madden (Dublin Westinghouse). Greg Oravetz (Tipperary Yoplait) led in the main bunch a further 26 seconds later.
McCormack was keen to try to get his first stage victory of the race and was part of a ten-man group that had earlier gone clear during the stage. He went after Relf when the Dublin South rider attacked; however light rain had started falling one lap before this and the roads were slippery. The race leader hit the deck on a corner and was delayed.
By chance his father J.J. McCormack was standing at that point of the course and he helped him back on his bike. Whilst the accident cost him his place with the other nine front-runners, he finished in the main bunch that crossed the line 40 seconds after Relf, triumphing overall.
All of McCormack's rivals in the top ten were also in this main bunch, meaning the GC positions were unchanged. Heuze and Barr were second and third, with Thomson, Niall McWilliams (Young Ireland), Thierry Delorme (Plancoet Lec France), Anthony O'Gorman (Limerick Burgerland), Phil Leigh (Bowland

Lancashire), Shane Clarke (Ireland Snowcream) and Bobby Power filling the remainder of those top ten positions.
Oravetz won the points competition by a small margin over Gerald Irvine, and Spratt beat Oravetz to take the King of the Mountains classification.
Plancoet Lec France were best international team, finishing a dominant 23 minutes 27 seconds up on Ireland Snowcream. Down were best in the county ranking, beating Longford by 33 minutes 21 seconds.

**Stage 10 Dun Laoghaire Criterium 25 Mls.** 1 F.Relf (Dublin South) 25 miles in 52 mins 51 secs 2 S.Spratt (Tipperary-Yoplait) at 14 secs 3 C.McCann (Ireland Snowcream) 4 P.Madden (Dublin Westinghouse) both same time 5 G.Oravetz (Tipperary-Yoplait) at 40 secs 6 R.Rutgers (Holland) 7 G.Thomson (Longford) 8 B.McCormack (Garda Lada) 9 G.Irvine (Ireland Snowcream) 10 D.Stenson (Dublin Westinghouse) all same time

**General Classification:** 1 P.McCormack (Longford) ) 31.00.11. 2 O.Heuze (Plancoet Lec France) at 2.44 3 J.Barr (Down) at 2.51 4 G.Thomson (Longford) at 4.17 5 N.McWilliams (Young Ireland) at 6.11 6 T.Delorme (Plancoet Lec France) at 7.47 7 A.O'Gorman (Limerick Burgerland) at 8.38 8 P.Leigh (Bowland Lancashire) at 9.15 9 S.Clarke (Ireland Snowcream) at 11.23 10 B. Power (Tipperary-Yoplait) at 11.35 11 M.Walsh (Dublin-Panasonic) at 16.06 12 L.Roche (Young Ireland) at 16.36

**Points:** 1 G.Oravetz 67 2 G.Irvine (Ireland Snowcream) 65 3 G.Thomson 55

**Mountains:** 1 S.Spratt 44 2 G.Oravetz 39 3 P.McCormack 36

**International Team:**
1 Plancoet Lec France 93 hours 21 mins 13 secs 2 Ireland Snowcream at 23.27 3 Young Ireland at 27.14

**County Team:** 1 Down 93.38.45 2 Longford at 33.21 3 Tipperary at 35.50

*Paul McCormack, 1987 winner*

## 1988

There was a new record entry of 149 for the '88 RÁS and there was also the largest ever entry from overseas with teams from Czechoslovakia, New Zealand, Holland, Brittany, Scotland the USA and two British regional squads.
There were two Irish national selections, the Olympic selections making up Ireland Snowcream while there was also a Young Ireland Snowcream. The remainder of the field was made up of 19 county teams.
To mark the Dublin Millennium celebrations there was an extra stage included with the race starting on Friday for the first time in years.
This extra Dublin stage was a criterium based in the oldest part of the city, around Christchurch Cathedral, Lord Edward Street, the Quays, Parliament Street and Wine tavern Street.

### STAGE 1

The opening criterium was a very spectacular event, especially as the big field swooped down the short hill past Christchurch Cathedral. Appropriately for a stage celebrating the city's 1000th birthday victory went to a Dublin rider, Julian Dalby, although he was riding for the Meath Avonmore team.
The stage comprised 20 laps of a 1.2 miles circuit and the decisive move came early when J.J. Henry (Brittany) went away with Steve Cole (Chilterns) and Andy Hurford (an Englishman riding for Limerick). On the third laps the trio were joined by Dalby and another Dubliner Gary Thompson (Dublin Fosters), the pair bridging a 20 second gap.
All other attempts to get across were brought back by the fast moving bunch the leaders, except Hurford, who shipped a chain on the final lap, contested the sprint. Fourteen seconds later Cormac McCann (Ireland Snowcream) led in the bunch.
**Stage 1 Dublin Criterium 24 Mls.** 1 J.Dalby (Meath Avonmore) 59.06 2 J.J.Henry (Brittany) 3 S.Cole (Chilterns) 4 G.Thompson (Dublin Fosters) all same time 5 C.McCann (Ireland Snowcream) at 14 secs 6 S.Hubert (Brittany) 7 V.Berka (Czechoslovakia) 8 S.Spratt (Ireland Snowcream) 9 P.Leitch (Garda Lada) 10 K.Adams (California) all same time

### STAGE 2

Josef Perny (Czechoslovakia) won Saturday's second stage, 107 miles from Mullingar (where the races had started following a transfer from Dublin) to Castlebar.
The stage was run off at high speed and there were a succession of breakaways, one containing almost 50 riders, but the speed made it difficult to stay away and all were

brought back.
Approaching the finish four riders went clear as they entered the 3 mile circuit which had to be covered two and a half times. The four were Perny, Andy Hurford (Limerick), Raymond Power (Tipperary) and Ray Ronan (Wicklow).
Perney and Hurford attack and got away with the other two getting swept up by the bunch. The two managed to stay out in front with the Czech taking the sprint.
Another Czech, Jan Virney was next home, 22 seconds behind just ahead of Ger Madden (Cork). Race-leader Dalby came in with the bunch over 2 minutes down.
**Stage 2 Mullingar - Castlebar 107 Mls.** 1 J.Perny (Czechoslovakia) 4.00.56 2 A.Hurford (Limerick) s.t. 3 J.Virney (Czechoslovakia) at 22 secs 4 G.Madden (Cork) 5 B.Reidy (Kerry) 6 S.Cole (Chilterns) 7 J.McQuaid (Dublin Fosters) 8 N.McWilliams (Young Ireland Snowcream) 9 B.Osborne (Cork) 10 R.Lodge (Chilterns) all same time
**General Classification:** 1 J.Perny (Czechoslovakia) 5.00.52 2 A.Hurford (Limerick) s.t. 3 S.Cole (Chilterns) at 22 secs 4 J.Virney (Czechoslovakia) 5 G.Madden (Cork) 6 B.Reidy (Kerry) all same time

## STAGE 3

Sunday's stage was another long one, 103 miles to Clifden and it was another very fast one with an average speed of 27.6 mph 81 miles covered in the first three hours.
Despite the speed three riders managed to stay out in front for the first 30 miles of the stage: Ian Chivers (Young Ireland Snowcream); Stephen Spratt (Ireland Snowcream) and Vladimir Berka who was looking after the yellow jersey's interests and not doing any work but coming to the front to take the KOM prime at 24 miles.
Four riders then joined the leaders including '83 winner Phil Cassidy (Ireland Snowcream) and then another three made it across leaving 10 at the front but they were not working well and at 52 miles the race was all together again.
Immediately eleven riders went away including previous year's winner Paul McCormack (Ireland Snowcream), Frank Relf (Dublin East), Donie Conroy (Kerry), Michael Griffith (New Zealand), Andy Hurford (Limerick), Jeff Wright (CC Bowland), Paul Nolan (Meath Avonmore), John McQuaid (Dublin Fosters), Chris McCann (Antrim) with Berka again along for the ride.
Working well the group built up a lead of 3.05 before it started to come down in the final 20 miles as the bunch put on the pressure.
With 9 miles remaining Conroy attacked and was joined first by Chris McCann then McQuaid, Relf and McCormack. These five were together as they reached the finishing circuit in Clifden.
For a couple of years it became popular to have stages ending with several laps of a finishing circuit. Depending on the composition of the race this could cause enormous problems in sorting out the finishing order and various measures were tried to help improve this situation. On this occasion times were being taken as the riders went on to the circuit after which they were only riding for the stage placings.

On the two laps of the circuit Relf dropped back and in the final sprint up the hill McQuaid just edged past McCann on the line with McCormack 3rd, Conroy 4th and Relf 5th. Hurford led in the remains of the break at 1.11.

**Stage 3 Castlebar - Clifden 103 Mls.** 1 J.McQuaid (Dublin Fosters) 3.42.43 2 Chris.McCann (Antrim) 3 P.McCormack (Ireland Snowcream) 4 D.Conroy (Kerry) 5 F.Relf (Dublin East) all same time 6 A.Hurford (Limerick) at 1.11 7 J.Wright (CC Bowland) 8 P.Nolan (Meath Avonmore) 9 Cormac.McCann (Ireland Snowcream) 10 P.Leitch (Garda) all same time

**General Classification:** 1 J.McQuaid (Dublin Fosters) 8.43.21 2 P.McCormack (Ireland Snowcream) at 16 secs 3 Chris.McCann (Antrim) at 48 secs 4 A.Hurford (Limerick) at 49 secs 5 F.Relf (Dublin East) at 59 secs 6 J.Perny (Czechoslovakia) at 1.46 7 N.McWilliams (Young Ireland) at 1.28 8 R.Ronan (Wicklow) at 2.01 9 J.Wright (CC Bowland) at 2.08 10 J.J.Henry (Brittany) at 2.09 12 Cormac.McCann (Ireland Snowcream) at 2.16

**Points:** 1 J.McQuaid 24 2 A.Hurford 10 3 S.Cole 24

**Mountains:** 1 A.Hurford 10 2 J.J.Henry 10 3 G.Thompson 10

**Team:** 1 Ireland Snowcream 2 Young Ireland Snowcream 3 CC Bowland

## STAGE 4

Defending champion Paul McCormack (Ireland Snowcream) won the 99 miles stage to Ennis in a sprint from an 11-man group which included race leader McQuaid who retained the jersey with the same 16 second margin over McCormack with Andy Hurford now third at 48 seconds.

The race started with a 10 miles circuit back through Clifden which included the tough climb at Skye Road where mountains leader Jean Jacques Henry (Brittany) took maximum points.

Little damage was done however and coming back through Clifden the bunch were all together. Shortly afterwards came the move of the day when 11 riders went away and this group would stay out in front all the way to the finish. as well as the yellow jersey and McCormack the group included Ian Chivers (Young Ireland); Martin Quinn (Antrim); Raymond Power (Tipperary); Paul Madden (Young Ireland); Andy Hurford (Limerick); John Sheehan (Dublin Telecom); Stephen Hubert (Brittany) and Shane Clarke (Dublin East).

At Galway they had a 1.45 lead on a chasing group and five riders left the group: Cormac McCann. Leslie McKay, Mick Kinsella and two American riders. At Gort they had got to 1.20 of the leaders but lost time from there to the finish eventually coming in 2.43 behind while behind the high speed was fragmenting the bunch.

In the sprint McCormack won from Raymond Power with McQuaid third.

**Stage 4 Clifden - Ennis 99 Mls.** 1 P.McCormack (Ireland Snowcream) 3.42.43 2 R.Power (Tipperary) 3 J.McQuaid (Dublin Fosters) 4 S.Clarke (Dublin East) 5 S.Hubert (Brittany) 6 J.Sheehan (Dublin Telecom) 7 A.Hurford (Limerick) 8

I.Chivers (Young Ireland) 9 M.Quinn (Antrim); 10 P.Madden (Young Ireland) all same time

**General Classification:** 1 J.McQuaid (Dublin Fosters) 12.38.32 2 P.McCormack (Ireland Snowcream) at 16 secs 3 A.Hurford (Limerick) at 49 secs 4 J.Sheehan (Dublin Telecom) at 2.23 5 I.Chivers (Young Ireland) 6 P.Madden (Young Ireland) all same time 7 R.Power (Tipperary) at 2.41 8 Chris.McCann (Antrim) at 4.31 9 F.Relf (Dublin East) at 4.38 10 S.Hubert (Brittany) at 4.42 11 Cormac.McCann (Ireland Snowcream) at 4.59 12 M.Kinsella at 5.10

**Points:** 1 J.McQuaid 37 2 P.McCormack 33 3 A.Hurford 33

**Mountains:** 1 J.J.Henry 17 2 V.Berka 15 3 S.Cole 14

**Team:** 1 Young Ireland Snowcream 30.05.18 2 Ireland Snowcream at 1.39 3 Dublin Fosters at 4.05

## STAGE 5

Richard O'Gorman (Cork) won the 105 miles stage to Killarney in a sprint from an 8-man group which had gone away just over 20 miles from the finish. Race leader John McQuaid just managed to hang on to the jersey and after the stage his lead was down to 9 seconds over Ian Chivers (Young Ireland) who had finished 3rd on the stage.

Chivers was somewhat lucky to end up in this position as his gears had jammed during the stage and in frustration he threw his bike over the hedge. When his team gave him a replacement there was no suitable back wheel and they had to climb over the hedge to retrieve the wheel from the faulty machine.

However he quickly got back and at one point was leader on the road before McQuaid fought back in the closing miles.

At Limerick they were all together when Declan Lonergan took the prime. Shortly afterwards 26 riders went away and built up a lead of over a minute. However on the climb at Knockfinnish they were recaptured and the bunch went over the top together with Cookstown rider Gareth Talbot, Guesting for Glasgow, taking maximum KOM points.

Before Castleisland the winning break of eight went clear. Included were O'Gorman, and Young Ireland Snowcream pair Paul Madden and Chivers, Vladimir Berka (Czechoslovakia), Alistair Martin (Antrim), Andy Hurford (Limerick), Sean Bracken (Dublin West) Ray Ronan (Wicklow) and Martin Coll (Glasgow).

At Farranfore their lead was 1.15 over a 5-man chasing group with the bunch at 2.40. However by the time they reached the timing point at the entrance to the finishing circuit the bunch had reduced their deficit to 1.14.

**Stage 5 Ennis - Killarney 105 Mls.** 1 R.O'Gorman (Cork) 3.48.46 2 V.Berka (Czechoslovakia) 3 I.Chivers (Young Ireland) 4 A.Martin (Antrim) 5 S.Bracken (Dublin West) 6 R.Ronan (Wicklow) 7 M.Coll (Glasgow) 8 P.Madden (Young Ireland) all same time 9 B.Mitrejean (Brittany) at 45 secs 10 K.Kimmage (Dublin Lada) s.t.

**General Classification:** 1 J.McQuaid (Dublin Fosters) 16.29.32 2 I. Chivers (Young Ireland) at 9 secs 3 P.Madden (Young Ireland) at 16 secs 4 P.McCormack (Ireland Snowcream) s.t. 5 A.Hurford (Limerick) at 49 secs 6 J.Sheehan (Dublin Telecom) at 2.23 7 R.Power (Tipperary) at 2.41 8 R.O'Gorman (Cork) at 3.52 9 S.Bracken (Dublin West) s.t. 10 Chris.McCann (Antrim) at 4.31 11 F.Relf (Dublin East) at 4.38 12 R.Ronan (Wicklow) at 4.39
**Points:** 1 J.McQuaid 37 2 P.McCormack 32 3 A.Hurford 33
**Mountains:** 1 V.Berka 20 2 J.J.Henry 17 3 S.Cole 14
**Team:** 1 Young Ireland Snowcream 49.33.50 2 Ireland Snowcream at 6.07 3 Dublin Fosters at 8.33

## STAGE 6

There was a popular home win for Cork rider Anthony Dineen at the end of the shortest stage of the week, 87 miles from Killarney to Clonakilty.
Paul McCormack (Ireland Snowcream) finished 6th, 7 seconds behind the winner and moved from 4th to second but there was no major movement in the general classification, McQuaid still leading by a few seconds more: 15, with Chivers losing 10 seconds to lie third at 19 seconds equal on time with teammate Paul Madden.
The stage started with the climb up Ladies View to Moll's Gap where Steve Cole took the KOM prime to improve his position in the mountains classification.
At this point there was a leading group of 15 and on the descent they were joined by 12 more.
Over the third climb at Cousune Gap the lead was 3 minutes but the bunch were chasing hard and approaching the finish the lead was down to 1.45.
Michael Kinsella (Dublin East) and Andy Hurford (Limerick) got away and on the first of the 5 kms. circuit they had a 40 second lead but were soon brought back.
On the final circuit 17 riders got away and opened a small gap which they managed to hold to the finish where Dineen jumped away early to win by 2 seconds over R. Lodge (Chilterns) while Cormac McCann (Ireland Snowcream) also escaped to take 3rd at 9 seconds with Vladimir Berka (Czechoslovakia) lead in the rest at 11 seconds.
**Stage 6 Killarney - Clonakilty 87 Mls.** 1 A.Dineen (Cork CMP) 3.17.07 2 R.Lodge (Chilterns) at 2 secs 3 Cormac.McCann (Ireland Snowcream) at 9 secs 4 V.Berka (Czechoslovakia) at 11 secs 5 G.Talbot (Glasgow) 6 P.McCormack (Snowcream Ireland) 7 R.Ronan (Wicklow) 8 Chris.McCann (Antrim) 9 K.Adams (California) 10 J.Wright (CC Bowland) all same time
**General Classification:** 1 J.McQuaid (Dublin Fosters) 19.46.50 2 P.McCormack (Ireland Snowcream) at 15 secs 3 I.Chivers (Young Ireland) at 19 secs 4 P.Madden (Young Ireland) s.t. 5 A.Hurford (Limerick) at 49 secs 6 R.Power (Tipperary) at 2.15 7 R.O'Gorman (Cork) at 3.52 8 S.Bracken (Dublin West) at 4.02 9 Chris.McCann (Antrim) at 4.31 10 R.Ronan (Wicklow) at 4.39 11 S.Hubert (Brittany) at 4.44 12 F.Relf (Dublin East) at 4.48
**Points:** 1 P.McCormack 43 2 J.McQuaid 41 3 V.Berka 35

**Mountains:** 1 S Cole 27 2 V.Berka 20 3 J.J.Henry 17
**International Team:** 1 Young Ireland Snowcream 59.26.14 2 Ireland Snowcream at 5.45 3 CC Bowland (Britain) at 12.30
**County Team:** 1 Dublin Fosters 59.34.29 2 Dublin East at 2.12 3 Kerry at 6.04

## STAGE 7

After good weather all week Thursday's 110 miles stage from Clonakilty to Dungarvan was run off in torrential rain and high winds and there were no less than 21 retirals. Of the 159 who had started out from Dublin only 93 remained in the race.
The stage went to Gary Thompson (Dublin Fosters) who led in a 7-man group, which included the race leader, 1.07 ahead of the chasers McQuaid, who had said before the stage that he expected to lose the jersey in the last day TT to Paul Madden, ended the day in a much stronger position, 1.23 ahead of Paul McCormack (Ireland Snowcream) with third-placed Chivers at 1.26. Madden, who had looked a potential overall winner had terrible luck puncturing several times and dropping to 19th overall.
McQuaid had rode well to improve his position doing most of the driving after getting across to the break and he also had to survive two crashes.
Eight riders were involved in a crash, including the yellow jersey, and stage 2 winner Josef Perny (Czechoslovakia) had to abandon. McQuaid, however, was able to quickly rejoin the race with the help of Thompson.
He was in trouble again when he crashed in the finishing sprint along with Michael Kinsella (Dublin East) and Philip Leigh (CC Bowland) but, because of the last kilometre rule, they lost no time.
This left only four of the break upright contesting the sprint which went to Thompson from Czech Vladimir Berka, Bruno Mitrejean (Brittany) and R. Chamberlain (Britain). Kinsella, Leigh and McQuaid remounted to take the next three places. Shane Clark (Dublin East) led in the chasers 1.07 down.
**Stage 7 Clonakilty - Dungarvan 110 Mls.** 1 G.Thompson (Dublin Fosters) 4.27.42 2 V.Berka (Czechoslovakia) 3 B.Mitrejean (Brittany) 4 M.Kinsella (Dublin East) 6 P.Leigh (CC Bowland) 7 J.McQuaid (Dublin Fosters) all same time 8 L.Robert (Brittany) at 1.07 9 M.Walsh (Dublin Fosters) 10 P.McCormack (Ireland Snowcream) all same time
**General Classification:** 1 J.McQuaid (Dublin Fosters) 24.14.32 2 P.McCormack (Ireland Snowcream) at 1.23 3 I.Chivers (Young Ireland) at 1.26 4 A.Hurford (Limerick) at 1.26 5 V.Berka (Czechoslovakia) at 5.01 6 M.Kinsella (Dublin East) at 5.10 7 R.Power (Tipperary) at 5.19 8 Chris.McCann (Antrim) at 5.38 9 S.Hubert (Brittany) at 5.51 10 P.Leigh (CC Bowland) at 6.16 11 N.McWilliams (Young Ireland) at 6.28 12 G.Wright (CC Bowland) at 6.56
**Points:** 1 J.McQuaid 50 2 V.Berka 49 3 A.Hurford 39
**Mountains:** 1 S.Cole 31 2 V.Berka 26 3 J.Wright 24

**International Team:** 1 Young Ireland Snowcream 72.57.54 2 CC Bowland at 3.13. 3 Brittany at 4.32
**County Team:** 1 Dublin Fosters 75.59.42 2 Tipperary at 10.46 3 Dublin East at 13.12

## STAGE 8 (a) and (b)

On the Friday morning there was a 12 miles time-trial which was won by Stephen Spratt (Ireland Snowcream) 21 seconds ahead of Young Ireland's Declan Lonergan. Biggest improver was Andy Hurford (Limerick) who finished 3rd, 1.14 faster than McQuaid, moving up to 3rd overall. McQuaid also lost time on close rivals Paul McCormack and Ian Chivers.
**Stage 8a Dungarvan 12 Mls. TT:** 1 S.Spratt (Ireland Snowcream) 29.20 2 D.Lonergan (Young Ireland) 29.41 3 A.Hurford (Limerick) 29.49 4 P.McCormack (Ireland Snowcream) 30.03 5 P.Leitch (Garda Lada) 30.18 6 R.Ronan (Wicklow) 30.32 7 S.Delaney (Tipperary) 30.32 8 A.Cook (GB Chilterns) 30.45 9 S.Hubert (Brittany) 30.46 10 I.Chivers (Young Ireland) 30.49 11 N.McWilliams (Young Ireland) 30.55 12 J.McQuaid (Dublin Fosters) 30.56
On the afternoon stage the tired field toured along for the first 40 miles only turning on the speed in the final hour. This gave a chance of some glory to Denis McCarthy (Garda Lada), last man on GC who went away at the start and at one time had a lead of 7 minutes. However any chance he had of staying away went when Spratt went in pursuit catching McCarthy before he in turn was caught by a chasing group of 15 which in turn was reeled in by the bunch.
A group went away on the finishing circuit to take the stage honours, Jeff Wright (CC Bowland) winning the sprint from Antrim's Chris McCann. Bruno Mitrejean (Brittany) was next with the other McCann brother Cormac (Ireland Snowcream) 4th. As the bunch had arrived at the finishing circuit together they all got the same time.
**Stage 8b Dungarvan - Wexford 76 Mls.** 1 J.Wright (CC Bowland) 2.54.46 2 Chris.McCann (Antrim) 3 B.Mitrejean (Brittany) 4 Cormac.McCann (Ireland Snowcream) 5 G.Talbot (Glasgow) 6 N.McWilliams (Young Ireland) 7 S.Spratt (Ireland Snowcream) 8 S.O'Hare (Armagh) 9 G.Thompson (Dublin Fosters) 10 S.Hubert (Brittany) all same time
**General Classification:** 1 John McQuaid
**Points:** 1 J. McQuaid 50 2 V.Berka 49 3 P.McCormack 48
**Mountains:** 1 S.Cole 31 2 V.Berka 26 3 J.Wright 24
**International Team:** 1 Young Ireland Snowcream 85.15.43 2 CC Bowland at 6.33 3 Brittany at 8.31
**County Team:** 1 Dublin Fosters 85.18.48 2 Tipperary at 10.17 3 Dublin East at 14.44

## STAGE 9

Paul McCormack took over the lead after the 9th stage, 80 miles from Wexford to Wicklow but was accused by deposed leader John McQuaid, who dropped to 3rd at 34 secs. of unfair tactics.

While the penultimate day of the RÁS is often a major mountain stage, on this occasion it was fairly flat until near the finish when they had to tackle the short but very steep Devil's Glen. McQuaid had the misfortune to have gear trouble just at this point while he and McCormack were at the front of the group starting the climb. He asked his friend McCormack not to take advantage while he changed bikes but after losing 20 seconds he never got back to the Ireland Snowcream rider.

McCormack denied attacking and said he just kept riding at his normal rhythm but reckoned he would have got away from him on the climb in any case.

The stage was won by Waterford rider Declan Lonergan who beat Frenchman Loic Robert and R. Chamberlain (CC Bowland) in a 3-up sprint. McCormack finished in a group led in by Niall McWilliams (Young Ireland) 9 seconds behind but it was over a minute before the group containing the yellow jersey arrived and the accusations and denials started.

**Stage 9 Wexford - Wicklow 80 Mls.** 1 D.Lonergan (Young Ireland Snowcream) 3.10.02 2 L.Robert (Brittany) 3 R.Chamberlain (CC Bowland) all same time 4 N.McWilliams (Young Ireland) at 9 secs 5 J.Wright (CC Bowland) 6,V.Berka (Czechoslovakia) 7 R.O'Gorman (Cork) 8 Chris.McCann (Antrim) 9 J.Quinn (Cork) 10 P.McCormack (Ireland Snowcream) all same time

**General Classification:** 1 P.McCormack (Ireland Snowcream) 30.41.27 2 A.Hurford (Limerick) at 20 secs 3 J.McQuaid (Dublin Fosters) at 34 secs 4 I.Chivers (Young Ireland) at 50 secs 5 V.Berka (Czechoslovakia) at 4.49 6 R.Power (Tipperary) at 5.10 7 Chris.McCann (Antrim) at 5.19 8 N.McWilliams (Young Ireland) at 5.34 9 S.Hubert (Brittany) at 6.10 10 M.Kinsella (Dublin East) at 6.20

## STAGE 10 (a) and (b)

There have been several editions of the race with two stages on the final day but invariable the morning stage was a time-trial. On this occasion, however there was a 72 miles mountain stage in the morning to be followed by a criterium in the afternoon.

The morning stage was over two laps, each including climbs at Sally Gap and Glenmacnass Waterfall. The severity of the terrain split the field into several groups, the largest of which contained only 20 riders at the finish. However the leading group contained all the chief contenders so there was no real change in the overall.

The only significant result of the morning stage was in the mountains competition where CC Bowland rider Jeff Wright took over the lead from another British rider Steve Cole (Chilterns). Loic Robert (Brittany) took maximum points on one of the

climbs and was second on another to move up to second in the classification. Czech Vladimir Berka also improved to third with Cole dropping back to fourth.
The group containing all the leaders stayed together to the finish where Berka won the stage from Cookstown's Gareth Talbot (Glasgow) and Niall McWilliams (Young Ireland)

**Stage 10a Wicklow - Bray 72 Mls.** 1 V.Berka (Czechoslovakia) 2.59.53 2 G.Talbot (Glasgow) 3 N.McWilliams (Young Ireland) 4 J.McQuaid (Dublin Fosters) 5 S.Cole (Chilterns) 6 B.Mitrejean (Brittany) 7 P.Leitch (Dublin Garda) 8 F.Relf (Dublin East) 9 R.Ronan (Wicklow) 10 L.Robert (Brittany) all same time

The Ireland Snowcream team, with the unofficial assistance of the second Ireland team: Young Ireland Snowcream, controlled the afternoon 1 hour plus five laps criterium in Dun Laoghaire for most of the stage, ensuring McCormack had a fairly comfortable ride on his way to a second successive win, only the third rider after O Hanlon and Flanagan to achieve a second RÁS victory.
A break was allowed to go away in the final laps when Gareth Talbot and Niall McWilliams, second and third in the morning, went away. On the final lap they were caught by Ciaran McKenna (Dublin Fosters) and Steve Cole (Chilterns) setting up a 4-man sprint from which McWilliams won from Talbot, McKenna and Cole. Davy McCall (Antrim) came home 4 seconds behind while Declan Lonergan (Young Ireland) led in the bunch just 2 seconds later.

**Stage 10b Dun Laoghaire Criterium 30 Mls.** 1 N.McWilliams (Young Ireland Snowcream) 1.07.15 2 G.Talbot (Glasgow) 3 C.McKenna (Dublin Fosters) 4 S.Cole (Chilterns) all same time 5 D.McCall (Antrim) at 4 secs 6 D.Lonergan (Young Ireland) at 6 secs 7 V.Berka (Czechoslovakia) 8 P.Leitch (Dublin Garda) 9 R.Ronan (Wicklow) 10 B.Mitrejean (Brittany) all same time

**General Classification:** 1 P.McCormack (Ireland Snowcream) 34.28.41 2 A.Hurford (Limerick) at 20 secs 3 J.McQuaid (Dublin Fosters) at 34 secs 4 I.Chivers (Young Ireland Snowcream) at 50 secs 5 V.Berka (Czechoslovakia) at 4.49 6 R.Power (Tipperary) at 5.10 7 Chris.McCann (Antrim) at 5.19 8 N.McWilliams (Young Ireland) at 5.28 9 M.Kinsella (Dublin East) at 6.20 10 J.Wright (CC Bowland) at 6.55 11 P.Leitch (Garda Lada) at 7.19 12 R.Chamberlain (CC Bowland) at 7.37 13 B.Mitrejean (Brittany) at 9.39 14 P.McQuaid (Dublin Fosters) at 10.40 15 L.Robert (Brittany) at 11.29

**Points:** 1 V. Berka 82 2 J. McQuaid 66 3 N. McWilliams 61

**Mountains:** 1 J. Wright (Britain Bowland) 59 2 L. Robert (Brittany) 57 3 V. Berka (Czechoslovakia) 53

**International Team:** 1 Young Ireland Snowcream 103.38.16 2 Ireland Snowcream at 25.53 3 Brittany at 28.41

**County Team:** 1, Dublin Fosters MBK 103.51.20 2 Dublin East at 15.08 3 Tipperary at 40.03

Race Average Speed 26.5

*Paul McCormack, 1988*

## 1989

The USSR were back for the '89 RÁS and the question in most people's minds was would they be as dominant as the Russian teams on the previous visits. The riders, all from Latvia, insisted on not being called Russian and indeed within a couple of years the break-up of the Soviet Union saw members of this very team take part in World Championships and Olympic Games in Latvian teams.
The rest of the international challenge was made up of a Great Britain team, New Zealand, France, Holland and the Isle of Man and there were several British regional squads.
'86 winner Stephen Spratt who had been racing in the USA was entered on the Meath Avonmore team while '84 winner Stephen Delaney was listed as Guesting on the Down team but ended up riding for Dublin IRC. A very strong Ulster Cycling Federation team was entered as Antrim and a notable guest on that team was NICF rider Andrew Moss from Ballymena RC, a winner of the 5-day Tour of the North.

## STAGE 1

Rik Rutgers (Holland) won the opening stage, 88 miles from Dublin to Dundalk beating Robert Vinovsky (USSR) and Ger Madden (Cork) in the sprint.
The break of the day went after 55 miles when ten riders went clear on the long drag up from Collon, with most of the top teams represented with the notable exception of the Irish National squad.
The lead went to 1.10 and stayed there as a succession of small groups went away from the main bunch which was eventually reduced to about 40 riders. Behind the break were a group, which contained most of the pre-race favourites and it looked as if the leaders would be caught. However with Rutgers, Vinovsky, Donie Conroy (Kerry) and Joe Barr (Down) working hard in the front group they actually started to increase their lead which was up to 2 minutes as they started the climb of the Windy Gap in the Cooley Mountains.
Madden and Conroy went away on the climb with Madden forging on alone to a minute's lead but he was caught before Dundalk where six leaders arrived together from whom Rutgers comfortably won the sprint.
The next group lost valuable time coming in 3.20 behind the leader.
**Stage 1 Dublin - Dundalk 88 Mls.** 1 R.Rutgers (Holland) 3.17.30 2 R.Vinovsky (USSR) 3 G.Madden (Cork) 4 J.Tanner (Great Britain) all same time 5 D.Conroy (Kerry) at 10 secs 6 S.Delaney (Dublin IRC) at 16 secs 7 S.Clarke (Dublin Abrakebabra) at 2.50 8 J.Sheehan (Dublin Abrakebabra) at 3.19 9 D.McCall (Antrim) 10 P.Keogh (Dublin Telecom) s.t.
**Points:** 1 R. Rutger 2 R.Vinovsky (USSR) 3 G.Madden (Cork)
**Mountains:** 1 G. Madden.

## STAGE 2

Ballymena's Andrew Moss (Antrim) came home on his own to win the 110 miles stage to Boyle, 47 seconds ahead of Arvis Piziks (USSR) whose team-mate Dainis Ozols came home in third place, a further 25 seconds back. Vinovsky, second on Saturday, took over the yellow jersey although on equal times with stage one breakaway companions John Tanner (G.B.) and Ger Madden (Cork).

The Antrim team were in all the moves and shortly after the stage began Sean O'Hare went out on his own opening a 1 minute gap which he sustained for over 10 miles but with no signs of anyone joining him he sat up and waited on the bunch.

Tanner (G.B.) and Philip Hodge (New Zealand) then had a go and were out in front for 20 miles before being joined by first 3 and then another 4 riders but they were all absorbed by the bunch just after the climb at Cuilcagh Mountain.

Then six went away including Ozols who decided to try on his own and he soon had 45 seconds on his recent companions with the bunch at 1.15.

With 20 miles remaining there were a series of attacked from the bunch and a large group of 33 riders eventually came together at the front with a 1.45 advantage on the bunch. As the race entered the beautiful Lough Kee Forest Park a few miles before the finish Moss took off and time-trialled to the line opening up a 47 secs gap on Piziks who left the bunch followed at intervals by first Ozols and then Julian Dalby (Ireland) who escaped to take the next three places before John Sheehan (Dublin Abrakebabra) led in a group of 12, ten seconds ahead of the bunch in which there was a big crash in the finishing straight.

**Stage 2 Dundalk - Boyle 110 Mls.** 1 A.Moss (Antrim) 4.46.25 2 A.Piziks (USSR) at 47 secs 3 D.Ozols (USSR) at 1.12 4 J.Dalby (Ireland) at 1.19 5 J.Sheehan (Dublin Abrakebabra) at 1.26 6 M.McLynskey (Dublin Telecom) 7 P.Keogh (Dublin (Telecom) 8 R.Vinovsky (USSR) 9 L.McKay (Dublin Fosters) 10 D.Stenson (Dublin IRC) all same time

**General Classification:** 1 R.Vinovsky (USSR) 8.05.17 2 J.Tanner (G.B.) 3 G.Madden (Cork) both same time 4 D.Conroy (Kerry) at 10 secs 5 S.Delaney (Dublin IRC) at 16 secs 6 R.Rutgers (Holland) at 2.47 7 S.Clarke (Dublin Abra.) at 2.50 8 D.Ozols (USSR) at 3.09 9 J.Dalby (Ireland) at 3.16 10 J.Sheehan (Dublin Abra.) at 3.19 11 P.Keogh (Dublin Telecom) 12 D. McCall (Antrim) all same time

## STAGE 3

A group of 15 riders fought out the sprint after a very fast 100 miles stage to Tuam but it was for second place as Declan Lonergan (Dublin Fosters) had left the leaders 15 miles from the finish to come home 56 clear of Andris Iarmolis (USSR) who won the sprint from John Sheehan (Dublin Abrakebabra).

Great Britain rider John Tanner, who finished 6th took over the lead on G.C. by 16 seconds from past winner Stephen Delaney with Vinovsky third at 1.39.

A break went early and there were panic buttons ringing in the USSR camp when the lead went to over 4 minutes. A long chase eventually same the break brought back after 70 miles the signal for a fierce series of attacks which saw the bunch splint into six groups at one time.
The first group on the road was 16-strong and with 15 miles remaining Lonergan jumped away and like Moss the day before opened up nearly a minute over the final miles to take the stage.
**Stage 3 Boyle - Tuam 100 Mls.** 1 D.Lonergan (Dublin Fosters) 3.49.24 2 A.Iarmolis (USSR) at 56 secs 3 J.Sheehan (Dublin Abra.) 4 A.Piziks (USSR) 5 J.Carey (Dublin Abra.) 6 J.Tanner (G.B.) 7 M.van Baarle (Netherlands) 8 R.O'Gorman (Cork) 9 Chris.McCann (Antrim) 10 F.Relf (Ireland) all same time
**General Classification:** 1 J.Tanner (Great Britain) 11.54.41 2 S.Delaney (Dublin IRC) at 16 secs 3 R.Vinovsky (USSR) at 1.39 4 D.Conroy (Kerry) at 1.41 5 D.Lonergan (Dublin Fosters) at 2.23 6 R.Rutgers (Holland) at 3.12 7 J.Sheehan (Dublin Abra.) at 3.19 8 F.Relf (Ireland) s.t. 9 P.Callaly (Dublin Abra.) at 3.34 10 G.Madden (Cork) at 4.26 11 S.Clarke (Dublin Abra.) at 4.31 12 R. O'Gorman (Cork) at 4.34
**Mountains:** 1 I.Chivers (Antrim) 2 P.Hodge (New Zealand) 3 D.Ozols.

## STAGE 4

Tanner became the first rider of the week to hold on to the yellow jersey after the 104 miles stage to Tipperary Town which was won by Dainis Ozols (USSR).
Like the previous two stages it was a long break in the closing stages as Ozols went clear on a climb with 25 miles remaining and at the finish he had a lead of 21 seconds over Richard O'Gorman (Cork) and Frank Relf (Ireland).
Paul Millar (New Zealand), Terry Jackson (Southend) and Brian Lenihan (Cork) went away early on and quickly built up a 3 minute lead on a 5-man chasing group which included John Sheehan (Dublin Abra.) and Joe Barr (Antrim).
When the two groups merged they worked well together and their lead went up to 4.30 which made Sheehan race leader on the road by over a minute.
The bunch started chasing with the G.B. and Dutch teams doing most of the driving and after 55 miles the lead was down to 1 minute at which stage Millar and Jackson went off again on their own.
At the foot of the climb they were one minute ahead of the chasing four who were soon overhauled by the bunch.
It was at this point that Ozols jumped away on his own and passing the two leaders he pressed ahead and opened a lead of 30 seconds. behind him three groups in turn left the bunch and these groups joined into a chasing group of 10 but despite their efforts Ozols held out to the finish.
The bunch stopped working and their deficit went to over 3 minutes although a late rally saw this reduced to 2.03 by the finish.

The chasers spilt over the final miles O'Gorman out sprinting Relf 21 seconds down while Sheehan led in Alistair Martin (Antrim) at 27 seconds with the rest at 44 and several other small groups finished before the arrival of the main bunch.

**Stage 4 Tuam - Tipperary Town 104 Mls.** 1 D.Ozols (USSR) 3.48.03 2 R.O'Gorman (Cork) at 21 secs 3 F.Relf (Ireland) s.t. 4 J.Sheehan (Dublin Abra.) at 27 secs 5 A.Martin (Antrim) s.t. 6 F.Guyon (France) at 44 secs 7 T.McManus (Dublin Telecom) 8 B.Lenihan (Cork) 9 M.Walsh (Dublin Fosters) all same time 10 M.Van Baarle (Holland) at 1.26

**General Classification:** 1 J.Tanner (Great Britain) 15.44.47 2 S.Delaney (Dublin IRC) at 16 secs 3 F.Relf (Ireland) at 1.37 4 R.Vinovsky (USSR) at 1.39 5 D.Conroy (Kerry) at 1.41 6 J.Sheehan (Dublin Abra.) at 1.43 7 D.Lonergan (Dublin Fosters) at 2.23 8 D.Ozols (USSR) at 2.45 9 RO'Gorman (Cork) at 2.52 10 A.Martin (Antrim) at 2.58

**Mountains:** I.Chivers 16.

**Points:** John Sheehan 50

**Team:** USSR 47.22.47.

## STAGE 5

If the home riders were beginning to believe the USSR team was not quite up to the quality of previous Soviet squads in the RÁS they were put right on the 100 miles stage to Cahirciveen, which included the first real climbing of the race, when they hit back to take the top two places on G.C.

They missed out on the stage however which went to Mario van Baarle (Holland) who came home 17 seconds ahead of Vinovsky who took over the lead. Stage 2 winner Andrew Moss (Antrim) was third in the same time as Vinovsky.

It was a great day for the Antrim team who finished all five of their riders in the top 14 on the stage with Alistair Martin moving to third overall. They also led the team classification from the USSR.

After a transfer to Kanturk the stage started and so did the rain which persisted through the day. An early break of three riders led through Castleisland where Ger Madden (Cork) took the prime. When they were caught five riders went away and these were joined a few miles later by Ozols and Richard O'Gorman (Cork).

Back in the bunch leader Tanner broke a pedal and had to change bikes twice before getting back to the bunch. A series of chasing groups left the bunch and eventually there was a big chasing group of 27, 30 seconds behind the leaders with the bunch at 45 seconds as they came through Cahirciveen for the first time after 70 miles but then the gap started to increase.

A long line of bedraggled riders struggled through the mist up the side of a Kerry mountain led by yellow jersey Tanner but the race was slipping from his grasp as the time checks came back: 2, 3, 4 and finally 5 minutes, all in the space of ten miles.

The final 20 miles included two major climbs and on the first Ozols went off on his own to be joined by van Baarle and teammate Gert Teunisse, Vinovsky, Shane Clarke (Dublin Abra.) and Antrim trio Moss, Martin and Cormac McCann.
With 5 miles left van Baarle took off to win the stage but it was almost six minutes before Tanner came home with a group falling back to seventh overall.
**Stage 5 Kanturk - Cahirciveen 100 Mls.** 1 M.van Baarle (Holland) 4.23.52 2 R.Vinovsky (USSR) at 17 secs 3 A.Moss (Antrim) s.t. 4 S.Clarke (Dublin Abra.) at 40 secs 5 D.Ozols (USSR) 6 Cormac.McCann (Antrim) 7 G.Teunisse (Holland) 8 S.Spratt (Meath Avonmore) 9 A.Martin (Antrim)all same time 10 S.Nevin (Dublin Fosters) at 2.01
**General Classification:** 1 R.Vinovsky (USSR) 20.10.35 2 D.Ozols (USSR) at 1.29 3 A.Martin (Antrim) at 1.42 4 S.Clarke ((Dublin Abra.) at 3.15 5 A.Moss (Antrim) at 3.36 6 M.van Baarle (Holland) at 3.37 7 J.Tanner (G.B.) at 3.42 8 Cormac.McCann (Antrim) s.t. 9 S.Delaney (Dublin IRC) at 3.58 10 F.Relf (Ireland) at 4.09
**Points:** D.Ozols
**Mountains: 1** D.Ozols 2 I.Chivers
**Team:** 1 Antrim 2 USSR

## STAGE 6

The pride of Irish cycling lay humbled by the shores of Bantry Bay after a whitewash by the USSR team whose climbing ability dominated the 87 miles stage from Cahirciveen to Bantry.
They filled the first four places and two of them: Vinovsky and Piziks came home 5.30 ahead of Ozols while their fourth member Iarmolis led in seven riders 6.23 behind the stage winner. The USSR team now had four riders in the top six overall.
With the climbs coming right after the start of the stage the Yellow jersey was much in evidence on the first climb to Ballaghasheen and he was third across the top behind his teammate Ozols and Ian Chivers (Ireland).
After a hair-raising descent they started up Ballaghbeama with the order the same at the top. After the descent there were two groups on the road in front of the remains of the bunch, separated by 50 seconds and a few miles later they merged leaving 13 at the front including the entire USSR team. Moss and Martin of Antrim, Chivers and Paul McQuaid (Ireland), Francis Guyon (France), Terry Jackson (Southend), Paul Madden (Kerry), Rob Langley (G.B.) and Ger Madden (Cork).
A minute behind them there was a bunch of 20 with a group of 15 a further minute back. While the groups remained the same, the gaps continued to grow throughout the stage.
There were two more climbs: Knouckaganish at 52 miles followed by the 1st category Healy Pass where the race leader took off along with Pizkis, never to be seen again.
Just to rub it in Ozols went away in the final miles taking 33 seconds out of the chasers.

**Stage 6 Cahirciveen - Bantry 87 Mls.** 1 R.Vinovsky (USSR) 3.41.20 2 A.Piziks (USSR) s.t. 3 D.Ozols (USSR) at 5.50 4 A.Iarmolis (USSR) at 6.23 5 F.Guyon (France) 6 G.Madden (Cork) 7 P.Madden (Kerry) 8 R.Langley (G.B.) 9 I.Chivers (Ireland) 10 P.McQuaid (Ireland) all same time
**General Classification:** 1 R.Vinovsky (USSR) 23.51.55 2 D.Ozols (USSR) at 7.19 3 A.Martin (Antrim) at 8.14 4 A.Piziks (USSR) at 9.46 5 A.Moss at 9.56 6 A.Iarmolis (USSR) at 13.03 7 S.Clarke (Dublin Abra.) at 14.15 8 G.Madden (Cork) at 14.31 9 J.Tanner (G.B.) at 14.42 10 Cormac.McCann (Antrim) s.t.
**Points:** 1 R.Vinovsky 73 2 A.Moss 45
**Mountains:** 1 D.Ozols 70 2 I.Chivers 48
**Team:** 1 USSR 71.47.30 2 Antrim at 16.37 3 Cork at 39.44

## STAGE 7 (a) and (b)

There were two short road stages on Friday, 62 miles in the morning and 48 in the afternoon and there appeared to be some chinks in the Soviet armour as race leader Robert Vinovsky lost 6 minutes of his lead and ended the day 1.58 in front.
While the flatter stages might have led the riders to expect a bit of a rest after the mountains, the high speed saw riders getting dropped from the bunch for the first time since the start of the race.
Stephen Nevin (Dublin Fosters) the current leader of the classic league, had a good win in the morning coming home on his own 1.26 ahead of a group of eight who were led in by Jim Carey (Dublin Abrakebabra) from Ozols. The Antrim team kept up their pressure and had two in the break, Cormac McCann 4th and Alistair Martin, strengthening his overall third position that was 9th.
Race leader Vinovsky came home with the bunch over 4 minutes down.
**Stage 7a Bantry - Mallow 62 Mls.** 1 S.Nevin (Dublin Fosters) 2.17.24 2 J.Carey (Dublin Abra.) at 1.29 3 D.Ozols (USSR) 4 C.McCann (Antrim) 5 P.McQuaid (Ireland) 6 P.Callaly (Dublin Abra.) 7 A.O'Hara (Dublin Panasonic) 8 B.Lenihan (Cork) 9 A.Martin (Antrim) all same time 10 T.Jackson (Southend) at 2.43
In the afternoon four riders went away immediately after the start: John Sheehan (Dublin Abra.), I.Chivers (Ireland), D.Lonergan (Dublin Fosters) and Fionn O'Sullivan (Dublin Panasonic).
A series of small groups went off the front and these came together in a big chasing group of around 30 riders. The yellow jersey was a marked man and couldn't get away from the bunch and he, in his turn, was keeping close watch on third placed Martin. The pair eventually finished in the bunch 3.50 down.
Sheehan punctured and was dropped from the break and Lonergan dropped back after 35 miles. Eight of the chasers got across to the leaders including fourth placed Piziks and 5th placed Moss. Piziks attacked and went away with Fionn O'Sullivan who he dropped on the finishing circuit coming home on his own 37 seconds ahead of the Dubliner. Ozols led in the rest of the break 1.04 behind his teammate.

**Stage 7b Mallow - Youghal 48 Mls.** 1 A.Piziks (USSR) 1.49.55 2 F.O'Sullivan (Dublin Panasonic) at 37 secs 3 D.Ozols at 1.04 4 P.Hodge (New Zealand) 5 I.Chivers (Ireland) 6 P.Callaly (Dublin Abra.) 7 A.Moss (Antrim) all same time 8 M.Walsh (Dublin Fosters) at 1.55 9 T.Dillon (Dublin) 10 D.Conroy (Kerry) all same time

**General Classification:** 1 R.Vinovsky (USSR) 28.07.13 2 D.Ozols (USSR) at 1.58 3 A.Martin (Antrim) at 4.15 4 A.Piziks (USSR) at 6.14 5 A.Moss (Antrim) at 9.30 6 C.McCann (Antrim) at 10.33 7 A.Iarmolis (USSR) at 11.52 8 P.McQuaid (Ireland) at 11.56 9 G.Madden (Cork) at 13.26 10 R. O'Gorman (Cork) at 15.13 11 S.Clarke (Dublin Abrakebabra) at 15.15 12 I.Chivers (Ireland) at 15.54

**Mountains:** 1 D.Ozols 70 2 I.Chivers 48

**Team:** 1 USSR 84.23.20 2 Antrim 84.40.21 3 Cork 85.06.37 4 Ireland 85.15.15

## STAGE 8

The Soviets emphasised their supremacy on the penultimate stage which included Mount Leinster with Andris Iarmolis coming home on his own in Carlow 5.25 in front of his teammate Arvis Piziks, performances which put them into the top four places on general classification.

Robert Vinovsky was in yellow, 1.58 ahead of Danis Ozols with Piziks now third at 3.34 and Iarmolis fourth at 3.45. Newtownards rider Alastair Martin (Antrim) was the best Irish rider, 5th at 4.19.

Iarmolis left the field at Craignamanagh with 35 miles of the 106 miles stage from Youghal still remaining. He took the tough climb of Mount Leinster in his stride

Before this Ger Madden (Cork), Sean McVittie (Isle of Man) and Enda Murray (Meath) were away and had a lead which at one stage was 8.40.

The Soviets attacked at Waterford and this lead rapidly came down. The race leader and Antrim's Alastair Martin were in a crash and while Martin got back quickly the yellow jersey had a hard chase.

Iarmolis went off on his own and caught the leaders dropping all three on the long climb of Mount Leinster. Madden was second over the top but he punctured and was then caught and dropped by Piziks. It was a pursuit from there to the finish with the two Soviets out ahead all the way.

The finish was a procession of single finishers with John Tanner (G.B.) coming in 1.24 after Piziks, Frank Relf (Ireland) 7 seconds later, and then Clarke (Dublin Abra.) another 57 seconds back, 4 seconds ahead of McCann. Then came a group of eight at 8.07 led in by Pat Gerard (Dublin Orwell).

**Stage 8 Youghal - Carlow 106 Mls.** 1 A.Iarmolis (USSR) 4.57.46 2 A.Piziks (USSR) at 5.25 3 J.Tanner (G.B.) at 6.51 4 F.Relf (Ireland) at 7.00 5 S.Clarke (Dublin Abrakebabra) at 7.57 6 C.McCann (Antrim) at 8.01 7 P.Gerrard (Dublin Orwell) 8 F.Guyon (France) 9 (Dublin IRC) 10 P.Callaly (Dublin Abra.) all same time

**General Classification:** 1 R.Vinovsky (USSR) 25.13.06 2 D.Ozols (USSR) at 1.58 3 A.Piziks (USSR) at 3.34 4 A.Iarmolis (USSR) at 3.45 5 A.Martin (Antrim) at 4.19 6 A.Moss (Antrim) at 8.30
**Points:** 1 D.Ozols
**Mountains:** 1 D.Ozols
**Team:** 1 USSR

## STAGE 9 (a) and (b)

There was drama at the start of the morning time when the race leader failed to start. X-rays taken after Saturday's stage showed that he had ridden 70 miles with two broken bones in his foot and it was no wonder he was in great pain as he received the yellow jersey after the stage.
The team had said all week that Ozols would take the lead in the time-trial but he was already leader when he started. However the way he rode it is more than likely that he could have wiped out his team-mate's advantage although the distance might not have been enough. That said he was almost 2 minutes faster than his teammate Piziks, second overall, who finished second in the TT...
Declan Lonergan was third 1.45 behind Ozols.
**Stage 9a Carlow 17.8 Mls. TT:** 1 D.Ozols (USSR) 39.36 2 A.Piziks (USSR) 41.17 3 D.Lonergan (Dublin Fosters) 41.21 4 A.Iarmolis (USSR) 41.38 5 T.Jackson (Southend) 41.49 6 F.Relf (Ireland) 42.07
The race finished with a 1 hour criterium in Dun Laoghaire and at half distance Cormac.McCann (Antrim) and Leslie McKay (Dublin Fosters) opened up a 20 second gap.
A group of seven went in pursuit with the bunch chasing hard. On the penultimate lap McCann attacked but McKay held him and edged past him in the sprint.
Declan Lonergan and Piziks left the chasing group of seven and just failed to get up to the leading pair. Piziks was 3rd at 3 seconds with Lonergan at 15 while Bernie McCormack (Dublin Telecom) got away on the final lap to take 5th just ahead of Paul Madden (Kerry) who led in the remains of the group at 46 seconds while the bunch were not far behind at 52 secs.
With the top three on overall the Soviets easily won the team classification. Next came Antrim who had the next three places on GC and won the county team by 46 minutes from Cork.
**Stage 9b Dun Laoire Criterium:** 1 L.McKay (Dublin Fosters) 1.07.29 2 C.McCann (Antrim) s.t. 3 A.Piziks (USSR) at 3 secs 4 D.Lonergan (Dublin Fosters) at 15 secs 5 B.McCormick (Dublin Telecom) at 40 secs 6 P.Madden (Kerry) at 46 secs
**General Classification:** 1 D.Ozols (USSR) 35.03.07 2 A.Piziks (USSR) at 2.23 3 A.Iarmolis (USSR) at 3.49 4 A.Martin (Antrim) at 5.25 5 A.Moss (Antrim) at 9.27 6 Cormac.McCann (Antrim) at 10.40 7 P.McQuaid (Ireland) at 12.30 8 T.Jackson (Southend) at 16.24 9 S.Clarke (Dublin Abrakebabra) at 16.28 10 I.Chivers (Ireland) at 17.09 11 R.O'Gorman (Cork) at 17.29 12 J.Tanner (Great Britain) at 18.29

**Points:** 1 A.Piziks 127 2 D.Ozols 111 3 A.Iarmolis 82
**Mountains:** 1 D.Ozols
**International Team:** 1 USSR 3.24.24 2 Ireland 106.04.11 3 Great Britain 106.35.22
**County Team:** 1 Antrim 105.30.13 2 Cork Ballyclough 106.16.27 3 Dublin Orwell 106.43.20

1989 winner, Dainis Ozoles (USSR)

## 1990

The trend of increasing entries continued in the 1990 RÁS when there was another record entry of 160.
The ten visiting teams included Great Britain (BCF), Holland, Scotland, Isle of Man, USA, Belgium, France with regional cross-Channel teams from Manchester and Bristol.
Reigning Irish champion Paul Slane could not get a release from his French club and his place on the Ireland team was taken by another Belfast rider Ian Chivers.

### STAGE 1

Herve Boussard (France) came home 16 seconds clear of his teammate Marc Peronin to take the opening stage, 78 miles from Dublin to Mullingar.
In a typical opening stage a succession of very large breakaways went up the road but although there were three large groups which finished in front of the main bunch, less than three minutes covered most of the field.
By Navan 28 miles a leading group of nine had been joined by another similar group to leave 18 at the head of affairs. Included were no less than four French riders while the Ireland team had John Sheehan and Declan Lonergan.
A second big group which included the rest of the Irish team went in pursuit and by the finish they were just 50 seconds down with yet another big group in front of the peleton.
There were three laps of a 3-mile finishing circuit in Mullingar and it was on the first lap that the two Frenchmen got away, Boussard leaving his teammate on the final lap to take the stage. Peronin managed by three seconds to hold of the chasers led in by Sheehan. Australian Patrick Jonker, riding for the French team was fourth.
**Stage 1 Dublin - Mullingar 78 Mls.** 1 H.Boussard (France) 2.25.13 2 M.Peronin (France) at 16 secs 3 J.Sheehan (Ireland) at 19 secs 4 P.Jonker (France) 5 D.Lonergan (Ireland) 6 K.de Muynck (Belgium) 7 C.Maye (Meath Avonmore) 8 Rob.Power (Tipperary FBD) 9 P.Leigh (Lancaster) 10 T.Vilatte (France) all same time
**Points:** 1 H.Boussard 25 2 M.Peronin 20 3 J.Sheehan 16
**Team:** 1 France 7.16.14 2 Tipperary FBD at 1.15 3 Ireland at 1.17

### STAGE 2

The French made it two-in-a-row when Marc Peronin led in Klaus de Muynck (Belgium) a minute ahead of Scotland's Roddy Riddle at the end of the 111 miles second stage to Westport.

There was a pattern of continual attacks for the first 50 miles of the stage but none of the many breaks was allowed to establish a useful lead.
John Nolan (Meath) took the prime at Tarmonbarry after 32 miles while at Frenchpark 56 miles Ian Bryant (G.B.) was first.
At Charlestown 74 miles a group of 20 riders was holding a small lead when they were joined by another group. As they joined four attacked but it was only when another group came up to the quartet that there was a combination at the front that could begin to draw away.
Before Castlebar 100 miles four riders left the leaders but Declan Lonergan (Ireland) punctured leaving three at the front. Near the finish Riddle was dropped but just managed to hang on for third leaving the French and Belgian riders to fight it out for the stage.
With Peronin only 16 seconds behind his teammate starting the stage he moved into the lead by 3 seconds from De Muynck with Boussard dropping back to third at 1.02.
**Stage 2 Mullingar - Westport 111 Mls.** 1 M.Peronin (France) 3.43.12 2 K.de Muynck (Belgium) s.t. 3 R.Riddle (Scotland) at 1 min 4 B.Power (Tipperary FBD) at 1.03 5 D.Lonergan (Ireland) at 1.18 6 R.de Smet (Belgium) 7 H.Boussard (France) 8 J.Dalby (Dublin Telecom) 9 P.Keogh (Dublin Telecom) 10 K.Kimmage (Meath Avonmore) s.t.
**General Classification:** 1 M.Peronin (France) 6.08.41 2 K.de Muynck (Belgium) at 3 secs 3 H.Boussard (France) at 1.02 4 D.Lonergan (Ireland) at 1.21 5 J.Sheehan (Ireland) at 1.45 6 P.Leigh (Lancaster) at 1.47 7 T Vilatte (France) at 2.14 8 K.Kimmage (Meath Avonmore) at 2.18 9 A.O'Gorman (Dublin Giant) s.t. 10 F.Relf (Ireland) s.t.
**Points:** 1 M.Peronin 45 2 H.Boussard 34 3 K.de Muynck 30
**Team:** 1 France 18.29.19 2 Ireland at 2.06 3 Tipperary at 3.42

## STAGE 3

The French paid the price of success when, like so many others who attracted too much early attention in the RÁS, they found themselves so heavily marked that they were trapped in the bunch which came home a huge 13 minutes behind the stage winner, Kevin Kimmage while Belgian Klaus de Muynch took over the yellow jersey by a useful 2.15 from Frank Relf (Ireland).
The 93 miles run to Ennis was the third without any climbs and was relatively uneventful for everyone except those in a big group which went away early on and just went further and further ahead with no great reaction from the bunch.
Eight riders went away at Party 14 miles and six miles further on at Ballinrobe they were joined by another 11 and this 19 stayed together for the next 70 miles.
The prime at Headford went to Patrick van Rafeigem (Belgium) and that at Gort went to Relf. The break split into several groups over the final miles with an 8-man group at the front from which Kimmage won the sprint for the stage from Robert

Power (FBD Tipperary) and H.Groen (Holland) but De Muynck, who finished 7th in the same time was the big winner moving into a good lead.

**Stage 3 Westport – Ennis 85 Mls.** 1 K.Kimmage (Meath Avonmore) 3.22.44 2 Rob.Power (Tipperary FBD) 3 H.Groen (Holland) 4 F.Relf (Ireland) 5 P.Callaly (Dublin Giant) 6 I.Chivers (Ireland) 7 K.de Muynck (Belgium) 8 B.Lenihan (Cork CMP) all same time 9 D.Conroy (Meath Avonmore) at 7 secs 10 M.Cahill (Dublin Euromech) at 1.39

**General Classification:** 1 K.de Muynck (Belgium) 9.31.28 2 K.Kimmage (Meath Avonmore) at 2.15 3 F.Relf (Ireland) s.t. 4 Rob.Power (Tipperary FBD) at 2.42 5 H.Groen (Holland) at 2.52 6 I.Chivers (Ireland) at 3.47 7 P.Callaly (Dublin Giant) at 3.49 8 A.O'Gorman (Dublin Giant) at 3.54 9 D.Lonergan (Ireland) at 5.28 10 B.Lenihan (Cork CMP) at 5.35

**Points:** 1 M.Peronin 45 2 K.de Muynck 39 3 H.Boussard 34

**Team:** 1 Ireland 28.43.47 2 Meath Avonmore at 3.50 3 Tipperary FBD at 5.46

## STAGE 4

Ian Chivers from Ballyrobert, outside Belfast, riding for the Ireland team, took over the lead after the 92 miles stage from Listowel which was won by team-mate Declan Lonergan.

Chivers had finished with the leading group on the opening three stages and on this, the first of the mountain stages he went away in a group of ten early in the stage. As well as Chivers and Lonergan there was past winners Stephen Spratt (Tipperary) and Phil Cassidy (Meath Avonmore) and working well they had a lead of 1.15 at Tralee which had stretched to 2 minutes as they approached the Connor Pass. Raymond Power (Tipperary) led over the Pass from Spratt and Lonergan.

On the descent several groups of riders came up to the leaders and by Dingle, 58 miles, a big lead group of 23 had a 5 minute lead on the bunch which contained the yellow jersey. A group of nine went away from the leaders and they opened up a 4 minute lead by the finish where Lonergan won the sprint from French rider M.Peronin.The yellow jersey bunch came in 5.40 down and Muynck dropped to second overall at 1.29.

**Stage 4 Listowel - Killorglin 92 Mls.** 1 D.Lonergan (Ireland 3.52.47 2 M.Peronin (France) 3 D.Power (Cork CMP) all same time 4 Ray.Power(Tipperary FBD) at 4 secs 5 J.Wolfkam (Holland) 6 S.Spratt(Tipperary FBD) 7 I.Chivers (Ireland) 8 P.Leigh (Lancaster) all same time 9 P.Cassidy (Meath Avonmore) at 15 secs 10 D.Long (Tipperary FBD) at 3.51

**General Classification:** 1 I.Chivers (Ireland) 13.28.06 2 K.de Muynck (Belgium) at 1.29 3 D.Lonergan (Ireland) at 1.37 4 P.Leigh (Lancaster) at 1.41 5 Ray.Power (Tipperary FBD) at 3.15 6 K.Kimmage (Meath Avonmore) at 3.44 7 F.Relf (Ireland) s.t. 8 J.Wolfkam (Holland) at 4.08 9 Rob.Power (Tipperary FBD) at 4.11 10 H.Groen (Holland) at 4.21

**Points:** 1 M.Peronin 65 2 D.Lonergan 49 3 K.de Muynck 39

**Mountains:** 1 Ray.Power 15 2 S.Spratt 12 3 D.Long 10
**Team:** 1 Ireland 40.27.32 2 Tipperary FBD at 4.21 3 Meath Avonmore at9.21

## STAGE 5

Declan Power (Cork CPM) won the fifth stage, 96 mile stage to Macroom in a two-up sprint from Patrick Jonker (France). Ian Chivers came home in the main bunch at 1.50 and became the first leader of the week to hold on to the yellow jersey.
An eight-man group went away shortly after the start and were joined by ten more before the first climb of the day at Moll's Gap. The leaders split on the climb and Brian Smith (Dublin Euromech) led eleven riders over the top including Chivers, Conor Henry and David Wilson (Antrim), John Cosgrove (Lancashire), Declan Power (Cork CMP), Patrick Jonker (France) and Richard Prebble (Southend).
On the descent Henry, Cosgrove and Prebble went away and at the top of the next climb at Turner's Rock Tunnel they had a lead of 30 seconds when Henry punctured and was caught by the chasers. Power and Jonker got across to the two in front and the four of them stayed away until the finishing circuit in Macroom where they split with Power and Jonker going away to finish 44 seconds ahead of third placed Cosgrove with Prebble another 24 seconds behind in fourth place.
**Stage 5 Killorglin - Macroom 96 Mls.** 1 D.Power (Cork CMP) 3.46.51 2 P.Jonker (France) s.t. 3 J.Cosgrove (Lancashire) at 44 secs 4 R.Prebble (Southend) at 1.08 5 Rob.Power (Tipperary FBD) at 1.23 6 M.Peronin (France) 7 K.de Muynck (Belgium 8 M.Coll (Scotland) 9 P.Callaly (Dublin Giant) 10 M.Walsh (Dublin Fosters) all same time
**General Classification:** 1 I.Chivers (Ireland) 17.16.20 2 K.de Muynck (Belgium) at 1.29 3 D.Lonergan (Ireland) at 2.23 4 P. Leigh (Lancaster)
at 2.27 5 Ray Power (Tipperary FBD) at 3.15 6 Rob.Power (Tipperary FBD) at 4.11 7 P.Cassidy (Meath Avonmore) at 4.23 8 K.Kimmage (Meath Avonmore) at 4.30 9 D.Power (Cork CMP) at 5.14 10 S.Spratt (Tipperary FBD) at 5.17
**Points:** 1 M.Peronin 75 2 D.Lonergan 49 3 K.de Muynck 48
**Mountains:** 1 Ray.Power 25 2 S.Spratt 20 3 P.Jonker 19
**Team:** 1 Ireland 51.54.47 2 Tipperary FBD at 1.48 3 Meath Avonmore at 8.20

## STAGE 6

20-year-old Barry Sutton from Ennis was first across the line on the sixth stage, 101 miles to Macroom but his joy was short-lived when he was penalised 10 seconds for allowing himself to be paced by his team car and the stage was awarded to second placed Martin Coll (Scotland).
A similar fate befell third across the line, John Cosgrove (Lancaster) who was fined 30 seconds elevating Bobby Power (Tipperary FBD) to second. Cosgrove was one of six riders so penalised.

Ian Chivers retained the yellow jersey holding his lead of 1.29 over De Muynck with another Ireland rider Declan Lonergan third at 2.23 taking over the green points jersey after leader Marc Peronin abandoned after a crash.
The action started when Raymond Power attacked at the Musheramore Mountain prime shattering the bunch as he took the prime and increased his KOM lead. The race regrouped on the descent and Dave Moloney (Dublin Fosters) went off on his own. He was joined by Patrick Goodwin (Manchester) and John Cosgrove (Lancaster) and then by Steve Hazlett (Scotland) and Conor Henry (Antrim) before Lismore where they led by over 2 minutes.
Over the Vee they were still clear by 1.50 with Henry taking maximum points. Cosgrove punctured but got back and then Henry punctured at Clogheen but he also got back to the break.
The bunch closed down fast as they approached the finish and only Cosgrove was still ahead as they reached the town. Coll attacked in sight of the finish but Sutton came round him to win the sprint with Cosgrove next across the line.
**Stage 6 Macroom - Clonmel 101 Mls.** 1 M.Coll (Scotland) 4.12.43 2 B.Power (Tipperary FBD) 3 P.O'Keeffe (Dublin IRC) 4 T.Vilatte (France) 5 S.Hazlett (Scotland) 6 D.Peelo (Dublin Euromech) 7 G.Madden (Wicklow) 8 D.McQuaid (Dublin Fosters) all same time 9 B.Sutton (Clare Rebel Menswear) at 10 secs 10 B.Quinn (Limerick) at 17 secs
**General Classification:** 1 I.Chivers (Ireland) 21.29.22 2 K.de Muynck (Belgium) at 1.29 3 D.Lonergan (Ireland) at 2.23 4 P.Leigh (Lancaster) at 2.47 5 Ray.Power (Tipperary FBD) at 3.15 6 Rob.Power (Tipperary FBD) at 4.11 7 P.Cassidy (Meath Avonmore) at 4.23 8 K. Kimmage (Meath Avonmore) at 4.30 9 D.Power (Cork CMP) at 5.14 10 S.Spratt (Tipperary FBD) at 5.17
**Points:** 1 D.Lonergan 51 2 K.de Muynck 48 3 D.Power 44
**Mountains:** 1 Ray.Power 35 2 P.Jonker 27 3 S.Spratt 20
**Team:** 1 Ireland 64.33.53 2 Tipperary FBD at 1.29 3 Meath Avonmore at 8.20

## STAGE 7 (a) and (b)

There was a spectacular big bunch finish into Thurles where point's leader Declan Lonergan (Ireland) took his second stage of the week ahead of Antrim pair Gary Scott and Andrew Callan. Earlier in the day Anthony O'Gorman (Dublin Giant) had won the 5 kms time-trial from Clonmel up to Powers the Pot by 4 seconds from Patrick Jonkers.
There was no change in the top three after the two stages but Lonergan gained 23 seconds on the race leader, his teammate Ian Chivers.
After their exertions in the morning, the 59 miles afternoon stage was not very difficult although there was a climb at Slievenamuck.
There was no significant break and the bunch arrived intact at Thurles where Andrew Callan led out the sprint for his teammate Gary Scott who came round him but Lonergan was the faster.

**Stage 7 Clonmel - Powers the Pot 5 Km. TT:** 1 A.O'Gorman (Dublin Giant) 14.37 2 P.Jonker (France) 14.41 3 J.Wolfkam (Holland) 14.43 4 Ray.Power (Tipperary FBD) 14.47 5 D.Lonergan (Ireland) 15.08 6 S. Spratt (Tipperary FBD) 15.11 7 P.McQuaid (Dublin Fosters) 15.17 8 R.de Smet (Belgium) 15.20 9 K.Kimmage (Meath Avonmore) 15.23 10 J.Dalby (Dublin Telecom) 15.25
**Stage 7b Clonmel - Thurles 59 Mls.** 1 D.Lonergan (Ireland) 2.21.25 2 G.Scott (Antrim) 3 A.Callan (Antrim) 4 J.Dalby (Dublin Telecom) 5 R.de Smet (Belgium) 6 K.Kimmage (Meath Avonmore) 7 R.Riddle (Scotland) 8 S.Healy (Dublin Euromech) 9 P.Keogh (Dublin Telecom) 10 K.de Muynck (Belgium) all same time
**General Classification:** 1 I.Chivers (Ireland) 24.06.18 2 K.de Muynck (Belgium) at 1.29 3 D.Lonergan (Ireland) at 2.00 4 Ray.Power (Tipperary FBD) at 2.31 5 P.Leigh (Lancaster) at 2.47 6 Rob.Power (Tipperary FBD) at 4.08 7 K.Kimmage (Meath Avonmore) at 4.22 8 S.Spratt (Tipperary FBD) at 4.57 9 J.Wolfkam (Holland) at 5.05 10 P.Callaly (Dublin Giant) at 5.28
**Points:** 1 D.Lonergan 82 2 K.de Muynck 54 3 D.Power 44
**Mountains:** 1 P.Jonker 47 2 Ray.Power 46 3 S.Spratt 31
**Team:** 1 Tipperary FBD 72.25.03 2 Ireland at 41 secs 3 Meath Avonmore at 10.46

## STAGE 8

Saturday's 98 miles stage from Dublin to Arklow over the mountains was won by Frank Relf (Ireland) at the head of a 7-man break.
This group went away early and also there was Bobby Power and Damien Long (Tipperary FBD), Patrick Jonker and Thierry Vilatte (France), Tom Shanahan (Limerick), Jos Wolfkam (Holland), Gerard O'Sullivan (Longford) and Michael McLynskey (Dublin Telecom).
At Mount Leinster Wolfkam attacked along with Relf, the Dutchman taking the prime. Relf, looking after Chivers' interests marked any attacks and with six miles to go he attacked and went clear to take the stage by 24 seconds.
Behind them the Irish team controlled things and nobody that was any threat to the leader was allowed to get away and Chivers came home safely in a group 50 seconds behind the stage winner.
**Stage 9 Thurles - Arklow 98 Mls.** 1 F.Relf (Ireland) 4.12.18 2 D.Long (Tipperary FBD) at 24 secs 3 P. Jonker (France) at 26 secs 4 M.McLynskey (Dublin Telecom) at 32 secs 5 T.Vilatte (France 6 G.O'Sullivan (Longford 7 J.Wolfkam (Holland) all same time 8 D.Lonergan (Ireland) at 44 secs 9 R.Riddle (Scotland) s.t. 10 K.Kimmage (Meath Avonmore) s.t.
**General Classification:** 1 I.Chivers (Ireland) 28.19.20 2 K.de Muynck (Belgium) at 1.29 3 D.Lonergan (Ireland) at 2.00 4 Ray.Power (Tipperary FBD) at 2.31 5 P.Leigh (Lancaster) at 2.47 6 Rob.Power (Tipperary FBD) at 4.08 7 K.Kimmage (Meath Avonmore) at 4.22 8 J.Wolfkam (Holland) at 4.53 9 S.Spratt (Tipperary FBD) at 4.57 10 P.Callaly (Dublin Giant) at 5.28
**Points:** 1 D.Lonergan 90 2 P.Jonker 59 3 K.de Muynck 54

**Mountains:** 1 P.Jonker 57 2 Ray.Power 46 3 S. Spratt 31
**Team:** 1 Tipperary FBD 85.03.49 2 Ireland at 17 secs 3 Meath Avonmore at 11.06

## STAGE 9

The final stage was a 1 hour, 15 minutes criterium in Dun Laoghaire and barring accidents, Chivers, supported by a strong team, was home and dry.

After 40 minutes of racing 13 riders got away and Chivers was there along with his main rivals De Muynck and Lonergan. Also in this group were Kevin Kimmage (Meath Avonmore), Roddy Riddle (Scotland), Patrick Jonker (France) Julian Dalby (Dublin Telecom) and Gary Scott (Antrim).

With four laps left Riddle and Jonker attacked and opened a gap. Dalby and De Muynck tried to get across but at the finish the two leaders had 12 seconds in hand over the two chasers and Riddle took the sprint. Dalby beat De Muynck for third spot while Chivers led in the remainder of the break, 23 seconds behind in 5th place.

With Chivers and Lonergan in the break Ireland just managed to knock Tipperary FBD off the top team spot by a mere 6 seconds.

**Stage 9 Dun Laoghaire Criterium:** 1 R.Riddle (Scotland) 1.10.41 2 P.Jonker (France) s.t. 3 J.Dalby (Dublin Telecom) at 12 secs 4 K.de Muynck (Belgium) s.t. 5 I.Chivers (Ireland) at 15 secs 6 J.Sheehan (Ireland) at 23 secs 7 K.Kimmage (Meath Avonmore) 8 D.Lonergan (Ireland) 9 I.Bryant (Britain) 10 D.Long (Tipperary FBD) all same time

**General Classification:** 1 I.Chivers (Ireland) 29.30.16 2 K.de Muynck (Belgium) at 1.26 3 D.Lonergan (Ireland) at 2.08 4 Ray.Power (Tipperary FBD) at 2.54 5 P.Leigh (Lancaster) at 3.22 6 Rob.Power (Tipperary FBD) at 4.16 7 K.Kimmage (Meath Avonmore) at 4.30 8 J.Wolfkam (Holland) at 5.28 9 S.Spratt (Tipperary FBD) at 5.32 10 P.Callaly (Dublin Giant) at 6.03

**Points:** 1 D.Lonergan 97 2 P.Jonker 79 3 K.de Muynck 68

**Mountains:** 1 P.Jonker 57 2 Ray.Power 46 3 S.Spratt 31

**Team:** 1 Ireland 88.37.10 2 Tipperary FBD at 6 secs 3 Meath Avonmore at 11.51

*1990 winner, Ian Chivers, Ireland*

## 1991

There was an entry of 145 for the '91 RÁS including Ian Chivers, the '90 winner back leading an all-star Ireland team which included Robert Power, Declan Lonergan and David Hourigan.
Included were teams from Great Britain, Australia, Holland, Belgium, Czechoslovakia and Scotland. Five cross-channel regional team were entered and there was a composite International Guest squad. Twenty Irish county teams completed the field.

### STAGE 1

The race got underway with an 81-miles stage to Enniscorthy which was won by Gethin Butler riding for the British Cycling Federation team.
There was climbing right from the start with a King of the Mountains prime at The Embankment after the race passed through Tallagh. The prime was taken by Dutch-born Australian Patrick Jonkers, the '90 King of the Mountains.
A group of twelve formed over this climb with Jonkers emphasising his climbing ability by also taking the KOM primes at Slieve Corragh and the Wicklow Gap. These climbs took their toll and by Arklow (51 miles) their numbers were down to eight as Butler attacked and went away to a lead of 1.30 as the remainder of the break were swept up by the bunch.
A group of 11 went in pursuit of Butler and got to within 20 seconds of the leader. Bobby Power (Tipperary) and Tyrone Belleek Pottery pair Donal O'Halloran and Cormac McCann tried to get across to the lone leader but the finish came just too soon and GB rider winning by 8 seconds from O'Halloran with McCann at 17, Power at 18 while Darren Lawson (Australia) led in the remains of the break at 35 secs.
**Stage 1 Dublin - Enniscorthy 81 Mls.** 1 G.Butler (Great Britain) 2.59.51 2 D.O'Halloran (Tyrone Belleek Pottery) at 8 secs 3 C.McCann (Tyrone) at 17 secs 4 B.Power (Tipperary) at 18 secs 5 D.Lawson (Australia) at 35 secs 6 M.Bell (G.B.) s.t.

### STAGE 2

The Ireland team had their first success on the 105 miles stage to Middleton, won by Robert Power. However it was Donal O'Halloran, riding as a guest on the Tyrone Belleek Pottery team, who took over the lead by 4 seconds from Stephen Spratt (Tipperary FBD).
A 16-man break went away early in the stage and at one point their lead had grown to six minutes. However this set alarm bells ringing and in the inevitable all-out chase the break was caught with only six miles to go.

Immediately another group went away but it too was swallowed up, all except Power and Spratt who managed to hold on, Power winning by 3 seconds from Spratt who in turn was 19 seconds ahead of the bunch led in by Czech Jan Vasek. O'Halloran finished 8th in the same time to hold his lead.
**Stage 2 Enniscorthy - Middleton 105 Mls.** 1 R.Power (Ireland) 4.29.56 2 S.Spratt (Tipperary FBD) at 3 secs 3 J.Vasek (Czechoslovakia) at 22 secs 4 K.Kimmage (Meath Avonmore) 6 B.McLoughlin (Cork) 7 O.Murphy (Down O'Rourke's) 8 D.O'Halloran (Tyrone Belleek) all same time
**General Classification:** 1 D.O'Halloran (Tyrone Belleek Pottery) 7.30.21 2 S.Spratt (Tipperary FBD) at 4 secs 3 C.McCann (Tyrone Belleek) at 9 secs 4 R.Power (Ireland) at 25 secs 5 R.de Smet (Belgium) at 27 secs 6 J.Wolfkam (Holland) s.t.
**Points:** D.O'Halloran 21.
**Mountains:** P.Jonkers 22.
**Team:** Tyrone Belleek Pottery.

## STAGE 3 (a) and (b)

In one of those typical RÁS stages where a break turns the general classification upside down, O'Halloran came in with the main group six minutes down, losing the jersey to Jan Wolfkamp (Holland), who had been lying sixth overnight. The stage went to Patrick Jonkers (International Selection).
Earlier, in the morning's 10 miles time-trial, O'Halloran looked in command when, riding Sean Kelly's time-trial bike, he won the stage by 1 second from Declan Lonergan (Ireland) with Stephen Spratt third, only 5 seconds back in a very close contest.
This improved O'Halloran's position overall but it mattered little when all of the top three missed out on the afternoon's 77-mile stage to Limerick when around 30 riders took a huge amount of time out of the bunch.
O'Halloran was unlucky to puncture in the middle of the action when the bunch had split into five distinct groups under the pressure of the chase. He rode well, jumping across from group to group but couldn't bridge the final gap to the leading thirty.
Four riders left the leaders with 10 miles to go: Phil Cassidy (Meath Avonmore), van Baarle (Holland), Marcel Lena (Australia) and Jonkers, these last two going away again while Cassidy and van Baarle were caught.
The Australian manager was delighted with Jonkers' form for, although he was not on the Aussie RÁS team, he was on their team for the British Milk Race, two week later.
**Stage 3a Middleton 10 Mls. TT:** 1 D.O'Halloran (Tyrone Belleek Pottery) 23.13 2 D.Lonergan (Ireland) 23.14 3 S.Spratt (Tipperary FBD) 23.18
**Stage 3b Middleton - Limerick 77 Mls.** 1 P.Jonkers (International Selection) 3.17.27 2 M.Lena (Australia) s.t. 3 K.Kimmage (Meath Avonmore) at 20 secs 4 G.Madden (Cork) 5 P.de Frenne (Belgium) 6 N.Holmes (Cork) 7 G.Wilson

(Australia) 8 G.Ford (G.B.) 9 D.Easton (Down O'Rourke's) 10 D.Hourigan (Ireland) all same time

**General Classification:** 1 J.Wolfkamp (Holland) 11.12.43 2 D.Hourigan (Ireland) at 5 secs 3 G.Butler (G.B.) at 17 secs 4 S.Nevin (Dublin Emmelle) at 1.00 5 P.McQuaid (Dublin Emmelle) at 1.01 6 K.Kimmage (Meath Avonmore) at 1.02 7 O.Murphy (Down O'Rourke's) s.t. 8 G.Wilson (Australia) at 1.05 9 P.Jonkers (Inter.Sel.) at 2.00 10 T.Jackson (Southend) s.t.

## STAGE 4

British Cycling Federation rider Gethin Butler regained the yellow jersey, which he had worn after the opening stage, even though he only finished tenth on the stage, 2.17 behind stage winner Declan Lonergan (Ireland), on the 107 miles stage from Limerick to Clifden.

The Preston rider came in with a 20-man group which had been out in front for virtually the whole stage and it was only in the final 10 kilometres that four of this group got away to take the major honours.

After racing got underway Andrew Roche (Mayo), Colm Maye and Donie Conroy (both Meath), Tim Schools (Lancaster) and Mike Bell (BCF) went clear and by Sixmilebridge 10 miles they had been joined by Lonergan, Joe Barr (Tyrone Belleek Pottery), and two past Rás winners Stephen Spratt (Tipperary) and Phil Cassidy (Ireland).

At Tulla (20 miles) they were caught by another group including Ian Chivers (Ireland), Denis Easton (Down O'Rourke's), Paul and Darragh McQuaid (Dublin Emmelle) and S. Allards (Holland). Sixteen miles later, at Gort, O'Halloran, Richard Hare (Southend) and John Nolan (Meath) got up making it 20 riders at the front with a lead of 3.30 minutes. However the bunch was still chasing and by Galway 57 miles the gap was down to 1.05.

With ten to go Lonergan, Bell, Nolan and Maye split from the front and quickly built up a 1 minute lead. They stayed this way until the final four miles when Lonergan took off chased by Bell. At the finish Lonergan had 1 minute to spare over Bell with the two Meath riders another 19 seconds behind. Roche led in the remainder of the break 2.17 down on the stage winner.

**Stage 4 Limerick - Clifden 107 Mls.** 1 D.Lonergan (Ireland) 4.22.00 2 M.Bell (GB) at 1.03 3 C.Maye (Meath) at 1.32 4 J.Nolan (Meath) s.t. 5 A.Roche (Mayo) at 2.17 6 T.Schools (Lancaster) 7 D.Easton (Down O'Rourke's) 8 I.Chivers (Ireland) 9 D.O'Halloran (Tyrone Belleek) 10 G.Butler (GB).

**General Classification:** 1 G.Butler (GB) 15.37.17 2 P.McQuaid (Dublin Emmelle) at 55 secs 3 J.Wolfkamp (Holland) at 1.37 4 P.Cassidy (Ireland) at 2.11 5 D.Hourigan (Ireland) at 3.00 6 S.Spratt (Tipperary) s.t. 7 J.Barr (Tyrone Belleek) at 3.07 8 I.Chivers (Ireland) at 3.37 9 D.Lonergan (Ireland) at 3.39 10 P.Jonkers (Inter. Sel.) at 4.10

**Teams:** 1 Meath 2 Ireland 3 Tyrone Belleek

## STAGE 5

Kevin Kimmage (Meath Avonmore) won the fifth stage, 91 miles from Clifden to Ballina in a sprint from a 5-man group. As a result he moved up to fifth overall behind Gethin Butler who retained the yellow jersey.
Kimmage was first in action after 55 miles at Westport when he went away in company with Pat Callaly (Dublin Les Jeunes) and David Hourigan (Ireland) but they didn't work well together and the Great Britain team at the head of the field brought them back.
Kimmage tried again at Castlebar (66 miles). He was joined again by Callaly and Czech rider Radek Tersaj with two GB riders, Mike Bell and Paul Barrett along to look after Butler's interests.
Despite the two GB riders sitting in the five stayed away and Kimmage was still strong enough to win the sprint. Declan Lonergan (Ireland) led in the chasers 1.09 behind the winner.
**Stage 6 Clifden - Ballina 91 Mls.** 1 K.Kimmage (Meath Avonmore) 3.44.38 2 P.Barrett (GB) 3 R.Tersaj (Czechoslovakia) 4 P.Callaly (Dublin Les Jeunes) 5 M.Bell (GB) all same time 6 D.Lonergan (Ireland) at 1.09 7 C.McCann (Tyrone Belleek) s.t.
**General Classification:** 1 G.Butler (GB) 19.23.04 2 P.McQuaid (Dublin Emmelle) at 55 secs 3 J.Wolfkamp (Holland) at 1.37 4 P.Cassidy (Ireland) at 2.11 5 K.Kimmage (Meath Avonmore) at 2.35 6 D.Hourigan (Ireland) at 3.00 7 J.Barr (Tyrone Belleek) at 3.07 8 S.Spratt (Tipperary) s.t. 9 I.Chivers (Ireland) at 3.37 10 D.Lonergan (Ireland) at 3.39 11 P.Jonkers (Int. Sel.) at 3.39 12 O.Murphy (Down O'Rourke's) at 4.19

## STAGE 6

There was no change at the top of the leader-board after Thursday's sixth stage which was won by Australian Jason Phillips from a six-man group.
The story of the day was a break by two lowly-placed riders, vet. Sean Lally and Garda Jim Cassidy who went away just after the start and by the time the race passed through Sligo, after 37 miles, they held a lead of over 13 minutes as the main bunch rolled along.
However the size of the gap spurred the peleton and a break of six went in pursuit: Phillips, Tim Schools (Lancaster), Milan Soula (Czechoslovakia), Conor Henry (Tyrone Belleek), Donie Conroy (Meath) and Patrick Goodwin (Manchester Irish Heritage).
At the front Cassidy had been dropped by Lally and was caught and passed by the break. However Lally managed to hang until the final miles when he was dropped and passed by several riders to finish a brave 13th.
Five more got away from the bunch but just failed to catch the leaders whose lead was just17 seconds at the end.

**Stage 6, Ballina - Letterkenny, 106m.:** 1 R.Phillips (Australia) 4.48.12 2 T.Schools (Lancaster) 3 M.Soula (Czech.) 4 C.Henry (Tyrone) 5 D.Conroy (Meath) 6 P.Goodwin (Manchester) all same time 7 C.McCann (Tyrone) at 17 secs 8 K.Eeckhoudt (Belgium) 9 P.de Frenne (Holland) 10 R.de Vink (Holland) all same time

**General Classification:** 1 G.Butler (BCF) 24.23.04 2 P.McQuaid (Dublin Emmelle) at 53 secs 3 J.Wolfkamp (Holland) at 1.37 4 P.Cassidy (Ireland) at 2.11 5 K.Kimmage (Meath Avonmore) at 2.35 6 D.Hourigan (Ireland) at 3.00 7 J.Barr (Tyrone) at 3.07 8 S.Spratt (Tipperary) s.t. 9 I.Chivers (Ireland) at 3.37 10 D.Lonergan (Ireland) at 3.39 11 P.Jonkers (Int. Sel.) at 3.39 12 O.Murphy (Down O'Rourke's) at 4.19

## STAGE 7

Milan Soula (Czechoslovakia) won the seventh stage, 84 miles from Letterkenny to Donegal but Gethin Butler finished in a chasing group, 1.59 in arrears to retain the yellow jersey.

Previous day's winner Kevin Kimmage (Meath Avonmore) finished fourth in the same time as Soula and moved into second place, only 36 seconds down on the GB rider. Declan Lonergan (Ireland) was also in the break and moved to third 1.40 behind.

Butler had to fight hard to retain the lead chasing the five-man break for the last 30 miles with Australian Patrick Jonkers.

Defending champion Ian Chivers had been in an early seven-man break and when that was brought back he went again in the 13-man group which was the basis of all the successful moves. However mechanical trouble after Glenties saw him drop back to the bunch, his chance of a second successive win gone.

At Kilcar, with 60 miles completed, the five leaders took a wrong road and Butler and Jonkers, who were chasing took a different wrong road but the bunch, now well down at 7.50 stayed on course. The commissaires stopped the race and restarted it with the gaps as they had been at the last time-check before the mishap. The five leaders stretched their lead and the bunch trailed in nearly ten minutes down.

**Stage 7 Letterkenny - Donegal 84 Mls.** 1 M.Soula (Czechoslovakia) 3.30.05 2 P.Callaly (Dublin Les Jeunes) 3 A.Roche (Mayo) 4 K.Kimmage (Meath Avonmore) 5 D.Lonergan (Ireland) all same time 6 P.Jonkers (Inter. Sel.) at 1.59 7 G.Butler (G.B.) s.t. 8 R.Power (Ireland) at 3.43 9 C.McCann (Tyrone Belleek) 10 D.Hourigan (Ireland) s.t.

**General Classification:** 1 G.Butler (GB) 27.45.20 2 K.Kimmage (Meath Avonmore) at 36 secs 3 D.Lonergan (Ireland) at 1.40 4 P.McQuaid (Dublin Emmelle) at 3.01 5 J.Wolfkamp (Holland) at 3.21 6 D.Hourigan (Ireland) at 4.43

## STAGE 8

In a great result for the big home crowd Kevin Kimmage (Meath Avonmore) , a member of the Navan Avonmore club, took over the lead with just two stages to go when he finished second to Declan Lonergan (Ireland) in a six-man break which came into Navan with a lead of almost two minutes. Yellow jersey Butler dropped back to second, 1.34 behind Kimmage.
There was a transfer from Donegal Town and the race started in Enniskillen. After an early break had been recaptured, Phil Cassidy (Meath) attacked at Butler's Bridge taking five riders with him.
In the break were Kimmage, Lonergan, Cassidy, Brendan McLaughlin (Cork), Z. Meloun (Czechoslovakia) and Southend pair Brian Long and Terry Jackson. When their lead was 30 seconds Lonergan bridged the gap in impressive style just as the yellow jersey punctured.
Although Butler quickly regained the bunch all hell broke loose as rider after rider tried unsuccessfully to emulate Lonergan in getting across to the leaders who stretched their lead to 1.30.
Cassidy dropped back with two kilometres to go and at the finish sprinter Lonergan beat Kimmage to take his second stage of the week.
**Stage 7 Enniskillen - Navan 104 Mls.** 1 D.Lonergan (Ireland) 4.0.31 2 K.Kimmage (Meath Avonmore) 3 B.McLaughlin (Cork) 4 B.Long (Southend) 5 Z.Melour (Czechoslovakia) 6 T.Jackson (Southend) all same time 7 P. Cassidy (Meath) at 1.57 8 P.de Frenne (Belgium) at 2.00 9 C.McCann (Tyrone Belleek) s.t.
**General Classification:** 1 K.Kimmage (Meath Avonmore) 31.36.27 2 G.Butler (G.B.) at 1.34 3 D.Lonergan (Ireland) at 1.04 4 P.McQuaid (Dublin Emmelle) at 4.03 5 J.Wolfkamp (Holland) at 4.45 6 P.Jonkers (Inter. Sel.) at 5.33 7 D.Hourigan (Ireland) at 6.08 8 I.Chivers (Ireland) at 6.45 9 M.Soula (Czech.) at 7.05 10 O.Murphy (Down O'Rourke's) at 7.37

## STAGE 9 (a) and (b)

Before Sunday morning's 10-miles time-trial there was some speculation as to whether time-trial specialist Butler might regain some or all of his 1.34 deficit on Kimmage but although he beat the Meath rider the distance was much too short for him and he only regained 5 seconds. Not only that but he lost his second place to Lonergan who moved to within 28 seconds of the jersey.
The stage, his third of the week, went to Declan Lonergan (Ireland) by 16 seconds from this teammate David Hourigan with the Czech Soula a further 5 seconds behind in third. Then came Butler, 31 seconds behind Lonergan with Kimmage in close attendance fifth.
Lonergan was now the biggest threat to Kimmage, especially with his sprinting ability in the afternoon's final stage, a one-hour criterium on a one-mile circuit in Dun Laoghaire which he duly won to make his score for the week four stages,

equalling the record of Gene Mangan (1958), Jiri Zelenka (1968), Yuri Lavrouchkin (1970), Alexander Gysiatnikov (1970), Batty Flynn (1971), and Shay O Hanlon who did it twice, 1962 and 1965.
Kimmage had the benefit of a strong Meath Avonmore team for that final hour's racing and they never gave Lonergan any leeway and he had to settle for the stage and a place on the podium as runner-up.
Kimmage was the third member of his family to achieve success in the RÁS. His father Christy won two stages in 1963 and his brother Paul won a stage in 1983.
**Stage 9a Navan 10 Mls. TT:** 1 D.Lonergan (Ireland) 20.49 2 D.Hourigan (Ireland) 21.05 3 M.Soula (Czech.) 21.10 4 G.Butler (Great Britain) 21.20 5 K.Kimmage (Meath Avonmore) 21.25 6 J.Wolfkamp (Holland) 21.25
**Stage 9b Dun Laoire Criterium:** 1 D.Lonergan (Ireland) 59.04 2 P.de Frenne (Belgium) 3 R.Terfaj (Czech.) 4 C.McCann (Tyrone Belleek) 5 J.Cosgrave (Dublin Eolas) 6 B.McLoughlin (Cork) all same time
**General Classification:** 1 K.Kimmage (Meath Avonmore) 33.06.56 2 D.Lonergan (Ireland) at 28 secs 3 G.Butler (G.B.) at 1.19 4 P.McQuaid (Dublin Emmelle) at 4.44 5 J.Wolfkamp (Holland) at 4.45 6 D.Hourigan (Ireland) at 5.48 7 P.Jonkers (International Selection) at 6.21 8 M.Soula (Czechoslovakia) at 8.05 9 P.Callaly (Dublin Les Jeunes) at 8.05 10 I.Chivers (Ireland) at 8.25 11 O.Murphy (Down O'Rourke's) at 8.29
**Points:** 1 D.Lonergan 91 2 K.Kimmage 73 3 C.McCann 57
**Mountains:** 1 M.Soula 32 2 J.Vasek 29 3 P.Jonkers 27
**Team:** 1 Ireland 99.29.03 2 Meath Avonmore 99.41.54 3 BCF 99.46.26

*1991 winner, Kevin Kimmage, Ireland*

## 1992

Italy, Germany, Belgium, Wales, the Isle of Man, Manchester, Lancaster and Southend joined 21 Irish county selection in the '92 RÁS which started on Saturday May 9, the earliest ever for the event.
There was controversy before the event when the riders most likely to be in the final selection for the Barcelona Olympics were selected to ride the British Milk Race when many though the home event should have first call on the top Irish riders.
The Italian team were top amateurs but unknown to most in Ireland. Only in later years would it be realised just how good they were as Wladimir Belli went on to lead the Festina team in the Tour De France while Giuseppi Guerini would win stages in the Giro d'Italia and Tour de France and lead the Deutche Telekom team in the French Tour in 1999 when he won the coveted l'Alp d'Huez stage of the Tour despite being knocked off his bike by a photographer in the final kilometre.

### STAGE 1

There was a tie on time after the opening stage, 100 miles from Dublin to Carrick-on Shannon between Robert Power (Ireland Golden Vale) and Guiseppe Guerini (Italy) even though neither of them had won the stage. The yellow jersey was presented to Robert Power who took the lead by virtue of a better stage placing.
Bobby Power (Tipperary) won the stage by two seconds from another Tipperary rider and past winner Stephen Spratt, riding for the Dublin Emmelle team with Robert Power and Guerini a further second behind, third and 4th respectively. However it was the hot-spot sprints en route which carried time bonuses from 5 seconds down to 1 which decided the destination of the jersey.
Robert Power started the action after Leixlip when he went clear with Finn O'Sullivan (Kerry) and their break got to almost a minute but their lead rapidly shrunk as the field approached the first sprint at Enfield where O'Sullivan beat Power, the pair earning 5 and 4 seconds bonus before being recaptured.
Seventeen riders went away with Geoff McNamara out sprinting Colm Bracken at Mullingar after 35 miles. The break's advantage had grown to a huge 4.50 at Longford with 25 miles to go where Guerini took maximum bonus at the prime from Bracken.
A group of twenty-eight went in pursuit but couldn't make any impression on the leaders who had over 5 minutes in hand at the finish, virtually ruling out anyone else in the chase for overall honours.
With five miles to go Robert Power attacked with Spratt and they were joined by Guerini and Bobby Power who then attacked but was countered by Spratt so leaving the four to contest the sprint. The rest of the original lead group split on the run-in and finished spread out over some 90 seconds.

**Stage 1 Dublin - Carrick-on-Shannon 100 Mls.** 1 B.Power (Tipperary) 3.26.59 2 S.Spratt (Dublin Emmelle) at 2 secs 3 R.Power (Ireland Golden Vale) at 3 seconds 4 G.Guerini (Italy) at 4 secs 5 P.Kennedy (Meath Avonmore) at 32 secs 6 D.Easton (Dublin Emmelle) 7 C.Bracken (Galway Nth. Telecom) 8 S.Kennedy (Dublin Mail Marketing) 9 A.Mooney (Isle of Man) 10 D.Klaar (Germany) all same time
**General Classification:** 1 R.Power (Ireland Golden Vale) 3.26.56 2 G.Guerini (Italy) s.t. 3 B.Power (Tipperary) at 2 secs 4 S.Spratt (Dublin Emmelle) at 5 secs 5 C.Bracken (Galway Nth Telecom) at 25 secs 6 P.Kennedy (Meath Avonmore) at 29 secs 7 D.Klaar (Germany) at 31 secs 8 A.Mooney (Isle of Man) at 33 secs 9 D.Easton (Dublin Emmelle) at 34 secs 10 S.Kennedy (Dublin Mail Marketing) s.t.

## STAGE 2

Continental riders had a clean sweep on the 99 miles second stage to Oughterard taking the top four places with Italian Gianmatteo Fagnini winning by 12 seconds, while Guerini took over the lead.
Yellow jersey Power seemed to be safe for another day when he was in the chasing group of 17 with only a few miles to go. However he was involved in a crash which was the signal for the Italians to attack.
Guerini and Wladimir Belli got away and joined up with their compatriot Fagnini who had been away with Belgian Philip de Baets since the two climbs after Cong. Their break had seemed doomed until the arrival of the other two Italians and the quartet stayed out in front.
Near the finish Fagnini attacked again to win by 12 seconds from De Baets. Belli was third with Guerini finishing fourth in the same time but 46 seconds ahead of Power, who came in with the chasers, led in by Colm Bracken (Galway Nth. Telecom), to take over the lead.
**Stage 2 Carrick-on-Shannon - Oughterard 99 Mls.** 1 G.Fagnini (Italy) 4.11.50 2 P.de Baets (Belgium) at 12 secs 3 W.Belli (Italy) 4 G.Guerini (Italy) all same time 5 C.Bracken (Galway Nth. Telecom) at 58 secs 6 G.De Vlaeminck (Belgium) s.t.
**General Classification:** 1 G.Guerini (Italy) 7.38.58 2 R.Power (Ireland Golden Vale) at 46 secs 3 C.Bracken (Galway Nth. Telecom) at 1.11 4 P.Daly (Kilkenny) at 2.12 5 P.Kennedy (Meath Avonmore) at 2.52 6 D.Easton (Dublin Emmelle) at 2.58

## STAGE 3

The 1986 RÁS winner Stephen Spratt from Dungarvan, riding for Dublin Emmelle, won the third stage, 86 miles to Ennistymon in a sprint from Belfast's Cormac McCann (Tyrone Flogas).
The two broke away from a 12-man break after Ballyvaughan, on the climb of the Corkscrew, with less than 20 miles to go.
Despite finishing 2.13 behind the winner in tenth place, Colm Bracken (Galway Nth. Telecom) took the yellow jersey by 22 seconds from Spratt.

Bracken was in the chasing group led in by Robert Power (Ireland) but he crashed. However as the incident occurred in the final kilometre he was given the same time as the rest of the group.

**Stage 3 Oughterard - Ennistymon 86 Mls.** 1 S.Spratt (Dublin Emmelle) 3.38.16 2 C.McCann (Tyrone Flogas) at 1 sec 3 R.Power (Ireland Golden Vale) at 2.07 4 P.Kennedy (Meath Avonmore) at 2.13 5 D.McQuaid (Dublin Emmelle) 6 P.Doyle (Kerry Lee Strand) 7 J.Meredith (Wales) 8 D.Hourigan (Ireland) 9 P.Cassidy (Meath Avonmore) 10 C.Bracken (Galway Nth. Telecom) all same time

**General Classification:** 1 C.Bracken (Galway Nth. Telecom) 11.20.38 2 S.Spratt (Dublin Emmelle) at 22 secs 3 G.Guerini (Italy) at 57 secs 4 P.Kennedy (Meath Avonmore) at 1.41 5 R.Power (Ireland) at 1.43 6 B.Power (Tipperary) at 2.26

**Team:** 1 Dublin Emmelle 34.14.23 2 Meath Avonmore 34.17.55 3 Tipperary 34.18.09

## STAGE 4

Stephen Spratt (Dublin Emmelle) moved into the lead by a 1.41 margin over Colm Bracken (Galway Nth. Telecom) after the 108 miles stage to Killorglin which was won by Declan Lonergan of the Ireland Golden Vale team.

A sizeable group built up a good lead but this came down rapidly over the final miles as the leaders splintered. Three past winners were in the break and finished in the top six. 1983 winner Phil Cassidy was second, 9 seconds behind Lonergan at the uphill finish in Killorglin.

'86 winner Spratt was next, 11 seconds back. Next came Philip de Baets (Belgium) at 1.20, six seconds in front of Ian Chivers, the winner two years previously who had been with the leaders put punctured with 10 miles to go.

John Cosgrove led in another three at 1.29 and this pattern continued with several more small groups sprinting in before the arrival of the bunch.

It was a good day for the Ireland team with three riders in the top eight while the Italians had no riders up with the leaders.

**Stage 4 Ennistymon - Killorglin 108 Mls.** 1 D.Lonergan (Ireland Golden Vale) 4.49.03 2 P.Cassidy (Meath Avonmore) at 9 secs 3 S.Spratt (Dublin Emmelle) at 11 secs 4 P.de Baets (Belgium) at 1.20 5 I.Chivers (Ireland) at 1.26 6 J.Cosgrove (Lancaster) at 1.29 7 B.Power (Tipperary) 8 D.Hourigan (Ireland) all same time 10 B.Monaghan (Dublin Bell Orwell) at 1.32

**General Classification:** 1 S.Spratt (Dublin Emmelle) 16.10.14 2 C.Bracken (Galway Nth. Telecom) at 1.41 3 G.Guerini (Italy) at 2.38 4 P.Kennedy (Meath Avonmore) at 2.51 5 B.Power (Tipperary) at 3.32 6 R.Power (Ireland) at 3.24 7 P.Daly (Kilkenny) at 4.19 8 D.Easton (Dublin Emmelle) at 5.36 9 S.Kennedy (Dublin Mail Marketing) at 5.36 10 G.McNamara (Tipperary) at 5.51 11 A.Mooney (Isle of Man) at 6.35 12 J.Barr (Tyrone Flogas) at 7.50

## STAGE 5

Rufin de Smet (Belgium) won the fifth stage, 93 miles from Killorglin to Skibereen, coming home 46 ahead of Joe Evans (Wales) who outsprinted Cormac McCann (Tyrone Flogas) at the head of an eight-man group.
There was no change at the head of the GC will all the top-placed riders safely in the main bunch over 2 minutes behind the winner.
The action started after 20 miles when Ian Chivers (Ireland Golden Vale) went away with Joe Evans (Wales) and Gary Scott (Tyrone Flogas). These three stayed out in front for most of the stage but in the final miles they were caught by a 6-man chasing group.
These six included De Smet who attacked with five miles to go opening up a good gap by the finish.
Chivers, who led over three of the four climbs during the stage, took over the lead in the mountains classification from race-leader Spratt.
**Stage 5 Killorglin - Skibereen 93 Mls.** 1 R.de Smet (Belgium) 4.11.21 2 J.Evans (Wales) at 46 secs 3 C.McCann (Tyrone Flogas) 4 I.Chivers (Ireland Golden Vale) 5 G.Scott (East Tyrone) 6 A.Roche (Isle of Man); 7 D.Goodwin (Manchester Irish Heritage) 8 S.Bracken (Dublin IRC) 9 N.Downey (Dublin Bell Orwell) 10 J.Meredith (Dublin Bluebell) all same time
**General Classification:** 1 S.Spratt (Dublin Emmelle) 20.24.38 2 C.Bracken (Galway Nth. Telecom) at 1.41 3 G.Guerini (Italy)) at 2.38 4 P.Kennedy (Meath Avonmore) at 2.51 5 B.Power (Tipperary) at 3.22 6 R.Power (Ireland) at 3.24 7 P.Daly (Kilkenny) at 4.19 8 D.Easton (Dublin Emmelle) at 5.36 9 S.Kennedy (Dublin Mail Marketing) s.t. 10 G.McNamara (Tipperary) at 5.51
**Points:** 1 S. Spratt
**Mountains:** 1 I.Chivers
**Team:** 1 Dublin Emmelle

## STAGE 6

Andy Roche (Isle of Man) won the sixth stage from Skibereen to Dungarvan out sprinting Richard Wooles of Wales and Ian Chivers (Ireland Golden Vale) at the end of a 100-mile breakaway.
Stephen Spratt (Dublin Emmelle) retained the yellow jersey.
**Stage 6 Skibereen - Dungarvan, 115 Mls.** 1 A.Roche (Isle of Man) 4.40.54 2 R.Wooles (Wales) 3 I.Chivers (Ireland Golden Vale) all same time
**General Classification:** 1 S.Spratt (Dublin Emmelle)

## STAGE 7

Philip de Baets (Belgium) won the 105 miles stage from Dungarvan to Gorey which saw Giuseppi Guerini cut the lead of Stephen Spratt by almost a minute coming into

Saturday's crucial mountain stage.
The Italians put on the pressure on the big climb of the day over Mount Leinster where 20 riders went away. However the gradient took its toll and the leading group was cut down to just nine.
Guerini was behind with Spratt in the bunch but attacked and rode across to his team-mates in the break. With the bunch chasing hard the lead steadied at around 30 seconds but Spratt had the misfortune to puncture near the finish losing another 30 seconds.
**Stage 7 Dungarvan - Gorey 105 Mls.** 1 P.de Baets (Belgium) 3.58.07 2 R.Wooles (Wales) 3 F.O'Sullivan (Kerry) 5 L.McKay (Dublin) 6 I.Chivers (Ireland Golden Vale) all same time
**General Classification:** 1 S.Spratt (Dublin Emmelle) 29.08.03 2 G.Guerini (Italy) at 1.39 3 B.Power (Tipperary) at 3.22 4 R.Power (Ireland) at 3.24 5 R.Wooles (Wales) at 4.20 6 S.Kennedy (Dublin) at 5.36 7 I.Chivers (Ireland) at 6.13

## STAGE 8

The penultimate stage from Gorey to Naas, 67 hard miles through the Wicklow mountains saw a superb show from the Italians with Wladimir Belli taking the stage from team-mate Giuseppi.Guerini who took over the yellow jersey at 8 seconds from Spratt who finished 10th, in a group led in by Belgium's Rufin de Smet in third place, 1.47 behind the two Italians.
The Belgians, who had worked for the Italians all week, kept it together until the start of the first climb, the first category Aughavannagh where Belli rode away with his team-mates Guerini and Pelidrini on his wheel. Race leader Spratt responded and joined the leading trio but on the steep slopes he couldn't hold them and dropped back along with Pelidrini.
Over the top the lead was 1 minute on a chasing group which included Spratt and Pelidrini, Robert Power (Ireland), Jason Meredrith (Dublin Bluebell), Stephen Maher (Tipperary), Andy Roche (Isle of Man), Rufin de Smet (Belgium), Patrick Goodwin (Manchester Irish Heritage) and Welsh pair Martin Jones and Richard Wooles.
Over the next climb at Drumgoff the lead had gone-up to 1.18 over the chasers who had lost Maher with a puncture. Over the Wicklow Gap it was still growing at 2.00 with the gap over the final KOM prime, Slieve Corragh 2.10.
On the flat run-in to the finish the chasers cut into the lead of the leading duo. Spratt needed to cut their advantage to 1.39 to stay in yellow and he almost made it as the group came home just 8 seconds too late.
**Stage 8 Gorey - Naas 67 Mls.** 1 W.Belli (Italy) 2.48.43 2 G.Guerini (Italy) s.t. 3 R.de Smet (Belgium) at 1.47 4 D.Pelidrini (Italy) 5 R.Wooles (Wales) 6 J.Meredith (Dublin Bluebell) 7 P.Goodwin (Manchester Irish Heritage) 8 A.Roche (Isle of Man) 9 M.Jones (Wales) 10 S.Spratt (Dublin Emmelle) all same time
**General Classification:** 1 G.Guerini (Italy) 31.58.25 2 S.Spratt (Dublin Emmelle) at 8 secs 3 R.Power (Ireland Golden Vale) at 3.32 4 R.Wooles (Wales) at 4.28 5

P.Goodwin (Manchester I.H.) at 7.07 6 D.Pelidrini (Italy) at 7.50 7 S.Kennedy (Dublin Mail Marketing) at 10.01 8 B.Power (Tipperary Carrick) at 10.08 9 I.Chivers (Ireland) at 10.38 10 S.Maher (Tipperary) at 11.27 11 A.Roche (Isle of Man) at 11.50 12 W.Belli (Italy) at 12.48
**Points:** 1 R.Wooles 53 2 P.de Baets 50 3 S.Spratt 48
**Mountains:** 1 W.Belli 57 2 D.Pelidrini 51 3 I.Chivers 51
**Team:** 1 Italy 96.09.45 2 Wales at 23.30 3 Ireland Golden Vale at 28.12

## STAGE 9

In one of the most controversial stages ever of the RÁS, Stephen Spratt (Dublin Emmelle) dramatically got away from race leader Giuseppi Guerini during the final stage, a 1 hour criterium in Dun Laoghaire to win by 22 seconds. Phil de Baets (Belgium) won the stage, his second of the week.
What made it controversial was the tactics of a big number of Irish riders who combined against the Italian team, who had made few friends during the week. It resulted in the unprecedented issuing of a communiqué from the race commissaires who condemned the dangerous and unsporting tactics of some Irish riders as they hampered Guerini and his team-mates as they tried to ride in pursuit of Spratt. Five Irish riders drew penalties of 30 seconds each for dangerous riding.

*1992 winner, Stephen Spratt*

With the Italian team exuding class, it had been generally expected that the final stage would be the usual last day promenade with no surprises. However when Spratt attacked after 20 minutes of the hour's racing he found plenty of riders in the break willing to ride their hearts out for him while back in the bunch the Italian team found the blocking tactics of the home riders made their chase very difficult. After the race the Italians protested but as Spratt was not involved in the tactics behind they had no chance of succeeding.

It was a pity the final stage left a bad taste as Spratt was a worthy winner and but for a puncture near the finish on Friday, he would have only lost 30 seconds instead of a minute and would not have lost the lead by a mere 8 seconds the following day.

**Stage 9 Dun Laoire Criterium:** 1 P.de Baets (Belgium) 1.00.13 2 R.Wooles (Wales) 3 C.McCann (Tyrone) 4 J.Dalby (Dublin) 5 R.de Smet (Belgium) 6 I.Chivers (Ireland) all same time

**General Classification:** 1 S.Spratt (Dublin Emmelle) 32.58.41 2 G.Guerini (Italy) at 22 secs 3 R.Power (Ireland) at 3.57 4 R.Wooles (Wales) at 4.21 5 P.Goodwin (Manchester Irish Heritage) at 7.32 6 D.Pelidrini (Italy) at 8.15 7 S.Kennedy (Dublin Mail Marketing) at 10.02 8 I.Chivers (Ireland Golden Vale) at 10.30

**Points:** 1 R.Wooles 62 2 P.de Baets 60 3 S.Spratt 48

**Mountains:** 1 W.Belli 57 2 D.Pelidrini 51 3 I.Chivers 51

**Team:** 1 Italy 2 Wales 3 Ireland

## 1993

Thirteen overseas teams were included in the field for the '93 RÁS including a first-time visit for a Japanese team, a reciprocal visit for the Irish team who took part in the Tour of Hokkaido.

There were also entries from Spain, Germany, Belgium, USA, Scotland, Wales, Isle of Man and several English regional teams.

These was a certain amount of controversy before the race that organiser Dermot Dignam had accepted an entry from the English professional team Neilson Tivoli Assos who included ex-world pursuit champion and Six-Day star Tony Doyle.

One of the pre-race favourites Mark Kane from Belfast had to withdraw from the Ireland team due to a chest infection and his place was taken by a young rider from Dublin, Eamon Byrne, who had shown good form when he took stage places of second and fifth in the French Ruban Granitier stage race.

## STAGE 1

The opening stage went to the visitors when Mark McKay, riding for the Liverpool Diamond Back) team won the sprint from the leading group at the end of the 80 miles run from Dublin to Cavan town.

With time bonuses available at three hot-spot sprint en-route this did not automatically give him the race lead but McKay had also shown his sprinting ability at the primes and had already picked up a near maximum 14 seconds before the final sprint.

it was the first of the hot-spots at Navan which was the catalyst which caused the formation of the winning break as 26 riders opened a gap.

In the chase behind there was another split with 21 riders leaving the main bunch to form a chasing group but they were 1.30 behind the leaders at the finish.

The only mountain prime of the day at Oldcastle went to David Hourigan (Ireland).

**Stage 1 Dublin - Cavan 80 Mls.** 1 M.McKay (Liverpool Diamond Back) 2.48.51 2 D.Hourigan (Ireland) 3 K.Riddle (Scotland) 4 D.Wilson (Scotland) 5 S.Colloby (Wales) 6 B.Graham (Antrim) 7 G.Butler (Lancaster) 8 B.Monaghan (Antrim) 9 I.Chivers (Dublin Bell) 10 C.Stracke (Germany Hamburg) all same time

**General Classification:** 1 M.McKay (Liverpool) 2.48.37 2 C.Stracke (Germany Hamburg) at 9 secs 3 P.Colby (USA) at 10 secs 4 K.Riddle (Scotland) at 11 secs 5 B.Monaghan (Antrim) at 12 secs 6.T.Timius (Germany Hamburg) s.t. 7 D.Hourigan (Ireland) at 13 secs 8 D.Wilson (Scotland) at 14 secs 9 S.Colloby (Wales) s.t. 10 B.Graham (Antrim) s.t.

**Points:** 1 M.McKay 15 2 D.Hourigan 14 3 K.Riddle 13

**Mountains:** 1 D.Hourigan 5 2 K.Riddle 4 3 I.Chivers 3

**Team:** 1 Germany Hamburg 8.26.33 2 Scotland at 1.06 3 Ireland at 1.50

## STAGE 2

The pros, who had missed the winning break on stage one, made their mark on Stage 2, 110 miles from Cavan to Dungloe in Donegal with John Tanner (Neilson Tivoli Assos) winning the stage while Neil Hoban was 4th and Tony Doyle 11th.However the race leader McKay was in close attendance finishing second, 1 second in arrears, to retain the yellow jersey.

For the first 50 miles there a series of attacks which all failed to build up a worthwhile lead but on the first climb of the day at Seraghy, before Castlederg, taken by David Hourigan (Ireland), a split appeared in the bunch and several small groups went off the front, eventually merging into a big 36-strong break.

A strong side wind and the tough open Donegal countryside continually splintered the bunch and at one time there were ten separate groups on the road. Splits were also taking place in the big group in front, Andrew Moss (Kerry Lee Strand) staying out in front on his own for ten miles.

On the KOH climb at Duchcharaigh McKay led over the top on his own but on the descent to Dungloe he was caught by Tanner who got away from him on the uphill sprint in Dungloe. Stephen Maher (Tipperary) led in the next group, 1.24 behind.

**Stage 2 Cavan - Dungloe 110 Mls.** 1 J.Tanner (Neilson Tivoli Assos) 4.15.04 2 M.McKay (Liverpool) at 1 sec 3 S.Maher (Tipperary) at 1.24 4 N.Hoban (Neilson) at 1.25 5 D.Hourigan (Ireland) 6 F.O'Sullivan (Kerry Lee Strand) 7 I.Chivers (Dublin Bell) 8 K.Hasikawa (Japan) 9 J.Hahn (Germany Hamburg) 10 P.Giles (Dublin Bell) all same time

**General Classification:** 1 M.McKay (Liverpool) 7.03.42 2 J.Tanner (Neilson) at 1.19 3 D.Hourigan (Ireland) at 1.37 4 I.Chivers (Dublin Bell) at 1.38 5 G.Butler (Lancaster) s.t. 6 B.Power (Tipperary) at 2.21 7 D.Wilson (Scotland) at 2.27 8 B.Monaghan (Antrim) s.t. 9 T.Timius (Germany Hamburg) at 2.28 10 F.O'Sullivan (Kerry) at 2.44

**Points:** 1 M.McKay 29 2 D.Hourigan 25 3 I.Chivers 16

**Mountains:** 1 D.Hourigan 13 2 M.McKay 10 3 M.Azkoita (Spain) 8

**Team:** 1 Germany Hamburg 21.19.20 2 Ireland at 2.04 3 Dublin Bell Helmets at 3.13

## STAGE 3

David Hourigan (Ireland) finished second on the 86.5 miles stage to Sligo in the same time as Neil Hoban (Neilson Tivoli Assos) but the Ireland rider did enough to take over the yellow jersey by 19 seconds from Hoban's teammate John Tanner.

These three were part of a 15-man break which went from the drop of the flag outside Dungloe. This caused a fierce reaction in the peleton and at Glenties, after 20 miles, there were four separate groups on the road in front of the bunch which was already 4 minutes behind the leaders.

There was no let-up throughout the stage and at the finish over half-an-hour separated the winner from the tail enders. Yellow jersey McKay finished with a group which came in six minutes behind and he dropped to 12th.
At the front Hoban attacked on the run-in to the finish taking with him Hourigan, Drew Wilson (Scotland), Stephen Maher (Tipperary) and Pat Callaly (Ireland) and in a close sprint the professional just got the verdict.
**Stage 3 Dungloe - Sligo 86.5 Mls.** 1 N.Hoban (Neilson Tivoli Assos) 3.16.34 2 D.Hourigan (Ireland) s.t. 3 D.Wilson (Scotland) at 1 sec 4 S.Maher (Tipperary) at 3 secs 5 P.Callaly (Ireland) at 5 secs 6 R.Riddle (Scotland) at 37 secs 7 A.Lawson (USA) s.t. 8 J.Tanner (Neilson) s.t. 9 C.McCann (Antrim) at 39 secs 10 P.Doyle (Kerry Lee Strand) s.t.
**General Classification:** 1 D.Hourigan (Ireland) 10.21.53 2 J.Tanner (Neilson) at 19 secs 3 I.Chivers (Bell Dublin) at 40 secs 4 D.Wilson (Scotland) at 51 secs 5 N.Hoban (Neilson) at 1.07 6 F.O'Sullivan (Kerry) at 1.46 7 S.Maher (Tipperary) at 3.01 8 P.Callaly (Ireland) s.t. 9 K.Riddle (Scotland) at 3.06 10 E.Byrne (Ireland) at 3.07
**Points:** 1 D.Hourigan 39 2 M.McKay 29 3 N.Hoban 27
**Mountains:** 1 D.Hourigan 13 2 M.McKay 10 3 M.Azkoita (Spain) 8
**Team:** 1 Ireland Black and Decker 31.11.50 2 Scotland at 2.02 3 Neilson Tivoli Assos at 5.56

## STAGE 4

Hourigan retained the lead after the 120 miles stage from Sligo to Nenagh which was won by Phillip Collins (Dublin IRC) but for a time it looked like local rider Stephen Maher (Tipperary) would take the jersey and indeed he was leader on the road until the final lap round the town.
The climb of the Curlew Mountains came shortly after the start and Mark McKay (Liverpool) led Hourigan over the top to come within two points of the lead in that competition.
After the descent a 16 man group went away at Boyle and with no big threats to the top men on overall present they were allowed to gradually increase their lead but after 50 miles Maher, who had started the day 3 minutes off the lead had taken the lead on the road. However the chase was not frantic as both Ireland and the Neilson pros. would probably have been happy to see some other team defending for a day of two.
However when the lead kept increasing until it was over 6 minutes alarm bells started ringing and they started to chase in earnest and the gap came down quickly.
Near the finish pursuit and time-trial specialist Collins managed to get a gap on the rest of the break and used his ability against the watch to hold off the chasers to the finish.
The break still had 3.15 in hand as they started the 6 kilometre finishing circuit but Maher, who had been working very hard, lost 23 seconds on Collins by the finish

coming in 5th and when the yellow jersey came home 2.35 later he had missed out on the lead by 26 seconds, ending up in fourth position.
Although Hourigan's lead was down to 12 seconds, the Irish team tactics meant they now had two riders at the top of the GC.
**Stage 4 Sligo - Nenagh 118.5 Mls.** 1 P.Collins (Dublin IRC) 4.41.25 2 T.Timius (Germany Hamburg) at 2 secs 3 E.Byrne (Ireland) at 3 secs 4 J.Hahn (Germany) at 6 secs 5 S.Maher (Tipperary) at 23 secs 6 M.Fitzgerald (Tipperary) at 1.19 7 T.Evans (Antrim) 8 S.Coloby (Wales) 9 J.Cosgrove (Lancaster) 10 P.Goodwin (Manchester) all same time
**General Classification:** 1 D.Hourigan (Ireland) 15.06.16 2 E.Byrne (Ireland) at 12 secs 3 J.Tanner (Neilson Tivoli Assos) at 19 secs 4 S.Maher (Tipperary) at 26 secs 5 I.Chivers (Dublin Bell) at 40 secs 6 D.Wilson (Scotland) at 51 secs 7 N.Hoban (Neilson) at 1.07 8 T.Timius (Germany) at 1.35 9 F.O'Sullivan (Kerry) at 1.46 10 J.Hahn (Germany) at 1.55
**Points:** 1 D.Hourigan 39 2 S Maher 35 3 M.McKay 29
**Mountains:** 1 D.Hourigan 17 2 M.McKay 15 3 M.Azkoita (Spain) 8
**Team:** Ireland Black & Decker 45.22.04 2 Scotland at 4.57 3 Germany Hamburg at 7.08

## STAGE 5

Andrew Lawson (USA) won the fifth stage, 89 miles from Nenagh to Listowel but Eamon Byrne of the Ireland Black & Decker team, who finished in 11th place, 10 seconds behind Lawson, took over the lead by 28 seconds from 1990 winner Ian Chivers (Dublin Bell) who finished just in front of Byrne in 10th place.
After the first KOM climb at Bollingbrooke, taken by Cormac McCann (Antrim Peugeot) from Germany's Tomas Timmius the race splintered with a big break of 32 riders going away and by Limerick they had a lead of over 1 minute.
At Foynes, 15 miles from the finish, Mark McKay attacked and split the lead group leaving 12 at the front. With 3 miles to go Lawson attacked and opened a gap and at the line he had 4 seconds to spare from Gethin Butler (Lancaster).
**Stage 5 Nenagh - Listowel 89 Mls.** 1 A.Lawson (USA) 3.09.41 2 G.Butler (Lancaster) at 4 secs 3 F.O'Sullivan (Kerry) at 7 secs 4 K.Hasikawa (Japan) 5 R.Riddle (Scotland) 6 M.McKay (Liverpool) 7 N.Hoban (Neilson Tivoli) 8 A.Yoshiyuki (Japan) 9 J.Hahn (Germany) all same time 10 E.Byrne (Ireland Black & Decker) at 10 secs
**General Classification:** 1 E.Byrne (Ireland Black & Decker) 18.16.19 2 I.Chivers (Dublin Bell) at 28 secs 3 N.Hoban (Neilson Tivoli) at 52 secs 4 D.Hourigan (Ireland) at 1.03 5 D.Wilson (Scotland) at 1.15 6 J.Tanner (Neilson Tivoli) at 1.22 7 S.Maher (Tipperary) at 1.29 8 F. O'Sullivan (Kerry) at 1.31 9 J.Hahn (Germany) at 1.40 10 T.Timius (Germany) at 2.38.
**Points:** 1 M.McKay 39 2 D.Hourigan 39 3 N.Hoban 36 4 S.Maher 36
**Mountains:** 1 D.Hourigan 18 2 M.McKay 17 3 T.Timius 10

**Teams:** 1 Ireland Black & Decker 54.53.28 2 Scotland at 4.54 3 Germany Hamburg at 7.05

## STAGE 6

There was no change on the general classification after stage 6, 94 miles from Listowel to Blarney which was won by Stephen Healy of the Wicklow team who won the sprint from his two breakaway companions Gary Thomas (Wales) and Ballymena's Andrew Moss, riding for the Kerry team.
There was little action until Millstreet where John Heraty (Galway) took the special Eurovision prime (the Eurovision Song Contest was taking place in Millstreet on Saturday evening).
Just outside the town Mark McKay (Liverpool) went away to take the KOM primes at Tullig Hill and Muchera Mountain, as the weather suddenly changed from a pleasant summer day into wintry fog and sleet, to take over the lead in the mountains classification from Ireland's Hourigan.
He dropped back on the descent where a group of seven went clear but they too were recaptured at Dripsey before Healy, Thomas and Moss made their successful break.
**Stage 6 Listowel - Blarney 94 Mls.** 1 S.Healy (Wicklow) 3.25.26 2 G.Thomas (Wales) at 2 secs 3 A.Moss (Kerry Lee Strand) s.t. 4 R.Riddle (Scotland) at 11 secs 5 K.Riddle (Scotland) at 12 secs 6 D.Hourigan (Ireland Black & Decker) 7 P.Doyle (Kerry Lee Strand) 8 B.Quinn (Galway Northern Telecom) 9 K.Hasikawa (Japan) 10 S.Maher (Tipperary (Carraig Hotel) all same time
**General Classification:** 1 E.Byrne (Ireland Black & Decker) 21.42.27 2 I.Chivers (Dublin Bell) at 28 secs 3 N.Hoban (Neilson Tivoli) at 52 secs 4 D.Hourigan (Ireland) at 1.03 5 J.Tanner (Neilson Tivoli) at 1.22 6 S.Maher (Tipperary) at 1.29 7 J.Hahn (Germany) at 1.40 8 G.Butler (Lancaster) at 3.23 9 P.Callaly (Ireland Black & Decker) at 3.25 10 D.Wilson (Scotland) at 4.03
**Points:** 1 D.Hourigan 49 2 S.Maher 42 3 M.McKay 39
**Mountains:** 1 M.McKay 47 2 P.Collins 20 3 K.Kimmage 20
**Teams:** 1 Ireland Black & Decker 65.11.52 2 Scotland at 4.53 3 Neilson Tivoli Assos at 9.27

## STAGE 7

There was a success for the Neilson Tivoli professional team when past world professional pursuit champion Tony Doyle came home on his own to win the 106 miles from Middleton to Enniscorthy run off in torrential rain for much of the stage.
In second place, 48 seconds behind, came Doyle's teammate John Tanner who led the bunch up the steep hill to the finish but with all the main contenders present there was no change in the overall classification with Eamon Byrne beginning to look like holding on for the two remaining days.

The field stayed together for the first 68 miles until the first cat. climb at Mountain Grove. A group of 35 went away on the descent and it was from this big break that Doyle attacked with 21 miles to go in the company of Gethin Butler (Lancaster).
When their lead had grown to 1 minute Doyle attacked again and using his well-known skill as a solo rider time-trialled to the finish.
**Stage 7 Middleton - Enniscorthy 106** 1 T.Doyle (Neilson Tivoli) 4.17.28 2 J.Tanner (Neilson Tivoli) at 49 secs 3 A.Roche (Isle of Man) 4 B.Quinn (Galway) 5 R.Clark (Tipperary Westgate) 6 F.O'Sullivan (Kerry Lee Strand) 7 A.Yoshiyuki (Japan) 8 D.Hourigan (Ireland) 9 D.McQuaid (Dublin Emmelle) 10 J.Hahn (Germany) all same time
**General Classification:** 1 E.Byrne (Ireland Black & Decker) 26.00.44 2 I.Chivers (Dublin Bell) at 28 secs 3 N.Hoban (Neilson Tivoli) at 52 secs 4 D.Hourigan (Ireland) at 1.03 5 J.Tanner (Neilson Tivoli) at 1.22 6 S.Maher (Tipperary) at 1.29 7 J.Hahn (Germany) at 1.40 8 G.Butler (Lancaster) at 3.23 9 P.Callaly (Ireland) at 3.25 10 K.Riddle (Scotland) at 4.09
**Points:** 1 D.Hourigan 57 2 S.Maher 42 3 M.McKay 39
**Mountains:** 1 M.McKay 52 2 K.Kimmage 35 3 P.Collins 33
**Team:** 1 Ireland Black & Decker 78.06.43 2 Scotland at 4.53 3 Neilson Tivoli Assos at 8.38

## STAGE 8

The penultimate stage was through the Wicklow Mountains to Blessington and Byrne survived in yellow even increasing his lead to 54 seconds over Neil Hoban (Neilson Tivoli) as Chivers dropped back to third at 1.17.
After the prime at Gorey, won by Paul Ennis (Mayo) eleven riders got away before the first KOM prime at the Devil's Glen where Christy Kimmage (Dublin) was first over.
Kimmage also took the next two primes at Luggala and Sally Gap but mountains leader Mark McKay was also picking up points for the minor placings and when he won the final prime of the day at Ballyward he tied up the mountains classification.
Kimmage and Abe Yoskiyuki dropped the others on the first climb but they were caught on the final climb after which there was a general regroupment.
On the run-in to the finish seven riders went clear to gain nearly a minute on the bunch. Kevin Kimmage (Meath) won by 1 second from Gethin Butler (Lancaster) with Ken Hasikawa (Japan) at 5 seconds. However Byrne in 5th place was looking every more secure.
**Stage 8 Enniscorthy - Blessington 90 Mls.** 1 K.Kimmage (Meath Avonmore) 3.36.32 2 G.Butler (Lancaster) at 1 sec 3 K.Hasikawa (Japan) at 5 secs 4 B.Quinn (Galway) 5 E.Byrne (Ireland Black & Decker) 6 P.Colby (USA) all same time 7 N.Hoban (Neilson Tivoli) at 7 secs 8 R.Riddle (Scotland) at 21 secs 9 F.O'Sullivan (Kerry Lee Strand) at 54 secs 10 A.Lawson (USA) s.t.

**General Classification:** 1 E.Byrne (Ireland Black & Decker) 29.37.21 2 N.Hoban (Neilson Tivoli) at 54 secs 3 I.Chivers (Dublin Bell) at 1.17 4 D.Hourigan (Ireland) at 1.52 5 J.Tanner (Neilson Tivoli) at 2.11 6 S.Maher (Tipperary) at 2.18 7 J.Hahn (Germany Hamburg) at 2.29 8 G.Butler (Lancaster) at 3.19 9 P.Callaly (Ireland) at 4.14 10 F.O'Sullivan (Kerry Lee Strand) at 5.08
**Points:** 1 D.Hourigan 57 2 N.Hoban 46 3 F.O'Sullivan 45
**Mountains:** 1 M.McKay 74 2 A.Yoshiyuki 48 3 C.Kimmage 40
**Team:** 1 Ireland Black & Decker 88.58.12 2 Neilson Tivoli Assos at 8.40 3 Scotland at 10.49

## STAGES 9 (a) and (b)

Phil Collins (Dublin IRC) collected a notable scalp when he beat favourite Tony Doyle (Neilson Tivoli) by 5 seconds to win Sunday morning's 10 miles time-trial at Blessington.
Hourigan and Tanner took the next two places but Byrne rose to the occasion finishing 5th, 33 seconds behind Collins but increasing his lead over second placed Hoban by another 5 seconds. Biggest loser was Ian Chivers who dropped to 6th.
The race finished off with 20 laps of a one-mile circuit in Dun Laoghaire which included five hot-spot sprints each carrying time bonuses. If Hoban could pick up some time he could still slip away to steal the race from the Dubliner.
He started off well winning the first sprint. However Byrne was obviously not going to give him any leeway and took second place, limiting his loss to 1 second.
John Nolan (Meath) took the next with Byrne again second while Hoban only managed third. The professional won the next but he needed time which was fast running out and he couldn't get away from the bunch.
Then Andy Lawson (USA) went away on his own and although he looked like being caught on the final lap he held on to take his second stage of the race and with Byrne and Hoban both finishing in the bunch the 19-year old Dubliner had triumphed.
**Stage 9a Blessington 10 Mls. TT:** 1 P.Collins (Dublin) 20.53 2 T.Doyle (Neilson Tivoli) 20.58 3 D.Hourigan (Ireland) 21.14 4 J.Tanner (Neilson Tivoli) 21.20 5 E.Byrne (Ireland) 21.26 6 R.Riddle (Scotland) 21.27 7 N.Hoban (Neilson Tivoli) 21.31 8 A.Roche (Isle of Man) 21.36 9 E.McMahon (Kerry Lee Strand) 21.42 10 S.Maher (Tipperary) 21.46
**General Classification:** 1 E.Byrne (Ireland Black & Decker) 29.58.47 2 N.Hoban (Neilson Tivoli) at 59 secs 3 D.Hourigan (Ireland) at 1.40 4 J.Tanner (Neilson Tivoli) at 2.05 5 S.Maher (Tipperary) at 2.38 6 I.Chivers (Dublin Bell) at 3.04 7 J.Hahn (Germany Hamburg) at 3.43 8 G.Butler (Lancaster) at 3.55 9 P.Callaly (Ireland) at 4.44 10 F.O'Sullivan (Kerry Lee Strand) at 6.44
**Points:** 1 D.Hourigan 70 2 N.Hoban 55 3 J.Tanner 54
**Mountains:** 1 M.McKay 74 2 A.Yoshiyuki 48 3 C.Kimmage 40
**Team:** 1 Ireland Black & Decker 90.02.48 2 Neilson Tivoli Assos at 7.53 3 Scotland at 14.43

**Stage 9b Dun Laoghaire Criterium:** 1 A.Lawson (USA) 42.37 2 J.Tanner (Neilson Tivoli) at 1 sec 3 R.Riddle (Scotland) 4 M.Maguire (Dublin IRC) 5 J.Cosgrove (Lancaster) 6 C.McCann (Antrim Peugeot) 7 N.Hoban (Neilson Tivoli) 8 R.Clarke (Tipperary) 9 P.Giles (Dublin Bell) 10 K.Kimmage (Meath) all same time
**General Classification:** 1 E.Byrne (Ireland Black & Decker) 30.41.20 2 N.Hoban (Neilson Tivoli) at 55 secs 3 D.Hourigan (Ireland) at 1.55 4 J.Tanner (Neilson Tivoli) at 2.09 5 S.Maher (Tipperary) at 2.43 6 I.Chivers (Dublin Bell) at 3.09 7 J.Hahn (Germany) at 3.48 8 G.Butler (Lancaster) at 4.00 9 P.Calally (Ireland) at 4.48 10 F.O'Sullivan (Kerry Lee Strand) at 6.49
**Points:** 1 D.Hourigan (Ireland) 75 2 J.Tanner (Neilson) 60 3 N.Hoban (Neilson) 64
**Mountains:** 1 M.McKay (Liverpool) 56 2 A.Yoshiyuki (Japan) 48 3 C.Kimmage (Dublin) 43.
**Team:** 1 Ireland Black & Decker 91.10.42 2 Neilson Tivoli Assos 92.19.50 3 Scotland 92.24.25
**County Team:** 1 Kerry Lee Strand 92.41.13

*Eamon Byrne, Ireland Winner 1993*

## 1994

There was a record entry of 167 for the 1994 RÁS and after the usual pre-race withdrawals, 147 started the prologue time-trial.
The sixteen overseas teams included Great Britain, USA, Germany (2), Belgium, Holland, Scotland, and the trend of increasing entries of cross-Channel teams was maintained.

### STAGE 1 (a) and (b)

The race opened with a 3.1 miles prologue TT in Phoenix Park which was won by Rob Harris of the Great Britain team. He had a margin of 17 seconds over Declan Lonergan (Ireland Lee Strand).
George Espinoza (USA) was third in front of another two of the Irish team, Philip Collins and Robert Power. Another American, Colby Pearce was 6th, Stephan Schruff (Germany Koln Bayer) 7th, Tommy Evans (Antrim) 8th, Alex Weil (USA) 9th and Mark Kane (Antrim) 10th.
The afternoon stage was a fast 100 kms. to Drogheda which included an 8 kms finishing circuit and it was won by David Hourigan who outsprinted Belfast rider Paul Slane, riding for Meath East.
A medical control after the stage of which the result was not known until the week after the race showed that Hourigan's sample contained methyl testosterone and he was banned for three months. He was the first rider tested positive in Ireland. Slane was retrospectively awarded the stage.
The pace from Dublin was flat out and it was only approaching the finishing circuit at Drogheda that 13 riders got away. Over the finishing circuit they increased their lead and at the finish they were 39 seconds ahead of lone chaser Matthew Stephens (Great Britain) with a further 11-man group led in by Paul Kennedy at 1.05 11 seconds ahead of the main bunch.
Of the leading group Tommy Evans (Antrim) had the best time from the morning's prologue and he took the yellow jersey by 10 seconds from Hourigan with GB pair Steve Farrell and Matthew Stephens 4th and 5th also on 10 seconds.
**Stage 1(a) Dublin Prologue 3.1 Mls. TT:** 1 R.Harris (Great Britain) 6.21.50 2 D.Lonergan (Ireland Lee Strand) 6.38.14 3 G.Espinoza (USA) 6.38.83 4 P.Collins (Ireland Lee Strand) 6.41.43 5 Rob.Power (Ireland Lee Strand) 6.42.11 6 C.Pearce (USA) 6.42.29 7 S.Schruff (Germany Koln Bayer) 6.43.91 8 T.Evans (Antrim) 6.44.78 9 A.Weil (USA) 6.45.88 10 M.Kane (Antrim) 6.46.27
**Points:** 1 R.Harris 15 2 D.Lonergan 14 3 G.Espinoza 13
**Team:** 1 Ireland Lee Strand 20.01 2 USA at 4 secs 3 Great Britain at 8 secs
**Stage 1(b) Dublin - Drogheda 62 Mls.** 1 D.Hourigan (Cork Buckleys Solicitors) 2.15.29 2 P.Slane (Meath East) (Slane later credited with the stage win after

Hourigan's disqualification) 3 E.Vereecken (Holland Giant) 4 S.Farrell (G.B.) 5 R.McCauley (Wicklow Coors) 6 T.Evans (Antrim Giant) 7 S.Bracken (Dublin IRC) 8 D.Stam (Holland Giant) 9 I.Chivers (Antrim Giant) 10 I.Gilkes (Manchester Irish Heritage) all same time

**General Classification:** 1 T.Evans (Antrim Giant) 2.22.13 2 D.Hourigan (Cork) at 10 secs 3 S.Farrell (GB) s.t. 4 M.Stephens (GB) s.t. 5 D.Stam (Holland Giant) at 21 secs 6 G.Butler (Lancaster) at 22 secs 7 I.Chivers (Antrim Giant) at 25 secs 8 D.McQuaid (Dublin Diamond Back) s.t. 9 P.Slane (Meath East) at 26 secs 10 I.Gilkes (Manchester Irish Heritage) at 27 secs

**Points:** 1 D.Hourigan 20 2 T.Evans 18 3 S.Farrell 16

**Mountains:** S.Maher 5 2 R.McCauley 4 3 D.McQuaid 3

**Team:** 1 Great Britain 7.07.52 2 Antrim Giant at 27 secs 3 Cork Buckley at 1.02

## STAGE 2

Robert Power (Ireland Lee Strand) won the second stage, 102 miles from Drogheda to Boyle but Evans held on to the jersey by his 10 second margin over Hourigan, Farrell and Matthews.

Evans had to fight to keep the jersey as at one time Power was leader on the road when a 4-man break which included him was over-4 minutes ahead.

Also there were Stephen Maher (Tipperary), Ben Wilson (Stretford Baywest) and Rob Lyne (Bristol). Four minutes was their maximum lead but this caused a reaction in the bunch and the lead dropped dramatically over the final 25 miles.

When it was down to 40 seconds Power decided he could do better on his own and attacked, leaving the other three to be swallowed up by the bunch. He gamely hung on over the final miles to win by 24 seconds which, with the gaps still so small, was only good enough to move him to 14th overall, although he took the green points jersey, equal with Lonergan on 26. Stephan Schruff (Germany Koln Bayer) led in the mass bunch sprint.

**Stage 2 Drogheda - Boyle 102 Mls.** 1 Rob.Power (Ireland Lee Strand) 3.47.23 2 S.Schruff (Germany Koln Bayer) at 24 secs 3 E.Becker (Germany Hamburg) 4 D.Lonergan (Ireland Lee Strand) 5 E.Verecken (Holland Giant) 6 W.Oschwald (Germany Koln Bayer) 7 P.Slane (Meath East) 8 S.Calland (Stretford Baywest) 9 P.Butler (Tipperary Carraig Hotel) 10 D.Stam (Holland Giant) all same time

**General Classification:** 1 T.Evans (Antrim Giant Cycles) 6.10.00 2 D.Hourigan (Cork Buckleys Solicitors) at 10 secs 3 S.Farrell (Great Britain) s.t. 4 M.Stephens (Great Britain) s.t. 5 D.Stam (Holland) at 21 secs 6 G.Butler (Lancaster) at 22 secs 7 I.Chivers (Antrim Giant) at 25 secs 8 D.McQuaid (Dublin Diamond Back) s.t. 9 P.Slane (Meath East) at 26 secs 10 I.Gilkes (Manchester Irish Heritage) at 27 secs

**Points:** 1 Rob.Power 26 2 D.Lonergan 26 3 E.Verecken 24

**Mountains:** 1 S.Maher 5 2 R.McCauley 4 3 D.McQuaid 3

**Team:** 1 Great Britain 18.31.13 2 Antrim Giant at 27 secs 3 Cork Buckleys at 1.02

## STAGE 3

Eric Becker (Germany Hamburg) won Monday's 111 miles run from Boyle to Westport but it was Danny Stam (Holland Giant Cycles) who took over the jersey, Evans, despite fighting back to save it once on the stage, dropping back to 9th.
He led a chase which saw his group catch a 30-strong breakaway which went away at half distance, staying away for 25 miles. Earlier Stephen Calland (Stretford Baywest) had taken the only mountain prime of the day to go equal with Maher at the head of this classification.
After the Evans group joined the leaders at the 90 miles mark another 15 went clear and soon had a minute in hand. This 15 split with five miles to go, leaving six at the front: Becker and Stam were there along with George Espinoza (USA), B. Wilson (Stretford Baywest), M. Rogers (Bristol Mobile Windscreen) and Lee Davis (G.B.).
Stam rode flat out to get the jersey and sat up in the sprint losing 3 seconds. Espinoza, who was third on the stage moved to second overall, 46 seconds behind the Dutchman with Lancaster's Gethin Butler a further 4 seconds back.
A notable casualty of the stage was one of the pre-race favourites, Rob Harris, the British champion who abandoned with tendonitis.
**Stage 3 Boyle - Westport 111 Mls.** 1 E.Becker (Germany Hamburg) 3.51.25 2 B.Wilson (Stretford Baywest) s.t. 3 G.Espinoza (USA) s.t. 4 M.Rogers (Bristol Mobile Windscreen) s.t. 5 L.Davis (Great Britain) s.t. 6 D.Stam (Holland Giant) at 3 secs 7 D.Lonergan (Ireland Lee Strand) at 25 secs 8 K.Riddle (Scotland) at 27 secs 9 D.Easton (Dublin Diamond Back) at 30 secs 10 B.Quinn (Tipperary Carraig Hotel) at 47 secs
**General Classification:** 1 D.Stam (Holland Giant) 10.01.49 2 G.Espinoza (USA) at 46 secs 3 G.Butler (Lancaster) at 50 secs 4 I.Gilkes (Manchester Irish Heritage) s.t. 5 I.Chivers (Antrim Giant) at 53 secs 6 B.Wilson (Stretford Baywest) at 1.10 7 D.Lonergan (Ireland) at 1.11 8 E.Becker (Germany Hamburg) at 1.12 9 T.Evans (Antrim Giant) at 1.13 10 L.Davis (G.B.) at 1.17
**Points:** 1 D.Lonergan 35 2 E.Becker 28 3 Rob.Power 26
**Mountains:** 1 S.Maher 5 2 S.Calland 5 3 G.Espinoza 4 R.McCauley 4
**Team:** 1 Holland Giant 30.09.33 2 Antrim Giant at 28 secs 3 Ireland Lee Strand at 49 secs

## STAGE 4

Tuesday's 92 miles stage from Westport to Ennis was a good one for the Dutch, winning the stage with Arthur Farenhour while Danny Stam kept his overall lead.
The Amsterdam rider had to fight off a strong challenge by the Ireland and Antrim teams and at one point '98 winner Ian Chivers (Antrim) was leader on the road and at the end of the day he had moved to second, just 15 seconds in arrears while Ireland's Declan Lonergan lay third at 33 seconds.

Nineteen riders went away after 10 miles and when the gap went to 1 minute Chivers was leader on the road. The jersey saw the danger and went in pursuit with a group which eventually caught the leaders.
Several other groups made it to the front group which swelled to over 40 riders as the much reduced bunch slipped further back to come in over 4 minutes down at the finish.
Nine riders went away from the lead group with Chivers again in attendance but the finish came too soon for the Antrim rider to take the lead. Farenhout, riding shotgun on the break for the jersey had an armchair rider and easily won the sprint from Lonergan with Conor Henry (Ireland Lee Strand) third. The stage was run off at a high average speed of 28.5 mph.
**Stage 4 Westport - Ennis 92 Mls.** 1 A.Farenhout (Holland Giant) 3.13.11 2 D.Lonergan (Ireland Lee Strand) s.t 3 C.Henry (Ireland) Lee Strand) s.t. 4 R.Riddle (Scotland) s.t. 5 D.McQuaid (Dublin Diamond Back) s.t. 6 C.Pearce (USA) s.t. 7 N.Martin (Manchester Irish Heritage) s.t. 8 I.Chivers (Antrim Giant) s.t. 9 L.Davis (G.B.) at 5 secs 10 S.Schruff (Germany Koln) at 38 secs
**General Classification:** 1 D.Stam (Holland Giant) 13.15.38 2 I.Chivers (Antrim Giant) at 15 secs 3 D.Lonergan (Ireland Lee Strand) at 33 secs 4 L.Davis (G.B.) at 44 secs 5 G.Espinoza (USA) at 46 secs 6 G.Butler (Lancaster) at 50 secs 7 I.Gilkes (Manchester) s.t. 8 D.McQuaid (Dublin Diamond Back) at 1.00 9 B.Wilson (Stretford Baywest) at 1.10 10 E.Becker (Germany Hamburg) at 1.12 11 C.Henry (Ireland Lee Strand)
**Points:** 1 D.Lonergan 49 2 S.Schruff 29 3 E.Becker 28
**Mountains:** 1 S.Maher 5 2 S.Calland 5 3 G.Espinoza 4 R.McCauley 4
**Team:** 1 Holland Giant 39.50.22 2 Ireland Lee Strand at 11 secs 3 Dublin Diamond Back at 52 secs

## STAGE 5

Richie McCauley (Wicklow) put his climbing skills to maximum use when he won a tough 83 miles stage to Castleisland. McCauley came home a second clear of Stephen Maher (Tipperary) and Matt Stephens (Great Britain).
However Stam survived the climbs to retain his yellow jersey and now leads George Espinoza (USA) by 17 seconds with Lee Davis (Great Britain at 22.
The sting was in the tail of the stage for when the race arrived in Castleisland they had to complete three laps of a finishing circuit which included the 1st category climb to Crag Cave.
This climb split the field to pieces and there were lots of changes on GC. Chivers, Lonergan and Gilkes dropping back while Espinoza, Davis, Gethin Butler (Lancaster) and Steve Farrell (Great Britain) improving their positions, all moving to within 30 seconds of the leader.
**Stage 5 Ennis - Castleisland 83 Mls.** 1 R.McCauley (Wicklow Coors) 3.05.09 2 S.Maher (Tipperary) at 1 sec 3 M.Stephens (Great Britain) s.t. 4 R.Riddle (Scotland)

at 7 secs 5 S.Farrell (G.B.) at 10 secs 6 E.McMahon (Dublin Diamond Back) at 11 secs 7 P.McQuaid (Dublin Diamond Back) at 12 secs 8 P.Collins (Ireland Lee Strand) s.t. 9 G.Espinoza (USA) at 34 secs 10 P.Giles (Dublin Cycleways) at 40 secs
**General Classification:** 1 D.Stam (Holland Giant) 16.21.50 2 G.Espinoza (USA) at 17 secs 3 L.Davis (Great Britain) at 22 secs 4 G.Butler (Lancaster) at 28 secs 5 S.Farrell (G.B.) at 30 secs 6. D.Lonergan (Ireland Lee Strand) at 33 secs 7 E.McMahon (Dublin Diamond Back) at 35 secs 8 I.Chivers (Antrim Giant) at 39 secs 9 R.Riddle (Scotland) at 41 secs 10 S.Maher (Tipperary) at 44 secs
**Points:** 1 D.Lonergan 49 2 G.Espinoza 33 3 E.Becker 29 4 S.Schruff 29
**Mountains:** 1R.McCauley 39 2 S.Maher 28 3 S.Farrell 18
**Team:** 1 Dublin Diamond Back 49.08.07 2 Ireland Lee Strand at 11 secs 3 Manchester Irish Heritage at 2.14

## STAGE 6

With the top ten all within 44 seconds it was an almost impossible task for Stam to continue a successful defence of the jersey and he finally succumbed on the sixth stage, 81 miles from Castleisland to Cahirciveen, dropping to 4th, 37 seconds behind the new leader Lee Davis (Great Britain).
The stage was won by Erik Becker (Germany Hamburg) but Davis finished 7th in the sprint from the leading 13 man break which came home 56 second ahead of the next group which contained the race leader.
The route, through some of the highest peaks in the Kerry Mountains wrought havoc on the peleton and the day saw some 25 retirals.
Twelve riders went away at Farranfore after 6 miles but they were recaptured just before the 1st category climb of Ballaghasheen where Richie McCauley led over the top to increase his King of the Mountains lead...
The bunch split into three groups on the climb but passing through Cahirciveen for the first time most of them had regrouped.
The next climb was at Raheen Cross where Leslie McKay (Dublin Fingal) and Phil Collins (Ireland Lee Strand) were first over followed 20 seconds later by McCauley and Matt Stephens (G.B.) while Conor Henry (Ireland Lee Strand) led over a nine-man group 15 seconds later.
These three groups merged on the descent and stayed together to the finish where they had opened a gap of 56 seconds over the next group which included the race leader.
**Stage 6 Castleisland - Cahirciveen 81 Mls.** 1 E.Becker (Germany Hamburg) 3.10.11 2 D.Lonergan (Ireland Lee Strand) s.t. 3 S.Farrell (G.B.) s.t. 4 R.McCauley (Wicklow Coors) s.t. 5 L.McKay (Dublin Fingal) s.t. 6 C.Henry (Ireland Lee Strand) s.t. 7 L.Davis (Great Britain) s.t. 8 M.Stephens (Great Britain) s.t. 9 D.McQuaid (Dublin Diamond Back) at 3 secs 10 A.Moss (Cork Buckleys) s.t.
**General Classification:** 1 L.Davis (Great Britain) 19.32.23 2 S.Farrell (Great Britain) at 8 secs 3 D.Lonergan (Ireland Lee Strand) at 11 secs 4 D.Stam (Holland

Giant) at 37 secs 5 R.McCauley (Wicklow Coors) s.t. 6 D.McQuaid (Dublin Diamond Back) at 41 secs 7 E.Becker (Germany Hamburg) at 50 secs 8 C.Henry (Ireland Lee Strand) at 54 secs 9 I.Chivers (Antrim Giant) at 1.16 10 P.Collins (Ireland Lee Strand) s.t.

**Points:** 1 D.Lonergan 63 2 E.Becker 44 3 S.Farrell 40

**Mountains:** 1 R.McCauley 67 2 S.Maher 28 3 L.McKay 24

**Team:** 1 Ireland Lee Strand 58.38.54 2 Dublin Diamond Back at 51 secs 3 Great Britain at 5.24

## STAGE 7

Ballymena's Andrew Moss, Guesting for the Cork Buckley's team, made it a home victory for the fans coming into Macroom 3 seconds clear of Paddy Callaly (Meath Avonmore).

There was a change on general classification Steve Farrell taking over the jersey from his Great Britain teammate Davis who came in with a chasing bunch 21 seconds behind the winner.

The gaps at the front of the race continued to close up, Farrell leading by only 3 seconds from Lonergan with Davis at 7 seconds. 57 seconds still covered the top eight on GC.

The Ireland team spent the day on the attack with Henry and Robert Power in the first move which saw eight riders a minute ahead by the first climb at the Coomakista Pass where Bart Peelman led over from Gary Scott (Cork Buckleys).

However on the descent the field regrouped into a strong headwind. Holland's Arthur Farenhout attacked on the second KOM climb at Inchee and stayed away on his own for over 10 miles.

When he was caught nine riders were clear including Ireland's Henry and Lonergan with GB's Farrell along in the interests of the jersey. Moss left this group with three kilometres to go just holding on to the finish.

**Stage 7 Cahirciveen - Macroom 89 Mls.** 1 A.Moss (Cork Buckley Solicitors) 3.43.00 2 P.Callaly (Meath Avonmore) at 3 secs 3 S.Calland (Stretford Baywest) at 6 secs 4 P.Slane (Meath East) s.t. 5 G.Scott (Cork Buckleys) s.t. 6 J.Blackwell (Kerry) s.t. 7 D.Lonergan (Ireland Lee Strand) s.t. 8 S.Farrell (G.B.) s.t. 9 C.Henry (Ireland) s.t. 10 E.Becker (Germany Hamburg) at 21 secs

**General Classification:** 1 S.Farrell (Great Britain) 23.15.37 2 D.Lonergan (Ireland Lee Strand) at 3 secs 3 L.Davis (Great Britain) at 7 secs 4 D.Stam (Holland Giant) at 44 secs 5 R.McCauley (Wicklow Coors) s.t. 6 C.Henry (Ireland Lee Strand) at 46 secs 7 D.McQuaid (Dublin Diamond Back) at 48 secs 8 E.Becker (Germany Hamburg) at 57 secs 9 I.Chivers (Antrim) at 1.23 10 P.Collins (Ireland Lee Strand) s.t.

**Points:** 1 D.Lonergan 72 2 E.Becker 50 3 S.Farrell 48

**Mountains:** 1 R.McCauley 67 2 S.Farrell 32 3 L.McKay 24

**Team:** 1 Ireland Lee Strand 69.48.27 2 Dublin Diamond Back at 1.21 3 Great Britain at 5.39

## STAGE 8

After stage 8 the 42nd RÁS made history with the closest ever situation at the top of the General Classification going into the final stage with the top two riders tied on time.
Declan Lonergan took over the yellow jersey from Farrell by virtue of his higher points placing but the two were equal after Lonergan finished 3 seconds ahead of Farrell after an incredible final 25 miles of racing in which two other riders briefly held the lead on the road.
Coming into Carrick-on-Suir for the first time with a 25 miles loop to be completed, a break was away which included ex-leader Danny Stam (Holland Giant) and 1990 winner Ian Chivers.
At this point Stam was leader on the road but he cracked and dropped back leading Chivers as the new leader. Behind Great Britain and Ireland were playing poker, each hoping to make the other team do the chasing.
The British finally launched an all out chase which saw most of the break caught over the final miles. However Lonergan launched an attack in the final mile, finishing 8th, 42 seconds behind American winner George Espinoza. More importantly he took three seconds out of Farrell leaving the pair tied on time.
**Stage 8 Macroom - Carrick-on-Suir 114 Mls.** 1 G.Espinoza (USA) 4.33.20 2 R.Riddell (Scotland) s.t. 3 S.McDonald (Dublin) at 39 secs 4 I.Gilkes (Manchester) s.t. 5 B.Peelman (Belgium) s.t. 6 P.Callaly (Meath Avonmore) at 42 secs 7 E.Becker (Germany Hamburg) s.t. 8 D.Lonergan (Ireland Lee Strand) s.t. 9 P.Giles (Dublin) at 45 secs 10 R.McCauley (Wicklow Coors) s.t.
**General Classification:** 1 D.Lonergan (Ireland Lee Strand) 27.49.42 2 S.Farrell (Great Britain) s.t. 3 L.Davis (Great Britain) at 7 secs 4 R.Riddell (Scotland) at 40 secs 5 D.Stam (Holland Giant) at 44 secs 6 R.McCauley (Wicklow Coors) s.t. 7 C.Henry (Ireland) at 46 secs 8 E.Becker (Germany Hamburg) at 54 secs 9 I.Chivers (Antrim Giant) at 1.23 10 A.Moss (Cork Buckleys) at 1.34
**Points:** 1 D.Lonergan 80 2 E.Becker 59 3 S.Farrell 53
**Mountains:** 1 R.McCauley 67 2 L.McKay 34 3 S.Farrell 32
**Team:** 1 Ireland Lee Strand 83.32.39 2 Dublin Diamond Back at 3.24 3 Great Britain at 13.40

## STAGE 9

The final stage was 70 miles starting in Naas and finishing in Swords where there were eight laps of a 4-mile circuit. To complicate matters there were hot spot sprints on the circuit which carried time bonuses of 3, 2 and 1 second which, given the state of the general classification had assumed enormous importance.

There was drama when Lonergan puncture at 50 miles, just before the race, still intact at this stage, was due to arrive in Swords. however the entire Irish team of Conor Henry, Phil Collins and Raymond Power waited and soon had the leader back in the bunch.
He arrived in time to contest the first hot-spot sprint on lap two when he gained two seconds to lead Farrell on actual time, in the final sprint on lap six he took another second in third place, just ahead of Farrell who finished out of the bonuses in 4th place...
The Irish team were then quite happy to see a 2-man break go away with George Espinoza (USA) getting his second stage out sprinting Leslie McKay with the 100-strong bunch led in by Erik Becker 30 seconds later.
**Stage 9 Naas - Swords 70 Mls.** 1 G.Espinoza (USA) 2.29.13 2 L.McKay (Dublin Fingal) at 4 seconds 3 E.Becker (Germany Hamburg) at 30 secs 4 R.Riddle (Scotland) s.t. 5 X.Bender (Germany Koln Bayer) s.t. 6 W.Oschwald (Germany Koln Bayer) s.t. 7 P.Kennedy (Meath Avonmore) s.t. 8 E.Verecken (Holland Giant) s.t. 9 P.Slane (Meath East) s.t. 10 R.McCauley (Wicklow Coors) s.t.
**General Classification:** 1 D.Lonergan (Ireland Lee Strand) 30.19.22 2 S.Farrell (G.B.) at 3 secs 3 L.Davis (Great Britain) at 10 secs 4 R.Riddle (Scotland) at 40 secs 5 R.McCauley (Wicklow Coors) at 43 secs 6 D.Stam (Holland Giant) at 47 secs 7 C.Henry (Ireland Lee Strand) at 49 secs 8 E.Becker (Germany Hamburg) at 57 secs 9 I.Chivers (Antrim Giant) at 1.26 10 A.Moss (Cork Buckleys) at 1.37
**Points:** 1 D.Lonergan 80 2 E.Becker 72 3 G.Espinoza 63
**Mountains:** 1 R.McCauley 67 2 L.McKay 34 3 S.Farrell 32
**Team:** 1 Ireland Lee Strand 91.01.48 2 Dublin Diamond Back at 3.24 3 Great Britain at 13.40

*1994 winner, Declan Lonergan*

## 1995

One hundred and sixty-four riders entered in 1995 RÁS which started on May 20, 147 actually taking the start in O'Connell Street. For the first time since their triumph in 1963, there was a team from Poland and there were also teams from Great Britain, Japan, South Africa, Germany, USA, France, Wales and Scotland.
Eight English regional teams, an Irish national team and 19 Irish county teams completed the entry as well as three individual entries.

### STAGE 1

Poland took up where they had left off 32 years before when Piotr Chmielewski won the opening stage, 85 miles from Dublin to Killeshandra. However he did not take the yellow jersey which went to Michael Fitzgerald of the Ireland Lee Strand team who led the Pole by 2 seconds by virtue of time bonuses picked up at the hot spot primes in Navan, Kells and Oldcastle.
In the 15-man break approaching the finish, Fitzgerald led Chmielewski by 8 seconds but the Pole opened a small gap and was timed 2 seconds ahead of Finn O'Sullivan (Dublin Fingal) who in turn had another 2 seconds on the rest of the break led in by Richard Prebble (Great Britain) from Jeff Wright (Lancaster Orange) with Fitzgerald fifth.
**Stage 1 Dublin - Killeshandra 85 Mls.** 1 P.Chmielewski (Poland) 3.11.13 2 F.O'Sullivan (Dublin Fingal) at 2 secs 3 R.Prebble (Great Britain) s.t. 4 J.Wright (Lancaster Orange) 5 M. Fitzgerald (Ireland Lee Strand) s.t. 6 M.Stephens (North Wirral Velo) s.t. 7 M.Kane (Ireland Lee Strand) s.t. 8 P.McQuaid (Ireland Lee Strand) s.t. 9 T.Jousset (France) s.t. 10 J.Cosgrove (Lancaster Orange) s.t.
**General Classification:** 1 M.Fitzgerald (Ireland Lee Strand) 3.11.08 2 P.Chmielewski (Poland) at 2 secs 3 J.Wright (Lancaster Orange) at 4 secs 4 F.O'Sullivan (Dublin Fingal) at 7 secs 5 R.Prebble (GB) s.t. 6 M.Stephens (North Wirral) at 9 secs 7 M.Kane (Ireland Lee Strand) s.t. 8 P.McQuaid (Ireland Lee Strand) s.t. 9 T.Jousset (France) s.t. 10 J.Cosgrove (Lancaster) s.t.
**Points:** 1 P.Chmielewski 15 2 F.O'Sullivan 14 3 R.Prebble 13
**Mountains**: 1 J.Wright 5 2 W.Wright (Wales) 4 3 P.Chmielewski 3
**Team:** 1 Great Britain 9.33.49 2 Ireland Lee Strand at 2 secs 3 Dublin Fingal at 2.19

### STAGE 2

Brian Quinn (Limerick) won the second stage when 19 riders blasted the race apart coming home a massive 7 minutes over their nearest pursuers.
Quinn and Eamon Byrne (Meath Avonmore) started the action as soon as the start flag was dropped and as small groups of riders battled across to the leaders, the front

group gradually grew until it was 29 strong.
As the fierce pace took its toll ten of the leaders dropped back leaving 19 to fight out the sprint with the rest of the field seemingly already out of the hunt for overall honours with a week still to go.
The Ireland Lee Strand team had a good day placing all their riders in the successful move and they took over the yellow jersey which went on the shoulders of Michael Fitzgerald who held a 7 second advantage over Fionn O'Sullivan (Dublin Fingal) with Ireland riders Mark Kane, Phil Cassidy and Paul McQuaid taking the next three places ahead of Antrim Giant Cycles pair Tommy Evans and Barry Monaghan.
**Stage 2 Killeshandra - Tuam 92 Mls.** 1 B.Quinn (Limerick) 3.40.40 2 C.Newton (North Wirral) s.t. 3 M.Illingworth (Great Britain) s.t. 4 W.Oschwald (Germany Bayer) s.t. 5 M.McKay (Liverpool Stena) s.t. 6 F.O'Sullivan (Dublin Fingal) s.t. 7 M.Fitzgerald (Ireland Lee Strand) s.t. 8 M.Bileskwi (Poland) s.t. 9 P.Cassidy (Ireland Lee Strand) s.t. 10 M.Kane (Ireland Lee Strand) s.t.
**General Classification:** 1 M.Fitzgerald (Ireland Lee Strand) 6.51.48 2 F.O'Sullivan (Dublin Fingal) at 7 secs 3 M.Kane (Ireland Lee Strand) at 9 secs 4 P.Cassidy (Ireland Lee Strand) s.t. 5 P.McQuaid (Ireland Lee Strand) s.t. 6 T.Evans (Antrim Giant) s.t. 7 C.Newton (North Wirral Velo) at 1.19 8 B.Glaser (Germany) at 1.22 9 B.Quinn (Limerick) at 1.23 10 M.McKay (Liverpool) at 1.24
**Points:** 1 F.O'Sullivan 24 2 M.Fitzgerald 20 3 B.Quinn 15
**Mountains:** 1 R.McCauley 5 2 J.Wright 5 3 F.O'Sullivan 4
**Team:** 1 Ireland Lee Strand 20.35.51 2 Antrim Giant Cycles at 11.06 3 Liverpool Stena at 15.01

## STAGE 3

Dubliner Fionn O'Sullivan (Dublin Fingal) took over the lead on the 105 miles stage to Tuam which was won by Great Britain rider Matthew Illingworth.
It was a "RÁS Special" day when a big break turned the GC upside down. Big losers were Ireland Lee Strand who had seemed in control with 4 riders in contention but saw two of them drop our of contention: Mark Kane and race leader Fitzgerald who dropped to 15th, 6.24 in arrears.
For a long time it looked like Chris Newton (North Wirral Velo) would take over the yellow jersey but a late fight back saw O'Sullivan back in contention and he went into the lead by 2 seconds from Tommy Evans (Antrim Giant) with the Ireland Lee Strand pair Phil Cassidy and Paul McQuaid while Newton moved up to 5th 1.12 down.
Approaching the finish, Illingworth, Ray Eden (indiv.) and Bilewski (Poland) opened up a 10 second gap on the rest of the leading group which they held to the line where the GB rider won the sprint.
**Stage 3 Tuam - Tipperary 105 Mls.** 1 M.Illingworth (Great Britain) 4.20.13 2 R.Eden (Guests) s.t. 3 M.Bilewski (Poland) at 10 secs 4 P.Chmielewski (Poland) s.t. 5 T.Jousset (France) s.t. 6 R.McCauley (Wicklow Coors) s.t. 7 D.Williams

(Liverpool Stena) s.t. 8 B.Quinn (Limerick) s.t. 9 F.O'Sullivan (Dublin) s.t. 10 M.McKay (Liverpool Stena) s.t.

**General Classification:** 1 F.O'Sullivan (Dublin Fingal) 11.12.18 2 T.Evans (Antrim Giant) at 2 secs 3 P.Cassidy (Ireland) s.t. 4 P.McQuaid (Ireland) s.t. 5 M.Illingworth (GB) at 1.08 6 C.Newton (North Wirral) at 1.12 7 B.Glaser (Germany) at 1.15 8 B.Quinn (Limerick) at 1.16 9 M.McKay (Liverpool) at 1.17 10 E.Byrne (Meath) at 1.19

**Points:** 1 F.O'Sullivan 31 2 M.Illingworth 28 3 P.Chmielewski 27

**Mountains:** 1 M. Illingworth 8 2 R.McCauley 5 3 J.Wright 5

**Team:** 1 Ireland Lee Strand 33.43.31 2 Great Britain at 11.03 3 North Wirral Velo at 13.48

## STAGE 4

Polish champion Piotr Chmielewski, who had been first on the opening stage had his second success when he was first into Dingle after the 108 miles run from Tipperary town.

Navan's Phillip Cassidy the 1983 RÁS winner, moved into top position equal on time with his teammate Paul McQuaid on a great day for the Ireland team after their reverses on the previous stage.

The climb of the 1st category Connor Pass, only 5 miles from the finish, was always going to play an important role and it was on the climb that the Pole got away riding strongly to finish 47 secs ahead of Jeff Wright (Lancaster Orange). Matt Stephens (North Wirral Velo) was at 51 seconds while Mark McKay (Liverpool Stena Sealink) led in the rest of the break 56 seconds down.

The next group came in a further 39 seconds back led in by Brian Quinn (Limerick). Included was Tommy Evans (Antrim Giant) who dropped a place overall to 3rd, 36 seconds behind the Ireland pair.

**Stage 4 Tipperary - Dingle 108 Mls.** 1 P.Chmielewski (Poland) 4.20.51 2 J.Wright (Lancaster Orange) at 47 secs 3 M.Stephens (North Wirral Velo) at 51 secs 4 M.McKay (Liverpool Stena Sealink) at 56 secs 5 Y.Nakajima (Japan) s.t. 6 R.Eden (Guests) s.t. 7 P.McQuaid (Ireland) s.t. 8 P.Cassidy (Ireland) s.t. 9 B.Quinn (Limerick) at 1.35 10 M.Bilewski (Poland) s.t.

**General Classification:** 1 P.Cassidy (Ireland) 15.34.07 2 P.McQuaid (Ireland) s.t. 3 T.Evans (Antrim) at 39 secs 4 M.McKay (Liverpool) at 1.15 5 C.Newton (North Wirral) at 1.49 6 B.Glasner (Germany) at 1.52 7 B.Quinn (Limerick) at 1.53 8 D.WIlliams (Liverpool) at 1.57 9 F.O'Sullivan (Dublin Fingal) at 2.41 10 M.Illingworth (Great Britain) at 2.51

**Points:** 1 P.Chmielewski 42 2 F.O'Sullivan 31 3 B.Quinn 30

**Mountains:** 1 P.Chmielewski 18 2 M.Illingworth 18 3 M.Stephens 16

**Team:** Ireland Lee Strand 46.50.52 2 Great Britain at 12.06 3 North Wirral Velo at 14.22

## STAGE 5

London cycle courier Ray Eden, riding the RÁS as an individual entry, won the 102 miles stage to Clonakilty while race leader Phil Cassidy (Ireland) improved his overall lead to 1.10 over Bjorn Glasner (Germany) who moved up to second place.
Loser on the day were second and third placed Paul McQuaid (Ireland) and Tommy Evans (Antrim Giant) who missed the big 28-man break losing over 2 minutes and slipping down the GC to 5th and 7th respectively.
The field split to pieces on the rolling roads of north Cork and the 28-man group which formed at the front opened up a substantial lead over several chasing groups. Six miles form the finish Glasner attacked and took with him Eden. Glasner had most to gain and did the lion's share of the work and the fresher Eden won the sprint, the two coming home 42 seconds ahead of the remainder of the break. led in by Fionn O'Sullivan (Dublin Fingal).
Eden, a relative newcomer to cycle racing, worked as a cycle courier in London and tried his luck at mountain biking before moving to the road, quickly achieving considerable success, especially in time-trials at longer distances. He wrote to race director Dermot Dignam requesting a ride in the RÁS and soon showed he was worthy of his place.
**Stage 5 Dingle - Clonakilty 102 Mls.** 1 R.Eden (Guests) 4.03.00 2 B.Glasner (Germany) s.t. 3 F.O'Sullivan (Dublin Fingal) at 42 secs 4 J.Cosgrove (Lancaster Orange) s.t. 5 J.Wright (Lancaster Orange) s.t. 6 B.Quinn (Limerick) s.t. 7 W.Oschwald (Germany Bayer) s.t. 8 P.Kennedy (Meath Avonmore) s.t. 9 R.Clarke (Tipperary Carraig) s.t. 10 M.O'Reilly (Cork Blarney) s.t.
**General Classification:** 1 P.Cassidy (Ireland) 19.37.49 2 B.Glasner (Germany) at 1.10 3 M.McKay (Liverpool Stena Sealink) at 1.15 4 B.Quinn (Limerick) at 1.53 5 P.McQuaid (Ireland) at 2.11 6 F.O'Sullivan (Dublin Fingal) at 2.41 7 T.Evans (Antrim) at 2.50 8 R.McCauley (Wicklow Coors) at 2.58 9 E.Byrne (Meath Avonmore) at 3.17 10 D.Williams (Liverpool Stena) at 4.08
**Points:** 1 R.Eden 44 2 F.O'Sullivan 44 3 P.Chmielwski 42
**Mountains:** 1 J.Wright 36 2 M.Stephens 28 3 P Chmielewski 18
**Team:** 1 Ireland Lee Strand 59.17.21 2 North Wirral Velo at 1.10 3 Liverpool Stena at 2.49

## STAGE 6

Dave Williams (Liverpool Stena Sealink) won the 98 miles stage to Clonmel to move to second overall behind the new leader, Paul McQuaid (Ireland) who finished 5th on the stage, 8 seconds behind the Merseysider.
Ireland sacrificed Cassidy who stayed in the bunch marked by 2nd and 3rd overall Glasner and McKay while a group of 39 rode away from the bunch. Soon McQuaid and Evans were lying 1st and 2nd overall on the road but when McQuaid attacked on

the climb of the Vee with 25 miles to go, the Banbridge man just failed to make it across to the final selection.
At the finish five riders including the new leader McQuaid were led into Clonmel by Williams who moved up to second while Evans came in with the chasers to move to 3rd.
**Stage 6 Clonakilty - Clonmel 98 Mls.** 1 D.Williams (Liverpool Stena Sealink) 3.41.18 2 M.Stephens (North Wirral Velo) at 1 sec 3 Y.Nakajima (Japan) s.t. 4 P.Collins (Dublin IRC) at 8 secs 5 P.McQuaid (Ireland) s.t. 6 S.Maher (Tipperary) at 2.20 7 M Bilewski (Poland) at 2.22 8 M.Fitzgerald (Ireland) at 2.26 9 W.Oschwald (Germany) s.t. 10 J.Cosgrove (Lancaster Orange) s.t.
**General Classification:** 1 P.McQuaid (Ireland) 23.21.26 2 D.Williams (Liverpool) at 1.49 3 T.Evans (Antrim Giant) at 2.57 4 R.McCauley (Wicklow Coors) at 3.05 5 E.Byrne (Meath Avonmore) at 3.24 6 M.Stephens (North Wirral) at 5.06 7 P.Cassidy (Ireland) at 6.26 8 B.Glasner (Germany) at 7.36 9 M.McKay (Liverpool) at 7.41 10 B.Quinn (Limerick) at 8.19
**Points:** 1 P.Chmielewski 47 2 R.Eden 44 3 F.O'Sullivan 44
**Mountains:** 1 M.Stephens 42 2 J.Wright 36 3 Y.Nakajima 27
**Team:** 1 Ireland Lee Strand 70.32.34 2 Liverpool Stena at 9.00 3 Poland at 13.16

## STAGE 7 (a) and (b)

The Friday morning time-trial, over the 13 miles from Clonmel to Carrick-on-Suir was won by British 25 miles time-trial champion Richard Prebble (Great Britain) by 48 seconds from Ray Eden (guests).
The race leader increased his advantage over Williams to 1.18. 1993 winner Eamon Byrne was third in the TT and kept up his challenge by moving to 4th overall at 2.25 while Antrim's Tommy Evans also slightly cut back his deficit on time to 2.28 but after the two stages had dropped to 5th on GC.
The afternoon's short 58 miles stage to Wexford changed little in the overall standings with most of the leaders finishing in the bunch. The stage run off in atrocious weather saw some history when Yashuhiro Nakajima gave Japan its first stage win when he finished 3 seconds ahead of Lancaster's Jeff Wright.
They were part of a 4-man group which got away on the hilly run-in to the finish in Wexford. Another small group went off the front of the bunch in pursuit from which Bilewski (Poland) came home 5th 23 seconds behind. In the break Ritchie McCauley (Wicklow Coors) picked up quite a haul of mountain points on the small climbs that he just failed to take over the lead in the mountains classification. His efforts were rewarded with a move to third overall, 1.28 down on McQuaid.
**Stage 7a Clonmel - Carrick-on-Suir 13 Mls. TT:** 1 R.Prebble (Great Britain) 27.42 2 R.Eden (Guests) 28.30 3 E.Byrne (Meath Avonmore) 29.31 4 A.Naylor (Liverpool Stena) 29.33 5 P.Chmielewski (Poland) 29.34 6 M.Sutcliffe (Dublin IRC) 29.35 7 J.Blackwell (Kerry) 29.42 8 B.Glasner (Germany) 29.46 9 M.Kane (Ireland) 29.53 10 D.Williams (Liverpool Stena) 29.59

**General Classification:** 1 P.McQuaid (Ireland Lee Strand) 23.51.56 2 D.Williams (Liverpool Stena) at 1.18 3 E.Byrne (Meath Avonmore) at 2.25 4 T.Evans (Antrim) at 2.28 5 R.McCauley (Wicklow Coors) at 3.41 6 M.Stephens (North Wirral) at 6.11 7 B.Glasner (Germany) at 6.52 8 P.Cassidy (Ireland) at 6.55 9 M.McKay (Liverpool) at 7.50 10 P.Chmielewski (Poland) at 10.36
**Points:** 1 P.Chmielewski 58 2 R.Eden 58 3 F.O'Sullivan 44
**Mountains:** 1 M.Stephens 42 2 J.Wright 36 3 Y.Nakajima 27
**Team:** 1 Ireland Lee Strand 72.03.32 2 Liverpool Stena at 8.13 3 Poland at 15.36
**Stage 7b Carrick on Suir - Wexford 58 Mls.** 1 Y.Nakajima (Japan) 2.17.04 2 J.Wright (Lancaster Orange) at 3 secs 3 B.Monaghan (Antrim Giant) at 4 secs 4 M.Stephens (North Wirral Velo) at 6 secs 5 M.Bilewski (Poland) at 23 secs 6 B.Glasner (Germany) s.t. 7 C.Kimmage (Carlow Dan Morrissey) s.t. 8 M.McKay (Liverpool Stena) at 26 secs 9 R.McCauley (Wicklow Coors) at 27 secs 10 R.Eden (Guests) at 1.08
**General classification:** 1 P.McQuaid (Ireland Lee Strand) 26.11.40 2 D.Williams (Liverpool Stena) at 1.18 3 R.McCauley (Wicklow Coors) at 1.28 4 E.Byrne (Meath Avonmore) at 2.25 5 T.Evans (Antrim) at 2.28 6 M.Stephens (North Wirral) at 3.37 7 B.Glasner (Germany) at 4.35 8 M.McKay (Liverpool) at 5.36 9 P.Chmielewski (Poland) at 9.10 10 M.Bilewski (Poland) at 10.5
**Points:** 1 R.Eden 64 2 P.Chmielewski 59 3 M.Stephens 52
**Mountains:** 1 J.Wright 59 2 M.Stephens 54 3 Y.Nakajima 47
**Team:** 1 Ireland Lee Strand 79.03.33 2 Liverpool Stena at 5.10 3 Poland at 11.04

## STAGE 8

Paul McQuaid rode strongly on the 4-climb mountain stage from Wexford to Newbridge to keep his yellow jersey into the final day with its second split stage of the week.
A potentially dangerous 30 man break was away over the climbs containing the Pole Chmielewski who would go on to his third stage win of the week and Nakajima of Japan and Matt Stephens (North Wirral) who was lying third 3.37 behind.
The Irish team worked well in support of the race leader and the lead was never allowed to grow enough to threaten the jersey and were limited at the finish to just over 1 minute.
**Stage 8 Wexford - Newbridge 95 Mls.** 1 P.Chmielewski (Poland) 3.46.38 2 Y.Nakajima (Japan) s.t. 3 M.Stephens (North Wirral Velo) at 2 secs 4 B.Glasner (Germany) at 1.08 5 R.Eden (Guests) at 1.10 6 F.O'Sullivan (Dublin Fingal) at 1.12 7 M.Firth (Scotland) at 1.20 8 M.Bilewski (Poland) at 1.44 9 J.Wright (Lancaster Orange) s.t. 10 S.Baker (Dublin IRC) s.t.
**General Classification:** 1 P.McQuaid (Ireland Lee Strand) 30.00.02 2 D.Williams (Liverpool Stena) at 1.18 3 R.McCauley (Wicklow Coors) at 1.34 4 M.Stephens (North Wirral Velo) at 1.55 5 E.Byrne (Meath Avonmore) at 2.31 6 T.Evans (Antrim

Giant Cycles) at 2.34 7 B.Glasner (Germany) at 3.59 8 M.McKay (Liverpool Stena) at 5.42 9 P.Chmielewski (Poland) at 7.26 10 M.Bilewski (Poland) at 10.51
**Points:** 1 R.Eden 75 2 P.Chmielewski 74 3 M.Stephens 65
**Mountains:** 1 J.Wright 76 2 Y.Nakajima 76 3 M. Stephens 70
**Teams:** 1 Ireland Lee Strand 90.35.65 2 Liverpool Stena at 5.10 3 Poland at 9.14

## STAGES 9 (a) and (b)

In Sunday morning's 8 miles time-trial Richard Prebble (Great Britain) had another stage win against the watch beating Ray Eden by 32 secs with Phil Collins (Dublin IRC) third.
McQuaid, who finished 14th in 18.40, limited his losses over his nearest rival Williams to 18 seconds leaving him in a strong position going into the afternoon's final stage, a criterium in Swords.
In the afternoon he stayed safely in the bunch surrounded by his team-mates mainly concerned with keeping out of danger. The final stage had four sprints carrying time bonuses but with a minute in hand McQuaid was in no danger barring accidents as long as the Ireland team were able to prevent either Williams or Stephens, the only real danger men, getting away.
The stage, despite almost continual attacking throughout the hour, finished in a sprint, contested by most of the 93 who started the final stage, which was won by Wolfgang Oschwald (Germany) from Michael Fitzgerald (Ireland).
**Stage 9a Newbridge 8 Mls. TT:** 1 R.Prebble (Great Britain) 17.17 2 R.Eden (Guests) 17.49 3 P.Collins (Dublin IRC) 18.04 4 B.Glasner (Germany) 18.10 5 D.Williams (Liverpool Stena) 18.22 6 P.Chmielewski (Poland) 18.24 7 M.Sutcliffe (Dublin IRC) 18.29 8 S.Colloby (Wales) 18.34.26 9 J.Hunter (Derry Clarke Bros.) 18.34.81 10 A.Naylor (Liverpool Stena) 18.34.96
**General Classification:** 1 P.McQuaid (Ireland Lee Strand) 30.18.42 2 D.Williams (Liverpool Stena) at 1.00 3 M.Stephens (North Wirral Velo) at 1.50 4 R.McCauley (Wicklow Coors) at 2.20 5 E.Byrne (Meath Avonmore) at 2.26 6 T.Evans (Antrim) at 2.39 7 B.Glasner (Germany) at 3.29 8 M.McKay (Liverpool Stena) at 6.00 9 P.Chmielewski (Poland) at 7.10 R.Eden (Guests) at 11.24
**Points:** 1 R.Eden 75 2 P.Chmielewski 74 3 M.Stephens 65
**Mountains:** 1 J.Wright 76 2 Y.Nakajima 76 3 M. Stephens 70
**Team:** 1 Ireland Lee Strand 91.32.31 2 Liverpool Stena at 4.29 3 Poland at 11.38
**Stage 9b Balbriggan - Swords 44 Mls.** 1 W.Oschwal (Germany) 1.26.42 2 M.Fitzgerald (Ireland Lee Strand) s.t. 3 R.Riddle (Scotland) s.t. 4 C.Bracken (Galway) s.t. 5 K.Zajdel (Poland) s.t. 6 J.Cosgrove (Lancaster Orange) s.t. 7 P.Kennedy (Meath Avonmore) s.t. 8 K.Bannon (Wicklow Coors) s.t. 9 B.Monaghan (Antrim Giant) s.t. 10 C.Watson (Down) s.t.
**General Classification:** 1 P.McQuaid (Ireland Lee Strand) 31.45.24 2 D.Williams (Liverpool Stena) at 1.00 3 M.Stephens (North Wirral Velo) at 1.50 4 R.McCauley (Wicklow Coors) at 2.18 5 E.Byrne (Meath Avonmore) at 2.26 6 T.Evans (Antrim)

at 2.38 7 B.Glasner (Germany) at 3.29 8 M.McKay (Liverpool Stena) at 6.00 9 P.Chmielewski (Poland) at 7.10 R.Eden (Guests) at 11.24
**Points:** 1 R.Eden 89 2 P.Chmielewski 84 3 M.Stephens 69
**Mountains: 1** J.Wright 76 2 Y.Nakajima 76 3 M.Stephens 70
**Teams:** 1 Ireland Lee Strand 95.52.37 2 Liverpool Stena Sealink at 4.29 3 Poland at 11.38

*Paul McQuaid, Ireland – Winner 1995*

## 1996

Of the 154 riders entered in 1996, 141 made it to the start line and this included eight international selections: Ireland, Japan Cycleways, South Africa, Germany, The Netherlands, Great Britain, USA and Scotland.
The increasing popularity of the event with cross-Channel riders was evidenced by the presence of no less than eight English teams. Eighteen Irish county squads completed the line-up.

### STAGE 1

Donegal rider Paul Giles, riding for the Derry Clarke Bros team, won the opening stage of the '96 event, 73 miles from Dublin to Kilkenny.
Giles, who had been racing all season in Belgium, missed the original 10-man break which went away at Naas but got up to the leaders at Castlecomer along with Fionn O'Sullivan (Dublin Fingal), Gary Beneke (South Africa) and Ben Luckwell (unatt.).
O'Sullivan then attacked and took with him Giles, Beneke and two of the original break Barry Monaghan (Derry Clarke Bros.) and Peter Daly (Ireland Abrakebabra). When they reached Kilkenny where they had two circuits of the town to do, their lead over the chasers was 1.10.
There were several attacks from the leaders on the circuit the end result of which was a series of splits. Giles was clearly the strongest and came home on his own, while Beneke outsprinted O'Sullivan 11 seconds behind the winner. With the hot-spot sprint bonuses, another Derry rider Barry Monaghan moved up to third overall, 4 seconds behind Giles.
**Stage 1 Dublin - Kilkenny 73 Mls.** 1 P.Giles (Derry Clarke Bros) 2.27.45 2 G.Beneke (South Africa) at 11 secs 3 F.O'Sullivan (Dublin Fingal) s.t. 4 B.Monaghan (Derry Clarke Bros) s.t. 5 P.Daly (Ireland Abrakebabra) s.t. 6 P.Butler (Tipperary) at 33 secs 7 J.P.Furus (Germany) s.t. 8 M.Fitzgerald (Ireland) s.t. 9 J.Fullard (South Africa) s.t. 10 C.Bracken (Dublin Ravens) s.t.
**General Classification:** 1 P.Giles (Derry Clarke Bros) 2.27.45 2 P.Daly (Ireland) at 3 secs 3 B.Monaghan (Derry Clarke Bros.) at 4 secs 4 G.Beneke (South Africa) at 11 secs 5 F.O'Sullivan (Dublin Fingal) s.t. 6 S.Stirzaker (NE England Kenbay) at 20 secs 7 D.Booth (South Africa) at 26 secs 8 K.Bannon (Wicklow) at 28 secs 9 M.Pitchford (Lincolnshire) at 30 secs 10 M.Lyttle (Antrim UCF) at 31 secs
**Points:** 1 P.Giles 15 2 G.Beneke 14 3 F.O'Sullivan 13
**Mountains:** 1 S.Stirzaker 5 2 P.Daly 4 3 D.Booth 3
**Team:** 1 Derry Clarke Bros 7.23.59 2 Ireland Abrakebabra at 33 secs 3 South Africa s.t.

## STAGE 2

The 103 miles stage to Millstreet, Co. Cork was won by Jaques Fullard (South Africa) best of four riders who split from a leading group of 10 which had been away for most of the stage.
Yellow jersey Giles had quite a bit of mechanical trouble and came in with a chasing group of 20, 49 seconds behind Fullard and dropped to 5th overall, 32 seconds behind the new leader, Peter Daly of the Ireland Abrakebabra team.
The 10-man break went away early and built up a lead of over 2 minutes. A chasing group of 20 left the bunch and got to within 1 minute of the leaders at Mallow, 20 miles from the finish.
At the front Fullard, Daly, Ciaran Power (Galway Thermo King) and John Cosgrove (NE England Kenbay Cycles) left the front group who shortly afterwards were absorbed by the chasers.
Approaching the finish Fullard jumped and held a 12 second advantage to the line. Daly, who had been giving it everything to get the jersey, dropped back and lost another couple of seconds on the run-in.
**Stage 2 Kilkenny - Millstreet 103 Mls.** 1 J.Fullard (South Africa) 4.08.59 2 C.Power (Galway Thermo King) at 12 secs 3 J.Cosgrove (NE England Kenbay) s.t. 4 P.Daly (Ireland Abrakebabra) at 14 secs 5 P.Griffin (Kerry) at 49 secs 6 J.Wright (NE England Kenbay Cycles) s.t. 7 P.Butler (Tipperary) s.t. 8 R.Hennes (Germany) s.t. 9 B.Kennealy (Tipperary) s.t. 10 D.O'Shea (Kerry) s.t.
**General Classification:** 1 P.Daly (Ireland) 6.37.01 2 J.Fullard (South Africa) at 16 secs 3 C.Power (Galway) at 28 secs 4 J.Cosgrove (NE England) s.t. 5 P.Giles (Derry Clarke Bros) at 32 secs 6 B.Monaghan (Derry Clarke Bros) at 36 secs 7 F.O'Sullivan (Dublin Fingal) at 43 secs 8 D.Booth (South Africa) at 58 secs 9 P.Butler (Tipperary) at 1.05 10 R.Hennes (Germany) s.t.
**Points:** 1 P.Daly 23 2 J.Fullard 22 3 P.Butler 19
**Mountains:** 1 D.Peelo 14 2 J.Wright 13 3 P.Daly 10
**Team:** 1 South Africa 19.53.07 2 Derry Clarke Bros at 16 secs 3 North-East Hardisty Cycles at 34 secs

## STAGE 3

English ex-professional Ben Luckwell, riding as an individual entry, won the 94 miles stage to Nenagh out sprinting breakaway companion Marcus Lemm (Germany), the two coming home 1.24 ahead of Roddy Riddle (Scotland) who took over at the top of the GC.
These three along with Christy Kimmage (Carlow Dan Morrissey) and Richard Moore (Scotland) got clear early on. With Riddle only 1.06 behind yellow jersey Daly, the Scots pair drove hard all day but paid the price when on the climb at

Portroe, 12 miles from the finish, they couldn't hold the attack of Luckwell and Lenn.

Riddle however continued riding strongly, coming home in third place 1.24 behind but with enough time in hand to take the jersey by 1.42 from Ciaran Power (Galway Thermo King) who left a large chasing group along with Gethin Butler (NE England Kenbay) catching and passing Moore before the finish.

It was a disastrous day for Daly and the Ireland team who came home in the bunch 6.11 behind the winner, Daly dropping to 5th at 3.42.

**Stage 3 Millstreet - Nenagh 94 Mls.** 1 B.Luckwell (Indiv.) 3.40.41 2 M.Lemm (Germany) s.t. 3 R.Riddle (Scotland) at 1.24 4 C.Kimmage (Carlow Dan Morrissey) at 3.18 5 G.Butler (NE England Kenbay) at 3.43 6 C.Power (Galway Thermo King) s.t. 7 R.Moore (Scotland) at 4.52 8 P.Butler (Tipperary) at 6.11 9 M.Sutcliffe (Dublin IRC) s.t. 10 R.Hennes (Germany) s.t.

**General Classification:** 1 R.Riddle (Scotland) 10.10.11 2 C.Power (Galway) at 1.42 3 G.Butler (NE England) at 2.19 4 M.Lemm (Germany) at 3.19 5 P.Daly (Ireland) at 3.42 6 J.Fullard (South Africa) at 3.58 7 J.Cosgrove (NE England) at 4.10 8 B.Monaghan (Derry Clarke Bros) at 4.18 9 F.O'Sullivan (Dublin Fingal) at 4.25 10 D.Booth (South Africa) at 4.40

**Points**: 1 P.Butler 27 2 C.Power 24 J.Fullard 23

**Mountains:** 1 D.Peelo (Dublin) 14 2 J.Wright (NE England) 13 3 P.Daly 10

**Team:** 1 Scotland 30.40.47 2 England at 1.02 3 South Africa at 2.56

## STAGE 4

Before the start of the race the Derry team, in essence a team from the Ulster Cycling Federation sponsored by Clarke Bros. had looked to be a very strong combination. Included was David McCann who since his return from riding across the United States had won every major event he entered including the 3-day Tour of Ulster, the weekend before the RÁS.

The team's expected move came on the fourth stage, 103 miles to Castlebar and Derry pair Tommy Evans and David McCann came home together 29 seconds ahead of a group led in by previous day's winner Ben Luckwell. This put the two Derry riders into second and third overall, both 59 seconds behind new leader Marcus Lemm (Germany) who had finished in 5th place in the Luckwell group.

Evans and McCann had left an 8-man group which had gone away shortly after the start. After Tuam 25 riders split off the front of the bunch and went in pursuit. The remainder of the bunch showed no real appetite for a hard chase and continually lost time, eventually coming home 20 minutes down.

The 25 strong group didn't make any inroads on the leaders and only limited their losses coming in 7 minutes down.

**Stage 4 Nenagh - Castlebar 103 Mls.** 1 T.Evans (Derry Clarke Bros) 4.00.07 2 D.McCann (Derry Clarke Bros) s.t. 3 B.Luckwell (Indiv.) at 29 secs 4 D.O'Shea (Kerry) s.t. 5 M.Lemm (Germany) s.t. 6 M.O'Reilly (Wicklow) s.t. 7 F.O'Sullivan

(Dublin Fingal) at 1.19 8 M.Dinkleman (Lincolnshire) at 1.56 9 K.Bannon (Wicklow) at 7.00 10 J.Wright (NE England) s.t.
**General Classification:** 1 M.Lemm (Germany) 14.14.06 2 D.McCann (Derry) at 59 secs 3 T.Evans (Derry) s.t. 4 D.O'Shea (Kerry) at 1.28 5 F.O'Sullivan (Dublin Fingal) at 1.56 6 M.O'Reilly (Wicklow) at 2.39 7 R.Riddle (Scotland) at 3.12 8 C.Power (Galway) at 5.54 9 B.Luckwell (Indiv.) at 5.00 10 G.Butler (NE England) at 5.31
**Points:** 1 B.Luckwell 28 2 J.Fullard 28 3 P.Butler 27
**Mountains:** 1 D.Peelo 14 2 J.Wright 13 3 P.Daly 10
**Team:** 1 Derry Clarke Bros 42.51.20 2 Germany at 7.29 3 Tipperary at 14.00

## STAGE 5

It was Derry Clarkes again on stage 5 when opening stage winner Paul Giles, had a very popular win into his home county at Letterkenny.
Before racing got underway Ben Luckwell had a meeting with the race commissaires at which he was found guilty on each of two counts of assisting the Derry team. He was fined £200 on each count plus a 10 second penalty,
Other teams had complained of the close association between the English ex-pro riding as an Individual, and the Derry squad with whom he had been staying throughout the week, even wearing team clothing. It was however his riding which seemed to be calculated to contribute to the team's success that the commissaires were investigating. As one stage it looked that he might even be expelled from the event.
Ironically, only for some bad luck on the opening stage, Luckwell could very well have been leading the race on his results on the succeeding stages.
A six-man break went away early on and stayed away all day. In the group were Giles, Rafel Hennes (Germany), Peter Daly (Ireland), Jaques Fullard (South Africa), Denis O'Shea (Kerry) and Fionn O'Sullivan (Dublin Fingal).
As O'Shea and O'Sullivan were in the top six overall, it looked like they could move to the top of the leader board but over the last 20 miles the bunch steadily eat into the lead which at the end was only 21 seconds. Giles easily won the sprint up the long hill of Letterkenny's main street which split the leaders, O'Shea losing 9 and O'Sullivan 12 seconds.
**Stage 5 Tubbercurry - Letterkenny 96 Mls.** 1 P.Giles (Derry Clarke Bros) 3.16.34 2 R.Hennes (Germany) s.t. 3 P.Daly (Ireland) at 3 secs 4 J.Fullard (South Africa) at 6 secs 5 D.O'Shea (Kerry) at 9 secs 6 F.O'Sullivan (Dublin Fingal) at 12 secs 7 M.Fitzgerald (Ireland Abrakebabra) at 21 secs 8 J.Furus (Germany) s.t. 9 C.Power (Galway Thermo King) s.t. 10 P.Butler (Tipperary) s.t.
**General Classification:** 1 M.Lemm (Germany) 17.13.01 2 D.McCann (Derry) at 59 secs 3 T.Evans (Derry) s.t. 4 D.O'Shea (Kerry) at 1.16 5 F.O'Sullivan (Dublin Fingal) at 1.47 6 M.O'Reilly (Wicklow) at 2.39 7 R.Riddle (Scotland) at 3.12 8

C.Power (Galway) at 4.54 9 B.Luckwell (Indiv.) at 5.00 10 G.Butler (NE England) at 5.31 11 M.Dinkleman (Lincolnshire) at 5.56 12 P.Daly (Ireland) at 6.36
**Points:** 1 J.Fullard 40 2 R.Hennes and P.Daly both 36
**Mountains:** 1 P.Daly 14 2 J.Wright 13 3 M.Lemm 5
**Team:** 1 Derry Clarke Bros 53.41.42 2 Germany at 1.39 3 Ireland at 17.15

## STAGE 6

Race leader Marcue Lemm (Germany) held on to his yellow jersey on a tough stage round the Inishowen peninsula to Buncrana which included the notorious climb of the Gap of Mamore in the last 10 miles.
The stage winner was Jeff Wright (NE England) who won in a sprint from a three-man break which included Peter Daly (Ireland) and Ben Luckwell (Indiv.) These three went away with a breakaway group on the climb of Ballagh Mountain after 50 miles where Wright took the KOM prime.
The three built up a lead of 1.45 on a chasing group which included yellow jersey Lemm and Derry pair Evans and McCann. Lemm and McCann got up to the leaders on the Gap of Mamore but an immediate counter attack saw Wright, Luckwell and Daly get away and they sped down the fast descent to the finish in Buncrana where Roddy Riddle (Scotland) came home on his own 39 seconds behind the winner with the remains of the break at 1.20.
**Stage 6 Letterkenny - Buncrana 87 Mls.** 1 J.Wright (NE England) 3.31.35 2 P.Daly (Ireland) s.t. 3 B.Luckwell (Indiv.) s.t. 4 R.Riddle (Scotland) at 39 secs 5 R.Hennes (Germany) at 1.20 6 M.Lemm (Germany) s.t. 7 A.Naylor (Great Britain) s.t. 8 D.McCann (Derry Clarke Bros) s.t. 9 T.Evans (Derry Clarke Bros) s.t. 10 B.Doherty (Antrim) at 3.13
**General classification:** 1 M.Lemm (Germany) 21.03.56 2 D.McCann (Derry) at 59 secs 3 T.Evans (Derry) s.t. 4 R.Riddle (Scotland) at 2.31 5 B.Luckwell (Indiv.) at 3.50 6 F.O'Sullivan (Dublin Fingal) at 4.46 7 M.O'Reilly (Wicklow) at 5.12 8 P.Daly (Ireland) at 5.16 9 J.Wright (NE England) at 6.39 10 D.O'Shea (Kerry) at 7.13
**Points:** 1 P.Daly 50 2 R.Hennes 47 3 B.Luckwell 41
**Mountains:** 1 J.Wright 63 2 P.Daly 52 3 B.Luckwell 27
**Team:** 1 Derry Clarke Bros 63.23.45 2 Germany at 19.36 3 Ireland at 20.23

## STAGE 7

Derry's Tommy Evans went into yellow after the leader Marcus Lemm cracked under Derry pressure on the 101 miles stage to Donegal Town, won by Ireland's Peter Daly from Jeff Wright (NE England).
Evans came home third, 1.14 behind to take the overall lead by 1.48 from his teammate David McCann.

Derry employed their usual tactic of sending Denis Easton away in the early break which soon was over 2 minutes ahead. Included was Jeff Wright (NE England) who took the mountain prime at Meenaroy to go further ahead of Daly in the mountains category. This prompted a chase by the Germans and the break was brought back.
However the leader was soon in trouble again as a 15-man group moved ahead on the steep Glengesh Pass. Included was Evans who was soon leader on the road. On the climb Wright broke his chain leaving the way clear for Daly to take back the mountains lead by taking maximum points. Over the top the group's lead had grown to over 3 minutes.
Wright, despite two bike changes, got back to the leaders and won the next two climbs to regain the KOM moving 5 points clear of the Ireland rider.
In the bunch McCann got away from Lemm on the climbs and cut the lead of Evans to 2 minutes by the finish.
On the third climb, Wright and Daly, engaged in their battle for the climbers prize, went clear of the leaders and maintained their advantage to the finish where Daly won the sprint.
**Stage 7 Buncrana - Donegal 101 Mls.** 1 P.Daly (Ireland Abrakebabra) 4.32.43 2 J.Wright (NE England Kenbay) at 2 secs 3 T.Evans (Derry Clarkes) at 1.14 4 A.Naylor (Great Britain) s.t. 5 C.Power (Galway Thermo King) s.t. 6 F.O'Sullivan (Dublin Fingal) s.t. 7 B.Luckwell (Indiv.) s.t. 8 L.McKay (Ireland Abrakebabra) s.t. 10 A.Hederman (Tipperary) s.t.
**General Classification:** 1 T.Evans (Derry) 25.38.52 2 D.McCann (Derry) at 1.48 3 B.Luckwell (Indiv.) at 2.51 4 P.Daly (Ireland) at 3.03 5 R.Riddle (Scotland) at 3.20 6 F.O'Sullivan (Dublin Fingal) at 3.47 7 J.Wright (NE England) at 4.28 8 M.O'Reilly (Wicklow) at 6.01 9 D.O'Shea (Kerry) at 6.14 10 A.Naylor (Great Britain) at 7.00
**Points:** 1 P.Daly 65 2 J.Wright 54 3 B.Luckwell 50
**Mountains:** 1 J.Wright 88 2 P.Daly 83 3 B.Luckwell 51
**Team:** 1 Derry Clarke Bros 77.14.56 2 NE England Kenbay at 19.59 3 Ireland Ababrakebabra at 25.31

## STAGE 8

Tommy Evans had an anxious time on the penultimate stage to Newry when teammate David McCann was in a break 1.51 ahead and clear leader on the road. However the Banbridge man led a chase which saw the leader's advantage reduced over the final miles and he retained the lead by 25 seconds.
The 91 survivors of the original 151 stayed together until the climb at Sion Finn, after Fintona when a break went clear which included McCann, Jeff Wright (NE England Kenbay), Ben Luckwell, J.P. Furis (Germany, Lee Davis and Andy Naylor (Great Britain), Y. Numata (Japan), Seamus O'Sullivan (Wicklow), D. Booth (South Africa) and Roddy Riddle (Scotland).

At Aughnacloy the break had their maximum advantage of 1.51 on a chasing group of 25 riders which included the yellow jersey. The chasers reduced the deficit which remained at around 1 minute for most of the remainder of the stage.
Approaching the finish at Newry, Jeff Wright, who had been active throughout sewing up the King of the Mountains classification, attacked on the climb on the new bypass and held on to win by 9 seconds from McCann who led in the rest of the break.
**Stage 8 Donegal - Newry 103 Mls.** 1 J.Wright (NE England) 3.40.36 2 D.McCann (Derry Clarke Bros) at 9 secs 3 B Luckwell (Indiv.) s.t. 4 J.P.Furis (Germany) s.t. 5 L.Davis (Great Britain) s.t. 6 A.Naylor (Great Britain) s.t. 7 Y.Numata (Japan) s.t. 8 S.O'Sullivan (Wicklow) s.t. 9 D.Booth (South Africa) s.t. 10 R.Riddle (Scotland) s.t.
**General Classification:** 1 T.Evans (Derry) 29.21.00 2 D.McCann (Derry) at 25 secs 3 B.Luckwell (Indiv.) at 1.28 4 R.Riddle (Scotland) at 1.57 5 J.Wright (NE England) at 2.56 6 P.Daly (Ireland) at 3.03 7 F.O'Sullivan (Dublin) at 3.47 8 A.Naylor (G.B.) at 5.37 9 M.O'Reilly (Wicklow) at 6.01 10 D.O'Shea (Kerry) at 6.14
**Points:** 1 J. Wright 69 2 P.Daly 65 3 B.Luckwell 63
**Mountains:** 1 J.Wright 107 2 P.Daly 83 3 B.Luckwell 63
**Team:** 1 Derry Clarke Bros 88.19.30 2 NE England Kenbay at 20.17 3 Ireland at 40.15

## STAGE 9

It rained on the final stage of the '96 RÁS, just as it had rained on each of the other eight stages, but it didn't dampen the joy of Tommy Evans who survived a final late challenge from teammate David McCann on the 76 miles stage from Newry to Swords.
The race stayed more or less intact until they reached Swords where there were ten laps of a 2 mile circuit to be completed. When Michael Fitzgerald (Ireland Abrakebabra) and Marcus Lemm (Germany) went away on the circuit, McCann went with them and as the gap grew to 10 seconds, Evans looked in danger.
However they were soon brought back by the bunch and the Banbridge man was safe, becoming one of the few riders to win both the Junior Tour of Ireland and the RÁS.
Super sprinter Michael Fitzgerald gave the Ireland team the final stage victory of the RÁS coming in 5 seconds ahead of Marcus Lemm while Hennes led in the bunch 30 seconds behind.
It was a triumph for the Derry Clarke Bros. team who took the top two places, the team race by 21 minutes and finished all five riders in the top 30. In addition they had three stage wins, two to Giles and one to Evans.
**Stage 9 Newry - Swords 76 Mls.** 1 M.Fitzgerald (Ireland Abrakebabra) 3.35.00 2 M.Lemm (Germany) at 5 secs 3 R.Hennes (Germany) at 30 secs 4 C.Power (Galway) s.t. 5 R.Hobby (Great Britain) s.t. 6 N.Smith (Lincolnshire) s.t. 7 M Dinkleman

(Lincolnshire) s.t. 8 A.Naylor (Great Britain) s.t. 9 G.Patterson (Scotland) s.t. 10 K.Brannigan (Mayo) s.t.

**General Classification:** 1 T.Evans (Derry Clarke Bros) 32.22.05 2 D.McCann (Derry) at 24 secs 3 B.Luckwell (Indiv.) at 1.28 4 R.Riddle (Scotland) at 1.57 5 J.Wright (NE England) at 2.56 6 P.Daly (Ireland) at 3.03 7 F.O'Sullivan (Dublin) at 3.46 8 A.Naylor (G.B.) at 5.37 9 M.O'Reilly (Wicklow) at 6.01 10 D.O'Shea (Kerry) at 6.11 11 G.Butler (NE England Kenbay) at 7.48 12 M.Pitchford (Lincolnshire) at 11.37 13 B.Emerson (USA Team Sony Music) at 12.04 14 L.Davis (G.B.) at 12.41 15, M.McNeena (Galway Thermo King) at 12.57

**Points:** 1 J.Wright 73 2 B.Luckwell 68 3 P.Daly 65

**Mountains:** 1 J.Wright 107 2 P.Daly 83 3 B.Luckwell 64

**Team:** 1 Derry Clarke Bros. 97.22.45 2 NE England Kenbay at 20.17 3 Ireland at 39.40 4 Great Britain at 53.56 5 Lincolnshire 98.35.57 6 Galway Thermo King 98.36.30

*Tommy Evans*
*Winner 1996*

## 1997

The were a record 187 entries for the '97 RÁS and although this was reduced by non-starters, it was still a record 164 who started the opening 73 miles stage to Roscommon.
Teams entered included for the first time The Philippines as well as Japan, France, Germany, The Netherlands, Belgium, Great Britain, Scotland, Wales plus eleven cross-Channel teams. The home entry consisted of the national team and seventeen county selections.
'96 winner Tommy Evans was not on the original list of entries but after a good ride in the Tour of Ulster he changed his mind and asked for a late entry and, when a vacancy occurred on the Ireland team, he was drafted in.

### STAGE 1

Jeff Wright (England NE Hardisty), who had been the strong-man in the closing stages of the '96 RÁS, winning the penultimate stage into Newry as well as the King of the Mountains, started the '97 edition where he had left off winning the opening stage to Roscommon and taking over the yellow jersey, not automatic for the stage-winner as three hot-spot sprints on the opening stage each carried bonuses of 5, 3 and 1 seconds.
Wright was in a group of three which got away in the final 20 miles and he won the sprint from Gregorz Gwiazdowski, the Polish champion riding for the crack French ACCB squad. Mike Harrison (England NW) finished third in the same time.
A small chasing group was led in 22 seconds later by Jeroem Slagter (Holland Top Team Tegeltoko) from Phil West (Great Britain) and Matthew Postle (Wales). Andy Mathieson (Scotland) was next and completing the multi-national line-up David Peelo (Dublin Hildebrand) was the first Irish rider in 8th place.
**Stage 1 Dublin - Roscommon 73 Mls.** 1 J.Wright (England NE Hardisty) 2.39.37 2 G.Gwiazdowski (France ACBB) s.t. 3 M.Harrison (England NW Centre) s.t. 4 P.West (Great Britain) at 22 secs 5 M.Postle (Wales) s.t. 6 A.Mathieson (Scotland) s.t. 7 D.Peelo (Dublin Hillebrand) s.t. 8 S.Calvez (France ACBB) s.t. 9 D.O'Loughlin (Mayo) s.t. 10 P.Kil (Holland Top Team Tegeltoko) at 28 secs
**General Classification:** 1 J.Wright (England NE Hardisty) 2.39.34 2 M.Harrison (England NW Centre) at 1 sec 3 G.Gwiazdowski (France ACBB) at 3 secs 4 S.Calvez (France ACBB) at 22 secs 5 J.Slagter (Holland Tegeltoko) s.t. 6 L.Davis (Great Britain) at 24 secs 7 P.West (Great Britain) at 25 secs 8 M.Postle (Wales) 9 A.Mathieson (Great Britain) 10 D.Peelo (Dublin Hillebrand) 11 D.O'Loughlin (Mayo) all same time 12 D.Hourigan (Limerick) at 26 secs
**Points:** 1 J.Wright 15 2 G.Gwiazdowski 14 3 M.Harrison 13

**Team:** 1 France Team ACBB 7.59.41 2 England NW Centre at 6 secs 3 England NE Hardisty Cycles s.t.
**County Team:** 1 Dublin JF Hillebrand 8.00.09 2 Mayo NCF s.t. 3 Ciarrai Baltic Trading at 6 secs

## STAGE 2

Dutchman Jeroem Slagter (Holland Top Team Tegeltoko) took over the yellow jersey with a 3 second lead over Matthew Postle (Wales) after the 103 miles stage to Clifden.
Slagter won the 103 miles haul in the rain from Roscommon coming in with a leading group 3.34 in front of the main bunch which contained race leader Jeff Wright (England NE Hardisty).
While less than a minute covered almost the entire 164-strong field on Saturday, the hills and rain dictated a different story and it was a succession of groups coming in at the finish in Clifden some over half-an hour down.
The action started early and a 17-strong group were already going away at the first prime at Ballygar 11 miles where Cian Lynch (Dublin Hillebrand) was the winner. At the next prime at Moylough 23 miles Lynch was first again while the group had almost a minute in hand.
Over the next few miles this stretched to 1.30 while a 10-man chasing group were in between the leaders and the main bunch. However it was the three King of the Mountains primes in the last 30 miles which did all the damage.
On the first of these the field, including the break disintegrated and Morgan Fox (Meath Avonmore) led a 12-strong group over the top of the first climb. Fox took the next two as well to give him a good start in the KOM competition. However he was a casualty entering Clifden when he fell. Luckily it was inside the last Kilometre so he didn't lose any time.
The leaders were reduced to nine by the finish where the Dutchman won the sprint to take over at the top. Holland Team Tegeltoko now have the lead in both the individual and team competitions and are looking strong with many big names having lost a lot of time.
**Stage 2 Roscommon - Clifden 103 Mls.** 1 J.Slagter (Holland Tegeltoko) 3.53.11 2 G.Butler (England NE Hardisty) s.t. 3 K.Donnelly (Dublin IRC) s.t. 4 M.Postle (Wales) s.t. 5 T.du Garle (France ACBB) s.t. 6 A.Naylor (Stoke Clarke Ambrosia) s.t. 7 A.Roche (Kerry Baltic Trading) s.t. 8 P.Kil (Holland Tegeltoko) s.t. 9 C.Power (Ireland Supermilk) s.t. 10 P.Daly (Ireland Supermilk) at 7 secs
**General Classification:** 1 J. Slagter 6.33.07 2 M.Postle at 3 secs 3 G. Butler at 9 secs 4 P.Kil 5 K.Donnelly 6 A.Roche 7 T.du Garle 8 A.Naylor 9 C.Power 10 M.Fox all same time 11 P.Daly at 16 secs 12 K.Dawson (G.B.) at 1.26
**Points:** 1 M.Postle 23 2 J.Wright 15 3 J.Slagter 15
**Mountains:** 1 M.Fox 20 2 P.Daly 11 3 M.Fitzgerald 10
**International Team:** 1 Holland 19.42.24 2 Ireland at 1.05 3 Wales at 2.32

**County Team:** 1 Meath Avonmore 19.45.02 2 Ciarrai Baltic Trading at 3.19 3 Dublin IRC at 5.53

## STAGE 3

Pelle Kil (Holland Top Team Tegeltoko) finished sixth into Lisdoonvarna. He took over the yellow jersey from teammate Jeroem Slagter who came in with the main bunch over three minutes down dropping to 14th overall, 1.55 down.
The stage was won by Gregorz Gwiazdowski (Team ACBB) from Ray Eden (Yorkshire Planet X) with Olympic champion Bart Brentjens (Holland Top Team Tegeltoko) third. Kil was equal on time with Matthew Postle (Wales) but took the jersey on better placings.
Denis O'Shea (Kerry Baltic Trading) took the first prime at Oughterard from a 7-man group which had a lead of 30 seconds but a few miles further on at Moycullen they were all together with Andy Mathieson (Scotland) winning the prime
At Kinvara 70 miles five riders including Gwiadowski broke away and were soon joined by four more including Brentjen and these nine at one time had a 2 minute lead. Behind them a chasing bunch of 25 riders broke away from the bunch from which Slagter couldn't escape, suffering the fate of many early RÁS leaders in the past.
At the King of the Mountains climb of Ballylacken on the coast road between Ballyvaughan and Lisdoonvarna, Gwiazdowski took first place and powered away on his own to come home 28 seconds ahead.
**Stage 3 Clifden - Lisdoonvarna 100 Mls.** 1 G.Gwiazdowski (Team ACBB) 3.44.27 2 R.Eden (Yorkshire Planet X) at 28 secs 3 B.Brentjens (Holland Tegeltoko) s.t. 4 K.Dawson (Great Britain) s.t. 5 I.Gilkes (Great Britain) at 48 secs 6 P.Kil (Holland Tegeltoko) at 52 secs 7 L.Davis (Great Britain) at 56 secs 8 D.Peelo (Dublin Hillebrand) s.t. 9 A.Doyle (Carlow Dan Morrissey) at 58 secs 10 M.L'Hoir (Belgium Giant) s.t.
**General Classification:** 1 P.Kil (Holland Tegeltoko) 10.18.35 2 M.Postle (Wales) s.t. 3 G.Butler (England NE Hardisty) at 6 secs 4 A.Naylor (Stoke Clarke Ambrosia) s.t. 5 A.Roche (Kerry Baltic Trading) s.t. 6 C.Power (Ireland Supermilk) s.t. 7 P.Daly (Ireland Supermilk) at 13 secs 8 K.Dawson (Great Britain) at 53 secs 9 G.Gwiazdowski (Team ACBB) at 1.16 10 I.Gilkes (Great Britain) at 1.36 11 M.Fox (Meath Avonmore) at 1.39 12 D.Rand (Wales) at 1.46
**Points:** 1 G.Gwiazdowski 29 2 P.Kil 24 3 M.Postle, 23
**Mountains:** 1 M.Fox 20 2 P.Daly 11 3 M.Fitzgerald 10
**International Team:** 1 Holland Tegeltoko 30.59.36 2 Ireland Supermilk at 8 secs 3 Great Britain at 1.10
**County Team:** 1 Meath Avonmore 31.02.50 2 Ciarrai Baltic Trading at 5.42
3 Dublin Hillebrand at 5.53

## STAGE 4

Matthew Postle of Wales took over yellow jersey and the list of those in with a chance of potential victory was greatly diminished with only seven riders within two minutes of the leader after the 106 miles stage to Tralee which was won by Mark McKay (Stoke Clarke Ambrosia). He led in a 9-man group which went away on the only climb of the day, a 2nd category at Glenaruddery, taken by Dave Rand (Wales). They broke from a 40-man lead group which formed at the front when three breaks merged after Limerick. Yellow jersey Pelle Kil (Holland Top Team Tegeltoko) was back in the main bunch which finished over 3 minutes behind.

Big shock of the day was the retiral after only 3 miles of Gregor Gwiazdowski, the Pole riding for Team ACBB who won the previous stage in such convincing fashion that he was thought the likely winner. The Polish champion who has signed for trade team Codifis next season developed bronchial problems overnight and was coughing up blood. He decided to start but soon climbed off.

**Stage 4 Lisdoonvarna - Tralee 107 Mls.** 1 Mark McKay (Stoke Clarke Ambrosia) 3.49.41 2 B.Brentjens (Holland Tegeltoko) s.t. 3 C.Power (Ireland Supermilk) s.t. 4 B.Hart (Perth Durham Pine) s.t. 5 M.Postle (Wales) s.t. 6 A.Naylor (Stoke) s.t. 7 G.Butler (England NE Hardisty) s.t. 8 D.Rand (Wales) at 5 secs 9 M.Fitzgerald (Tipperary) at 1.08 10 B.Moore (Ireland Supermilk) s.t.

**General Classification:** 1 M.Postle (Wales) 14.08.16 2 A.Naylor (Stoke) at 6 secs 3 G.Butler (England NE) s.t. 4 C.Power (Ireland Supermilk) s.t. 5 A.Roche (Kerry Baltic Trading) at 1.14 6 P.Daly (Ireland Supermilk) at 1.21 7 D.Rand (Wales) at 1.51 8 K.Dawson (Great Britain) at 2.01 9 B.Brentjens (Holland Tegeltoko) at 2.08 10 I.Gilkes (Great Britain) at 2.44 11 M.Fox (Meath) at 2.47 12 P.Kil (Holland) at 2.58

**Points:** 1 M.Postle 34 2 B.Brentjens 27 3 A.Naylor 24 P.Kil 24

**Mountains:** 1 M.Fox 20 P.Daly 11 3 D.Rand 10 M.Fitzgerald 10

**International Team:** 1 Ireland Supermilk 42.31.03 2 Wales at 1.38 3 Holland Tegeltoko at 1.42

**County Team:** 1 Meath Avonmore 42.40.19 2 Ciarrai at 40 secs 3 Antrim UCF at 6.08

## STAGE 5

For the first day since the FBD RÁS started the leader held on to his yellow jersey but it was touch and go for Matthew Postle (Wales) as at one time during the 85 miles stage from Killarney to Killorglin, round the Ring of Kerry, Postle was 3.20 behind Karl Donnelly (Dublin IRC) who was then leader on the road.

However the bunch, which contained all the top placed riders, worked hard to cut into that lead over the final 30 miles and Donnelly only moved up to 5th overall, now lying 36 seconds behind the Welshman.

Team Tegeltoko, had lost Olympic MTB champion Bart Brentjens overnight when the organization threw him out when they discovered he was committed to riding in the Dutch Mountain Bike Championship on the final Sunday had planned to leave the race after Thursday. However the Dutch were immediately into the action and Jeroem Slagter went away on the first climb of the day with Kerry's John Blackwell (Kerry Baltic Trading) seeking a stage win in his home town.
Slagter led over the first climb at Ladies' View and he was to take maximum points on all four climbs racing to a strong lead in the King of the Mountains competition.
On the climb to the third KOM at Gortadown the two leaders were caught by a group of nine. This was to be the move of the day although two more riders managed to get across, Tuesday's winner Mark McKay (Stoke Clarke Ambrosia) and Karl Donnelly both bridging the gap with solo efforts.
On the descent of the Coomakista pass the break's lead reached its maximum of 3.20, leaving Donnelly leader on the road by 8 seconds. Another group split from the main field and got to within 1.10 of the leaders but then fell back and were lucky not to be absorbed by the main bunch in full flight approaching the finish.
On the hard sprint up the hill in Killorglin, Micheal Fitzgerald (Tipperary Premier), who two weeks ago had a 1st and 2nd in stages of the prestigious Ruban Granitier in France, easily won by a second from McKay with Blackwell having to be satisfied with third before his home crowd.
**Stage 5 Killarney - Killorglin 85 Mls.** 1 M.Fitzgerald (Tipperary Premier) 3.29.38 2 M.McKay (Stoke Clarke Ambrosia) at 1 sec 3 J.Blackwell (Kerry Baltic Trading) at 3 secs 4 L.Davis (Great Britain) s.t. 5 T.Evans (Ireland Supermilk) s.t. 6 D.O'Loughlin (Mayo NCF) s.t. 7 R.Eden (Yorkshire Planet X) s.t. 8 J.Slagter (Team Tegeltoko) s.t. 9 C.Newton (Perth Durham Pine) s.t. 10 S.Bray (Wales) s.t.
**General Classification:** 1 M.Postle (Wales) 17.40.33 2 A.Naylor (Stoke) at 6 secs 3 G.Butler (England NE) s.t. 4 C.Power (Ireland Supermilk) s.t. 5 K.Donnelly (Dublin IRC) at 36 secs 6 A.Roche (Kerry Baltic Trading) at 1.14 7 P.Daly (Ireland Supermilk) at 1.21 8 M.McKay (Stoke Clarke Ambrosia) at 1.42 9 D.Rand (Wales) at 1.51 10 K.Dawson (Great Britain) at 2.01 11 M.Fitzgerald (Tipperary Premier) at 2.09 12 J.Slagter (Team Tegeltoko) at 2.17
**Points:** 1 M.Postle 34 2 M.Fitzgerald 31 3 M.McKay 29
**Mountains:** 1 J.Slagter 57 2 M.Fox 34 3 J.Blackwell 31
**International Team:** 1 Ireland Supermilk 53.05.18 2 Holland Tegeltoko at 1.26 3 Wales at 1.38
**County Team:** 1 Ciarrai Baltic Trading 53.15.14 2 Meath Avonmore at 1.42 3 Tipperary Premier at 3.20

## STAGE 6

For the first time in this year's race an Irish rider was in the leader's yellow jersey when the race left Bandon on the 94 miles to Tramore. Ciaran Power (Ireland Supermilk) took over at the top but only on virtue of points when he finished 8th in a

bunch sprint of 100 riders to put him equal on time with Andy Naylor (Stoke Clarke Ambrosia) and Gethin Butler (England NE Hardisty) but in the lead on count back of placings.
Story of the day was the eclipse of overnight race leader Matthew Postle (Wales) who had looked comfortable in yellow for two stages but was in trouble when the bunch split on the first climb of the day at Ladies View finding himself distanced with about 50 other riders who, try as they might, never got back, giving up the fight after holding the bunch at 30 seconds for miles, eventually losing nearly 18 minutes.
The stage was won by Ian Gilkes of the Great Britain team, who jumped away before the final corner to win by 4 seconds with Tipperary Premier pair Raymond Clarke and Micheal Fitzgerald next. A few miles out it looked like Power might take the jersey on time as he was in a 7-man group which went away on the final climb.
They never had much of a lead as the Stoke Clarke Ambrosia and England NE Hardisty teams led a furious chase. At the 5kms to go board the break still had 15 seconds in hand but were swallowed up soon after. However Power still had enough left to beat his two close rivals in the sprint and take the jersey.
**Stage 6 Killorglin - Bandon 84.5 Mls.** 1 I.Gilkes (Great Britain) 3.21.20 2 R.Clarke (Tipperary Premier) at 4 secs 3 M.Fitzgerald (Tipperary Premier) 4 P.Kil (Holland Tegeltoko) same time 5 B.Fleming (Great Britain) at 6 secs 6 L.McKay (Ireland Supermilk) same time 7 P.West (Great Britain) at 9 secs 8 C.Power (Ireland Supermilk) 9 S.Calvez (France ACBB) 10 K.Bannon (Wicklow Coors) same time
**General Classification:** 1 C.Power (Ireland Supermilk) 21.02.08 2 A.Naylor (Stoke Clarke Ambrosia) 3 G.Butler (England NE Hardisty) all same time 4 K.Donnelly (Dublin IRC) at 30 secs 5 A.Roche (Kerry Baltic Trading) at 1.08 6 P.Daly (Ireland Supermilk) at 1.15 7 M.McKay (Stoke Clarke Ambrosia) at 1.36 8 K.Dawson (Great Britain) at 1.55 9 M.Fitzgerald (Tipperary Premier) at 1.58 10 J.Slagter (Holland Tegeltoko) at 2.11 11 I.Gilkes (Great Britain) at 2.29 12 P.Kil (Holland Tegeltoko) at 2.47
**Points:** 1 M.Fitzgerald 44 2 P.Kil 36 3 M.Postle 34
**Mountains:** 1 J.Slagter 57 2 B.Smith 50 3 R.Clarke 38
**International Team:** 1 Ireland Supermilk 63.09.42 2 Great Britain 63.12.29 3 Stoke Clarke Ambrosia 63.13.21
**County Team:** 1 Kerry Baltic Trading 63.19.41 2 Tipperary Premier 63.22.51 3 Antrim UCF 63.27.27

## STAGE 7

Andy Roche (Kerry Baltic Trading) was the new man in yellow when he finished 7th behind stage winner Stephane Calvez (France ACBB), 1.42 ahead of overnight leader Ciaran Power (Ireland Supermilk). Roche who has lived all his life on the Isle of Man declared for Ireland last season and holds an Irish racing licence. He qualified because his grandparents came from Co. Kerry.

The Ireland Supermilk team sent Peter Daly and '96 winner Tommy Evans away in a 17-man move whose lead reached 3.20 by half distance which left Daly leader on the road by over 1.5 minutes. As the race moved on to the twisting hilly coastal road after Dungarvan this lead melted away as the race erupted into some furious racing with the situation changing by the mile.
On the climb at Dunabrattin Roche crossed to the leading group. The final miles saw a succession of breaks including one by Tommy Evans who was only caught with 3 kilometres to go. Gethin Butler (England NE Hardisty) managed to get away from Power and now lies second 14 seconds down with the Ireland rider equal third on time with Andy Naylor (Stoke) at 34 seconds.
**Stage 7 Bandon - Tramore 95 Mls.** 1 S. Calvez (France ACBB) 4.06.02 2 P.West (GB) at 2 secs 3 L.Davis (GB) s.t. 4 D.Mulroy (England NW Centre) at 7 secs 5 J.Wright (England NE Hardisty) at 9 secs 6 R.Moore (Scotland) s.t. 7 A.Roche (Kerry Baltic Trading) s.t. 8 D.Healy (Dublin Hillebrand) at 11 secs 9 C.Kimmage (Mayo NCF) at 12 secs 10 P.Kil (Holland Tegeltoko) at 12 secs
**General Classification:** 1 A.Roche (Kerry Baltic Trading) 25.09.27 2 G.Butler (England NE Hardisty) at 14 secs 3 C.Power (Ireland Supermilk) at 34 secs 4 A.Naylor (Stoke Clarke Ambrosia) same time 5 M.McKay (Stoke Clarke Ambrosia) at 38 secs 6 K.Donnelly (Dublin IRC) at 1.04 7 I.Gilkes (GB) at 1.31 8 P.Kil (Holland Tegeltoko) at 1.42 9 P.Daly (Ireland Supermilk) at 1.45 10 M.Fitzgerald (Tipperary Premier) at 2.02 11 K.Dawson (Great Britain) at 1.55 12 J.Slagter (Holland Tegeltoko) at 2.41
**Points:** 1 M.Fitzgerald 44 2 P.Kil 42 3 P.West 35
**Mountains:** 1 J.Slagter 57 2 B.Smith 53 3 R.Clarke 38
**International Team:** 1 Great Britain 75.30.58 2 Ireland Supermilk 75.31.48 3 Stoke Clarke Ambrosia 75.34.05
**County Team:** 1 Kerry Baltic Trading 75.41.20 2 Tipperary Premier 75.44.29 3 Dublin Hillebrand 75.49.22

## STAGE 8

Andy Roche was in big trouble on the penultimate stage when he lost contact with the leaders on the climb of Mount Leinster but bravely fought back to regain the leaders with only three miles of the stage to go. Michael Smith (Antrim) won the stage ahead of defending RÁS winner Tommy Evans, having a great run over the closing stages.
Early on 14 riders including Roche, Evans, Smith, Gethin Butler (England NE Hardisty), Kevin Dawson (Great Britain), Matthew Postle and Julian Wynn (Wales) and Brian Smith (Stoke Clarke Ambrosia) went away and had a lead of 2.40.
At the start of the long climb the race blew apart with groups scattered all up the slopes. Roche stayed in contact over the prime at The Height, won by Smith and Corrabut Gap won by Wynn from Smith but between there and the summit the jersey lost contact dropping back to the chasers.

At the bottom of the descent with 25 miles to the finish Roche's challenge looked over as he has now 1.50 down on Butler who was leader on the road. But the Manxman, who had Kerry grandparents and who opted to ride on an Irish licence, showed his mettle and inspired a chase which saw him get back to his main rival in the final miles.
In the sprint it was an Ulster double with Smith edging out Evans from a 4-man group which had a lead of 1.47 over the yellow jersey bunch.
**Stage 8 Tramore - Carlow 95 Mls** 1 M.Smith (Antrim UCF) 3.50.01 2 T.Evans (Ireland Supermilk) s.t. 3 K.Dawson (Great Britain) at 1 sec 4 B.Smith (Stoke Clarke Ambrosia) at 4 secs 5 M.Fitzgerald (Tipperary Premier) at 1.47 6 C.Power (Ireland Super Milk) 7 P.Kil (Holland Tegeltoko) 8 D.Rand (Wales) 9 S.Baker (Dublin IRC) 10 D.Peelo (Dublin Hildebrand) all same time
**General Classification:** 1 A.Roche (Kerry Baltic Trading) 29.01.15 2 G.Butler (England NE Hardisty) at 14 secs 3 K.Dawson (Great Britain) at 20 secs 4 C.Power (Ireland Supermilk) at 34 secs 5 A.Naylor (Stoke Clarke Ambrosia) s.t. 6 M.McKay (Stoke Clarke Ambrosia) at 38 secs 7 K.Donnelly (Dublin IRC) at 1.04 9 I.Gilkes (Great Britain) at 1.31 10 T.Evans (Ireland Supermilk) at 1.37 11 P.Kil (Holland Tegeltoko) at 1.42 11 P.Daly (Ireland Supermilk) at 1.45 12 M.Fitzgerald (Tipperary Premier) at 2.02
**Points:** 1 M.Fitzgerald 55 2 P.Kil 52 3 C.Power 37
**Mountains:** 1 B.Smith 93 2 J.Winn 77 3 J.Slagter 57
**International Team:** 1 Great Britain 87.04.36 2 Ireland Supermilk 87.05.25 3 Stoke Clarke Ambrosia 87.07.46
**County Team:** 1 Dublin Hildebrand 87.24.46 2 Tipperary Premier 87.28.23 3 Kerry Baltic Trading 87.32.22

## STAGE 9 (a) and (b)

Andy Roche, the Manxman with Kerry grandparents, survived an incredible last day challenge from Mark McKay (Stoke Clarke Ambrosia) to win the RÁS by a mere 5 seconds when the event finished in Swords.
McKay a past RÁS yellow jersey who won the King of the Mountains both in the RÁS and the British Milk Race, stormed up the hill at The Butts in the morning's 11.2 miles TT, catching his 2-minute man and winning the stage by 27 seconds. Second was Roche who had been written off by most race followers on Saturday when he wad dropped on Mount Leinster.
But Roche, who declared for Ireland last season and has already ridden on an Irish team, showed great fighting qualities to come back from being 1.50 down with 25 miles to go and save the jersey.
Fancied rider before the TT was Gethin Butler (England NE Hardisty) who was lying second at 14 seconds. However he cracked in the TT and was caught by Roche, dropping out of contention to 9th place.

McKay's TT left him just 11 seconds down and there was a maximum 15 seconds time bonuses to be won in the afternoon criterium in five hot spot sprints. Roche's jersey looked very shaky when McKay romped away to take the first and reduce his deficit to 8 seconds.

In the next sprint McKay was pipped in the sprint but picked up 2 seconds leaving the gap 6 seconds with three sprints left. But in a cruel twist of fate McKay punctured on the next sprint lap and while he was scoreless, Roche took the maximum getting back three precious seconds and had made his victory almost certain.

McKay could still tie the race with two more sprint wins but he only managed a 2nd and 3rd and that was how it finished, with just five seconds separating them after 10 stages and 800 miles of racing. In the bunch sprint to the line, Micheal Fitzgerald (Tipperary Premier) beat teammate Ray Clarke for his second stage of the week, clinching the point's jersey.

**Stage 9a Carlow 11.2 Mls. TT:**
1 M.McKay (Stoke Clarke Ambrosia) 26.34 2 A.Roche (Kerry Baltic Trading) 27.01 3 K.Dawson (Great Britain) 27.08 4 P.Daly (Ireland Supermilk) 27.20 5 L.Davis (Great Britain) 27.23 6 T.Evans (Ireland Supermilk) 27.24

**Stage 9b Swords Criterium:** 1 M.Fitzgerald (Tipperary Premier) 40.57 2 R.Clarke (Tipperary Premier) 3 L.McKay (Ireland Supermilk) 4 T.Evans (Ireland Supermilk) 5 P.West (Great Britain) 6 P.Griffin (France ACBB) 7 S.Calvez (France ACBB) 8 J.Wright (G.B.) 9 M.McKay (Stoke Clarke Ambrosia) 10 T.du Garle (France ACBB) all same time

*Andrew Roche, Winner 1997*

**General Classification:** 1 A.Roche (Kerry Baltic Trading) 30.09.11 2 M.McKay (Stoke Clarke Ambrosia) at 5 secs 3 K.Dawson (Great Britain) at 29 secs 4 C.Power (Ireland Supermilk) at 1.05 5 K.Donnelly (Dublin IRC) at 1.37 6 T.Evans (Ireland Supermilk) at 1.59 7 P.Daly (Ireland Supermilk) at 2.06 8 I.Gilkes (Great Britain) at 2.48 9 G.Butler (England NE Hardisty) at 2.55 10 L.Davis (Great Britain) at 3.12 11 P.Kil (Holland Tegeltoko) at 4.06 12 M.Fitzgerald (Tipperary Premier) at 4.24 13 D.Finnegan (Meath Avonmore) at 4.28 14 R.Eden (Yorkshire Planet X) at 5.19 15 S.Bray (Wales) at 5.28
**Points:** 1 M.Fitzgerald 70 2 M.McKay 56 3 P.Kil 52
**Mountains:** 1 B.Smith (Stoke Clarke Ambrosia) 93 2 J. Winn (Wales) 77 3 J.Slagter (Holland Tegeltoko) 57
**International Team:** 1 Great Britain 90.30.35 2 Ireland Supermilk 90.30.35 3 Stoke Clarke Ambrosia 90.36.28 4 England NE Hardisty 90.52.59 5 Wales 90.54.44 6 Yorkshire Planet X 91.00.49
**County Team:** 1 Dublin Hillebrand 90.55.43 2 Tipperary Premier 91.01.16 3 Kerry Baltic Trading 91.02.35
**Ben McKenna Young Rider competition:** 1 C.Power 2 D.Finnegan 3 P.Healion (Dublin IRC)
164 riders started, 124 finished.
Total Distance: 1255.7 kms ( 780.9 miles). Speed: 41.8 kph (26.0 mph)

# 1998

There was another big entry for the 1998 RÁS and with the usual last minute dropouts 151 riders started off on the opening stage which for the first time since 1957 ended back in the capital, the 67.5 miles stage consisting of a loop out through Meath before finishing back in the Phoenix Park.
'97 winner Andy Roche was absent from the line-up opting to ride on the Irish team in the inaugural Pru-Tour, a 9-day event in Britain whose opening weekend-overlapped the end of the RÁS.
This new event was mainly professional (the UCI had abolished the distinction between professional and amateur but the term professional was still generally applied to elite riders who were on full-time trade teams) but included the top British amateur squads, a factor which probably robbed the RÁS of some contenders for overall victory. No British Cycling Federation team was invited because the Federation would have its top riders in the home event. Nevertheless seven English teams were entered for the RÁS.
Also in the line-up were teams from Belgium, Germany, Japan, Netherlands, South Africa, France, Estonia and

## STAGE 1

Within ten miles of the racing start at Finglas a group of 13 went away and by the first hot-spot sprint at Slane they had a lead of 55 seconds. Sigvard Kukk (Estonia) took the five seconds bonus at the hot-spot and sprinting strongly went on to take the other two bonus sprints at Navan and Knockmaroon.
Entering the Phoenix Park the group had over 2 minutes lead over the bunch but the leaders split on the 3-miles lap, 5 riders opening up a 34 seconds gap by the finish where Kukk won the stage from David O'Loughlin (Mayo) , Kosie Loubser (South Africa), Tommy Evans and Ciaran Power (both Ireland).
Another Estonian Alges Massikmets led in the rest of the original group ahead of Mel Sutcliffe (Dublin Usher Insulation). A crash in the finishing straight brought down several riders including Irish champion Morgan Fox riding for his Belgian club team.
With no stage time bonuses the  hot-spot sprints gave Kukk at 12 second lead over '96 winner Tommy Evans with O'Loughlin a further 2 seconds back. Loubser and Power were a further 15 seconds in arrears but there was then a 41 second gap to 6th placed Neil McDonald (South Africa).
**Stage 1 Dublin - Dublin 67.5m.** 1 S.Kukk (Estonia) 2.17.38 2 D.O'Loughlin (Mayo) 3 K.Loubser (South Africa) 4 T.Evans (Ireland) 5 C.Power (Ireland) all same time 6 A.Massikmets (Estonia) at 34 secs 7 M.Sutcliffe (Dublin Usher Insulation) 8

F.Zwanveld (Netherlands) 9 U.Hardier (Germany) 10 Y.Ando (Japan Cycleways) 11 D.Booth (South Africa) 12 N. McDonald (South Africa) 13 P.Cassidy (Meath Avonmore) all same time

**General Classification:** 1 S.Kukk 2.17.23 2 T.Evans at 12 secs 3 D.O'Loughlin at 14 secs 4 K.Loubser at 15 secs 5 C.Power at 15 secs 6 N.McDonald at 41 secs 7 D.Booth at 42 secs 8 A.Massikmets at 46 secs 9 F.Zwanveld 10 Y.Ando, all same time 11 P.Cassidy (Meath Avonmore) at 47 secs 12 M.Sutcliffe (Dublin Usher) at 49 secs

**Points:** 1 S.Kukk 15 2 D.O'Loughlin 14 3 K.Loubser 13

**International Team:** 1 South Africa 6.54.02 2 Ireland 6.55.46 3 Estonia 6.56.20

**County Team:** 1 Mayo 6.58.38 2 Dublin Usher Insul 6.59.12 3 Meath Avonmore s.t.

## STAGE 2

The visiting riders again took the honours on the 92 miles from Mullingar to Tubercurry with Britain's Jeff Wright (Bentek Drilling) taking the stage while South Africa's Kosie Loubser took over the race lead.

Race leader Sigvard Kukk (Estonia) finished in the main bunch, 59 seconds down and dropped to 4th at 44 seconds Tommy Evans (Ireland) a place further back at 56 seconds.

The bunch stayed together for the first 40 miles before 13 riders went away, including Phil Cassidy (Meath Avonmore) and Yasuhiro Ando (Japan) both of whom had been in the break on Saturday. When their lead went to over 1.40 at Boyle the alarm bells rang and a hard chase by the bunch saw them reeled in on the descent of the Curlew Mountains.

This was the signal for another attack by David O'Loughlin (Mayo), Wright, Loubser, Uwe Hardier (Germany) and the four went 1 minute clear leaving O'Loughlin leader on the road. However the Mayo rider cramped on the run-in falling back to a chasing group but his efforts moved him up to second.

On the run-in two groups broke away in pursuit of the leaders, the first getting to within 9 seconds at the finish where Wright won the closest of sprints from Loubser in a high-speed downhill finish.

**Stage 2 Mullingar - Tubercurry 92 Mls.** 1 J.Wright ((UK Bentec Drilling) 3.12.54 2 K.Loubser (South Africa) s.t. 3 U.Hardier (Germany) at 2 secs 4 W.Moore (Meath Avonmore) at 9 secs 5 J.Slagter (Netherlands) 6 D.Williams (UK Bentec) 7 B.Kenneally (Ireland) all same time 8 W.Veenstra (Netherlands) at 28 secs 9 W.Randle (Manchester) 10 H.Szonn (Germany) all same time

**General Classification:** 1 K.Loubser 5.30.32 2 D.O'Loughlin at 31 secs 3 U.Hardier at 36 secs 4 S.Kukk at 44 secs 5 T.Evans at 56 secs 6 C.Power at 59 secs 7 N.McDonald (South Africa) 1.25 8 D.Booth (South Africa) at 1.26 9 A.Maasikmets at 1.30 10 F.Zwaneveld (Netherlands) s.t. 11 Y.Ando (Japan) s.t. 12 P.Cassidy (Meath Avonmore) at 1.31

**Points:** 1 K.Loubser 27 2 U.Hardier 20 3 D.O'Loughlin 16

**Mountains:** 1 J.Fullard (South Africa) 5 2 P.Cassidy 4 3 Y.Ando 3
**International Team:** 1 South Africa 16.32.42 2 Ireland at 1.53 3 Estonia at 3.17 4 Germany at 4.41 5 Netherlands at 4.48 6 UK Bentec Drilling at 6.07
**County Team:** 1, Mayo 16.39.50; 2, Meath Avonmore at 11 secs; 3, Dublin Usher Insul. at 1.01.

## STAGE 3

Kousie Loubser (South Africa) retained the yellow jersey when he finished the 106 miles stage to Westport in the chasing group, 1.21 down on winner Dave Willisma (UK Bentec Drilling).
The visiting riders continue their domination and there was not one Irish rider in the 8-man winning break. Tommy Evans in 6th place, 56 down was unlucky not to improve as it was he who initiated the winning break 12 miles after the start in Tubercurry. However a puncture put him back to the chasing group.
A feature was the race's first visit to Achill Island where they had three tough climbs. The eight leaders stayed together over them, the King of the Mountains primes going to Jerome Slagter (Netherlands), Stephane Rifflet (France) and Wayne Randle (Manchester). However the most consistent climber was Yashuhiro Ando (Japan) who took the lead in the mountains classification.
On the run-in to the finish Randle kept attacking but was always countered. A crash in the last kilometre saw the group finish all in separate times but the last kilometre rule meant most of them got the same time. Dave Williams was first up the hill into Westport to give the UK Bentec Drilling team their second stage in a row.
**Stage 3 Tubercurry - Westport 107 Mls.** 1 D.Williams (UK Bentec Drilling) 4.01.02 2 J.Slagter (Netherlands) at 2 secs 3 C.Roshier (Surrey Racing League) 4 S.Rifflet (France) 5 Y.Ando (Japan) 6 W.Randle (Manchester) 7 F.Shiogami (Japan) 8 D.Haueisen (Germany) at 46 secs 9 S.Kukk (Estonia) 10 T.Evans (Ireland)
**General Classification:** 1 K.Loubser (South Africa) 9.32.55 2 Y.Ando (Japan) at 11 secs 3 D.O'Loughlin (Mayo) at 31 secs 4 U.Hardier (Germany) at 36 secs 5 S.Kukk at 44 secs 6 T.Evans at 56 secs 7 C.Power (Ireland) at 59 secs 8 D.Booth (South Africa) at 1.26 9 F.Zwaneveld (Netherlands) at 1.30 10 P.Cassidy (Meath Avonmore) at 1.31 11 M.Sutcliffe (Dublin Usher) at 1.33 12 D.Williams (UK Bentec) at 1.40
**Points:** 1 K.Loubser 27 2 D.Williams 25 3 J.Slagter 25
**Mountains:** 1 Y.Ando 27 2 S.Rifflet 25 3 W.Randle 24
**International Team:** 1 South Africa 28.41.51 2 Ireland at 1.53 3 Estonia at 3.17 4 Germany at 3.22 5 Netherlands at 3.29 6 Japan at 3.31
**County Team:** 1 Mayo 28.46.59 2 Meath Avonmore at 11 secs 3 Dublin Usher Insul. at 1.01

## STAGE 4

There was no change in the top six overall on the stage from Westport to Kilrush, at 116 miles the longest of the race. Peter Lernout (Belgium Jonge) won the stage in a 2-up sprint from Stephane Rifflet (France) but Kosie Loubser (South Africa) came in with the main group 49 seconds behind the winner to keep the lead.
Although Tommy Evans and Ciaran Power of the Ireland team remained in 5th and 6th position respectively within a minute of the leader, the Irish riders were noticeable by their absence from the winning moves and the important break of the day which had 15 riders but included only three Irish, none on the national team.
One of the three was Irish champion Morgan Fox showing for the first time since his stage one crash. His Belgian team made a big effort and had three in the break including the winner.
The rider who stood to gain most if the break had held its maximum 2 minute advantage was previous stage winner Dave Williams who would have taken over the jersey but the lead was greatly reduced by the chasers over the final miles.
On the run-in the leading group started to split as first three riders Lernout, Rifflet and Colin Roshier (Surrey) got away chased by lone German Heiko Szonn and then another six, including Randle, who finished 21 seconds behind with the rest at 35 just 28 seconds ahead of the fast closing bunch.
**Stage 4 Westport - Kilrush 116 Mls.** 1 P.Lernout (Belgium) 4.19.14 2 S.Rifflet (France) 3 C.Roshier (Surrey) at 2 secs 4 H.Szonn (Germany) at 9 secs 5 J.Fullard (South Africa) at 21 secs 6 M.Fox (Belgium) 7 W.Veenstra (Netherlands) 8 D.Williams (UK Bentec Drilling) 9 R.Hobby (Lincoln) 10 J.Wright (UK Bentec Drilling) all same time
**General Classification:** 1 K.Loubser (South Africa) 13.52.58 2 Y.Ando (Japan) at 11 secs 3 D.O'Loughlin (Mayo) at 31 secs 4 U.Hardier (Germany) at 36 secs 5 S.Kukk (Estonia) at 44 secs 6 T.Evans (Ireland) at 56 secs 7 C.Power (Ireland) at 59 secs 8 S.Rifflet (France) at 1.12 9 D.Williams (UK Bentec Drilling) s.t. 10 D.Booth (South Africa) at 1.26 11 F.Zwaneveld (Netherlands) at 1.30 12 P.Cassidy (Meath Avonmore) at 1.31
**Points:** 1 D.Williams 33 2 S.Rifflet 31 3 K.Loubser 27
**Mountains:** 1 Y.Ando 27 2 S.Rifflet 25 3 W.Randle 24
**International Team:** 1 South Africa 41.41.32 2 Ireland at 2.21 3 Netherlands at 3.29 4 Estonia at 3.45 5 Germany at 3.55 6 Japan at 3.59
**County Team:** 1 Mayo 41.47.01 2 Meath Avonmore at 11 secs 3 Dublin Usher Insul at 1.01

## STAGE 5

Tommy Evans was the toast of the Irish when the diminutive Banbridge rider winner in '96, led a three-man break into Castletownbeare to take the stage and move to

second place overall only 12 seconds behind new leader Sigvard Kukk, winner of the opening stage.
The Estonian and Irish national teams had looked the strongest on that opening stage but both had played a cagey game taking no part in most of the breaks on the three intervening stages. However with six mountain primes the time for bluffing was over and it was Ireland and Estonia who ended the stage the big winners while South Africa, Japan and Belgium, who had been making the running since Sunday lost out.
On the first major climb to Ladies View, out of Killarney it was Evans who went away taking with him Kukk and Wayne Randle (Manchester) the ex-professional who had daily been getting closer to the lead.
Randle took the KOM Prime and went on to take the four remaining primes to build up a substantial lead in the mountains classification, 28 points ahead of Evans. Their lead fluctuated between 1 and 2 minutes for most of the day while behind a 9-man group went in pursuit, this group including another Ireland rider Ciaran Power.
The leading three flew down the serpentine bends of the Healy Pass to stretch their lead which was 1.30 with 10 kms. to go. In the chasing group Eugene Moriarty (Kerry) crashed and broke his wrist, but the remaining eight cut into the lead on the run-in with the gap down to 42 seconds at the line. The third group on the road had several riders go over the edge on the descent of the Healy, one of them Shane Connaughton being taken to hospital. This group finished at 3.18 so the number left in the race with a realistic chance overall was down to less than a dozen.
At the finish Evans went for a long sprint opening up a sufficient gap to be able to sit up and acknowledge the cheers of the crowd as he crossed the line.
**Stage 5 Listowel - Castletownbeare 91 Mls.** 1 T.Evans (Ireland) 3.31.57 2 S.Kukk (Estonia) 3 W.Randle (Manchester) all same time 4 I.Mandoja (Estonia) at 42 secs 5 P. Griffin (Carlow) 6 D.Finnegan (Meath) 7 M.Lovatt (UK Bentec Drilling) 8 H.Szonn (Germany) 9 A.Kakinuma (Japan) 10 C.Power (Ireland)
**General Classification:** 1 S.Kukk (Estonia) 17.25.39 2 T.Evans (Ireland) at 12 secs 3 C.Power (Ireland) at 57 secs 4 S.Rifflet (France) at 1.10 5 W.Randle (Manchester) at 1.17 6 H.Szonn (Germany) at 3.46 7 D.Williams (UK Bentec Drilling) s.t. 8 D.Finnegan (Meath) at 3.49 9 A.Kakinuma (Japan) s.t. 10 P.Griffin (Carlow) s.t. 11 M.Lovatt (UK Bentec Drilling) s.t. 12 K.Loubser (South Africa) at 4.02
**Points:** 1 D.Williams 37 2 S.Kukk 36 3 S.Rifflet 36
**Mountains:** 1 W.Randle 84 2 T.Evans 46 3 S.Kukk, 41
**International Team:** 1 Ireland 52.23.44 2 Estonia at 1.24 3 UK Bentec Drilling at 5.15 4 France at 7.13 5 Germany at 7.48 6 Japan at 7.52
**County Team:** 1 Meath Avonmore 5.37.50 2 Carlow Dan Morrissey at 41 secs 3 Mayo at 3.53

## STAGE 6

There were no changes at the top after the 96 mile stage to Mallow and Kukk kept his yellow jersey.

With the top men busy marking each other, there was an opportunity for the Irish County riders to make their mark and it was from this group that the stage winner came, Paul Griffin (Carlow Morrissey) out sprinting two previous stage winners Jeff Wright and Wayne Randle, both of the UK Bentek Drilling squad who, like Carlow, had three riders in the 15-man break.
As a result UK Bentek took over the lead in the international team classification from Ireland while Carlow did likewise in the county team listings. Another feature of the day was retirals several due to injury including Irish champion Morgan Fox and previous yellow jersey Kosie Loubser (South Africa). In a crash near the finish, two riders both broke legs, Bester (South Africa) and Szonn (Germany). The field was reduced to 136 with three stages remaining.
The break of the day went away on the Pass of Keimenagh, the third climb of the day and they soon had a lead of 2 minutes. Dave Williams made a great effort to get across to the leaders and when the lead then went to over 3 minutes, he was a danger to the leaders and the resulting chase saw the lead cut back by the finish. However Williams moved up to 6th and stage-winner Griffin to 7th and there are now 9 riders within 3 minutes of Kukk.
The winning move came as the leaders passed the 5k. to go sign Griffin and the two UK Bentec riders going clear. It looked odds on another English win as both were good sprinters with stage wins to their credit, Wright having won five. However Griffin, who won the Irish Classic League in '96, was a clear winner, as the three crossed the line, 7 seconds ahead of Michael O'Donnell (Wicklow Coors).
The bunch containing all the top riders on GC came home 2.08 behind Griffin.
**Stage 6 Castletownbeare - Mallow 95 Mls.** 1 P.Griffin (Carlow Morrissey) 3.40.34 2 J.Wright (UK Bentec Drilling) 3 D.Williams (UK Bentec Drilling) all same time 4 M.O'Donnell (Wicklow Coors) at 7 secs 5 M.Lovatt (UK Bentec Drilling) at 9 secs 6 G.Dodd (Surrey Racing League) 7 P.Moriarty (Kerry Irish Baltic) 8 M.Kiernan (Carlow Morrissey) 9 J.Onesime (France) 10 P.Cassidy (Meath Avonmore) all same time
**General Classification:** 1 S.Kukk (Estonia) 21.08.21 2 T.Evans (Ireland) at 12 secs 3 C.Power (Ireland) at 57 secs 4 S.Rifflet (France) at 1.10 5 W.Randle (Manchester) at 1.17 6 D.Williams (UK Bentec Drilling) at 1.38 7 P.Griffin (Carlow Morrissey) at 1.41 8 M.Lovatt (UK Bentec Drilling) at 1.50 9 U.Hardier (Germany) at 2.39 10 J.Wright (UK Bentec Drilling) at 2.39 11 D.Finnegan (Meath Avonmore) at 3.49 12 A.Kakinuma (Japan) at 3.49
**Points:** 1 D.Williams 50 2 S.Kukk 36 3 J.Wright 36 4 S.Rifflet 36
**Mountains:** 1 W.Randle 84 2 T.Evans 46 3 S.Kukk, 41
**International Team:** 1 UK Bentec Drilling 63.30.50 2 Ireland at 1.00 3 Estonia at 2.24 4 Germany at 4.50 5 France at 6.14 6 Japan at 8.52
**County Team:** 1 Carlow Dan Morrissey 63.41.03 2 Meath Avonmore at **2**.54 3 Mayo at 8.46

## STAGE 7

Sigvard Kukk (Estonia) hung onto his lead over Evans but his position became even more precarious as Ciaran Power (Ireland) was now only 17 seconds behind and 4th place Stephane Rifflet (France) is at 27 secs.
With Evans second at 12 secs. Ireland played their ace in the hole on the 96.5 miles stage to New Ross sending third placed Power away in an early break along with David Hourigan (Limerick) and Rifflet, putting the pressure on the Estonians to do all the chasing.
The plan seemed to have worked when the break's lead went to over three minutes on the climb at the Pike, after Dungarvan. A 15-strong break then broke away in pursuit but the leader, closely marked by Evans, was still back in the main field.
It was on the final 12 miles from Waterford that Kukk showed his mettle, powering a third chasing group which cut into this deficit. By the finish his group had got to within 49 seconds of the stage winner and with Power, tiring after his efforts losing valuable seconds in the final mile, he lost out on taking over at the top by 17 seconds.
The second group on the road also closed on the three leaders over the final mile and when the gap closed to less than 30 seconds, Michael Fitzgerald (Dublin Usher Insulation) and Jeroen Slagter (Netherlands) jumped across to the leaders.
Fitzgerald, who was Irish champion in '96, waited for a few minutes to get his breath back and attacked, opening up a slight lead on the one-mile loop round the town and he crossed the line 6 seconds ahead of Hourigan, Slagter and Rifflet, with Power a further 3 seconds down. Richard Hobby (Lincoln) led in the rest of the chasers 18 seconds behind the winner.
**Stage 7 Mallow - New Ross 96.5 Mls.** 1 M.Fitzgerald (Dublin Usher Insulation) 3.49.12 2 D.Hourigan (Limerick) at 6 secs 3 J.Slagter (Netherlands) 4 S.Rifflet (France) all same time 5 C.Power (Ireland) at 9 secs 6 R.Hobby (Lincoln) at 18 secs 7 C.Farrell (Meath) 8 D.O'Loughlin (Mayo) 9 K.de Valkeneer (Belgium) 10 M.Lovatt (UK Bentec Drilling) all same time
**General Classification:** 1 S.Kukk (Estonia) 24.58.22 2 T.Evans (Ireland) at 12 secs 3 C.Power (Ireland) at 17 secs 4 S.Rifflet (France) at 27 secs 5 W.Randle (Manchester) at 46 secs 6 M.Lovatt (UK Bentec Drilling) at 1.19 7 D.Williams (UK Bentec Drilling) at 1.38 8 P.Griffin (Carlow) at 1.53 9 J.Wright (UK Bentec) at 2.50 10 U.Hardier (Germany) at 2.51 11 R.Hobby (Lincoln) at 3.27 12 J.Slagter (Netherlands) at 3.33
**Points:** 1 D.Williams 50 2 S.Rifflet 48 3 J.Slagter 41
**Mountains:** 1 W.Randle 84 2 S.Rifflet 49 3 T.Evans 46
**International Team:** 1 UK Bentec Drilling 75.49.51 2 Ireland at 51 secs 3 Estonia at 3.38
**County Team:** 1 Carlow Morrissey 75.11.30 2 Meath Avonmore at 2.11 3 Mayo at 8.15

## STAGE 8

Ireland team manager Ritchie Beattie tried again the move that almost succeeded on Friday and this time it worked.
Third placed Ciaran Power went away early with a 7-man group before the first of the day's four climbs and by the foot of the 1st category climb at Drumgoff the six had a lead of over 3 minutes with Power clearly leader on the road.
Evans, second for most of the week, sacrificed his chance of a second RÁS win in the interests of the team when he marked leader Kukk who tried in vain to bring back the leaders.
When the Estonian finally cracked on the climb at Drumgoff Evans gamely tried to get up to the Power group but although he gained 2.10 over the last 30 miles, he was still 50 seconds behind at the finish in Ballymore Eustace and he had to settle for second, 45 seconds behind his teammate.
Jeff Wright (UK Bentec Drilling) attacked from the leading group in the final kilometre and came home for his second stage win (his fifth RÁS win in all). Michael Smith (Mayo), winner on the final Saturday the previous year, won the second place sprint, 6 secs behind.
**Stage 8 New Ross - Ballymore Eustace 93 Mls.** 1 J.Wright (UK Bentec Drilling) 3.47.54 2 M.Smith (Mayo) at 6 secs 3 J.Desjardins (France) 4 D.Finnegan (Meath Avonmore) 5 C.Power (Ireland), all same time 6 W.Randle (Manchester) at 56 secs 7 S.Rifflet (France) 8 T.Evans (Ireland) 9 P.Moriarty (Kerry Irish Baltic) 10 D.Booth (South Africa) all same time
**General Classification:** 1 C.Power (Ireland) 28.46.39 2 T.Evans (Ireland) at 45 secs 3 S.Rifflet (France) at 1.00 4 W.Randle (Manchester) at 1.19 5 J.Wright (UK Bentec Drilling) at 2.27 6 S.Kukk (Estonia) at 2.45 7 P.Griffin (Carlow Morrissey) at 3.21 8 D.Finnegan (Meath Avonmore) at 3.32 9 R.Hobby (Lincoln) at 4.00 10 J.Slagter (Netherlands) at 4.14 11 D.Williams (UK Bentec Drilling) at 4.32 12 Y.Ando (Japan) at 4.37
**Points:** 1 S.Rifflet 57 2 J.Wright 51 3 D.Williams 50
**Mountains:** 1 W.Randle 84 2 J.Wright 57 3 S.Rifflet 49
**International Team:** 1 Ireland 86.26.22 2 UK Bentec Drilling at 4.58 3 France at 9.37
**County Team:** 1 Meath Avonmore 86.45.36 2 Carlow Morrissey at 45 secs 3 Mayo at 12.20

## STAGE 9

Michael Fitzgerald (Dublin Usher Insulation), winner into New Ross on Friday and who won the last stage in a bunch sprint in '97, did it again, out sprinting 118 riders in a spectacular charge down O'Connell Street.

With almost all the 133 riders finishing on the same time, there was no change on general classification so Ciaran Power (Ireland) held on to the yellow jersey with his teammate Tommy Evans second at 45 seconds.
For the new Irish National Team Director Ritchie Beattie it was a triumph in his first big race as manager. He refused to be pressured into a premature attack on the jersey early in the week when the visiting teams seemed to be winning everything, waiting until the first big mountain stage on Wednesday to launch the attacks which put Evans within 12 seconds of the lead with Power third, giving him two cards to play which he did perfectly.
A record 133 riders started the final stage, 25 laps in the centre of Dublin. Despite the high speed only a handful were dropped. In the final third of the race Power went away in a break which held a slender lead for a couple of laps and when they were caught, Evans went with a similar move but they were all together again in time for the mass sprint where Fitzgerald squeezed past two Dutch riders just on the line.
Ireland won the international team from UK Bentec and France. Meath took the county team Stephane Rifflet (France) the points classification and Manchester's Wayne Randle the mountains. The total race distance was 1260 kilometres with the winner's average speed 26.45 mph.
**Stage 9 Dublin Criterium 28 Mls.** 1 M.Fitzgerald (Dublin Usher Insulation) 58.10 2 H.Fledderus (Netherlands) 3 W.Veenstra (Netherlands) 4 S.Kukk (Estonia) 5 C.Farrell (Meath) 6 S.Whelan (Dublin McNally) 7 P.Griffin (Carlow Morrissey) 8 J.Fullard (South Africa) 9 G.Adamson (UK Bentec Drilling) 10 P.Lernout (Belgium) all same time **General Classification:** 1 C.Power (Ireland) 29.44.49 2 T.Evans (Ireland) at 45 secs 3 S.Rifflet (France) at 1.00 4 W.Randle (Manchester) at 1.19 5 J.Wright (UK Bentec Drilling) at 2.27 6 S.Kukk (Estonia) at 2.45 7 P.Griffin (Carlow Morrissey) at 3.21 8 D.Finnegan (Meath Avonmore) at 3.32 9 R.Hobby (Lincoln) at 4.00 10 J.Slagter (Netherlands) at 4.14 11 D.Williams (UK Bentec) at 4.23 12 Y.Ando (Japan) at 4.37 13 P.Moriarty (Kerry Irish Baltic) at 5.11 14 M.Lovatt (UK Bentec Drilling) at 5.35 15 U.Hardier (Germany) at 5.36
**Points:** 1 S.Rifflett 61 2 J.Wright 51 3 D.Williams 50
**Mountains:** 1 W.Randle 84 2 J.Wright 57 3 S.Rifflet 49
**International Team:** 1 Ireland 89.20.52 2 UK Bentec Drilling at 4.58 3 France at 9.37 4 Netherlands at 13.58 5 Germany at 14.22 6 Japan at 16.03.
**County Team:** 1 Meath Avonmore 89.40.06 2 Carlow Morrissey at 45 secs 3 Mayo at 12.50

*Ciaran Power, Winner 1998*

# 1999

One hundred and forty-one of the 165 entries lined up for the '99 event with visiting teams from Estonia, France, Netherlands, USA/Europe composite, Belgium, Wales and first time visitors Egypt.
Once again there was a strong British presence headed by the professional Linda McCartney Foods, a big team with continental ambitions who had split their riders between the RÁS and the British week-long Pru-Tour which again clashed with the RÁS, starting the day the Irish event finished.
Missing from the RÁS was '98 winner Ciaran Power who was on the Irish team for the Pru-Tour along with past RÁS multi-stage winner Michael Fitzgerald. Past winner Tommy Evans was listed on the Ireland team (sponsored by Clarke Contracts with whom he had won in '96) but he dropped out following a crash in the Lincoln Grand Prix. His place was taken by '83 winner Phil Cassidy, currently enjoying excellent form.
The Irish team had also lost Aidan Duff who crashed out of the Tour of Ulster, two weeks previous and with the riders absent in the Pru Tour, the Irish team, who had won five of the last 10 events, was generally thought to be a weak one.

## STAGE 1

Two of the strongest teams in the race made their mark on the opening stage. The Netherlands Prowinn squad won the stage with Pelle Kil, a yellow jersey in '97 while the McCartney's took the jersey with Ben Brooks who had picked up 10 seconds in time-bonuses during the 95 miles run from Dublin to Waterford.
The first of these hot-spots was a Naas where the field was all together when Brooks took maximum points from Colm Bracken (Dublin IRC Usher). A fourth at Kilcullen and third at Borris was enough to give him the jersey.
A group of twelve went clear at Timolin after 30 miles and they were joined by another 11 riders at Bagnelstown 55 miles. This group stayed away but split on the run-in to the finish when Kil, Dermot Finnegan (Meath Avonmore), Brian Kenneally (Wicklow Anglo Irish Bank) and Colby Pearce (USA/Europe) went away.
In the final kilometre Kil attacked holding on to win by 2 seconds from Pearce with Finnegan third and Kenneally fourth in the same time.
**Stage 1 Dublin - Waterford 99 Mls.** 1 P.Kil (Netherlands Prowin) 3.19.21 2 C.Pearce (USA/Europe) at 2 secs 3 D.Finnegan (Meath Avonmore) 4 B.Kenneally (Wicklow.Ang. Ir. Bank) 5 J.Griffiths (Wales) 6 M.Lovatt (Cheshire Peugeot) 7 S.O'Sullivan (Wicklow) 8 B.Brooks (Linda McCartney Foods) 9 E.Putsep (Estonia) 10 P.Cassidy (Ireland Clarke Contracts) all same time

**General Classification:** 1 B.Brooks (Linda McCartney) 3.19.13 2 E.Moriarty (Ireland Clarke Contracts) at 5 secs 3 S.O'Sullivan (Wicklow) at 6 secs 4 P.Kil (Netherlands) at 8 secs 5 C.Pearce (USA/Europe) s.t. 6 E.Putsep (Estonia) at 8 secs 7 D.Finnegan (Meath Avonmore) at 10 secs 8 B.Kenneally (Wicklow) 9 J.Griffiths (Wales) 10 M.Lovatt (Cheshire Peugeot) 11 P.Cassidy (Ireland) 12 J.Clarke (Linda Mc Cartney) all same time
**Mountains:** 1 E.Moriarty (Ireland) 12 2 S.O'Sullivan 12 3 P.Kil 9
**Points:** 1 P.Kil 15 2 C.Pearce 14 3 D.Finnegan 13
**Team:** 1 Netherlands 9.58.07 2 Linda McCartney at 2 secs 3 Ireland at 2 secs

## STAGE 2

Jon Clay (Linda McCartney) took over the yellow jersey from teammate Brooks after winning the 104m. stage from Waterford to Charleville in a 2-up sprint from Brian Kenneally (Wicklow) and to lead him on overall by the same margin with Dermot Finnegan (Meath Avonmore) who was third in the stage holding the same place on GC at 15 secs.
However behind them the race had been blown apart by constant attacking and the main group which contained over 80 of the remaining 139 riders, including the yellow jersey, finished over 17 minutes down and are now out of the running for overall honours.
A big break of 25 riders went away early and this was chased by several smaller group who all came together and then caught the leaders at the start of the 1st cat. climb of The Vee, but on the long climb this big front group lost 17 riders and there were 22 who came over the top where Jeff Wright took maximum points to take the lead in the mountains classification.
The split which came on the descent to Lismore saw 9 riders go away in the vital break of the day. They pushed up their lead to over 1 minute at the 16 kms to go sign and shortly afterwards Kenneally and Clay made their move. Kenneally only had to hold the professional to take overall lead but Clay was too strong, opening a 2 second gap in the sprint.
**Stage 2 Waterford - Charleville 104 Mls.** 1 J.Clay (Linda McCartney) 4.02.44 2 B.Kenneally (Wicklow) at 2 secs 3 D.Finnegan at 15 secs 4 R.Downing (Linda McCartney) at 23 5 J.Wright (Cheshire Peugeot) 7 E.Putsep (Estonia) 8 R.Reynolds-Jones (Linda McCartney) all same time 9 E.Moriarty at 30 secs 10 R.Hobby (Lincoln) at 1.53
**General Classification:** 1 J.Clay (Linda McCartney) 4.02.44 2 B.Kenneally (Wicklow) at 2 secs 3 D.Finnegan (Meath) at 15 secs 4 C.Pearce (USA/Europe) at 21 secs 5 E.Putsep (Estonia) at 22 secs 6 E.Moriarty (Ireland Clarke Contracts) at 25 secs 7 P.Cassidy (Ireland Clarke Contracts) at 1.53 8 R.Downing (Linda McCartney) at 3.35 9 J.Wright (Cheshire Peugeot) s.t. 10 R.Reynolds-Jones (Linda McCartney) at 4.23 11 D.Commault (France) at 4.39 12 D.McCann (Armagh Planet X) at 5.00
**Points:** 1 B.Kenneally 26 2 D.Finnegan 26 3 C.Pearce 23

**Mountains:** 1 J.Wright 18 2 D.Finnegan 18 3 E.Moriarty (Ireland) 17
**International Team:** Linda McCartney 22.07.07 2 Ireland at 10.48 3 USA/Europe at 18.41
**County Team:** 1 Wicklow 22.17.49 2 Armagh at 11.53 3 Meath Avonmore at 12.32

## STAGE 3

It was a Dutch clean sweep on the 87 miles stage to Killaloe as Harm Jansen led his Netherlands Prowin team-mates Pelle Kil and Erik Dagelet up the hill to the ancient capital of Ireland at Brian Brou's old palace at Kincora, 30 seconds ahead of Belfast David McCann (Armagh Planet X).
There were however, no changes in the general classification as some 120 riders arrived in a large group, 59 seconds behind the winner with only Jeff Wright and David McCann of the top 12 showing any improvement.
It was a case of locking the stable door as far as the bunch was concerned. After letting the big break go on Sunday to finish over 17 minutes ahead, they would let nothing go yesterday and countless attacks never managed to get a working lead before being hauled back.
Adrian Hedderman (Carlow Dan Morrisey) took the first prime in Tipperary Town after 36 miles and Patrick Marrey (Kildare Hire Equipment) the next at Borrisoleigh 56 miles but most of the 139 riders left in the race were together as they tackled the two KOM climbs in the last 12 miles.
Bill Moore (Meath Avonmore) led over the first, a 3rd category at Newtown, from Sayed Masry (Egypt) with the Dutchmen Dagelet and Kil next moving into position for their assault. Two miles further on they went over the 2nd category at Portroe where Dagelet led from Masry, Moore with Kil and Jansen next.
With three up with the leaders Saturday's stage winner Kil attacked on the descent and when he had opened a gap his team-mates jumped across to him and the three of them rode a superb team-time-trial over the remaining 5 miles to open a 30 second gap by the finish.
**Stage 3 Charleville - Killaloe 87 Mls.** 1 H.Jansen (Netherlands Prowin) 3.30.33 2 P.Kil (Netherlands) 3 E.Dagelet (Netherlands) same time 4 D.McCann (Armagh Planet X) at 40 secs 5 M.Lovatt (Cheshire Peugeot) 6 P.Griffin (Carlow) 7 S.Steiner (USA/Europe) 8 B.Moore (Meath) same time 9 J.Wright (Cheshire) at 48 secs 10 S.Masry (Egypt) at 52 secs
**General Classification:** 1 J.Clay (Linda McCartney) 10.53.39 2 B.Kenneally (Wicklow) at 2 secs 3 D.Finnegan (Meath) at 15 secs 4 C.Pearce (USA/Europe) at 21 secs 5 E.Putsep (Estonia) at 22 secs 6 E.Moriarty (Ireland) at 25 secs 7 P.Cassidy (Ireland) at 1.53 8 J.Wright (Cheshire) at 3.24 9 R.Downing (Linda McCartney) at 3.35 10 R.Reynolds-Jones (Linda McCartney) at 4.23 11 D.Commault (France) at 4.39 12 D.McCann (Armagh) at 4.41
**Points:** 1 P.Kil 29 2 B.Kenneally 26 3 D.Finnegan 26
**Mountains:** 1 J.Wright 19 2 D.Finnegan 18 3 E.Moriarty 17

**International Team:** 1 Linda McCartney Foods 32.41.43 2 Ireland Clarke Contracts at 10.48
**County Team:** 1 Wicklow Anglo Ir. Bank 32.52.25 2 Armagh Planet X at 11.34

## STAGE 4

David McCann (Planet X Pro-Vision) won the fourth stage of the FBD Milk RÁS, 88 miles from Killaloe to Ballinrobe coming home on his own 17 seconds ahead of Paul Healion (Dublin IRC Usher) with a chasing group led in by Peter van Hoof (Belgium) 40 seconds down.
Victory for the Belfast rider was especially sweet as he thought he had won the previous stage only to discover that three Dutch riders had slipped away over the top of the climb near the finish and were out of sight on the twisting descent into Killaloe.
This time he made no mistake going away from the leading group in the final 10 kilometres and used his considerable skills as a time-triallists to hold a 14 second lead over the remaining miles to the finish.
Jon Clay (Linda McCartney Foods), the race leader starting out came in with a big group 4 minutes behind McCann and dropped to 3rd at 2.56. The McCartney's found, like many teams before, that it doesn't pay to be too prominent in the early stages because they become heavily marked and end up prisoners in the bunch.
What looked like being the easiest stage of the week, a relatively short 88 miles over mainly flat roads, was turned upside down by strong cross winds which caused the peleton to fragment into five groups within 30 miles of the start and at Gort, where Aidan Hedderman (Carlow Dan Morrissey) took the prime, the main bunch was over 5 minutes down on a big leading break with three chasing groups in between. These chasers eventually merged into a 40-strong group which Clay led in 3.58 behind McCann.
In the group 40 seconds behind McCann was Erki Putsep (Estonia) and he has taken over the yellow jersey with a lead of 1.08 over Philip Cassidy (Ireland Clarkes Contracts).
**Stage 4 Killaloe - Ballinrobe 88 Mls.** 1 D.McCann (Armagh Planet X Pro-Vision) 3.26.33 2 P.Healion (Dublin IRC) at 1 secs 3 P.van Hoof (Belgium) s.t. 4 A.Lyons (Cheshire) 5 J.Griffiths (Wales) all same time 6 P.Cassidy (Ireland Clarke) at 17 7 N.Fabien (France) at 40 secs 8 B Doherty (Armagh Planet X) 9 D.O'Loughlin (Ireland Clarke) 10 G.Dodd (Surrey Racing League).
**General Classification:** 1 E.Putsep (Estonia) 14.21.14 2 P.Cassidy (Ireland Clarke) at 1.08 3 J.Clay (Linda McCartney) at 2.56 4 B.Kenneally (Wicklow) at 2.58 5 D.Finnegan (Meath Avonmore) at 3.11 6 C.Pearce (USA/Europe) at 3.17 7 E.Moriarty (Ireland Clarke) at 3.21 8 D.McCann (Armagh) at 3.39 9 E.Dagelet (Netherlands) at 4.42 10 R.Hobby (Lincoln) at 4.43 11 P.Healion (Dublin IRC) at 5.05 12 I.Chivers (Dublin Orwell) at 5.41
**Points:** 1 P.Kil 29 2 D.McCann 27 3 B.Kenneally 26

**Mountains:** 1 J.Wright 19 2 E.Dagelet 19 3 D.Finnegan 18
**International Team:** 1 Ireland Clarke Contracts 43.17.05 2 Estonia at 7.14 3 Linda McCartney at 10.02
**County Team:** 1 Wicklow Anglo Ir. Bank 43.28.05 2 Armagh Planet X at 11 secs 3 Meath at 8.066 4 Antrim at 31.24

## STAGE 5

There were no significant changes on the fifth stage to Sligo which was won by Harm Jansen (Netherlands Prowinn) who held a slender lead over the final kilometres to come home a mere 6 seconds in front of the bunch.
It was just behind him that the real drama occurred as most of the 135 riders in the field sprinted for the line. Colm Bracken (Dublin Usher IRC) touched the Belgian van Hoof and lost his line clipping the crash barriers and coming down, his bike careering across the road. This caused a big high-speed crash which saw three riders finish underneath the lorry carrying the finish podium.
One of these was Denis Easton (Armagh Planet X Pro-vision) who was placed sixth despite crossing the line on the ground as was Padraig Marrey (Kildare) 7th and Aiden Crowley (Wicklow) 11th. Incredibly there were no major injuries and all those involved were able to walk away from the scene.
Right at the start of the stage there was more bad news for the Armagh team as Tuesday's stage-winner David McCann retired as his knee, which has been causing him trouble for the past two seasons, was giving him pain after his efforts of the past two days and he didn't want to risk permanent damage on the longest stage of the race.
Despite the length of the stage and the two climbs en route, the peleton stayed together all day, largely due to the high speed being set, 47 kilometres in the first hour, which made it very hard for any breaks to gain any time. Eleven riders did stay clear for about 15 kilometres but the flying bunch soon had them back.
It was only after the final climb at Strandhill, that Jansen opened a small gap which he gamely maintained over the final 10 kilometres.
**Stage 5 Ballinrobe - Sligo 108 Mls.** 1 H.Jansen (Netherlands Prowin) 4.08.18 2 P.van Hoof (Belgium) at 6 secs 3 P. Kil (Netherlands) 4 D.Finnegan (Meath Avonmore) 5 S.Whelan (Dublin Swords McNally) 6 D.Easton (Armagh Planet X Pro-Vision) 7 P.Marrey (Kildare Hire Equip) 8 R.Downing (Linda McCartney) 9 G.Dodd (Surrey Racing League) 10 S.Duclos (France) all same time
**General Classification:** 1 E.Putsep (Estonia) 18.29.38 2 P.Cassidy (Ireland Clarke) at 1.08 3 J.Clay (Linda McCartney) at 2.56 4 B.Kenneally (Wicklow) at 2.58 5 D.Finnegan (Meath Avonmore) at 3.11 6 C.Pearce (USA/Europe) at 3.17 7 E.Moriarty (Ireland Clarke) at 3.21 8 E.Dagelet (Netherlands) at 4.42 9 R.Hobby (Lincoln) at 4.43 10 P.Healion (Dublin IRC) at 5.05 11 I.Chivers (Dublin Orwell) at 5.41 12 E.Moriarty (Ireland Clarke)
**Points:** 1 P.Kil 42 2 H.Jansen 30 3 P.van Hoof 27

**Mountains:** 1 E.Dagelet 24 2 J.Wright 21 3 E.Moriarty 21
**International Team:** 1 Ireland Clarke Contracts 55.42.17 2 Estonia at 7.14 3 Linda McCartney at 10.02
**County Team:** 1 Wicklow Anglo Ir. Bank 55.33.17 2 Armagh Planet X at 11 secs 3 Meath at 8.06; 4 Antrim at 31.24

## STAGE 6

Harm Jansen (Netherlands Prowinn) took his Second FBD Milk RÁS stage in a row from Donegal to Killybegs over a mountainous 98 miles but the contrast could not have been greater than the previous day into Sligo.
It finished in a mass sprint but after a battering over climbs like Glengesh Pass it was a succession of small groups who arrived with some 80 minutes between the first and last rider to finish.
Jansen arrived at the finish in company with Jeff Wright (Cheshire Peugeot) and sprinted away in the final 300 metres to open a 3 second gap. The two had been together since before the major climb at Glengesh with Wright taking three King of the Mountain climbs to establish a strong lead in the climber's category, 56 points to 33 of the Dutchman Dagelet.
Estonian Erki Putsep just managed to hang onto the overall lead but Phil Cassidy (Ireland Clarke Contracts) moving to within 18 seconds after a stage on which he launched a continual assault on the jersey.
He led a break right from the start up the Barnesmore Gap where Seamus O'Sullivan (Wicklow) was first over from Richard Hobby (Lincoln) and the ever-present Cassidy. The break of 11 riders held a lead of just under a minute for some 20 miles but an all-out chase by the bunch saw them recaptured.
The second KOM prime was the 2nd cat. Climb at Meenirroy where Raymond Clarke (Ireland Clarke) led over from Alges Massikmets (Estonia). between there and Glengesh a break of 24 went away and it was from this group that Jansen and Wright escaped. At one stage their lead was over a minute but this was reduced to 46 seconds at the line.
Cassidy came in with the chasing group but the group containing the Yellow jersey was a further 50 seconds behind just close enough to keep the jersey with the Estonian.
**Stage 6 Donegal - Killybegs 98 Mls.** 1 H.Jansen (Netherlands Prowin) 3.39.02 2 J.Wright (Cheshire Peugeot) at 3 secs 3 Derek Finnegan (Meath Avonmore) at 46 secs 4 J.Clay (Linda McCartney) 5 R.Downing (Linda McCartney) 6 A.Massikmets (Estonia) 7 R.Hobby (Lincoln) 8 E.Dagelet (Netherlands) 9 C.Pearce (USA/Europe) 10 Dermot Finnegan (Meath Avonmore) all same time
**General Classification:** 1 E.Putsep (Estonia) 22.10.16 2 P.Cassidy (Ireland Clarke) at 18 secs 3 J.Clay (Linda McCartney) at 2.06 4 B.Kenneally (Wicklow) at 2.08 5 Dermot Finnegan (Meath Avonmore) at 2.21 6 C.Pearce (USA/Europe) at 2.27 7 E.Moriarty (Ireland Clarke) at 3.21 8 E.Dagelet (Netherlands) at 3.52 9 R.Hobby

(Lincoln) at 3.53 10 I.Chivers (Dublin Orwell) at 4.51 11 R.Downing (Linda McCartney) at 6.11 12 S.O'Sullivan (Wicklow) at 6.33
**Points:** 1 H.Jansen 45 2 P.Kil 42 3 J.Wright 32
**Mountains:** 1 J.Wright 56 2 E.Dagalet 33 3 H.Jansen 32
**International Team:** 1 Ireland Clarke Contracts 55.42.17 2 Estonia at 7.14 3 Linda McCartney at 10.02
**County Team:** 1 Wicklow Anglo Ir. Bank 55.33.17 2 Armagh Planet X at 11 secs 3 Meath at 8.06 4 Antrim at 31.24

## STAGE 7

Having exposed Putsep's vulnerability on Thursday, Cassidy was on the attack from the start of the seventh stage to Cootehill.
Over the first KOM at Black Gap before Pettigo a six-man break including Cassidy already had a lead of over a minute. The prime was taken by Estonian Alges Massikmets who was along as policeman for the jersey. Cassidy was over in third place.
The near gale force tailwind saw the race 20 minutes ahead of schedule as they tackled the two KOM primes at Mount Finn and the speed was splitting the race into a series of groups with the yellow jersey dropping back in the third group on the road. Brian Kenneally (Wicklow) and John Clay (Linda McCartney) who had both seemed possible winners throughout the week were also finding the going tough and both dropped down the field. They would both retire the following day, Clay with food poisoning and Kenneally with a chest cold.
Young Dermot Finnegan, who would have been Cassidy's teammate on the Navan Avonmore team had Cassidy not been drafted into the Ireland squad made it across to the leaders and the 19-year-old's performance moved him up to 2nd overall 2.11 behind his club mate.
Mountains leader Jeff Wright (Cheshire Peugeot) was defending his jersey well and was up in the leading break and first over Mount Finn and Carnmore to establish a commanding lead in that competition.
The Estonians had some consolation for losing the jersey as Masskimets took the stage from Wright and Richard Hobby (Lincoln) with Cassidy sitting up in the sprint, happy in the knowledge that he had done enough to take the lead by a comfortable margin.
**Stage 7 Killybegs - Cootehill 100 Mls.**1 A.Maasikmets (Estonia) 3.41.48 2 J.Wright (Cheshire Peugeot) 3 R.Hobby (Lincoln) all same time 4 P.Cassidy (Ireland Clarke) at 2 secs 5 M.Lovatt (Cheshire Peugeot) at 10 secs 6 T.Cuppens (Belgium) 7 R.Kodanipork (Estonia) 8 R.Downing (Linda McCartney) 9 S.O'Sullivan (Wicklow) 10 D.Finnegan (Meath) all same time
**General Classification:** 1 P.Cassidy (Ireland Clarke) 25.52.24 2 D.Finnegan (Meath Avonmore) at 2.11 3 C.Pearce (USA/Europe) at 2.24 4 R.Hobby (Lincoln) at 3.33 5 E.Putsep (Estonia) at 4.44 6 R.Downing (Linda McCartney) at 6.01 7 S.O'Sullivan

(Wicklow) at 6.23 8 E.Moriarty (Ireland Clarke) at 8.05 9 E.Dagelet (Netherlands) at 8.36 10 B.Moore (Meath Avonmore) 9.07 11 A.El Nady (Egypt) at 10.52 12 M.Lovatt (Cheshire Peugeot) at 12.16
**Points:** 1 J.Wright 46 2 H.Jansen 45 3 P.Kil 42
**Mountains:** 1 J.Wright 87 2 A.Maasikmets 54 3 E.Dagelet 33
**International Teams:** 1 Ireland Clarke 77.56.45 2 Estonia 3 Egypt
**County Teams:** 1 Meath Avonmore 78.13.08 2 Armagh Planet X 3 Wicklow Anglo Ir.Bank

## STAGE 8

Cassidy had a bad night on Friday when he was sick all night but didn't show any signs of weakness to his rivals on another tough stage through Down, Armagh and Louth, which included five climbs, and held onto his advantage when the stage finished in Drogheda.
The stage provided another win for Dutchman Harm Jansen, who joined the select band of riders to have won four stages in one RÁS.
The bunch was all together starting the first climb of the day at Keady Mountain after 33 miles where Morgan Fox (Belgium) led the ever present Wright over the top.
Five miles further on at Newtownhamilton it was again Fox. Wright was 4th scoring his last points of the competition but he had an unbeatable lead of 31 points over the Estonian Maasikmets.
The very steep climb at Windy Gap, out of Omeath fragmented the bunch and a break of some dozen riders went away but after the descent they lost their impetus and were swept up in a general regroupment.
It was on the final climb at King William's Glen that Jansen, who was clear with teammate Kil and Anthony Malarczyk (Wales) made his move, sprinting for the prime and then keeping it going to win in Drogheda by 4 seconds from the Welsh rider with Kil a further second back. Cassidy came in with a large group 16 seconds behind the stage winner.
**Stage 8 Cootehill - Drogheda 102 Mls.** 1 H.Jansen (Netherlands Prowin) 4.03.10 2 A.Malarczyk (Wales) at 4 secs 3 P.Kil (Netherlands) at 5 secs 4 P.Griffin (Carlow Dan Morrissey) 5 R.Hobby (Lincoln) s.t. 6 J.Wright (Cheshire Peugeot) at 16 secs 7 Derek Finnegan (Meath Avonmore) at 16 secs 8 R.Downing (Linda McCartney) 9 A.Maasikmets (Estonia) 10 B.Moore (Meath Avonmore) all same time
**General Classification:** 1 P.Cassidy (Ireland Clarke) 29.55.50 2 Dermot Finnegan (Meath Avonmore) at 2.11 3 C.Pearce (USA/Europe) at 2.27 4 R.Hobby (Lincoln) at 3.27 5 E.Putsep (Estonia) at 4.44 6 R.Downing (Linda McCartney) at 6.01 7 S.O'Sullivan (Wicklow) at 6.23 8 E.Dagelet (Netherlands) at 8.36 9 E.Moriarty (Ireland Clarke) at 8.48 10 B.Moore (Meath Avonmore) at 9.07 11 A.El Nady (Egypt) at 10.52 12 M.Adbelfattah (Egypt) at 11.21
**Points:** 1 H.Jansen 60 2 J.Wright 56 3 P.Kil 55
**Mountains:** 1 J.Wright 102 2 A.Maasikmets 71 3 H.Jansen 47

**International Team:** 1 Ireland Clarke Contracts 90.07.46 2 Estonia at 3.45 3 Egypt at 18.20
**County Team:** 1 Meath Avonmore 90.23.26 2 Armagh Planet X Pro-Vision at 1.14.01 3 Wicklow Anglo Ir.Bank at 1.14.06

## STAGE 9

The final stage was held over 50 minutes plus three laps on a Dublin city centre circuit taking in O'Connell Street and Parnell Square.
The bunch stayed together over the 25 laps with 27 miles covered in the hour and it was won by Belgian Peter van Hoof, who had finished second winning the bunch sprint into Sligo when the spectacular finish line pile-up had occurred. This had established him as firm favourite should the stage come down to a big bunch finish and sure enough he edged out Pelle Kil (Netherlands) but the Dutchman had done enough to take over the point's jersey from his teammate Harm Jansen who on Saturday had won his fourth stage of the week.
**Stage 8 Dublin Criterium 27 Mls.** 1 Peter van Hoof (Belgium) 1.00.14 2 P. Kil 3 P.Griffin 4 S.Whelan (Dublin Swords) 5 R.Downing 6 Derek Finnegan 7 N.Fabien (France) 8 A.Maasikmets 9 R.Clarke (Ireland Clarke Contracts) 10 Dermot Finnegan (Meath Avonmore) all same time
**General Classification:** 1 P.Cassidy (Ireland Clarke Contracts) 30.56.04 2 Dermot Finnegan (Meath Avonmore) at 2.11 3 C. Pearce (USA/Europe) at 2.27 4 R.Hobby (Lincoln) at 3.27 5 E.Putsep (Estonia) at 4.44 6 R.Downing (Linda McCartney) at 6.01 7 S.O'Sullivan (Wicklow) at 6.23 8 E.Dagelet (Netherlands Prowin) at 8.36 9 E.Moriarty (Ireland Clarke) at 8.48 10 B.Moore (Meath Avonmore) at 9.07 11 A.El Nady (Egypt) at 10.52 12 M.Adbelfattah (Egypt) at 11.21
**Points:** 1 P.Kil 69 2 H.Jansen 65 3 R.Downing 58
**Mountains:** 1 J.Wright 102 2 A.Maasikmets 71 3 H.Jansen 47
**International Team:** 1 Ireland Clarke Contracts 93.08.28.17 2 Estonia at 3.45 3 Egypt at 18.20
**County Team:** 1 Meath Avonmore 93.24.08 2 Armagh Planet X Pro-Vision at 1.14.01 3 Wicklow Anglo Ir.Bank at 1.14.06
**Ben McKenna Trophy (Irish riders under 23):** 1 P.Healion (Dublin Usher IRC) 2 J.Mannix (Kerry Baltic Trading) 3 D.Finnegan (Meath Avonmore)
**Second Category riders:** 1 J.Mannix (Kerry Baltic Trading) 2 J.Fenlon (Carlow Dan Morrissey) 3 R.O'Leary (Dublin Usher IRC).

*Philip Cassidy, Winner 1999*

## 2000

The first RÁS of the new Millennium saw a record entry of 200, which, despite the usual last minute dropouts saw a record number of 172 starters.
The visiting teams also saw some last minute changes with Egypt and Latvia staying at home and Sweden coming in along with Belgium, The Netherlands, Germany, Estonia, USA (2), Wales, Scotland (2), and six English selections. The remainder was made up of an Ireland team and 23 county teams.
Defending champion Phillip Cassidy was on the Ireland International Cargo Systems team along with '96 winner Tommy Evans. 38-year-old Cassidy went into the race strongly fancied after an extraordinary season where he had dominated the home scene winning a string of races includes the 5-day Tour of the North and the 3-day Tour of Ulster only weeks before.

### STAGE 1

No matter how often the RÁS has been lost on the opening stage, riders never seem to learn the lesson and after the opening 89 miles to Longford all but 18 of the 172 starters had effectively lost their chance of winning the premier prize.
Riders like Cassidy, Evans, and all but seven of the visiting teams found themselves over four minutes down after an 18-man break finished that margin ahead.
The stage was won by Tjarco Cuppens (Belgium DMC) but he didn't get the yellow jersey which went to Julian Winn (Wales) who finished second but picked up 9 seconds in time bonuses by finishing second at the Delvin hot spot sprint and winning at the Edgeworthstown prime.
Added to his 4 seconds in finishers bonuses, given for the first time in many years (but only on stage 1), that gave him a 1 second margin over the Belgian who had only picked up a second place during the stage plus 3 seconds, his wining margin over Winn at the finish.
The Ireland team had two: Eugene Moriarty and Fergus McCauley in the lead group and manager Ritchie Beattie was upbeat about leap-frogging some more riders up the classification during the week. Sweden, Wales and Tipperary also had two riders but big losers were the Dutch, widely fancied after their performance in '99 who had nobody included.
The big break formed after Navan and although their lead hung around 1 minute for some time the gap started to grow and continued to do so through the second half of the stage which was run off at over 25 mph. In the final kilometre Cuppens jumped away to win by 3 seconds but it was 1 second short of what he needed to take the jersey.
**Stage 1 Dublin - Longford 143 Kms.** 1 T.Cuppens (Belgium DMC) 3.32.28 2 J.Winn (Wales) at 3 secs 3 T.Nilsson (Sweden) 4 E.Moriarty (Ireland Int.Cargo Sys)

5 D.Eston (Antrim Planet X) 6 A.Duff (Carlow Dan Morrissey) 7 D.O'Loughlin (Mayo NCF) 8 E.O'Donoghue (Tipperary Kieran Bourke) 9 F.McCauley (Ireland) 10 P.Moriarty (Dublin Skip Hire) all same time
**General Classification:** 1 J.Winn (Wales) 3.32.18 2 T.Cuppens (Belgium) at 1 second 3 E.Moriarty (Ireland) at 6 secs 4 T.Nilsson (Sweden) at 7 secs 5 G.Butler (England Surrey Racing) s.t. 6 R.Jahn (Germany Telekom) at 11 secs 7 D.Easton (Antrim) at 12 secs 8 D.O'Loughlin (Mayo) s.t. 9 A.Duff (Carlow) at 13 secs 10 E.O'Donoghue (Tipperary) 11 F.McCauley (Ireland) 12 P.Moriarty (Dublin Skip) all same time

## STAGE 2

Brian Kenneally (Tipperary Kieran Bourke) won the 102 miles second stage from Longford to Newport with a 30 miles solo effort which saw him finish 51 seconds ahead of two chasers: John Tanner (England Pro-Vision Powerbar) and David McCann (Derry Clarke Contracts).
Another Power-Vision rider Mark Lovatt would wear the yellow jersey on stage 3 to Oughterard after Julian Winn (Wales) who led after the opening stage finished in the bunch and dropped to 10th overall.
All the breaks for the first 70 miles came to nothing and they were all together as they approached the first climb at Lake Levally where Samuel Faruhn (Germany Telekom) was first over from Chris Greene (Armagh) and Kenneally.
A few miles further on at the climb of the Windy Gap, used for the first time in the Rás, Kenneally had gone clear and descending like a demon he opened up a gap of over 2 minutes by Westport. McCann and Tanner went in pursuit as a further dozen riders went away from the bunch.
On the run-in to Newport the two chasers closed the gap but Kenneally still had a minute in hand entering the town.
Of the 18 riders who finished 4 minutes ahead of the bunch on Saturday's stage to Longford there were only two now equal on time with Lovatt at the top of the classification: Stephen O'Sullivan (Derry Clarke Contracts) and Krisstofer Ingeby (Sweden). Eight were still within 13 seconds but Kenneally, who moved up to 9th after his efforts was 2.41 down and the main body of the race including pre-race favourites like Phil Cassidy and Tommy Evans were already over 7 minutes behind with an awful lot to do.
**Stage 2 Longford - Newport 163 Kms.** 1 B.Kenneally (Tipperary Kieran Bourke) 4.06.53 2 J.Tanner (England Pro-Vision) at 48 secs 3 D.McCann (Derry Clarke) s.t. 4 H.Haymes (GB Prickett) at 1.20 5 S.O'Sullivan (Derry Clarke) 6 S.Faruhn (Germany Telekom) 7 M.Lovatt (England Pro-Vision) 8 K.Ingeby (Sweden) all same time 9 J.Wright (GB Prickett) at 1.23 10 C.Bracken (Dublin Usher) at 1.33
**General Classification:** 1 M.Lovatt (England Pro-Vision Powerbar) 7.40.44 2 S.O'Sullivan (Derry Clarke Contracts) 3 K.Ingeby (Sweden) all same time 4 E.Moriarty (Ireland) at 6 secs 5 G.Butler (England Surrey Racing) at 7 secs 6 R.Jahn

(Germany Telekom) at 11 secs 7 D.O'Loughlin (Mayo) at 12 secs 8 P.Moriarty (Dublin Skip) at 13 secs 9 B.Kenneally (Tipperary) at 2.41 10 J.Winn (Wales) at 2.54 11 T.Cuppens (Belgium) at 2.55 12 T.Nilsson (Sweden) at 3.01

**Points:** 1 T.Cuppens (Belgium) 15 2 B.Kenneally (Tipperary) 15 3 J.Winn (Wales) 14

**Mountains;** 1 S.Faruhn (Germany) 19 2 B.Kenneally (Tipperary) 18 3 J.McCarthy (Kerry)

**International Team:** 1 Sweden 23.06.39 2 Wales at 3.13 3 England Pro-Vision at 3.16

**County Team:** 1 Carlow Dan Morrissey 23.10.53 2 Tipperary at 14 secs 3 Derry Clarke at 1.56

## STAGE 3

Julian Winn (Wales) who lost the yellow jersey on Sunday, struck back to win the 75 miles stage from Newport to Oughterard leading in Wayne Randle (England Pro-Vision) and David McCann (Derry Clarke Contracts).

Yellow jersey Mark Lovatt (England Pro-Vision) finished 5th, five second behind Winn and now led by 13 seconds from Paddy Moriarty (Dublin Skip Hire) with Stephen O'Sullivan (Derry Clarkes) third at 36 seconds.

The relatively short 75 miles stage was expected to be something of a rest day but the hard roads and hills saw big gaps open in the bunch and the main bunch including pre-race favourite Phil Cassidy came in 10 minutes behind.

For the first half of the stage the race stayed intact but when a three man group including yellow jersey Lovatt got across to a leading group of ten just before the climb from Leenaun to Derrynacleigh it was the signal for all out action which saw several more groups come up to the leaders while others dropped back.

On the run-in from Maam Cross a lead group of twelve, including the race leader and '96 winner Tommy Evans (Ireland) opened a gap and in the final mile Winn, Randle and McCann broke away to sprint for the stage.

**Stage 3 Newport - Oughterard 121 Kms.** 1 J.Winn (Wales) 3.02.31 2 W.Randle (England Pro-Vision) 3 D.McCann (Derry Clarke) all same time 4 P.Moriarty (Dublin Skip Hire) at 5 secs 5 M.Lovatt (Pro-Vision) 6 M.Albertson (Sweden) 7 J.Tanner (Pro-Vision) 8 S.Faruhn (Germany Telekom) 9 T.Evans (Ireland Int. Cargo) 10 P.Kil (Netherlands) all same time

**General Classification:** 1 M.Lovatt (England Pro-Vision) 10.43.20 2 P.Moriarty (Dublin Skip Hire) at 13 secs 3 S.O'Sullivan (Derry Clarke) at 36 secs 4 G.Butler (England Surrey) at 43 secs 5 D.O'Loughlin (Mayo) at 48 secs 6 K.Ingeby (Sweden) at 2.14 7 E.Moriarty (Ireland) at 2.20 8 J.Winn (Wales) at 2.49 9 A.Duff (Carlow) at 3.07 10 D.McCann (Derry Clarke) at 3.24 11 J.Tanner (Pro-Vision) at 3.29 12 R.Jahn (Germany) at 3.39

**Points:** 1 J.Winn 29 2 D.McCann 26 3 M.Lovatt 25

**Mountains:** 1 S.Faruhn 24 2 B.Kenneally 18 3 J.McCarthy 12

**International Team:** 1 Sweden 32.17.17 2 England Pro-Vision at 21 secs 3 Wales at 7.14
**County Team:** 1 Derry Clarke Contracts 32.24.36 2 Carlow Dan Morrissey at 5.21 3 Tipperary at 7.49.

## STAGE 4

There was a complete reshuffle at the top of the leader board after a dramatic 120 miles stage from Oughterard to Listowel, won by Sweden's Krisstofer Ingeby who attacked in the final mile to come home 9 seconds clear of a nine-man group.
In the group was young Mayo rider David O'Loughlin who took over the yellow jersey by 1.17 from the Swede with Kerry's Eugene Moriarty (Ireland), who was given a great reception by his home town crowd moving up to third overall after finishing 5th on the stage.
Mark Lovatt (England Pro-Vision Powerbar) who started in the yellow jersey missed the break and although he got away in a chasing group he still lost almost 5 minutes and dropped to 7th overall at 3.55. However his losses were small compared to some with two large groups of around 70 riders each coming in 20 and 30 minutes respectively behind the stage winner. The speed was reflected in the average speed which was 26.21 mph despite the last 50 miles being into a headwind.
It was an all out attack by the Ireland team which done the damage. Three of their riders, Philip Cassidy, Eugene Moriarty and Tommy Evans went almost from the start and forced a big break at the front of the bunch containing 28 riders. Setting a furious pace the leaders covered 31 miles in the first hour.
Riders who had been caught napping including yellow jersey Lovatt, Paddy Moriarty (Dublin Skip) and Derry's David McCann went in pursuit and almost got across but the leaders kept up the pace and the gap gradually widened to 2 minutes where is stayed for a long time before stretching again over the final miles to almost 5.
**Stage 4 Oughterard - Listowel 192 Kms.** 1 K.Ingeby (Sweden) 4.33.17 2 J.Winn (Wales) at 9 secs 3 M.Salumets (Estonia) 4 W.Randle (England Pro-Vision) 5 E.Moriarty (Ireland) 6 R.Riddle (Scotland Union Transport) 7 A.Duff (Carlow Dan Morrissey) 8 J.Wright (GB Prickett) 9 D.O'Loughlin (Mayo NCF) 10 T.Evans (Ireland) all same time
**General Classification:** 1 D.O'Loughlin (Mayo) 15.17.34 2 K.Ingeby (Sweden) at 1.17 3 E.Moriarty (Ireland) at 1.32 4 J.Winn (Wales) at 2.01 5 A.Duff (Carlow) at 2.19 6 W.Randle (Pro-Vision) at 3.21 7 M.Lovatt (Pro-Vision) at 3.55 8 P.Moriarty (Dublin Skip Hire) at 4.08 9 S.Faruhn (Germany Telekom) at 4.37 10 G.Butler (England Surrey) at 4.38 11 T.Cuppens (Belgium) at 5.43 12 T.Evans (Ireland) at 6.20
**Points:** 1 J.Winn 43 2 W.Randle 29 3 D.McCann 26
**Mountains:** 1 S.Faruhn 33 2 J.Winn 21 3 B.Kenneally 18
**International Team:** 1 Sweden 46.03.35 2 England Pro-Vision at 3.47 3 Ireland at 4.19

**County Team:** 1 Kildare 46.31.28 2 Meath East at 14.56 3 Derry Clarke Contracts at 15.08

## STAGE 5

There was little change overall after the 'Ring of Kerry' stage, 106 miles from Listowel to Kenmare which was won in fine style on his own by Gethin Butler of the England Surrey Racing team.

Butler was chased home 30 seconds later by David McCann (Derry Clarke Contracts) who with two third placings on stages 2 and 3 was beginning to make an assault on the green jersey.

David O'Loughlin (Mayo NCF) kept the lead but his jersey looked anything but safe halfway through the stage when he was in the bunch 2.40 behind a 16-man group which contained Aidan Duff (Carlow Dan Morrissey), lying 4th overall at 1.58, who was race leader on the road.

The action started on the climb out of Tralee which saw some 50 riders out the back but on the descent there was a general regroupment and most of them regained the bunch.

On the succession of small climbs after Killorglin three riders, David McCann, Phillip Cassidy (Ireland) and Brian Kenneally (Tipperary Kieran Bourke) went away and when their break became established a succession of small groups got across to them leaving 26 at the front with their lead growing to a maximum of 2.40.

On the category 1 climb of the Coomakista Pass ex-yellow jersey Mark Lovatt (England Pro-Vision Powerbar) towed a three-man group across to the leaders but as they turned into a tailwind on the descent the bunch really got its tail up and relentlessly reduced the lead.

With 15 kms to go Butler went away and the GB multi time-trial champion never looked like being caught. David McCann went in pursuit but only got to within 40 seconds, the chasers were at another 10 seconds and the bunch were at 1.11.

**Stage 5 Listowel - Kenmare 171 Kms.** 1 G.Butler (England Surrey Racing) 4.21.57 2 D.McCann (Derry Clarke Contracts) at 40 secs 3 M.Lovatt (Pro-Vision) at 50 secs 4 R.Riddle (Scotland Union Transport) 5 R.Kodanipork (Estonia) 6 B.Moore (Ireland) 7 A.Kay (York Cycleworks) 8 M.Carlson (Sweden) 9 R.Cahill (Cork Triton Ventilux) 10 H.Haymes (GB Prickett) all same time

**General Classification:** 1 D.O'Loughlin (Mayo NCF) 19.40.42 2 K.Ingeby (Sweden) at 1.17 3 E.Moriarty (Ireland) at 1.32 4 A.Duff (Carlow) at 1.58 5 J.Winn (Wales) at 2.01 6 W.Randle (Pro-Vision) at 3.21 7 G.Butler (Surrey Racing) at 3.27 8 M.Lovatt (Pro-Vision) at 3.34 9 P.Moriarty (Dublin Skip Hire) at 3.47 10 S.Faruhn (Germany Telekom) at 4.37 11 R.Riddle (Scotland) at 5.59 12 T.Evans (Ireland) at 6.20

**Points:** 1 J.Winn 43 2 D.McCann 40 3 M.Lovatt 38

**Mountains:** 1 S.Faruhn 39 2 D.McCann 32 3 J.Winn 29

**International Team:** 1 Sweden 59.12.38 2 England Pro-Vision at 3.47 3 Ireland at 4.19
**County Team:** 1 Kildare 59.40.52 2 Derry Clarke at 14.37

## STAGE 6

There was an Ulster one-two on the 90 miles run from Kenmare to Mitchelstown. David McCann (Derry Clarke Contracts) who had already had a second and two thirds broke away from the leaders with a mile to go to take the victory. The sprint from the remainder of the seven-man group was won by Tommy Evans (Ireland Int. Cargo Systems).
In a complete shake-up at the top of the general classification Julian Winn (Wales), who had worn the yellow jersey on Sunday, got it back to lead by 1.20 from Wayne Randle (England Pro-Vision Powerbar) whose teammate Mark Lovatt, another ex-yellow jersey was third at 1.33. '96 RÁS winner Evans moved up to 8th at 4.19 with McCann 9th at 4.41 also led both the points and mountains classifications.
It was the Pro-Vision trio who done all the damage going away on the first climb of the day, the category 2 at Inchee Mountain where Paddy Moriarty (Dublin Skip Hire) led Evans, Ray Clarke (Derry Clarkes), Winn, Tanner and Randal across the prime. All these except Clarke were in the vital breakaway group along with McCann and Lovatt.
The race split into a series of bunches over the succession of climbs in the next 30 miles with yellow-jersey David O'Loughlin (Mayo) in the first chase group which lost time throughout the stage eventually coming in over 4 minutes down, O'Loughlin dropping back to 5th overall at 2.27.
The Swede Krisstofer Ingeby dropped to 6th at 3.44 but the biggest loser on the day was Aidan Duff (Carlow Dan Morrissey), strongly fancied after he led on the road on Wednesday's stage but now back in 23rd place at 16.02.
**Stage 6 Kenmare - Mitchelstown 144 Kms.** 1 D.McCann (Derry Clarke Contracts) 3.24.02 2 T.Evans (Ireland) at 6 secs 3 M.Lovatt (England Pro-Vision Powerbar) 4 J.Tanner (Pro-Vision) 5 P.Moriarty (Dublin Skip Hire) 7 W.Randle (Pro-Vision) 7 J.Winn, all same time 8 F.McCauley (Ireland) at 4.31 9 A.Crowley (Kildare Cahill Cycles) at 4.33 10 J.McCarthy (Kerry) at 4.34
**General Classification:** 1 J.Winn (Wales) 23.06.51 2 W.Randle (Pro-Vision); at 1.20 3 M.Lovatt (Pro-Vision) at 1.33 4 P.Moriarty (Dublin Skip) at 1.46 5 D.O'Loughlin (Mayo) at 2.27 6 K.Ingeby (Sweden) at 3.44 7 E.Moriarty (Ireland) at 3.59 8 T.Evans (Ireland) at 4.19 9 D.McCann (Derry Clarke) at 4.41 10 J.Tanner (Pro-Vision) at 5.23 11 G.Butler (England Surrey) at 5.54 12 S.Faruhn (Germany Telekom) at 7.04
**Points:** 1 D.McCann 55 2 J.Winn 52 3 M.Lovatt 51
**Mountains:** 1 D.McCann 56 2 J.Winn 54 3 S.Faruhn 41
**International Team:** 1 England Pro-Vision 69.28.49 2 Ireland at 9.25 3 Sweden at 9.37

**County Team:** 1 Kildare Cahill Cycles 70.06.39 2 Derry Clarke at 30.16 3 Dublin Skip at 35.09

## STAGE 7

There was no change at the top of the general classification the seventh stage of, 94 miles from Mitchelstown to Enniscorthy, won by John Tanner of the England Pro-Vision Powerbar team from Ray Clarke (Derry Clarke Contracts).
David O'Loughlin ((Mayo NCF) made a brave bid to regain the yellow jersey which he lost to Julian Winn (Wales) on Thursday. He initiated a break shortly after the start of the stage and when he was joined by eleven others including Tanner, Clarke, Philip Brown and Roddy Riddle (Scotland), JP Hilliard (Dublin Skip), Eddie O'Donoghue and Adrian Hedderman (Tipperary), Matthias Carlsson (Sweden), Gregor Willwohl (Germany), Hamish Haymes (GB Prickett) and Tommy Evans (Ireland) they set about building up a lead which had grown to 2.30 by Carrick-on-Suir after 40 miles.
This left the young Mayo rider race leader on the road which rang alarm bells back in the Welsh camp where the whole team went to the front to try and reduce the deficit. With the lead quickly coming down Ray Clarke decided to go it alone and attacked coming out of New Ross with 20 miles to go. He was chased by Tanner and Brown but it took the pair a long time to catch the ex-Irish champion. On the long drag up to the finish in Enniscorthy Clarke went again but Tanner judged his effort just right and swept past 20 metres from the line. The trio just survived as Magnus Albertsson (Sweden) led in the fast closing bunch 10 seconds behind Tanner.
David McCann (Derry Clarke) maintained his lead in both the green points and polka dot mountains classifications.
**Stage 7 Mitchelstown - Enniscorthy 150 Kms.** 1 J.Tanner (England Pro-Vision Powerbar) 3.27.33 2 R.Clarke (Derry Clarke Contracts) at 1 sec 3 P.Brown (Scotland) s.t. 4 M.Albertson (Sweden) at 10 secs 5 T.Nilsson (Sweden) 6 E.Moriarty (Ireland) 7 M.Salumets (Estonia) 8 D.McCann (Derry Clarke) 9 J.Winn (Wales) 10 F.McCauley (Ireland) all same time
**General Classification:** 1 J.Winn (Wales) 26.34.24 2 W.Randle (Pro-Vision) at 1.20 3 M.Lovatt (Pro-Vision) at 1.33 4 P.Moriarty (Dublin Skip) at 1.46 5 D.O'Loughlin (Mayo) at 2.27 6 K.Ingeby (Sweden) at 3.44 7 E.Moriarty (Ireland) at 3.59 8 T.Evans (Ireland) at 4.19 9 D.McCann (Derry Clarke) at 4.41 10 J.Tanner (Pro-Vision) at 5.13 11 G.Butler (England Surrey) at 5.54 12 S.Faruhn (Germany Telekom) at 7.04
**Points:** 1 D.McCann 63 2 J.Winn 59 3 M.Lovatt 51
**Mountains:** 1 D.McCann 63 2 J.Winn 59 3 S.Faruhn 41
**International Team:** 1 England Pro-Vision 79.51.18 2 Ireland at 9.35 3 Sweden at 9.47
**County Team:** 1 Kildare Cahill Cycles 80.29.18 2 Derry Clarke at 30.07 3 Dublin Skip at 35.09 4 Antrim Planet X at 66.15

## STAGE 8

The race was finally lost and won in the Wicklow Mountains on Saturday.
The usual break went away with riders anxious to get to the mountains with some time in hand but it was on the steep slopes of the first climb at Aughavanna that the race took shape.
David Peelo (Dublin Usher) led Gethin Butler (Surrey Racing) over the prime and the pair stayed together on the descent. Immediately they tackled the Drumgoff climb to the Shay Elliott Memorial and there Butler took off on his own. Peelo was second over with David McCann (Clarke Contracts) leading a chasing group along with the yellow jersey.
After the long climb of the Wicklow Gap Butler was still out on his own with McCann, Winn and Peelo leading over the chasers. Butler stayed away over the final climb of the day, the Cat. 2 Slieve Corragh.
As the chasing group was about to catch Butler McCann and teammate Stephen O'Sullivan attacked and surprisingly, after his efforts, Butler was able to latch on and the trio came home 1.15 ahead of the remains of the break at the finish in Tullow where O'Sullivan came home 1 second ahead of McCann with Butler tailed off 7 seconds behind.
**Stage 8 Enniscorthy – Tullow 156 Kms.** 1 Stephen O'Sullivan (Derry Clarke Contracts) 3.51.24 2 D.McCann (Derry Clarke Contracts) at 1 sec 3 G.Butler (England Surrey Racing) at 7 secs 4 P.Kil (Netherlands) at 1.15 5 T.Evans (Ireland) at 1.17 6 R.Riddle (Scotland) 7 M.Lovatt (Pro Vision) 8 P.Moriarty (Dublin Skip Hire) 9 A.Meehan (Kildare) 10 Dermot Finnegan (Meath Avonmore) all same time
**General classification:** 1 J.Winn (Wales) 30.27.14 2 W.Randle (Pro Vision) at 1.11 3 M.Lovatt (Pro Vision) at 1.24 4 P.Moriarty (Dublin Skip) at 1.37 5 D.O'Loughlin (Mayo NCF) at 2.18 6 D.McCann (Derry Clarke) at 3.16 7 K.Ingeby (Sweden) at 3.35 8 T.Evans (Ireland) at 4.10 9 G.Butler (Surrey) at 4.35 10 J.Tanner (Pro-Vision) at 5.04 11 R.Riddle (Scotland) at 8.17 12 P.Kil (Netherlands) at 10.25
**Points:** 1 D.McCann 77 2 J.Winn 65 3 J.Tanner 61
**Mountains:** 1 D.McCann 86 2 J.Winn 59 3 G.Butler 58

## STAGE 9

The race ended with an hour long criterium on O'Connell Street. Nothing changed on the final day despite lone breakaways by McCann, O'Loughlin and Evans.
Winn came home safely in the bunch behind Tommy Evans, showing new talents as a big bunch sprinter, beating his teammate Eugene Moriarty and most of the 132 survivors in the frantic dash for the line. The two salvaged something for an Irish team which had one of their worst results for years.
Best of the International teams was the England Pro Vision outfit, without a doubt the strongest team of the race, while the Kildare Cahill Cycles team had 30 minutes in hand over a 3-man Derry Clarke Contracts in the county award. The Derry team,

however, had a god RÁS with two stages as well as McCann's win in both the points and mountains classifications.

David O'Loughlin, who had made a brave bid for overall honours took the Ben McKenna Memorial competition for the best under 23 rider and Tim Barry (Cork Triton Ventilux) was the best second category rider in 33rd place at 29.08.

**Stage 9 Dublin Criterium 40 Kms.** 1 T.Evans (Ireland International Cargo Systems) 56.26 2 E. Moriarty (Ireland) 3 M.Salumets (Estonia) 4 G.Willwohl (Germany Telekom) 5 J.Tanner (Pro-Vision) 6 C.Bracken (Dublin Usher Insulations) 7 P. Brown (Scotland Union Transport) 8 A.Crowley (Kildare Cahill Cycles) 9 G.Butler (England Surrey Racing) 10 J.Winn (Wales) all same time

**General classification:** 1 J.Winn (Wales) 31.23.40. 2 W.Randle (England Pro Vision) at 1.11 3 M.Lovatt (Pro Vision) at 1.24 4 P.Moriarty (Dublin Skip Hire) at 1.37 secs 5 D.O'Loughlin (Mayo NCF) at 2.18 6 D.McCann (Derry Clarke) at 3.16 7 K.Ingeby (Sweden) at 3.35 8 T.Evans (Ireland) at 4.10 9 G.Butler (Surrey) at 4.35 10 J.Tanner (Pro-Vision) at 5.04 11 R.Riddle (Scotland) at 8.17 12 P.Kil (Netherlands) at 10.25 13 S.Faruhn (Germany) at 10.50 14 E.Moriarty (Ireland) at 11.49 15 A.Kay (England York Cycleworks) at 13.34

**Points:** 1 D.McCann 77 2 J.Winn 65 3 J.Tanner 61

**Mountains:** 1 D.McCann 86 2 J.Winn 65 3 G.Butler 58

**Ben McKenna Memorial competition (best under 23):** 1 D.O'Loughlin 2 J.McCarthy (Kerry) at 30.40 3 S.Prendergast (Dublin Usher) at 50.18

**International Team**: 1 England Pro Vision 94.18.38 2 Sweden at 9.47 3 Ireland at 21.43

**County Team:** 1 Kildare Cahill Cycles 95.08.25 2 Derry Clarke Contracts at 30.00 3 Dublin Skip Hire at 51.47

**Second category:** 1 T.Barry (Cork Triton Venelux) 2 J.Crowley (Kerry) 3 A.Donnellan (UCD)

*Julian Winn (Wales, 2000 Winner*

# 2001

It was back to eight days in 2001, a condition imposed by the Union Cycliste International in accepting the RÁS as an event on the International Calendar.
The event had been on the international calendar for a couple of years at the start of the nineties but the costs were prohibitive and Dermot Dignam had taken it back to its semi-international status with the foreign entry made up of club or regional teams.
More recently, however, the international body had brought in grading of international races which made full international status less costly. The UCI had also abolished amateurs and professionals and had brought in a points classification for both nations and riders.
Riders would earn points in UCI ranked events and only the top 30 countries in terms of points earned by their riders automatically qualified for the elite World Championships and the Olympic Games.(There are other methods of qualifying through B World Championships and individual riders with enough points).
With Ireland just outside this top 30 there was a feeling that an international tour at home would provide more opportunities for our cyclists to gain UCI points and improve this position.
The race went on the calendar ranked 2.6, the lowest ranking which can earn points with some 160 on offer on General Classification, stage wins plus mountains and points classifications.
This of course made the race more attractive to foreign teams including lower ranked trade teams who were seeking to improve their standings.
As a result there was a record entry of 190 (189 started, the Japanese team arriving with one rider short). There were four trade teams (still generally referred to as professionals): Team Jet Fuel Coffee from Canada; Team HSBC from South Africa; Team Deutsche Telekom from Germany and Team Legia Bazylisek from Poland.
In total there were 17 visiting teams representing the above plus Wales, defending with Julian Winn; another German team: RG Hamburg; Japan; Netherlands; Sweden; the USA; Scotland and three English teams: Surrey; York and Southend. Great Britain, which had been absent for the previous few years because of the clash with the PRU-Tour at home were back with a crack squad which included the Olympic bronze medal pursuit team which had recently dominated the classic Tour des Mines stage race in France which they had won with Chris Newton.
The remainder of the field was made up of 20 Irish county teams plus an Ireland team who had national champion and new pro. David McCann; past winner Tommy Evans; ex-pro. Morgan Fox; '98 World Junior Champion Mark Scanlon and Aidan Duff who had been having a good season in France.

## STAGE 1

It was first blood for the Ireland Shannon Oaks Hotel team when David McCann won the opening stage over 96.3 miles from Navan in his trademark style, attacking from a leading group in the final miles and time-trialling to the finish. He won stages in '99 and 2000 in the exact same fashion.

With time bonuses on offer at three hot-spot sprints during the stage, McCann was second at Strokestown picking up 2 seconds and combined with 3 seconds for the stage win and his three second gap at the line, he led the previous year's winner Julian Winn (Wales) and two other riders: Dirk Reichl (Deutsche Telekom) and '99 winner Phil Cassidy (Meath Cycleways) by 4 seconds on general classification.

McCann was in the break of the day which went away with 50 kms of the stage remaining. The 11 riders which included Cassidy and race favourite Aussie Dave McKenzie (G.S. Ficonseils) worked well and raced to a lead of over 2 minutes.

Notable absentees from the break were the Great Britain team and when they realised the danger their all-star quintet went to the front and set such a ferocious pace that the bunch and around 50 riders lost over 5 minutes by the finish.

The bunch closed quickly on the leaders and at the 5kms board the gap was down to 40 seconds and continued to close. McCann, realising the danger attacked with 3 kms. remaining and as the bunch swallowed up the rest of the break he hung on and had time to sit up and take a victory salute as he crossed the line 3 seconds ahead of the thundering bunch led in by David Kopp of the Deutsche Telekom team with Philip West (Great Britain) getting up for third.

There were only two 3rd category climbs on the stage and Dirk Reichl (Deutsche Telekom) led by a point from Krzystof of the Polish pro. Legia - Bazyliszek squad. McCann led the points and Ireland Shannon Oaks the team race by virtue of McCann 4 second advantage.

A new under-23 classification, sponsored by the Irish Sports Council was headed by Dirk Reichl while Carlow led the county teams.

**Stage 1 Navan - Ballaghaderreen 155 Kms.** 1 D.McCann (Ireland Shannon Oaks) 3.26.09 2 D.Kopp (Deutsche Telekom) at 3 secs 3 P.West (Great Britain) 4 A.Greipel (Deutsche Telekom) 5 M.Fox (Ireland) 6 M.Scanlon (Ireland) 7 J.Papp (Team Cliff Bar) 8 T.Wienenroth (Team RG Hamburg) 9, M.Fitzgerald (Derry Classic Walls) 10 D. Chassot (GS Ficonseils) all same time

**General Classification:** 1 D.McCann 3.26.04 2 J.Winn (Wales) 3 D.Reichl (Deutsche Telekom) 4 P.Cassidy (Meath Cycleways) all same time 5 P.West (G.B.) at 7 secs 8 A.Crowley (Meath Cycleways) s.t. 9 A.Greipel at 8 secs 10 M.Fox (Ireland) s.t.

**Under 23:** 1 D.Reichl 2 D.Kopp 3 A.Greipel

**Points:** 1 D.McCann 15 2 D.Kopp 14 3 P.West 13

**Mountains:** 1 D.Reichl 8 2 K.Zasada (Legia) 7 3 C.Newton 5

**International Team:** 1 Ireland Shannon Oaks 10.18.33 2 Deutsche Telekom at 3 secs 3 GS Ficonseils s.t.

**County Team:** 1 Carlow Dan Morrissey 10.18.36

## STAGE 2

Dirk Reichl of the German Team Deutsche Telekom won the second stage, 84.46 miles from Ballaghaderreen to Portumna and took over the yellow jersey from David McCann who came in with the main bunch, 34 seconds behind a 15-man break.
The Ireland team sent Morgan Fox away with the big break after 40 kilometres, hoping he might get the stage, but he finished 4th and took the green Points jersey.
When the break's lead got to nearly 2 minutes the Irish team decided to start chasing. With 10 kilometres left the gap was 1.05 and by the finish they had cut it back to 34 seconds.
From a racing point of view it was an uneventful stage with no hot sports or mountains primes to be contested on the flat run which was into the wind for most of the way. Main interest on the day came from crashes of which there were five which were responsible for some retirals. There was one non-starter and 4 non finishers leaving 184 in the race.
**Stage 2 Ballaghaderreen – Portumna 131 Kms.** 1 D.Reichl (Team Deutsche Telekom) 3.06.39 2 H.Odlin (Team Melerengi) 3 K.Zasada (Team Legia Bazyliszek) 4 M. Fox (Ireland Shannon Oaks) 5 S.Cummings (Great Britain) 6 C.Knees (Team Deutsche Telekom) 7 J.Crookham (Team Jet Fuel Coffee) 8 M.Salinski (Team Legia Bazyliszek) 9 D.Chassot (GS Ficonseils) 10 N.White (Team HSBC), all same time
**General Classification:** 1 D.Reichl 6.32.47 2 M.Fox at 4 secs 3 D.Chassot 4 J.Crookham 5 K.Zasada 6 P.Manning (G.B.) 7 M.Salinski (Legia) 8 H.Odlin 9 C.Knees 10 J.Griffiths (Wales) 11 N.White 12 F.Modin (Malerengi) all same time
**Under 23:** 1 D.Reichl 2 M.Salinski 3 C.Knees
**Points:** 1 M. Fox 23 2 D.Reichl 15 3 D.McCann 15
**Mountains:** 1 D.Reichl 8 2 K.Zasada 7 3 D.McKenzie (GS Ficonseils) 7
**International Team:** 1 Team Deutsche Telekom 9.20.31 2 Team Malerengi 3 Team Legia Bazyliszek all same time
**County Team:** 1 Antrim UCF 19.39.41 2 Carlow Dan Morrissey at 34 secs 3 Derry Classic Walls s.t.
**2nd Cat:** 1 C.McGuinness (Naas) 6.33.25 2 M.Slattery (Kerry) 3 J.Crowley (Kerry) all same time.

## STAGE 3

There was no major change overall on the third stage from Nenagh to Castleisland which resulted in another triumph for the Deutsche Telekom team as David Kopp won the sprint from over 100 riders.
His teammate Dirk Reichl kept the yellow jersey from a big group of riders all equal on time at 4 seconds with over 100 riders within 40 seconds of the leader. By virtue of sprint placings Morgan Fox (Ireland Shannon Oaks) moved to 2nd.

The long 114 miles stage with three climbs had been expected to produce a shake up but although bunch splits saw two big groups totalling 70 riders finishing up to 30 minutes behind, all the big hitters were in the main peleton.
The German team seemed to be well in control of affairs and although a 5-man group was away for around 40 miles, it always seemed likely that they would be caught before the finish.
The first KOM prime, a 2nd category at Bolingbrooke was taken by Julian Winn (Wales) ahead of Stefan Schumacher (Deutsche Telekom) and Dave McKenzie (GS Ficonseils).
The positions were reversed at the 1st cat. Climb of Carrigeenina which gave Schumacher enough points to take over the climber's jersey.
After the descent the five man group went away: Ray Clarke (Derry Classic Walls), Eddie O'Donoghue (Carlow Dan Morrissey); Chris Young (Deeside Olympic) and Welsh pair Anthony Malarczyk and James Griffiths.
Griffiths dropped back leaving four at the front and Clarke led over the final climb at Ballydesmond from Malarczyk and Young.
With 25 kms to go Clarke decided to go it along and for the next 15 kilometres he stayed out in front, at one time more than a minute ahead. However the flying bunch swept up the remainder of the break and then Clarke at the 10 kms to go board setting it up for a spectacular sprint in front of a big crowd in the main street.
**Stage 3 Nenagh – Castleisland 184 Kms.** 1 D.Kopp (Deutsche Telekom) 2 D.McKenzie (GS Ficonseils) 3 E.Moriarty (Meath Cycleways) 4 M.Fox (Ireland Shannon Oaks) 5 N.Exstrom (Team Malerengi) 6 K.McMahon (Dublin Iarnrod Eireann) 7 T.Evans (Ireland Shannon Oaks) 8 P.West (Great Britain) 9 P.Griffin (Dublin Iarnrod Eireann) 10 J.Winn (Wales) all same time
**General Classification:** 1 D.Reichl (Deutsche Telekom) 11.00.04 2 M.Fox at 4 secs 3 D.Chassot (GS Ficonseils) 4 K.Zasada (Legia Baz.) 5 J.Crookham (Jet Fuel Coffee) 6 P.Manning (Great Britain) 7 M.Salinski (Legia Baz.) 8 H.Odlin (Team Malerengi) 9 C.Knees (Deutsche Telekom) 10 J.Griffiths (Wales)
**Points:** 1 M.Fox 35 2 D.Kopp 29 3 P.West 21
**Mountains:** 1 S.Schumacher 23 2 J.Winn 22 3 D.Mckenzie 21
**International Team:** 1 Deutsche Telekom 33.00.58 2 Team Malerengi 3 Team Legia Baz. all same time

## STAGE 4

The first climb in the Kerry Mountains, the Conor Pass was the catalyst which finally blew the race apart and it was all change at the top in Killorglin.
Mark Scanlon of the Ireland Shannon Oaks team won the stage from a big breakaway group but David Chassot of the Swiss GS Ficonseils team took over at the top of the General classification although equal on time with six other riders.
Stephen Cummings (Great Britain) attacked just after the start and the fast early pace saw a group of riders dropped before Tralee after only 11 miles. Cummings stayed

away for 25 miles with Phil Cassidy (Meath Cycleways) and Erik Saunders (GS Ficonseils) between him and the peleton.
They were all together again by the start of the first category climb of the Conor Pass and three riders went away: David McKenzie (GS Ficonseils) led Marek Blazej (Legia Bazylisek) and Christian Knees (Deutschd Telekom) over the top with a group of around fifty 15 seconds down but behind the race had split into five bunches.
The three leaders stayed away over the next climb at Lispole 47 miles after which they were joined by a chasing group which included Scanlon, David O'Loughlin (Mayo Connacht Gold) and Michael McNena (Galway Telecom).
Over the final 20 miles several small groups of riders came up to join the leading bunch with 19 riders contesting the sprint in Killorglin up the short sharp hill to the finish where Scanlon won easily.
Deutsche Telekom, who had led most of the classifications at the start of the stage were the biggest losers with only David Kopp in the first 10 but he finished 3rd to take over the green Points jersey. Race leader Dirk Reichl came home with the next group 36 seconds behind Scanlon.
McKenzie led the mountains and Marek Salinski of Poland the under-23 classification. Deutsche Telekom have lost the team lead to the Polish Legia Bazylisek squad with Great Britain next.
**Stage 4 Castleisland – Killorglin 119 Kms.** 1 M.Scanlon (Ireland Shannon Oaks) 2.47.49 2 D.McKenzie (GS Ficonseils) 3 D.Knopp (Deutsche Telekom) 4 M.McNena (Galway Telecom) 5 P.Griffin (Dublin Iarnrod Eireann) 6 D.O'Loughlin (Mayo Connacht Gold) 7 J.Welniak (Legia Bazylisek) 8 P.Manning (Great Britain) 9 P.Wedge (Canada Jet Fuel Coffee) 10 L.Davis (Velo Esocce Montpelier) all same time
**General Classification:** 1 D.Chassot (GS Ficonseils) 13.47.57 2 J.Crookham (Canada Jet Fuel Coffee) 3 M.Salinski (Legia Bazylisek) 4 P.Manning (Great Britain) 5 C.Knees (Deutsche Telekom) 6 B.de Waard (Holland B.C.R.0. 7 D.Kopp (Deutsche Telekom) all same time 8 M.Scanlon (Ireland) at 32 secs 9 P.Griffin (Dublin Iarnrod Eireann) at 34 secs 10 J. Welniak (Legia Bazylisek) s.t.
**Under 23:** 1 M.Salinski 13.47.57 2 C.Knees 3 B.de Waard all same time
**Points:** 1 D.Kopp 42 2 M.Fox (Ireland) 35 3 D.McKenzie 28
**Mountains:** 1 D.McKenzie 41 2 J.Winn 30 3 S.Schumacher 28
**International Team:** 1 Poland Legia Bazylisek 41.24.25 2 Germany Deutsche Telekom at 46 secs 3 Great Britain at 57 secs
**County Team:** 1 Dublin Skip Hire 41.35.49 2 Antrim UCF at 12 secs 3 Carlow Dan Morrissey at 46 secs
**Second Cat:** 1 M.Slattery (Kerry) 13.49.17 2 C.McGuinness (Naas) at 5.23 3 J.McCarthy (Kerry) at 12.35

## STAGE 5

Christian Knees scored yet another stage win for the Deutsche Telekom team on the 5th stage, 93.2 miles from Killorglin to Skibbereen.

Paul Manning (Great Britain) took the Yellow jersey but it was still very tight at the top with Knees equal on time with the leader and four more only 7 seconds adrift. The first 50 were still covered by 1.27 so it was still anybody's race.

It was a day that promised much with ten King of the mountains climbs, three of them 1st category but the strength of the field was such that a very large bunch of around 80 riders were never more than 3.30 down and the big teams turned on the power in the final miles to once more make it a virtual bunch sprint at the finish.

A group of five had been away for most of the day: Ray Clarke (Derry Classic Walls), Denis O'Shea (Kerry), Nicholas White (South Africa HSBC) and Meath Cycleways pair Eugene Moriarty and double RÁS winner Phil Cassidy.

Clarke made a determined assault on the mountains classification and ended the day leading White by 76 points to 72 with previous leader Dave McKenzie and O'Shea well back in equal third place on 41.

Cassidy gave his all riding for Moriarty and blew up on the climb of Mount Gabriel losing 18 minutes over the final 15 miles. When he crossed the line he collapsed from exhaustion and had to be taken away in an ambulance but was able to start again next morning.

Meanwhile behind a 5-man chasing group including Tommy Evans (Ireland Shannon Oaks), Erik Saunders (Switzerland GS Ficonseils), Marek Blazej (Poland Legia Bazylisek), Josh Hall (Canada Jet Fuel Coffee) and Mark Lovatt (Southend) almost got across to the leaders but they were swept up in the bunch charge for the finish.

The four leaders almost managed to hang on but Knees, Manning, Jukla Heinikainen (Sweden Malerengi) got past them in the final sprint with David Kopp (Deutsche Telekom) heading in the huge bunch just 7 seconds down on the stage winner.

Kopp still led the points by 9 points from Ireland's Morgan Fox; Knees had the U-23 jersey and Matt Slattery (Kerry) still led the second category riders. Poland Legia Bazyliszek led Deutsche Telekom by 39 seconds while Dublin Skip headed the county teams.

**Stage 5 Killorglin – Skibbereen 150 Kms.** 1 C.Knees (Deutsche Telekom) 3.44.52 2 J.Hainikainen (Sweden Malerengi) 3 P.Manning (Great Britain) 4 E.Moriarty (Meath Cycleways) all same time 5 R.Clarke (Derry Classic Walls) at 4 secs 6 N.White (South Africa HSBC) at 5 secs 7 D.Kopp (Deutsche Telekom) at 7 secs 8 A.Greipel (Deutsche Telekom) 9 M.Fox (Ireland Shannon Oaks) 10 J.McIntyre (Velo Esocce Montpeliers) all same time

**General Classification:** 1 P.Manning (Great Britain) 17.32.49 2 C.Knees (Deutsche Telekom) s.t. 3 D.Chassot (GS Ficonseils) at 7 secs 4 J.Crookham (Jet Fuel Coffee) 5 M.Salinski ((Legia Bazylisek) 6 B.de Waard (Holland BRC Kennemerlan) all same time 7 D.Kopp (Deutsche Telekom) at 39 secs 8 P.Griffin (Dublin Iarnrod Eireann)

at 41 secs 9 D.McKenzie (GS Ficonseils) 10 M.Scanlon (Ireland Shannon Oaks) 11 J.Welniak (Legia Bazylisek) 12 P.Wedge (Jet Fuel Coffee) all same time
**Under 23:** 1 C.Knees 17.32.49 2 M.Salinski at 7 secs 3 B.de Waard s.t.
**Points:** 1 D.Kopp 51 2 M.Fox 42 3 D.McKenzie 30
**Mountains:** 1 R.Clarke 76 2 N.White 72 3 eq. D.McKenzie and D.O'Shea 41
**International Team:** 1 Poland Legia Bazylisek 52.39.22 2 Germany Deutsche Telekom at 39 secs 3 Switzerland G.S. Ficonseils at 1.20
**County Team:** 1 Dublin Skip Hire 52.50.46 2 Carlow Dan Morrissey at 46 secs 3 Derry Classic Walls at 12.01
**Second Cat:** 1 M.Slattery (Kerry) 17.34.16 2 J.Crowley (Kerry) at 30.52 3 A.Buckley (Waterford) at 31.14

## STAGE 6

There was another change of lead after the yellow jersey Paul Manning (Great Britain) was penalised 10 seconds for a hand sling from a teammate allowing Christian Knees (Deutsche Telekom) who had been equal on time with Manning to take the lead by 7 seconds.
The British team, the Olympic bronze-medal winning track team pursuit squad from Sydney, had not been aware that the hand sling, in response to a Telekom attack, was illegal, but manager John Herety was and they accepted Commissaire President Gerry McDaid's ruling without protest.
Once again the race ended with almost 100 riders within 10 seconds of the winner despite a stage run off at an average speed of 28.5 m.p.h. Seven riders did manage to grab a few seconds but is didn't impact on the top five placings with four riders still equal on time, 5 seconds behind the new leader. Manning dropped to 6th by virtue of his 10 second penalty.
The stage was won by Jeremy Maartens (South Africa HSBC) by 2 seconds from Mark Lovatt (Southend) and Anthony Malarczyk (Wales) with another three riders David O'Loughlin (Mayo Connacht Gold), James Griffiths (Wales) and Dominique Perras (Switzerland GS Ficonseils) a further 3 seconds back and the bunch led in by Green jersey David Kopp at 10 seconds.
The seven-man break had come together over the final few miles following an attack by Perras. He was joined first by Griffiths, and then at intervals by the others.
With 10 kms remaining Maartens stopped working in the break. At 5 kms. the lead was 25 seconds and at 2 kms. it was down to 16. Malarczyk Mckenzie and Lovatt attacked but Maartens went with them and at the kilometre mark he left them to ride home on his own.
The stage had started at a furious pace with 60 miles covered in the first two hours. At 66 miles Jason Macintyre (Velo Ecosse Montpeliers) went off on his own and stayed out in front for over 20 miles but was brought back at Youghal with 20 miles to go.

On a day with seven small climbs Ray Clarke (Derry Classic Walls) retained the climbers jersey with 80 points to the 76 of Nick White (South Africa HSBC) with Eugene Moriarty (Cycleways) coming into the reckoning on 65. Kopp retained the Points, Knees the under-23 and Matt Slattery (Kerry) the second category rider classification.

**Stage 6 Skibberreen – Dungarvan 164 Kms.** 1 J.Maartens (South Africa HSBC) 3.34.17 2 M.Lovatt (Southend) at 2 secs 3 A.Malarczyk (Wales) 4 D.McKenzie (Switzerland GS Ficonseils) all same time 5 D.O'Loughlin (Mayo Connacht Gold) at 5 secs 6 J.Griffiths (Wales) 7 D.Perras (GS Ficonseils) all same time 8 D.Kopp (Germany Deutsche Telekom) at 10 secs 9 E.Moriarty (Meath Cycleways) 10 H.Odlin (Sweden Malerengi) all same time

**General Classification:** 1 C.Knees (Deutsche Telekom) 21.07.16 2 D.Chassot (GS Ficonseils) at 7 secs 3 J.Crookham (Jet Fuel Coffee) 4 M.Salinski ((Legia Bazylisek) 5 B.de Waard (Holland BRC Kennemerlan) all same time 6 P.Manning (Great Britain) at 10 secs 7 J.Maartens (South Africa HBSC) at 31 secs 8 D.McKenzie (GS Ficonseils) at 33 secs 9 A.Malarczyk (Wales) s.t. 10 D.O'Loughlin (Mayo Connacht Gold) at 36 secs 11 D.Kopp (Deutsche Telekom) at 39 secs 12 P.Griffin (Dublin Iarnrod Eireann) at 41 secs

**Under 23:** 1 C.Knees 21.07.16 2 M.Salinski at 7 secs 3 B.de Waard s.t.

**Points:** 1 D.Kopp 59 2 D.McKenzie 42 3 E.Moriarty 35

**Mountains:** 1 R.Clarke 80 2 N.White 76 3 E.Moriarty 65

**International Team:** 1 Poland Legia Bazylisek 63.22.43 2 Germany Deutsche Telekom at 39 secs 3 Switzerland GS Ficonseils at 1.07

**County Team:** 1 Dublin Skip Hire 63.34.07 2 Carlow Dan Morrissey at 46 secs 3 Meath Cycleways at 14.57

**Second Cat:** 1 M.Slattery (Kerry) 21.08.43 2 D.O'Shea (Kerry) at 49.25 3 J.Crowley (Kerry) at 57.12

## STAGE 7

Throughout the week the strong teams had been able to count on pulling back any breaks in the final 30 miles but it was always going to be a different story on Saturday which saw six climbs, three of them first category on Mount Leinster in the last hour of the stage.

As the field tackled the first of the 1st cat. primes at The Heights, Mountains leader Ray Clarke (Derry Classic Walls) led his closest challenger Nicholas White (South Africa HSCB) off the front but as the climbing continued Clarke dropped back as Paul Manning (Great Britain) made it across to White who picked up enough points on the next two 1st cats. to wrap up the mountains classification.

The two worked well and after the descent their lead was over a minute. With 10 kilometres to go David McCann (Ireland Shannon Oaks) went away from the chasing group in company of Jaroslaw Welniak (Poland Legia Baz.) but although they stayed

away to take the next two places, the leaders still had 1.05 in hand at the line where Manning, sure of the yellow jersey, did not contest the sprint.
It was a very satisfying result for Manning who had lost the jersey in controversial circumstances on Friday. Manning, led the GC by 41 seconds from White, ending a run of bad luck for the GB team who had never won the RÁS but several times saw victory snatched away on the final stages.
**Stage 7 Dungarvan – Bunclody 171 Kms.** 1 N.White (South Africa HSBC) 3.47.48 2 P.Manning (Great Britain) s.t. 3 D.McCann (Ireland Shannon Oaks) at 1.05 4 J.Welniak (Poland Legia Baz.) s.t. 5 J.Winn (Wales) at 1.18 6 S.Skiba (Poland Legia Baz) 7 J.Crookham (Canada Jet Fuel Coffee) 8 D.McKenzie (Switzerland GS Ficonseils) 9 P.Griffin (Dublin Iarnrod Eireann) 10 L.Davis (Velo Ecosse Montpeliers) all same time
**General Classification:** 1 P.Manning (Great Britain) 24.55.13 2 N.White (South Africa HSBC) at 41 secs 3 C.Knees (Germany Deutsche Telekom) at 1.08 4 D.Chassot (Switzerland GS Ficonseils) at 1.15 5 J.Crookham (Canada Jet Fuel Coffree) s.t. 6 J.Welniak (Poland Legia Bazylisek) at 1.36 7 D.McKenzie (GS Ficonseils) at 1.41 8 D.O'Loughlin (Mayo Connacht Gold) at 1.44 9 P.Griffin (Dublin Iarnrod Eireann) at 1.49 10 P.Wedge (Jet Fuel Coffee) s.t. 11 S.Skiba (Legia Bazylisek) s.t. K.Dawson (Southend) s.t. 13 L.Davis (Velo Ecosse Montpeliers) s.t. 14 P.Moriarty (Dublin Skip) s.t. 15 D.McCann (Ireland Shannon Oaks Hotel) at 2.14 16 D.Perras (GS Ficonseils) at 2.30 17 J.Winn (Wales) at 2.31 18 K.Gallagher (Antrim UCF) at 2.35
**Under 23:** 1 C.Knees 2 M.Salinski 3 B.de Waard.
**Points:** 1 D.Kopp 59 2 D.McKenzie 50 3 E.Moriarty 35
**Mountains:** 1 N.White 130 2 R.Clarke 108 3 E.Moriarty 68
**International Team:** 1 Poland Legia Bazylisek 77.19.48 2 Switzerland GS Ficonseils at 1.20 3 Canada Jet Fuel Coffee at 3.40
**County Team:** 1 Carlow Dan Morrissey 75.39.44 2 Dublin Skip Hire at 17.37 3 Dublin Iarnrod Eireann at 3.05
**Second Category:** 1 M.Slattery (Kerry) 2 D.O'Shea (Kerry) 3 C.Farrell (Meath Avonmore)

## STAGE 8

After eleven years of trying, Great Britain finally won the RÁS when Olympic rider Paul Manning successfully defended the yellow jersey on the final stage, a 50 minutes plus 3 lap's criterium in Dublin city centre.
The stage ended in a big bunch sprint won by David Kopp (Germany Deutsche Telekom) who had led the Green jersey point's classification for most of the week.
The stage was run off at very high speed which doomed any breakaway attempts. Over the final three laps the well drilled Telekom squad controlled the head of the peleton setting up their sprinter perfectly to use his finishing speed and he duly obliged by a length from Sweden's Ekstrom. Eugene Moriarty was best of the Irish

in 5th place while Tommy Evans, who had won the same stage a year before was 9th.

It was not a great RÁS for the Irish riders with only four of them picking up UCI points for GC placings: David O'Loughlin 8th; Paul Griffin 9th, Paddy Moriarty 14th and David McCann 15th. The German Deutsche Telekom team won three stages with South Africa and Ireland getting two apiece, Belfast's David McCann and Sligo's Mark Scanlon scoring for the home team.

The average race speed for the week was a record 26.78 mph. 157 of the 189 starters finished.

**Stage 8 Dublin Criterium 40 Kms.** 1 D.Kopp (Deutsche Telekom) 47.17 2 N.Ekstrom (Sweden Malerengi) 3 M.Lange (South Africa) 4 A.Greipel (Deutsche Telekom) 5 E.Moriarty (Meath Cycleways) 6 H.Odlin (Sweden Malerengi) 7 F.de Jager (Holland BRC Kennemerlan) 8 P.West (Great Britain) 9 T.Evans (Ireland Shannon Oaks) 10 E.O'Donoghue (Carlow Dan Morrissey) all same time

**General Classification:** 1 P.Manning (Great Britain) 25.52.31 2 N.White (South Africa HSBC) at 41 secs 3 C.Knees (Germany Deutsche Telekom) at 1.08 4 D.Chassot (Switzerland GS Ficonseils) at 1.15 5 J.Crookham (Canada Jet Fuel Coffree) s.t. 6 J.Welniak (Poland Legia Bazylisek) at 1.36 7 D.McKenzie (GS Ficonseils) at 1.41 8 D.O'Loughlin (Mayo Connacht Gold) at 1.44 9 P.Griffin (Dublin Iarnrod Eireann) at 1.49 10 P.Wedge (Jet Fuel Coffee) s.t. 11 S.Skiba (Legia Bazylisek) s.t. 12 K.Dawson (Southend) s.t. 13 L.Davis (Velo Ecosse Montpeliers) s.t. 14 P.Moriarty (Dublin Skip) s.t. 15 D.McCann (Ireland Shannon Oaks Hotel) at 2.14 16 D.Perras (GS Ficonseils) at 2.30 17 J.Winn (Wales) at 2.31 18 K.Gallagher (Antrim UCF) at 2.35

**Under 23:** 1 C.Knees 2 M.Salinski 3 B.de Waard

**Second Category:** 1 M.Slattery (Kerry) 2 D.O'Shea (Kerry) 3 C.Farrell (Meath Avonmore)

**Points:** 1 D.Kopp 74 2 D.McKenzie 50 3 E.Moriarty 46

**Mountains:** 1 N.White 130 2 R.Clarke 108 3 E.Moriarty 68

**International Team:** 1 Poland Legia Bazylisek 77.41.39 2 Switzerland GS Ficonseils at 1.20 3 Canada Jet Fuel Coffee at 3.40

**County Team:** 1 Carlow Dan Morrissey 78.01.35 2 Dublin Skip Hire at 17.37 3 Dublin Iarnrod Eireann at 3.05

*Paul Manning, Britain, 2001 winner*

# 2002

2002 was the 50th anniversary RÁS with 200 riders entered for the race, once again held over eight days to comply with the UCI requirements for granting full international status.
A row broke out in the weeks before the race between organiser Dermot Dignam and the Irish Department of Justice and Law Reform's refusal to grant visas to the Nigerian team
As a result of this refusal 195 riders were on the start list and for the first time visiting riders outnumbered the home contingent, 20 teams of five (without the Nigerians) against 19 county teams
Visiting teams came from Great Britain, Canada, South Africa, Wales, Poland, Denmark, France, Germany (2),Japan, Scotland, Isle of Man, USA and six English regional teams
It was looking odds-on another overseas victory although the Cycling Ireland team had two former winners in their line-up, US based pro. Ciaran Power and Tommy Evans. The very strong defending GB squad had 2001 winner Paul Manning in their line-up along with Chris Newton who had started favourite the previous year before being forced into early retirement
Also strongly fancied were the Lancashire Team Compensation group whose riders John Tanner, Mark Lovatt and Keith Dawson had been dominating the British Premier Calendar and who had cleaned up on two visits to Ireland for the RÁS Mumhaim and the UCI ranked Shay Ellliot Memorial in Bray
To mark the 50th anniversary the race was dedicated to Joe Christle, the first race director who held that position for many years.
Individual stages were also dedicated to deceased riders and officials who had strong connections to the event. Noel McGuill, killed in the 1972 event, Ando Christle and Donal Roche killed in traffic accidents while officiating in 1954 and 1963. Jim Killeen, President of the NCA during the formative years of the race and three past winners, Paddy Flanagan, Ben McKenna and Joe O'Brien

## STAGE 1

Chris Newton of the Great Britain team won the opening stage 97 miles from Dublin to Ballinamore, Co. Leitrim
The Olympic medallist came home on his own, 20 seconds ahead of a big group of 26 riders and having already picked up 6 seconds in time bonuses at the intermediate Hot Spots sprints, he led on general classification by 25 seconds from John Tanner (Lancaster Compensation Group) with Ciaran Power (Team Ireland Stena), who won

the sprint for second place, lying second but equal on time at 27 seconds with a group of other riders

The Irish riders missed out badly on the day with only Power and fellow US based professional David O'Loughlin making the big break. The bunch came in over 4 minutes behind and with so many good riders having finished in the lead group, it was difficult to see anyone outside the 27 having any realistic chance of overall honours

The first 30 miles were run off in atrocious weather which flooded the roads in places and punctures were numerous among the 184 starters. The first serious break of nine riders went away after 30 miles and they in turn were chased by two further groups of nine and when they all came together and were prepared to work, they took a lot of time out of the bunch

The sun came out for the second half of the stage but by them the race had turned head on into gale force winds which discouraged the chasers. As they came through Ballinamore with a lap of 6-mile circuit to be completed the 27 were split into four groups covered by about 20 seconds but they all came together on the circuit before Newton made his successful move

Newton had started the 2001 race as favourite after winning the Circuit des Mines in France but had to retire after the first day with a pulled muscle, his team-mate Paul Manning going on to give Great Britain their first ever win

**Stage 1 Dublin - Ballinamore 156 Kms.** 1 C.Newton (Great Britain) 3.36.04 2 C.Power (Team Ireland Stena) at 20 secs 3 N.Swithenbank (Lancs M.K. Cycles) 4 L.Bojsen (Denmark Distrikt Jyll) 5 J.Tanner (Lancs Compensation Group) 6 H.Pritchard (Wales) 7 B.Brooks (NW England Cycle Centre) 8 A.Hojgaard (Denmark Distrikt Jyll) 9 I.McLeod (South Africa Team HSB) 10 G.Dodd (Surrey League)

**General Classification:** 1 C.Newton (G.B.) 3.35.55 2 J.Tanner (Lancs. Compensation Group) at 25 secs 3 C.Power (Team Ireland Stena) at 27 secs 4 T.Buckle (G.B.) 5 H.Pritchard (Wales) 6 G.Dodd (Surrey League) all same time 8 B.Brooke (NE Eng.) at 28 secs 9 A.Hojgaard (Denmark) 10 L.Bojsen (Denmark) all same time

**Points:** 1 C.Newton 15 2 C.Power 14 3 N.Swithenbank 13

**International Team:** 1 Great Britain 10.48.52 2 Denmark Distrikt Jyll) at 20 secs

**County Team:** 1 Mayo Connacht Gold 11.03.16 2 Meath Lee Strand s.t.

## STAGE 2

John Tanner (Lancashire Compensation Group) won the 101 miles second stage from Ballinamore to Nenagh, Co. Tipperary but failed by 12 seconds to take the yellow jersey from Newton

The riders toiled all day into a gale which saw them come home almost an hour behind schedule. However it tended to keep the bunch together and despite dozens of breakaways getting established, there was usually a general regroupment within a few miles

Early on a break of six including Dermot Nally (Ireland Stena) made the first serious looking move but after a flurry of counter attacks they were all together again after 40 kms. The first KOM of the race, a fairly mild 3rd cat.was taken by Timo Wolk (Germany Team Stevens - Jeantex)

Julian Winn (Wales) the 2000 Rás winner went away along with Lancs. Compensation Group's Mark Lovatt, Rory Wylie (Southend), Tashiro (Japan) and Ian McLeod (South Africa HBSC) in a useful looking move and a few miles further on they were joined by a chasing group of 13 which included Tanner, Paul Manning (GB) and Nicholas White (South Africa HBSC)

This group got a lead of 1.50 and with the pace of the chase behind the bunch split into two but once again they all came together around the 55 miles mark

The pattern continued and it was from a big leading group that past double winner Phil Cassidy (Meath Lee Strand Cycleways), Kevin Dawson (Lancs Compensation Group) and Frederic Pedersoly (France La Pomme) went away. The Frenchman dropped back to the chasers but Cassidy and Dawson kept at it and got a lead of 1.15

With 12 kms to go Tanner and Ben Brooks (NW England Cycle Centre) went in pursuit and joined the two leaders before the 5kms. to go sign. Behind them the bunch were in full cry with the GB riders leading the chase and they mopped up everybody except the four leaders who just survived to the finish by less than 15 seconds

Tanner came home 1 second in front of Cassidy with Brooks at 2 seconds and Dawson at 5 seconds while Huw Pritchard of Wales led in a huge bunch of around 145 riders just 13 seconds behind the stage winner with Newton just behind in sixth place

**Stage 2 Ballinamore - Nenagh 163 Kms.** 1 J.Tanner (Lancs Team Compensation Group) 4.45.14 2 P.Cassidy (Meath Lee Strand Cycleways) at 1 sec 3 B.Brooks (NW England Cycle Centre) at 2 secs 4 K.Dawson (Lancs Compensation Group) at 5 secs 5 H.Pritchard (Wales) at 13 secs 6 C.Newton (Great Britain) 7 D.Rollin (Canada Team Sympatico) 8 C.Power (Team Ireland Stena Line) 9 C.Bracken (Dublin Usher Insulation) 10 D.Rudnicki (Poland Team Legia) all same time

**General Classification:** 1 C.Newton (GB) 8.21.22 2 J.Tanner (Lancs Compensation Group) at 12 secs 3 B.Brooks (NW England) at 17 secs 4 K. Dawson (Lancs Compensation Group) at 21 secs 5 C.Power (Ireland Stena) at 27 secs 6 H.Pritchard (Wales) 7 G.Dodd (Surrey League) 8 T.Buckle (GB))all same time 9 N.Swithenbank (Lancs MK Cycle) 10 A.Hojgaard (Denmark Distrikt Jyll) all same time 11 L.Bojsen (Denmark) at 29 secs 12 I.McLeod (South Africa HSBC) s.t

## STAGE 3

Just when it looked like the Irish were being shut out, an extraordinary stage saw Philip Cassidy (Meath Lee Strand Cycleways) come home first with Ciaran Power

(Ireland Stena Line) second and going into the yellow jersey by a healthy margin of 3.54 with the other Irish professional in the race David O'Loughlin (Mayo Connacht Gold) taking over second spot

Chris Newton (Great Britain) who started the day in yellow came home with a big chasing group but they were nearly 5 minutes down and he was now third 4.43 behind Power

Once more it was rain and gales all the way although the sun came out for the last ten miles. The conditions saw the race split into five groups with two big groups of around 20 riders each coming in over half-an-hour down

Cassidy went from the drop of the flag along with O'Loughlin on a seemingly suicide mission. Going along as policeman for the Ireland team was Timmy Barry who was not contributing to the work. Despite the conditions they immediately started building up a lead and after 5 kms of racing they were 1 minute ahead

When the were told that a chasing group was coming up they sat up and waited and they were joined by Ray Clarke (Meath Lee Strand), Denis Lynch (VC La Pomme), Anthony Malarczyk (Wales) and Power

Even with the increased numbers it seemed like a hopeless mission into the wind but by Limerick, after 40 kms, the lead had grown to 1.35 and this lead continued to grow. They were still together at the KOM climb off the Barnagh Gap at 55 miles where Clark, Barry and Malarczyk dropped back as Lynch led Cassidy over the top

Ten miles later at the Kilconlea KOM Cassidy led from Power and the Meath man also took the next at Glansherin as their lead had grown too nearly 5 minutes on a chasing group while the yellow jersey was over 7 minutes down

Cassidy attacked at Castleisland inside the last 20 miles and only Power could hold his wheel and the two sped away from Lynch and O'Loughlin who lost nearly 4 minutes over the final miles but still had enough in hand to come home 22 seconds ahead of a big group led in again by Huw Pritchard of Wales from Newton who with his team had staged quite a recovery to get up to this group, an effort which saw two of the GB riders, including last year's winner Paul Manning dropped in the final miles. In the sprint up the hill in Killorglin, Power, knowing he had taken over the overall lead, seemed happy to see Cassidy take the honours

Cassidy said the team had decided to go for the stage because Lee Strand their sponsors were based in the area. He said the weather was in their favour because it made it hard for everyone, whether in the break or in the bunch.

**Stage 3 Nenagh - Killorglin 155 Kms.** 1 P.Cassidy (Meath Lee Strand Cycleways) 3.43.51 2 C.Power (Ireland Stena Line) s.t. 3 Denis Lynch (France VC La Pomme) at 3.48 4 D.O'Loughlin (Mayo Connacht Gold) at 3.52 5 H.Pritchard (Wales) at 5.10 6 C.Newton (G.B.) 7 J.Winn (Wales) 8 H.Nowak (Poland Legia) 9 D.Rudnicki (Poland Legia) 10 I.McLeod (South Africa HBSC)

**General Classification:** 1 C.Power (Team Ireland Stena Line) 12.05.40 2 D.O'Loughlin (Mayo Connacht Gold) at 3.54 3 C.Newton (G.B.) at 4.43 4 J.Tanner (Lancs Compensation Group) at 4.55 5 B.Brooks (NW England Cycle Centre) at 5.00 6 K.Dawson (Lancs Compensation Group) at 5.04 7 H. Pritchard (Wales) at

5.10 8 G.Dodd (Surrey League) s.t. 9 A.Hojgaard (Denmark Distrikt) at 5.11 10 N.Swithenbank (Lancs MK Cycle) s.t.
**Points:** 1 C.Power 36 2 C.Newton 35 3 H.Pritchard 32
**Mountains:** 1 P.Cassidy 14 2 D.Lynch 10 3 C.Power 10

## STAGE 4

Power successfully defended the yellow jersey on the tough stage round the Ring of Kerry from Killorglin to Castletownbeare, 106 miles with 7 climbs, two of them premier category
Chris Newton (Great Britain) whom Power deposed on Tuesday had a good day finishing second, 39 seconds ahead of Power reducing his deficit to 4.04, lying second following the shock withdrawal of second placed David O'Loughlin (Mayo Connacht Gold) before the start of the stage, a victim of food poisoning
The stage was won by Andrew Randell giving the professional Canada Team Sympatico their first success of the race. It was a controversial victory as Newton claimed he was pushed towards the barriers but the commissaires studied the film and judged that the Canadian had held his line and the protest was disallowed
There was an early break which included Julian Winn (Wales) who took the first KOM prime at Seefin. However they were all back in the bunch when the race was neutralised after 18 miles because of road works
After the restart a break went away before Cahirciveen and several small groups made their way up to the leading group which numbered 15 as they tackled the Category 1 climb of the Coomakista Pass where Paul Griffin (Ireland Stena) took the maximum 15 points
The break stayed together over the climb but lost some riders on the road from Kenmare to the foot of the Healy Pass where the leaders held a lead over the bunch of just 1 minute. At this stage there were only two groups on the road but the bunch fragmented on the tough climb with a large group, including the yellow jersey, going off the front of the bunch
In the break Winn, who had been scoring all day took top points for a 10 point lead in the mountains competition. Newton was also there, crossing the top in 4th place
The very tricky descent of the Healy Pass with its numerous S bends saw a series of crashes one rider somersaulting over a stone wall, but all got up and continued. The yellow jersey group was closing on the leaders all the way in but at the finish they were still 39 seconds adrift
**Stage 4 Killorglin - Castletownbeare 171 Kms.** 1 A.Randell (Canada Team Sympatico) 4.21.26 2 C.Newton (Great Britain) 3 H.Nowak (Poland Team Legia) 4 D.Rudnicki (Poland Team Legia) 5 J.Winn (Wales) 6 H.Menad (France VC La Pomme) 7 A.Hojgaard (Denmark Distrikt) 8 C.Brondberg (Denmark) 9 S.Cummings (Great Britain) all same time 10 G.Zoledziowski (Poland Team Legia) at 6 secs
**General Classification:** 1 C.Power (Ireland Stena) 16.27.45 2 C.Newton (G.B.) at 4.04 3 A.Hojgaard (Denmark Distrikt) at 4.32 4 H.Nowak (Poland Team Legia) at

4.33 5 A.Randell (Canada Team Sympatico) 6 H.Menad (France VC La Pomme) 7 S.Cummings (G.B.) all same time 8 J.Tanner (Lancs. Compensation Group) at 4.55 9 B.Brooks (NW England Cycle Centre) at 5.00 10 K.Dawson (Lancs. Compensation Group) at 5.04 11 I.McLeod (South Africa Team HSBC) at 5.12 12 Jean-Francois Laroche (Canada Team Sympatico) s.t.
**Ben McKenna Trophy U23**: 1 H.Nowak 16.32.18 2 S.Cummings (GB) s.t. 3 I.McLeod at 39 secs
**Points:** 1 C.Newton 49 2 C.Power 39 3 H.Pritchard 32
**Mountains:** 1 J.Winn 41 2 D.Spence 31 3 P.Griffin 27
**International Team:** 1 Great Britain 49.37.13 2 Lancaster Comp. Group at 1.17 3 Denmark Distrikt Jyll at 7.14
**County Team:** 1 Meath Lee Strand Cycleways 50.11.22 2 Tipperary Dan Morrissey at 23.04 3 Dublin Skip Hire at 33.19
**Second Category** 1 S. Kelly (Cork Stafford Fuels) 17.00.40 2 M.Power (Tipperary) 3 P.O'Leary (Dublin Usher) all same time

## STAGE 5

Dariusz Rudnicki of the Polish professional Legia squad showed a remarkable turn of speed to beat top sprinters, Chris Newton and Ciaran Power at the end of the 5th stage from Castletownbere to Middleton
The 104.8 miles stage was completed in a time of 3.37.53, an average speed of 28.8 mph. The strong, at times gale force south west wind that has been blowing since the race began was now on the riders backs but this was no relief for the weaker riders who were soon shot out the back by the speed and there were ten retirals bringing the field down to 145
Ride of the day was by GB rider Tim Buckle. After mountains leader Julian Winn (Wales) took the first KOM prime at Traflask, Buckle beat Alexander Ross (Scotland) and Winn for the next at Loughavaul and just kept going
Aided by the tailwind he was averaging 35 mph for long periods and at one time his lead reached 1.35 and he was to stay out in front for 55 miles before a concerted chase by the peleton saw his brave effort come to an end. He was, however, awarded the daily Cuchullain Crystal Merit Award
With 23 miles remaining the bunch were all together when Yellow jersey Power went to the front to take the final climb at Coolculitha and he was immediately followed by second placed Chris Newton (GB) and the effort by the pair split the bunch into three with the strongest 50 in the front group
Banbridge's Tommy Evans was doing sterling work for the Ireland Stena team riding at the front and keeping up a tremendous pace to discourage any attacks, an effort which drew praise from the race leader at the finish saying 'the lads really looked after me and Tommy Evans was on the front for the whole last 20 kms. sheltering me from the crosswind. It was amazing.'

So it all came down to a final mass gallop up the main street in Middleton and Rudnicki showed himself to be a remarkable sprinter holding off the late challenge of Newton and Power. There were no big changes at the top of the GC

**Stage 5 Castletownbeare - Middleton 168 Kms.** 1 D.Rudnicki (Poland Legia) 3.37.53 2 C.Newton (G.B.) 3 C.Power (Ireland Stena) 4 H.Nowak (Poland Legia) 5 R.Muir (Scotland Visit Scotland) 6 E.Moriarty (Meath Lee Strand Cycleways) 7 G.Zoledziowski (Poland Team Legia) 8 I.McLeod (South Africa HBSC) 9 A.Randell (Canada Team Smypatico) 10 S.Cummings (GB) all same time

**General Classification:** 1 C.Power (Ireland Stena) 20.05.38 C.Newton (G.B.) at 4.04 3 A.Hojgaard (Denmark Distrikt) at 4.32 4 H.Nowak (Poland Team Legia) at 4.33 5 A.Randell (Canada Team Sympatico) 6 S.Cummings (G.B.) all same time 7 H.Menad (France VC La Pomme) 8 J.Tanner (Lancs. Compensation Group) at 4.55 9 K.Dawson (Lancs. Compensation Group) at 5.04 10 B.Brooks (NW England Cycle Centre) at 5.10 11 I.McLeod (South Africa Team HSBC) at 5.12 12 Jean-Francois Laroche (Canada Team Sympatico) s.t.

**Ben McKenna Trophy U23:** 1 H.Nowak 20.10.11 2 S.Cummings (GB) s.t. 3 I.McLeod at 39 secs

**Points:** 1 C. Newton 63 2 C.Power 49 3 D.Rudnicki 39

**Mountains:** 1 J.Winn 63 2 D. Spence 50 3 T.Buckle 45

**International Team:** 1 Great Britain 60.30.52 2 Lancaster Comp. Group at 1.17 3 Denmark Distrikt Jyll at 7.14

**County Team:** 1 Meath Lee Strand Cycleways 61.05.01 2 Tipperary Dan Morrissey at 29.08 3 Dublin Skip Hire at 36.33

**Second Category:** 1 F.O'Leary (Dublin Usher) 20.40.23 2 M.Power (Tipperary) 3 S.Kelly (Cork Stafford Fuels) all same time

## STAGE 6

Paul Manning (Great Britain) won the sixth stage, 96.5 miles from Dungarvan to Arklow, coming home 11 seconds ahead of a 9-man chasing group led in by his teammate Chris Newton.

Race leader Ciaran Power (Ireland Stena Line) finished safely in the chasing group and maintains his overall lead by 4.03 from Newton who managed to pull back just one second in the sprint

The G.B. team had decided to blow the race apart from the off and the five of them went to the front and with the gale on their backs the speed was unbelievable, touching 50 mph at times. The stage was the second fastest in 50 years, 96.5 miles in 3.02.31, an average of 31.73 mph

The start from Dungarvan was straight into the drag up The Pike and in pouring rain riders were getting dropped almost immediately. A big group of 28 split off the front with the whole GB team, Power, Paul Griffin of Ireland Stena, Denis Easton riding for Meath Avonmore, Ray Clarke (Meath Lee Strand), Rory Wylie (NW Cycle Centre), Ian McLeod (South Africa HSBC), John Tanner and Mark Lovatt (Lancs

Compensation Group), Dariusz Rudnicki and Hubert Nowak (Poland Legia), Paddy Moriarty (Dublin Skip) and Hichem Menad (VC La Pomme)
With a steady 45 mph being maintained something had to give and this group split, 14 going ahead. It was then that Power found himself isolated with Newton, Cummings and Manning (GB) along with the Compensation Group pair Lovett and Tanner, Ari Hojgaard (Denmark), Moriarty, Nowak and Rudnicki, McLeod and Julian Winn of Wales who was second on the only climb of the day at The Pike to increase his lead in the mountains competition
At New Ross the peleton were already nearly 4 minutes down and before Enniscorthy, with the gap still growing the break lost Cummings and Rudnicki leaving 12 at the front with their maximum lead of 8.40. The bunch started to pull this back but at the finish it was still 7.16
On the Arklow Bypass Power attacked in a strong cross-wind but was quickly joined by Manning who sat in defending Newton's position. With 2 kms. to go as they turned into the wind Power sat-up but Manning attacked and stayed out in front. He was visibly weakening up the hill to the finish but managed to hold on for the stage
**Stage 6 Dungarvan - Arklow 155 Kms.** 1 P.Manning (Great Britain) 3.02.31 2 C.Newton (G.B.) at 11 secs 3 M.Lovatt (Lancs. Compensation Group) at 12 secs 4 H.Nowak (Poland Team Legia) 5 C.Power (Ireland Stena) 6 I.McLeod (South Africa HBSC) 7 J.Tanner (Lancs. Compensation Group) 8 H.Pritchard (Wales) 9 A.Hojgaard (Denmark) 10 J.Winn (Wales) all same time
**General Classification:** 1 C.Power (Team Ireland Stena Line) 23.08.31 2 C.Newton (G.B.) at 4.03 3 A.Hojgaard (Denmark) at 4.32 4 H.Nowak (Poland Team Legia) at 4.33 5 H.Menad (France VC La Pomme) 6 J.Tanner (Lancs. Compensation Group) at 4.55 7 I.McLeod (South Africa Team HSBC) at 5.12 8 M.Lovatt (Lancs. Compensation Group) s.t. 9 J.Winn (Wales) at 11.35 10 K.Dawson (Lancs. Compensation Group) at12.08 11 B.Brooks (NW England Cycle Centre) at 12.14 12 J.F.Laroche (Canada Team Sympatico) at 12.16
**Ben McKenna Trophy U23:** 1 H.Nowak 20.10.11 2 S.Cummings (GB) s.t. 3 I.McLeod at 39 secs
**Points:** 1 C.Newton 63 2 C.Power 49 3 D.Rucnicki 39
**Mountains:** 1 J.Winn 63 2 D.Spence 50 3 T.Buckle 45
**International Team:** 1 Great Britain 60.30.52 2 Lancaster Comp. Group at 1.17 3 Denmark Distrikt Jyll at 7.14
**County Team:** 1 Meath Lee Strand Cycleways 61.05.01 2 Tipperary Dan Morrissey at 29.08 3 Dublin Skip Hire at 36.33
**Second Category:** 1 F.O'Leary (Dublin Usher) 20.40.23 2 M.Power (Tipperary) 3 S.Kelly (Cork Stafford Fuels) all same time

## STAGE 7

Saturday's penultimate stage was in the Wicklow Mountains leader Julian Winn (Wales) broke away with last year's RÁS winner Paul Manning. (G.B.) on the first climb. Winn took the points but on the second climb at Luggala Manning rode away from Winn to take the KOM points. Keeping out in front he took maximum points from all other climbs on the stage. It was a very similar ride to Manning's a year previous but on that occasion he was riding for outright victory which was this time out of reach.

Power was in a small chasing group with Newton and at the top of the Sally Gap they were 1.35 in arrears but this had grown to 4.00 by the penultimate climb of Wicklow Gap. However Manning started to tire and was caught shortly after the final climb

At 5 kilometres to go Power attacked and immediately Newton, Nowak and Persoli responded. At the finish Manning led out his teammate Newton who took his second stage win just holding off the race leader.

**Stage 7 Arklow – Baltinglass 153 Kms.** 1 C.Newton (Great Britain) 3.54.36 2 C.Power (Team Ireland Stena Line) 3 M.Lovatt (Lancaster Compensation Group) 4 H.Nowak (Poland Team Legia) 5 J.Tanner (Lancaster Compensation Group) 6 H.Menad (France VC La Pomme) all same time 7 G.Butler (Surrey League RT) at 3 secs 8 P.Manning (Great Britain) at 6 secs 9 J.Winn (Wales) at 3 mins 5 secs 10 G.Zoledziowski (Poland Team Legia) same time

**General Classification:** 1 C.Power 27.02.57 2 C.Newton at 4.03 3 H.Nowak (Poland Team Leggia) at 4.33 4 H.Menad (France VC La Pomme) at 4.43 5 J.Tanner (Compensation Group) at 4.55 6 M.Lovatt (Compensation Group) at 5.12 7 A.Hojgaard (Denmark Distrikt Jyll) at 7.42 8 I.McLeod (South Africa HSBC) at 8.17 9 G.Butler (Surrey League) at 12.19 10 J.Winn (Wales) at 14.40

**Points:** 1 C.Newton 92 2 C.Power 76 3 H.Nowak 61 4 J. Tanner 47 5 D.Rudnicki (Poland Team Legia) 42

**Mountains:** 1 J.Winn 115 2 P.Manning 87 3 D.Spence 62 4 T.Buckle 45; 5 C.Power 49.

**International Team:** 1 Great Britain 2 Lancaster Compensation Group 3 Poland Team Legia

**County Team:** 1 Meath Lee Strand Cycleways 2 Dublin Skip Hire 3 Kerry Earl of Desmond.

## STAGE 8

Ciarán Power became only the sixth rider in the 50 years history of the FBD Milk RÁS to win the event more than once when he came home safely in second place on the final stage in the Phoenix Park

Power needed just needed to stay out of trouble on the final stage of 1 hour plus 3 laps in the Park. The Team Ireland Stena squad kept up a fast pace discouraging attacks and they successfully countered any attacks and the stage finished in a big bunch sprint with most of the 140 riders left in the race taking part. Like on Saturday Newton just held off a strong challenge from the Yellow jersey for the stage win.

**Stage 8 Phoenix Park Criterium 55 Kms.** 1 C.Newton (Great Britain) 1.12.45 2 C.Power (Team Ireland Stena Line) 3 D.Rudnicki (Poland Team Legia) 4 E.Moriarty

(Meath Lee Strand Cycleways) 5 K.McMahon (Kerry Earl of Desmond) 6 H.Pritchard (Wales) 7 B.Miller (Canada Team Sympatico) 8 A.Crowley (Meath Lee Strand Cycleways) 9 T.Suzuki (Japan Cycleways) 10 C.Bracken (Dublin Usher Insulation) all same time

**General Classification:** 1,C.Power 28.15.42 2 C.Newton at 4.03 3 H.Nowak (Poland Team Leggia) at 4.33 secs 4 H.Menad (France VC La Pomme) at 4.43 secs 5 J.Tanner (Compensation Group) at 4.55 6 M.Lovatt (Compensation Group) at 5.12 7 A.Hojgaard (Denmark Distrikt Jyll) at 7.42 8 I.McLeod (South Africa HSBC) at 8.17 9 G.Butler (Surrey League) at 12.19 10 J.Winn (Wales) at 14.40

**Points:** 1 C.Newton 107 2 C.Power 88 3 H.Nowak 61 4 J.Tanner 47 5 D.Rudnicki 42

**Mountains:** 1 J.Winn 115 2 P.Manning 87 3 D.Spence 62 4 T.Buckle 45 5 C.Power 49

**International Team:** 1 Great Britain 2 Lancaster Compensation Group 3 Poland Team Legia

**County Team:** 1 Meath Lee Strand Cycleways 2 Dublin Skip Hire 3 Kerry Earl of Desmond.

*2002 Winner, Ciaran Power*

# 2003

The 51st RÁS had a field of 155 entries, the first reduction in some years. Like the previous year the percentage of Irish riders was down, leading to much speculation as to whether the race in its UCI ranked mode was getting beyond the abilities of Irish county riders. There were 12 Irish county teams who with the Irish national team made a total of 65 home riders.
Great Britain, winners in 2001 were back with Paul Manning, winner on that occasion and World Points Champion Chris Newton, second last time and hoping to improve.
Ireland, sponsored by the Irish Sports Council, had defending champion Ciaran Power. With him were Vincent Gleeson, Andrew Donnellan, '96 winner Tommy Evans and in form US-based pro. David O'Loughlin, winner of six races since the start of the season including the UCI ranked Archer Grand Prix in England where he had beaten Chris Newton.
After a couple of years in the south of the country, this time the emphasis was on the north with three stage finishes in County Donegal.

## STAGE 1

Tommy Evans, riding for the Ireland team, won the opening stage, 84 miles from Dublin to Roscrea, Co. Tipperary.
The Banbridge rider came home together with Danish rider Ari Hojgaard and comfortably won the sprint. With the 10 seconds winner's bonus he took the first yellow jersey as no single rider had amassed sufficient bonus seconds on the three hot-spot sprints en route to pose any threat to the stage winner.
For most of the stage it looked like it would end in a bunch sprint of the 151 starters as the field struggled into a fierce headwind all the way making it virtually impossible for any breaks to make much headway, especially with so many strong teams ready to take up the chase.
The first hot-sport at Newbridge went to David Harrigan (Australia Team Down Under) from Aidan Crowley (Meath Lee Strand). They were still all together at the next hot-spot at Mountmellick which went to Jonas Holmkvist (Sweden Team Bianchi) but it was yet another country Kazakhstan, which took the next with Maxim Iglinskiv.
This prime doubled as a 3rd category KOH climb at The Cut in the Slieve Bloom Mountains where Iglinskiv went away on his own. He stayed out in front for a time and as the bunch chased him down the winning move started when Hojgaard attacked and was chased by Evans, 2001 winner Paul Manning (Great Britain) and Paddy Moriarty (Dublin Skip Hire).

As they got up to the Dane, Moriarty dropped back leaving three at the front with some 25 kilometres to go. They worked well together getting a gap of 41 seconds at Borris-in-Ossory despite the best efforts of the bunch.
Over the final kilometres Manning blew and as they entered the finishing straight, Evans, a noted fast finisher jumped and opened a good gap which Hojgaard could not close. Cody Stevenson of the Australian Team Down Under led in the big bunch just 20 seconds later.
**Stage 1 Dublin - Roscrea 135 Kms.** 1 T.Evans (Ireland Irish Sports Council) 2.36.27 2 A.Hojgaard (Denmark Jyll) s.t. 3 C.Stevenson (Australia Team Down Under) at 20 secs 4 C.Newton (Great Britain) 5 A.Bazayev (Kazakhstan) 6 M.Yates (Australia Team Down Under) 7 J.Holmkvist (Sweden Team Bianchi) 8 M.Iglinskiv (Kazakhstan) 9 A.Myerson Hodges (USA Team Sportbook.com) 10 P.Manning (Great Britain) all same time.
**General Classification:** 1 T.Evans 3.26.27 2 A.Hojgaard at 4 secs 3 D.Harrigan (Team Down Under) at 25 secs 4 C.Stevenson at 26 secs 5 J.Holmkvist at 27 secs 7 A.Myerson Hodges s.t. 8 A.Crowley (Meath Lee Strand) at 28 secs 9 M.Yates at 29 secs 10 T.Lovkvist (Sweden Team Bianchi) at 29 secs 11 C.Newton (Great Britain) at 30 secs 12 A.Bazayev (Kazakhstan) s.t.
**Under 23:** J.Holmkvist
**Points:** 1 T. Evans 15 2 A.Hojgaard 14 3 C.Stevenson 13
**Mountains:** 1 M.Iglinskiv 2 D.Harrigan (Team Down Under) 3 T.Lovkvist (Sweden Bianchi)
**International Team:** Ireland Irish Sport Council
**County Team:** Meath Lee Strand.
**County Rider:** E.O'Donoghue (Dublin Usher Insulation)

## STAGE 2

On day two from Roscrea to Clifden Tommy Evans (Ireland Irish Sports Council) came home in the leading group to retain the yellow jersey of race leadership.
The stage was won by Jonas Holmkvist (Sweden Team Bianchi) in a sprint from a 23-man group. This group finished over 5 minutes ahead of the next rider while the main bunch came home nearly a quarter of an hour down.
The 118 miles stage was one of the hardest in the history of the race with very strong winds either on their face or on their side. Combined with the torrential rain, often of hailstones, the race was blown apart with some riders just making it in before the 1 hour 30 minutes time-limit (25%).
There were a couple of notable breaks early on, the first containing Ireland's David O'Loughlin and the next including Evans but the big teams never lost their grip and the race was all together by Galway with 50 miles to go. However group after group was losing contact and at that point there were only 40 left at the front, and this kept dwindling until only 23 were left for the sprint into Clifden.

It was a good day for Ireland as apart from Evans they had defending champion Ciaran Power and Mayo professional David O'Loughlin with the leaders and they also lead the team classification. Keith Gallagher, the 2001 Ulster road race champion riding as a guest with Kildare North was leading county rider finishing 4th on the stage and moving to 7th overall, 30 seconds behind Evans who still led Dane Ari Hojgaard by 4 seconds.

**Stage 2 Roscrea - Clifden 188 Kms.** 1 J.Holmkvist (Sweden Bianchi) 5.13.14 2 A.Bazayev (Kazakhstan) 3 I.McLeod (South Africa Team HSBC 4 K.Gallagher (Kildare North) 5 C.Power (Ireland Irish Sports Council) 6 S.Kelly ((Mayo Galway Bay) 7 P.Griffin (Dublin Iarnrod Eireann) 8 H.Haymes (England North West) 9 A.Hogjaard (Denmark Jyll) 10 J.Tanner Lancaster Life Repair) all same time.

**General Classification:** 1 T.Evans (Ireland Irish Sports Council) 8.39.41 2 A.Hogjaard (Denmark Jyll) at 4 secs 3 J.Holmkvist (Sweden Bianchi) at 27 secs 5 T.Lovkvist (Sweden Bianchi) at 29 secs 6 A.Bazayev (Kazakhstan) at 30 secs 7 K.Gallagher (Kildare North) 8 C.Newton (Great Britain) 9 P.Manning (Great Britain) 10 S.Kelly (Mayo Galway Bay) 11 C.Power (Ireland Irish Sports Council) 12 J.Tanner (Lancaster Life Repair Group) all same time.

**Under 23:** J.Holmkvist

**Points:** A.Bazayev 25 2 J.Holmkvist 24 3 A.Hojgaard 21

**Mountains:** 1 M.Iglinskiv 2 D.Harrigan (Australia Team Down Under) 3 T.Lovkvist (Sweden Bianchi Scandinavia)

**International Team:** Ireland Irish Sports Council

**County Team:** Dublin Iarnrod Eireann

**County Rider:** K.Gallagher

## STAGE 3

It was another good day for the Ireland - Irish Sport Council team on the 89 miles third stage from Clifden to Ballina with the previous year's winner Ciaran Power taking the stage while teammate Evans retained the yellow jersey.

Most of the top men on general classification were with a big lead group of around 50 riders who sprinted for the stage so there were no major changes overall. However Armagh rider Keith Gallagher, who was with the leaders punctured and lost time dropping out of the top placings.

Ride of the day was by Mark Lovatt (Lancaster Team Life Repair Group) who went away on his own at Westport with 50 miles to go and despite the high winds, often in his face, he held a slender lead which was never more than 1.40, and was only caught with three kilometres to go.

The high winds and rain were there again for the third day although it brightened up a bit for the second half of the stage. All hell broke loose in the first 5 miles when, after a stiff climb right from the start, there was a big crash on the winding descent in wet and slippery conditions.

This caused a split in the bunch and a group went away and looked like they might run away with the race. Gallagher was with them but a puncture saw him lose contact. During an hour's flat out effort by break and chasers several groups got across to the leaders and the lead group swelled to around 50 and they kept it going as the bunch dropped further and further behind.
The race would now head into County Donegal for three stages with the extremely steep Gap of Mamore coming close to the finish on Thursday and the equally notorious Glengesh Pass on Friday. It was still wide open, 30 seconds covering the top 20 with Ireland, Great Britain, Kazakhstan, Sweden Bianchi, South Africa HSBC, Australia Team Down Under, Denmark, USA Team Sportsbook.com and Lancaster Team Life Repair all represented.
**Stage 3 Clifden - Ballina 145 Kms.** 1 C.Power (Ireland Irish Sports Council) 3.27.24 2 E.Moriarty (Meath Lee Strand Cycleways) 3 M.Elliott (London Irish) 4 P.Manning (Great Britain) 5 J.Holmkvist (Sweden Bianchi Scandinavia) 6 C.Stevenson (Australia Team Down Under) 7 Y.Barker (Wales Stena Line) 8 D.O'Loughlin (Ireland Irish Sports Council) 9 A.Bazayev (Kazakhstan) 10 J.Holmkvist (Sweden Bianchi) all same time.
**General Classification:** 1 T.Evans (Ireland Irish Sports Council) 12.07.05 2 A.Hojgaard (Denmark Jyll) at 4 secs 3 J.Holmkvist (Sweden Bianchi) at 27 secs 4 T.Lovkvist (Sweden Bianchi) at 29 secs 5 A.Bazayev (Kazakhstan) at 30 secs 6 P.Manning (Great Britain) 7 C.Newton (Great Britain) 8 C.Power (Ireland Irish Sports Council) 9 P.Griffin (Dublin Iarnrod Eireann) 10 D.O'Loughlin (Ireland Irish Sports Council) 11 J.Tanner (Lancaster Life Repair Group) 12 K.Page (Great Britain) all same time
**Under 23:** J.Holmkvist
**Points:** 1 J.Holmkvist 35 2 A.Bazayev 32 3 C.Power 26
**Mountains:** 1 D.Harrigan (Team Down Under) 8 2 T.Lovkvist (Team Bianchi) 6 3 M.Lovatt (Lancaster Team Life Repair) 5
**International Team:** Ireland Irish Sports Council
**County Team:** Dublin Iarnrod Eireann
**County Rider:** E.Moriarty

## STAGE 4

The Lancaster Team Life Repair Group who were unlucky not to take a stage on Tuesday when Mark Lovatt was captured just before the finish after being away for 50 miles on his own, tried the same tactic again on Wednesday's 107 miles run to Letterkenny with British Time Trial champion Kevin Dawson and this time were rewarded with a stage win when he came home on his own, 49 seconds ahead of the remainder of the small breakaway group from which he had escaped.
Once again all the top men finished in the bunch which came in at 2.11 and there was no change overall.

Dawson was in the thick of the action all day as were Eugene Moriarty (Meath Lee Strand) and Brian Ahern (Kildare HireEquip) and all three made it into the final shake-up.
Action started just after the start and these three were among the 20 riders who went clear. It looked like the winning break for a long time but eventually they were recaptured at Bundoran after 60 miles of racing.
The next serious move started on the long drag of the Barnesmore Gap after Donegal Town and once again included Dawson, Moriarty and Ahern along with Patrick Kohler (Germany RG Gutersloh/Neheim) and Andrew Medyannikov (Kazakhstan).
These five, who included no danger men on general classification, were allowed to build up a lead of over 2 minutes and it was at Ballybofey, with 15 miles to go that Dawson took off and showing the power that had taken him to a British Best All Rounder TT crown, time-trialled it to the finish.
Ahern dropped back from the remaining five leaving three to sprint for the runner-up spot which went to Kohler from Medyannikov with Moriarty in the top six for the second day. Ahern managed to hang on for fifth.
A crash in the final kilometre saw some gaps in the bunch both at the front and at the back but the panel of commissaires decided that they should all receive the bunch time but that their placings would stand.
**Stage 4 Ballina - Letterkenny 172 Kms.** 1 K.Dawson (Team Life Repair Group) 4.09.12 2 P.Kohler (Germany RG Gutersloh/Neheim) at 49 secs 3 A.Medyannikov (Kazakhstan) at 50 secs 4 E.Moriarty (Meath Lee Strand Cycleways) at 59 secs 5 B.Ahern (Kildare Hire Equip) at 2.11 6 J.Holmkvist (Sweden Bianchi) at 2.30 7 M.Iglinskiv (Kazakhstan) 8 A.Bazayev (Kazakhstan) 9 D.Finnegan (Meath Donnelly) 10 S.Bierman (Germany RG Gutersloh/Neheim) all same time
**General Classification:** 1 T.Evans (Ireland Irish Sports Council) 18.18.28 2 A.Hojgaard (Denmark Jyll) at 4 secs 3 J.Holmkvist at 27 secs 4 T.Lovkvist (Sweden Bianchi) at 29 secs 5 A.Bazayev (Kazakhstan) at 30 secs 6 P.Manning (Great Britain) 7 P.Griffin (Dublin Iarnrod Eireann) 8 C.Newton (Great Britain) 9 C.Power (Ireland Irish Sports Council) 10 D.O'Loughlin (Ireland Irish Sports Council) all same time
**Under 23:** J.Holmkvist
**International Team:** Ireland Irish Sport 48.57.31 2 Sweden Bianchi at 20 secs 3 Great Britain at 20 secs
**County Team:** Tipperary Dan Morrissey 49.40.37 2 Dublin Iarnrod Eireann at 4.24 3 Meath Lee Strand Cycleways at 8.54.
**Mountains:** 1 D.Harrigan 8 2 A.Medyannikov 3 T.Lovkvist 6
**Points:** 1 J.Holmkvist 35 2 A.Bazayev 32 3 C. Power 26.
**County Rider:** E.Moriarty
**Second Category:** T.Greene (Kildare North)

## STAGE 5

The first serious climbing of the race saw the Irish dropping out of contention with Tommy Evans, who led for four stages, now their best rider in 9th place over 5 minutes down while Power and David O'Loughlin, in whom high hopes had been placed, were 20th and 21st, now a quarter of an hour behind.
Chris Newton (Great Britain), who had lost out to Power in 2002, launched a fierce attack on the Gap of Mamore and he took the stage and the yellow jersey.
With Evans heavily marked Ireland pinned their hopes on O'Loughlin who was away all day with the leaders. The form rider before the race, he was confidently expected to make his bid for the Yellow jersey on the Gap of Mamore, but he completely blew on the lower slopes and lost 17 minutes in the final 10 miles coming in along with the other big Irish hope, defending champion Power.
O'Loughlin was in the break of 18 which went away after 20 miles along with Chris Newton and Paul Manning (Great Britain), Maxim Iglinskiv and Andrew Medyannikov (Kazakhstan), Tobias Lergard (Sweden Bianchi), Mark Lovatt and John Tanner (Lancaster Life Repair Group), Ian McLeod and Daniel Spence (South Africa HSBC), Ari Hojgaard (Denmark Jylland-Fyn), Yanto Barker (Wales Stena Line), Roger Morgan (Surrey Team gbcycles.co.uk), Josh Beck USA Team Sportsbook.com), Hamish Haymes (England North West Div.) and two Irish county riders Eugene Moriarty and Ray Clarke (both Meath Lee Strand Cycleways).
Apart from an early 3rd cat climb at Maghera, Iglinskiv took all the King of the Mountain primes to lead climber's category by 7 points from teammate Medyannikov.
These two went away from the leaders staying out in front over all the climbs but on the Gap of Mamore Newton attacked splitting the group and only Tobias Lergard could stay with him while. O'Loughlin was dropped and completely blew up.
Iglinskiv waited on his teammate after the final climb and probably lost the stage as a result as Newton and then Lergard caught the two just before the finish with Newton winning by a second from Iglinskiv and 5 seconds from Lergard who was now second overall, 5 seconds behind the leader. With 12 to Hojgaard and 38 to Lovatt. Only 8 riders were now within 2 minutes of the leader.
**Stage 5 Letterkenny - Buncrana 145 Kms.** 1 C.Newton (Great Britain) 3.24.46 2 M.Iglinskiv (Kazakhstan) at 1 sec. 3 A.Medyannikov (Kazakhstan) at 5 secs 4 T.Lergard (Sweden Bianchi) s.t. 5 M.Lovatt (Lancaster Team Life Repair Group) 6 A.Hojgaard (Denmark Jyll) 7 E.Moriarty (Meath Lee Strand) at 1.15 8 Y.Barker (Wales Stena Line) 9 H.Haymes (England N. West Div.) 10 J.Tanner (Lancaster Team Life Repair Group) all same time
**General Classification:** 1 C.Newton (Great Britain) 18.18.28 2 T.Lergard (Sweden Bianchi) at 5 secs 3 A.Hojgaard (Denmark Jyll) at 12 secs 4 M.Lovatt (Lancaster Team Life Repair Group) at 38 secs 5 P.Manning (Great Britain) at 1.15 6 J.Tanner (Lancaster Team Life Repair Group) at 1.15 7 H.Haymes (England N. West Div.) s.t.

8 I.McLeod (South Africa HSBC) at 2.09 9 T.Evans (Ireland Irish Sports Council) 10 T.Lovkvist (Sweden Bianchi) at 6.02
**Under 23:** T.Lovkvist
**Points:** 1 J.Holmkvist 45 2 A.Bazayev 40 3 E.Moriarty 35
**Mountains:** 1 M.Iglinskiv 45 2 A.Medyannikov 38 3 C.Newton 19
**International Team:** 1 Great Britain 59.19.27 2 Sweden Bianchi at 6.20 3 Lancaster Life Repair Group at 15.01
**County Team:** 1 Meath Lee Strand Cycleways 10.27.39 2 Tipperary Dan Morrissey at 23.23 3 Dublin Iarnrod Eireann at 23.25
**County Rider Stage:** E.Moriarty.
**Second Category:** T.Greene (Kildare North)

## STAGE 6

After losing his yellow jersey on Wednesday, Tommy Evans was on the attack from the drop of the flag next day and was in front all day over the 103 miles from Buncrana to Donegal over some very tough roads including the notorious Glengesh Pass.
He looked on course for a second stage win but pulled his foot out of the pedal and was just pipped on the line by green jersey points leader Jonas Holmkvist of the Swedish Bianchi Scandinavia team whose team-mate, in the under-23 leader's jersey, Thomas Lovkist was 1 second behind in third place.
Despite all his efforts the Banbridge man only improved his overall standing by one place to 8th overall, 5.05 behind Great Britain's Chris Newton. Evans' team-mate O'Loughlin failed to start the stage.
An early break containing Evans stayed away all day although there were riders coming up and dropping back over the various climbs. Their best advantage was over 2 minutes but they were almost caught on the run-in to Donegal Town before Evans attacked again and stretched the lead to 40 seconds and the three leaders managed to hold 24 seconds of this to the line.
The climbers from Kazakhstan were again in their element in the mountains and Assan Bazayev took three of the KOM primes including Glengesh while Evans was first over at Bogagh. Bazayev has now moved to just two points behind the mountains leader, his team-mate Maxim Iglinskiv with yet another of the team Andrey Madyannikov third just 6 points off the lead.
Stage winner Jonas Holmkvist now looks unbeatable in the green jersey sprinters competition with 60 points 17 ahead of county rider Eugene Moriarty (Meath Lee Strand Cycleways) who took the Cuchullain best county rider award for the third time. Despite his successes, however, early time losses leave Moriarty only third overall in the County Rider classification behind namesake Paddy Moriarty (Dublin Skip).
Unlike the usual RÁS pattern the penultimate stage would not be a big day for the climbers but at 113 miles it is the second longest and has KOM primes at Oggal Hill

and Bellavalley Junction and there was still scope for a surprise but Great Britain team looked to be in control although the strain of defending the jersey was telling as they lost the lead in the team classification to the Swedes with Kazakhstan third and Ireland fourth.

**Stage 6 Buncrana - Donegal Town 166 Kms.** 1 J.Holmkvist (Sweden Bianchi) 4.07.38 2 T.Evans (Ireland Irish Sports Council) s.t. 3 T.Lovkvist (Sweden Bianchi) at 1 sec 4 M.Lovatt (Lancaster Life Repair Group) at 24 secs 5 D.Spence (South Africa Team HSBC) s.t. 6 C.Power (Ireland Irish Sports Council) at 28 secs 7 M.Iglinskiv (Kazakshtan) 8 E.Moriarty (Meath Lee Strand Cycleways) 9 M.Elliott (London Irish Team Sdeals/Jbc) 10 C.Newton (Great Britain) all same time

**General Classification:** 1 C.Newton (Great Britain) 23.52.09 2 T.Lergard (Sweden Bianchi) at 5 secs 3 A.Hojgaard (Denmark Jyll) at 12 secs 4 M.Lovatt (Lancaster Team Life Repair Group) at 34 secs 5 J.Tanner (Lancaster Team Life Repair Group) at 1.15 6 H.Haymes (England N. West Div.) s.t. 7 I.McLeod (South Africa HSBC) at 2.09 9 T.Evans (Ireland Irish Sports Council) at 5.05 9 T.Lovkvist (Sweden Bianchi) at 5.35 10 A.Bazayev (Kazakhstan) s.t.

**Under 23:** T.Lovkvist

**Points:** 1 J.Holmkvist 60 2 E.Moriarty 43 3 A.Bazayev 40

**Mountains:** 1 M.Iglinskiv 45 2 A.Bazayev 43 3 A.Medyannikov 39

**International Team:** 1 Sweden Team Bianchi Scandinavia 71.49.10 2 Kazakhstan at 9.47 3 Great Britain at 12.06

**County Team:** 1 Meath Lee Strand Cycleways 72.48.02 2 Dublin Iarnrod Eireann at 26.48 3 Tipperary Dan Morrissey at 29.57

**County Rider Stage**: E.Moriarty.

**Second Category:** T.Brady (Meath Donnelly Avonmore)

## STAGE 7

The long stage from Donegal to Oldcastle gave Ciaran Power (Ireland Irish Sports Council) his second stage of the week and some compensation for his failure to defend the title and make it three RÁS wins.

An early break went clear before Ballyshannon and stayed out in front all day. Included were Power; Yanto Barker (Wales Stena Line); Patrick Kohler (Germany Rg Gutersloh/Neheim) and Jaaron Poad (Australia Team Down Under).

With the top men on GC keeping a close watch on each other, the four, who posed no threat to the top positions, were allowed to build up a substantial lead which reached a maximum of over 5 minutes at Cavan Town

With around 30 miles to go. Barker was dropped on the descent from Bellavalley Gap leaving three in front.

A series of attacks over the final 15 miles saw first Poad dropped and then Kohler, Power coming in on his own, 16 seconds ahead of the German. Poad still had a good margin and finished comfortable in third place 1.34 down while his team-mate Cody Stevenson led home the bunch sprint 4.09 behind the stage winner.

**Stage 7 Donegal - Oldcastle 180 Kms.** 1 C.Power (Ireland Irish Sports Council) 4:01:54 2 P.Kohler (Germany Rg Gutersloh/Neheim) at 16 secs 3 J.Poad (Australia Team Down Under) at 1:34 4 C.Stevenson (Australia Team Down Under) at 4:09 5 J.Holmkvist (Sweden Bianchi) s.t. 6 E.Moriarty (Meath Lee Strand Cycleways) s.t. 7 E.O'Donoghue (Dublin Usher Insulations) s.t. 8 B.Ahern Kildare Hirequip) s.t. 9 M.Iglinskiv (Kazakhstan) s.t. 10 A.Hodges Myerson (USA Team Sportsbook.com)
**General Classification:** 1 C.Newton (Great Britain) 27.58.12 2 T.Lergard (Sweden Bianchi Scandinavia) at 5 secs 3 A.Hojgaard (Denmark Jylland-Fyn) at 12 secs 4 M.Lovatt ( Lancaster Life Repair Group) at 34 secs 5 J.Tanner (Lancaster Life Repair Group) at 1:15 6 H.Haynes (England North West) s.t. 7 I.McLeod (South Africa Team HSBC) at 2:09 8 T.Evans (Ireland Irish Sports Council) at 5:05 9 T.Lovkvist (Sweden Bianchi Scandinavia) at 5:35 10 P.Moriarty (Dublin Skip) at 6:03
County Rider Overall: P.Moriarty (Dublin Skip)
**Under 23:** T.Lovkvist
**Points:** 1 J.Holmkvist 71 2 E.Moriarty 53 3 C.Power 51
**Mountains:** 1 M.Iglinskiv 45 2 A.Bazayev 43 3 A Medyannikov 39
**International Team:** 1 Sweden Bianchi Scandinavia 84.07.19 2 Kazakhstan at 9.47 3 Ireland Irish Sports Council at 13.19
**County Team:** 1 Meath Lee Strand Cycleways 85.06.11 2 Dublin Iarnrod Eireann at 27.44 3 Tipperary Dan Morrissey at 29.57
**County Rider Stage:** E.Moriarty.
**Second Category:** T.Brady (Meath Donnelly Avonmore)

## STAGE 8

Chris Newton (Great Britain), successfully defended his yellow jersey in the Phoenix Park where American, Adam Hodges Myerson won the coveted final stage, a 1 hour plus 3 laps circuit race, in a great sprint from past Vuelta points winner Malcolm Elliott.
After Newton took the Yellow jersey on the Mamore Gap on the stage into Buncrana he and the Great Britain team defended it from the front and on the finishing circuit in the Phoenix Park where they were never away from the front of the bunch
On the final lap he was close to the front. Malcolm Elliott, looked likely to win the bunch sprint but it was Adam Hodges Myerson who was a surprise winner helped by USA Sportsbook.com team mate, Matt Svatek.
Elliott, riding for the London Irish Team Sdeals/jbc was not happy to lose the sprint. 'There were a lot of elbows there. One of the Australians came through on my inside and I lost my line and that cost me the win,' he said.
Newton said that after winning three stages and finishing second overall last year he had set his mind on winning the race but he did not think it would be this year.
'During the week John (Herety) called us together and asked us if we were really interested in winning the race. There had been a lot of banter and we were just trying

to keep our minds off the weather. We discussed it with him and everything changed after that,' he said. 'It is a unique race and a very difficult race to win.

Ciaran Power put the finishing touches to the week by finishing third in the sprint ahead of Listowel man Eugene Moriarty (Meath Lee Strand Cycleways) who has been to the podium practically every day this week to collect the daily Cuchullain Crystal prize for the best county rider.

Power, whose overall ambitions ended in the Donegal Mountains, said he was pleased with the week.

'Two stage wins and third today – I have to be happy with that,' he said, 'and Tommy (Evans) had a stage win and would have had two but for the fact that his foot slipped out of the pedal. So, overall, we can regard it as a good week.'

Evans was the man of the Irish team winning a stage and wearing the yellow jersey for four days. He lost out when Ireland pinned their hopes on David O'Loughlin on the Mamore stage but the Mayo man failed to deliver.

**Stage 8 Phoenix Park Criterium 55 Kms.** 1 A.Hodges Myerson 1.11.58 2 M.Elliott (London Irish Team Sdeals/Jbc) s.t. 3 C.Power s.t. 4 C.Stevenson s.t. 5 E.Moriarty s.t. 6 J.Holmkvist (Sweden Bianchi Scandinavia) s.t. 7 J.Ljungblad (Sweden Bianchi Scandinavia) s.t. 8 A.Bazayev (Kazakhstan) s.t. 9 R.Clarke (Meath Lee Strand Cycleways) s.t. 10 D.Worthington (Surrey Team gbcycles.co.uk) s.t.

**General Classification:** 1 C.Newton (Great Britain) 29.10.10 2 T.Lergard (Sweden Bianchi Scandinavia) at 5 secs 3 A.Hojgaard (Denmark Jylland-Fyn) at 12 secs 4 M.Lovatt (Lancaster Life Repair Group) at 34 secs 5 J.Tanner (Lancaster Life Repair Group) at 1.15 6 H.Haymes (England North West) s.t. 7 I.McLeod (South Africa Team HSBC) at 2.09 8 T.Evans (Ireland Irish Sports Council) at 5.05 9 T.Lovkvist (Sweden Bianchi Scandinavia) at 5.35 10 P.Moriarty (Dublin Skip) at 6.03

**Under 23:** 1 T.Lovkvist 29.15.45 2 J.Holmkvist at 1.24 3 A.Medyannikov at 1.37.

**Points:** 1 J.Holmkvist 81 2 E.Moriarty 64 3 C.Power 64

**Mountains:** 1 M.Iglinskiv 45 2 A.Bazayev 43 3 A Medyannikov 39

**International Team:** 1 Sweden Bianchi Scandinavia 87:43:13 2 Kazakhstan at 9.47 3 Ireland-Irish Sports Council at 13.19.

**County Team:** 1 Meath Lee Strand Cycleways 88.42.05 2 Dublin Iarnrod Eireann at 27.44 3 Tipperary Dan Morrissey at 29.57.

**County Rider:** 1 P.Moriarty 29.16.13 2 P.Griffin (Dublin Iarnrod Eireann) at 1.21 3 E.Moriarty at 8.29.

**County Rider Stage:** E.Moriarty.

**Second Category:** 1 T.Brady (Meath Donnelly Avonmore) 31.01.40 2 M.McLeavey (Dublin Skip) at 8.14 3 F.Kelly (Wicklow) at 16.38

*Chris Newton, 2003 Winner*

# 2004

A strong turn out of fifteen foreign squads travelled for the 2004 FBD Milk RÁS, including the Scandinavian Bianchi Nordic team managed by former Giro'Italia runner-up Tommy Prim and a Slovenia Perutnina Ptuj lineup led by Valter Bonca another Giro rider.
Other overseas teams also seemed destined to be a threat. These included the Germany Team Comnet Senges team, a national selection from Kazakhstan, a very strong-looking Yorkshire – Murphy and Gunn selection (including former top European pro Malcolm Elliott and the 2000 FBD Milk RÁS winner Julian Winn) plus the Wales Stena Line and Great Britain squads.
Reassuringly for those hoping for a second Irish win in five years, the home challenge was also solid. The Thorntons Recycling Team Ireland squad was the strongest and would have two clear leaders. David O'Loughlin came to the race after early victories in the Shay Elliot Memorial, the Lincoln Grand Prix and the mountains classification in the Tour of Ulster, while David McCann had ridden strongly against professional teams in the Tour de Langkawi, placing 14$^{th}$. Tommy Evans, Denis Lynch and Eugene Moriarty looked set to play a strong supporting role. Aside from the riders in the Green jerseys, Spanish-based professional Dermot Nally was Guesting with the Galway team and was likely to be a factor, as was Kerry's Paul Griffin.
Of note was the fact that the race would feature the first father and son combination in its history. Former double champion Philip Cassidy and his son Mark would both ride for the Meath Lee Strand team.

## STAGE 1

The FBD Milk RÁS' graduation to the international calendar in 2001 initially seemed to lead to a more controlled style of racing, thanks to the tight discipline and riding style of the professional teams in attendance, but day one of the 2004 race harked back to the old, more anarchic days. Although it was just 132 kilometres in length, the opening stage from Dublin to Trim resulted in a fairly substantial time gap by the time Valter Bonca (Slovenia Perutnina Ptuj) beat Peter Renang (Scandinavia Bianchi Nordic), Mark Lovatt (Yorkshire – Team Murphy and Gunn) and David O'Loughlin (Ireland – Thornton's Recycling) to the line.
Two big breaks defined the day's action. Eight riders went clear inside the first sixteen kilometres of the stage, with an initial surge by Mikael Segarsall (Scandinavia Bianichi Nordic) and Uwe Senegewald (Germany ComNet Senges) being joined by Denis Lynch (Ireland - Thornton's Recycling), Glenn Bak and Tobias Lergard (both Scanindavia Bianchi Nordic), Branko Filip (Slovenia Perutnina

Ptuj), Jens Schiwedler (Germany Stevens Van Hacht) and the 1983 and 1999 FBD Milk RÁS winner Philip Cassidy (Meath Lee Strand).

The octet stayed clear for over half of the stage, opening up a lead of two minutes before the bunch started to respond. In that time Lergard soaked up King of the Mountains and intermediate sprint points/seconds which would see him end the day in the climber's jersey and sixth place overall. However they were hauled back by the peleton.

The next big move was more decisive. After approximately 80 kilometres of racing David O'Loughlin (Ireland-Thornton's Recycling), Anthony Malarczyk (Wales Stena Line), Petter Renang (Scandinavia Bianchi Nordic), Valter Bonca (Slovenia Perutnina Ptuj) and Mark Lovatt (Yorkshire Murphy and Gunn) wrested clear of the bunch. With twelve miles to go they had over two and a half minutes lead and it was certain that one of those would win.

Renang forged clear with two miles remaining but Bonca bridged across and then kept going, hitting the line two seconds clear of his rival. Lovatt and O'Loughlin finished a further ten seconds back, Malarczyk conceded another six, and the bunch trailed in almost two minutes down. Just one day had elapsed but the race had already a clear leader board.

**Stage 1 Dublin - Trim 132 Kms.** 1 V.Bonca (Slovenia Perutnina) 3.01.18 2 P.Renang (Scandinavia Bianchi Nordic) at 2 secs 3 M.Lovatt (Yorkshire Murphy & Gunn) at 12 secs 4 D.O'Loughlin (Ireland Thornton Recycling) s.t. 5 A.Malarczyk (Wales Stena Line) at 18 secs 6 V.Dmitryev (Kazakhstan) at 1.56 7 M.Stare (Slovenia) s.t. 8 M.Fitzgerald (Galway) s.t. 9 T.Wiedenroth (Germany Stevens Von Hacht) s.t. 10 S.Lacey (Kerry) s.t.

**General Classification:** 1 V.Bonca 3.01.08 2 P.Renang at 6 secs 3 M.Lovatt at 18 secs 4 D.O'Loughlin at 22 secs 5 A.Malarczyk at 28 secs 6 T.Lergard (Scandinavia) at 2.00 7 B.Filip (Slovenia) at 2.01 8 Denis Lynch (Ireland) at 2.03 9 J.Schiwedler (Germany Stevens) at 2.05 10 V.Dmitryev at 2.06

**Under 23:** 1 V.Dmitryev 3.03.14 2 S.Lacey s.t. 3 P.O'Brien s.t.

**Points:** 1 V.Bonca 15 2 P.Renang 14 3 M.Lovatt 13

**Mountains:** 1 T.Lergard 14 2 B.Filip 12 3 J.Schiwedler 7

**International Team:** 1 Slovenia 9.07.46 2 Scandinavia at 2 secs 3 Ireland at 12 secs

**County Team:** 1 Kerry 9.09.42 2 Cork Kanturk s.t. 3 Galway s.t.

## STAGE 2

After the big time gap on day one, it was predictable that a tighter control would be held on the race on the 171 kilometre second stage from Trim to Oranmore. And so it proved; 21 year old Dutch victor Stefan Cohnen (Germany ComNet Senges) won on his own, but he was just eight seconds clear of a big chasing group led home by David McCann (Ireland – Thornton's Recycling) and the former Tour de France rider and Vuelta a España points jersey winner Malcolm Elliott (Yorkshire – Murphy and Gunn).

It was an extremely active day, with attack after attack going from the start of the sun-roasted stage. Double FBD Milk RÁS winner Philip Cassidy got the hostilities underway as soon as the flag dropped with a characteristic early surge. However luck was not with him; he punctured after about a mile of freedom, was passed by the bunch and then ran into the back of a car in the cavalcade while chasing back on. He was cut and bruised, but the Meath Lee Strand rider was fortunately able to continue in the race.

Several other moves followed but perhaps the biggest danger to Valter Bonca's yellow jersey came around the halfway point. Denis Lynch (Ireland – Thornton's Recycling) was clear after an earlier attack and was joined by team-mate Tommy Evans, a determined Cassidy, Tobias Lergard (Scandinavia Bianchi Nordic) and Spain-based Irish pro Dermot Nally, who was riding the race on the Galway county team. However they too were reeled in.

A subsequent move by David O'Loughlin (Ireland – Thornton's Recycling) and Brian Ahern (Dublin Orwell Dundrum Shopping Centre) saw the two riders joined by Lynch. They remained clear for 30 kilometres but were hauled back. O'Loughlin and Lynch then made it into a subsequent 31-man move which also failed to last the pace. Indeed, the elastic didn't fully break until Cohnen made his move with about twelve kilometres to go.

He rode strongly between there and the line and took a well-deserved win, while race leader Valter Bonca finished safely in the chasing group and maintained his advantage over his closest rivals. Tobias Lergard (Scandinavia Bianchi Nordic) remained in the king of the mountains jersey, while Paul Griffin overtook Bonca in the points classification.

**Stage 2 Trim - Oranmore 171 Kms.** 1 S.Cohnen (Germany ComNet Senges) 3.54.12 2 D.McCann (Ireland) at 8 secs 3 M.Elliott (Yorkshire) s.t. 4 C.Gunn (USA/Britain) s.t. 5 P.Griffin (Kerry) s.t. 6 G.Briggs (Britain U23) s.t. 7 D.Nally (Galway) s.t. 8 P.O'Brien (Cork Kanturk Credit Union) s.t. 9 V.Vdovinov (Kazakhstan) s.t. 10 S.Lacey (Kerry) s.t.

**General Classification:** 1 V.Bonca 6.55.28 2 P.Retang at 6 secs 3 M.Lovatt at 18 secs 4 D.O'Loughlin at 22 secs 5 A.Malarczyk at 28 secs 6 S.Cohnen at 1.58 7 T.Lergard at 2.00 8 B.Filip at 2.01 9 Denis Lynch at 2.03 10 P Griffin at 2.06

**Under 23:** 1 S.Cohnen 6.57.28 2 P.O'Brien at 8 secs 3 S.Lacey at 8 secs

**Points:** 1 P.Griffin 16 2 V.Bonca 15 3 S.Cohnen 15

**Mountains:** T.Lergard 14 2 B.Filip 12 3 J.Schiwedler 7

**International Team:** 1 Slovenia 20.50.46 2 Scandinavia at 2 secs 3 Ireland at 12 secs

**County Team:** 1 Kerry 20.52.42 2 Tipperary s.t. 3 Galway at 2.42

## STAGE 3

While he'd lived in Valencia since six years of age and can remember very little of his time in Cork city before that, Dermot Nally had a victorious homecoming to the

South-west County when he soloed to victory in Charleville.
The Paternina-Costa Del Almeria professional took the first pro win of his career in the colours of the Galway team, darting away of a large breakaway group inside the final kilometre and reaching the line two seconds clear. Valeriy Dmitryev (Kazakhstan) was second ahead of a disappointed Malcolm Elliott (Yorkshire – Murphy and Gunn), the latter having the consolation of taking the Green points jersey plus a place in the top ten overall.
The 171 kilometre stage from Oranmore began in an aggressive fashion when Paul Healion (Dublin Usher IRC) sparked off a seven-man breakaway which quickly gained time over the bunch. Healion's companions were Valeriy Dmitryev (Kazakhstan), Jamie Norfolk (Wales Stena Line), Mikael Segarsall (Scandinavia Bianchi Nordic), Massimo Demarin (Slovenia Perutnina Ptuj), Jens Schiwedler (Germany Stevens Von Hacht) and Kevin Dawson of the Yorkshire Murphy and Gunn team. They were joined shortly afterwards by two reinforcements, Ireland - Thornton's Recycling rider David McCann and Daniel Lynch (Cork Kanturk Credit Union).
The gap was over a minute by Gort (26 kilometres) and continued to go up as they crested three third category summits, with Segarsall, Lynch and Schiwedler taking the top points at Killenena, Aylevaun and Ogonell respectively. The latter's solo effort on the final climb earned him the mountains jersey at the end of the stage. Surprisingly, McCann looked to be under pressure on the climbs and stated afterwards that he was on an unexpected off-day.
Due to a lack of cooperation, the bunch closed to within ten seconds of the move at Birdhill, 84 kilometres into the stage. The break did pull away again but first Nally and then Kimmo Kananen (Scandinavia Bianchi Nordic) took advantage of this, bridging across. That made it eleven up front, although this dropped to ten when Lynch punctured.
Denis Lynch (Ireland – Thornton's Recycling), Malcolm Elliott (Yorkshire – Murphy and Gunn), plus the Kerry train of Sean Lacey, Ritchie Cahill and Vincent Gleeson then got across just after Caherconlish, while Tommy Evans (Ireland – Thornton's Recycling), Ivan Andreeyev (Kazakhstan) and Richard Eastham (North East England Bannatyne) swelled the group number up to 18 when they joined with twenty kilometres to go.
A big sprint looked to be the most likely outcome but Nally had the strength and timing to get that solo win. Valter Bonca (Slovenia Perutnina Ptuj) came in as part of the main bunch, 1 minute and 19 seconds back, and had enough in hand to hold onto his yellow jersey. The day's action did however make things tighter at the top, with fourteen others ending the day within a minute of the lead.
**Stage 3 Oranmore - Charleville 152 Kms.** 1 D.Nally (Galway) 3.37.05 2 V.Dmitryev (Kazakhstan) at 2 secs 3 M.Elliott (Yorkshire) s.t. 4 K.Kananen (Scandinavia) s.t. 5 D.McCann (Ireland) s.t. 6 Denis Lynch (Ireland) s.t. 7 S.Lacey (Kerry) at 5 secs 8 J.Norfolk (Wales) at 6 secs 9 K.Dawson (Yorkshire) s.t. 10 P.Healion (Dublin Usher IRC) at 7 secs

**General Classification:** 1 V.Bonca (Slovenia) 10.33.52 2 P.Renang (Scandinavia) at 6 secs 3 M.Lovatt (Yorkshire) at 18 secs 4 D.O'Loughlin (Ireland) at 22 secs 5 A.Malarczyk (Wales) at 28 secs 6 Denis Lynch (Ireland) at 46 secs 7 D.Nally (Galway) at 47 secs 8 K.Kananen (Scandinavia) at 49 secs 9 M.Elliott (Yorkshire) s.t. 10 D.McCann (Ireland) s.t.
**Under 23:** 1 S.Lacey 10.34.44 2 I.Andreeyev at 13 secs 3 S.Cohnen at 1.06
**Points:** 1 M.Elliott 26 2 D.McCann 25 3 D.Nally 24
**Mountains:** 1 J.Schiwedler 18 2 T.Lergard 14 3 B.Filip 12
**International Team:** 1 Ireland 31.42.29 2 Yorkshire at 1.11 3 Scandinavia at 1.13
**County Team:** 1 Kerry 31.44.18 2 Tipperary at 3.36 3 Galway at 4.59

## STAGE 4

Although he had felt out of sorts on the previous day's stage, David McCann showed that his FBD Milk RÁS challenge was very much alive when he took an excellent win on the first real mountain stage of the race. The Ireland – Thornton's Recycling rider hit the line in Cahirciveen 26 seconds clear of stage three winner Dermot Nally (Galway), who led in the yellow jersey group. In doing so the Belfast man jumped from tenth to fourth place overall.
The marathon 181 kilometre stage from Charleville to Cahirciveen featured nine categorised climbs including, inside the final 26 kilometres of racing, the second category ascent of Cill Urlat and the first category Coonanaspic.
McCann's victory was all the more impressive as he was away for almost 100 kilometres in a breakaway group. This included riders such as Kimmo Kananen (Scandinavia Bianchi Nordic), fourth the previous day, former RÁS winner Julian Winn (Yorkshire – Murphy and Gunn), plus Irishmen Daniel Lynch (Cork Kanturk Credit Union) and John O'Shea (Tipperary Dan Morrissey). The ten opened up a maximum lead of over four minutes on the peleton, which was headed by race leader Valter Bonca' s Slovenia Perutnina Ptuj team plus the Kazakhstan squad of Petter Renang, second overall
The break was finally mopped up before Glenbeigh, 113.4 kilometres into the stage, with the last two riders - Winn and Hew Pritchard (Wales) caught after the third category climb at Mount Foley (128 kilometres). Almost instantly, Eugene Moriarty (Ireland – Thornton's Recycling) and Tim Barry (Tipperary Dan Morrissey) jumped away, and were joined by David O'Loughlin (Ireland – Thornton's Recycling) with less than 40 kilometres to go.
A huge chase behind by the Scandinavia Bianchi Nordic team split the peleton into smaller groups. Moriarty was dropped from the break and on the climb of Raheen, 30 kilometres from the finish; O'Loughlin and Barry were reeled in as a large front group pressed ahead of the rest.
O'Loughlin was however strong enough to join with McCann, Valentin Iglinsky (Kazakhstan), Evan Oliphant (Great Britain Under 23), Anthony Malarczyk (Wales – Stena Line), Petter Renang and Tobias Lergard (Scandinavia Bianchi Nordic), race

leader Valter Bonca and Massimo Demarin (Slovenia Perutnina Ptuj), Stefan Cohnen (Germany ComNet Senges), John Tanner and Malcolm Elliott (Yorkshire – Murphy and Gunn), Brian Ahern (Dublin Orwell Dundrum SC) and Dermot Nally (Galway). Bonca then drove the pace up the first category Coonanaspic, dropping all bar O'Loughlin and Petter Renang (Scandinavia Bianchi Nordic). McCann was able to bridge across just before the descent, and the four then entered the final twenty kilometres with a lead of 23 seconds over Lergard, Cohnen and Nally. O'Loughlin attacked but was closed down by Bonca. However the Slovenian had no answer when McCann countered, and the strong time triallists finished 26 seconds clear of Nally and the other riders in the growing chasing group.

**Stage 4 Charleville - Caherciveen 181 Kms.** 1 D.McCann (Ireland) 4.27.16 2 D.Nally (Galway) at 26 secs 3 V.Iglinskiy (Kazakhstan) s.t. 4 D.O'Loughlin (Ireland) s.t. 5 M.Elliott (Yorkshire) s.t. 6 V.Bonca (Slovenia s.t. 7 E.Oliphant (Britain U23) s.t. 8 Denis Lynch (Ireland) s.t. 9 T.Lergas (Scandinavia) s.t. 10 J.Tanner (Yorkshire) s.t.

**General Classification:** 1 V.Bonca (Slovenia) 15.01.34 2 P.Renang (Scandinavia) at 6 secs 3 D.O'Loughlin (Ireland) at 22 secs 4 D.McCann (Ireland) at 23 secs 5 Denis Lynch (Ireland) at 46 secs 6 D.Nally (Galway) at 47 secs 7 M.Elliott (Yorkshire) at 49 secs 8 M.Lovatt (Yorkshire) at 1.37 9 A.Malarczyk (Wales) at 1.47 10 T.Lergard (Scandinavia) at 2.00

**Under 23:**1 S.Cohnen 15.03.40 2 S.Lacey at 5 secs 3 V.Iglinskiy at 1.09

**Points:** 1 D.McCann 40 2 D.Nally 38 3 M.Elliott 37

**Mountains:** 1 T.Lergard 43 2 B.Filip 33 3 P.Renang 28

**International Team:** 1 Ireland 45.05.09 2 Yorkshire at 2.56 3 Slovenia at 5.18

**County Team:** 1 Kerry 45.16.30 2 Galway at 6.52 3 Meath M Donnelly at 9.08

## STAGE 5

Evoking memories of his days as one of the fastest professionals in the peleton, 42 year old veteran Malcolm Elliott thundered up the Millstreet finishing straight to win stage five of the FBD Milk RÁS. The Yorkshire - Murphy and Gunn rider beat 81 other riders on the uphill drag to the line, holding off two Irish county riders, Brian Ahern (Dublin Orwell – Dundrum Shopping Centre) and Kerry's Paul Griffin.

The 152 kilometre stage started in Cahirciveen and was marked by much aggression by the Ireland – Thornton's Recycling squad, who were keen to put pressure on race leader Valter Bonca (Slovenia Perutnina Ptuj). Daniel Lynch began their assault shortly after the start in Cahirciveen when he went clear with six others in a short-lived break.

After the move was reeled in, double FBD Milk RÁS winner Philip Cassidy attacked going through Waterville, 15 kilometres into the stage. Shortly afterwards, O'Loughlin and Julian Winn (Yorkshire – Murphy and Gunn) raced clear of the main field on the first category Coomakista climb and passed Cassidy, the duo opening up a big lead over the Slovenia Perutnina Ptuj-led peleton.

O'Loughlin and Winn were over a minute clear at the top but the Irish rider eventually sat up when it became clear that the gap was not going to further widen. Winn persisted, hoping that the bunch would ease back once GC threat O'Loughlin was back in the fold, but he too was eventually reeled in while going through Sneem.

King of the Mountains Tobias Lergard and his Scandinavia Bianchi Nordic team-mate Kimmo Kananen were next to get clear, with Lergard soon pressing on ahead alone. He gobbled up maximum points on the first category Inchee Mountain (98.4 kilometres) and the category three County Bounds (111.4 kilometres).

He was reeled back in by the peleton just after the summit, then Tommy Evans (Ireland – Thornton's Recycling) and two others pushed clear. RÁS leader Bonca jumped across to the group while behind about ten riders hit the dirt, amongst them O'Loughlin, Griffin and Elliott. The three were able to rejoin the group, although O'Loughlin had to switch to team-mate Eugene Moriarty's bike due to damage to his own.

Slovenia Perutnina Ptuj rider Massimo Demarin slipped away with 35 kilometres to go, trying to take the pressure off his team which had been stuck defending Bonca's lead all day. He was joined by Lynch and Kevin Dawson (Yorkshire – Murphy and Gunn), the former becoming race leader on the road when the break gained nearly a minute on the field

All three were however swept up by the Slovenia- and Kazakhstan led peleton in the final run in to Millstreet. There, Elliott made no mistakes in the uphill gallop to the line, charging home a length clear to become the oldest ever stage victor in the race. 36 year old Bonca retained his yellow jersey, proving it was a good day for the more experienced riders in the peleton.

**Stage 5 Cahirciveen - Millstreet 152 Kms.** 1 M.Elliott (Yorkshire) 4.00.09 2 B.Ahern (Dublin Orwell) 3 P.Griffin (Kerry) 4 T.Cuppens (Germany ComNet) 5 G.Briggs (Britain U23) 6 M.Schweizer (Germany ComNet) 7 T.Evans (Ireland) 8 E.Oliphant (Britain U23) 9 A.Hedderman (Cork Kanturk) 10 A.Crowley (Meath Lee Strand) all s.t.

**General Classification:** 1 V.Bonca (Slovenia) 19.01.43 2 P.Renang (Scandinavia) at 6 secs 3 D.O'Loughlin (Ireland) at 22 secs 4 D.McCann (Ireland) at 23 secs 5 Denis Lynch (Ireland) at 46 secs 6 D.Nally (Galway) at 47 secs 7 M.Elliott (Yorkshire) at 49 secs 8 M.Lovatt (Yorkshire) at 1.37 9 A.Malarczyk (Wales) at 1.47 10 T.Lergard (Scandinavia) at 2.00

**Under 23:** 1 S.Cohnen 19.03.49 2 S.Lacey at 5 secs 3 V.Iglinskiy at 1.09

**Points:** 1 M.Elliott 52 2 D.McCann 44 3 D.Nally 39

**Mountains:** 1 T.Lergard 63 2 B.Filip 43 3 J.Winn 29

**International Team:** 1 Ireland 57.05.36 2 Yorkshire at 2.56 3 Slovenia at 5.18

**County Team:** 1 Kerry 57.16.57 2 Meath M Donnelly at 9.08 3 Cork Kanturk at 9.17

## STAGE 6

Underlining that he was a clear challenger for the overall win, David O'Loughlin triumphed atop Seskin Hill, the famous climb on the outskirts of Sean Kelly's hometown Carrick on Suir.

The Ireland – Thornton's Recycling rider plus his team-mates had been on the attack for much of the stage, putting the pressure on race leader Valter Bonca (Slovenia Perutnina Ptuj) shortly after the start in Millstreet and turning the screw as the 151 kilometre stage played out.

After twenty kilometres O'Loughlin got away with his team-mate Eugene Moriarty, plus Yorkshire - Murphy and Gunn duo John Tanner and Mark Lovatt. Moriarty lost his place up front twenty kilometres later but the other three riders persisted to eke out a maximum lead of three minutes, putting O'Loughlin firmly in yellow on the road.

As expected, Bonca's Slovenian Perutnina Ptuj team brought the gap down towards the end. Together with the Kazakhstan team they devoured the break's lead, reducing it to one minute and six seconds with ten kilometres to go. When Lovatt punctured it looked like curtains for the leaders, but while Tanner was caught and passed by a stomping Bonca and McCann on the steep, two kilometre rise to the line, a flying O'Loughlin had enough left to stay clear.

The Mayo rider crested the first category climb nineteen seconds ahead of the duo, taking his first-ever RÁS stage win. He and McCann ended the day second and third in the general classification, three and twenty-three seconds behind an increasingly vulnerable-looking Bonca.

**Stage 6 Millstreet - Carrick on Suir 151 Kms.** 1 D.O'Loughlin (Ireland) 3.25.47 2 V.Bonca (Slovenia) at 19 secs 3 D.McCann (Ireland) s.t. 4 J.Tanner (Yorkshire) at 25 secs 5 D.Nally (Galway) at 31 secs 6 S.Cohnen (Germany ComNet) s.t. 7 P.Griffin (Kerry) s.t. 8 R.Schild (Germany ComNet) at 35 secs 9 J.Veness (Surrey Racing League) s.t. 10 V.Iglinskiy (Kazakhstan) s.t.

**General Classification:** 1 V.Bonca (Slovenia) 22.27.49 2 D.O'Loughlin (Ireland) at 3 secs 3 D.McCann (Ireland) at 23 secs 4 D.Nally (Galway) at 59 secs 5 M.Elliott (Yorkshire) at 1.08 6 Denis Lynch (Ireland) at 1.10 7 A.Malarczyk (Wales) at 2.14 8 S.Cohnen (Germany ComNet) at 2.18 9 T.Lergard (Scandinavia) at 2.19 10 M.Lovatt (Yorkshire) at 2.28

**Under 23:** 1 S.Cohnen 22.30.07 2 S.Lacey at 51 secs 3V.Iglinskiy at 1.13

**Points:** 1 D.McCann 57 2 M.Elliott 56 3 D.Nally 51

**Mountains:** 1 T.Lergard 65 2 D.O'Loughlin 43 3 B.Filip 43

**International Team:** 1 Ireland 67.23.54 2 Yorkshire at 3.53 3 Scandinavia at 8.26

**County Team:** 1 Kerry 67.37.16 2 Cork Kanturk at 10.02 3 Dublin Wheelers at 10.12

## STAGE 7

Although David O'Loughlin started the day just three seconds adrift of the yellow jersey, it was his namesake and Ireland – Thornton's Recycling team-mate David McCann who ended the day atop the leader board and looking set for overall victory.
The Irish double whammy finally wrested the yellow jersey from Valter Bonca (Slovenia Perutnina Ptuj) during the mountainous 149 kilometre stage from Carrick on Suir to Tullow.
A flurry of attacks came after the start, with Ireland – Thornton's Recycling rider Denis Lynch being involved in one and team-mate Tommy Evans in another. Bonca's team-mates then rode tempo at the front, acting to discourage further attacks but also using up precious energy.
This suited the challengers just fine and a stalemate of sorts transpired until the start of the first category ascent of The Heights. At the bottom of the climb mountains leader Tobias Lergard (Scandinavia Bianchi Nordic) attacked and bolstered his advantage when he crested the summit of that and the similarly-ranked Corrabutt (97.5 km) slightly ahead.
Behind, McCann and Bonca forged clear of the fragmenting peleton, cresting the summit just behind Lergard and slightly ahead of O'Loughlin and Dermot Nally (Galway).
A small regrouping happened on the false flat between the top of the Corrabutt and the start of Mount Leinster. O'Loughlin kicked clear and hit the top of the climb ahead of Bonca and McCann. The three came together on the descent and were soon joined by Nally, Lergard and several other riders. McCann seized his chance on the descent, accelerating clear while O'Loughlin blocked Bonca's immediate pursuit.
At the 118 kilometre point McCann was clear leader on the road, 51 seconds ahead of Kimmo Kananen and Glenn Bak of the Scandinavia Bianchi Nordic team and 1 minute 12 seconds up on Bonca. The race leader's prospects improved when his team-mates rejoined the front group and managed to bring the gap down to eight seconds. However strong surges by the other Ireland – Thornton's Recycling riders turned the screw and Bonca's team cracked, enabling the gap to soar once again.
McCann finally hit the line in Tullow 27 seconds clear of Anthony Malarczyk (Wales – Stena Line) and Dermot Nally (Galway). Bonca, O'Loughlin and many of the other challengers came home 59 seconds back, leaving McCann firmly in the race lead with just one stage left to go.
**Stage 7 Carrick on Suir - Tullow 149 Kms.** 1 D.McCann (Ireland) 3.30.29 2 A.Malarczyk (Wales) at 27 secs 3D.Nally (Galway) s.t. 4 K.Kananen (Scandinavia) at 36 secs 5 K.Dawson (Yorkshire) s.t. 6 M.Elliott (Yorkshire) at 59 secs 7 E.Oliphant (Britain U23) s.t. 8 P.O'Brien (Cork Kanturk) s.t. 9 D.O'Loughlin (Ireland) s.t. 10 H.Pritchard (Wales) s.t.
**General Classification:** 1 D.McCann (Ireland) 25.58.41 2 V.Bonca (Slovenia) at 36 secs 3 D.O'Loughlin (Ireland) at 39 secs 4 D.Nally (Galway) at 1.03 5 M.Elliott (Yorkshire) at 1.44 6 Denis Lynch (Ireland) at 1.46 7 A.Malarczyk (Wales) at 2.18 8

S.Cohnen (Germany ComNet) at 2.54 9 T.Lergard (Scandinavia) at 2.55 10 M.Lovatt (Yorkshire) at 3.04
**Under 23:** 1 S.Cohnen 26.01.35 2 V.Iglinskiy at 1.13 3 E.Oliphant at 2.00
**Points:** 1 D.McCann 72 2 M.Elliott 66 3 D.Nally 64
**Mountains:** 1 T.Lergard 123 2 D.O'Loughlin 76 3 V.Bonca 68
**International Team:** 1 Ireland 77.57.19 2 Yorkshire at 4.29 3 Scandinavia at 9.02
**County Team:** 1 Kerry 78.21.30 2 Cork Kanturk at 5.07 3 Galway at 19.44

## STAGE 8

Taking his second stage victory of the race, former Tour of Spain points jersey winner Malcolm Elliott (Yorkshire – Murphy and Gunn) galloped home ahead of Kimmo Kananen (Scandinavia Bianchi Nordic) and Dublin Usher IRC's Paul Healion on the final stage of the FBD Milk RÁS in Dublin's Phoenix Park.
Race leader David McCann (Ireland – Thornton's Recycling) made sure of his overall victory when he kept out of trouble, finishing ninth in the sprint for the line and ending the eight day, 2.5 ranked UCI event 36 seconds ahead of Valter Bonca (Slovenia Perutnina Ptuj) and a further three up on his own team-mate David O'Loughlin. Dermot Nally (Galway) and Denis Lynch (Ireland – Thornton's Recycling) made it four Irish riders in the top six, the best home performance for several years.
McCann and the Irish team controlled the 57 kilometre stage perfectly; several riders tried to break the Green-jersey stranglehold, but didn't get very far. Aidan Crowley (Meath Lee Strand) Michael Schweizer (Germany ComNet Senges), Philip Cassidy (Meath Lee Strand) and Daniel Lynch (Cork Kanturk Credit Union) took the four Cycleways primes during the stage, but double RÁS winner Philip Cassidy was the only one who opened a significant gap between himself and the bunch. With just over four laps to go he went clear with Mikael Segarsall (Scandinavia Bianchi Nordic), built a lead of eleven seconds but was hauled back with just over two laps remaining.
That ensured a big bunch gallop. While Elliott's victory saw him edge ahead of McCann and win the green jersey competition, the Belfast man was not concerned. He was delighted to finally win the race eight years after placing second overall, and even stated that FBD Milk RÁS victory was a more important season goal for him than riding the Olympics.
Looking at the other classifications, Tobias Lergard (Scandinavia Bianchi Nordic) was best climber while Nally was top county rider overall. Stefan Cohnen (Germany ComNet Senges) and Donal Byrne (Dublin Orwell Shopping Centre) came out on top in the best under 23 and the best second category rider competitions. Finally, Kerry were tops in the county team award and the Ireland Thornton's Recycling riders were strongest international squad.
**Stage 8 Phoenix Park Circuit 59.5 Kms.** 1 M.Elliott (Yorkshire) 1.18.31 2 K.Kananen (Scandinavia) s.t. 3 P.Healion (Dublin Usher IRC) s.t. 4 M.Cavindish

(Britain U23) 5 C.Bracken (Galway) s.t. 6 A.Crowley (Meath Lee Strand) s.t. 7 M.Stare (Slovenia) s.t. 8 P.O'Brien (Cork Kanturk) s.t. 9 D.McCann (Ireland) s.t. 10 C.Sweetman (Meath M Donnelly)
**General Classification**: 1 D.McCann (Ireland) 27.17.12 2 V.Bonca (Slovenia) at 36 secs 3 D.O'Loughlin (Ireland) at 39 secs 4 D.Nally (Galway) at 1.03 5 M.Elliott (Yorkshire) at 1.44 6 Denis Lynch (Ireland) at 1.46 7 A.Malarczyk (Wales) at 2.18 8 S.Cohnen (Germany ComNet) at 2.54 9 T.Lergard (Scandinavia) at 2.55 10 M.Lovatt (Yorkshire) at 3.04
**Under 23:** 1 S.Cohnen 27.20.06 2 V.Iglinskiy at 1.13 3 E.Oliphant at 2.00
**Points:** 1 M.Elliott 81 2 D.McCann 79 3 D.Nally 64
**Mountains:** 1 T.Lergard 123 2 D.O'Loughlin 76 3 V.Bonca 68
**International Team:** 1 Ireland 81.52.52 2 Yorkshire at 4.29 3 Scandinavia at 9.02
**County Team:** 1 Kerry 82.17.03 2 Cork Kanturk at 5.07 3 Galway at 19.44

*David McCann, 2004 winner*

# 2005

The 2005 edition of the race saw a major change with FBD Insurance taking over as the sole title sponsor of the RÁS. Pleased with its association with the contest plus the successful growth of the RÁS after it became a world-ranking event, the company was happy to increase its involvement at a time when the National Dairy Council stepped aside as one of the backers.

A strong overseas line-up was guaranteed for the race. There were three former winners amongst those chasing victory, namely Julian Winn (Wales Stena Line), Paul Manning and Chris Newton (Recycling.co.uk). There were also riders from pro teams such as Estonia - Kalev Chocolate Classic Bicycles, Czech Republic - Elmarco KK Cube Dukla Liberec, Canada – Jet Fuel Coffee/Sympatico, Netherlands –Team B&E, and Norway – Team Sparebanken Vest, as well as the TIAA-CREF development team set up by former Tour de France rider Jonathan Vaughers. The overseas armada represented a real threat to Irish aspirations of overall victory.

Twelve months earlier David McCann and David O'Loughlin had finished first and third overall in the race, capping off an excellent week for the national squad. However in 2005 the duo were absent due to racing commitments with their pro teams, meaning that Belgian-based riders Stephen Gallagher and Paídi O'Brien would lead the charge on the Grant Thornton Ireland team. Other strong Irish riders were riding for other teams and would end up playing important parts in the race.

## STAGE 1

Having taken the Irish cyclo-cross championship for the first time earlier in the year, Roger Aiken proved his versatility when he won the rain-drenched opening stage of the FBD Insurance RÁS into Emyvale.

In doing so the Banbridge rider also gave a significant boost to the Sean Kelly Cycling Academy, launched earlier in the season and based in Merchtem, Belgium. Although Aiken was riding the FBD Insurance RÁS for the Louth Safe Cycling team, the sprint victory over three others – Morten Hegreberg (Norway – Sparebanken), Kevin Dawson (Yorkshire – Trinity Capital) and 2003 RÁS champion Chris Newton (GB – Recycling.co.uk) – was big news for the project.

The move of the day took place shortly after 2000 race victor Julian Winn (Wales Stena Line) took the first hot-spot sprint in Balrothery, which itself occurred 15 kilometres after the start in Dublin. A ten man break surged clear, comprising Rostilav Krotky (Czech Republic – Elmarco KK Cube), former stage winner Sigvard Kukk (Estonia – Kalev Chocolate), Morten Hegreberg, Gabriel Rasch (both Norway – Sparebanken Vest), Robert Partridge, Yanto Barker (both Wales – Stena Line),

Stuart Gillespie, Nathan Mitchell (both US – TIAA CREF), Eugene Moriarty (Meath Cycleways.com) and Tim Barry (Tipperary Dan Morrissey).
Former winner Chris Newton (GB – Recycling.co.uk) then jumped across by himself, making it eleven up front. This number grew yet further when Stephen Gallagher (Ireland Grant Thornton), Morten Christiansen (Norway – Sparebanken Vest), Evan Oliphant (Scotland), Alex Coutts (Wales Stena Line), Paul Manning, Robin Sharman (GB – Recycling.co.uk), Kevin Dawson (Yorkshire – Trinity Capital), Andrew Roche (Tipperary Worldwide Cycles), Andrew Randell (Canada – Jet Fuel Coffee), Denis Lynch (Cork – Kanturk), Jens Schwedler (Germany – Stevens Von Hacht), Malcolm Elliott (Yorkshire – Murphy and Gunn) and the day's eventual stage winner Roger Aiken (Louth-Safe Cycling) all bridged, although Gallagher, Partridge and several others lost contact again soon afterwards.
Hegreberg was first to the top of the Tully Esker category 3 climb, taking the King of the Hills points there and, even more importantly, a three second time bonus. This would prove crucial by the end of the stage.
Inside the final hour of racing, 2001 race winner Manning crashed out of the break. Elliott took the final hot spot sprint of the day in Anyalla, but crucially missed out on the winning move when Aiken, Hegreberg, Dawson and Newton clipped away with four kilometres remaining. The Norwegian was not quick enough to beat his Irish rival, but had the considerable consolation of taking the first yellow jersey of the race, thanks to his first and second placings in bonus sprints. Aiken ended the day in the stage winner's jersey and was just one second back overall; success, then, for both the Louth team and the Sean Kelly Racing Academy.
**Stage 1 Dublin - Emyvale 135 Kms.** 1 R.Aiken (Louth Safe Cycling) 2.53.19 2 M.Hegreberg (Norway Sparebanken Vest) s.t. 3 K.Dawson (Yorkshire Trinity Capital) s.t. 4 C.Newton (GB Recycling .co.uk) s.t. 5 E.Oliphant (Scotland) at 10 secs 6 M.Elliott (Yorkshire) s.t. 7 M.Christiansen (Norway) s.t. 8 S.Kukk (Estonia Kalev Chocolate) s.t. 9 Y.Barker (Wales Stena) s.t. 10 R.Sharman (GB Recycling) s.t.
**General Classification:** 1 M.Hegreberg (Norway) 2.53.08 2 R.Aiken (Louth) at 1 sec 3 K.Dawson (Yorkshire) at 7 secs 4 C.Newton (Britain) at 10 secs 5 M.Elliott (Yorkshire) at 18 secs 6 E.Oliphant (Scotland) at 20 secs 7 M.Christiansen (Norway) at 21 secs 8 S.Kukk (Estonia) s.t. 9 Y.Barker (Wales) s.t. 10 R.Sharman (Britain) s.t.
**Under 23:**1 S.Gillespie 2.53.29 2 M.Pozniak at 2.57 3 A.Mustonen at 2.57
**Points:** 1 R.Aiken 15 2 M.Hegreberg 14 3 K.Dawson 13
**Mountains:** 1 M.Hegreberg 5 2 E.Moriarty 4 3 E.Oliphant 3
**International Team:** 1 Norway 8.40.17 2 Britain at 2.57 3 Yorkshire at 2.57
**County Team:** 1 Louth 8.46.11 2 Tipperary Worldwide Cycles at 10 secs 3 Tipperary Dan Morrissey at 10 secs

## STAGE 2

Considering the lightning-fast finish he had displayed in the past, it was surprising that Chris Newton had finished fourth out of four in the sprint which decided stage one. However the Great Britain – Recycling.co.uk rider showed his form was more than solid when he outsprinted former Tour of Spain points victor Malcolm Elliott (Yorkshire – Trinity Capital) into Tubbercurry, grabbing the yellow jersey in the process.

The 160 kilometre stage began in Emyvale and saw the riders tackle two categorised climbs en route to the finish. The first of these came just five kilometres after the start and here Meath – Cycleways rider Eugene Moriarty soloed off the front to scoop maximum points.

The Kerryman had started the day in the King of the Mountains jersey but only by virtue of the fact that classification leader Hegreberg was wearing yellow. However, that prime win plus a later victory at the top of Bellavalley Gap saw him move a healthy ten points clear in that classification.

A number of attacks were fired off between those two climbs, with the most notable being a move by Mark Pozniak (Canada – Jet Fuel Coffee), Are Andresen (Norway – Sparebanken Vest) and 43 year old double RÁS winner Philip Cassidy (Meath – Cycleways.com), which temporarily opened a 15 second gap, and later a solo effort by Duncan Urquhart (Scotland). The British army solider struck out alone after 61 kilometres, some 12 kilometres from the start of the second category Bellavalley Gap, built a maximum lead of 45 seconds, but was recaptured before the top of the seven-kilometre climb.

On the descent, Donald Reeb (US – Guinness) raced clear on the descent and built a minute's lead. After approximately 40 minutes of solo riding he was chased by six others - Zach Bell (Canada – Jet Fuel Coffee), Gabriel Rasch (Norway – Sparebanken Vest), Malcolm Elliott (Yorkshire – Trinity Capital), Michael Steed (Kildare – Murphy Surveyors), Eoin Whelan (Louth – Safe Cycling) and Philip Cassidy (Meath – Cycleways.com). Steed was dropped but Gary Dodd (Surrey Racing League) took his place in the group, and then Conor Murphy (Ireland - Grant Thornton) and Chris Newton (GB – Recycling.co.uk) also got across. Others tried to join up but were unable to do so.

Along with Elliott and Newton, Rasch was also in the previous day's escape and so was in the running for yellow. However the Norwegian had the misfortune to puncture just before Newton, Elliott, Murphy and Cassidy turned the screw at 27 kilometres to go and blew the break apart.

The four worked together until Newton and Elliott forged ahead with approximately eight kilometres remaining, shedding the two Irish riders, and raced on into the finish in Tubbercurry together. Elliott led it out, but said afterwards that he had trouble getting into his top gear. Newton came around the 43 year old with less than 50 metres remaining and nabbed both the stage and the yellow jersey.

Stage one winner Roger Aiken (Louth – Safe Cycling) lost considerable time, crossing the line as part of the main bunch some 5 minutes and 51 seconds after the leading duo. Tim Barry (Tipperary – Dan Morrissey) finished eighth on the stage and became best placed Irishman overall in sixth.
**Stage 2 Emyvale - Tubbercurry 160 Kms.** 1 C.Newton (Britain) 4.11.11 2 M.Elliott (Yorkshire) s.t. 3 C.Murphy (Ireland Grant Thornton) at 1.12 4 P.Cassidy (Meath Cycleways) at 1.49 5 J.Tanner (Yorkshire) at 2.21 6 R.Sharman (Britain) s.t. 7 M.Lovatt (Yorkshire) s.t. 8 T.Barry (Tipp Dan Morrissey) s.t. 9 G.Dodd (Surrey Racing League) at 2.26 10 Y.Barker (Wales) s.t.
**General Classification:** 1 C.Newton (Britain) 7.04.29 2 M.Elliott (Yorkshire) at 8 secs 3 M.Hegreberg (Norway) at 2.16 4 K.Dawson (Yorkshire) at 2.23 5 R.Sharman (Britain) at 2.32 6 T.Barry (Tipp Dan Morrissey) s.t. 7 Y.Barker (Wales) at 2.37 8 G.Rasch (Norway) s.t. 9 C.Murphy (Ireland) at 4.20 10 S.Gillespie (US-TIAA-CREF) at 4.30
**Under 23:** 1 S.Gillespie 7.08.59 2 A.Coutts at 3.00 3 M.Pozniak at 4.29
**Points:** 1 C.Newton 27 2 M.Elliott 24 3 M.Hegreberg 17
**Mountains:** 1 E.Moriarty 19 2 R.Krotky 9 3 M.Urban 8
**International Team:** 1 Yorkshire 21.21.29 2 Norway at 3.04 3 Britain at 3.30
**County Team:** 1 Meath Cycleways 21.33.28 2 Tipperary Dan Morrissey at 29 secs 3 Meath M Donnelly at 3.31

## STAGE 3

In a virtual replay of the previous day's result, British rider Chris Newton once again out galloped former Tour of Spain point's victor Malcolm Elliott to win the third stage, a 156 kilometre leg from Tubbercurry to Lisdoonvarna.
Newton, Elliott and nine others shed the rest of the field on the day's final climb of Corkscrew Hill, racing clear over the top of the switch backed climb and plunging down towards the finish where they all sprinted it out.
The former world point's race champion underlined his superiority with a win in yellow, while the nearest chasers came in 41 seconds back.
Following two days of flat out racing, the third stage was somewhat more controlled. There were several attempts to break things up, though, including a brave but fruitless 60 kilometre effort by Mark Lovatt (Yorkshire Trinity Capital) and Paul Healion (Dublin Usher Insulations), plus a later move containing Stian Remme (Norway – Sparebanken Vest), Gary Hand (Scotland), Paul Sheppard (Wales – Stena Line), Mick Hennessy (Cork Nucleus), Rory Wyley (Tipperary Dan Morrissey) and John Mason (Tipperary Worldwide Cycles). This sextet opened up a forty second lead but were hauled back just before Corkscrew Hill, paving the way for the final break to go clear inside the last 12 kilometres.
In Lisdoonvarna, the successful escape – namely Newton, Elliott, Malte Urban (Germany – Stevens von Hacht), Morten Hegreberg (Norway – Sparebanken Vest), Tim Barry (Tipperary Dan Morrissey), Stephen Gallagher (Ireland – Grant

Thornton), Evan Oliphant (Scotland), Gabriel Rasch (Norway – Sparebanken Vest), John Tanner (Yorkshire – Trinity Capital), Yanto Barker (Wales Stena Line) and Robin Sharman (GB – Recycling.co.uk) – fought it out for the stage win, finishing in that order.

Barry remained best Irishman, moving up to fourth overall, while Eugene Moriarty (Meath – Cycleways) held onto his lead in the King of the Mountains competition.

**Stage 3 Tubbercurry - Lisdoonvarna 156 Kms.** C.Newton (Britain) 3.29.55 2 M.Elliott (Yorkshire) s.t. 3 M.Urban (Germany Stevens) s.t. 4 M.Hegreberg (Norway) s.t. 5 T.Barry (Tipp Dan Morrissey) s.t. 6 S.Gallagher (Ireland) s.t. 7 E.Oliphant (Scotland) s.t. 8 G.Rasch (Norway) s.t. 9 J.Tanner (Yorkshire) s.t. 10 Y.Barker (Wales) s.t.

**General Classification:** 1 C.Newton (Britain) 10.34.24 2 M.Elliott (Yorkshire) at 8 secs 3 M.Hegreberg (Norway) at 2.16 4 T.Barry (Tipp Dan Morrissey) at 2.32 5 R.Sharman (Britain) s.t. 6 Y.Barker (Wales) at 2.37 7 G.Rasch (Norway) s.t. 8 K.Dawson (Yorkshire) at 3.04 9 C.Murphy (Ireland) at 5.01 10 S.Gillespie (US-TIAA-CREF) at 5.11

Under 23: 1 S.Gillespie 10.39.35 2 A.Coutts at 3.00 3 B.Greenwood at 4.29

**Points:** 1 C.Newton 42 2 M.Elliott 38 3 M.Hegreberg 29

**Mountains:** 1 E.Moriarty 23 2 M.Urban 16 3 G.Hand 10

**International Team:** 1 Yorkshire 31.51.55 2 Norway at 3.04 3 Britain at 3.30

**County Team:** 1 Meath Cycleways 32.06.44 2 Tipp Dan Morrissey at 1.24 3 Meath M Donnelly at 4.07

## STAGE 4

Third time lucky. After being outsprinted by Chris Newton two days in a row, former Tour of Spain point's winner Malcolm Elliott showed the speed he is renowned for and triumphed in Templemore. The Yorkshire – Trinity Capital rider was quicker than 109 other riders, timing his move perfectly after an overconfident Newton jumped too early.

Elliott's victory was particularly sweet for the Yorkshire – Trinity Capital team, as Newton's Recycling.co.uk team had staged a last-gasp recapture of two of their riders. Mark Lovatt and Irishman Tommy Evans were clear right up to the closing stages, going eyeballs out to try to hold off the main bunch. Evans blew with two kilometres remaining, while Lovatt was caught just 100 metres from the line.

Evans was in the thick of it for much of the stage, originally going clear with Philip Cassidy (Meath – Cycleways.com), Scottish rider Duncan Urquhart and several others thirty kilometres into the 162 kilometre stage. This trio pressed on approximately 20 kilometres later, being joined soon afterwards by Lovatt, Zach Bell (Canada – Jet Fuel Coffee), Are Andresen (Norway – Sparebanken Vest) and John Charlesworth (NE England).

After the last climb, Lovatt, Evans, Cassidy and Charlesworth and Cassidy opened up a gap on the others and pulled together in a bid to hold off the pursuing main bunch. However on the final descent Cassidy and Charlesworth overshot a tight left hand bend and ended up in the ditch, as did pursuers Urguqhart and Andreson. And while all four riders were able to remount and finish the stage, it's quite likely that Evans, Lovatt, Cassidy and Charlesworth could otherwise have held off the peleton and fought out the stage win between them.

Elliott remained second overall after his victory, trailing Newton by eight seconds. He said afterwards that he'd try to attack but that another stage victory was a more realistic target than the final yellow jersey. Tim Barry (Tipperary Dan Morrissey) remained the best Irishman in fifth overall, while compatriot Eugene Moriarty was third on the stage and held onto the mountains jersey.

**Stage 4 Lisdoonvarna - Templemore 162 Kms.** 1 M.Elliott (Yorkshire) 4.02.58 2 C.Newton (Britain) s.t. 3 E.Moriarty (Meath Cycleways) s.t. 4 P.Healion (Dublin Usher IRC) s.t. 5 M.Hegreberg (Norway) s.t. 6 Y.Barker (Wales) s.t. 7 S.Kukk (Estonia) s.t. 8 A.Hinrichsen (Germany Stevens) s.t. 9 J.Tanner (Yorkshire) s.t. 10 R.Krotky (Czech Elmarco)

**General Classification:** 1 C.Newton (Britain) 14.37.22 2 M.Elliott (Yorkshire) at 8 secs 3 M.Hegreberg (Norway) at 2.16 4 R.Sharman (Britain) at 2.32 5 T.Barry (Tipp Dan Morrissey) s.t. 6 Y.Barker (Wales) at 2.37 7 G.Rasch (Norway) s.t. 8 K.Dawson (Yorkshire) at 3.04 9 C.Murphy (Ireland) at 5.01 10 S.Gillespie (US-TIAA-CREF) at 5.11

**Under 23:** 1 S.Gillespie 14.42.33 2 A.Coutts at 3.00 3 I.McGregor at 4.29

**Points:** 1 C.Newton 56 2 M.Elliott 53 3 M.Hegreberg 40

**Mountains:** 1 E.Moriarty 23 2 M.Hegreberg 17 3 M.Lovatt 17

**International Team:** 1 Yorkshire 44.00.49 2 Norway at 3.04 3 Britain at 3.30

**County Team:** 1 Meath Cycleways 44.15.38 2 Tipp Dan Morrissey at 1.24 3 Meath M Donnelly at 4.07

## STAGE 5

On a stage regarded as one of the hardest of the 2005 FBD Insurance Rás, close marking by the favourites meant that a total of fifty-four riders finished within 25 seconds of each other on the streets of Abbeyleix.

Top honours went to Norway – Sparebanken Vest rider Morten Christiansen, who benefited from a strong lead-out by team-mate Are Andresen to beat Irishmen Simon Kelly (Cork Nucleus), Roger Aiken (Louth – Safe Cycling) plus the others in their eight-man breakaway group to the line.

Five seconds later, Meath Cycleways.com rider Eugene Moriarty led home the main bunch for ninth. However the Kerryman lost his King of the Mountains jersey to 2000 Rás winner Julian Winn, who took three of the day's climbs. Chris Newton defended his race lead, and top Irishman Tim Barry (Tipperary Dan Morrissey) moved up a place to fourth overall.

Christiansen was one of seven riders who went clear inside the first twenty kilometres of the stage, a 143 kilometre race which began in Templemore and featured five categorised mountains. These ascents included the category 1 climbs of the Crag and the Butts.

The breakaway group contained Irishmen Philip Cassidy (Meath – Cycleways.com) and Paul Healion (Dublin – Usher Insulation), and was further bolstered when Winn and Stephen Gallagher (Ireland – Grant Thornton) got across on the climb of the Crag. Several others then joined after the fifty kilometres-elapsed sign, including Stephen O'Sullivan (Meath – Cycleways.com), John Mason and Andrew Roche (both Tipperary – Worldwide Cycles).

Under the pressure of a chase by Newton's GB – Recycling.co.uk squad and the top county team of Tipperary Dan Morrissey, the gap was down a manageable 1 minute and 20 seconds by the time the riders reached the bottom of The Butts (96.3 kilometres). Here Ireland – Grant Thornton rider Conor Murphy punctured and lost his ninth place overall.

Seeking the mountains jersey, Winn pushed the pace on this climb and the second category Uskerty Hill, dragging several others clear. However the front-runners were caught before the final climb of the day, that of Glenmagoo.

Several attacks followed, with the decisive move going at the 25 kilometres to go point. Kevin Miller (Canada – Jet Fuel Coffee), Rotislav Krotky (Czech Republic – Elmarco KK Cube), Christiansen and Lovatt quickly opened a twelve second gap. Stage one winner Aiken got across ten kilometres later, and then Andresen, Kelly and Denis Lynch (Cork Kanturk) made the junction, all going on to sprint it out for the win.

**Stage 5 Templemore - Abbeyleix 143 Kms.** 1 M.Christiansen (Norway) 3.23.13 2 S.Kelly (Cork Nucleus) s.t. 3 R.Aiken (Louth) s.t. 4 M.Lovatt (Yorkshire) s.t. 5 K.Miller (Canada Jet Fuel Coffee) s.t. 6 R.Krotky (Czech Elmarco) at 2 secs 7 Denis Lynch (Cork Kanturk) s.t. 8 A.Andresen (Norway) at 5 secs 9 E.Moriarty (Meath Cycleways) s.t. 10 C.Newton (Britain) s.t.

**General Classification:** 1 C.Newton (Britain) 18.00.40 2 M.Elliott (Yorkshire) at 8 secs 3 M.Hegreberg (Norway) at 2.16 4 T.Barry (Tipp Dan Morrissey) at 2.32 5 R.Sharman (Britain) s.t. 6 Y.Barker (Wales) at 2.37 7 G.Rasch (Norway) s.t. 8 K.Dawson (Yorkshire) at 3.04 9 S.Gillespie (US-TIAA-CREF) at 5.11 10 J.Tanner (Yorkshire) at 5.29

**Under 23:** 1 S.Gillespie 18.05.51 2 A.Coutts at 3.00 3 I.McGregor at 4.29

**Points:** 1 C.Newton 62 2 M.Elliott 57 3 M.Hegreberg 42

**Mountains:** 1 J.Winn 35 2 E.Moriarty 3 31 M.Lovatt 31

**International Team:** 1 Yorkshire 54.10.38 2 Norway at 3.04 3 Britain at 9.03

**County Team:** 1 Meath Cycleways 54.31.00 2 Tipp Dan Morrissey at 1.24 3 Meath M Donnelly at 4.07

## STAGE 6

Underlining the assured grip he had on the yellow jersey, Chris Newton exploded from the bunch on the steep rise up to the finish line in Rathdrum to scoop his third

stage victory of the race. In less than 700 metres the GB – Recycling.co.uk rider impressively carved out a five second gap over the chasing riders, with Morten Hegreberg (Norway – Sparebanken Vest), Nathan Mitchell (US – TIAA CREF) and Irishman Eugene Moriarty (Meath – Cycleways.com) next over the line.
Newton's closest rival Malcolm Elliott (Yorkshire – Trinity Capital) finished sixth and dropped to 14 seconds behind the race leader. While the race was by no means over, the yellow jersey-holder had scored an important psychological victory.
The 160 kilometre stage started in Abbeyleix and would take the riders over mainly flat terrain. Various breaks went clear early on but it was not until approximately 55 kilometres into the stage when the elastic broke. Brian Keane (Ireland – Grant Thornton), Kristian House (Britain – Fujibikes.com), Duncan Urquhart, Evan Oliphant (both Scotland), Stuart Gillespie (US – TIAA CREF), Kenny Williams (US – Ventilux First Mortgage), Tommy Evans (Yorkshire – Trinity Capital), Chris Belsham (East England Angliasport) and Eddie O'Donoghue (Dublin – Team Murphy and Gunn) were of no real threat to the yellow jersey and, despite some unexpected driving by the Norway – Sparebanken vest team of third-placed rider Morten Hegreberg, they stayed away for a substantial chunk of the day.
With about 30 kilometres remaining Tommy Evans decided that the break was not working well enough and forged clear with Evan Oliphant (Wales – Stena Line) and Chris Belsham (East England Angliasport). The peleton was just 34 seconds back with ten kilometres to go and, four kilometres later; this gap had dropped to just 15 seconds. Evans pressed ahead alone at that point, gambling everything on a solo move, but he was finally caught with four kilometres left.
The peleton then tore down the hairpin bends into Rathdrum and raced onto the final climb where, surging out of the bunch, Newton demonstrated he was the strongest rider in the race.
**Stage 6 Abbeyleix - Rathdrum 160 Kms.** 1 C.Newton (Britain) 4.01.09 2 M.Hegreberg (Norway) at 5 secs 3 N.Mitchell (US-TIAA-CREF) s.t. 4 E.Moriarty (Meath Cycleways) s.t. 5 Y.Barker (Wales) s.t. 6 M.Elliott (Yorkshire) at 6 secs 7 J.Tanner (Yorkshire) at 11 secs 8 T.Barry (Tipp Dan Morrissey) s.t. 9 R.Sharman (Britain) s.t. 10 S.Gallagher (Ireland) s.t.
**General Classification:** 1 C.Newton (Britain) 22.01.49 2 M.Elliott (Yorkshire) at 14 secs 3 M.Hegreberg (Norway) at 2.21 4 Y.Barker (Wales) at 2.42 5 T.Barry (Tipp Dan Morrissey) at 2.43 6 R.Sharman (Britain) s.t. 7 G.Rasch (Norway) at 2.59 8 K.Dawson (Yorkshire) at 3.33 9 S.Gillespie (US-TIAA-CREF) at 5.33 10 J.Tanner (Yorkshire) at 5.40
**Under 23:** 1 S.Gillespie 22.07.22 2 A.Coutts at 3.00 3 I.McGregor at 4.29
**Points:** 1 C.Newton 77 2 M.Elliott 67 3 M.Hegreberg 56
**Mountains:** 1 J.Winn 35 2 E.Moriarty 3 31 M.Lovatt 31
**International Team:** 1 Yorkshire 66.14.51 2 Norway at 3.01 3 Britain at 10.18
**County Team:** 1 Meath Cycleways 66.35.44 2 Tipp Dan Morrissey at 1.35 3 Meath M Donnelly at 4.10

## STAGE 7

With seven rated climbs, including the category one ascents of Slieve Mann, Sally Gap and Luggala, the penultimate stage of the FBD Insurance RÁS was set for a big showdown in the mountains of Wicklow. Chris Newton and his Recycling.co.uk team things under control, though, and despite a long-distance breakaway, things came down to a bunch sprint in Wicklow town.
There Morten Hegreberg (Norway – Sparebanken Vest) beat Malcolm Elliott (Yorkshire – Trinity Capital), Yanto Barker (Wales – Stena Line) plus 21 others to win the stage. Newton finished tenth and retained his race lead.
The route covered 138 kilometres between Rathdrum and Wicklow Town and was arguably the hardest of the race. There were a number of attacks after the start but mountains leader Julian Winn appeared in control of the situation and took top points on the day's first three climbs, reinforcing his advantage.
Following the third climb, the category one Barnameelia, Morten Christiansen (Norway – Sparebanken Vest) and Sean Lacey (Meath – M. Donnelly) went clear. They were joined soon afterwards by Duncan Urquhart (Scotland), Mark Lovatt (Yorkshire – Trinity Capital), Steve Kenny (NE England), Denis Lynch (Cork – Kanturk), Philip Finegan (Dublin – Usher Insulations), Bill Moore (both Meath – M. Donnelly) and Andrew Roche (Tipperary – Worldwide Cycles) in a nine-man move.
By the time this front group had reached the 50 kilometre point they had a lead of 2 minutes 24 seconds, and this soon inched up to its maximum of 2 minutes 32 seconds.
Approximately 40 kilometres later, the riders were on the long climb of Sally Gap and there the splintering yellow jersey group had closed to within 40 seconds of the fragmenting break. However, Newton's progress was delayed slightly when he punctured. He took a wheel from a team-mate and quickly rejoined, while up ahead Lynch led over the top of the climb and then pressed on with Urquhard and Lovatt. The latter then sealed his victory in the King of the Mountains classification when he was first to the top of Luggala.
Behind, the yellow jersey group split on the climbs, but the overall contenders were all present and this group gradually reformed. With seven kilometres to go the three leaders had thirty seconds advantage; however, a furious chase behind saw them caught with two clicks to go and, following an unsuccessful break by the leading under 23 rider Stuart Gillespie (US - TIAA CREF), the scene was set for a big group sprint and Hegreberg's win. Eugene Moriarty (Meath – Cycleways.com) was best Irishman in fifth.
**Stage 7 Rathdrum - Wicklow 139 Kms.** 1 M.Hegreberg (Norway) 3.29 .36 2 M.Elliott (Yorkshire) s.t. 3 Y.Barker (Wales) s.t. 4 J.Tanner (Yorkshire) s.t. 5 E.Moriarty (Meath Cycleways) s.t. 6 2 S.Kelly (Cork Nucleus) s.t. 7 S.Kukk (Estonia) s.t. 8 S.Gallagher (Ireland) s.t. 9 R.Sharman (Britain) s.t. 10 C.Newton (Britain) s.t.

**General Classification:** 1 C.Newton (Britain) 25.31.25 2 M.Elliott (Yorkshire) at 14 secs 3 M.Hegreberg (Norway) at 2.21 4 Y.Barker (Wales) at 2.42 5 R.Sharman (Britain) at 2.43 6 T.Barry (Tipp Dan Morrissey) s.t. 7 G.Rasch (Norway) 2.59 8 J.Tanner (Yorkshire) at 5.40 9 S.Gillespie (US-TIAA-CREF) at 5.40 10 K.Dawson (Yorkshire) at 6.19
**Under 23:** 1 S.Gillespie 25.37.05 2 A.Coutts at 2.53 3 P.O'Brien at 7.20
**Points:** 1 C.Newton 83 2 M.Elliott 81 3 M.Hegreberg 71
**Mountains:** 1 M.Lovatt 72 2 J.Winn 60 3 M.Hegreberg 56
**International Team:** 1 Yorkshire 76.43.39 2 Norway at 3.08 3 Britain at 10.25
**County Team:** 1 Tipp Dan Morrissey 77.10.19 2 Meath Cycleways at 1.47 3 Dublin Usher IRC 18.25

## STAGE 8

Chris Newton (GB – Recycling.co.uk) finished safely in the main bunch on the last day of the race, making history in becoming the first overseas rider to ever win two editions. Yet another rider was even happier after the concluding stage.
32 year old Bill Moore shocked the sprint specialists when he thundered to an excellent victory, using his experience of racing on the Phoenix Park circuit to jump at exactly the right time and hold on until the line. The Meath – M. Donnelly rider netted his best career result when he beat Julian Winn (Wales – Stena Line), stage 7 winner Morten Hegreberg (Norway – Sparebanken Vest) plus the 153 other riders left in the race.
Mild, bright weather and a good crowd greeted the 156 starters on the final stage, a pancake flat circuit race held in Dublin's Phoenix Park. As expected, it was a controlled affair Chris Newton's GB – Recycling.co.uk team, the Norway-Sparebanken Vest squad and the Wales – Stena Line riders did what they could to keep things together and set things up for a sprint finish.
Several riders did succeed in getting a brief gap on the main field, but most of these efforts related to the four Cycleways primes which were up for grabs.
The first of these went to former KOH leader Eugene Moriarty (Meath – Cycleways.com), while the others were taken by Richard Kooijman (Netherlands – Kennemerland), Kristian House (Britain-Fujibikes) and Irishman Simon Kelly (Cork Nucleus). From there until the finish the Norway – Sparebanken Vest and the GB – Recycling.co.uk controlled things and ensured a bunch gallop.
Newton was expected to try to repeat his stage 8 victory of 2002 but instead he found himself in a bad position, at the front of the bunch with one lap to go. Conscious that he had to beat the GB Recycling.co.uk rider by at least three places to scoop the point's jersey, and psyched by his win here twelve months ago, Malcolm Elliott (Yorkshire – Trinity Capital) manoeuvred himself into position and was in the right place with 200 metres to go. However he was unable to engage the 12 sprocket in the sprint and, to add near-injury to that frustration, the 43 year old fast man was switched badly by another rider, losing spokes and almost crashing. He was 13th.

Things went perfectly for Moore, though, and he galloped to a superb victory. Newton did not contest the sprint, but was in no danger of losing the race he'd started the day 14 seconds ahead of Elliott, who was 15 places ahead of him going over the line and thus had the consolation prize of the point's jersey.

Lovatt took the mountains jersey, while Tim Barry was best Irishman in sixth place. He netted the county rider prize, Stuart Gillespie (US – TIAA CREF) won the under 23 classification and Barry Meehan (Tipperary Worldwide Cycles) was best second category rider.

The top international squad was Yorkshire – Trinity Capital and Barry's Tipperary Dan Morrissey lineup were first county team.

**Stage 8 Phoenix Park Circuit 40 Kms.** 1 B.Moore (Meath M Donnelly) 1.01.14 2 J.Winn (Wales) s.t. 3 M.Hegreberg (Norway) s.t. 4 S.Kelly (Cork Nucleus) s.t. 5 E.Moriarty (Meath Cycleways) s.t. 6 A.Crowley (Meath Cycleways) s.t. 7 R.Kooijhan (Netherlands) s.t. 8 Y.Barker (Wales) s.t. 9 C.Bracken (Kildare Murphy) 10 A.Hinrichsen (Germany Stevens) s.t.

**General Classification:** 1 C.Newton (Britain) 26.32.39 2 M.Elliott (Yorkshire) at 14 secs 3 M.Hegreberg (Norway) at 2.21 4 Y.Barker (Wales) at 2.42 5 R.Sharman (Britain) at 2.43 6 T.Barry (Tipp Dan Morrissey) s.t. 7 G.Rasch (Norway) 2.59 8 J.Tanner (Yorkshire) at 5.40 9 S.Gillespie (US-TIAA-CREF) s.t. 10 K.Dawson (Yorkshire) at 6.19

**Under 23:** 1 S.Gillespie 26.38.19 2 A.Coutts at 2.53 3 P.O'Brien at 7.20

**Points:** 1 M.Elliott 84 2 M.Hegreberg 84 3 C.Newton 83

**Mountains:** 1 M.Lovatt 72 2 J.Winn 60 3 M.Hegreberg 56

**International Team:** 1 Yorkshire 79.47.21 2 Norway at 3.01 3 Britain at 10.25

**County Team:** 1 Tipp Dan Morrissey 80.14.01 2 Meath Cycleways at 1.47 3 Dublin Usher IRC 18.25

*2005 winner, Chris Newton*

## 2006

In terms of the general classification, Irish riders were less successful in 2005 than they had been a year earlier. This was due in part to the absence of some of the country's big professionals. However hopes were high that they would play a bigger part in the 2006 event. National road race champion David O'Loughlin (Ireland Grant Thornton) was back after a year's absence and former double champion Ciarán Power was also in the race, riding for the Éireann Dan Morrissey squad.
Power had posted a career best performance in the 2004 Olympics when he finished 13th in the bunch sprint, despite having been away for several laps in a break. He was highly motivated by his showing and intended building on the ride, but instead began suffering with the effects of a blood flow problem in his legs.
Finally pinpointed as Iliac artery endofibrosis, the condition was corrected in early 2006 and Power set about returning to top form. He felt that his condition was not good enough to win the FBD Insurance RÁS, but said he would target stage victories in the race.
As had become the norm, there was a strong line-up of overseas teams in the race, including riders from as far afield as the American and Australian continents. The defending champion Chris Newton was back at the helm of an impressive Great Britain Recycling.co.uk squad. Another strong challenge was likely to come from the USA – TIAA CREF squad, fronted by 2001 world under 23 time trial champion Danny Pate and former US Postal Service rider Mike Creed.
The Canada – Team Symmetrics line-up and the Australia – FRF Couriers Carravello team also travelled a long distance, while several strong squads came from mainland Europe. These included the Belgium – Sean Kelly Racing Team, which comprised three Irish riders and two Belgians, the Poland – Legia Bazylisek line-up, Norway Sparebanken Vest and Germany - Team Stevens. The Doncaster Stena Line squad was also expected to play a big part.

### STAGE 1

Tommy Evans had taken five RÁS stage wins over the years but lost out on adding to that tally when a premature celebration at the finish in Enniscorthy allowed 2005 race winner Chris Newton to edge by.
The 1996 RÁS champion was part of a breakaway group which escaped inside the final 30 kilometres of the stage. With less than two clicks to go, Newton's Britain – Recycling.co.uk team-mate Rob Sharman soloed clear but Evans (Dublin IRC Usher Insulations) overhauled him approximately 600 metres from the line. He thought he had won but in thrusting his arm skywards, it gave a fast-closing Newton just enough

of a chance to lunge past and take victory by a tyre-width. The double RÁS champion also landed the first yellow jersey of the race.
The 121 kilometre stage from Tallaght to Enniscorthy was run off in brutal weather conditions, 144 riders braving the elements while sporting fixtures were being cancelled all around the country. The second category climb of the Embankment came after just 1.2 kilometres of racing and 2002 race winner Ciarán Power (Éireann Dan Morrissey) was first to the top, also taking the Hot Spot Sprint there.
Next to attack was 2001 US under 23 champion Mike Friedman (USA TIAA-CREF), who launched an attack shortly after the summit and quickly opened a lead of 15 seconds. By Naas, 28 kilometres after the start, he had 1 minute and 15 seconds over three riders – including Ireland-Grant Thornton's Paídi O'Brien - but the chasers were recaptured soon afterwards. The American was riding strongly and picked up three bonus seconds at the Hot Spot Sprint in Kilcullen. However he was finally hauled back at the 58 kilometre point.
Martin Prazdnovsky (Norway Sparebanken Vest) went on a solo move and later joined up with Bartlomiej Matysiak (Poland Legia Bazylisek) and Tommy Evans (Dublin IRC Usher Insulations). The trio pulled away before the 100 kilometre point and opened up a minute's lead by Bunclody, 22 kilometres from the finish.
Evan Oliphant (Britain Recycling.co.uk) tried but failed to get across, then seven others – Newton and Sharman, Joe McDonnell (Australia FRF Couriers Caravel), Jehudi Schoonacker (Belgium M. Donnelly Sean Kelly), Brad Fairall (Canada Symmetrics), Morten Hegreberg (Norway Sparebanken Vest) and Dan Bowman (USA TIAA CREF) – successfully bridged with about eleven kilometres remaining.
A strong chase by the Ireland Grant Thornton team and Power's Éireann Dan Morrissey squad closed the gap to 150 metres with just two kilometres remaining, but a stall gave the break another chance. Sharman and then Evans played their cards but Newton ultimately triumphed. Two seconds later McDonnell and Matysiak scraped home for third and fourth, the peleton swamping the remainder of the break as they crossed the line.
A disappointed Evans ended the day second overall, four seconds back, while Power was third due to time bonuses picked up. He also held the mountains jersey after placing first and second on the day's KOM primes.
**Stage 1 Dublin - Enniscorthy 121 Kms.** 1 C.Newton (Britain Recycling) 2.48.37 2 T.Evans (Dublin IRC Usher) s.t. 3 J.McDonnell (Australia FRF) at 2 secs 4 B.Matysiak (Poland Legia) s.t. 5 B.Hill (Germany Stevens) s.t. 6 M.Hegreberg (Norway Sparebanken) s.t. 7 R.Sharman (Britain Recycling) s.t. 8 J.Marden (Australia FRF) s.t. 9 C.Stevenson (Australia FRF) 10 J.Schoonacker (Ireland (M.Donnelly S.Kelly)s.t.
**General Classification:** 1 C.Newton (Britain) 2.48.27 2 T.Evans (Dublin Usher) at 4 secs 3 C.Power (Eireann Dan Morrissey) at 5 secs 4 J.McDonnell (Australia FRF) at 8 secs 5 M.Hegreberg (Norway Sparebanken) at 9 secs 6 M.Friedman (USA TIAA-CREF) s.t. 7 L.Modzelewski (Poland Legia) s.t. 8 B.Matysiak (Poland Legia) at 11

secs 9 P.O'Brien (Ireland Grant Thornton) s.t. 10 B.Hill (Germany Stevens) at 12 secs

**Under 23:** 1 L.Modzelewski 2.48.36 2 B.Matysiak at 2 secs 3 P.O'Brien s.t.

**Points:** 1 C.Newton 15 2 T.Evans 14 3 J.McDonnell 13

**Mountains:** 1 C.Power 14 2 L.Modzelewski 8 3 B.Matysiak 6

**International Team:** 1 Britain Recycling 8.25.55 2 Australia FRF at 2 secs 3 Germany Stevens s.t.

**County Team:** 1 Dublin IRC Usher 2 Meath MyHome.ie 3 Kerry Earl of Desmond

## STAGE 2

Redisplaying the solo strength which won him the world under 23 time trial championship in Lisbon in 2001, American rider Danny Pate raced to a superb win on day two of the 2006 FBD Insurance RÁS.

The USA TIAA-CREF rider attacked three breakaway companions six kilometres from the end of the wind-buffeted 180 kilometre stage from Enniscorthy to Cobh, powering up the final climb to take both the victory and the yellow jersey.

Martin Prazdnovsky (Norway Sparebanken Vest) finished 27 seconds back in second place, with Wayne Randle (Britain Doncaster Stena Line) and Robin Sharman 34 and 41 seconds behind.

A total of 142 riders lined out the 180 kilometre second stage, the longest of the race, which took the FBD Insurance RÁS field from Enniscorthy to Cobh. Two category three climbs, a category two ascent and the steep uphill finish were all on the menu, the day made harder by strong, cold winds.

Various attacks went early on, most notably a 15 man group which included some strong foreign riders plus Irishmen Ryan Connor (Ireland Grant Thornton), David O'Loughlin (Ireland Grant Thornton), Brian Kenneally (Meath MyHome.ie/Cycleways) and King of the Mountains leader Ciarán Power (Éireann Dan Morrissey). The latter won the category 3 prime at Glenmore, boosting his points.

However many other strong riders, including race leader Newton, gradually made their way across to the break and swelled it to an unmanageable number.

The reshuffling began once again and Wayne Randle (Britain Doncaster Stena Line), Tamas Lengyel, Martin Prazdnovsky (both Norway Sparebanken Vest) and Danny Pate (USA TIAA-CREF) eventually slipped away, marked by Newton's team-mate Rob Sharman (Britain Recycling.co.uk).

By the time Prazdnovsky took the prime at the top of the Sweep climb, 116 kilometres after the start, the leaders were a full 2 minutes and 49 seconds up on a Power-led chasing group. This gap went up to over five minutes and when the attacks started inside the final 20 kilometres, it was clear that one of those in the break would win.

Pate and Randle put in a couple of good surges before the former finally broke the elastic with about six kilometres remaining and opened up a winning advantage.

Prazdnovsky, Randle and Sharman were second, third and fourth while Pate's team-mate, an impressive Mike Friedman, was fifth, 3 minutes and seven seconds back. He chased for many kilometres alone, having come out of a chase group which was five minutes in arrears.

Newton led home the chasers for sixth. Hee and Irish challengers such as Tommy Evans (Dublin IRC Usher Insulations), David O'Loughlin (Ireland Grant Thornton), Brian Kenneally (Meath MyHome.ie/Cycleways) and Simon Kelly (Ireland Murphy and Gunn/Newlyn Group) had a tough task on their hands if they wanted to win the race as they had all conceded 3 minutes and 41 seconds to Pate.

**Stage 2 Enniscorthy - Cobh 180 Kms.** 1 D.Pate (USA TIAA-CREF) 4.31.15 2 M.Prazdnovsky (Norway) at 27 secs 3 W.Randle (Doncaster) at 34 secs 4 R.Sharman (Britain) at 41 secs 5 M.Friedman (USA TIAA-CREF) at 3.10 6 C.Newton (Britain) at 3.41 7 M.Hegreberg (Norway) s.t. 8 B.Matysiak (Poland) s.t. 9 T.Evans (Dublin IRC) at 3.45 10 J.Schoonacker (Ireland (M.Donnelly S.Kelly) s.t.

**General Classification:** 1 D.Pate (USA TIAA-CREF) 7.19.54 2 M.Prazdnovsky (Norway) at 27 secs 3 W.Randle (Doncaster) at 34 secs 4 R.Sharman (Britain) at 41 secs 5 M.Friedman (USA TIAA-CREF) at 3.07 6 C.Newton (Britain) at 3.29 7 T.Evans (Dublin IRC Usher) at 3.37 8 M.Hegreberg (Norway) s.t. 9 B.Matysiak (Poland) at 3.41 10 J.McDonnell (Australia FRF) s.t.

**Under 23:** 1 B.Matysiak 7.23.35 2 R.Partridge at 3.23 3 M.Concannon s.t.

**Points:** 1 C.Newton 25 2 R.Sharman 21 3 T.Evans 21

**Mountains:** 1 C.Power 20 2 D.Pate 16 3 M.Prazdnovsky 15

**International Team:** 1 Norway 22.07.35 2 Britain Recycling at 12 secs 3 USA TIAA-CREF at 2.28

**County Team:** 1 Dublin IRC Usher 22.32.39 2 Meath MyHome.ie at 2 secs 3 Cork Murray Ford at 1.57

## STAGE 3

If it seemed like game over for many of the overall contenders after day two of the race, the third stage showed just how unpredictable and exciting the FBD Insurance RÁS can be.

Joshua Marden (Australia FRF Couriers) proved quickest in the 28 man sprint which decided the honours, the 23 year old beating Lukasz Modzelewski and Irishman Mehall Fitzgerald (Meath MyHome.ie/Cycleways) on the uphill drag to the line.

Danny Pate (USA TIAA-CREF) had began the day in yellow but he, Martin Prazdnovsky (Norway Sparebanken Vest), Wayne Randle (Britain Doncaster Stena Line) and Rob Sharman (Britain Recycling.co.uk) all finished in a small group 3 minutes and 30 seconds back. Those riders had occupied the first four places overall but paid for their efforts from the day before, being out-manoeuvred by the other race favourites approximately 50 kilometres from the finish. Pate's team-mate Mike Friedman placed fourth on the stage and took over at the top of the general classification.

The third stage of the FBD Insurance RÁS started in bright weather and took the riders 173 kilometres from Cobh to An Daingean/Dingle.
Several breakaways slipped clear, including a large group containing Mike Friedman (USA TIAA-CREF), David O'Loughlin and Ryan Connor (both Ireland Grant Thornton), Tommy Evans (Dublin IRC Usher Insulations). These were all brought back and then an eight-man group went away after 50 kilometres of racing.
Thirty kilometres later this break split on the category 3 County Bounds climb and Evan Oliphant (Britain Recycling.co.uk), Mark Lovatt (Britain Doncaster Stena Line), Peter Herzig (Australia FRF Couriers) and Fabian Brzezinski (Germany Stevens) surged ahead. They were joined by six others on the outskirts of Killarney, after 106 kilometres of racing, and the gap at this point was a considerable 2 minutes and 40 seconds.
Ray Clarke (Eireann Dan Morrissey) was one of those who bridged across and he soloed clear shortly after the summit of the category three Crohane climb, 114 kilometres into the stage. Behind, many of the big guns in the race escaped from the bunch and started closing up to those behind Clarke. Crucially, the first four in the general classification had missed out and this provided ample motivation for the merging breaks to ride hard.
Clarke was finally caught about 36 kilometres from the end of the stage, and at this point there was a big group of about 30 riders at the head of the race. The gap to the main bunch was a minute, with Pate's USA – TIAA CREF squad, the Poland Legia Bazylisek team and the Ireland M. Donnelly Sean Kelly selection trying unsuccessfully to get back on terms.
Herzig won the prime on the cat three An Draighneain climb and Morten Hegreberg took the final one of the day, An Bharog Bheag. At this point, 13.5 kilometres from the finish, a group of chasers was 2 minutes and 30 seconds back, while the peleton was three minutes in arrears. Pate looked set to lose his jersey and so it proved, with Friedman taking fourth on the stage behind Marden and succeeding his team-mate at the top of the leader board.
Hegreberg's consistency on the climbs saw him move equal on points with Power in the mountains classification, but the latter stayed in the polka-dot jersey on count back.
**Stage 3 Cobh - An Daingean 172.5 Kms.** 1 J.Marden (Australia FRF) 4.42.49 2 L.Modzelewski (Poland Legia) s.t. 3 M.Fitzgerald (Meath MyHome.ie) s.t. 4 M.Friedman (USA TIAA-CREF) s.t. 5 P.Healion (Ireland Murphy & Gunn) 6 C.Newton (Britain) s.t. 7 P.Herzig (Australia FRF) s.t. 8 S.Kelly (Ireland Murphy & Gunn) s.t. 9 M.Hegreberg (Norway) s.t. 10 T.Evans (Dublin IRC Usher) s.t.
**General Classification:** 1 M.Friedman (USA TIAA-CREF) at 12.05.50 2 C.Newton (Britain) at 22 secs 3 D.Pate (USA TIAA-CREF) at 23 secs 4 T.Evans (Dublin IRC Usher) at 30 secs 5 M.Hegreberg (Norway) s.t 6 S.Kelly (Ireland Murphy & Gunn) at 38 secs 7 D.O'Loughlin (Ireland Grant Thornton) s.t. 8 K.House (Britain Recycling) s.t. 9 B.Kenneally (Meath MyHome.ie) s.t. 10 M.Prazdnovsky (Norway) at 50 secs
**Under 23:** 1 R.Partridge 12.09.47 2 P.O'Brien at 6 secs 3 B.Matysiak at 14 secs

**Points:** 1 C.Newton 35 2 T.Evans 27 3 M.Hegreberg 26
**Mountains:** 1 C.Power 20 2 M.Hegreberg 20 3 P.Herzig 19
**International Team:** 1 Britain Recycling 36.16.14 2 Norway at 3.18 3 USA TIAA-CREF at 5.46
**County Team:** 1 Meath MyHome.ie 36.44.45 2 Dublin IRC Usher at 3.35 3 Cork Murray Ford at 5.32

## STAGE 4

Lacking some racing miles due to an operation earlier in the year, Ciarán Power (Éireann Dan Morrissey) came into the 2006 RÁS with one aim in mind. The former double champion knew he didn't have the condition to win overall, but stage victories were very much a target. He achieved his goal on stage four, outsprinting breakaway companion Lukasz Modzelewski (Poland Legia Bazylisek) to the line in Listowel.
Third on the stage was Ireland – Grant Thornton rider David O'Loughlin. He crossed the line four seconds behind Power and missed out on taking over the yellow jersey by just one frustrating second. Race leader Mike Friedman (USA – TIAA CREF) had missed an important break and he and 2005 champion Chris Newton (Britain – Recycling.co.uk) finished almost eight minutes down, losing out on any hope of overall victory. Instead, Friedman's team-mate Danny Pate reclaimed the yellow jersey he had lost one day earlier.
138 riders lined out in damp, cold conditions for the 150 kilometre race from An Daingean (Dingle) to Listowel. The stage was seen as perhaps the hardest of the race, with seven categorised climbs and many undulating roads coming along the way.
Several attacks were fired off early on, with the battle for the King of the Mountains jersey being one of the big catalysts. Power and Peter Herzig (Australia FRF Couriers) both scored well but the latter got the upper hand, taking over the lead in that classification.
Mark Lovatt (Britain Doncaster Stena Line) attacked after the summit of the third climb of the day, the category three Casadh na Graige, and was later joined by Herzig, leading second category rider John McCarthy (Kerry Earl of Desmond), Denis Lynch and his Cork Murray Ford Developments team-mate Michael Fitzgerald.
Power and Greg Reian (Germany Stevens) subsequently got across. Meanwhile several others realised the danger and began a long chase, this group including O'Loughlin, his Ireland – Grant Thornton team-mates Conor Murphy and Simon Kelly (Ireland Grant Thornton), Kristian House (Britain Recycling.co.uk), Morten Hegreberg (Norway Sparebanken Vest), Danny Pate, Tommy Evans (Dublin IRC Usher Insulations) and Modzelewski.
They had plenty of motivation to work, as those lying third to eight on GC were there while yellow jersey Mike Friedman and defending RÁS champion Chris Newton,

second overall going into the stage, had missed out. The chasers eventually joined up with the leaders just before the Maum climb, after about 108 kilometres of racing.
Several of them were dropped on the first category ascent, and over the top Modzelewski broke clear. Herzig took second, boosting his KOM lead over Power. There was a regrouping of sorts inside the final 20 kilometres of racing, and approximately six clicks later Modzelewski and Power jumped away and opened a ten second lead over a five man chasing group, namely House, O'Loughlin, Hegreberg, Pate and Evans.
O'Loughlin eventually left this group but couldn't quite catch them by the line. He ended the day just one second off yellow but said afterwards that it was perhaps better not to have the responsibility of defending the lead so early.
**Stage 4 An Daingean - Listowel 149.8 Kms.**1 C.Power (Eireann Dan Morrissey) 3.42.42 2 L.Modzelewski (Poland) at 1 sec 3 D.O'Loughlin (Ireland Grant Thornton) at 4 secs 4 T.Evans (Dublin IRC Usher) at 18 secs 5 D.Pate (USA TIAA-CREF) s.t 6 K.House (Britain Recycling) s.t. 7 M.Hegreberg (Norway) s.t 8 C.Stevenson (Australia FRF) at 1.03 9 G.Reian (Germany Stevens) s.t. 10 J.McCarthy (Kerry Earl of Desmond) s.t.
**General Classification:** 1 D.Pate (USA TIAA-CREF) 15.49.13 2 D.O'Loughlin (Ireland Grant Thornton) at 1 sec 3 T.Evans (Dublin IRC Usher) at 7 secs 4 M.Hegreberg (Norway) s.t 5 K.House (Britain Recycling) at 15 secs 6 S.Kelly (Ireland Murphy & Gunn) at 1.00 7 P.Herzig (Australia FRF) at 1.16 8 W.Randle (Doncaster) at 4.45 9 G.Reian (Germany Stevens) at 6.24 10 R.Sharman (Britain) at6.52
**Under 23:** 1 P.O'Brien 15.57.04 2 L.Modzelewski at 2.56 3 R.Partridge at 3.15
**Points:** 1 T.Evans 39 2 C.Newton 35 3 M.Hegreberg 35
**Mountains:** 1 P.Herzig 52 2 C.Power 42 3 L.Modzelewski 23
**International Team:** 1 Norway 47.36.54 2 Britain Recycling at 2.03 3 Australia FRF at 4.14
**County Team:** 1 Dublin IRC Usher 48.11.03 2 Cork Murray Ford at 42 secs 3 Meath MyHome.ie at 2.365

## STAGE 5

Following four days of upheavals in the general classification, the fifth stage of the FBD Insurance RÁS was one defined by relative stability in the overall standings of the eight-day race. Eventual honours went to Jaroslaw Welniak, the 28 year old outsprinting his Poland Legia Bazylisek team-mate Bartlomiej Matysiak and Ireland Grant Thornton's Ryan Connor to the line.
Race leader Danny Pate (USA TIAA-CREF) came in as part of the main group, 4 minutes and 41 seconds after Welniak, but defended his lead. Closest rival David O'Loughlin remained one second back overall.
The 179 kilometre was run off in bright conditions and took the riders from Kilrush to the Gaeltacht area of An Cheathrú Rua. There was an aggressive start to the stage

and after about twelve kilometres, a group of ten riders got clear. They were Robert Partridge (Britain Recycling.co.uk), Ryan Connor (Ireland Grant Thornton), Mark Cassidy (Ireland M. Donnelly Sean Kelly), Ryan Connor (Ireland Stevens), Are Andresen (Norway Sparebanken Vest), Michal Pawlyta (Poland Legia Bazylisek), Jaroslaw Welniak (Poland Legia Bazylisek), Lucas Euser (USA TIAA CREF), Stephen O'Sullivan (Meath MyHome.ie Cycleways) and Ray Clarke (Éireann Dan Morrissey).

Others tried to bridge but were unable to cross the steadily-increasing gap between break and bunch. However coming up to the 50 kilometre mark Joshua Marden (Australia FRF Couriers Caravel), Bartlomiej Matysiak (Poland Legia Bazylisek) and Brian Kenneally (Meath MyHome.ie Cycleways.com) got clear and joined up with the leaders after the descent of Corkscrew hill.

At Clarinbridge (101.7 km), twelve chasers were 3 minutes and 33 seconds back, with the peleton 6 minutes and 54 seconds in arrears. Kenneally had started the day best placed overall of those in the break, lying 14th at 7 minutes and 47 seconds in the general classification, and soon got very close to being the race leader on the road. This prompted acceleration behind and the gap then started to gradually come back down.

Welniak, Connor and Euser forged ahead on the day's sole categorised climb, the second category ascent of Seanafeistin, and then on the undulating terrain afterwards the first two of those pressed ahead with Matysiak.

Connor was aiming for the stage win and attacked several times on the run-in to An Cheathrú Rua, but each time he was brought back by the two team-mates. Welniak had seemed the weaker of the two in the closing stages but sprinted strongly to get by Matysiak and Connor, who had led out the gallop, thus winning the stage. Clarke was next home, 1 minute and 23 seconds behind the stage winner.

**Stage 5 Kilrush - An Cheathru Rua 178.2 Kms.** 1 J.Welniak (Poland) 4.18.57 2 B.Matysiak (Poland) at 1 sec 3 R.Connor (Ireland Grant Thornton) at 3 secs 4 R.Clarke (Eireann Dan Morrissey) at 1.23 5 J.Marden (Australia FRF) at 1.29 6 M.Cassidy (Ireland M.Donnelly S.Kelly) at1.31 7 R.Partridge (Britain Recycling) s.t. 8 F.Schroder (Germany Stevens) s.t. 9 A.Andresen (Norway) s.t. 10 9 B.Kenneally (Meath MyHome.ie) at 1.34

**General Classification:** 1 D.Pate (USA TIAA-CREF) 20.12.51 2 D.O'Loughlin (Ireland Grant Thornton) at 1 sec 3 M.Hegreberg (Norway) at 7 secs 4 T.Evans (Dublin IRC Usher) s.t. 5 K.House (Britain Recycling) at 15 secs 6 S.Kelly (Ireland Murphy & Gunn) at 1.00 7 P.Herzig (Australia FRF) at 1.16 8 B.Kenneally (Meath MyHome.ie) at 4.40 9 W.Randle (Doncaster) at 4.45 10 A.Andresen (Norway) at 5.45

**Under 23:** 1 B.Matysiak 20.19.31 2 P.O'Brien at 1.11 3 R.Partridge at 1.16

**Points:** 1 C.Newton 39 2 T.Evans 39 3 M.Hegreberg 35

**Mountains:** 1 P.Herzig 52 2 C.Power 42 3 L.Modzelewski 23

**International Team:** 1 Norway 60.44.38 2 Britain Recycling at 2.01 3 Australia FRF at 4.12

**County Team:** 1 Meath MyHome.ie 61.21.26 2 Dublin IRC Usher at 31 secs 3 Cork Murray Ford at 1.13

## STAGE 6

For the first time in many years, a split stage was held in the FBD Insurance RÁS. Taking place on the sixth day of the race, the first of these was a 24 kilometre team time trial starting and finishing in An Cheathrú Rua.

The Britain Recycling.co.uk team was quickest, covering the distance in a time of 31 minutes and 31 seconds. USA TIAA-CREF and Norway Sparebanken Vest were second and third, with the Ireland-Grant Thornton team of David O'Loughlin finishing a disappointing sixth. He had started the day just one second behind Danny Pate and dropped to fifth overall.

Following their victory, the Recycling.co.uk team were both surprised and somewhat annoyed to learn that Kristian House would not be in yellow that afternoon. Instead, the race lead went to Tommy Evans. His Dublin Usher Insulations team had been a full two minutes and four seconds slower than the quickest time but a somewhat controversial race regulation designed not to disadvantage strong riders on small county teams came into play.

Under the rule - which had been announced well before the race began - the fastest county team was to be given the same time as the quickest International squad. As winners of each category, they had zero time added to their general classification standings while the next teams incurred a fifteen second penalty. Each team thereafter would be given a further five seconds. The finishing placings rather than actual times were used to determine the increase in overall time after the stage.

The net result was that Evans jumped from fourth to first overall, moving eight seconds clear of Kristian House (Recycling.co.uk) and the previous race leader, Danny Pate (USA TIAA – CREF). The third place recorded by Norway Sparebanken Vest saw Morten Hegreberg drop a place and thirteen seconds to fourth, while David O'Loughlin's Ireland Grant Thornton team finished back in sixth in the International ranking. He consequently went from second, one second behind Pate, to fifth, 29 seconds off the new leader Evans.

**Stage 6 An Cheathru Rua TTT.** 1 Britain Recycling 2 Dublin IRC Usher 3 USA TIAA-CREF 4 Meath MyHome.ie 5 Norway 6 Kildare Murphy Surveys 7 Poland 8 Kerry Earl of Desmond 9 Australia FRF 10 Meath M Donnelly

**General Classification:** 1 T.Evans (Dublin IRC Usher) 20.12.58 2 K.House (Britain) at 8 secs 3 D.Pate (USA TIAA-CREF) s.t. 4 M.Hegreberg (Norway) at 20 secs 5 D.O'Loughlin (Ireland Grant Thornton) at 29 secs 6 S.Kelly (Ireland Murphy & Gunn) at 1.33 7 P.Herzig (Australia FRF) at 1.39 8 B.Kenneally (Meath MyHome.ie) at 4.48 9 W.Randle (Doncaster) at 5.23 10 R.Sharman (Britain) at 6.45

**Under 23:** 1 B.Matysiak 20.19.57 2 R.Partridge at 50 secs 3 P.O'Brien at 1.20

**Points:** 1 C.Newton 39 2 T.Evans 39 3 M.Hegreberg 35

**Mountains:** 1 P.Herzig 52 2 C.Power 42 3 L.Modzelewski 23

**International Team:** 1 Norway 61.16.39 2 Britain Recycling at 1.13 3 Australia FRF at 4.37
**County Team:** 1 Dublin IRC Usher 61.55.14 2 Meath MyHome.ie at 38 secs 3 Cork Murray Ford at 3.19

## STAGE 7

Ciarán Power made it two stage wins in the 2005 FBD Insurance RÁS when he raced to a fine victory in Westport. At the end of the 83 kilometre stage the Éireann Dan Morrissey rider outsprinted Jehudi Schoonacker (Ireland M. Donnelly Sean Kelly) and Ryan Connor (Ireland Grant Thornton). He also reclaimed the lead in the King of the Mountains classification.
Following the morning's team time trial, Tommy Evans had started the afternoon leg in the yellow jersey of race leadership. However relentless attacks isolated the Dublin IRC Usher Insulations rider, who also suffered additional difficulties when a spoke broke. Kristian House (Britain Recycling.co.uk) and Danny Pate (USA TIAA-CREF) had started the stage level on time, and both finished in a group 1 minute and 10 seconds behind Power. Crucially, they were 46 seconds ahead of Evans and House moved into yellow.
As was expected from such a short stage, the pace was flat-out from the start. This forced a split very early on, with eighteen riders going clear. All of the major contenders were here with the exception of Morten Hegreberg (Norway Sparebanken Vest), but he rejoined as part of a chase group.
The GC contenders started marking each other and this manoeuvring gave six riders the opportunity to slip clear. Evan Oliphant (Britain Recycling.co.uk), Wayne Randle (Britain Doncaster Stena Line), Martin Prazdnovsky (Norway Sparebanken Vest), Lukasz Modzelewski (Poland Legia Bazylisek), Mike Friedman (USA A TIAA-CREF) and Power went ahead, and were soon joined by Matthew Ward (Dublin IRC Usher Insulations), Connor and Schoonacker.
The latter attacked with approximately 15 kilometres remaining and was joined by Power and Connor. They reached the finish together where Power proved quickest, outsprinting Schoonacker and Conor to take his second victory this week. He had also been first to the top of the day's two category three climbs, moving level with Peter Herzig (Australia FRF Couriers) on KOM points but taking the jersey on count back.
42 seconds after Power's win, Modzelewski outsprinted Ward, Randle and Prazdnovsky for fourth. Friedman and Hagman were slightly adrift, but the big news was what was happening out the road.
While team-mate Ward was up in the break, his team leader Evans was losing his yellow jersey. Pate, House, Hegreberg and O'Loughlin had managed to distance him and put 46 seconds into him by the finish. This was enough to see House take over at the top, the Britain Recycling.co.uk rider being level on time with Pate but ahead on count back.

O'Loughlin had attacked many times on the run-in to the finish but was unable to shake off the others. He ended the day 21 seconds behind House and Pate, with Hegreberg just 12 seconds off the race lead in third.

**Stage 7 An Cheathru Rua - Westport 83 Kms.** 1 C.Power (Eireann Dan Morrissey) 2 J.Schoonacker (Ireland M.Donnelly S.Kelly) s.t. 3 R.Connor (Ireland Grant Thornton) at 5 secs 4 L.Modzelewski (Poland) at 42 secs 5 M.Ward (Dublin IRC Usher) s.t. 6 W.Randle (Doncaster) s.t. 7 M.Prazdnovsky (Norway) s.t. 8 M.Friedman (USA TIAA-CREF) at 45 secs 9 A.Hagman (Surrey Racing League) at 50 secs 10 D.Pate (USA TIAA-CREF) at 1.10

**General Classification:** 1 K.House (Britain) 22.09.37 2 D.Pate (USA TIAA-CREF) s.t. 3 M.Hegreberg (Norway) at 12 secs 4 D.O'Loughlin (Ireland Grant Thornton) at 21 secs 5 T.Evans (Dublin IRC Usher) at 38 secs 6 P.Herzig (Australia FRF) at 1.55 7 S.Kelly (Ireland Murphy & Gunn) at 2.18 8 W.Randle (Doncaster) at4.47 9 M.Friedman (USA TIAA-CREF) at 6.44 10 B.Matysiak (Poland at 6.51

**Under 23:** 1 B.Matysiak 22.16.28 2 R.Partridge at 1.43 3 P.O'Brien at 2.13

**Points:** 1 M.Hegreberg 40 2 L.Modzelewski 40 3 C.Newton 39

**Mountains:** 1 C.Power 52 2 P.Herzig 52 3 L.Modzelewski 23

**International Team:** 1 Norway 61.16.39 2 Britain Recycling at 1.13 3 Australia FRF at 4.37

**County Team:** 1 Meath MyHome.ie 67.57.46 2 Dublin IRC Usher at1.31 3 Kildare Murphy Surveys at 13.11

## STAGE 8

Under 23 classification leader Bartlomiej Matysiak won an 82-man bunch sprint which decided the penultimate stage of the race, a 168 kilometre leg from Westport to Clara.

The Poland Legia Bazylisek competitor sprinted in a bike-length clear of the previous day's stage victor Ciaran Power (Eireann Dan Morrissey) and his own team-mate Lukasz Modzelewski. Race leader Kristian House was ninth and with his closest challenger Danny Pate – who started the day level on time but separated by stage placings – taking 16th, the Britain Recycling.co.uk rider earned a small buffer which would offer a clear advantage if the final general classification went to count back.

The stage took place on a flat route and, thanks to a strong tailwind plus aggressive racing, was run off at a very fast speed of 46 km/h. Soon after the start a break of nine riders went clear. Although Brad Fairall (Canada Symmetrics), Fabian Brzezinski (Germany Stevens), Michael Fitzgerald (Cork Murray Ford Develops.) and John Mason (Meath MyHome.ie/Cycleways) dropped back along the way, Roger Aiken (Ireland Grant Thornton), Peter McDonald (Australia FRF Couriers Caravel), Jehudi Schoonacker (Ireland M. Donnelly Sean Kelly), Brandon Crichton (Canada Symmetrics) and Tim Barry (Éireann Dan Morrissey) persisted and stayed clear for most of the stage.

Behind, House's Britain Recycling.co.uk team and the Polish riders were doing the bulk of the driving, limiting the maximum gap to 1 minute 31 seconds. Shortly after the 20 kilometre to go point, previous race leader Tommy Evans attacked hard and opened up a small lead. He was hauled back, after which he, David O'Loughlin (Ireland Grant Thornton) and Paul Healion (Ireland Murphy and Gunn/Newlyn Group) each took turns to surge again.
The net effect of these accelerations was that the bunch was getting closer and closer to the break. With ten kilometres to go the gap was just 18 seconds and riders out front began to sit up. Roger Aiken and Peter McDonald persisted, with the latter then going clear by himself. He rode strongly but was eventually caught with four kilometres to go, paving the way for a bunch sprint and Matysiak's victory.
**Stage 8 Westport - Clara 168 Kms.** 1 B.Matysiak (Poland) 3.38.46 2 C.Power (Éireann Dan Morrissey) 3 L.Modzelewski (Poland) 4 J.Marden (Australia FRF) 5 B.Hill (Germany Stevens) 6 M.Hegreberg (Norway) 7 C.Stevenson (Australia FRF) 8 M.Fox (Ireland Murphy & Gunn) 9 K.House (Britain) 10 M.Fitzgerald (Meath MyHome.ie) all s.t
**General classification:** 1 K.House (Britain) 25.48.23 2 D.Pate (USA TIAA-CREF) s.t. 3 M.Hegreberg (Norway) at 12 secs 4 D.O'Loughlin (Ireland Grant Thornton) at 21 secs 5 Tommy Evans (Dublin IRC Usher) at 38secs 6 P.Herzig (Australia FRF) at 1.55 7 S.Kelly (Ireland Murphy & Gunn) at 2.18 8 W.Randle (Britain Doncaster Stena Line) at 4.47 9 B.Matysiak (Poland) at 6.51 10 C.Power (Éireann Dan Morrissey) at 6.52
**Under 23:** 1 B.Matysiak 25.55.14 2 R.Partridge at 1.43 3 P.O'Brien at 2.13
**Points:** 1 L.Modzelewski 53 2 B.Matysiak 52 3 M.Hegreberg 50 **Mountains:** 1 C.Power 52 2 P.Herzig 52 3 L.Modzelewski 23 **International Team:** 1 Norway 78.02.48 2 Britain Recycling at 2.31 3 Australia FRF at 6.22
**County Team:** 1 Meath MyHome.ie 78.54.04 2 Dublin IRC Usher at 1.31 3 Kildare Murphy Surveyors at 13.11

## STAGE 9

After 1232 kilometres of racing, Kristian House (Britain Recycling.co.uk) came out on top of the tightest battle in the race's history. He and closest competitor Danny Pate (USA TIAA-CREF) completed the eight-day event in exactly the same time, but the Britain Recycling.co.uk competitor got the verdict by virtue of his better stage placings.
Morten Hegreberg (Norway Sparebanken Vest) won the final 155 kilometre stage to Skerries and took third place overall, 12 seconds down, while David O'Loughlin (Grant Thornton Ireland) and Tommy Evans (Dublin IRC Usher Insulations) also finished in the leading group of 19 riders and were best Irishmen overall in fourth and fifth. They had started the day just 21 and 38 seconds back respectively but

while they launched numerous attacks on House, they were unable to open any lasting advantage.
Simon Kelly (Murphy and Gunn/Newlyn Group) finished second to Hegreberg at the crowd-thronged finish and placed sixth in the general classification.
The final stage took the riders from the start town of Clara and would see them tackling four categorised climbs, namely Pluckhimin, Cross of the Cage and then two ascents of the Black Hills. The final two came on a 14 kilometre finishing circuit in and around Skerries
There were several attacks after the start, with the most significant of these beginning when Ryan Connor (Ireland Grant Thornton) struck out after about 15 kilometres. He was joined by Ray Clarke (Éireann Dan Morrissey) and then by Simon Saunders (Surrey Racing League), although the latter was dropped around Trim (62.6 km). The gap at this point was 1 minute and 41 seconds.
Connor led Clarke over the day's first climb, Pluckhimin, and shortly afterwards Power beat Herzig for third and thus moved back into the lead of the King of the Mountains competition. Several kilometres after the climb, previous race leader Mike Friedman (USA – TIAA CREF) attacked, passing the two leaders but being himself recaptured by the bunch soon afterwards.
Roger Aiken (Ireland Grant Thornton) and Paul Healion got away just before the day's second climb, Cross of the Cage. (118.6 km). Power took third and the summit and then kept going to join the break. The bunch was closing fast but the Waterford rider had enough time to grab the first prime of the Black Hills, making sure of his win in that classification.
Many attacks followed, including efforts by O'Loughlin and Evans, and this reduced the front group to 19 riders. They sprinted it out for the stage win in Skerries, where Hegreberg triumphed in the gallop and House secured the final overall victory ahead of Pate.
Hegreberg ended the eight-day race as winner of the points classification, Bartlomiej Matysiak (Poland Legia Bazylisek) was top under 23 competitors and Tommy Evans took the county rider award.
Norway Sparebanken Vest and Meath MyHome.ie Cycleways.com were best in the international and county team classifications.
**Stage 9 Clara - Skerries 155 Kms.** 1 M.Hegreberg (Norway) 3.28.10 2 S.Kelly (Ireland Murphy & Gunn) 3 B.Matysiak (Poland) 4 T.Evans (Dublin IRC Usher) 5 K.House (Britain) 6 M.Prazdnovsky (Norway) 7 C.Power (Éireann Dan Morrissey) 8 J.Schoonacker (Ireland M.Donnelly S.Kelly) 9 D.Pate (USA TIAA-CREF) 10 W.Randle (Britain Doncaster Stena Line) all s.t.
**General Classification:** 1 K.House (Britain) 29.16.33 2 D.Pate (USA TIAA-CREF) s.t. 3 M.Hegreberg (Norway) at 12 secs 4 D.O'Loughlin (Ireland Grant Thornton at 21 secs 5 Tommy Evans (Dublin IRC Usher) at 38 secs 6 S.Kelly (Ireland Murphy & Gunn) at 2.18 7 P.Herzig (Australia FRF) s.t. 8 W.Randle (Britain Doncaster Stena Line) at 4.47 9 B.Matysiak (Poland) at 6.51 10 C.Power (Éireann Dan Morrissey) at 6.52

**Under 23:** 1 B.Matysiak 29.23.24 2 P.O'Brien at 2.36 3 R.Connor s.t.
**Points:** 1 M.Hegreberg 65 2 B.Matysiak 65 3 C.Power 58
**Mountains:** 1 C.Power 63 2 P.Herzig 56 3 L.Modzelewski 23
**International Team:** 1 Norway 88.27.18 2 Britain Recycling at 2.54 3 Australia FRF at 7.08
**County Team:** 1 Meath MyHome.ie 89.19.43 2 Dublin IRC Usher at 1.08 3 Kildare Murphy Surveyors at 13.52

*2006 winner, Kristian House pictured with Philip Fitzsimons and Adrian Taheny*

# 2007

As the closest-fought edition in the history of the race, the 2006 FBD Insurance RÁS was also one of the most exciting. Race organiser Dermot Dignam was aiming to guarantee another suspenseful contest the following year and so a carefully-crafted route was unveiled early in the 2007 season.
While there were difficult climbs such as the first category Mamore Gap – believed by many to be one of the toughest climbs in the country – and a total of nineteen categorises ascents, the route was a balanced one which would seek to avoid major time gaps early on. This plus the inclusion of a tough 174 kilometre final stage meant that the final outcome would, in theory, go down to the wire once again.
A strong line-up of teams took part in the race, including the Britain Stena Line Reycling.co.uk team of former double champion Chris Newton, the Germany Thuringer Energy outfit of Tony Martin, the Czech Republic Sparta Praha, Australia FRF Couriers NSWIS, Estonia Kalev Chocolate, Germany Stevens Von Hacht, US Kodak Gallery Sierra Nevada and US Kelly Benefit Strategies teams plus a Netherlands under 23 selection. This latter line-up included Ricardo and Alain Van der Velde, sons of former professional Johan Van der Velde who finished third overall in the 1982 Tour de France.
On the Irish side, the charge was led by internationally-oriented squads such as the Ireland Subway Eat Fresh team of David McCann, Dermot Nally, Paul Griffin, Mark Scanlon and Martyn Irvine, and a Continental-level Murphy & Gunn-Newlyn-M. Donnelly-Sean Kelly selection which included Paídi O'Brien, Mark Cassidy, Stephen Gallagher, Simon Kelly and the Dane Glenn Bak.
There was of course the usual complement of county teams, who would have their own ferocious scrap for honours during the eight-day event.

## STAGE 1

Estonian rider Mart Ojavee and Irishman Paídi O'Brien both showed their speed when they placed first and second on the 157 kilometre opening leg from Naas to Templemore.
Galloping in at the head of a 119 man bunch, the Kalev Chocolate team rider got the better of the Murphy and Gunn/Newlyn Group/M. Donnelly Sean Kelly competitor O'Brien and Petr Pucelik (Czech Republic Sparta Praha). This earned him the first yellow jersey of the eight-day race.
Former world junior champion Mark Scanlon (Ireland Subway) rode encouragingly well despite a lack of racing this season, netting fifth.
The stage was marked by a long distance breakaway featuring six riders - Andrei Mustonen (Estonia Kalev Chocolate), Ricardo Van der Velde (Netherlands), Simon

Kelly (Ireland - Murphy and Gunn/Newlyn Group/M. Donnelly Sean Kelly), Michael Johansen (Denmark Vision Bikes), Jesse Anthony (US Kodak Gallery Sierra Nevada) and Ondrej Pavek (Czech Republic Sparta Praha). They went clear in the first five kilometres, built a maximum lead of approximately four minutes before the day's sole categorised climb of The Cut and resisted the efforts of several others to bridge across, most notably Dominique Perras (USA Kelly Benefit Strategies), Martyn Irvine (Ireland) and Roger Aiken (Armagh Big Picture Development).
Towards the end of the stage the bunch began to haul them back and, with the gap dropping quickly, Johansen, Mustonen and Anthony forged ahead of the others. However their move was neutralised just before the ten kilometre to go board.
Several riders tried to get clear on the final run in to the finish, including Alain Van der Velde (Netherlands), but there was no denying a bunch sprint.
Mart Ojavee (Estonia Kalev Chocolate) came out best there, earning him the first yellow jersey of the race. Van der Velde's first, second and second places in the bonus sprints saw him end the day three seconds back in second overall, while O'Brien was one second further back in third.
**Stage 1 Naas - Templemore 157 Kms.** 1 M.Ojavee (Estonia Kalev Chocolate) 3.52.44 2 P.O'Brien (Ireland Murphy & Gunn) 3 P.Pucelik (Czech Rep) 4 D.Rollin (US Kodak) 5 M.Scanlon (Ireland Subway) 6 Y.Kusters (Netherlands) 7 R.Chaigneau (Netherlands) 8 B.Hill (Germany Stevens) 9 R.Birkenfeld (Germany Stevens) 10 M.Cassidy (Ireland Murphy & Gunn) all s.t.
**General Classification:** 1 M.Ojavee (Estonia Kalev Chocolate) 3.52.34 2 R.van der Velde (Netherlands) at 3 secs 3 P.O'Brien (Ireland Murphy & Gunn) at 4 secs 4 P.Pucelik (Czech Rep) at 6 secs 5 J.Anthony (US Kodak) s.t. 6 O.Pavek (Czech Rep) at 8 secs 7 M.Johansen (Denmark Vision Bikes) at 9 secs 8 S.Kelly (Ireland Murphy & Gunn) s.t. 9 D.Rollin (US Kodak) at 10 secs 10 M.Scanlon (Ireland Subway) s.t.
**Under 23:** 1 R.van der Velde 3.52.37 2 J.Anthony at 3 secs 3 Y.Kusters at 7 secs
**Points:** 1 M.Ojavee 15 2 P.O'Brien 14 3 P.Pucelik 13
**Mountains:** 1 J.Anthony 10 2 R.van der Velde 8 3 M.Johansen 6
**International Team:** 1 Netherlands 11.38.12 2 Australia FRF s.t 3 Ireland Murphy & Gunn s.t.
**County Team:** 1 Dublin Murphy & Gunn 11.38.12 2 Meath MyHome.ie s.t. 3 Waterford Comeragh s.t.

## STAGE 2

Brian Kenneally completed his comeback to the top echelon of Irish cycling when he won the second stage of the FBD Insurance RÁS, soloing to victory at the end of the race from Templemore to Loughrea. He finished two seconds clear of eleven breakaway companions, amongst them new yellow jersey Ricardo Van der Velde (Netherlands), and was over a minute clear of the peleton.
Meath MyHome.ie/BDBC rider Kenneally first won a stage in the race seven years previously. He was tipped for a pro career then but the pieces never really fell into

place. He spent some time away from the sport, gradually got back into top shape and took a number of strong wins in the run up to the 2007 FBD RÁS.

The 147 kilometre stage featured three categorised ascents; the cat two Curreeney Cross, plus the third cat Lecarrow and Killamena climbs. Various attacks went early on, including a move by 2003/2005 RÁS champion Chris Newton (Britain Stena Line/Recycling.co.uk), but these were all hauled back.

The crucial break started approximately after 95 kilometres of racing when René Birkenfeld (Germany Stevens Von Hacht), Ricardo Van der Velde (Netherlands) and Justin Spinelli (USA Kelly Benefit Strategies) went clear just before category three Lecarrow climb. Overnight mountains jersey leader Jesse Anthony (US Kodak Gallery Sierra Nevada) bridged alone and then at the105 kilometre point, nine others made it across.

They were Paul Griffin (Ireland Subway), Van der Velde, Yvo Kusters and Dennis Kreder (all Netherlands), Mark Cassidy (Ireland Murphy and Gunn/Newlyn Group/M. Donnelly Sean Kelly), Peter McDonald (Australia FRF Couriers NSW IS), Benjamin Justesen (Denmark Vision Bikes), Dominique Rollin (US Kodak Gallery Sierra Nevada), Anthony, Spinelli, Birkenfeld, Ryan Roth (US Kelly Benefit Strategies) and Brian Kenneally (Meath MyHome.ie/BDBC). Tony Martin (Germany Thuringer Energy) missed this chase group but showed his strength when he soloed across a 24 second gap.

Justesen was dropped with about 26 kilometres remaining. The gap was 37 seconds at this point but, despite a hard chase by the peleton, it had jumped up to 53 seconds with ten kilometres to go. Kenneally made his move inside the final couple of kilometres and hit the line two seconds ahead of Martin and Roth.

Van der Velde crossed the line in tenth but with overnight leader Mart Ojavee finishing 1'06 back in 31st place, the 20 year old Dutch rider took over at the top of the general classification. He also retained his lead in the best under 23 classification, while Anthony and Rollin ended the day as leaders of the mountains and points competitions.

**Stage 2 Templemore - Loughrea 147 Kms.** 1 B.Kenneally (Meath MyHome.ie) 3.22.21 2 T.Martin (Germany Thuringer Energy) at 2 secs 3 R.Roth (USA Kelly Benefit) s.t. 4 D.Rollin (US Kodak) s.t. 5 R.Birkenfeld (Germany Stevens) s.t. 6 P.Griffin (Ireland Subway) s.t. 7 P.McDonald (Australia FRF) s.t. 8 M.Cassidy (Ireland Murphy & Gunn) s.t. 9 Y.Kusters (Netherlands) s.t. 10 R.van der Velde (Netherlands) s.t.

**General Classification:** 1 R.van der Velde (Netherlands) 7.15.00 2 J.Anthony (US Kodak) at 3 secs 3 B.Kenneally (Meath MyHome.ie) at 5 secs 4 D.Rollin (US Kodak) at 7 secs 5 R.Birkenfeld (Germany Stevens) s.t. 6 Y.Kusters (Netherlands) s.t. 7 M.Cassidy (Ireland Murphy & Gunn) s.t. 8 P.McDonald (Australia FRF) s.t. 9 T.Martin (Germany Thuringer) s.t. 10 P.Griffin (Ireland Subway) s.t.

**Under 23:** 1 R.van der Velde 7.15.00 2 J.Anthony at 3 secs 3 Y.Kusters at 7 secs

**Points:** 1 D.Rollin 24 2 R.Birkenfeld 18 3 Y.Kusters 17

**Mountains:** 1 J.Anthony 27 2 R.van der Velde 23 3 R.Birkenfeld 9

**International Team:** 1 Netherlands 21.45.31 2 US Kodak at 54 secs 3 USA Kelly at 1.47
**County Team:** 1 Meath MyHome.ie 21.47.27 2 Dublin Murphy & Gunn at 1.06 3 Tipperary Dan Morrissey s.t.

## STAGE 3

Canadian Dominique Rollin (US Kodak Gallery Sierra Nevada) showed his considerable speed when he outsprinted Paídi O'Brien (Ireland Murphy and Gunn/Newlyn Group/M. Donnelly Sean Kelly), Paul Griffin (Ireland Subway) plus 31 other riders to the line in Sligo.
Overnight leader Ricardo Van der Velde, the 20 year old son of former top professional Johan, and his under 23 Netherlands team had a tough day in the saddle, being unable to control the race. Van der Velde finished 19 minutes and 55 seconds behind Rollin and his yellow jersey passed onto the shoulders of American rider Jesse Anthony.
The stage started off very aggressively with several big groups going clear. While these initial forays didn't materialise into anything long-lasting, they had the effect of softening up Van der Velde and his Netherlands team. About fifty kilometres after the start a more serious split formed when 21 riders surged clear; these were later joined by two other groups, making it 44 up front. Most of the race favourites were represented there, but Van der Velde missed out.
Approximately 80 kilometres from the finish four riders then pressed on ahead. They were Irishman Roger Aiken (Armagh Big Picture Developments), Petr Pucelik (Czech Republic Sparta Praha), Alo Jakin (Estonia Kalev Chocolate) and Australian Nathan Jones (Kildare Newbridge Remax). These opened up a lead of 1 minute and 15 secs but were recaptured with about seven kilometres to go, setting things up for the subsequent 34 man sprint and Rollin's victory.
Stage 2 Victor Brian Kenneally moved up one place to second overall. He ended the day two seconds off Anthony's race lead, while Mark Cassidy son of double RÁS winner Philip Cassidy was fifth.
It was a good day for Irish riders, but an even better one for the US Kodak Gallery Sierra Nevada team; in addition to the stage win, Anthony and Rollin had between them captured the jerseys for the overall, points, mountains and under 23 classifications.
**Stage 3 Loughrea - Sligo 171 Kms.** 1 D.Rollin (US Kodak) 3.55.10 2 P.O'Brien (Ireland Murphy & Gunn) 3 P.Griffin (Ireland Subway) 4 P.McDonald (Australia FRF) 5 Y.Kusters (Netherlands) 6 B.Ahern (Dublin DTC Orwell) 7 M.Cassidy (Ireland Murphy & Gunn) 8 R.Roth (USA Kelly) 9 D.Bowman (USA Kelly) 10 Alain.van der Velde (Netherlands) all s.t
**General Classification:** 1 J.Anthony (US Kodak) 11.10.13 2 B.Kenneally (Meath MyHome.ie) at 2 secs 3 D.Rollin (US Kodak) at 4 secs 4 Y.Kusters (Netherlands) s.t. 5 M.Cassidy (Ireland Murphy & Gunn) s.t. 6 P.McDonald (Australia FRF) s.t. 7

T.Martin (Germany Thuringer) s.t. 8 P.Griffin (Ireland Subway) s.t. 9 R.Roth (USA Kelly) s.t. 10 J.Spinelli (USA Kelly) at 57 secs
**Under 23:** 1 J.Anthony 11.10.13 2 Y.Kusters at 4 secs 3 M.Cassidy s.t.
**Points:** 1 D.Rollin 39 2 Y.Kusters 28 3 P.O'Brien 28
**Mountains:** 1 J.Anthony 29 2 R.van der Velde 23 3 R.Birkenfeld 10
**International Team:** 1 Netherlands 33.31.01 2 US Kodak at 54 secs 3 USA Kelly at 1.47
**County Team:** 1 Meath MyHome.ie 33.54.37 2 Dublin IRC Usher at 9.19 3 Tipperary Dan Morrissey s.t.

## STAGE 4

Stage one winner Mart Ojavee (Estonia Kalev Chocolate) took his second stage victory of the race on the streets of Dungloe, outsprinting Dominique Rollin (US Kodak Gallery Sierra Nevada) and Tomas Hruby (Czech Republic Sparta Praha) on the uphill finishing straight.
Rollin's team-mate Jesse Anthony finished in this main bunch of 59 riders, successfully defending the yellow jersey. Brian Kenneally (Meath Myhome.ie/BDBC) remained two seconds behind in second place overall.
There were countless attacks on the 138 kilometre stage from Sligo to Dungloe but, despite the battles and skirmishes on the road to Dungloe, the overall contenders all kept tabs on each other.
After passing through the seaside resort town of Bundoran, a move started which would eventually see a group containing double FBD RÁS winner Chris Newton (Britain Stena Line Recycling.co.uk), Dermot Nally (Ireland Subway Eat Fresh), Stephen Gallagher (Ireland Murphy and Gunn/Newlyn Group/M. Donnelly Sean Kelly) and others stay away until 50 kilometres into the stage.
Other breaks then went clear and were hauled back, with a big threat to Anthony's lead coming when Mark Cassidy (Ireland Murphy and Gunn/Newlyn Group/M. Donnelly Sean Kelly) infiltrated a large group and became race leader on the road. This too was reeled in, though.
The day's most significant escape was then sparked off by an attack by Mark Lovatt (Team Sportscover) at the 88 kilometre point. He was joined by Graham Briggs (Britain Stena Line/Recycling.co.uk), then Silvar Kibur (Estonia Kalev Chocolate) and Dominique Perras (USA Kelly Benefit Strategies) also made the junction. Glenn Bak (Ireland Murphy and Gunn/Newlyn Group/M. Donnelly Sean Kelly) was the last rider to get across, making it five up front.
The latter attacked from the group with 25 kilometres to go but was caught by the other four 15 clicks later. Then with four kilometres remaining the peleton got back on terms, setting things up for a bunch gallop and Ojavee's victory. Stephen Gallagher (Ireland Murphy & Gunn-Newlyn-M. Donnelly-Sean Kelly) was best Irishman in sixth.

Rollin remained in the green jersey while race leader Anthony stayed top in the mountains and under 23 classifications.

**Stage 4 Sligo - Dungloe 138 Kms.** 1 M.Ojavee (Estonia) 3.14.04 2 D.Rollin (US Kodak) 3 T.Hruby (Czech Rep) 4 M.Barth (Germany Thuringer) 5 Y.Kusters (Netherlands) 6 S.Gallagher (Ireland Murphy & Gunn) 7 B.Raby (US Kodak) 8 A.Mustonen (Estonia) 9 E.Moriarty (Meath MyHome.ie) 10 N.Graf (Germany Thuringer) all s.t.

**General Classification:** 1 J.Anthony (US Kodak) 14.24.17 2 B.Kenneally (Meath MyHome.ie) at 2 secs 3 D.Rollin (US Kodak) at 4 secs 4 Y.Kusters (Netherlands) s.t. 5 P.McDonald (Australia FRF) 6 M.Cassidy (Ireland Murphy & Gunn) s.t. 7 T.Martin (Germany Thuringer) s.t. 8 P.Griffin (Ireland Subway) s.t. 9 R.Roth (USA Kelly) s.t. 10 J.Spinelli (USA Kelly) at 57 secs

**Under 23:** 1 J.Anthony 14.24.17 2 Y.Kusters at 4 secs 3 M.Cassidy s.t.

**Points:** 1 D.Rollin 53 2 Y.Kusters 39 3 M.Ojavee 30

**Mountains:** 1 J.Anthony 29 2 R.van der Velde 27 3 R.Birkenfeld 15

**International Team:** 1 Netherlands 43.13.13 2 US Kodak at 54 secs 3 USA Kelly at 1.47

**County Team:** 1 Meath MyHome.ie 43.36.49 2 Dublin IRC Usher at 9.19 3 Tipperary Dan Morrissey at 10.50

## STAGE 5

Making their move on what was probably the hardest day of the race, the Germany Thuringer Energie duo of Nico Graf and Tony Martin raced to success in Buncrana. Graf beat Paídi O'Brien (Ireland Murphy and Gunn/Newlyn Group/M. Donnelly Sean Kelly) and Riccardo Van der Velde (Netherlands) to win the gruelling mountain stage, while Martin finished 42 seconds back in fifth and took over in the yellow jersey from Jesse Anthony (US Kodak Gallery Sierra Nevada).

O'Brien replaced compatriot Brian Kenneally (Meath Myhome.ie/BDBC) in second place overall, keeping the home challenge strong after the latter dropped to tenth. Anthony slipped to third after being unable to follow Martin and Chris Newton (Britain Recycling.co.uk) when they put the hammer down on the day's toughest mountain.

The 131 kilometre stage from Dungloe to Buncrana featured a total of six categorised climbs, including the cat one ascent of Mamore Gap and, as expected, had a pronounced effect on the general classification.

After a very aggressive start a group of twenty-nine riders went clear approximately ten kilometres into the stage. These and a chasing group merged soon after the race leader Jesse Anthony (US Kodak Gallery Sierra Nevada) fortified his hold on the mountains jersey when he beat closest challenger Ricardo Van der Velde (Netherlands) to the top of the category 3 Peirse Mor.

Shortly after the day's second climb of Carabit (where Van der Velde beat Anthony for second across the prime line), the Dutchman clipped away alone, realising that

he needed to open up some distance over Anthony in a bid to maximise his chances of taking the mountains jersey. He was soon joined by four others, namely Paídi O'Brien (Ireland Murphy and Gunn/Newlyn Group/M. Donnelly Sean Kelly), Jason Hegert (Australia FRF Couriers), Nico Graf (Germany Thuringer Energie) and Yannick Tiedt (Germany Stevens Von Hacht), and this quintet opened a steadily-increasing lead.
The group was briefly sent the wrong way in Letterkenny, some 50 kilometres after the start of the stage, but got back on course and had enough time in hand to maintain their advantage over a large chase group. Most of the race favourites were in this second bunch and by the time the break reached the 20 kilometre to go point, they were still a full two minutes 40 seconds behind.
Van der Velde was climbing very strongly and taking the primes, thus moving into the lead in that classification. He showed his uphill ability when he dropped Graf and O'Brien on the wall-like Mamore Gap and continued alone over the top of the day's final climb, that of Old Mountain. However Graf and O'Brien caught and passed him inside the final two kilometres, going on to fight out the stage between them.
Further back, the yellow jersey group had exploded on the slopes of the Mamore Gap, with Chris Newton – who won there four years ago – and Martin ripping clear of the others and chasing hard all the way to the line. They came in 42 seconds behind Graf and O'Brien, Newton taking the sprint for fourth. Irish duo David McCann and Stephen Gallagher placed sixth and seventh, while the race leader Jesse Anthony finished 1'22 behind Graf in tenth place.
Martin duly took over the race lead, with O'Brien ending the day 17 seconds back.
**Stage 5 Dungloe - Buncrana 131 Kms.** 1 N.Graf (Germany Thuringer) 3.12.17 2 P.O'Brien (Ireland Murphy & Gunn) at 1 sec 3 R.van der Velde (Netherlands) at 4 secs 4 C.Newton (Britain) at 42 secs 5 T.Martin (Germany Thuringer) s.t. 6 D.McCann (Ireland Subway) at 1.13 7 S.Gallagher (Ireland Murphy & Gunn) s.t. 8 G.Bak (Ireland Murphy & Gunn) at 1.21 9 P.Gretsch (Germany Thuringer) s.t. 10 J.Anthony (US Kodak) at 1.22
**General Classification:** 1 T.Martin (Germany Thuringer) 17.37.20 2 P.O'Brien (Ireland Murphy & Gunn) at 17 secs 3 J.Anthony (US Kodak) at 36 secs 4 P.McDonald (Australia FRF) at 40 secs 5 C.Newton (Britain) at 1.02 6 D.Rollin (US Kodak) at 1.04 7 M.Cassidy (Ireland Murphy & Gunn) at1.05 8 D.McCann (Ireland Subway) at 1.35 9 S.Gallagher (Ireland Murphy & Gunn) s.t. 10 B.Kenneally (Meath MyHome.ie) at 1.38
**Under 23:** 1 T.Martin 17.37.20 2 J.Anthony at 36 secs 3 M.Cassidy at 1.05
**Points:** 1 D.Rollin 53 2 P.O'Brien 42 3 Y.Kusters 39
**Mountains:** 1 R.van der Velde 74 2 J.Anthony 40 3 P.O'Brien 24
**International Team:** 1 Netherlands 52.54.04 2 Germany Thuringer at 1 sec 3 Ireland Murphy & Gunn at 33 secs
**County Team:** 1 Meath MyHome.ie 53.36.56 2 Tipperary Dan Morrissey at 26.36 3 Dublin IRC Usher at 33.28

## STAGE 6

Dominique Rollin took the sixth leg of the FBD Insurance RÁS in Derry, riding powerfully on the uphill drag to the line and landing his second stage victory of the race.

The Canadian jumped away from his 13 breakaway companions with about a kilometre remaining, getting a gap and holding off Marcel Barth (Germany Thuringer Energie), young Irishman Mark Cassidy (Ireland Murphy and Gunn/Newlyn Group/M. Donnelly Sean Kelly) plus the rest of the group.

Race leader Tony Martin and closest challengers Paídi O'Brien (Ireland Murphy and Gunn/Newlyn Group/M. Donnelly Sean Kelly) and Jesse Anthony (US Kodak Gallery Sierra Nevada) all missed the move but remained to the fore in the general classification. The latter was however bumped down one place to fourth due to the time gained in the break by Peter McDonald (Australia FRF Couriers).

At 96 kilometres the stage from Buncrana was the shortest of the race. That was a small consolation for the Irish team, some of whom had their bikes stolen from the team van during the night and who had to race on borrowed machines.

After a number of early attacks, the decisive move went around about the 28 kilometre point. Nine riders slipped away, namely king of the mountains leader Ricardo Van der Velde (Netherlands), Stephen Gallagher (Murphy and Gunn/Newlyn Group/M. Donnelly Sean Kelly), Peter McDonald (Australia FRF Couriers NSWIS), Ondrej Pavek (Czech Republic Sparta Praha), Michael Johansen (Denmark Vision Bikes), Marcel Barth (Germany Thuringer Energie), Marcel Barth (Germany Thuringer Energie), Dominique Rollin (US Kodak Gallery Sierra Nevada), Yannick Tiedt (Germany Stevens Von Hacht) and Isaac Speirs (Dublin Murphy and Gunn/Newlyn Group).

They were joined approximately 15 kilometres later by Thomas Bendixen (Denmark Vision Bikes), Dominique Perras (USA Kelly Benefit Strategies), Nathan Jones (Kildare Newbridge Remax), Mark Cassidy (Ireland Murphy and Gunn/Newlyn Group/M. Donnelly Sean Kelly) and Brian Kenneally (Meath MyHome.ie/BDBC).

With 25 kilometres to go the peloton was 1 minute 31 seconds adrift then but a number of teams including the Netherlands, Germany Thuringer Energie and Britain Stena Line Recycling.co.uk combined to try to close the move down?

However the gap remained over twenty seconds with a kilometre to go, making it certain that one of the break would triumph. Rollin surged clear at that point and held off Barth on the steep rise to the line. Cassidy took third ahead of Van der Velde. Tomas Hruby (Czech Republic Sparta Praha) was first home of the bunch, placing 15th, some 22 seconds behind.

Meanwhile several other riders, including second-placed O'Brien plus David McCann and Dermot Nally of the Ireland Subway Eat Fresh team, crashed inside the slippery, technical final kilometre. As per standard rules, they were given the same time as the main bunch.

**Stage 6 Buncrana - Derry 96 Kms.** 1 D.Rollin (US Kodak) 2.12.14 2 M.Barth (Germany Thuringer) at 1 sec 3 M.Cassidy (Ireland Murphy & Gunn) at 3 secs 4 R.van der Velde (Netherlands) s.t. 5 S.Gallagher (Ireland Murphy & Gunn) at 4 secs 6 T.Bendixen (Denmark Vision Bikes) s.t. 7 I.Speirs (Dublin Murphy & Gunn) at 6 secs 8 M.Lovatt (Team Sportscover) s.t. 9 O.Pavek (Czech Rep) s.t. 10 D.Perras (USA Kelly) at 8 secs

**General Classification:** 1 T.Martin (Germany Thuringer) 19.49.58 2 P.O'Brien (Ireland Murphy & Gunn) at 17 secs 3 P.McDonald (Australia FRF) at 24 secs 4 J.Anthony (US Kodak) at 36 secs 5 D.Rollin (US Kodak) at 40 secs 6 M.Cassidy (Ireland Murphy & Gunn) at 44 secs 7 C.Newton (Britain) at 1.02 8 S.Gallagher (Ireland Murphy & Gunn) at 1.15 9 B.Kenneally (Meath MyHome.ie) at 1.22 10 D.McCann (Ireland Subway) at 1.35

**Under 23:** 1 T.Martin 19.49.58 2 J.Anthony at 36 secs 3 M.Cassidy at 44 secs

**Points:** 1 D.Rollin 68 2 P.O'Brien 42 3 Y.Kusters 39

**Mountains:** 1 R.van der Velde 76 2 J.Anthony 40 3 P.O'Brien 24

**International Team:** 1 Germany Thuringer 59.31.36 2 Netherlands at 1 sec 3 Ireland Murphy & Gunn at 14 secs

**County Team:** 1 Meath MyHome.ie 60.14.34 2 Tipperary Dan Morrissey at 26.52 3 Dublin IRC Usher at 33.44

## STAGE 7

Clearly on a roll, Canadian rider Dominique Rollin took his second consecutive stage win – and his third of the race – when he beat 87 riders to the line in Newcastle.

The US Kodak Gallery Sierra Nevada rider got the better of Mart Ojavee (Estonia Kalev Chocolate) and Ondrej Pavek (Czech Republic Sparta Praha) at the end of the 165 kilometre stage from Derry. Race leader Tony Martin (Germany Thuringer Energie) finished in this main bunch and maintained his 17 second advantage over Paídi O'Brien (Ireland Murphy and Gunn/Newlyn Group/M. Donnelly Sean Kelly).

Following a relatively controlled first hour and a half of racing, a number of short-lived moves went clear. The aggressors included riders such as Mark Walters (US Kodak Gallery Sierra Nevada),

Stephen Gallagher (Ireland Murphy and Gunn/Newlyn Group/M. Donnelly Sean Kelly), David McCann (Ireland Subway Eat Fresh) and former race leader Jesse Anthony (US Kodak Gallery Sierra Nevada). One of the most persistent was Roger Aiken (Armagh Big Picture Developments), who was from the area and clearly motivated to do well.

With approximately 30 kilometres remaining he tried once again, tearing through Banbridge at the head of the race and building a 21 second lead. He was joined by Dermot Nally (Ireland Subway Eat Fresh), Dennis Kreder (Netherlands) and Brian Kenneally (Meath MyHome.ie/BDBC), then by Mark Cassidy (Ireland Murphy and Gunn/Newlyn Group/M. Donnelly Sean Kelly) and Chris Newton (Britain Recycling.co.uk). The bunch soon got back on terms, though.

Ricardo Van der Velde (Netherlands) sealed his win in the King of the Mountains classification when he took third on the final climb of the day, the third category climb of Devils Elbow. This topped out 9.9 kilometres from the finish and the promising young rider soloed clear after the summit, staying away for a couple of kilometres. However a bunch sprint seemed inevitable and so it proved, Rollin solidifying his lead in the green jersey competition with yet another stage win.
Aidan Crowley (Meath MyHome.ie/BDBC) was ninth on the stage, finishing as both the first Irishman and the best county rider.
**Stage 7 Derry - Newcastle 165 Kms.** 1 D.Rollin (US Kodak) 3.38.53 2 M.Ojavee (Estonia) 3 O.Pavek (Czech Rep) 4 M.Barth (Germany Thuringer) 5 B.Hill (Germany Stevens) 6 R.Chaigneau (Netherlands) 7 T.Hruby (Czech Rep) 8 R.van der Velde (Netherlands) 9 A.Crowley (Meath MyHome.ie) 10 J.Anthony (US Kodak) all s.t.
**General Classification:** 1 T.Martin (Germany Thuringer) 23.28.51 2 P.O'Brien (Ireland Murphy & Gunn) at 17 secs 3 P.McDonald (Australia FRF) at 24 secs 4 J.Anthony (US Kodak) at 36 secs 5 D.Rollin (US Kodak) at 40 secs 6 M.Cassidy (Ireland Murphy & Gunn) at 44 secs 7 C.Newton (Britain) at 1.02 8 S.Gallagher (Ireland Murphy & Gunn) at 1.15 9 B.Kenneally (Meath MyHome.ie) at 1.22 10 D.McCann (Ireland Subway) at 1.35
**Under 23:** 1 T.Martin 23.28.51 2 J.Anthony at 36 secs 3 M.Cassidy at 44 secs
**Points:** 1 D.Rollin 83 2 M.Ojavee 44 3 P.O'Brien 43
**Mountains:** 1 R.van der Velde 83 2 J.Anthony 45 3 P.O'Brien 24
**International Team:** 1 Germany Thuringer 70.28.15 2 Netherlands at 1 sec 3 Ireland Murphy & Gunn at 14 secs
**County Team:** 1 Meath MyHome.ie 71.11.31 2 Tipperary Dan Morrissey at 26.52 3 Dublin IRC Usher at 33.44

## STAGE 8

Digging deep into his reserves of strength and determination, Brian Kenneally held off a fast-closing main bunch to win the final stage of the 2007 FBD Insurance RÁS
The Meath MyHome.ie/BDBC rider was clear with David McCann (Ireland Subway Eat Fresh) in the closing kilometres of the 174 kilometre leg to Skerries, and then dropped the national road race champion the final time up the Black Hills.
With one kilometre to go he had an 18 second lead over a fast-closing main bunch. A strong headwind on the finishing stretch saw this gap plummet but Kenneally had just enough left to hit the line a bike length clear of Andrei Mustonen (Estonia Kalev Chocolate) and Glenn Bak (Ireland Murphy and Gunn/Newlyn Group/M. Donnelly Sean Kelly).
Tony Martin (Germany Thuringer Energie) placed tenth and won the race overall, finishing 17 seconds ahead of Paidi O'Brien (Ireland Murphy and Gunn/Newlyn Group/M. Donnelly Sean Kelly) in the general classification. Peter McDonald (Australia FRF Couriers NSWIS) was 24 seconds back in third.

McCann had gone clear approximately 15 minutes into the stage, building a good lead with Nick Waite (US Kelly Benefit Strategies) and Peter Herzig (Australia FRF Couriers NSWIS). They were 2 minutes and 20 seconds clear at Newry, 34 kilometres after the start, but their progress was disrupted when they had to wait for Herzig after he punctured. The group then got additional reinforcements 80 kilometres into the stage when Dominique Rollin (US Kodak Gallery Sierra Nevada) and Mart Ojavee (Estonia Kalev Chocolate) bridged.
Herzig and Waite were dropped soon afterwards, and Rollin lost his place on the climb of Pluckhimin (category 3, 118.7 km). However he got back up to the front with Alain Van der Velde (Netherlands), Dermot Nally (Ireland Subway Eat Fresh) and Brian Kenneally (Meath MyHome.ie/BDBC). McCann and Kenneally then pushed on ahead on the first ascent of the Black Hills, which topped out 23 kilometres from the end.
The Irish road race champion had been riding very strongly all day but he ran out of steam on the final lap, slipping backwards on that same climb with just nine kilometres remaining. Kenneally due deep into the strong headwind and just about hung on to take the victory, while Martin wheeled across the line as the final overall victor.
Murphy and Gunn/Newlyn Group/M. Donnelly Sean Kelly rider Mark Cassidy had started the day sixth overall but was forced to pull out during the stage due to stomach problems.
Rollin won the green points jersey and Ricardo Van der Velde (Netherlands) took the mountains classification. Martin was also best young rider, Kenneally was best Irish county team entrant and Brian Ahern (Dublin Dundrum Town Centre Orwell Wheelers) was top second category competitor.
Kenneally's Meath MyHome.ie/BDBC lineup topped the county team classification and the young Netherlands squad won out in the international team award.
**Stage 8 Newcastle - Skerries 174 Kms.** 1 B.Kenneally (Meath MyHome.ie) 3.58.22 2 A.Mustonen (Estonia) 3 G.Bak (Ireland Murphy & Gunn) 4 J.Soukup (Czech Rep) 5 M.Walters (US Kodak) 6 J.Anthony (US Kodak) 7 T.Hruby (Czech Rep) 8 Z.Krizek (Czech Rep) 9 J.Hegert (Australia FRF) 10 T.Martin (Germany Thuringer) all s.t.
**General Classification:** 1 T.Martin (Germany Thuringer) 27.27.13 2 P.O'Brien (Ireland Murphy & Gunn) at 17 secs 3 P.McDonald (Australia FRF) at 24 secs 4 J.Anthony (US Kodak) at 36 secs 5 C.Newton (Britain) at 1.02 6 S.Gallagher (Ireland Murphy & Gunn) at 1.15 7 B.Kenneally (Meath MyHome.ie) at 1.22 8 D.Rollin (US Kodak) at 1.30 9 D.McCann (Ireland Subway) at 1.35 10 P.Gretsch (Germany Thuringer) at 1.43
**Under 23:** 1 T.Martin 27.27.13 2 J.Anthony at 36 secs 3 P.Gretsch at 1.43
**Points:** 1 D.Rollin 83 2 M.Ojavee 44 3 P.O'Brien 43
**Mountains:** 1 R.van der Velde 83 2 J.Anthony 45 3 D.McCann 26
**International Team:** 1 Netherlands 82.23.22 2 Ireland Murphy & Gunn at 13 secs 3 US Kodak at 2.33

**County Team:** 1 Meath MyHome.ie 83.07.59 2 Tipperary Dan Morrissey at 27.34 3 Dublin IRC Usher at 32.53

*2007 Winner, Tony Martin (Germany)*

# 2008

The 2008 FBD Insurance RÁS once again started outside the Capital in the heartland of Meath cycling Navan, home of the famed Navan Road Club who have produced so many Overall and stage winners in the history of the RÁS than any other club. 140 riders lined up for the start a 142 kilometre stage from Navan to Ballinamore. The route included two category three climbs, in Kells (14.2 kilometres) and at Slieve an gCallaigh (29.3 kilometres), as well as hot spot sprints there and at Newtownforbes (104.2 kilometres) where vital seconds were up for grabs which could prove so crucial to the wearer of the first yellow Jersey. Temperatures were mild and the day was bright with a few scattered clouds overhead as the peleton left Navan on their journey round Ireland

## STAGE 1

The route included two category three climbs, in Kells (14.2 kilometres) and at Slieve an gCallaigh (29.3 kilometres), as well as hot spot sprints there and at Newtownforbes (104.2 kilometres).
Early attacks included solo moves by Ismael Kip (Netherlands), Daniel Davies (Britain S of E Primera Sport) and Neill Delahaye (Dublin IRC Ushers), the latter getting fifteen seconds and staying out front until just after the hot spot sprint/King of the Mountains in Kells.
The next move of significance was sparked off when Alex Higham (Britain Plowman Craven) went clear and was joined by 2004 race victor David McCann (Ireland) and Stephen Gallagher (Ireland An Post M. Donnelly Grant Thornton Sean Kelly). They were however hauled back by the peleton
On the climb of Slieve an gCallaigh, six riders forged ahead. Levi Heimans (Netherlands), Jaroslaw Dabrowski (Poland), Amir Zargari (Iran Islamic Azad University), Christer Rake (Norway Sparebanken Vest), Jean Marc Maurin (France Province Alpe Cote d'Azur) and Johannes Sickmuller (Germany Stevens von Hacht) opened up a gap but were then brought back.
It did however enable Dabrowski and Rake to take first and third at the prime, with Kieran Page (Ireland Pezula) and Kristian House (Britain Team Stena Rapha Condor Recycling.co.uk) getting up for second and fourth.
Shortly afterwards, nine riders got away and opened up a maximum lead of 35 seconds. These were Miceal Concannon (Ireland), Wojciech Dybel (Poland), Dean Downing (Britain Stena Line Rapha Condor Recycling.co.uk), Alex Higham (Britain Plowman Craven), Paídi O'Brien, Stephen Gallagher (both Ireland An Post M. Donnelly Grant Thornton Sean Kelly), Kieran Page (Ireland Pezula Racing), Stian

Remme (Norway Sparebanken Vest) and Nicolas Ligier (France Provence Alpes Cote d'Azur).
They were recaptured; with Tim van der Zanden (Netherlands) and Eugene Moriarty (Meath/MyHome BDBC) then going away just before Ballyjamesduff (which came 51.3 kilometres into the stage). At the 64 kilometre point they were caught by seven others, namely Rob Partridge (Britain Team Stena Line Rapha Condor Recycling.co.uk), Alex Higham (Britain Plowman Craven), Daniel Lloyd (Ireland An Post M. Donnelly Grand Thornton Sean Kelly), Derek Burke (Ireland Pezula Racing), Morten Hegreberg (Norway Sparebanken Vest), Simon Kelly (Dublin IRC Ushers) and Sean Lacey (Dublin Eurocycles).
The peleton was 29 seconds back at this point and the gap continued to grow. Once past the midway point of the stage, Jean Marc Maurin (France Provence Alpes Cote d'Azur) set off alone from the peloton and started chasing. He was 50 seconds back, with Barry Sutton (Meath Cycleways@53degreesnorth) 1 minute and 13 seconds behind, and the main bunch at 1 minute 40 seconds.
These chasers were both reeled in, but the bunch's deficit nevertheless went up to 2 minutes and 15 seconds.
Iran was riding at the front and then the Ireland National team, the Ireland An Post M. Donnelly Grant Thornton Sean Kelly squad and the Ireland Pezula Racing outfit began to drive hard. The latter two had riders – Daniel Lloyd and Derek Burke – in the move but it was decided that the composition was not right and thus the decision was taken to chase.
Partridge took the final hot spot sprint in Newtownforbes ahead of Hegreberg and Lloyd. Shortly afterwards, when heading through Rooskey with 28 kilometres left to go, the gap was down to 28 seconds.
Van der Zanden, Higham and Lloyd then attacked and opened up a decisive lead over their former breakaway companions. However the peleton continued to draw closer and a resigned Lloyd then sat up with about twelve kilometres left to race. Van der Zanden and Higham pressed on but they were finally reeled in by the bunch inside the final eight kilometres. A number of attacks were then fired off, including a move containing former race winner Andrew Roche (Isle of Man Microgaming Dolan). However it seemed that a bunch sprint was destined to happen and so it proved, 110 riders hitting the line together in Ballinamore. Hanson was quickest, holding off a strong Kos in their dual to the line. De Schrooder also showed his pace when he nabbed third, while Nestor, McDonald and O'Brien were sixth, seventh and eleventh respectively.
**Stage 1 Navan - Ballinamore 130 Kms.** 1 K.Hanson (Isle of Man) 3.06.32 2 P.Kos (Netherlands) s.t. 3 B.de Schrooder (Ireland An Post) s.t. 4 M.Komar (Poland) s.t. 5 D.Downing (Britain Stena Rapha) s.t. 6 M.Nestor (Dublin Eurocycles) s.t. 7 S.McDonald (Meath Cycleways@53degrees s.t. 8 R.Pioline (France Provence Alpes Cote) s.t. 9 M.Hegreberg (Norway Sparebanken) s.t. 10 J.M.Maurin (France Provence Alpes Cote) s.t. 11 P.O'Brien (Ireland An Post) s.t. 12 B.Janiaczyk

(Poland) s.t. 13 J.James (Britain Kinesis) s.t. 14 H.Nybo (Norway Sparebanken) s.t. 15 E.Moriarty (Meath MyHome.ie) s.t.

**General Classification:** 1 K.Hanson (Isle of Man) 3.06.22 2 P.Kos (Netherlands) at 4 secs 3 B.de Schrooder (Ireland An Post) at 6 secs 4 M.Hegreberg (Norway Sparebanken) at 7 secs 5 N.Delahaye (Dublin IRC Ushers) s.t. 6 R.Partridge (Britain Stena Rapha) s.t. 7 J.Dabrowski (Poland) s.t. 8 K.Page (Pezula) at 8 secs 9 S.Gallagher (Ireland An Post) s.t. 10 D.Lloyd (Ireland An Post) at 9 secs 11 C.Rake (Norway Sparebanken) s.t. 12 M.Komar (Poland) at 10 secs 13 D.Downing (Britain Stena Rapha) s.t. 14 M.Nestor (Dublin Eurocycles) s.t. 15 S.McDonald (Meath Cycleways@53degrees) s.t.

**Under 23:** 1 P.Kos 3.06.26 2 C.Rake at 5 secs 3 M.Nestor at 6 secs

**Points:** 1 K.Hanson 15 2 P.Kos 14 3 B.de Schrooder 13

**Mountains:** 1 N.Delahaye 5 2 J.Dabrowski 5 3 K.Page 4

**International Team:** 1 France Provence Alpes Cote 9.19.36 2 Ireland An Post s.t. 3 Poland s.t.

**County Team:** 1 Meath MyHome.ie 9.19.36 2 Tipperary Dan Morrissey s.t. 3 Dublin Eurocycles s.t.

## STAGE 2

Although British rider Dean Downing was the stage winner, day two was also a good one for Irish cycling supporters as Stephen Gallagher took over the yellow jersey of race leader in the FBD Insurance RÁS.

The Ireland An Post M. Donnelly Grant Thornton Sean Kelly team rider made it into the crucial breakaway move and sprinted in just behind Dean Downing (Britain Stena Line Rapha Condor Recycling.co.uk) and Evan Oliphant (Britain Plowman Craven) at the end of the 167 kilometre stage from Ballinamore to Claremorris. However, having started the day two seconds ahead of them in ninth overall, he took over from American rider Ken Hanson (Isle of Man Microgaming Dolan team) as race leader.

Downing and Oliphant end the day one and two seconds behind respectively in the general classification, while Gallagher's team-mate Mark Cassidy netted fourth on the stage and is now fourth overall.

Each of these riders were part of a 57 man front group which formed after a very aggressive first half to the stage. Then, after approximately 100 kilometres of racing, National cyclo cross champion Roger Aiken (Ireland) plus another rider clipped away.

They were soon joined by twelve others, resulting in a leading bunch comprising of Aiken, Jaroslaw Dabrowski (Poland), Dean Downing and Rob Partridge (Britain Stena Line Rapha Condor Recycling.co.uk), Alex Higham (Britain Plowman Craven), Evan Oliphant (Britain Plowman Craven), Mark Cassidy and Stephen Gallagher (Ireland An Post M. Donnelly Grant Thornton Sean Kelly), Kieran Page (Ireland Pezula Racing), Havard Nybo (Norway Sparebanken Vest), Martin Grashev

(Bulgaria Nessebar), Stevens Aubert and Renaud Pioline (France Provence Alpes Cote d'Azur) plus Andrew Bye (Britain Surrey Racing League). This group opened up a lead of almost three minutes over the disorganised group behind, with the Pezula team's efforts to get back on terms being frustrated by the reluctance of other squads to commit to the chase.
Although the lead was gradually whittled down, it was clear that one of them would win the stage when the leaders passed the ten kilometre to go point with a lead of two minutes. Two clicks later Oliphant played his card, attacking hard and then being joined by Downing and Gallagher.
Downing himself kicked clear with three kilometres to go but the other two were able to get back on terms. However he had no problem in taking the sprint, beating Oliphant and Gallagher to the line. The latter had the considerable consolation of taking his – and the Irish-registered An Post team's – first ever yellow jersey in the race
Cassidy was closing up towards the end and crossed the line four seconds behind Downing, while the rest of the break came in shortly after that. Most of the race favourites finished in as part of a large group 1 minute and 29 seconds down. Apart from featuring the race leader Ken Hanson (Isle of Man Microgaming Dolan), the group had Irish hopes David McCann (Ireland national team), Ciarán Power and David O'Loughlin (Team Pezula), as well as last year's runner-up Paídi O'Brien (Ireland An Post M. Donnelly Grant Thornton Sean Kelly). Foreign riders who missed out included past race winners Chris Newton, Kristian House (both Britain Stena Line Rapha Condor Recycling.co.uk) and Andrew Roche (Isle of Man Microgaming Dolan), as well as several other strong contenders. Their deficit is not insurmountable, bit missing such a big move has made winning the RÁS a whole lot harder.
**Stage 2 Ballinamore - Claremorris 167 Kms.** 1 D.Downing (Britain Stena Rapha) 3.55.48 2 E.Oliphant (Britain Plowman Craven) at 1 sec 3 S.Gallagher (Ireland An Post) s.t. 4 M.Cassidy (Ireland An Post) at 4 secs 5 M.Grashev (Bulgaria Nessebar) at 8 secs 6 R.Pioline (France Provence Alpes Cote) s.t. 7 A.Higham (Britain Plowman Craven) at 9 secs 8 J.Dabrowski (Poland) s.t. 9 S.Aubert (France Provence Alpes Cote) at 11 secs 10 H.Nybo (Norway Sparebanken) s.t. 11 R.Partridge (Britain Stena Rapha) s.t. 12 A.Bye (Britain Surrey Racing League) at 21 secs 13 R.Aiken (Ireland) at 23 secs 14 K.Page (Pezula) s.t. 15 N.Coleman (Britain Plowman Craven) at 1.29
**General Classification:** 1 S.Gallagher (Ireland An Post) 7.02.19 2 D.Downing (Britain Stena Rapha) at 1 sec 3 E.Oliphant (Britain Plowman Craven) at 2 secs 4 M.Cassidy (Ireland An Post) at 5 secs 5 J.Dabrowski (Poland) at 7 secs 6 R.Pioline (France Provence Alpes Cote) at 9 secs 7 M.Grashev (Bulgaria Nessebar) s.t. 8 R.Partridge (Britain Stena Rapha) s.t. 9 A.Higham (Britain Plowman Craven) at 10 secs 10 H.Nybo (Norway Sparebanken) at 12 secs 11 S.Aubert (France Provence Alpes Cote) s.t. 12 A.Bye (Britain Surrey Racing League) at 22 secs 13 K.Page (Pezula) s.t. 14 R.Aiken (Ireland) at 24 secs 15 K.Hanson (Isle of Man) at 1.20

**Under 23:** 1 M.Grashev 7.02.28 2 P.Kos at 1.15 3 C.Rake at 1.20
**Points:** 1 D.Downing 26 2 R.Pioline 18 3 K.Hanson 15
**Mountains:** 1 J.Dabrowski 8 2 A.Higham 5 3 N.Delahaye 5
**International Team:** 1 Ireland An Post 21.08.34 2 Britain Plowman Craven at 5 secs 3 Britain Stena Rapha at 6 secs
**County Team:** 1 Dublin IRC Ushers 21.19.45 2 Kerry Total Cleaning at 7.58 3 Dublin Eurocycles s.t.

## STAGE 3

Once again benefiting from bright, dry conditions, 137 riders lined out for the start of the third stage of the FBD Insurance RÁS. The 133 kilometre leg took the riders from Claremorris to Lisdoonvarna and with the first category Doonagore climb coming just 7.5 kilometres from the line, it was sure to shake up the general classification.

This would be preceded by the category three ascent of Ballinalacken, coming fractionally under 20 kilometres from the finish.

There was plenty of aggressive riding from the drop of the flag and ten minutes after the start, Patrick Kos (Netherlands) went clear and was joined by Ireland National team riders Miceal Concannon and Robin Seymour. Jean Marc Maurin (France Provence Alpes Cote d'Azur) tried to get across but was unable to do so, going back to the bunch. Philip Finegan (Meath MyHome.ie/BDBC) also suffered the same fate. The gap went up to one minute and seven seconds, but came back down to 35 seconds around Tuam due to the efforts of the Ireland An Post M. Donnelly Grant Thornton Sean Kelly team of race leader Stephen Gallagher to split the field in the crosswinds. The break was hauled back several kilometres later. Following an unsuccessful attempt by Barry Sutton (Cycleways@53degreesnorth), Roger Aiken (Ireland), Levi Heimans (Netherlands) and Stephen O'Sullivan (Meath MyHome.ie/BDBC) to open up a decisive lead, Derek Burke (Pezula Racing) and Neill Delahaye (Dublin IRC Usher Insulations) went clear approximately 65 kilometres into the stage. They were soon joined by Tim van der Zanden (Netherlands).

The significance and danger of the break increased significantly when the strong Belgian rider Benny de Schrooder (An Post M. Donnelly Grant Thornton Sean Kelly) and double RÁS champion Ciarán Power (Pezula Racing) attacked, chased, and eventually joined the move heading into Kinvara, 67.5 kilometres after the start. The peleton was 40 seconds back at this point.

Although Burke was dropped soon afterwards, the break's chances were boosted significantly when Roger Aiken (Ireland), double RÁS winner Chris Newton (Britain Team Stena Line Rapha Condor Recycilng.co.uk) and Morten Hegreberg (Norway Sparebanken Vest) attacked the bunch and narrowed the gap. They were joined by 2004 victor David McCann (Ireland) and Paídi O'Brien (Ireland An Post M.

Donnelly Grant Thornton Sean Kelly), with the two groups merging approximately 88 kilometres into the stage.

At this point the nine-man group was one minute and ten seconds ahead of the Plowman Craven-led main field. The peloton succeeded in reducing the gap to 41 seconds along the stunning coastline towards Fanore, but the break then started to pull clear again. With 25 kilometres remaining it was 45 seconds ahead of four chasers – Amir Zargari (Iran Islamic Azad University), Mark Cassidy (Ireland An Post M. Donnelly Grant Thornton Sean Kelly), Kieran Page (Pezula) and Andrew Bye (Britain Surrey Racing League) – and a minute up on the main field. Wojciech Dybel, Mateusz Komar (both Poland), Rob Partridge (Britain Stena Line Rapha Condor Recycling.co.uk), Ole Quast (Germany Stevens Von Hacht) and Chris McNamara (Britain Surrey Racing League) also gave chase and merged with the Cassidy group, making it nine chasing nine. This latter group then swelled to twelve when S. Mostafa Razaei Khormizi (Iran Islamic Azad University), Dale Appleby (Britain Stena Line Rapha Condor Recycling.co.uk) and Alex Higham (Britain Plowman Craven) got across.

With approximately 18 kilometres to go, McCann and Newton attacked hard and were then joined briefly by De Schrooder. The Belgian slipped back but the other two persisted, pulling further and further away of their former breakaway companions.

Mark Cassidy had started the day five seconds behind Stephen Gallagher in fourth overall, but with McCann and Newton adding to their advantage up the road, it was possible that one or other of them could take yellow.

They went over the top of the third category climb of Ballinalacken in that order, the summit coming approximately 15 kilometres from the line, with Hegreberg and Higham netting third and fourth. At the top of Doonagore – which came seven kilometres later - Newton and McCann had built their lead to one minute and five seconds over the lone chaser Razaei Khormizi, with the fragmenting chase group a little further behind.

Newton jumped hard inside the final 500 metres, opening up a two second lead on McCann by the line and adding to his list of stage successes in the race. The former Irish National champion was followed home one minute and four seconds later by Komar, with Power and Partridge one and two seconds further back, respectively. The rest of the chasing group was an additional second in arrears. The race referees spent quite some time examining the finishing images to determine if there were sufficient gaps in this group to give separate times – something that could have potentially seen Partridge take the race lead over Cassidy – but finally it was confirmed that the young Irish rider was indeed in yellow.

As regards the other classifications, Dean Downing (Britain Stena Line Rapha Condor Recycling.co.uk) remained in the point's jersey, Newton took over in the mountains competition and Appleby ended the day as leading under 23 rider. Stephen O'Sullivan (Meath MyHome.ie/BDBC) was first county team rider and Brendan Lacey (Kerry Total Cleaning Supplies) topped the list of second category

competitors.
Newton and Partridge's good showing saw the Britain Stena Line Rapha Condor Recycling.co.uk squad move into the lead in the International team standings, and Dublin IRC Usher Insulations remained at the top of the county team lists.
**Stage 3 Claremorris - Lisdoonvarna 133 Kms.** 1 C.Newton (Britain Stena Rapha) 3.25.08 2 D.McCann (Ireland) at 2 secs 3 M.Komar (Poland) at 1.04 4 C.Power (Pezula) at 1.05 5 R.Partridge (Britain Stena Rapha) at 1.06 6 A.Bye (Britain Surrey Racing League) at 1.07 7 A.Zargari (Iran Islamic Azad University) s.t. 8 S.M.Khormizi Razaei (Iran Islamic Azad University) s.t. 9 M.Hegreberg (Norway Sparebanken) s.t. 10 B.de Schrooder (Ireland An Post) s.t. 11 P.O'Brien (Ireland An Post) s.t. 12 D.Appleby (Britain Stena Rapha) s.t. 13 C.McNamara (Britain Surrey Racing League) s.t. 14 K.Page (Pezula) s.t. 15 M.Cassidy (Ireland An Post) s.t.
**General Classification:** 1 M.Cassidy (Ireland An Post) 10.28.39 2 R.Partridge (Britain Stena Rapha) at 3 secs 3 A.Higham (Britain Plowman Craven) at 5 secs 4 A.Bye (Britain Surrey Racing League) at 17 secs 5 K.Page (Pezula) s.t. 6 C.Newton (Britain Stena Rapha) at 18 secs 7 D.McCann (Ireland) at 20 secs 8 R.Aiken (Ireland) at 24 secs 9 B.de Schrooder (Ireland An Post) at 1.21 10 D.Downing (Britain Stena Rapha) at 1.22 11 M.Hegreberg (Norway Sparebanken) s.t. 12 M.Komar (Poland) s.t. 13 C.Power (Pezula) at 1.23 14 S.Gallagher (Ireland An Post) s.t. 15 P.O'Brien (Ireland An Post) at 1.25
**Under 23:** 1 D.Appleby 10.30.04 2 M.Grashev at 7 secs 3 O.Quast at 9 secs
**Points:** 1 D.Downing 26 2 M.Komar 25 3 B.de Schrooder 19
**Mountains:** 1 C.Newton 19 2 D.McCann 17 3 S.M.Khormizi Razaei 14
**International Team:** 1 Britain Stena Rapha 31.26.17 2 Ireland An Post at 1.02 3 Ireland at 2.31
**County Team:** 1 Dublin IRC Ushers 31.45.34 2 Kerry Total Cleaning at 5.46 3 Dublin Eurocycles at 8.11

## STAGE 4

After three days of good weather, the fourth stage of the FBD Insurance RÁS got underway in wet conditions in the town of Corofin. 135 riders lined out for the 156 kilometre stage to Tralee, which featured three third category climbs in the final 60 kilometres.
Paídi O'Brien (Ireland An Post M. Donnelly Grant Thornton Sean Kelly) and Ciarán Power (Ireland Pezula Racing) attacked very soon after the stage start, and were joined by Paul Healion (Dublin McNally Swords). However the bunch had no intention of letting those riders getting any sort of advantage, and soon closed it down. Just before that happened, Simon Richardson (Britain Plowman Craven) bridged but his effort proved to be in vain due to the break's recapture. Healion was at it again several kilometres later, going clear with Roger Aiken (Ireland) and Neill Delahaye (Dublin IRC Usher Insulations). They were joined by eleven others, namely Jaroslaw Dabrowski (Poland national team), Kristian House

(Britain Stena Line Rapha Condor Recycling.co.uk), Simon Richardson (Britain Plowman Craven), Benny de Schrooder (Ireland An Post M. Donnelly Grant Thornton Sean Kelly), Ciarán Power (Ireland Pezula Racing), Morten Hegreberg and Havard Nybo (Norway Sparebanken Vest), Johannes Sickmuller (Germany Stevens von Hacht), Kit Gilham (Britain Kenesis), Joe Fenlon (Tipperary Dan Morrissey) and Denis Lynch (Cork Kanturk Town), and this group opened up a lead of 50 seconds. Double RÁS winner Ciarán Power had been sick during the first couple of days of the race and was hoping to start mounting a challenge for his third title. However he punctured out of the break. His Pezula Racing team then started contributing to the chase and this brought the gap right down.

Aiken, Dabrowski, House, Richardson, de Schrooder and Nybo then clipped away before the break was caught, with Power and yellow jersey Mark Cassidy (Ireland An Post M. Donnelly Grant Thornton Sean Kelly) and Ciarán Power (Ireland Pezula Racing) jumping across. However the peloton recognised the danger and closed down the move.

After 50 kilometres of racing, the riders reached the city of Limerick and here a small group of several riders got clear, these including Dean Downing (Britain Stena Line Rapha Condor Recycling.co.uk) and Benny de Schrooder (Ireland An Post M. Donnelly Grant Thornton Sean Kelly). The break was hauled back but around this time, race leader Cassidy hit a rock on the road and crashed hard. He lay on the ground for several minutes, receiving medical attention, and then painfully remounted his bike. Two riders were clear at this point, Abbas Saeidi Tanha (Iran Islamic Azad University) and a lone chaser Neil Coleman (Britain Plowman Craven), but the peloton rode slowly along in a gesture of sportsmanship and this enabled Cassidy to eventually return 64 kilometres after the start. His injuries would however prove to be too much for him to continue, the 23 year old being taken to hospital with a suspected fractured elbow. This was eventually diagnosed as very bad bruising, but he was out of the race. By that point Tanha was six minutes clear and while Coleman was chasing hard, he was still 1 minute and 32 seconds down. The latter was eventually caught before Abbeyfeale (111 kms), while Tanha was reeled in soon afterwards. They had managed to take first and second at the day's first king of the mountains climb, the category three ascent of Barnagh Gap (99.8 kilometres), with Simon Richardson (Britain Plowman Craven) and Martin Grashev (Bulgaria Nessebar) nabbing third and fourth.

Prior to the start of the next climb, the third category ascent at Glanshearon, Wojciech Dybel (Poland), Bogdan Stoytchev (Bulgaria Nessebar), Roger Aiken (Ireland national team) and Tiedt Yannick (Germany Stevens von Hacht) broke away.

They were joined by S. Mostafa Razaei Khormizi (Iran Islamic Azad University), Simon Richardson (Britain Plowman Craven), Stephen Gallagher (Ireland An Post M. Donnelly Sean Kelly) and Kit Gilham (Britain Kinesis). The first two riders

yesterday, Chris Newton (Britain Stena Line Rapha Condor Recycling.co.uk), then bridged together.
Levi Heimans (Netherlands) and Dean Downing (Britain Stena Line Rapha Conor Recycling.co.uk) were the last two to get across, making it twelve ahead of the bunch.
Razaei Khormizi was first to the summit of the climb, the prime coming 27 kilometres from the end of the stage. Newton, Yannick and Richardson were next over the top
Dybel and Razaei Khormizi (Iran Islamic Azad University) then attacked after the climb and pushed on ahead, opening up an 18 second lead over the rest of the bunch and a 56 second advantage over the peloton. They were first and second at the category three Barr na Gaoithe prime, then sat up and went back to the break. The gap was just thirty seconds with ten kilometres remaining but the bunch was unable to haul it back. With less than three kilometres to go Newton punctured out of the break, losing his chance for a second successive stage win and, more importantly, the opportunity to take over the race lead. He had been the best-placed rider in the move.
McCann had started the day two seconds behind him and broke clear of the group inside the final two kilometres. While his advantage at the finish would give him the yellow jersey on count back, he said that he was thinking first and foremost of the stage victory.
Dybel, Stoytchev, Richardson and Downing finished two seconds behind the former national road race champion, while Heimans, Yannick, Aiken, Gallagher and Razaei Khormizi were a further two seconds back. Ken Hanson (Isle of Man Microgaming Dolan) led home the main bunch 24 seconds after McCann crossed the line. Newton at the back of this group but, as per UCI rules, he was given the same finishing time as the break. He ended the day locked on time with McCann but a count back of their stage placings saw the jersey go to the Ireland rider. Aiken and Partridge were third and fourth overall, with Downing and team-mate Newton leading the points and mountains classifications respectively.
A third competitor from the Britain Stena Line Rapha Condor Recycling.co.uk squad, Dale Appleby, was in the white jersey as Irish Sports Council best young rider.
**Stage 4 Corofin - Tralee 156 Kms.** 1 D.McCann (Ireland) 3.53.36 2 W.Dybel (Poland) at 2 secs 3 B.Stoytchev (Bulgaria Nessebar) s.t. 4 S. Richardson (Britain Plowman Craven) s.t. 5 D.Downing (Britain Stena Rapha) s.t. 6 L.Heimans (Netherlands) s.t. 7 T.Yannick (Germany Stevens Von Hacht) s.t. 8 R.Aiken (Ireland) s.t. 9 S.Gallagher (Ireland An Post) s.t. 10 S.M.Khormizi Razaei (Iran Islamic Azad University) s.t. 11 K.Gilham (Britain Kinesis) at 8 secs 12 K.Hanson (Isle of Man) at 24 secs 13 M.Komar (Poland) s.t. 14 E.Moriarty (Meath MyHome.ie) s.t. 15 R.Birkenfeld (Germany Stevens Von Hacht) s.t.
**General Classification:** 1 D.McCann (Ireland) 14.22.35 2 C.Newton (Britain Stena Rapha) s.t. 3 R.Aiken (Ireland) at 6 secs 4 R.Partridge (Britain Stena Rapha) at 7 secs

5 A.Higham (Britain Plowman Craven) at 9 secs 6 A.Bye (Britain Surrey Racing League) at 56 secs 7 D.Downing (Britain Stena Rapha) at 1.04 8 S.Gallagher (Ireland An Post) at 1.05 9 S.M.Khormizi Razaei (Iran Islamic Azad University) at 1.07 10 K.Page (Pezula) at 1.11 11 B.de Schrooder (Ireland An Post) at 1.25 12 M.Komar (Poland) at 1.26 13 P.O'Brien (Ireland An Post) at 1.29 14 D.Appleby (Britain Stena Rapha) s.t. 15 A.Zargari (Iran Islamic Azad University) s.t.
**Under 23:** 1 D.Appleby 10.30.04 2 M.Grashev at 7 secs 3 O.Quast at 9 secs
**Points:** 1 D.Downing 37 2 D.McCann 29 3 M.Komar 28
**Mountains:** 1 C.Newton 25 2 S.M.Khormizi Razaei 23 3 D.McCann 17
**International Team:** 1 Britain Stena Rapha 43.07.33 2 Ireland An Post at 1.24 3 Ireland at 2.29
**County Team:** 1 Dublin IRC Ushers 43.28.41 2 Meath MyHome.ie at 10.23 3 Kerry Total Cleaning at 17.42

## STAGE 5

Day five was one of mixed fortunes for the Irish competitors on this year's FBD Insurance RÁS, with David O'Loughlin puncturing whilst in the running for the stage victory and David McCann successfully defending his race leader's yellow jersey.
McCann faced a serious threat to his jersey when two general classification contenders made it into the day's crucial break. Simon Richardson (Britain Plowman Craven) and Kit Gilham had started the day as major threats to the yellow jersey, having started the day 2'35 and 2'41 back in 25th and 26th place overall. They, David O'Loughlin (Ireland Pezula Racing) and Patrick Kos (Netherlands) went clear before Farranfore, the first of five climbs on the stage. The group opened up a maximum lead of 4 minutes 45 seconds over the main bunch, working well together over the tough terrain. And although the gap did narrow towards the finish, Richardson and O'Loughlin had enough left in reserve to raise their game, ramp up their speed and finish over a minute clear.
"It was a beautiful stage, I loved every minute of it," said the Englishman afterwards. "It was super hard because of the wind and the climbs themselves, because of the wind, were almost nullified. I knew that with the time gaps we had, I was possibly looking at yellow at the end of today, so I gave it everything.
"It was super unfortunate that David punctured at the end…it is not the best way to win a stage, off the back of someone else's misfortune. I really don't know what his finish is like [if it had come to a sprint]. I think he had a lot of riding left in him, though, so it would have been tough."
Although the riders were clear for a long time during the stage, he said that towards the end he became relatively confident that they could stay away. "With about 30 or 40 kilometres to go, we were really not riding very fast and yet the time gap was not really coming down. I knew I had a couple of gears left and I had hoped that once we started riding that they would struggle to bring us back."

Kos cracked 36 kilometres from the end and then, eleven kilometres later, Richardson attacked. O'Loughlin bided his time, continuing to ride along with Gilham, then bridged across alone several kilometres later. As he had done when winning the Shay Elliott Memorial earlier this year, he was clear for much of the day and was looking to use his fast finish to take the victory. However that went out the window when he punctured inside the final three kilometres. He got a spare bike but didn't have enough time to get back to the front.
"I drilled it hard as soon as I got the bike change," he said. "I was closing on him but I just did not have enough road at the end so I sort of gave up in the last few hundred metres. Obviously I am very disappointed."
He's determined that he and the team will keep trying. "Ciaran (Power) was up there in a sprint today and he is in good form. He will be fighting for a stage win as well the rest of the week. Hopefully we will have more aggressive riding from here on and hopefully we will come away with a stage win.
"The Pezulas have been great this year. They gave us a good investment in Irish cycling and that helped greatly towards my track programme for the Olympics. It is all really positive and it is good for Irish cycling."
Richardson had started the day well placed overall and so was clearly a concern to McCann. However he finished 54 seconds off the yellow jersey, moving up to sixth overall but still needing more time. He's likely to try again in the remaining three days, but the 2004 Rás winner is relatively confident.
"I was not too concerned when the break went away," said McCann. "In some ways it might suit me to have another guy from a different team close behind but not leading. I was not really that worried when the time went up because I was pretty confident we could bring it back when we needed to."
There is likely to be a big showdown on Saturday. He feels up to the task. "Those are the hills where I have won the RÁS before – all around the Wicklow Mountains. I have won stages there and I have won the Shay Elliott, so this is my racing territory. I am looking forward to those hills."
Before then, he will have to get through tomorrow's 180 kilometre stage from Skibbereen to Clonmel. Six riders are within a minute or less of his race lead and there's plenty of opportunity for them to attack. However he's got confidence in the other riders in the green jersey.
"Robin Seymour, Micheal Concannon, Paul Griffin and Roger Aiken…on paper you might not think it, but this is one of the strongest teams I have been on. They are riding really well. They are just phenomenal. They are making my job a lot easier."
**Stage 5 Tralee - Skibereen 141 Kms.** 1 S.Richardson (Britain Plowman Craven) 3.35.01 2 D.O'Loughlin (Pezula) s.t. 3 M.Komar (Poland) at 1.41 4 C.Power (Pezula) s.t. 5 R.Ratajczyk (Poland) s.t. 6 K.Hanson (Isle of Man) s.t. 7 M.Hegreberg (Norway Sparebanken) s.t. 8 D.Downing (Britain Stena Rapha) s.t. 9 R.Pioline (France Provence Alpes Cote) s.t. 10 C.Cassidy (Meath Cycleways@53degrees) s.t. 11 E.Moriarty (Meath MyHome.ie) s.t. 12 B.Janiaczyk (Poland) s.t. 13 S.Kelly

(Dublin IRC Ushers) s.t. 14 R.Birkenfeld (Germany Stevens Von Hacht) s.t. 15 S.M.Khormizi Razaei (Iran Islamic Azad University) s.t.
**General Classification:** 1 D.McCann (Ireland) 17.59.17 2 C.Newton (Britain Stena Rapha) s.t. 3 R.Aiken (Ireland) at 6 secs 4 R.Partridge (Britain Stena Rapha) at 7 secs 5 A.Higham (Britain Plowman Craven) at 9 secs 6 S.Richardson (Britain Plowman Craven) at 54 secs 7 A.Bye (Britain Surrey Racing League) at 56 secs 8 D.Downing (Britain Stena Rapha) at 1.04 9 S.Gallagher (Ireland An Post) at 1.05 10 S.M.Khormizi Razaei (Iran Islamic Azad University) at 1.07 11 K.Page (Pezula) at 1.11 12 B.de Schrooder (Ireland An Post) at 1.25 13 M.Komar (Poland) at 1.26 14 P.O'Brien (Ireland An Post) at 1.29 15 A.Zargari (Iran Islamic Azad University) s.t.
**Under 23:** 1 D.Appleby 18.00.46 2 M.Grashev at 7 secs 3 O.Quast at 9 secs
**Points:** 1 D.Downing 45 2 M.Komar 41 3 M.Komar 3 D.McCann 29
**Mountains:** 1 K.Gilham 49 2 S.Richardson 41 3 P.Kos 38
**International Team:** 1 Britain Stena Rapha 53.57.39 2 Ireland An Post at 1.24 3 Ireland at 2.29
**County Team:** 1 Dublin IRC Ushers 54.18.47 2 Meath MyHome.ie at 10.23 3 Kerry Total Cleaning at 18.39

## STAGE 6

The longest stage of the FBD Insurance RÁS started in Skibbereen in bright conditions and very soon after the drop of the flag, a group of ten riders went clear. These were Miceal Concannon (Ireland national team), Stephen Gallagher (Ireland An Post M. Donnelly Grant Thornton Sean Kelly), Ciarán Power, Cameron Jennings and Derek Burke (Ireland Pezula Racing), Christer Rake (Norway Sparebanken Vest), Andrew Roche (Isle of Man Microgaming Dolan), Paul Healion (Dublin McNally Swords), Sean Lacey (Dublin Eurocycles) and Eugene Moriarty (Meath MyHome.ie/BDBC).
Concannon dropped back to the bunch in order to support the race leader David McCann, but his place at the front was taken by stage five winner Simon Richardson (Britain Plowman Craven), who bridged across alone.
The Ireland team of McCann and the Britain Stena Line Rapha Condor Recycling.co.uk squad of second-placed rider Chris Newton started riding at the front of the bunch but, whether it was due to a lack of full commitment or the horsepower of those up front, the break kept pulling clear.
The high overall placings of Richardson, Gallagher and McCann meant that there was a clear danger to McCann's lead, and the yellow jersey himself started riding as well. Richardson had started the day sixth overall, 54 seconds back, while Gallagher (9th) was one minute five seconds down and Power (23rd) was a further 57 seconds in arrears.
Fifty kilometres into the stage, the break was one minute and 24 seconds clear. Thirty-five kilometres later, this had gone up to three minutes. Healion had experienced mechanical trouble, chased back to the break, but was then dropped

several kilometres later. Burke also found himself heading back to the bunch after he punctured and was unable to rejoin

The eight-man break pressed onwards in sometimes-wet conditions, building its lead. With 35 kilometres left, it peaked at six minutes and two seconds. An attack and several-kilometre stint off the front by lone rider Chris McNamara (Britain Surrey Racing league) showed that the peloton was not riding as well as it could have been, and this was echoed when McCann himself attacked, showing his frustration with others who would not ride. However he was hauled back by the Plowman Craven team of Richardson, who looked set to take over the yellow jersey. Wojciech Dybel (Poland) and Renaud Pioline (France Provence Alpes Cote d'Azur) attacked from the peloton and, after their recapture, Dybel went once again with Pioline's team-mate Jean Marc Maurin. This was again brought back, after which a stubborn Dybel took off with his Poland team-mate Mateusz Komar. A group of seven riders set off in pursuit, but all nine were all reeled in.

With twenty kilometres to go it became clear that the break was not going to be seen again until after the finish. The time check there was two minutes and forty seconds; it was still considerable at the ten kilometres to go marker.

Approximately five clicks later Richardson, Gallagher, Power, Rake and Roche pushed on, leaving Moriarty, Lacey and Jennings behind. Power then attacked inside the final three kilometres, opening up a small lead over solo chaser Rake and holding him off to the line. The Norwegian finished three seconds back, with Gallagher six and Richardson plus Roche seven seconds down.

Moriarty, Lacey and Jennings were next across the line, the first two of these scrapping it out for the county prize, and then Dybel and Poland team-mate Blazej Janiaczyk finishes two minutes 26 seconds and two minutes 37 seconds in arrears. They had broken free of the main bunch, which was itself led home two minutes and 47 seconds after Power's victory by Dean Downing (Britain Stena Line Rapha Condor Recycling.co.uk).

McCann and Newton finished in this group and while they remained deadlocked on time, they dropped to fourth and fifth overall, one minute and 46 seconds back. Downing and Kit Gilham (Britain Kinesis) continued to lead the points and mountains classifications, while Dale Appleby (Britain Stena Line Rapha Condor Recycling.co.uk), Denis Dunworth (Kerry Total Cleaning Supplies) and Brendan Lacey (Kerry Total Cleaning Supplies) ended the day at the top of the Under 23, the county rider and the CI category two competitions. Ireland An Post M. Donnelly Grant Thornton Sean Kelly and Dublin IRC Usher Insulations were at the helm of the international and county teams' ranking

**Stage 6 Skibereen - Clonmel 180 Kms.** 1 C.Power (Pezula) 4.17.56 2 C.Rake (Norway Sparebanken) at 3 secs 3 S.Gallagher (Ireland An Post) at 6 secs 4 S. Richardson (Britain Plowman Craven) at 7 secs 5 A.Roche (Isle of Man) s.t. 6 E.Moriarty (Meath MyHome.ie) at 29 secs 7 S.Lacey (Dublin Eurocycles) at 30 secs 8 C.Jennings (Pezula) at 37 secs 9 W.Dyble (Poland) at 2.26 10 B.Janiaczyk (Poland) at 2.37 11 D.Downing (Britain Stena Rapha) at 2.47 12 L.Heimans (Netherlands) s.t.

13 D.McCann (Ireland) s.t. 14 R.Pioline (France Provence Alpes Cote) s.t. 15 R.Birkenfeld (Germany Stevens Von Hacht) s.t.

**General Classification:** 1 S.Richardson (Britain Plowman Craven) 22.18.14 2 S.Gallagher (Ireland An Post) at 10 secs 3 C.Power (Pezula) at 1.01 4 D.McCann (Ireland) at 1.46 5 C.Newton (Britain Stena Rapha) s.t. 6 R.Aiken (Ireland) at 1.52 7 R.Partridge (Britain Stena Rapha) at 1.53 8 A.Higham (Britain Plowman Craven) at 1.55 9 A.Bye (Britain Surrey Racing League) at 2.42 10 D.Downing (Britain Stena Rapha) at 2.50 11 S.M.Khormizi Razaei (Iran Islamic Azad University) at 2.53 12 K.Page (Pezula) at 2.57 13 B.de Schrooder (Ireland An Post) at 3.11 14 M.Komar (Poland) at 3.12 15 P.O'Brien (Ireland An Post) at 3.15

**Under 23:** 1 D.Appleby 22.21.29 2 M.Grashev at 7 secs 3 O.Quast at 9 secs

**Points:** 1 D.Downing 50 2 M.Komar 41 3 S.Richardson 39

**Mountains:** 1 K.Gilham 49 2 S.Richardson 41 3 P.Kos 38

**International Team:** 1 Ireland An Post 66.58.31 2 Britain Stena Rapha at 1.17 3 Britain Plowman Craven at 1.21

**County Team:** 1 Dublin IRC Ushers 67.20.56 2 Meath MyHome.ie at 8.05 3 Kerry Total Cleaning at 18.39

## STAGE 7

Finishing in a group 48 seconds behind the day's winner Wojciech Dybel (Poland national team), Irish rider Stephen Gallagher regained the yellow jersey he held earlier this week and looks poised to take the 2008 FBD Insurance RÁS when it finishes in Skerries tomorrow.

The 27 year old's Ireland An Post. M. Donnelly Grant Thornton Sean Kelly team had a superb day, placing Benny de Schrooder and Paídi O'Brien in an early fourteen-man move before he and Daniel Lloyd successfully bridged across with sixteen others. Gallagher had started the day second overall and the rider who was ten seconds ahead of him, race leader Simon Richardson (Britain Plowman Craven), missed the break. So too did the other riders in the top five, namely Ciarán Power (Ireland Pezula Racing), David McCann (Ireland national team) and Chris Newton (Britain Stena Line Rapha Condor Recycling.co.uk).

Roger Aiken (Ireland national team), who had started sixth overall, made it into the first move and was at that point race leader on the road. However Gallagher had started the day one minute and 42 seconds ahead of him and so once his group joined with those at the front, he knew he was riding back into the yellow jersey he had lost on Tuesday.

"It really couldn't have gone any better," said Gallagher after the stage. "Our tactic last night was pretty much how it ended up. Obviously with a four-man team it would be very difficult to try and control the race, but I think we did a great job today. We sent two guys up the road and obviously the danger was Roger being there.

"I think the worst case scenario was that we were going to leave Benny or Paídi up

there to try to take the yellow jersey [from Aiken] coming towards the finish. It was quite stop-start in the bunch behind and eventually Dan [Lloyd] jumped away. I said I'd try to get across to him and then the two of us could ride together and try to get across to the front break.
It was a textbook display of strategy. "It's not often that these tactics work out but today it went perfectly. We went across and when we got up to Paídi and Benny, we had three in the front including myself. The team rode an unbelievable race. To come across to the front break, Daniel Lloyd was riding into a headwind at 45 or 50 kilometres an hour. I was struggling to hold his wheel; he closed a two minute gap practically on his own. Then when we hit the climbs Paídi and Benny rode tempo on the hills and controlled it the whole way. I knew I had to watch riders like Roger and [Dean] Downing, but it was really good team-work."
Wojciech Dybel (Poland national team), Kit Gilham (Britain Kinesis) and Sayed . M. Razaei Khormizi (Iran Islamic Ahad University) broke clear on the day's final climb of Drumgoff, going on to fight it out for the stage win between them. Points leader Dean Downing led in Gallagher's group 48 seconds later, with Irish riders Paul Griffin (Ireland national team), Paídi O'Brien (Ireland An Post M. Donnelly Grant Thornton Sean Kelly) and Simon Kelly (Dublin IRC Usher Insulations) taking fifth, seventh and tenth.
After a very frustrating day early on, David McCann had a strong ride to get clear of the main bunch, catch and pass the group of yellow jersey Simon Richardson and finish five minutes and 21 seconds back. Richardson was seven minutes 18 seconds down.
The upended general classification saw Gallagher end the day one minute and 42 seconds ahead of Aiken, with Rob Partridge (Britain Stena Line Rapha Condor Recyling.co.uk) a further second back.
Alex Higham (Britain Plowman Craven) is one minute 45 seconds down in fourth place while Razaei Khormizi (Iran Islamic Ahad University) is an additional ten seconds behind.
**Stage 7 Clonmel - Roundwood 177 Kms.** 1 W.Dyble (Poland) 4.51.49 2 K.Gilham (Britain Kinesis) s.t. 3 S.M.Khormizi Razaei (Iran Islamic Azad University) s.t. 4 D.Downing (Britain Stena Rapha) at 48 secs 5 P.Griffin (Ireland) s.t. 6 K.Page (Pezula) s.t. 7 P.O'Brien (Ireland An Post) s.t. 8 M.Hegreberg (Norway Sparebanken) s.t. 9 B.de Schrooder (Ireland An Post) s.t. 10 S.Kelly (Dublin IRC Ushers) s.t. 11 A.Tanha Saeidi (Iran Islamic Azad University) s.t. 12 A.Zargari (Iran Islamic Azad University) s.t. 13 W.Sybrandy (Britain Surrey Racing League) s.t. 14 R.Pioline (France Provence Alpes Cote) s.t. 15 M.Grashev (Bulgaria Nessebar) s.t.
**General Classification:** 1 S.Gallagher (Ireland An Post) 27.11.01 2 6 R.Aiken (Ireland) at 1.42 3 R.Partridge (Britain Stena Rapha) at 1.43 4 A.Higham (Britain Plowman Craven) at 1.45 5 S.M.Khormizi Razaei (Iran Islamic Azad University) at 1.55 6 W.Dyble (Poland) at 2.30 7 D.Downing (Britain Stena Rapha) at 2.40 8 K.Page (Pezula) at 2.47 9 B.de Schrooder (Ireland An Post) at 3.01 10 P.O'Brien (Ireland An Post) at 3.05 11 A.Zargari (Iran Islamic Azad University) s.t. 12

D.Appleby (Britain Stena Rapha) s.t. 13 R.Pioline (France Provence Alpes Cote) at 3.08 14 M.Grashev (Bulgaria Nessebar) at 3.12 15 K.Gilham (Britain Kinesis) at 3.29

**Under 23:** 1 D.Appleby 27.14.06 2 M.Grashev at 7 secs 3 M.Schreurs at 7.50

**Points:** 1 D.Downing 62 2 M.Komar 41 3 S.Richardson 39

**Mountains:** 1 K.Gilham 49 2 S.M.Khormizi Razaei 53 3 S.Richardson 41

**International Team:** 1 Ireland An Post 81.36.22 2 Britain Stena Rapha at 1.17 3 Ireland at

**County Team:** 1 Dublin IRC Usher 82.23.14 2 Meath MyHome.ie at 23.46 3 Tipperary Dan Morrisey at 45.15

## STAGE 8

Stephen Gallagher and David O'Loughlin today capped off a fine week for Irish riders in the FBD Insurance RÁS, with the former securing the first home victory in four years and the latter taking the stage victory in Skerries. Gallagher had started the day comfortably clear of closest-challenger Roger Aiken (Ireland National team) and, together with his Ireland An Post M. Donnelly Grant Thornton Sean Kelly team-mates, kept close tabs on all of his rivals during today's 130 kilometre stage from Newbridge to Skerries.

Each of those main competitors finished in the peloton and therefore Gallagher ended the race with the same advantage he had started the stage with. Aiken took second, one minute and 42 seconds back, while Rob Partridge (Britain Stena Line Rapha Condor Recyling.co.uk) and Alex Higham (Britain Plowman Craven) were an additional one and three seconds back, respectively.

It's the biggest win thus far for both Gallagher and the An Post M. Donnelly Grant Thornton Sean Kelly team. "I had the yellow jersey earlier in the week but lost it. I was quietly confident that I could get it back, both because of the team that I had and because my form was quite good. I was never under too much pressure during the week and I was always holding back a little for these final two days, where I knew I was going to try to take the race lead."

"My form here is up there with the best condition I have had in the past," he stated. "Unfortunately I haven't had the best of luck in the last few years. I have had broken wrists, injuries to my knees and tendonitis. Like any athlete it goes on and on. A month or two off here and there adds up and up. I think everything has just gone right – the team has been good, my form has been good, things went our way. It doesn't often happen like that in cycling, as most cyclists will know. It is difficult to get it right but out team did it…it was a brilliant group effort."

O'Loughlin, meanwhile, was one of four riders who broke clear approximately 20 kilometres into the stage. He, Ireland Pezula Racings Cameron Jennings, Evan Oliphant (Britain Plowman Craven) and Blazej Janiaczyk (Poland national team) were completely committed and together eked out a maximum lead of almost six minutes over the peloton.

Despite strong head- and cross-winds, the quartet held onto much of their advantage and once onto the two laps of the tough finishing circuit in Skerries, they knew that the stage win would be fought out between them. Jennings sparked off the aggression when he tried to go clear inside the final 20 kilometres. This move was covered but it was actually intended to pave the way for a counter-attack by O'Loughlin. The Mayo rider shot clear and only Oliphant was able to get across to him. The two rode together to the finish, where O'Loughlin narrowly outsprinted the Scottish competitor. Janiaczyk and Jennings came in 37 seconds later for third and fourth, while a further 39 seconds later another Irish Pezula Racing rider, Ciarán Power, won the bunch sprint for fifth.

"The four of us got away early in the race and there was pretty even riding all the way," he said. "I told Cameron to put in an attack with 20 kilometres to go, to suss them out a bit because I didn't know if they were strong or not. He attacked, they didn't seem that strong and I took encouragement from that.

"I countered it and Oli [Evan Oliphant] came across to me. I threw in a few attacks but I couldn't get rid of him. I was a little bit worried because he is good in the sprint. But I kept it in on the left hand side because the wind was coming across the road. I also left it late enough because I knew that there was a strong enough wind there. That was it. He sort of came at me with 50 metres to go but I just got him on the last little bit.

The 30 year old was in the running for a stage win on day five but punctured inside the final three kilometres when clear with Simon Richardson (Britain Plowman Craven). Today's victory makes up for that. "That day was really frustrating because I didn't have a chance to sprint [for the stage win]. My form is only coming around now, I am definitely coming out of the week better than I went into it."

Despite a strong international line-up, three Irish riders held the yellow jersey – namely Gallagher, Mark Cassidy and David McCann, and McCann, Power and O'Loughlin took stage wins.

Other prizes went to Dean Downing (Britain Stena Line Rapha Condor, points classification), Kit Gilham (Britain Kinesis, King of the Mountains competition), Dale Appleby (Britain Stena Line Rapha Condor, best under 23), Stephen O'Sullivan (Meath MyHome.ie/BDBC, best Irish county rider) and Mark Power (Tipperary Dan Morrissey, best Irish second-category rider).

Gallagher's Ireland An Post M Donelly Grant Thornton line-up won the International team competition while Dublin IRC Usher Insulations was best of the county squads. David McCann was the last Irish winner of the FBD Insurance RÁS, taking his victory in 2004.

**Stage 8 Newbridge - Skerries 130 Kms.** 1 D.O'Loughlin (Pezula) 3.22.13 2 E.Oliphant (Britain Plowman Craven) s.t. 3 B.Janiaczyk (Poland) 3.22.50 4 C.Jennings (Pezula) s.t. 5 C.Power (Pezula) 3.23.29 6 D.Downing (Britain Stena Rapha) s.t. 7 M.Komar (Poland) s.t. 8 P.Healion (Dublin McNally Swords) s.t. 9 P.Kos (Netherlands) s.t. 10 S.O'Sullivan (Meath MyHome.ie) s.t. 11 M.Hegreberg (Norway) s.t. 12 R.Pioline (France Provence Alpes Cote) s.t. 13 O.Quast (Germany

Stevens Von Hacht) s.t. 14 E.Moriarty (Meath MyHome.ie) s.t. 15 K.Page (Pezula) s.t.

**General Classification:** 1 S.Gallagher (Ireland An Post) 30.34.30 2 R.Aiken (Ireland) at 1.42 3 R.Partridge (Britain Stena Rapha) at 1.43 4 A.Higham (Britain Plowman Craven) at 1.45 5 S.M.Khormizi Razaei (Iran Islamic Azad University) at 1.55 6 W.Dybel (Poland) at 2.30 7 D.Downing (Britain Stena Rapha) at 2.40 8 K.Page (Pezula) at 2.47 9 B.de Schrooder (Ireland An Post) at 3.01 10 P.O'Brien (Ireland An Post) at 3.05 11 A.Zargari (Iran Islamic Azad University) s.t. 12 D.Appleby (Britain Stena Rapha) s.t. 13 R.Pioline (France Provence Alpes Cote) at 3.08 14 M.Grashev (Bulgaria Nessebar) at 3.12 15 K.Gilham (Britain Kinesis) at 3.29

**Under 23:** 1 D.Appleby 30.37.35 2 M.Grashev at 7 secs 3 M.Schreurs at 7.50

**Points:** 1 D.Downing 72 2 C.Power 50 3 M.Komar 50

**Mountains:** 1 K.Gilham 81 2 S.M.Khormizi Razaei 53 3 D.O'Loughlin 46

**International Team:** 1 Ireland An Post 91.46.49 2 Britain Stena Rapha at 1.17 3 Ireland at 8.19

**County Team:** 1 Dublin IRC Ushers 92.33.41 2 Meath MyHome.ie at 23.46 3 Tipperary Dan Morrisey at 46.33

*2008 Winner, Stephen Gallagher (Ireland)*